The Buffalo Soldiers

The Buffalo Soldiers

The story of South Africa's 32-Battalion
1975 —1993

Col Jan Breytenbach

GALAGO

Books by Jan Breytenbach

Forged in Battle
They Live by the Sword
Eden's Exiles
The Plunderers
The Buffalo Soldiers

GALAGO BOOKS

Galago Books are published by Galago Publishing (1999) (Pty) Ltd
PO Box 404, Alberton, 1450, Republic South Africa
Web address: www.galago.co.za

Galago Books are distributed by Lemur Books (Pty) Ltd
PO Box 1645, Alberton, 1450, Republic South Africa
Tel: (Int + 2711 — local 011) 907-2029. Fax 869-0890
Email: lemur@mweb.co.za
The Galago logo is a registered trademark

First published by Galago as The Buffalo Soldiers, October 2002
Second edition October 2004 (trade paperback with corrections)
Reprinted April 2006

Typeset by Galago in 10 point Arial

Colour and black and white photographs reproduced
by Full Colour Graphics, Johannesburg

Colour corrections by Justyn and Madelain Davies

Printed and bound by CTP Book Printers, Cape

Electronic DD20: 355.496

Book design: Fran Stiff and Madelain Davies
Maps: Madelain Davies
Dust jacket design: Fran Stiff, Justyn and Madelain Davies
Dust jacket conceptualisation: Justyn and Madelain Davies
Dust jacket photography: Justyn Davies

This is the story— of a unique infantry battalion, its officers, NCOs and troops. It was an honour for me and those who followed me to have commanded such men in battle.

It was a rare joy to have experienced such loyalty and trust from men who fought shoulder to shoulder with, and often died shoulder to shoulder with, their commanders from 'racist' South Africa — commanders who could scarcely speak their language.

To the men of 32-Battalion, both black and white, Angolan and South African, this book is dedicated.

Officers Commanding: 32-Battalion

1976-1977	Colonel	Jan Breytenbach, DVR, SD, SM
1977-1978	Comdt	Gert Nel
1978-1982	Colonel	Deon Ferreira
1982-1987	Colonel	Eddie Viljoen, HC, SM, MMM
1987	Colonel	Jock Harris
1988-1993	Colonel	Michau Delport

Regimental Sergeant Majors: 32-Battalion

1976-1979	WO1	Pep van Zyl, PMM
1979-1982	WO1	Lars Ueckerman
1982-1983	WO1	P W van Heerden
1983-1984	WO1	Faan Joubert
1984-1986	T/WO1	Piet Nortje
1986-1991	WO1	Tallie Botha
1992-1993	WO1	Tienie Geldenhuys

Photographic and picture credits

A book of this nature is brought alive by photographs and maps. I want to thank some very special photographers who contributed immensely in this department. The late Connie van Wyk took virtually all the photographs dealing with *Operation Savannah*. Jakes Jacobs, Willy Ward and Sybie van der Spuy contributed some photos dealing with the role of the Recces in the establishment of 32-Battalion after *Operation Savannah*. Piet Nortje and Eeben Barlow provided photographs covering Omauni and the Reconnaissance Wing.

Cloete Breytenbach, my brother and a well known photo journalist, provided some pictures. Hannes Nortmann and Mike Rogers gave me pictures of the battles on the Lomba River in 1987. Anton Hart provided pictures of other aspects Other photographs were taken by the unit photographer or by that prodigiously productive happy snapper known as 'anonymous'.

I wish to thank Madelain Davies for professionally refining my maps illustrating battles and campaigns.

Acknowledgements

I wish to express my humble gratitude to those who willingly shared their personal experiences of their service in 32-Battalion with me. This book is about them and the valiant and unselfish sacrifices they and others made to build the unit into the most elite infantry unit that the South African Army has ever had. They are listed in alphabetical order and certainly not in order of importance:

Eeben Barlow, Des Burman, the late Mac da Trinidade, TT de Abrieu,Michau Delport, Duppie du Plessis, Neall Ellis, Deon Ferreira (Falcon),Piet Fourie, Pierre Franken,the late Martin Geldenhuys, the late Harry Gilliland, Ken Greeff (Wing Nuts), Jan Hougaard, Jakes Jacobs, Heinz Katzke, Sister 'Sakkie' Korff, Koos 'Krokodil' Kruger, Louis Lombard, Dick Lord, Padre Middlemost, Gert Nel, Tony Nienaber, Piet Nortje, Hannes Nortmann, Willem Rätte, Johan Schutte, Sybie van der Spuy, John Taylor, Piet 'Boer' van Zyl, the late Pep van Zyl, Eddie Viljoen (Echo Victor and a special friend), Willy Ward and last but definitely not least, Peter Williams.

I also wish to thank three very special ladies. They are Cheney Lombard, daughter of Eddie Viljoen, and Elizabeth (Liz) Laubscher, a former Recce wife, who both faced endless difficulties in dropping everything to transcribe my writings on to computer in double quick time. Ros, my wife, had the thankless task of continually calling up chapters from the computer to allow me to fiddle with them until I was satisfied. (I am not at all computer literate!). I thank her for her patience and understanding, because I know very well that I can be a difficult customer at times.

The last female who requires mention is Katrolletjie, a member of the species *felis lybica*. While I wrote, Katrolletjie monopolised my only office chair, which forced me to use a hard kitchen chair to avoid arguments. Despite that, she uncomplainingly and firmly remained at her post, on my best chair, until the small hours of many mornings keeping me company and keeping my spirits up while I wrote.

Contents

Chapter		Page
	Picture Credits	5
	Officers Commanding/Regimental Sergeant Majors	5
	Acknowledgements	6
	Colour, black and white pictures and maps	9
	Bibliography	12
	Foreword	13
1	The reluctant staff officer	15
2	The training mission	19
3	Shaping the unit	24
4	Is UNITA the enemy?	29
5	Towards the furnace of war	34
6	UNITA: The first clash	38
7	Pereira de Eça	44
8	Attack on Sa da Bandeira	50
9	Moçamedes	59
10	Regrouping	66
11	Catengue	68
12	Cubal	80
13	Benguela	86
14	Marking time	92
15	Nova Redondo	98
16	Cela	110
17	*Operation Savannah*: Thoughts in retrospect	123
18	Legio patria nostra	128
19	Learning to be guerrillas	141
20	Guerrilla tactics pay off	178

21   Living by the sword   198

22   My goodbye to 32-Battalion   203

23   Jacks of all trades   211

24   And masters of war   222

25   Recce Wing   235

26   'This is my guerrilla battalion' . . . General Viljoen   242

27   32-Battalion to the rescue   254

28   Enjoy this war — the peace will be worse: *Operation Modular*, 1987 .   272

29   *Operation Hooper* and so on   299

30   Back behind the enemy lines   311

31   The Western Front   315

32   Move to Pomfret   326

33   A new kind of war   332

34   Bolt from the blue   338

35   32-Battalion disbanded   343

36   And they died by the sword   348

     32-Battalion: Roll of Honour   351

     Organisation and equipment:: Enemy forces   353

     Organisation and equipment:: Own forces   355

     Glossary/Abreviations   357

     Index   358

Colour, black and white pictures and maps

No apologies are made for the sometimes poor quality of illustrating photographs, most of which are unique, having been shot under adverse active service conditions some 25 years ago with inexpensive cameras by men who never pretended to be anything other than amateur photographers.

1   Instructors' Unimog — M'pupa, Aug 1975 161
2   Mortar platoon under training on old World War-II 3 inch mortars. Platoon Commander, Sgt 'Oupa' van Dyk, in front of mortars (right) — M'pupa, Aug 1975 161
3   Commandant Delville Linford, commander of Battle Group Alpha, Aug 1975 161
4   UNITA control point attempts to halt Battle Group Bravo. Pointing aloft distinguished UNITA from FNLA (thumbs up) and MPLA (V sign) — Artur da Paiva, Oct 1975 162
5   Little Cathedral — Pereira de Eça, Oct 1975 162
6   Sgt Oupa van Dyk's mortars stonking road running south from the former Portuguese Artillery Barracks at Sa da Bandeira — Oct 1975 162
7   Paratroopers with Battle Group Bravo familiarising themselves with a captured B10 — Sa da Bandeira, Oct 1975 163
8   Aircraft shot up during the attack on Sa da Bandeira Airport — Oct 1975 163
9   Taking on the defiles from Vila de Arriaga to Moçamedes. Author's Land Cruiser is immediately in front of this vehicle, fourth from the front of the column — Oct 1975 163
10   A FAPLA delaying position clobbered while en route to Moçamedes from Vila de Ariaga. Sgt Mechie van der Merwe's infantry platoon in the background — Oct 1975 164
11   Capt Jack Dipenaar's Bravo Company clearing the old airport at Moçamedes — Oct 1975 164
12   Lt Connie van Wyk's Alpha Company leaves to secure Porto Alexandre. Note the motley assortment of vehicles — Oct 1975 164
13   Lt Connie van Wyk's ambush east of Catengue. FAPLA prisoners dig graves for 40 of their less fortunate comrades — Oct 1975 165
14   (L to R) Chris Hillelvardt, unknown, Sgt Mechie van der Merwe, Lt Connie van Wyk. Knocked out FAPLA vehicle burns in the background — Oct 1975 165
15   Infantry with armoured cars in support clear Cubal — Oct 1975 165
16   Crowds welcome Battle Group Bravo on its arrival at Lobito. Note FNLA banner and Vickers machine guns — Oct 1975 166
17   Battle Group Bravo enters Lobito led by Maj Toon Slabbert's Eland armoured cars — Oct 1975 166
18   Lt Connie van Wyk in front of FAPLA's HQ in Lobito after its capture. Sgt Robbie Ribeiro is wearing the cowboy hat — Oct 1975 166
19   FNLA leader, Daniel Chipenda, attempts to motivate Bravo Group's FNLA troops north of Lobito. Capt Jack Dippenaar second from right with back to camera and AK47 slung over right shoulder, Oct 1975 167
20   Bravo Group's HQ in the 'Pink House' at Novo Redondo, Oct 1975 167
21   FAPLA ammunition truck shot out on road to Ebo — October 1975 167
22   After lifting mines contrived from enemy shells from a small bridge on the Blue Route to Gabela, Lt Connie van Wyk effects repairs — Oct 1975 168
23   G2 140mm artillery pieces sent to Angola by the SADF to combat the enemy's B21 Stalin Organ multiple rocket launcher — Oct 1975 168
24   Tony Dippenaar, 'The Surgeon of Cela', at work — Oct 1975 168
25   Gunboat of the Portuguese Marines abandoned at Vila Nova da Armada and taken over by Sgt-Maj Willy Ward. Shown on a supply run to M'pupa. 169
26   Alongside at Vila Nova. Willy Ward is on the bridge and Sgt Brian Walls is next to the crane. The rest were from the Engineer Corps who crewed the boat. 169
27   Sgt Maj Willy Ward's FNLA company at Vila Nova D'Armada. Morning PT 169

28   Sgt Maj Willy Ward and 12 black soldiers captured 13 ex-French Foreign Legion mercenaries and 70 UNITA troops with all their equipment including an armoured car, when they attacked Vila Nova D'Armada. Those with arms are Bravo Group soldiers and the rest are UNITA prisoners. Note the 106mm anti-tank guns etc mounted on the Land-Rovers — 1976 170

29   (L to R) Sgt Danny Roxo, Sgt Robbie Ribeiro, Sgt Brian Walls, Cpl Jan van der Merwe and Sgt Sierro. With captured Land-Rover and 106mm anti-tank gun — 1976 170

30   Commdt Sybie van der Spuy's company, posing as FAPLA, on a deep penetration operation within southern Angola — 1976 170

31   UNITA forces at the 906km peg on the Benguela Railway. Jonas Savimbi with his hand out and his foot on 906 — 1976 171

32   Bravo Group finally reestablish contact with UNITA. Epelanca (far left) and his men discuss future arrangements with the SADF liaison officer, Commdt Flip du Preez (right) — 1976 171

33   UNITA group before they were reequipped by the SADF. Note the variety of weapons, even including a shotgun — 1976 171

34   The troop lines at Buffalo Base before the barracks were constructed — 1976 172

35   The Omauni operational base south of Beacons 24 to 35. A flourishing herd of beef cattle was kept at the base and Bushmen, shown in the picture, were hired to look after them. Sgt Maj Piet Nortje is just above the left hand Bushman 172

36   Omauni's pub the Winged Stagger. The milestone was liberated from Ondjiva during *Operation Protea* 172

37   Author on operations with Sgt Maj Tony Vieira's platoon north of Beacon 28 in Angola — 1976 173

38   After the fight. Troopie of Sgt Maj Tony Vieira's platoon searches body of dead SWAPO guerrilla — 1976 173

39   Recce Wing operators in the Winged Stagger after an operation. (L to R) Leon Myburgh, Eeben Barlow, Coeni Riekert, Peter Williams. Note Peter's Afro wig for disguise purposes 173

40   Capt Eeben Barlow's Recce Wing group. Note the preponderance of machine guns for increased fire power 174

41   Butterfly operation. Helicopter deploying fireforce 174

42   Donkeys utilised for logistical purposes — *Operation Forte* 174

43   Some of the FAPLA trucks captured at Savate. Savate can be seen in the background — May 1980 175

44   Soviet-supplied assault bridge captured at Savate — May 1980 175

45   Captured SWAPO under interrogation — *Operation Protea*, Aug 81 175

46   Rifle company formed up for kit inspection at Buffalo Base 176

47   March past of 32-Battalion with company banners leading. Capt 'Buttons' Heyns right — Buffalo Base 176

48   Commanders of 32-Battalion. (L to R) (Author) Col Jan Breytenbach, DVR, SD, SM, Brig Gert Nel, SM, Maj-Gen Georg Meiring, SM (Commander SWA Territorial Force), Col Deon Ferreira, Col Eddie Viljoen, HC, SM — Buffalo Base 176

49   A UNITA air portable short wheel base Land-Rover armed with 14.5mm anti-aircraft gun. Part of a group of five, two with 106mm anti-tank guns and three with 14.5mms to defend them. 50 were supplied by the CIA 257

50   Crossing a river — *Operation Alpha Centauri*, 1985 257

51   Author and 'friend' on the Quando River before deployment to Cuito Cuanavale for *Operation Alpha Centauri*, 1985 257

52   Preparation for *Operation Modular*. 32-Battalion's anti-tank platoon's firepower is increased by the addition of 106mm anti-tank guns (in photo)and Milan anti-tank guided missiles — 1987 258

53   Preparation for *Operation Modular*. Experimenting with Milan anti-tank missiles. Mounted on a tripod so as to be clear of long grass, 1987 258

54   Preparation for *Operation Modular*. 127mm Valkyrie multiple rocket launchers mounted on Buffels congregate, 1987 258

55   Ratel armoured cars going into the attack on the Lomba River — *Operation Modular*, 1987 259

56   This missile Ratel knocked out three T55 tanks. One is brewing to the right on the flood plain — *Operation Modular*, 1987 259

57   Maj Hannes Nortmann (right) and Capt Mac McCallum, later KIA, examine knocked out Soviet-supplied T55 tank on the Lomba River flood plain — *Operation Modular*, 1987 259

58   Another knocked out T55 260

59   And another knocked out T55 260

60   A 32-Battalion Support Company's 81mm mortar in ambush position — *Operation Modular*, 1987 260

61   Cmmdt Les Rudman borrowed an idea from *Operation Savannah*. A Vickers wagon — three Vickers machine guns mounted on a truck — *Operation Modular*, 1987 261

62   A South African Engineer-built bridge over the Lomba River. A Ratel armoured car crosses to follow up — *Operation Modular*, 1987 261

63   South African G6 155mm self propelled gun in 32-Battalion's echelon area. Because of the enemy's air supremacy it fired only at night and afterwards moved at least 100km to avoid being pinpointed — *Operation Modular*, 1987 261

64   Command vehicle of Combat Group Bravo. (Sitting) Major Doep du Plessis, (centre) 'Doc' and Sgt Maj Mike Rogers — *Operation Modular*, 1987 262

65   81mm mortar Unimog crossing river — *Operation Modular*, 1987 262

66   32-Battalion OP on high ground north of the Calueque Dam watching for an anticipated Cuban advance on Ruacana — 1988 262

67   Pomfret from the air. The mine dumps containing the deadly asbestos fibres can be seen all around the base 263

68   Death of an elite Regiment. 32-Battalion forms up on parade at Pomfret prior to disbandment 263

69   Two indignant ex-lieut 32-Bn platoon commanders. Jan Kruger (lt) marched on 32-Bn's disbandment parade, addressed the parade in Portuguese and harangued the reviewing officer. Dr Bothes Bothma (rt) with the 30 pieces of silver that Dr Willie Snyman tried to give Pres FW de Klerk 263

70   The colours of 32-Battalion showing its battle honours 264

71   Troops tending the war cemetery at Buffalo Base where the majority of 32-Battalion's honoured dead lay buried. It is neglected now and the jungle is reclaiming its own 264

72   The leadwood tree stump showing 32-Battalion's Roll of Honour at Buffalo Base. It was later moved to Pomfret 264

Maps

1   Map showing Task Force Zulu's opposed advance of 3 000km into Angola in 33 days 111

2   The Western Front: Operations in Angola 1977-1983 244

3   Operations on Angola's Eastern Front, 1976-1988. Note: *Operation Modular* became *Hooper*, then *Packer* and finally *Displace* 300

4   The Western Front: Deployments and clashes around Techipa and Calueque: May-June 1988 317

Bibliography

The Buffalo Soldiers could never have been written without the contributions of a large number of people. I also delved into records and books by other authors in order to expand my background knowledge, especially as regards the Cuito Cuanavale campaign of 1987-1988 and the behind-the-scenes manoeuvring that affected all operations between 1975 and 1988.

Although I have not quoted from the books I consulted, I nevertheless gained valuable insights that helped to structure this book.

The drama of battle was particularly useful in highlighting a number of remarkable characters through their own battlefield experiences. *The War for Africa*, written by Fred Bridgland, gave me valuable information, especially regarding the tension that became evident between command groups at various levels. Fred wove personal experiences into his narrative in such a way that the various battles came alive with the noise, chaos and destruction always associated with armed conflict.

War in Angola, by Helmoed-Römer Heitman, gives a factual blow-by-blow account of each of the many battles fought during operations *Modular*, *Hooper* and *Packer*. The detailed analysis clarified my own mind and provided an impressive backcloth against which to spin my own account. I want to thank Helmoed for presenting me with a signed copy of his excellent book — some years ago!

The last book I wish to cite is a more recent one — *The Silent War* by Peter Stiff. Peter too presented me with a signed copy, for which I am grateful. This excellent book deals with Special Forces, but as the reader soon picks up when reading *The Buffalo Soldiers*, Special Forces were closely associated with 32-Battalion, especially in the beginning. What was a great help was Peter Stiff's detailed documentation of the shenanigans going on in political and diplomatic circles which preceded, accompanied and wrapped up all the various campaigns from 1975 to 1988. It makes for interesting reading, and sometimes, disillusionment like when the intelligence organisations of a number of countries rushed to get involved in a new 'Scramble for Africa'.

Foreword

The Buffalo Soldiers is the story of South Africa's 32-Battalion, forged in battle from black guerrilla irregulars and white South African officers and NCOs during the South African military intervention in Angola in 1975. It was destined to become the most elite infantry unit in the South African Army's order of battle — it also became its most controversial.

The author, Col Jan Breytenbach, was its founding commander.

It is a soldier's story about warring in southern Angola and Namibia and about the enemies that 32-Battalion fought. It tells of insurgency and counter-insurgency, guerrilla warfare and counter-guerrilla warfare, almost conventional warfare and conventional warfare. It tells of a conflict that the world regarded as unpopular and unjust and in which South Africa was perceived as the aggressor.

The South African soldiers who fought in it, however, saw it as a conflict aimed at stopping what is now Namibia from falling into the hands of the Soviet and Cuban-backed SWAPO black nationalist political organisation. They believed that after Namibia South Africa would be the next target. They saw the conflict as an extension of the Cold War, a war that was 'Cold' on the frontiers in Europe, but very 'Hot' war in Angola, in other parts of Africa and in South-East Asia.

The Buffalo Soldiers is effectively the story of how the South Africans fought the Angolan War, for there was scarcely a combat fighting action during its course that did not involve 32-Battalion.

'Battalion' was a misnomer for towards the end of the Angolan War 32-Battalion was more a mini brigade with two infantry battalions, an anti-tank squadron of Ratel armoured cars with 90mm guns and anti-tank missiles, two artillery batteries and an anti-aircraft battery.

With the collapse of the Soviet Union imminent the war was finally resolved in 1989 by the democratic solution of UN supervised free and fair elections in Namibia. Since then, regrettably, there has been interference by the ruling party with the democratic constitution put in place in there which has eroded much of that hard won democracy.

With peace in place in Namibia the unit was withdrawn to South Africa and deployed to combat MK infiltrations into South Africa. After the ANC's unbanning in 1990, its troops were redeployed to deal with political troubles, principally between armed ANC self-defence units and armed units of the IFP. The intrusion into the townships of black foreigners who were prepared to deal with the troubles robustly and without fear or favour, did not suit either the ANC or the IFP as they could not be subverted to support local causes because they held no local tribal allegiances.

This resulted in 32-Battalion becoming something of a bargaining chip at the CODESA talks where a new political dispensation was being sought for South Africa. Despite having borne the brunt of South Africa's war in Angola with the blood of its troops, the National Party Government, to its lasting shame, ordered its arbitrary disbandment in March 1993 as an act of political appeasement and 32-Battalion ceased to exist.

1

The reluctant staff officer

To my disgust I had been transferred to Army Headquarters in Potgieter Street, Pretoria as Staff Officer 1 (SO) Special Operations. I had never had a staff job before except for a short period when I was SO2 Training at South West Africa Command Headquarters in Windhoek. This occupation, however, allowed me to travel far and wide in the expansive interior of South West Africa to visit commando units, organise training courses and generally enjoy myself in remote parts of that country then rarely visited by westerners. It was not a staff job that kept me chained to a desk shuffling papers and browsing through dreary and dusty files to track down long-lost correspondence.

I like to think that my attitude to staff work was the same as that of Field Marshal Earl Alexander when he was posted as a colonel to a staff post at the War Office in London. He shared an office with another senior staff officer (SSO). Like his colleague, he would have a pile of files dumped into his In tray at the start of each day. Diligently the young Alexander would start at the top and work his way down the stack, but halt for a leisurely lunch and the usual tea breaks. His fellow SSO noted, however, that at the end of each day Alexander would transfer all the uncompleted files into his 'Out' tray, dumping them on top of the last one he had previously dealt with. One day he remarked to Alexander: 'You cannot do that ! You are supposed to deal with and sign off all the files before putting them into the Out tray.

'Oh', replied Alexander, 'you'd be surprised at how many of them don't come back!'

I had been the first commander of 1-Reconnaissance Commando, the unit which became the forerunner of the Special Forces Brigade. My time had been spent selecting and training Special Forces operators, deploying them as teams and often leading penetration operations deep into enemy-controlled war zones.

I developed an almost fanatical love for the African bush. Quite bluntly, I abhorred anything that smelled of civilisation, particularly the tidiness and political and military correctness of Defence Headquarters at the higher echelons. Senior and general officers went to work carrying briefcases bulging with papers, policy documents and classified reports. They were firmly trapped in the web of civil service red tape and the rat race of officialdom.

I also unashamedly enjoyed the challenges unique to Special Forces operations which were marked by mutual comradeship and respect with the most professional body of soldiers in the whole SADF — if not the world. For me it was the greatest honour to be an accepted Special Forces operator amongst a body of perfectionists. To be yanked out of that environment into the coldly calculated bureaucracy of Army Headquarters filled me with despondency.

My posting came through unexpectedly at the end of 1974 while I was on annual leave at the coast. For the remaining three weeks of my leave — as my wife will testify — I was a zombie sunk in gloom and despair. Soldiering had lost its appeal for me.

Early in January I reported to Army Headquarters to man my desk as SO1 Special

Operations. They gave me an office in what used to be the Officers' Mess in the days of the *Staats Artillerie* of the old ZAR (*Zuid-Afrikaansche Republiek*), overlooking the main square in front of Army Headquarters in Pretoria. The office was on the third floor and the only window was fitted with sturdy steel bars.

From behind the bars I could see the generals and brigadiers coming and going through the main entrance. They looked impressive in their red caps and red tabs as they waited for their drivers to open the rear doors of their black limousines, perfunctorily returning a salute before stepping out purposefully to do battle with their overflowing In trays. (It is a requirement to start practising the perfunctory salute the very day one is issued with a set of red tabs.)

I was not at all sure what my job as SO1 (Special Operations) entailed because nobody had told me. So I started to devise ways and means to escape from Headquarters as often as possible. I went to Durban to assess a somewhat disappointing crop of new combat divers. I initiated the development of a proper combat diving course and I organised and controlled joint exercises between submarines and the Recces.

I explored the area known as Hell's Gate on Lake St. Lucia as a possible venue for training the operators of 1-Reconnaissance Commando in bushcraft, minor tactics, survival, weapons, demolitions and so forth. To my mind, the new location of 1-Reconnaissance Commando on the Bluff in Durban was inappropriate. I have always advocated locating combat units, especially Special Forces-type organisations, right next to or in the centre of their training areas.

The fellow who coined the phrase, 'train hard and fight easy' hit the nail on the head. To my mind, a Recce could not really become totally bush-wise in the smoke, noise, crowds and traffic jams of a major seaport. A Special Forces soldier should be able to step out of his front door into a training environment where he can immediately, and with as few restrictions as possible, hone his combat skills. I tried to neutralise the foolish decision made by the powers-that-be to post the Recces to an environment that would cut the umbilical cord between Special Forces operators and the African bush.

Not surprisingly, I sought every opportunity to visit courses run by the Commandos in Fort Doppies, far away to the north in the Western Caprivi's tropical savannah. Fort Doppies, of course, was the ideal training area. The only problem was that it was over 1 500km from Durban. It was impossible to maintain the continuity essential to improving combat skills.

General Fritz Loots was my boss. He did not have much sympathy for my frustrations as I stood behind my barred window like a caged animal, viewing the goings-on and plotting my next escape to the Caprivian bush. In fact, he sent a Dakota to bring me back from Fort Doppies when I disappeared for three weeks into the depths of the bush without informing him. He then ordered me to stop sneaking off and to stay in my office, grinding away at staff papers. I had to be at his beck and call at all times. That meant being stuck almost permanently behind my desk for the foreseeable future.

One day a group of five officers and senior NCOs stepped into my prison cell. They too had been posted to Army Headquarters and were looking for a suitable office from where they could practise their obscure trade. They were a time-and-motion study outfit, bright-eyed and bushy-tailed. They asked me for advice on suitable office space. Obviously they were looking forward to reorganising the Army in order to make it more efficient as a fighting machine.

'Commandant, we have looked all over the place but we can't find a suitable office anywhere', their leader said.

'What's wrong with this office?' I asked.

'Nothing, sir, nothing at all', replied the enthusiastic young man. 'Does it mean that we can have it?'

'Yes, of course', I replied.

'But what about you, where will you go?'

'Well, I have decided that I do not need an office. You can have this one', I replied.

'When can we move in?'

'Right away', I said and got up from behind my desk. I pulled my red beret over my right ear as required by paratrooper custom and walked out. 'You've got a marvellous view', I said as I shut the door behind me. I did not have to clear out my desk or the filing cabinet as there was nothing to clear out. The fruit of my staff work over eight months or so had amounted to a fat round zero.

But I had to find a resting place somewhere. I strolled into the Army Operations Room in the same building, run by my old friend Commandant Gert Nel, my counterpart as SO1 (Normal) Operations. Gert was a stickler for form and did things exactly the army way. He was somewhat nonplussed when I asked his permission to become a squatter in his Operations Room.

'What's happened to your office?' he asked.

'I gave it to the time-and-motion study boys', I responded.

'But you cannot do that!'

'Never mind Gert. Just give me a place where I can park myself. I won't disturb you', I promised.

The Operations Room was a rather splendid place, just like those World War-II operations rooms portrayed by Hollywood.

Gert and his operations staff sat at desks on a gallery held up by thick wooden pillars on one side of a huge well. They looked down into the well at a number of large-scale maps pinned to three walls opposite and below them. Plotters on the floor moved coloured pins and tactical signs around as deployments and incidents occurred in the SWA/Angola war theatre, the Rhodesian war theatre and the increasing disruptions in South Africa itself. It was where the Chief of the Army and his generals, brigadiers, colonels, officers commanding the various commands and Joint Planning Staffs were briefed and did most of their planning.

I could see that there would be no resting place for me on the gallery. Gert would never tolerate me up there. So I moved into the well where I found a corporal sitting behind a desk, entering incoming and outgoing classified signals in four big ledgers. To his surprise, he found a Recce commandant politely asking for just enough space on his desk to park a cowboy book. The commandant would provide his own chair. With some apprehension he consented to this strange request.

After that the corporal and I shared a desk. He retained about 80% percent while I utilised the remainder as a rest for my book. Every morning at briefing time, which commenced promptly at 08:00, I would ostentatiously open my book, taking no notice of the corporal who would be diligently entering signals into his registers.

Gert would brief the generals and other senior officers, indicating a variety of coloured pins and symbols on the relevant battle map with a long pointer. It was his task to bring them up to date on the latest operational developments at the various fronts.

These very senior officers used to look at me askance. Why was a senior officer so absent-mindedly engrossed in a book amongst all the excitement engendered by the maps? Gert regarded me with unconcealed disapproval. I am afraid that I was the bane of his life. The same situation would occur again later in our careers.

One day in August 1975, Major-General Constand Viljoen, the Chief of Staff Operations, came into the Operations Room alone. He wanted to be briefed on the latest developments in the SWA/Angola operational area. Gert, as usual, went through the whole rigmarole of recent incidents — most of them to do with mines — together with the latest enemy and own forces deployments, deployments of FAPLA,

UNITA and FNLA, plus a host of other material that made up a well-conducted briefing. I sat there a few paces away engrossed in my cowboy book, not even glancing at General Viljoen or Gert as he droned on.

General Viljoen asked Gert questions. Some, as usual, were quite awkward. Satisfied at last, he turned around and spotted me incongruously tucked behind a small desk next to a corporal whose eyes barely cleared a pile of very thick ledgers.

'Jan, what are you doing here?' he asked.

'Sweet bugger all, General', I replied somewhat truculently.

'What do you mean by that?'

I could see that the general was displeased with my response.

'Well, General, as you can see, I have nothing to do', I continued a little more carefully.

'Come and see me in my office at 14:00', he snapped brusquely and walked out.

Gert was convinced I would get the chop, or at least a rocket of no mean proportions.

I reported to the general's office, saluted and, reassuringly, was asked to sit down. He had either forgotten my rudeness or was about to give me a long fatherly talk.

'How would you like to train some FNLA from Chipenda's faction?' General Viljoen asked unexpectedly. 'It would be inside Angola.'

My heart skipped. At last, at long last, I would be able to get out of Army Headquarters.

'Nothing I would like better', I answered. 'When do I start?'

'Right away', said the general. 'You are leaving for Rundu tomorrow with the Flossie (C-130 transport plane). Report to General Loots to plan your training requirements as far as personnel is concerned.'

That was it. I was a free man. With a spring in my step I returned to Gert Nel's Operations Room.

I collected my cowboy book, thanked the corporal for his sympathetic understanding and Gert for his sorely tried patience. I then walked down the passage to General Loots' office to wheedle some Recce operators out of him for my new mission. I would never have to polish the seat of an army office chair ever again — or so I thought at the time.

With General Loots strangely cooperative, I selected a number of Special Forces operators from 1-Reconnaissance Commando as my core of instructors. I chose 11 in all. That made 12 with myself. Inevitably, we became known as the second Dirty Dozen in Special Forces circles. The first Dirty Dozen were the founding operators who had founded Special Forces some years before. I had also selected and commanded them.

It remains a tremendous privilege for me that I led the men who laid the foundations for the two most remarkable units in the history of the South African Defence Force. The first, of course, was — and still is — the South African Special Forces Brigade. The second was the soon to be formed 32-Battalion — sadly no longer in the Army's order of battle.

2

The training mission

Seventy-five kilometres north-east of Rundu, capital of the Kavango homeland in South West Africa, lies a small former Portuguese marine base called M'pupa in southern Angola. It is on the west bank of the Cuito River, a short distance from the M'pupa Falls. The base marks the downstream end of the navigable stretch of river between it and another former Portuguese marine base, Villa Nova D'Armada, which is about three days travel upstream by gunboat.

Portuguese marines patrolled this stretch of water during the guerrilla war which lasted from 1961 until the beginning of 1975 when their own communist-infiltrated armed forces brought the Portuguese metropolitan government to its knees. They patrolled the Cuito River against UNITA and MPLA guerrillas who crossed in gangs from the uninhabited east bank to the populated west bank. Their purpose was to either intimidate the population to gain support MPLA fashion, or to spread their message by indoctrination — a more acceptable way. Initially, at least, this was how Dr Jonas Savimbi elected to spread his UNITA gospel.

There were, of course, numerous armed clashes between MPLA and UNITA, with the Portuguese administration surreptitiously supporting UNITA. The Portuguese rarely, if ever, launched operations against Savimbi's people. In fact, there are indications that they even supplied them with arms and ammunition in certain parts of southern and eastern Angola. Around the end of 1974 and the beginning of 1975, the MPLA in southern Angola, under the leadership of Daniel Chipenda, their FAPLA commander, began to have doubts about the MPLA cause. A leadership struggle developed between him and Augustinho Neto, the president of MPLA. This eventually culminated in most of the MPLA in the south and east breaking away and throwing in their lot with the FNLA. FNLA was commanded by Holden Roberto from the safety of Zaïre (now Democratic Republic of Congo). Chipenda's ex-MPLA, now FNLA, operated from the same power base in the south of Angola that they had established when they were still competing with Savimbi's UNITA. There was certainly no love lost between the two movements, although they both had begun to fight MPLA as the common enemy.

The sudden Portuguese abdication quite naturally brought about a power struggle among the three liberation movements — MPLA, FNLA and UNITA. Each movement was intent on gaining as much ground as possible before 11 November 1975 — the date the Portuguese would hand over the country either to a coalition or to the strongest of the three. With this in mind, Jonas Savimbi and Holden Roberto teamed up against MPLA which was, militarily, in a weaker position after Chipenda's defection with most of FAPLA — the MPLA's army.

With the help of tho communist-infiltrated Portuguese armed forces, Cuban assistance was obtained to restructure, re-equip and retrain what was left of FAPLA In a short space of time a large and well-equipped FAPLA army was deployed throughout central Angola, most of southern Angola and parts of the east and the north. It was backed by the first contingents from the Cuban army which started to arrive in Angola towards the middle of 1975.

The situation in southern Angola became chaotic with towns frequently changing hands between the contestants who were performing like three boxers in the same ring. It became difficult for the South Africans on the southern banks of the Okavango and Cunene Rivers to determine which troops from which movement they were facing across the border. They could not tell whether they were actively hostile or whether they were SWAPO supporters, passive or otherwise. Most were wearing Portuguese camouflage and many, from all three movements, carried not only AK47s but also G3s — the standard rifle of the Portuguese army which had somehow fallen into their hands.

To add to the confusion hundreds of Flechas, former Bushmen Portuguese soldiers, were drifting aimlessly across the countryside, trying to find a home with any of the three movements. Most ended up in a Chipenda's FNLA, mainly because this particular faction had developed into a fairly slick gangster mob which preyed on banks, businesses and, quite often, the unfortunate white Portuguese settlers. Money and loot were to be had with FNLA, whereas UNITA only offered a highfalutin idealistic cause and MPLA (FAPLA), the harsh discipline of their Cuban mentors and taskmasters. Often they just killed off the Bushmen as lackeys of the former colonial government.

On an exceedingly hot and dry August afternoon in 1975, I flew towards M'pupa with the mission of making contact with FNLA. I was not at all sure whether M'pupa was still in the hands of Chipenda's men. The latest information, which was several weeks old, indicated that FNLA was the most recent occupant but it had changed hands several times during the past year. It was with a feeling of some trepidation that we approached the base, shimmering in the dry afternoon heat at the eastern end of a dusty airstrip which had been hacked out of the bush by the former Portuguese garrison.

The pilot was Commandant Jules Moolman, expertly in charge of the twin-engine Aztec. His intention was to fly over the base at a height that would enable us to have a look at the flag. FNLA's colours were red, white and yellow. Unfortunately, though, there was insufficient breeze to even stir the limp rag hanging from a pole at the entrance to the base. We could make out the red, but we were uncertain about the yellow or the white. The UNITA flag was red and green, so it could easily have been a UNITA garrison in occupation. This would be bad news for us because at the time many SWAPOs (South West Africa People's Organisation — the terrorist organisation operating in South West Africa against the South African forces) were to be found in UNITA ranks. White throats would surely be cut, especially if we arrived unannounced. Then there was the red and black banner of the MPLA. They would consider it a great privilege to rid Africa of four white capitalists, three of whom were hated racists from the south.

The three of us, myself, Major Coen Upton — a staff officer from the Sector Headquarters — and Pelissa — an Italian farming in Angola and on friendly terms with Chipenda — would carefully approach the base on foot to determine, from a distance, which organisation was in occupation. In the event of a shootout or if the wrong people were in situ, we would rush back to Jules and his Aztec and hope for a quick takeoff before collecting too many holes in our persons or in the plane.

There was a stirring among the troops on the far side as Jules crossed the western threshold of the runway. He put the Aztec down in a cloud of dust and with a somewhat firmer application than usual of his brakes, brought the plane to a stop less than halfway down the runway. Although a bush airstrip, the Portuguese had built it long enough to take their lumbering Noratlas transport aircraft.

The three of us scrambled out into the blasting furnace heat while Jules ensconced himself on a wing with an Uzi sub-machine gun to cover our afternoon stroll towards the base. He kept the engines running. With false bravado, Coen and I went right and left respectively, rifles at the ready, keeping as much cover as possible between ourselves and the base. Pelissa, as big as a tank, strode majestically down the centre of the runway, armed with his walking stick and a ten-gallon hat squarely on his head. He was evidently unafraid or completely convinced that the troops approaching us from the eastern end were FNLA.

The troops had split into two sections of about eight apiece on each side of the runway. With a caution that matched our own, they approached the Aztec and the three advancing white men. They were all armed. The way they were carrying their weapons at the ready and darting from cover to cover did not exactly fill me with confidence that we were meeting with an enthusiastic bunch of future comrades-in-arms.

I was more than apprehensive. I felt the heavy cold stone of fear settling in the pit of my stomach and I developed a distinct inclination to lag behind the other two. A glance over my shoulder at Jules, squatting on the wing of the Aztec with the Uzi in his hands, did not reassure me either. Most pilots I know are pretty useless with small arms, even though they may be damn good with a rocket-slung Mirage strike jet. I found myself wondering whether Jules had the safety catch off and whether he had remembered to put in a fully loaded magazine.

Gradually the approaching blacks, mostly in Portuguese-type camouflage, leapfrogged closer and closer. Pelissa continued to stride casually along the hot dusty runway, swinging his cane. Coen and I moved forward in unison, but with reluctance on my part. How Coen felt, I had no idea.

Suddenly a figure better dressed than the rest and wearing a black beret and typical calf-length Soviet army boots, disengaged himself from one section and strode purposefully towards Pelissa.

Soviet boots!

Not a hopeful sign, but it did not seem to disturb Pelissa. In fact, he increased his pace until the two were at embracing distance.

'Pelissa!'

'Domingos!'

There was much hugging and backslapping in the centre of the runway, accompanied by a stream of Portuguese. There were also audible sighs of relief as Coen and I applied safety catches and slung our rifles.

The two sections gathered around Pelissa and Domingos, shaking hands and spouting away in Portuguese. Coen and I were introduced. Jules climbed back into the Aztec and taxied to the eastern end of the runway. Hopefully, he had re-applied the safety catch on his Uzi. We all walked to the base to meet the remainder of the FNLA garrison.

The base was filthy. The approach was through a several-hundred-metre wide minefield of human excrement through which one had to step very gingerly. Millions of flies swarmed everywhere and the stench was overpowering. Papers, empty beer bottles, plastic containers and all sorts of rubbish littered the camp and the living quarters.

The only place that was reasonably clean was the headquarters building with its two or three offices, each with metal desks and some rickety chairs. There was even a typewriter on which a soldier was banging away at some order of the day in the name of Chipenda, probably exhorting FNLA to fight to the bitter end. The barracks were sturdy prefabs assembled by the former Marine occupants from metal panels bolted together. They were, however, in a disgusting state with virtually every door and window pane broken.

In the south-western corner there was a pretty, thatched, white-washed chapel. It was, however not used for its original purpose, but rather as a store room for the few bits of equipment the garrison had acquired by fair means or by foul extortion. Priests and religion had departed from this benighted land long before.

Domingos was the commander of the 300 FNLA troops quartered in the base. More FNLA were arriving from the north and the west almost daily as they sought to escape FAPLA's and UNITA's depredations.

Pelissa wasted no time in explaining to Domingos that my arrival spelt the end of their military problems — that I had come to take command of the FNLA, train them and lead them in a victorious campaign to wrest Angola from MPLA's iron grip. But this was in Portuguese, of course, so it went right over my head. I smiled in the interest of friendly relations while nodding my head in apparent agreement. Domingos was delighted. He put his arm around my shoulders, clapped me on the back and chattered away in Portuguese. Likewise I clapped him on his back, spouted away in English, shook hands and generally felt pleased with the fact that Domingos was so well disposed towards me and that contact with FNLA had been effected with so much bonhomie and friendliness on both sides.

'There will now be a parade', said Pelissa in broken English. 'You must attend the parade.'

Well, I thought, a turnout by the troops for me, a South African officer— to pay their respects — would not be out of place. It would be an honour.

There was much shouting. From the shade of the stinking barrack buildings, a few hundred blacks rose reluctantly from the prone siesta position. After stretching and yawning, the gallant FNLA forces of Chipenda shambled off to the hot and dusty parade ground. They were formed up, with about 40 of their so-called *commandantes*, in crooked lines to one flank.

When all was more or less ready, Domingos invited me to accompany him onto the parade ground. We strolled off, out of step, to take up a position opposite the main body. Pelissa fell in behind my right shoulder, from where he could brief me about what was going on and act as prompter when necessary.

Domingos called the parade to attention and to present arms.

He saluted.

I saluted.

The troops came to the Portuguese Army stand-easy position and Domingos began to harangue his men. He was interrupted by shouts of 'FNLA, O Yea!', which I gathered was the FNLA battle cry. Occasionally I heard Chipenda's name mentioned and once or twice Holden Roberto's. Towards the end my name also began to feature. I had been given the code name 'Carpenter'.

I began to get a distinct feeling that the situation was getting away from me. Suddenly the speech stopped, the troops were called to attention, they presented arms and Domingos threw me a long salute.

'You are now in command of Chipenda's FNLA in southern Angola,' said Pelissa from behind my right shoulder.

I gulped. I had come to make contact and ended up with an army. What would I tell the brigadier?

I returned the salute.

'*Viva* Carpenter!' and 'FNLA, O Yea!' followed.

I looked at my army — all 300 of them. They were undoubtedly the scruffiest, most underfed, worst-armed and most unwarlike body of troops I had ever seen in my life.

On my left stood the reasonably well-fed and well-clad *commandantes*, all armed with brand new 9mm FN pistols which they had obtained from heaven-knows-where. Pistols, of course, are pretty useless in a high intensity war — unless one wants to kill oneself when things get tough and the outlook is gloomy.

In front of me stood the troops. The better clad and armed group that had met us on the runway was to my right. They had about 20 or so rifles of various makes among them — G3s, AK47s and a few FNs. The farther left my eyes traversed, the more desperate the future of my newly acquired FNLA command appeared.

Few of the troops had proper footwear. Some wore the ridiculous and uncomfortable high-platform shoes favoured by lay-abouts in Angolan cities at the time. Their clothes were equally exotic. Some wore yellow, red or bright green trousers with sharply contrasting brightly coloured shirts. Baseball caps were commonplace. Quite a number stared at me through reflecting sunglasses, concealing their eyes from my scrutiny.

Many were barefoot with ulcerating sores on their feet and legs caused by malnutrition. All had that grey look of hunger about them. Pelissa told me they were down to their last two bags of mealie meal.

In the rear rank I spotted a dozen or so Bushmen, impassively staring to their front and showing no interest in the proceedings. They were obviously former Portuguese Flechas who had joined the enemy they had once hunted so successfully. There was no other way for them or their families to stay alive. However, the FNLA cause held no attraction whatsoever for them.

What I saw brought to mind the famous incident when The Duke of Wellington inspected and addressed his motley assortment of troops before the Battle of Waterloo.

'You may not frighten the French,' he said, 'but by God you frighten me!'

Also, Wellington's troops were much better fed, equipped, trained and disciplined than my untried mob with whom, according to Pelissa, I was about to conquer all of Angola.

After the march past — more of a shuffle past really — I left the parade ground and was promptly congratulated by Jules on my newfound status and appointment. He was highly amused and so was Coen. Only Pelissa was not grinning as he extended his sincere congratulations. He had informed the garrison that I would feed, clothe and arm them as a matter of the highest priority. He instructed them to send word to all FNLA in southern Angola to gather at M'pupa where I would ring in a new dawn of FNLA conquests and power.

We took off from M'pupa with Domingos and the *commandantes* waving a cheerful goodbye to their new commander. They were no doubt visualising bags of mealie meal, tons of meat, beautiful camouflage uniforms and brand-new rifles rolling up the next morning from Rundu.

I sat next to Jules grimly pondering how to go about equipping, training and disciplining a mob of virtual gangsters. Worst of all, how would I break the news to the brigadier that I was now the FNLA commander and obtain the goods from him to keep Pelissa's promises?

Pelissa was smiling from ear to ear. He and FNLA were back in business — especially as he owned five farms in Angola, four of which he had lost to MPLA. He had every intention, with my unwitting help, of getting his farms back.

3

Shaping the Unit

Brigadier Dawie Schoeman was an elderly gentleman and a successful farmer from Western Transvaal (now North West Province). He could be as stubborn as a thorn tree. I suppose one must be stubborn to survive as a farmer in the uncertain conditions prevalent in that part of South Africa.

Schoeman was a reserve officer who had been called up for duty. He was a man with a mind uncluttered by the bureaucratic nonsense that seems to clog the brains of most professional officers. He got down to the kernel of a problem quickly, discarding all the sideshows along the way as unnecessary and time-consuming. He could make a rapid decision. But he could also be difficult, especially if one acted outside his concept of what an operation should be. Unfortunately, it was not always clear in which direction he was going. This was not so much because of his lack of communication, but rather because everything that happened in Angola was considered highly classified.

Apart from being told to contact FNLA and arrange for their training, I had no idea what the future held for us, for FNLA, UNITA or Angola in general. I assumed that we would provide training and military aid to FNLA so that they could stake their claim to as large a part of the country as possible before 11 November 1975 when, by decree of the Portuguese Government, Angola would become independent.

Aid to UNITA, by my reckoning, was out of the question since they supported SWAPO. SWAPO was our particular enemy because it killed South African troops and civilians on our side of the border. It followed that UNITA was also an enemy that had to be dealt with. The best organisation for that was undoubtedly the FNLA — or so I thought. I was to discover later that the brigadier and I did not quite see eye to eye on this matter.

Meanwhile, the report-back went unexpectedly smoothly. Apparently I had operated within the guidelines of the brigadier's operational plan. He thought it was a joke that I should be commanding a black FNLA unit of uncertain potential, after having previously commanded a crack Special Forces unit. Arms and equipment, including suitable combat fatigues, would be forthcoming. The first priority, food for the starving troops, would be attended to right away.

Some operators from 1-Recce Commando had already reported to assist me with the training. I also got hold of Captain Jack Dippenaar, a paratrooper, and promptly passed the buck to him. He had to arrange for the drawing of rations, get hold of some vehicles, then transport the food and vehicles across the river at night at some remote point where, hopefully, nobody could see what we were about. Finally, he had to deliver it to M'pupa before the troops starved to death.

The Okavango is a big river and even in August before the start of the rainy season, it holds enough water to make it unfordable. It also meanders a lot, looping about in a very wide flood plain with many side channels, horseshoe lakes and swamps. Crossing such a river with vehicles is a difficult challenge if no known fords or prepared crossing sites exist.

Jack managed to wangle the use of some ten-ton trucks on the Angolan side, but we had to supply the diesel. Nevertheless, an engineering effort using assault craft was still needed to deliver the food, arms and ammunition to the north bank of the river. Only when this had been successfully accomplished did the fun and games really start. The heavily loaded trucks were supposed to be moved across the flood plain to firmer ground and then onto the road leading to Dirico.

It was around midday the next day that a mud-encrusted Jack Dippenaar reported to me in Rundu. All his vehicles were firmly stuck in the soft turf of a wide-open plain. Curious Angolan povo (people) had gathered around to marvel at the tons of mealie meal, tinned meat and other luxuries they had never even dreamed about. They had never seen so much food in their lives, coming as they did from this very impoverished part of the Cuando Cubango. Speculation, probably tinged with some hope, was rife. We hoped they would show less curiosity about what lay underneath the rations.

Opposite Rundu on the Angolan side was the small town of Calai. It was later almost razed to the ground. A strong FNLA contingent lived there. They comprised politicians, a few troops and all manner of other shady characters who made their living by smuggling commodities from the Kavango into Angola. There was also a small UNITA presence but they were forced to keep a very low profile. In fact, some of the UNITAs spent time in the local FNLA jail on a regular basis. UNITA members also disappeared from time to time, especially after upheavals involving supporters of the two organisations.

Jack was despatched to see the FNLA political leader of the area — who also controlled the black market — to provide a tractor for pulling out the trucks. This he agreed to do if we would supply him with some extra drums of diesel for his Land-Rover and possibly for other more shady purposes.

For the rest of the day Jack and his men dug and pulled the trucks from the mud. They then set course for Dirico, at the point where the Cuito and Kavango Rivers converge, before turning north on the west bank of the Cuito for M'pupa. The going was better along the river banks than by the existing short cut through the bush — a deeply rutted sand track — from Calai to M'pupa.

I gathered the rest of my men two days later. We took the short cut using my Toyota Land Cruiser and a Unimog to carry our personal gear. Towards afternoon we arrived at our destination to be met by a still starving mob that had by then increased to something close to 500 men. Jack and the food trucks were nowhere in sight.

Domingos was unhappy. The last of the mealie meal had been eaten two days before and he was convinced that some of the men were on the point of turning their toes up. The troops were listlessly lying about in the shade. This did look ominous, but it might also have been dramatically staged for my benefit.

Jack had to be found quickly and the only means available was the Unimog. About 15km south on the road to Dirico the first truck was found. It was stuck in the sand, but with the help of the Unimog it was extracted.

Later on, towards sundown, the first rations to reach M'pupa in weeks were driven through the main gate. It was almost a small-scale repetition of the famous Malta Convoy when only one fuel tanker made Grand Harbour — the rest having been sunk along the way — just in time for the few freshly refuelled fighter planes to beat off a massive German bomber raid. In our case, of course, it was starvation that was kept at bay. In the cool of the evening the truck was enthusiastically off-loaded. The first bags of mealie meal and some tinned meat went straight to the cookhouse. It was not long before the men were filling their empty bellies with vast helpings of porridge and bully beef.

It was not long before eating became of secondary importance. As the troops filled up with the hastily prepared scoff, the noise level increased until it appeared, to me anyway, as if they were all conversing at once at the tops of their voices, each determined to make himself heard above the din. In the months ahead, this noise level, especially in the early mornings when they woke up, was to give me fits of near hysteria. We whites quickly moved off to Pelissa's house on the river bank where we were clear of the noise, the flies and the stench that polluted the main base.

Jack brought in the rest of the trucks over the next 24 hours. By then the men had virtually finished the food from the first truck. Reinforcements in the way of rations were more than welcome.

*　　　*　　　*

We organised the troops into companies, platoons and sections. There were sufficient troops for two rifle companies, each with three rifle platoons and a support company with a mortar platoon, machine-gun platoon and an anti-tank platoon.

Jack Dippenaar commanded Bravo company with three young Recce corporals as platoon leaders. Lieutenant Connie van Wyk, another Recce, commanded Alpha company with three former Portuguese soldiers as platoon leaders. Sergeant 'Fingers' Kruger commanded the machine-gun platoon and Sergeant 'Oupa' van Dyk the mortar platoon. They were both Recce operators. I was still short of a leader for the anti-tank platoon. I had no headquarters staff because no one could be spared. I made do with one radio operator — a South African of Portuguese extraction — and appointed one of the former FNLA *commandantes* as my intelligence officer.

This intelligence officer was an old hand at guerrilla war. He had been trained in the Soviet Union and North Korea and had been in the bush almost continuously since 1961. He was getting rather tired of fighting, so it was small wonder he fancied himself as a staff officer. Judging by the impeccably serviced condition of his well-used AK47, though, he must have been a formidable fighter in his day. His idea of compiling and evaluating intelligence was to go off into the bush and gather the necessary information himself, probably from the local population. He would sometimes disappear for days on end, then reappear with hair-raising stories about how SWAPO was virtually all around us.

It took me some time to realise that FNLA made no distinction between SWAPO and UNITA. They were also clever enough to play the South Africans off against UNITA by emphasising the SWAPO factor.

I left my old spy, the ex-bush fighter, to his own devices to build up a reasonable intelligence picture of the whole area, particularly along the Okavango River line. I felt that the river line had to be secured to ensure our logistics, and that we had to be able to pinpoint and eradicate any armed threat to our supply line before it could materialise.

I was already getting trouble from the Cuangar region where FNLA troops on their way to M'pupa had been waylaid and beaten up. Some had been killed. Cuangar, by all accounts, was a nest of SWAPO on the Okavango River about 150km upstream from Rundu. This also made it a real threat to South West Africa.

Another SWAPO nest, according to my spy, was at Mucusso. That was also on the Okavango River, about 150km downstream from Rundu. I was already, in my own mind, planning operations along the river to clear my back door as a first stage to further potential operations, depending on the brigadier's plans.

Farther west, opposite Ruacana in the Owambo area, the brigadier had launched a splendid little operation inside Angola during which quite a number of UNITAs, and presumably SWAPOs, bit the dust. It was clear to me, at least, who South Africa's enemies were.

My greatest priority was training. I was given just two weeks to get my battalion up to scratch. Fortunately, this ridiculously short period was extended later by several weeks. Nevertheless, this forced me to concentrate my training on only a few important aspects and to cut out not only the frills but some important subjects as well.

I concentrated on weapons training and the art of the attack only. We hoped that later we would have time to take the troops through the other phases of war and the nitty-gritty of minor and guerrilla tactics, not to mention the training of specialists like signallers, assault pioneers, drivers and, most importantly, medics.

In spite of a much shortened syllabus, training was still an immense headache. The troops were unfit, knew very little and had not yet been properly equipped with uniforms and weapons. Many of the *commandantes* refused to undergo training alongside the troops because, according to them, they already knew everything we could teach. Many of them left after we divested them of their weapons and sometimes their Land-Rovers. We badly needed both weapons and vehicles. I considered all equipment to be the common property of Chipenda's army, not the property of individual *commandantes*. They were none too happy anyway, having lost their former status and the perks that went with it.

The mortar platoon was equipped with old World War-II-vintage three-inch mortars. The yokes were well-worn which could result in shots going virtually anywhere — including occasionally at the target. Despite such problems and language difficulties, Sergeant Oupa van Dyk did a splendid job in training 12 mortar crews. He had a marvellous sense of humour and would regale us nightly on his experiences of the day with his somewhat slow and awkward mortar crews. Yet he never gave up. Of course some drills had to be modified, including one that he introduced to personally check the laying of each mortar before it could be fired for effect. Oupa became very fit, running constantly to each of the 12 mortar tubes, checking on every one while firing was in progress. Without those checks, the results could have been disastrous — not for the enemy but for ourselves — remembering the worn state of the weapons and the limited capability of the crews.

Sergeant Fingers Kruger reluctantly took charge of the Vickers machine guns. Very few infantrymen have a love for this obsolete weapon. It is heavy and cumbersome, has far too many stoppages and generally looks what it is — a relic from the trenches of World War-I. We had 12 of those weapons in the platoon.

Later, the feelings of myself and Fingers towards the Vickers grew firstly into a reluctant acceptance then, later towards the end of the campaign, to downright enthusiasm and respect for its firepower and the role it could play. Infantrymen primarily regard the Vickers as a defensive weapon, but in our scheme of things we had little scope for defensive capabilities. We improvised our tactics and drills to use the machine guns in a more aggressive role. We mounted them on the Land-Rovers confiscated from the *commandantes* and practised quick deployment to the flanks from which targets could be engaged to support the infantry attacking on foot. It was an impressive sight to see 12 Vickers machine guns stuttering away with fire converging on the target and tracers and dust engulfing the fictional enemy. Our troops arrived at the opinion that we could take on all comers.

Eventually brand new FN rifles and fatigue uniforms arrived. The troops were in seventh heaven with all this new equipment, particularly the uniforms and boots. At least they were starting to look like soldiers, although they still had a long way to go before they became real operational troops. The mortar and machine-gun crews were less than happy because they had been palmed off with World War-II Sten guns as personal weapons.

A Sten looks crude and is in fact crudely welded together. It was designed by the British as a stopgap weapon for partisans and is often more dangerous to the uninitiated than it is to the enemy. It has the nasty habit of discharging a round when the butt is slammed on the ground or against any hard surface. Over the years many an inexperienced soldier has come to grief because of this characteristic.

Training started daily with a cross-country run. This was followed by weapons training until about 11:00. Then came section, platoon and company attack drills. It was early September and extremely hot, so a siesta in the heat of the day followed from about 12:00 till 15:00. Further attack drills took place until about 18:00 after which came the evening meal. Then, more often than not, there was night training. It was a heavy day for everyone, including the troops.

As energy and stamina improved with the consumption of large quantities of good food and hard training, discipline began to get out of hand. The remaining *commandantes* were incapable or unwilling to mete out punishment because of the unpredictability of what might result. It was not beyond the realms of possibility that the whole lot could turn against us or just decide to desert and head back into the bush.

The troops had a habit of going down to the river during siesta time to wash, catch fish or just lie around. In spite of numerous inspections for loose ammunition, they would always manage to squirrel away some rounds. Without fail, every afternoon was punctuated by the indiscriminate discharging of rifles. Whether they were shooting at birds, fish or each other, I never really found out.

There is nothing that upsets an instructor more than the uncontrolled discharge of weapons. I persistently warned them to stop firing their weapons as it was making the instructors nervous — so nervous, in fact, that we might assume we were under attack by the enemy. However, this little talk did nothing to help. So I arranged for a machine gun to be mounted at our camp from where we could overlook the river area and M'pupa. In future, I decided, fire would be returned with interest.

The very next day, as expected, indiscriminate shooting started up down by the river. Fingers replied with a long burst from his Vickers, the tracers streaking over the heads of the troops washing or swimming. The river cleared within seconds and there was a deathly hush for the rest of the afternoon. Not a single raised voice could be heard from the main base.

For two or three days things seemed to be under control. Then the shooting started again. Again I told that them we might assume we were under attack, but the next time there would be an assault on foot into the area from which the shots were coming. At first it fell on deaf ears. Then one afternoon we were returning to our camp in the Unimog. Suddenly there was a lot of shooting to our right with bullets flying all over the place.

'Right, dismount and attack. Keep your fire low.'

There were eight of us and we spread out in extended line and moved into the thick bush in the direction of the shooting. At the right moment we opened fire, this time not bothering to shoot above their heads. With war whoops, shouting and much shooting, we closed in on the 'enemy'. Ahead we could hear branches breaking as they took off in panic. All shooting ceased abruptly. We swept through the area and, to my relief, found no bodies lying around. Maybe our own shooting needed sharpening up.

This was the last time we suffered the indiscriminate discharge of weapons. It was also good to see the sudden alacrity with which orders were carried out, combined with a general improvement in discipline. The whinging and whining stopped completely, except from some of the *commandantes*.

It was also when the troops' loyalty began to shift from the old to the new *commandantes*. They had discovered that we meant business and that we were serious about knocking an operational battalion together that would be fit to fight wherever required.

4

Is UNITA the enemy?

A new *commandante*, evidently senior to Domingos in the FNLA hierarchy, appeared on the scene. He was known as 'Double O' or Oginga Odinga, obviously a war name he had adopted as a sign of admiration for the radical Kenyan politician of that name. As we shall see later, this did not auger well for the future.

Double O, however, was more effective than Domingos in that he took firm control of the troops in the camp. I appointed him as base commandant with the mission of cleaning up the place, administering it, seeing to the distribution and preparation of rations and generally maintaining discipline. He took no nonsense from anyone. At times he could be harsh. I am certain that he would have shot one or two culprits had we not been around to prevent it. He carried a big stick which made painful contact with many an FNLA bottom or back. I was personally satisfied with Double O in spite of his war name.

He brought with him additional FNLA troops, which allowed me to form a third company. I gave the command of the new Charlie company to Staff Sergeant Costa Marão, a Portuguese national and a former member of the DGS (Direcçáo-General de Seguranga — Director-General of Security, formerly PIDE (Polícia Internacional e de Defesa do Estado — International and State Defence Police). I took two of Connie van Wyk's platoon leaders, Sergeants Danny Roxo and Silva Sierro — another ex-DGS member — both Portuguese nationals, away from him and gave them to Costa Marão. To make up the deficit, I re-allocated a platoon leader from Jack Dippenaar's company to Connie van Wyk's. This left each of the three companies short of a platoon leader.

Over the rutted sand track from Calai in the south came a number of Land-Rovers and Land Cruisers, even a tractor, driven by a motley crew of former Portuguese troops. Pelissa, who had not been with us for a while, was leading the procession. He had returned to permanently re-occupy the house on his only remaining farm in Angola. He was accompanied by a young, black woman who turned out to be his common law wife. She was related to Chipenda, which accounted for Pelissa's close relationship with the FNLA leader.

The crew that came with him, about six or seven of them, looked like gangsters disguised in Portuguese camouflage. They were armed with AK47s, M1s, Berettas and even an Armalite or two. I discovered later that they were, in fact, truly gangsters who, under Pelissa's leadership, had robbed several banks in Nova Lisboa, Angola's second-largest city to the north. They served as Pelissa's bodyguards. He intended to expand his nefarious operations in south-eastern Angola. At the time, ivory and animal skins were available in abundance in those parts, as well as an inexhaustible supply of teak. Pelissa, by getting in first before any other returning Portuguese refugees could make a move, had staked his claims to many of the bountiful treasures in the region.

His eagerness to get training under way suddenly began to make sense. As the days passed I detected obvious signs that Pelissa's main concern was to secure south-eastern Angola for the FNLA and, in the process, for himself. He frequently interfered with the training and began to drop hints that we should consider driving the MPLA and UNITA out of the region. This, he reasoned, should secure Mavinga to the north-east, Vila Nova da Armada and Cuito Cuanavale upstream from M'pupa and even Rivungo on the Quando River.

At the time, we were installed in a wing of Pelissa's house while his wife and his foreman, D'Oliviera — rumoured to be his wife's lover — occupied the other wing. His bodyguards slept on the wide gauze-enclosed verandah.

Our personal rations began to disappear and invariably seemed to end up in Pelissa's kitchen. The wife made it plain that she objected to our presence. Pelissa's ill-fed bodyguards began to sponge on us. They claimed that Pelissa had failed to pay or feed them. While we felt sorry for them, our rations were insufficient to add them to the ration roll.

D'Oliviera also made things unpleasant and refused to attend to minor mechanical problems on our vehicles. Pelissa, by then, had re-opened and re-equipped his farm workshop with equipment and tools that he had no doubt looted from somewhere.

The last straw was the theft of our dieseline which we had kept at the house to refuel our vehicles. This prompted us to move out and re-establish ourselves in an old hunting camp, Coutado de M'pupa, which was across the Cuito River about four kilometres downstream. To get there meant crossing the river on a ferry which was propelled by ropes pulled by hand.

Already ensconced at Coutado de M'pupa was a former professional hunter together with his mulatto wife and two very naughty children. He bore the old Afrikaans name of Van Dyk, but he was Portuguese speaking and could speak neither English nor Afrikaans. He was obviously a descendant of the Dorsland Trekkers who had arrived in those parts in the latter part of the 19th Century.

We moved into two of the huts and arranged to supply Van Dyk with diesel and rations provided he shot the odd antelope to supply us with fresh meat. We had become somewhat tired of tinned food. Pelissa and his gang had already forcibly requisitioned Van Dyk's one and only drum of diesel, so he could no longer pump water from the river or run his Land-Rover. This ensured that during our stay in M'pupa, we had willing co-operation from Van Dyk and his family. Mrs van Dyk even made a point of baking delicious Portuguese paos (bread buns) for us and laundered our washing.

The last FNLA official to arrive was João accompanied by his common-law wife. They were both mulattoes. João was higher up in the FNLA hierarchy than Double O, so theoretically he should have replaced him. I could see, though, that he did not have it in him to control the troops and that they would probably resent him because of an irritatingly superior pose he adopted. I appointed him as my second-in-command, but retained Double O as camp commandant. João was allocated no particular duties. All he had to do was look important, which he did very well, and act as spokesman between myself, Pelissa and any other senior FNLA leader who might pitch up at M'pupa.

Shortly afterwards an Aztec, similar to the one flown by Jules, arrived unexpectedly at M'pupa. Unusually, it had come from the north and not the south. We rushed to the airstrip and met a rather large and sweaty African who introduced himself as Chipenda. Accompanying him was Kambuta — the party secretary of Chipenda's FNLA, an American called Cameron and a white Portuguese pilot. I had met Kambuta once or twice before in Rundu at conferences when the training and equipping of FNLA was discussed.

It was the first time I had met Chipenda. He looked impressive and was evidently an eloquent speaker. He also liked his whisky and reportedly suffered from high blood pressure, probably because of his love for wine, women and song. Kambuta introduced Cameron and we had a short but interesting exchange of words.

'I am sure Cameron is not your real name and no doubt you are CIA', I remarked rudely.

'Nor is your name Carpenter and, no doubt, you work for military intelligence', Cameron replied wryly.

Well, he was wrong as far as Military Intelligence was concerned.

Pelissa, not surprisingly, had arrived at the aircraft before us. We moved to the coolness of his house to discuss future plans. The conversation between Chipenda and myself amounted to very little because neither could speak the other's language. I gathered from Kambuta, though, that Chipenda had brought Cameron along to persuade him that American support of FNLA (Chipenda faction) was worthwhile.

In my discussions with Cameron, I gathered that US President Gerald Ford was supporting Holden Roberto. Cameron had direct access to Ford through US Secretary of State, Henry Kissinger. Cameron also said he could arrange the delivery to me of a module of weapons, ammunition, clothing and rations for 1 000 men for a period of six months. M'pupa airstrip was ideally situated to allow the delivery in total secrecy of supplies from Zaïre by C130 aircraft.

I accepted the proposal with alacrity. This was the first time I became aware of America's involvement with Holden Roberto's FNLA. I discovered that Roberto had been the US' long-standing protégée during the bush war against Portugal and that they were backing him as the future leader of an independent Angola.

Discussions were followed by a parade of my FNLA battalion. This time the troops were formed up less raggedly, in relatively straight ranks and with a more soldierly bearing. Increased rations had filled them out and the greyness of their skins had disappeared. The new uniforms and weapons must have impressed Chipenda because he launched into an impassioned speech. I gathered from João that he promised a new dawn for Angola, death to all FNLA's enemies, freedom of speech and religion, a capitalist society and the rest — in short, the typical speech of most African political leaders.

There were numerous 'FNLA, O Yeas!'

Chipenda beamed at me in farewell and headed for the Aztec. He was obviously proud of his new-look army. The party took off and disappeared to the north.

I neither saw nor heard from Cameron again.

I wrote a report of the visit and got a real stinker in reply — not from the brigadier, but direct from Pretoria.

'Who gave you the right to approach the Americans for aid or even to make contact with them?'

The fact that they came to see me and that I had not even known of their existence somehow escaped Pretoria's attention. I was firmly told to get on with my training and leave the negotiations with outsiders, especially the Americans, to people who knew what they were doing.

The promised equipment, in spite of my subsequent discreet enquiries, never materialised. I was in particular need of decent mortars, light machine guns, M79 grenade launchers and anti-tank weapons.

Whether it was my inadvertent contact with the Americans that killed the project or whether the Americans were not too impressed with my battalion, I never found out. I have a feeling that the Americans' close involvement with Roberto, to the exclusion of Chipenda, clinched the matter in the end. No doubt our promised supplies went to Roberto's FNLA, trained by a bunch of hooligan mercenaries who then led an abortive and morally disreputable invasion from the north. Cameron would have done far better for the CIA if he had kept his promises to us.

My intelligence officer reported some alarming news. UNITA was planning to take over Calai by force in the next day or two. They would advance from Cuangar, using the UNITA garrison there.

It was known that Johnny Katale, Cuangar's UNITA commander, was also a SWAPO officer. He had been diligently expanding SWAPO's influence in the Mpungu Vlei area of the Kavango just across the river. The South African Security Police were interested in Johnny and his activities. Curbing his influence would not only keep my back door, via Calai open — it would also remove the source of all SWAPO's influence along the river line.

The FNLA-supporting inhabitants of Calai were in uproar because if Katale succeeded in taking the town, indiscriminate slaughter would result. I dispatched Jack Dippenaar with his company and half my machine guns to secure the place against attack. I also informed my headquarters of what I was doing.

I followed Jack in my Land Cruiser. Calai was a small town surrounded by kraals. There were numerous approach routes from the east, west and north that the enemy could use. Adequately defending the place posed quite a problem. After conducting a general reconnaissance of the area, we discussed possible solutions to the defence problem. Finally we decided to ignore the outlying kraals and base the defence on the inner core of Calai itself. Platoon positions, each with a Vickers machine-gun section in support, were established to the east, north and west. A small reserve was formed. Flanks could be properly tied in because the perimeter was small enough for a single rifle company to defend.

Satisfied with our handiwork and our initiative, I crossed the river to Rundu to make a final report to the brigadier. He appeared to be disturbingly offhand about my deployments and my arrangements in general. In fact, after I had spoken to him, he completely ignored my report and began to tell me about the SADF supporting UNITA. Amongst the officers with him were Commandants Phillip du Preez and 'Kaas' van der Waals, an old friend from paratrooper days.

The discussion turned to the planning of an air supply of brand new 81mm mortars, rifles, light machine guns and so on to UNITA. They would be delivered to the airfield at Silva Porto where Kaas would be going to act as liaison officer with Savimbi. I was unhappy about this because I needed some of that equipment — particularly the mortars — for my own troops.

It became obvious that somewhere along the line FNLA had become of lesser importance than UNITA. Having been isolated and fully occupied with training at M'pupa for the past month or so, I had lost touch with the bigger picture of ongoing developments in Angola. My protestations about the alarming information that UNITA was supporting SWAPO made no impression on Brigadier Schoeman. Savimbi had become the new star in the firmament while Chipenda's was waning fast. The official outlook had shifted to the view that he was a gangster pretending to be a freedom fighter.

I could only agree with this assessment, but the battalion I commanded was rapidly being shaped into a genuine fighting force. Furthermore, the FNLA troops were swinging their loyalties to their new South African commanders and rapidly losing their attachment to the old order.

I stopped at Calai on my return trip to M'pupa. I decided to keep the troops there in position just in case Johnny Katale decided to go ahead with his plan to oust FNLA from the town.

At M'pupa we stepped up the training, especially that of Charlie company and the anti-tank platoon. For the latter, I had found a commander from amongst Pelissa's bodyguards who had decided to desert him and join our cause.

Shortly afterwards I received another summons to report to Rundu. This time I flew there and landed at the air base late one afternoon. Brigadier Schoeman was not available but I was told that Colonel Corky van Heerden wanted to speak to me.

I found him in the officers' quarters lying on his bed. From this prone position he proceeded to give me the most remarkable briefing of my military career. Combat Formation Zulu was in the process of being put together. It would be made up of two battle groups, Alpha and Bravo. Battle Group Alpha would comprise a battalion of mostly former Portuguese army Bushman Flechas commanded by my good friend Commandant Delville Linford. Battle Group Bravo was the new name for my FNLA battalion. Zulu would be used to launch an invasion into southern Angola within a week. Its task was to seek out and destroy the MPLA.

Operation Savannah was about to begin. UNITA would not, after all, be the enemy but our ally in this venture.

5

Towards the furnace of war

I told Captain Jack Dippenaar to stand down his company in its mission to defend Calai against a UNITA attack. Instead they were to concentrate on the northern bank of the Okavango River, directly opposite Rundu on the South West African side. I briefed my other company commanders and the FNLA *commandantes* as far as I could, allowing for the security aspects of the operation.

There were several long faces amongst the *commandantes*. One has to remember that less than a year before they had been part of FAPLA, the military wing of MPLA. Now they were about to be launched against their old comrades-in-arms instead of against UNITA which to most of them was still the real enemy.

My FNLA intelligence officer gave me a graphic description of FAPLA's strength, especially around Sa da Bandeira. It was there that the mysterious 122mm Stalin Organs, later to become known to us as Red Eyes, were deployed on high ground from where they could engage approaching forces at a range of at least 20km. These rockets, he assured me, were capable of killing anything from 50 to 100 troops on impact. I had vaguely heard of the 122mm Katyusha rockets, but knew nothing of their capabilities. I was nevertheless impressed by my intelligence officer's assessment of what we could expect. I looked at my platoon of old British three-inch mortars which could possibly reach 1000 metres. Understandably, I felt somewhat apprehensive about our chances. So, it seems, did some of my *commandantes*. Double O came to see me. He had received word that his son had died in Mavinga. Could he go there to sort out problems with his wife and family, bury his son and join us later, maybe at Sa da Bandeira?

Domingos wanted to go up river to say goodbye to some friends.

I never saw Double O again, although he would appear later in the Mavinga area and cause us numerous problems and some grief.

Unbeknown to Domingos, our departure was postponed for 24 hours. He turned up in his Land-Rover at M'pupa on the day of our departure, fully expecting that we had gone to war without him. He was somewhat surprised to find we were still there and not a little put out when I confiscated his Land-Rover for use by my anti-tank platoon. I left Domingos, who was obviously unwilling to go to war, in charge of the sick, lame, lazy and other non-combatants at M'pupa base. Already some dependants of the soldiers were settling in the area.

Domingos was frankly unhappy about his association with Battle Group Bravo. It was not from a lack of fighting spirit, but because he could not regard MPLA as the enemy. Later in the unit's history, he would come to the fore as one of my best platoon sergeants and prove himself a courageous fighter against SWAPO and FAPLA — his erstwhile comrades-in-arms.

The brigadier's staff had bought some civilian trucks from the Portuguese refugees. Many were stranded on the SWA/Angolan border with worthless Angolan escudos in their pockets and no means of paying their fares to metropolitan Portugal. By all accounts, these unfortunates were dealt with fairly by the South African Army, inasmuch as they were given reasonable prices in South African rands for their vehicles. At a later stage there would be much exploitation of similar helpless refugees. In their desire to leave Africa — after having suffered untold miseries and abuse at the hands of all three Angolan liberation movements — they took whatever was offered as long as it was in South African rands. Some refugees from deep inside Angola had started out with all their household goods loaded in their trucks. But by the time they arrived at the SWA border, they had nothing, having been robbed at roadblocks of everything but the clothes they were wearing.

As the families made their way southwards, it was usual for mothers and daughters to be raped at the check points, almost as a drill. While all this was going on, the Portuguese Army, under orders from its new communist-leaning superior officers in Portugal, disgracefully maintained a hands-off posture. Nowhere did they even lift a finger to protect their citizens from the undisciplined liberation movements who had gone mad with an insatiable lust to rob, rape, beat up and kill the former Portuguese colonists.

From such sources we acquired some splendid ten-ton, six-wheeled four-wheel drive trucks as unit transport. But we had become motorised on paper only, because we still had to collect the vehicles from Rundu. The brigadier sent a fleet of Unimogs to move my troops from M'pupa to the concentration area at Calai. In due course, close to 600 FNLA soldiers, equipped with brand new rifles and suitably attired in jungle-green fatigues, concentrated just across the river from Rundu. It was a point where many of the houses in Rundu were grouped together on the edge of a cliff that overlooked the Okavango River.

Because of a plethora of rumours and counter rumours during the past year about the ongoing conflict in southern Angola, the already nervous folk in Rundu could never be sure who was in occupation of Calai on the opposite bank at a given time. Understandably, for security reasons, they knew nothing about our imminent advance into Angola. Needless to say too, they were somewhat alarmed when they saw hundreds of unidentified black troops camping on the far side of the river.

With the black man's complete disregard for modesty, some ladies found it difficult to enjoy tea and cakes on their shady verandahs while the troops were bathing right under their delicate noses. I was summoned to Rundu Headquarters and told to move my mob away from the river and out of sight of the worthy Rundu burghers and their womenfolk. I was also told, in no uncertain terms, that South African troops would be deployed along the river bank and if any of my troops set a foot across the river on to South West African soil, they would promptly be shot.

So, except for the crazy few of us who were serving with them, Battle Group Bravo did not start the war with the South Africans holding them in high esteem. We had, however, come to regard the men with paternalistic fondness, so we were highly indignant at the obvious prejudice being directed against our new unit. I sought out the brigadier, complained to him and assured him that our troops were under disciplined control. Despite this I deemed it prudent to move them away from the river bank into an area of thick vegetation where the inhabitants of Rundu could not see them without using binoculars.

My biggest problem, though, had nothing to do with Rundu. It was keeping them away from the *kimbos* (kraals) around Calai. A pass system was adopted and patrols were mounted to police the area. This enabled us to keep contact between the troops and the local povo at a manageable level. It also ensured that no troops would be missing when we finally moved out.

It was a dark night when engineers rafted loads of rations and ammunition across the river to ready us for our march to the north. The engineering officer in charge had no idea of the identities of the white soldiers he was conferring with on the Angolan bank of the Okavango. I knew him well, but I deliberately spoke in broken English and he could not see my face because it was so dark. It was clear from what he said in Afrikaans to his own men that he believed we were Portuguese mercenaries. He was not at all flattering and it was clear he had no respect for the Portuguese as a fighting nation.

After this resupply, plans were finally made to move the Zulu invasion force westwards along the river to Katuitui. It was there that the Okavango River in its southward flow crosses into South West Africa. That would be the start point for the invasion. I had sufficient vehicles in Angola to transport Jack and his company to Katuitui via Cuangar. The remainder of Battle Group Bravo crossed the river into South West Africa early one morning. From there they were loaded into trucks and transported west along the course of the river to our start point.

I gave Jack Dippenaar strict instructions not to pick a fight with Johnny Katale and his UNITA at Cuangar as they were now our allies. If need be, Jack was to bypass Cuangar. As it turned out, Katale and his men were probably overwhelmed by the sight of Jack's company and the rest of Battle Group Bravo passing through town, FNLA banners flying and the troops mockingly singing FNLA songs at full blast. All the trucks were festooned with FNLA banners and FNLA songs could be heard up and down the convoy. Fortunately, nobody took it into their heads to fire the normal joyful shots into the air — a custom so prevalent only a few short weeks before. It appeared that our often crudely enforced discipline had begun to show positive results.

The population of Kavango was astonished. It must have come as a rude shock to see hundreds of well-armed Angolan soldiers driving through their country and behaving as if it belonged to them. Perhaps they thought that the war in Angola had gotten out of hand and that the FNLA had decided to invade South West Africa. In any event, they stood gaping alongside the road, some waving tentatively. Most, however, were clearly apprehensive as to what the future held for them. They regarded themselves as a neutral and peace-loving nation that wanted to remain aloof from the triangular civil war brewing north of the river.

We arrived at Katuitui late that afternoon. Jack had left the previous evening but he was nowhere in sight. This did not particularly worry me as the road on the north bank was atrocious and we had received no indication that he had met with trouble at Cuangar. We pulled off the road and prepared a night laager. It would be our last on South African-controlled territory for a long time.

Zulu Headquarters, comprising Colonel Corky van Heerden and his principal staff officer responsible for operational planning, Commandant Willie Kotze, arrived.

Delville Linford turned up with his Bushmen. The Bushmen clutched their rifles somewhat more tightly when they came face-to-face with their old enemies from the Portuguese war — my FNLA ex-MPLA troops. Many, I am sure, surreptitiously eased off the safety catches of their rifles, in case it turned out to be an elaborate ruse designed to decimate the formerly much feared Flechas of Battle Group Alpha. They obviously believed that their own white officers just did not understand and had been taken in by the wily 'long feet' — the name the Bushmen gave to all black African tribes who normally exploited them cruelly.

Delville had his work cut out convincing his men that my black troops were really on their side; that the force encamped opposite them was not FAPLA but FNLA. In this new war, only FAPLA was the enemy — no one else. Carpenter, they were told, would ensure that his troops kept their fingers off their triggers. Relax, Delville told them. FAPLA, the real enemy, still lay ahead to the north.

This FAPLA/FNLA/MPLA business confused the Bushmen thoroughly. Delville's explanation cut no ice with them either. An enemy remains an enemy forever and a friend remains a friend forever. There could be no compromise. They probably felt that the white men of Bravo Group should be pitied because they could not see the error of their ways. They found it difficult to believe that myself and a handful of whites would be foolish enough to go to war with 600 'terrorists'. They were convinced that my white officers and I would pretty soon end up getting our throats cut.

Our last evening was spent with Commandant Vossie Nel who was in charge of a refugee camp in Angola north of Katuitui. He invited the officers of Zulu Headquarters and Alpha and Bravo battle groups to dine with him. Vossie, with a few National Servicemen to help him, was responsible for feeding the refugees, providing them with medical attention and handling their documentation while they awaited passage to Portugal or for permission to settle in South Africa. Hundreds of Portuguese refugees clamoured for his assistance and his undivided attention. They frequently resorted to bribery in an attempt to speed up the processing or to secure an outcome favourable to their application. It was a thankless job.

Vossie had a tented camp on high ground overlooking the river. We arrived for dinner to find tables beautifully laid with silver, wine glasses and folded white napkins — an unheard of luxury when out in the African bush.

While we were enjoying pre-dinner drinks, a blonde vision in a white evening dress appeared from a tent and floated towards us. It turned out that Vossie had an attractive young nursing sister to assist him in his onerous work. She later became famous as the Angel of Calai. After a moment of stunned silence we recovered from our surprise. She immediately became the centre of attention and the men swarmed around her like bees around the proverbial honey pot. Delville, in his own inimitable style, soon staked out sole claim to this delectable distraction. The rest of us resumed our pre-dinner beers, ragging Vossie about the difficulties he faced while executing his assignment while poor fellows like us had to be content with dust, flies, FAPLA and other miseries.

Inwardly, though, we felt superior and thankful that the powers-that-be had not seen fit to saddle us with a bunch of Portuguese refugees. For us it would be the smoke and flames of the battlefield. The more wine we consumed, the mistier our eyes became in anticipation of the heroic battles ahead. For most of those present, it would be the first time they had seen a shot fired in anger.

The next morning we mounted our vehicles and commenced the invasion. Battle Group Alpha took the lead. We followed the track northwards to Caiundo, through the Portuguese refugee camp just beyond the border. The inmates turned out in their hundreds to cheer us on to victory, many shouting out slogans like 'Death to FAPLA and communism.' Perhaps they had visions of South Africa restoring Angola to them and with it, the pleasant life they had led as colonisers.

By then everybody, except for South Africans back home, knew that we were invading Angola. The Portuguese refugees had not been fooled and after a day or so, neither were the surprised inhabitants of the Kavango. South Africa, for the second time in its history, was invading a foreign territory. (The first invasion occurred during World War-I when the Union invaded the then German South West Africa).

6

UNITA
The first clash

When barely across the border we stopped near a place called Catambué. Delville Linford was having problems on the flood plain of the Okavango River in the area of Tandaue. The road between Caiundo and Katuitui had been under construction when the Portuguese pulled out of Angola, dropping their tools as they went. Fortunately, they left behind a perfectly sound bulldozer which Delville appropriated to pull his trucks through the thick mud of the flood plain. He was trying to bypass a particularly sandy and treacherous-looking stretch of road.

Disenchanted and frustrated, we walked up and down the river, had a wash and contemplated a swim but decided against it because of crocodiles. We also investigated a firewater still which the proprietor had abandoned when he saw hundreds of fierce-looking FNLA troops descending on his *kimbo*. Freshly picked monkey oranges and nuts, commonly used in local distilling, were scattered about. Unfortunately for us, there was no sign of the finished product. Some of my troops had probably got there first and liberated the stuff.

Colonel Corky van Heerden and his headquarters pulled up. His was quite elaborate compared to my mine, but it still seemed rather scant to perform the functions of a brigade headquarters. In addition to Willie Kotze — his principal staff officer — and a gunner, he had Shylock Mulder — his logistics officer — and an engineer. Dave was his intelligence officer.

At Pereira de Eça a communications officer, Major 'Uncle Sarel' Kruger, and a driver fluent in Portuguese and English joined Zulu. At Sa da Bandeira, Major Dries van Coller plus an assistant replaced Dave as the intelligence team. They had a very useful retired PIDE inspector attached to them as an interrogator. PIDE was known to be good at interrogation, but their methods were questionable. At the same time Captain Piet van Heerden took over from Shylock as logistics officer.

My headquarters comprised myself and Paul, my Portuguese-speaking radio operator-cum-driver. In wartime establishment tables, such individuals are classified as driver/operators or driver/op for short. Unfortunately, Paul was neither a driver nor a radio operator. He knew next to nothing about radios and frequently ignored the basic rudiments of safe driving. So I drove my cut-down sporty Toyota Land Cruiser myself because I could not bear to see it suffering abuse at Paul's hands. He sat in the front passenger seat, headsets of the various radios slung around his neck. More often than not he was asleep. I almost always had to awaken him when somebody called on one of the nets. This invariably resulted in Paul answering on the wrong net first, then frantically shouting into various microphones in turn until he eventually got it right.

We spent the night at Catambué. Corky was getting restless because the longer we took to get to our first objective, Pereira de Eça, the greater was the chance that MPLA would become aware of our surreptitious invasion. This would give them time to dig in and prepare the town against assault. We intended approaching from the north, which we hoped would be an unexpected direction. None of us, least of all myself, looked forward to fighting a battle to capture a well-defended town with badly trained and unproven troops.

Corky was instructed to move as far as Caiundo, then to Pereira de Eça by a lateral road still under construction. Higher headquarters assured him that the road was in excellent condition. They said the aim of our expansive right hook was to create the impression that an unidentified force was approaching the town from the north-east, and not a South African force thrusting north from South West Africa. The difficulties that Delville was experiencing in his efforts to open a route farther to the north to facilitate a rapid advance, however, boded ill for our future. It might give FAPLA time to tumble to our deception plan.

Corky told me to bypass Delville and make Caiundo before dark. We cheerfully set off and made good time to Tandaue where we came on Delville's vehicles struggling through the mud in a long, labouriously moving train. Tandaue is an *omuramba* that joins the Okavango River from the west. An inspection showed that off-road going was swampy. The *omuramba*'s bed and its flood plains, which were adjacent to the river's flood plain, acted as sponges from the start of the heavy summer rainfall in November until well after the rainy season ended. Even at the end of the dry season most of the flood plains remained veritable tank-traps with deep mud and isolated pools of water lurking unseen beneath a lush green grass cover.

We kept to the road. I gave strict instructions that nobody was to stop and aid vehicles stuck in the loose sand. They were to push on until we were through the bad patches. If any vehicles got stuck, Delville's bulldozer would pull them out. In the event, all vehicles made it without mishap.

We arrived at Caiundo before sunset and laagered on the eastern side of the bridge. It was in the hands of UNITA. Rumour had it that, with the knowledge and connivance of UNITA, there was a SWAPO base about 12km upstream on the eastern bank.

When Corky arrived I proposed a night attack on this base. I thought it would be a splendid way to shake my men down for the battles that lay ahead. Corky was not amused, maybe because we had been joined by UNITA's Major Katahale who would be our liaison officer with Jonas Savimbi's headquarters. (Major Katahale should not be confused with Johnny Katale from Cuangar.)

Major Katahale was well turned out. He looked smart in his camouflage fatigues and was more refined and educated than my FNLA riff-raff. He made it clear by his behaviour that he had no intention of associating with me, my officers or anybody else in the battle group. He rarely ventured far from Zulu headquarters. After meeting him, Delville also said some unflattering things about him. This was probably because Bushmen were even lower in Katahale's scale of contempt than my FNLA soldiers. He insisted there were no SWAPOs in the area. My offer to send out a patrol, just to be sure, was not taken up. Feeling rather disgruntled, I turned in for the night.

The next morning I was ordered to reconnoitre the far northern route of advance by going to Serpa Pinto and then on to Artur de Paiva. Serpa Pinto was in FNLA hands and Artur de Paiva was held by UNITA. I decided to take Paul and go alone by Land Cruiser. I would leave the rest to catch up later if Corky decided to use this longer approach to Pereira de Eça. Delville, meanwhile, was ordered to reconnoitre the shorter route to Pereira de Eça via Ionde, but it was still under construction and it was unlikely it could take the weight of our heavier lorries.

We set off at a great clip on a beautifully tarred road and reached Serpa Pinto in record time. We turned west and headed towards Artur de Paiva on to a good dirt road that ran parallel to the railway line from Moçamedes. The terrain was typical tropical savannah and much greener than farther to the south. There was also plenty of water. We passed numerous well-constructed *kimbos* with seemingly well fed and content residents. Most of them were flying UNITA flags, so we dared not stop for a chat because João and I were both sporting FNLA badges on our forage caps. At Cuchi I turned back for Serpa Pinto as I was getting low on fuel. I had established, however, that the road up to Artur de Paiva was in excellent condition.

Serpa Pinto, later known as Menongue, was a fair-sized town largely still untouched by the war. It is built on both banks of the Cuebe River which bisects the town. Chipenda, my boss, lived in a large pink house set in beautiful gardens with palms and all sorts of flowering tropical trees and shrubs. The river was at the end of a vast expanse of rolling lawn. Chipenda was not at home, but I had no intention of calling on him anyway. The 'Mafia gang' from Calai was there and so was the FNLA's secretary, Kambuta. We rustled up some diesel and left for Caiundo. We were seen off by cheerful, high-ranking FNLA officials who were already mentally counting the escudos they believed would stream into their personal coffers after we had dealt with MPLA.

I met Corky and Zulu Force en route to Serpa Pinto. Delville had returned with a negative report on the state of the Pereira de Eça road. Some of my troops were still in Caiundo so I pushed on south, collected the tail-end of my unit and headed north again for Cuchi. We caught up with the rest where they had laagered for the night just beyond Cuchi.

We spent an exceedingly cold night because Corky had placed the laager on the edge of an *omuramba* instead of on higher ground where it was warmer. We were glad to saddle up the next morning, painfully stiff from spending a night with inadequate bedding.

With Battle Group Bravo in the lead, we entered Artur de Paiva and encountered our first UNITA-manned roadblocks. Despite Paul's earnest explanations, the guards refused point-blank to let us through. We took matters into our own hands and barged straight through, scattering drums, barriers and UNITA troops in every direction. They dared not put up a fight because they were heavily outnumbered. We crossed the Okavango River once more — this time south-westwards over a magnificent steel bridge — turned south at a T-junction and headed for Pereira de Eça.

The road, although dusty, remained good. We passed Cassinga without stopping. If I had been aware that Cassinga would play a very important part later in my military career, I would have stopped for a good look at the terrain and town. As it turned out, I could hardly remember passing through the place.

We finally pulled into Tetchamutete for the night. It was the site of Angola's most productive iron mines. Tetchamutete had a large dam that served the mines which, at the time, were out of production. The muddy waters of the dam could not be sneered at, however, so we washed, topped up our water bottles and reconnoitred the nearby landing strip.

The terrain got drier as we turned south and water became scarcer with every kilometre of our rapid advance. The locals told us that we had nearly reached the limit of UNITA-controlled territory and that from Cuvelai on we would be entering MPLA country. We took extra care when we moved off the next morning, still in the vanguard of Zulu Force. Connie van Wyk and his number two — each in Land-Rovers fitted with two 30 calibre Brownings — and an infantry platoon for immediate support were in front as an advance patrol. My Land Cruiser with an escort of two Land-Rovers, each equipped with two Vickers machine guns, followed. Behind them and quite close to the front of the column came the mortar platoon because the range of our clapped-out three-inch mortars was so limited. The remaining companies followed in column with the echelon vehicles bringing up the rear. The column probably stretched over more than five kilometres.

I always advanced with maximum firepower up front. This enabled any resistance to our unconducted tour of Angola to be overcome speedily with a sudden burst of maximum violence — provided, of course, my machine gunners, mortar men and manoeuvre elements in the advance patrol were quick off the mark.

Our advance was relatively slow because we expected resistance around every corner. Any high ground that commanded the dirt road to the south was viewed with the greatest suspicion and some apprehension. The bush was tinder dry but thick. Visibility was rarely more than 100 metres. We could expect to come under fairly accurate fire at short ranges and I did not envy Connie out in front. Nevertheless, he seemed happy with his machine guns and in his element at the head of the column, despite it being inevitable that he would be the first to make contact with the enemy.

We reached Cuvelai after last light. The advance patrol reached the bridge that crossed the Cuvelai River just north of the town and settled down to watch the buildings on the far side. I deployed the rest of my force so it was ready for an all-out assault should it become necessary. The town was reportedly in the hands of FAPLA and I moved forward to look at it. There were rows of houses on each side of a single main road. It was well lit with street lamps. The bridge had already been checked for demolition charges but none had been found. I sent a patrol across to secure the southern end of the bridge. They reappeared shortly afterwards with a big unarmed soldier in camouflage uniform with both arms raised above his head.

With Paul acting as interpreter, he identified himself as a UNITA officer. The town, he said, was in UNITA's hands and his commander had sent him to make contact with us. I detached Sergeant Nel's platoon to accompany me for a meeting with our allies. The UNITA officer got in the passenger seat of my Land Cruiser and directed me to the old Portuguese barracks on the southern outskirts of town where the UNITA garrison was housed. He told me that the garrison had a strength of about 40. The nearest MPLA were in Mupa, the next town along the road to Pereira de Eça.

Nel entered the town with his troops in two columns, one on each side of the street. Everyone was alert. Rightly, they had no trust in anything that smacked of UNITA. Suddenly the streetlights went out and we were left in total darkness. This suited me, as the light enabled hostile eyes to watch my every move from their places of concealment in the darkness beyond.

We finally drew level with the barracks. It was in an open space on our left with two rows of virtually impenetrable sisal on our right. That put us in a perfect killing ground, for the sisal would cut off our retreat to where good cover was available. The street running north -south afforded no cover whatsoever.

Suddenly all hell broke loose with tracers streaming over our heads from barrack blocks about 50 metres to our left. Interspersed with this was the odd 60mm mortar bomb thumping into the fields behind us. Fortunately, they were firing far too high. I turned to shoot my UNITA companion who had obviously deliberately led us into an ambush, but he had gone. The only way he could have got away was to bulldoze a path through the sisal barrier, but I shall never know for certain.

My troops had dropped down out in the open on the crown of the road. I pulled them back behind the camber which gave them the barest minimum of protection. Their eyes, gleaming white in the darkness, seemed to be staring at me expectantly for a decision of some sort. Not a single one of them was returning fire. So much for our training!

'Shoot, you bastards! Look at the enemy, you dumb idiots — not at me! Shoot, damn you, shoot!'

My fury, expressed in English, must have penetrated the paralysis of their minds. Slowly our return fire began to build, high of course, but nevertheless at a satisfactory level. Everybody's morale began to pick up. Meanwhile, I was trying to make sense out of the enemy dispositions. A bothersome machine gun was firing at us from a small building set slightly back on UNITA's right flank. The thatched roofs of large buildings were ablaze to our front and the fires lit up the whole scene. They also illuminated our own attempts to find shelter behind the only pathetic cover available.

I had brought a rocket-launcher team with me. It was manned by the ex-Portuguese commando who led my anti-tank platoon. I instructed him to put a rocket into the small building that was sheltering the machine gun that had us pinned down.

There was a sudden almighty bang, accompanied by clouds of dust, smoke and flames. I thought that something heavy, possibly an 82mm mortar bomb, had fallen amongst us. I could see nothing, not even the blazing thatched roofs, as there was not even a breath of wind to clear the smoke and dust. Gradually though, I began to make out my intrepid rocketeer to my left. He was covered in dust, as no doubt I was too. He was kneeling, the rocket launcher placed firmly on the ground at an angle of 45°.

'What the hell are you doing? You must aim at the building!'

I pointed vigorously through the smoke towards the still-firing machine gun.

He told me in broken English that he was using high-angle fire as they used to do in the Portuguese Army.

'You are not in the bloody Portuguese Army. Now do as I tell you. See that building with the machine gun?'

'Yes!'

'Now aim your bloody launcher directly at the building and shoot!'

Rocket launchers have a characteristic backblast that cancels the recoil when a rocket is launched from the tube. The back of the tube is open and usually flared. This particular one was a 3.5 inch launcher, which generated a tremendous amount of flames and gas escaping from the rear. Standing behind one when it is fired is highly dangerous — men have been killed that way.

The gunner proceeded to reload. While I was looking at the burning buildings and noting that UNITA fire was decreasing, there was another tremendous bang with smoke, flame, dust and even pebbles flying about. This time I tasted blood in the back of my throat. My ears rang and my eyes, mouth and nose were clogged with dirt.

He had done it again!

I heard a distant thump as the rocket returned to earth from outer space.

'Get the hell out of here! Bugger off! Vamoose, you stupid bastard!'

The soldier picked up his rocket launcher and indignantly walked off down the road. The road was still under UNITA fire which proved, at least, that he had some guts. He vanished into the darkness and I never used him again in a combat capacity. I eventually got rid of him at Sa da Bandeira.

Meanwhile, our return fire was becoming effective. Even the machine gun had ceased firing and had pulled out. Most of the remaining fire seemed to be coming from a position beyond the burning buildings. The time had obviously come for an assault.

'*Advança!*' I shouted in my best carrying voice, full of determination and aggression.

I tentatively moved forward, but there was no movement in response by anybody up or down the line.

'*Advança*, you bastards!'

White eyes just stared at me.

Nel and I had no option but to move up and down the line. We literally had to pick them up one by one by the scruff of their necks and the seat of their pants. We would run forward and dump them, then go back for another one. This kicking, swearing and cajoling finally got them as far as the first line of buildings.

UNITA was now shooting from an embankment on the eastern side of the barracks. We took up positions, returned fire and managed to set a second line of buildings on fire. Starting the second phase of the assault proved less troublesome. It was probably the first real assault the troops had ever been in. UNITA had vanished into the darkness by the time we reached the embankment, leaving us in sole possession of the burning barracks.

We searched the place but found no dead bodies or discarded equipment. We only came across the odd item of uniform, some rations and lots of rubbish. There was a stink of burnt thatch, cordite and human excrement. This was normal on the outskirts of all bases, whether they belonged to UNITA, FNLA, FAPLA or SWAPO.

UNITA had deliberately led us into an ambush and I was livid. I reported it to Corky with the comment that I would welcome a word about it with Major Katahale. Meanwhile, I had heard from the local population that UNITA had withdrawn to a farming complex ten kilometres east of Cuvelai. I dispatched Sergeants Danny Roxo and Silva Sierro and two platoons with strict instructions to sort out UNITA once and for all.

The troops took up an all-round defensive position with our vehicles in the centre. We warmed ourselves at the burning buildings and reflected on UNITA's treachery. At first light Danny and Silva returned with their tired platoons. They had found no signs of UNITA.

Jack Dippenaar appeared with a RPG7 that one of his troops had found under a tree. It had apparently been abandoned by UNITA. So at least we had something to show for our exertions of the previous night. Then a troop from the anti-tank platoon pitched up. He wanted to know if anyone had seen his RPG7 that he had left under a tree. So much for our first venture into war loot.

And so ended our first contact of the *Operation Savannah* campaign, a skirmish with UNITA which did not ease our minds about them as allies in the months ahead. In fact, Corky had his work cut out keeping me away from the throat of the UNITA commander at Cuvelai who pitched up later that day to sheepishly pay respects to his new allies. In retrospect, probably nobody had bothered to tell him of the latest developments in Angola's three-sided civil war.

7

Pereira de Eça

We left Cuvelai at about eight the next morning with our foes of the previous night picking up the pieces and re-establishing themselves more or less as a viable garrison — only this time in burnt-out buildings. Served them right!

At least my troops had experienced their first taste of war and with the telling and retelling of the previous night's events, their stature increased enormously while that of UNITA decreased to vanishing point. FAPLA or anybody else would have had a wild cat by the tail if they had tangled with this FNLA bunch!

A positive aspect of the skirmish for my FNLA troops was that they had seen their white commanders were perfectly willing to take their place in the battle lines when the lead began to fly. Unlike their old FNLA *commandantes*, they did not make themselves comfortable in the rear and tell their men to get on with it. The result was that the first buds of loyalty, barely detectable but full of promise, had begun to poke through the surface. It must be said, though, it was a loyalty more to their new commanders than to the FNLA cause. Chipenda, in that pink house of his in Serpa Pinto, was beginning to become somewhat more distant and removed from his FNLA army.

We headed south for Mupa, a village boxed in between some high hills to the east and a dry river bed to the west. The hills were an obvious delaying position, well placed to hold up our advance and difficult to flank to the east because of extremely thick bush.

Nothing happened, however, as we drove cautiously into the village from the north. At the southern end by some stores, we unexpectedly came upon two Land-Rovers packed with FAPLA. Before we could even fire a shot, they debussed in an unseemly haste and disappeared into the bush. This resulted in the addition of two reasonably serviceable Land-Rovers to our fleet. They were most welcome as we had begun to realise that we would have to rely on what we could capture in this war. Our logistic supplies had not yet caught up with us and even when they did, it seemed doubtful they would satisfy much more than our most basic needs anyway.

We moved farther south, driving somewhat faster than the day before as a feeling of élan took hold of the men. The next town of consequence was Evale, reportedly a FAPLA stronghold.

With Lieutenant Connie van Wyk in the lead, we made for this town at a cracking pace. We passed a mission station. Then we drove into an ambush. An RPG7 rocket was fired at Connie's Land-Rover, but it failed to explode. It had been fired at a range of less than 15 metres and the missile needed to travel that distance before it armed. The only damage was a huge dent on the left side of the vehicle. A torrent of small-arms fire was coming Connie's way, however. He effectively returned fire from his Brownings and at the same time shouted for mortar support. Fire that he was unable to deal with was being directed at him from the right side of the road.

Oupa van Dyk dismounted and his mortars with their rickety yokes came into action.

They succeeded in frightening FAPLA without frightening our own troops. In the front of the column, FAPLA began to pack up and leave the battle scene, which substantially reduced fire on our advance patrol.

Meanwhile, I was about level with Connie. I was lying in a ditch alongside the road trying to regain a semblance of control over events. While deploying Jack Dippenaar and his company in case a sweep on both flanks became necessary, a tremendous firefight broke out to the rear. It was, quite honestly, the biggest and noisiest scrap I had ever heard in my life. Staff Sergeant Costa Marão, commander of Charlie company, said they were being attacked by FAPLA from both flanks and that Zulu Headquarters was also pinned down under enemy fire.

We were still engaged in dealing with FAPLA to our front. I had visions of our column being wiped out Vietnam-style, like the time the Viet Minh caught a mobile column of French troops in a pass and virtually exterminated them. I could not move because of the shower of lead flying about, so I decided to deal with Connie's situation before attending to Costa's problem.

Oupa Van Dyk's mortar fire soon drove FAPLA off along Connie's front and the shooting died down. I felt it was reasonably safe to move down the column to see for myself the situation to the rear. The fire on Charlie company's front was also beginning to slacken, so the enemy was probably running out of ammunition.

I located Corky and his headquarters. They were under fire and taking cover in a ditch alongside the road. Charlie company was spread out, roughly in two halves on both road shoulders, and they were furiously pumping rounds at each other. Fortunately, they had their eyes closed and their rifle barrels were pointed almost straight up into the sky.

There was not a FAPLA in sight.

It took some doing to get them to stop shooting at each other and at Zulu Headquarters. I could only achieve this by moving at a low crouch down the centre of the road.

'Cease fire!' I shouted at the top of my voice to both sides of the road.

'Cease fire!'

Finally both sides did so, but it was more from a lack of ammunition than from my efforts. I watched as they sheepishly got up and moved back to their trucks. I could not really blame Charlie company, although I was as mad as a snake. During our short period of training, they had been subjected to the least training of all. I could only have a 'clenched jaw' heart-to-heart talk with a thoroughly discomfited Sergeant Costa Marão.

The incident had unfortunate repercussions for Charlie company. While they served with me, it placed them in the almost permanent position of reserve company. They never really had a proper baptism of fire under incremental enemy resistance, like the other companies. Right at the end of our service in Angola, they faced a deluge of enemy fire which wiped the company out to a man, except for their company commander who was seriously maimed.

Corky was somewhat sarcastic about the unsolicited baptism of fire we had given Zulu Headquarters. But it did not seem to put his nose out of joint too much. I think he understood our problems, even if we did not understand his as commander of a largely untried force of Africans and Bushmen — surely a nightmare to any military commander who treats war as a serious business.

We swept the bush on both sides of the road and found a few dead and one wounded FAPLA whom we passed on to our doctor for treatment and to our intelligence team for interrogation. We collected a few PPSHs, AK47s and several Soviet helmets which soon reappeared on the heads of some of our troops. Sergeant Robbie Ribeiro was one of them. He looked quite silly with a large helmet falling over his ears as he peered at the world from under the brim with a perpetual grin on his face. Robbie was Connie van Wyk's driver and he was obviously enjoying the war.

We still had about ten kilometres to go to Evale and the advance resumed. We had obviously bumped into an outpost. The column cautiously snaked forward with Connie's converted Land-Rover in the lead on the left-hand side. He stood crouched behind his guns, swinging the barrels from side to side as the irrepressible Robbie drove in the ditch beside the road.

I drove on the right-hand side of the road, slightly behind Connie. I had no intention of attracting the first shots. Oupa moved his mortars in bounds, half the platoon at a time. Fingers Kruger remained close behind me with the two Land-Rovers and his Vickers machine guns on alert.

We moved forward slowly, eyes scanning the thick bush with apprehension, expecting a sudden burst of fire at any moment. I intended to get within two kilometres of Evale. If we had not yet bumped FAPLA by then, Jack Dippenaar's company would mount an assault on the town.

Just as I decided to stop and deploy Jack's company, Connie hit a contact on my side of the road. Luckily, he was in the ditch on the left of the road which gave him good cover. We spun into action. Oupa opened up with mortars while Fingers and Connie pumped devastating fire at the ambush with their machine guns.

Meanwhile, Jack dismounted and moved his platoons at the double into an assault formation on the right-hand side of the road. Our performance was becoming noticeably polished and the black troops had begun to move with alacrity and understanding, despite the language barrier.

Jack swept towards the town and I leapfrogged the fire support base — in other words the mortars and machine guns — to keep up with him. Charlie company, at the rear of the column, did not open fire at all. This was probably because they had no ammunition left.

Evale came into view and I noticed an MPLA flag flying briskly in the afternoon breeze above the most important-looking building. FAPLA fired some RPG7 rockets into the air which burst above our heads scattering shrapnel. Other than this, their fire was desultory and it ceased altogether when Jack's company hit the edge of town. His troops went through and cleared the houses on the right side of the main street. Connie took his leading platoon and cleared the few houses on the left.

FAPLA, meanwhile, had withdrawn and were no doubt heading for Pereira de Eça. We heard vehicles starting up and engine sounds disappearing rapidly in a southerly direction. This left us with Evale and a FAPLA flag in our hands. The flag would look good on the wall of a mess or a pub back home.

Corky ordered a halt and we laagered just south of Evale. There was no water. The bush was as dry as a bone and there were no wells in sight. It had been a hot and eventful day and we turned in for the night feeling very thirsty. Apart from the performance of Charlie company, I felt satisfied with the way the troops were settling down under fire.

Connie van Wyk had been an absolute marvel. Later he would be awarded the *Honoris Crux* for his actions that day. His calmness and rapid reaction with devastating firepower while under accurate fire himself at ranges of less than ten metres showed courage which deserved the decoration.

Delville Linford and Battle Group Alpha would be taking the lead the next morning, so I slept peacefully until 03:00 when my black troops started awakening. They were noisy as always as they made fires with which to braai the meat of goats they had caught the previous day. I tried to continue sleeping but it was no use. Long before daybreak I was sipping a mug of coffee and conferring with my company commanders.

Delville and his Bushmen passed us in clouds of dust just after daybreak to take the lead. We gave them sufficient time to get ahead, then mounted our trucks for the final approach to Pereira de Eça (now Ondjiva) — our first major target.

Delville moved cautiously to Anhanca, the next village, which was another possible delaying position for FAPLA. We were right at the back of the column, recovering our nerve for the severe test we were expecting to face at Pereira de Eça.

Towards sundown Zulu formed a laager five kilometres east of the objective. We intended to spend the night in an all-round defensive position. We would move out for the assault at first light and would launch our attack on the town at about 08:00.

Corky briefed us using a sand model and air photographs. The town was roughly two kilometres from east to west on both sides of a main street on which there were several rows of houses.

I was given the half of the town north of the main road with the airfield about eight kilometres beyond town as my final objective. It was vital this be taken as it was needed to facilitate the re-supply of Zulu Force. There were *kimbos* on the northern outskirts and in my sector. Pereira de Eça was the capital of Cunene Province and a rather large town for Angola. There were several substantial buildings in our sector, including a small cathedral and a multi-storeyed administration building.

Delville was given the southern half of the town. In addition he was tasked to send a strong patrol to Namacunde and Santa Clara to secure the tar road leading north from the South West African border. Commandant Gert van Niekerk, the commander of 2 Military Area (the designation for the Owamboland combat zone), would be waiting just across the border at Santa Clara to rendezvous with Delville and hand over two troops of armoured cars.

Having been a keen student of warfare all my life, it seemed to me that a mini El Alamein was in order. I intended to use two companies in the attack — Jack's would clear the town and Connie's would clear the *kimbos* to the north. Costa's Charlie company would be kept in reserve.

The employment of the mortars provided the resemblance to El Alamein. I had read about the old-fashioned rolling barrage and decided that this would be the role for Oupa van Dyk and his mortars. We would deliver a curtain of exploding steel behind which the attacking infantry could advance in relative safety. This, of course, was subject to the rickety mortar yokes which did not auger well for the accuracy one might usually expect when putting down a rolling barrage.

Being laagered so close to town I fully expected a FAPLA attack during the night, but nothing happened. We arose long before dawn and made preparations for what we believed would be a desperate fight. I have always regarded fighting in built-up urban areas with some trepidation.

At first light the companies advanced on foot to the start line. By 08:00, the so-called H hour, we crossed the start line in plain sight of the nearest buildings.

Oupa opened up with his mortars, dropping his bombs a mere 100 metres in front of the advancing infantry. A curtain of black smoke and deep red flashes marked the first salvo. To the left there was a general racket as Delville engaged FAPLA with rifles, light mortars and my Vickers platoon which had been detached to him. I followed closely behind the infantry in my Land Cruiser, trying to keep our advance coordinated with Delville's on the left.

The fight was not one-sided and my troops began to receive incoming mortar fire. At first they were quick to blame our own mortars and their dodgy yokes. Yet one could tell the difference in the explosions from the smoke. Scarcely 20 metres away from me, a bomb exploded in a cloud of white smoke and an instantaneous brilliant white flash that was typical of post-World War-II explosives. The blast cartwheeled one of my soldiers and he dropped lifelessly to the ground. The World War-II three-inch mortar bombs on the other hand, exploded with black smoke and deep red, almost orange, flashes. Delville was also being subjected to incoming mortar fire and I had my job cut out to convince him and his troops that it was not our mortars shooting off-target.

Glancing back at the start line, I saw Oupa running from tube to tube checking sight settings, clouting the odd mortar man around the ears and generally making sure that his platoon was performing well. Soon after this I leapfrogged them forward, six mortars at a time.

The town had seen fighting before between the various armed factions, so there was already a fair amount of damage. My mortars had certainly not improved the look of the place. Unfortunately some bombs had crashed through the cathedral's roof and had damaged the smallish but beautifully proportioned white-washed church, architecturally the only building in town worth looking at.

The enemy's resistance was weak to start with, apart from their mortar shelling, and the fighting soon died down, the silence broken only by the occasional clatter of automatics. Oupa had ceased firing and my troops had reached the western side of town suffering only a few casualties in the process.

I took Connie's company and secured the airport. We met with no resistance but found quite a few undamaged light aircraft parked on the apron. They would come in handy later. The airfield, with its tarred runway, was large enough to take the latest jet fighter planes. For the first time supplies could be flown in to us by C130 transports. This was a great boon to us as it would appreciably boost our limited logistical capabilities.

Delville cleared the road as far south as Santa Clara and it was not long before we saw the welcome sight of eight Eland armoured cars — basically the same as the Panhard — entering town from the south. It was a disappointment that they were a mixture of 90mm and 60mm cars — the latter carrying a mortar instead of a gun. I would have preferred them all to have been armed with the 90mm gun because of its devastating punch. I have always been a great admirer of firepower. The bigger the gun, the harder the enemy gets clobbered and the less the infantry are needed to sort him out afterwards. Apart from being a paratrooper, I am also a very wary infantryman.

We discovered a reasonably well-stocked hospital with a resident medic who claimed to be a doctor. A medical system was soon established to treat both our wounded and the local population. We could not evacuate FNLA wounded to South West Africa for security reasons, so it was essential they be left behind in Pereira de Eça where they could receive adequate attention.

Small quantities of weapons and ammunition were captured. More important were a few vehicles that we confiscated to expand the mobility of our units. We had been carrying both troops and equipment on the same vehicles. Loads had comprised a bottom layer of ammunition and explosives, a second layer of personal equipment and rations and a third layer of ready-to-use ammunition, water bottles and the day's rations. The troops were perched on top. The chaos that would have resulted if a truck loaded like that had taken a hit from an RPG7 can only be imagined.

En route to Zulu Headquarters I came on a Bushman soldier trying to start a virtually brand-new Lancia — part of the war loot of Delville's battalion. When I passed the same way later I found the beautiful Lancia completely wrecked against the side of a building. The Bushman had clearly been unable to cope with the intricacies of trying to drive a car for the first time in his life. Delville's reaction was unprintable.

The brigadier arrived by helicopter to brief us. We would replenish ammunition and fuel before moving on. For food we could live off the fat of the land — although the land around there was not particularly fat.

The next phase of the operation involved us proceeding to Sa da Bandeira. We would take Roçades and other towns en route in our stride. At Roçades a third battle group, Battle Group Charlie consisting primarily of armoured cars, would join Zulu Force.

Commandant Gert van Niekerk would continue his counter-insurgency operations in Owambo while Commandant Hans Moller would attack SWAPO bases in the area we had just covered. UNITA had evidently been forthcoming with information about such bases and had offered to provide guides to lead our forces to SWAPO. For the record, Hans had little success. It appeared to him that SWAPO had been forewarned by his UNITA guides, so the result turned out to be a lemon. (A lemon was an operation that produced no results, usually because the enemy escaped before contact could be made.)

The briefing session was memorable for one particular reason. It was hot and stuffy in the room where Brigadier Schoeman addressed us. He had a tendency to jump from one subject to the next without following any pattern or logical sequence. He carried on for several long hours. It was confusing and boring. Delville reacted by falling asleep while sitting in front of the brigadier and he slept soundly throughout the briefing. He awoke refreshed but completely in the dark as to our next move when everyone stood up at the end. This did not bother him unduly and he cheerfully departed for his headquarters after finding out from Corky the time and direction in which the advance would be resumed. Where we were going was unimportant.

We celebrated our first major success at Zulu Headquarters with several bottles of wine and turned in for the night. The next day Battle Group Bravo would again take the lead, but this time we would have two troops of armoured cars. The days of Connie heading the column in a soft-skinned, lightly armed and clapped out Land-Rover had come to an end. It was none too soon, as he surely would not have lasted out the war as Battle Group Bravo's permanent scout.

8

Attack on Sa da Bandeira

We did not leave early the next morning because of logistical problems. The B (logistics) echelon had been expanded by the addition of several more fuel tankers, both diesel and petrol, to cater for the petrol-guzzling armoured cars. The armoured cars also had to be integrated and a reorganisation of Zulu Force conducted.

I had an additional wireless net, an armoured car net, to cope with, which brought the total to three. Fortunately, the Zulu Command net was rarely used because we were mostly out of range of Corky and his headquarters.

We passed the airfield where SAAF C130s had already landed and were parked, and headed for Mongua — the next town of consequence. I would later become thoroughly acquainted with that part of Angola but at the time it seemed to be mostly dry bush with dried out *chanas* and *omurambas* interspersed with miserable little *kimbos* and tiny herds of bony cattle. The rains had not come, yet we were deep into October. Later, I would see this same bare, dry, table-top plain with its brittle, dead-looking bush become lush, green and waterlogged so that even Unimogs would sink up to their axles. Movement in the rainy season was restricted to the few all-weather roads like the one to Mongua, Roçades and beyond. It was tarred all the way to Luanda.

We sped along with a troop of armoured cars in the lead, followed by myself in the Land Cruiser, a platoon of infantry, a second troop of armoured cars and then the rest of the column. It was relaxing and even peaceful to drive along without constantly anticipating a burst of unfriendly bullets to rake one's unprotected hide. This time the armoured cars would be the first target, but they were far better equipped to survive.

Mongua came and went. It turned out to be a small village with six or seven buildings. We were fast approaching Roçades when Zulu Headquarters informed me that Battle Group Charlie had already taken charge there. Later that afternoon we cruised into the town and made our way to the picturesque fort. It was situated on high ground overlooking and dominating a long bridge that spanned the Cunene River.

We adopted an all-round defensive position on the eastern slope of the rise on which the fort was situated. I went to Zulu Headquarters where I met Major Toon Slabbert, the commander of Battle Group Charlie, and some of his officers.

Toon was a giant of a man with flaming red hair and beard. He was a rough diamond and an excellent fighting soldier. He was also the only man I had ever seen putting on an Eland 60 armoured car like a pair of underpants, instead of getting into it as other people do. He used the 60 as a command vehicle because his size made it impossible for him to ride in a 90 where space was taken up by the big 90mm gun.

I also met Aparicio and his ELP (Army to Liberate Portugal). Aparicio was a small, ex-Portuguese commando major who, after the Portuguese colonial empire had collapsed, tried to join my old unit. He could not pass the selection course , however, and had thrown in the towel after about two days. He then left the army and formed the ELP with which, according to him, he was going to liberate Portugal. ELP consisted of approximately 20 white and one mulatto Portuguese, all dressed in camouflage and hung with a profusion of hand grenades and machine-gun belts. Most of their G3 rifles had no stocks — an old Portuguese commando custom which meant that the rifle could not be fired from the shoulder. Usually, they just sprayed the target, and much of the surrounding area, by firing their weapons from the hip.

Aparicio and his ELP certainly looked picturesque in their gung-ho get-up with the historic Portuguese fort as a dramatic backdrop. One fully expected to see Warner Brothers appearing to shoot a war movie, full of heroics and camouflaged figures dashing through smoke and fire, teeth clenched in determination, eyes narrowed into cruel slits and with stuttering machine guns gripped in iron fists.

Zulu Force was becoming more weird as the war progressed. Aparicio had not exactly bubbled over with joy when he saw me. After all, I had rudely sacked him from Special Forces as unsuitable. He informed me that ELP would commence their liberation of Portugal in the south — in other words Angola — work their way northwards through Portuguese Guinea, the Cape Verde Islands, Madeira and finally Portugal itself. I assumed he intended to put Alexander the Great's exploits in the shade.

Part of Battle Group Charlie had been sent upriver to capture Peu Peu, reported to be a FAPLA stronghold. According to Brigadier Schoeman, intelligence indicated that hundreds of almost new military vehicles would fall into our hands there like manna from heaven. We needed them to ease our transport problems which were chronic. The group returned before last light with nothing to show for its efforts. There were no vehicles, no weapons, no fuel and no FAPLA. The place was deserted. The vehicles we had would have to serve us for the rest of the campaign, unless we could liberate some more elsewhere.

João, meanwhile, had decided to wander into town for a few drinks in the Portuguese equivalent of a local pub. While standing at the counter, beer in hand, three FAPLA soldiers walked in, also intent on having a couple of beers after a long and hot day's patrolling in the bush. They were unaware that during their absence the town had changed hands again. They were taken completely by surprise when João opened fire, killing two of them and wounding the third. The wounded man escaped and legged it to the fort to complain to his commander at what he thought was still FAPLA's Headquarters.

At the entrance gate the agitated man was confronted by white South African sentries. They could not understand a word of Portuguese. Not grasping who he was they directed him to Battle Group Bravo's laager. I was awakened by raucous screams of laughter. I was highly irritated. I got out of my sleeping bag to quieten my rowdy men. I found them standing in a circle and poking fun at a forlorn-looking soldier in the centre. I gathered that he was complaining that a stranger had shot at him and his mates and he wanted the comrades to go to the downtown pub to sort out the culprit. The laughter increased. Then slowly the penny dropped.

'You are FAPLA, comrade?' he asked one of my men.

'No, we are not FAPLA.'

'Who are you then?'

'FNLA!'

The troops were just about crawling with laughter.

The last I saw of him he was being escorted to Zulu Headquarters, probably to be attended to by the doctor and dealt with by interrogators — perhaps in reverse order.

We left Roçades (later to become known as Xangongo) the next day and headed for Humbe. It had been captured by Battle Group Charlie the previous day after they had followed the west bank of the Cunene River from Calueque in the south. Delville led the way with most of the armoured car squadron attached to him and progress was fast. We passed Cahama without seeing a sign of FAPLA and got to Tchibemba.

The next morning our forces were split up. Delville would head for Rotunda via Chiange, Jau and Huila and I would go there via João de Almeida. The armoured cars were divided between the two battle groups. I got the squadron headquarters and three troops and Delville took the other two troops.

The terrain changed and became broken and hilly as we moved northwards. We saw mountains on the northern horizon. We passed through small villages and townships and arrived at João de Almeida during late afternoon.

A fight broke out between the advance patrol and some FAPLA by the railway station which we quickly captured. I took Jack's company, with the armoured cars and four 81mm mortars in support, to seize the town itself.

Oupa van Dyk deployed his three-inchers alongside the 81mms and looked at them enviously. Those mortars, which had come with Battle Group Charlie, were manned by white South African troops. Oupa began to feel that he was beginning to lose business to a more up-to-date crowd. In the end the mortars were not required and Jack's company concentrated near the Dutch Reformed Church. This was the heart of the country settled by the old Dorsland Trekkers.

We discovered several storerooms at the railway station packed with rations, clothing and a limited amount of ammunition. It came in very handy, especially the rations, as we had more or less been forced to live off the land. We also seized two lorry-loads of what we suspected was Angolan beer. Unfortunately, it turned out to be ersatz wine, so sour that not even our troops would drink it.

Shortly after midday we pulled out of João de Almeida and headed into the hills to the north of town. The terrain was covered with thick vegetation and the going was tough as the road wound upwards through the hills towards the top of the plateau. It was ideal country for fighting a delaying battle and shortly afterwards we ran into FAPLA.

The armoured cars were unable to deploy off-road because of the broken and rocky terrain. This meant we were forced to fight on a two-armoured car front. Fingers Kruger, with his two Land-Rovers mounted with machine guns, soon came into his own by putting down a quick, heavy and sustained rate of fire. At the short ranges at which we had to fight, these guns were even more effective than the armoured cars. The leading platoon deployed rapidly under cover of the armoured cars' machine guns and the mortars. The Vickers guns raked long killing bursts of fire through the FAPLA position. Time was precious so we did not stop to do a body count.

We swept upwards through the hills, fighting three more times before we got clear of FAPLA's grip on our northward advance. During one fight we overran one of those famous Soviet-supplied 122mm rocket launchers. It was the first one we had seen and at first we did not recognise it. It was only when some of my FNLA *commandantes* became excited and explained what it was that we took notice. It comprised a single portable tube and was accompanied by rockets packed in boxes. We killed our first Cubans, probably crew members of the launcher, at this position.

FAPLA had surely suffered heavy casualties, because for several weeks afterwards, convoy crews moving between João de Almeida and Rotunda remarked on the stench of decaying bodies all the way up the pass. We had taken no casualties — mainly, I think, because we had immediately brought down a very high concentration of fire on the FAPLA positions, followed by a rapid assault before they could recover from the shock.

We reached Rotunda by sundown. A quick attack on the high ground beyond secured the crossroads and gave us defensible terrain for the night. This assault was led by Charlie company. They went through in grand style, although the resistance was light.

I laagered on the high ground and Zulu Headquarters drew into the centre. The Vickers machine guns were dismounted and allocated to different companies. The armoured cars were distributed all along the perimeter, adding their weight of fire to that of the infantry. We were not taking any chances. After all, we were only 20km from Sa da Bandeira and a night attack from that quarter was likely. Delville arrived later and extended our laager to the south. I established my headquarters on the stoep of a small house to the left of the main road and thankfully went to sleep. I felt dead tired after having been through three skirmishes and two company-size attacks that day.

Silence settled over the laager. I was awakened by one of my black soldiers. FAPLA had been heard moving about at the bottom of the next valley and an attack was expected. I heard nothing but ordered a stand-to all the same. This was quite unnecessary, for all my troops were standing-to already and anxiously peering into the pitch blackness of a moonless night.

I had just decided it was a false alarm when FAPLA opened fire with tracers from the high ground to the north and from the valley. Vehicles started driving towards us with their lights blazing which provided the 90mm armoured cars with some excellent targets to shoot at. Two vehicles caught fire and began to burn on the opposite slope. The Vickers machine guns joined in and so did Oupa's mortars. After some time the FAPLA attack died down completely.

One soldier was shot in the head and he was evacuated to my headquarters. He lay on a stretcher groaning throughout the rest of the night despite several injections of painkillers. His groaning kept me awake and I moved my sleeping bag to the yard behind the house so I could get some sleep. I was met by a growling Alsatian housed in a kennel. When I refused to budge, he quietened down and we were both soon asleep.

In the early hours of the morning I was awakened by an almighty bang. Somewhat disorientated, I jumped up and saw a 90mm armoured car blasting away at a vehicle that was trying to sneak away to the north on the opposite slope. Eventually the vehicle was hit and another funeral pyre was added to the other two. I went back to bed and slept the sleep of the very tired.

The next morning I was awakened by the sun and I made friends with the dog. I discovered a tap in the garden and used it to wash and shave. Unfortunately, the wounded soldier had died and his blanket-covered body was lying on the stoep.

I spotted tentative movement within the house which I had thought was deserted. The corner of a curtain lifted and eyes peered anxiously through the window at me. The situation must have reassured the person because the front door opened slowly and carefully. The lady of the house handed me a mug of milky, very sweet coffee. My own, which I had just brewed, tasted better, but I thought it would be rude to refuse to swallow the horrible syrupy stuff.

There was a small shop next to the house and I asked the Portuguese owner to open it so my troops could replenish their cigarettes. He hastily obliged. The troops queued up, clutching escudos with which to pay for their addiction. The owner beamed because he had thought at first we had wanted the shop opened so we could loot it.

Corky briefed us on the assault on Sa da Bandeira to be conducted later that day. I would attack the airfield on the south-eastern side of the town and clear the eastern suburbs. After securing these objectives I would halt my advance and continue into the city centre. Corky feared that my troops would get out of hand, go on a looting spree and sack the city.

Delville would approach Monte Cristo — a high mountain that looms over Sa da Bandeira from the south — in a roundabout way and assault the crest from the southern slopes. It was the dominating terrain and possession of the mountain would secure the whole of Sa da Bandeira. Delville was warned he could expect stiff resistance.

Delville would come down from the mountain the following day and clear the city. In the meanwhile, Battle Group Bravo would attack and secure the old Portuguese garrison and its surrounding area on the north-eastern side of the town.

Sa da Bandeira (now Lubango), a very large town by Angolan standards, was the main commercial centre of southern Angola and the capital of Huila province. It is beautifully situated in a valley surrounded by mountains to the south, west and north. The streets were well laid out and lined with avenues of trees and the buildings were substantial and well maintained. It had been beautified by the addition of parks, fountains and lots of flowering shrubs.

We approached Sa da Bandeira along the main road from the southeast with Monte Cristo to our left. Somewhere to the south, but out of our sight, Delville's Bushmen were preparing for an attack up the steep slopes to seize the summit of the mountain.

I detailed Sergeant Robbie Ribeiro and his platoon, with a troop of armoured cars in support, to take the airfield. While he was busy with that, the rest of Battle Group Bravo would hunker down and wait beside the road. It was dominated by the airfield and was the only approach road to town. Robbie was allowed only 15 minutes to complete his task. I expected the real fight to start when we reached the outskirts of town and I did not want to give FAPLA enough time to prepare a hot reception for us.

Robbie was to take the airfield by what one could term a coup de main. The armoured cars would storm the terminal building and bring it under fire of their 90mm guns. The infantry would dismount smartly from the armoured cars when they were almost on the doorstep. They would storm the building and clear it. They had to make absolutely sure that the control tower was in our hands. Pockets of resistance would be mopped up later. Robbie understood his mission and he left with his armoured cars in a cloud of exhaust smoke while the rest of us followed more sedately behind.

I watched from a distance as Robbie deployed according to plan. Flames and smoke belched from the terminal as the armoured cars thumped away with their 90mm guns. Little figures dismounted and stormed the wrecked buildings. Bursts of automatic fire could be heard. Then, one by one, the armoured cars turned their fire from the terminal to the airfield. The target had changed from the terminal building to some positions beyond. I could make out a line of infantry, rifles blazing, moving rapidly to the nearest edge of the airfield. It looked suspiciously to me as if Robbie was getting snarled up in a battle of somewhat greater proportions than expected.

Robbie's allotted time expired, and it became obvious he was meeting more resistance than I had bargained for. I could not raise him on the radio so I moved forward to investigate. My Land Cruiser crossed the boundary fence and we came under small-arms fire from different parts of the airfield. The armoured cars were still on the apron in front of the terminal building, seemingly hurling 90mm shells in all directions.

Robbie doubled past with his platoon on his way to the eastern side of the runway. He was grinning from ear to ear. He had discarded his Soviet helmet and was wearing a cowboy hat that he had no doubt looted from somewhere.

I asked how he was doing.

'No problem!' was the only English I could make out in his reply.

As he did not require reinforcements, I decided to leave him to get on with it.

Watching him clear the airfield was fascinating. There were several enemy positions round the perimeter and Robbie dealt with each in turn. The armoured cars would fire on a position and he and his platoon would storm it with tremendous élan. They were shouting and swearing, their rifles spitting away, until they reappeared triumphantly on the far side. Without a pause they would double to the next position and repeat the procedure.

'No problem! No problem!' he shouted, grinning and giving me the thumbs up every time he passed me. Robbie was obviously enjoying himself, but his command of the

English language required expansion.

FAPLA prisoners were brought in and congregated at the traffic circle on the main road by the turnoff to the airfield. Gradually the shooting died down. Robbie and his tired crew slowed from the double to a walk and eventually they stopped completely. The airfield was in our hands.

We had suffered only a few casualties including a white former Portuguese soldier who had been seriously wounded in the chest and some others with light wounds. FAPLA dead were strewn all across the airfield and the approaches to the terminal building. We counted more than 80 bodies and estimated that a battalion had been dug in around the perimeter. Robbie's coup de main had obviously caught them off balance.

We took about 30 FAPLA prisoners. They included a child of about ten who was carrying an FN rifle almost as big as himself. When he saw my Land Cruiser, he ran forward, fell on his knees and pleaded for his life. He said he had been press-ganged into service by FAPLA and that his father was an FNLA supporter languishing in jail in Moçamedes. That was also where his mother lived. I made him my batman and he joined Paul and myself in the Land Cruiser. His name was also João, but I called him Junior because I had too many Joãos in my organisation already..

The prisoners were passed on to Dries van Coller while we continued to expand our attack against the eastern suburb of Sa da Bandeira. I used Jack's and Connie's companies, giving each specific street blocks to clear. I kept Costa's company in reserve. Three troops of armoured cars were giving support as were my three-inch mortars with their fire on call. We had no intention of flattening a beautiful Sa da Bandeira suburb with high explosive shells. Delville had the 81mm mortars to support his assault on Monte Cristo and their fire was not available to Battle Group Bravo.

The assault went in rapidly against light resistance. It soon became obvious that the main defences had been centred around the airfield where Robbie had broken the back of FAPLA's resistance.

A car rushing from the city to the airfield came face-to-face with an armoured car with the 90mm gun pointing down its throat. The car turned swiftly, the driver intent on fleeing. But he was stopped by machine-gun fire. We found a black driver behind the wheel and two white Portuguese, a man and a woman, in the back seat. They were all dead. A dazed and slightly wounded Portuguese man was sitting by the side of the road. The commander of the armoured car felt awful because he had obviously shot civilians who had strayed into a combat zone at the wrong time. The wounded Portuguese was taken to a Shell service station which was being used as a collection point for casualties, prisoners and non-combatants who had been caught up in the fighting.

Our attack halted at the predetermined line. Across the river in a valley to the north we could see dozens of vehicles loaded with troops streaming from the barracks in town and escaping to the north-east. Major Toon Slabbert moved his armoured cars as far forward as the river which he was unable to cross. He opened fire on the barracks at maximum range. I wished that we had brought the 81mm mortars with us as their superior range would have created havoc among the fleeing columns. Toon's cars, however, did their best. Some shots fell inside the barracks compound, but this only served to speed up FAPLA's evacuation. We could not see evidence of serious damage to the barracks, so we thought it was rather unsporting of FAPLA to flee without offering at least token resistance.

In the meantime, Delville had also reached his objective at the top of Monte Cristo where he was faced with a minimum of resistance. His troops settled down around the magnificent statue of Christ, a replica of the one at Rio de Janeiro, and had a panoramic view of the men of Battle Group Bravo scurrying around at the foot of the mountain like ants. They remarked later on the magnificent view they enjoyed and expressed their appreciation of the warlike display we had laid on for their entertainment. They also complimented us on our battle drills which appeared faultless when viewed from such a lofty perch.

Down below we gave up shooting at the disappearing FAPLA as they were rapidly getting out of range. Instead, we began to consolidate our position for the night.

The Portuguese civilian captured at the vehicle shot up by the armoured car approached me and requested I give him a free pass to emigrate to Brazil. He said he was sick and tired of Angola. He identified himself as 'D'Oliveira' and said he had been working in town as a schoolteacher. I gave him permission to go home to his family but he refused, saying that FNLA would kill him. A short distance away an FNLA (formerly FAPLA) soldier conversant with English was eavesdropping on the conversation. When he realised that I was about to send D'Oliveira home, he approached me and protested vigorously. He insisted that D'Oliveira was no schoolteacher but a very high-ranking FAPLA officer.

It turned out that the soldier was correct. Under Major Dries van Coller's skilful interrogation, D'Oliveira admitted he was in charge of MPLA's propaganda machine. He had come from Benguela to motivate the local FAPLA who were in a state of panic because of our initial successes. It was a panic that was beginning to spread throughout the FAPLA army.

The Portuguese male killed in the car was the military advisor to FAPLA's military commander for the Huila Province and Benguela. He had come to Sa da Bandeira to plan its defences. He had piloted a light plane parked on the airfield which was captured during our attack. It was the sound of battle that caused these high-ranking cadres to break off their conference and try to make a run for it. But they were not quick enough — the airfield was already in our hands when they came face-to-face with our armoured car. The Portuguese woman was the FAPLA commander's wife and an important link in the MPLA hierarchy.

The armoured car commander felt much happier when I revealed the surprising details of his bag. So did my FNLA troops when D'Oliveira was eventually handed over as a prisoner to their political structure.

I had been out of radio contact for most of the day, so I returned to Zulu Headquarters at Rotunda to report our success. En route I managed to raise Willie Kotze.

'Who are you with?' he asked.

'I am alone', I replied.

I almost heard his sigh of relief over the intervening distance of several kilometres. Everyone there had pessimistically assumed me to be in full flight with my battalion.

I reported to Corky and he moved his headquarters from Rotunda to the terminal building at Sa da Bandeira's airfield. He was none too happy with the state of the buildings. The glass had been shot out, electricity and water installations wrecked, furniture and fittings were in splinters and large holes had been shot in the walls. There were bodies everywhere which added a smelly contribution to the general atmosphere of warlike desolation and wreckage. Corky put out some work parties to collect the dead and bury them in mass graves. Despite this early effort, bodies were continually being found over the next several days so there seemed to be no escape from the stench of rotting flesh.

Corky's HQ became a most insalubrious place to visit. The staff eventually got used to living with the smell but I never did. When visiting I tried to stop for as short a time as possible. Corky probably felt that I was ill-mannered but I found it difficult to tell him that his headquarters stank. It might have been taken the wrong way!

Included in our booty was a selection of serviceable aircraft. Only a few had been shot up during the assault by Robbie. A veritable treasure was found in the aircraft used by the FAPLA commander, his wife and D'Oliveira. There was a brand-new

AK47, a sub-machine gun, a pistol and many interesting documents and maps that kept Dries van Coller busy for days.

There was an almost new Aztec, a Queen Air and various single-engined light planes that belonged to the MPLA. They were legitimate war booty and it was not long before SAAF pilots were brought in to fly them back to South West Africa.

The next morning we crossed the river and went for the barracks compound. We advanced in copy-book style in long extended lines supported by the armoured cars and Oupa van Dyk's mortars. Oupa, as usual, had to continually move his mortars by bounds and was hard-pressed to keep up with the advance. Finally, when he was in range of the barracks, I allowed him to fire a few shots to see if there was any reaction. There was none.

The armoured cars closed in on the four corners of the high wall surrounding the barracks from where they could support us and also cut off the escape route of any FAPLA who tried to get away. Infantry rushed through the impressive main gates and spread out in the long, three-storeyed main building, clearing rooms as they went. A troop of armoured cars stormed through a central arch under the main building and deployed on the parade square at the back. They readied to fire at anything that moved or looked like FAPLA.

We found only a couple of confused old gentlemen in hard hats and brown overalls who were floating aimlessly around. They said that nobody had been in camp when they arrived for work that morning. They were labourers who had worked for the Portuguese artillery regiment when it was stationed there and for FAPLA more recently. Hopefully, they would be doing the same for FNLA in the immediate future.

Some people see the tide of war come and go and have the knack to adapt to whatever situation comes their way. They let fate roll over them without offering resistance and consider their abnormal way of life to be completely normal. Maybe they are right. Maybe we are the abnormal ones who invariably strive to change situations and peoples to suit ourselves — not always for the better.

Simultaneous with our move on the barracks, Delville Linford's troops descended from their mountain and cleared the central city area. They, like us, encountered no resistance.

On the edge of the parade ground were huge hanger-like warehouses crammed with weapons, ammunition, camouflage fatigues and rations. This was an amazing windfall, especially for the white troops manning the armoured cars who had been issued with only a pair of trousers and one shirt. In the next few days, everybody — Bushman, FNLA and white South African — was issued with brand new combat fatigues. The support company troops were also issued with PPSHs in lieu of their despised Sten guns.

There was a lot of rubbish lying around the main building which suggested a hasty departure. Nevertheless, it was comfortable and convenient so I decided to make it Battle Group Bravo's headquarters and use its accommodation for my officers. I moved into the large and plushly furnished office of the FAPLA commander with its heavy oak desk, deep armchairs, thick carpet and huge but empty bookcases lining the walls. It was on the second floor overlooking the parade ground through an ornate window.

We also found a pub downstairs to use as the officers' club. Alas, it carried no stock.

The troops moved into comfortable bungalows behind the headquarters. The vehicles were despatched to the vehicle park and the tiffies from the armoured car squadron took over existing workshop facilities. At last our vehicles could be properly seen to.

In front of the barracks was a large tarred square with an island in the centre. After our takeover of the barracks an armoured car was posted there, its 90mm gun pointing down the road that led into town. At about 08:00, after we had occupied the barracks, I strolled over to the armoured car to chat to the commander. While talking to him I noticed a car painted in a drab olive approaching from the direction of town. It drove up and stopped about two paces from the armoured car and me. It was being driven by a soldier in camouflage fatigues. In the rear seat were two officers also wearing fatigues. One had a splendid red-banded cap on his head.

I was completely off guard at first until I suddenly realised they were FAPLA and that they were armed! I hurriedly unslung my rifle and fired a couple of bursts into the back of the car. It was the driver's and his passengers' turn to be surprised. The driver took off in a cloud of dust — I suppose it was by reflex action — and he nearly ran over me in the process. He made a hurried U-turn and sped off towards town. The armoured car opened fire with its 30mm Browning and I chipped in with my rifle. We brought the car to a halt before it could turn a corner and get to cover. We followed up in the armoured car but found only the driver dead behind the wheel. From the blood around, it seemed that one passenger had been badly hit, perhaps killed, and had been dragged away by the other one. A few days later a badly injured civilian with gunshot wounds turned up and was admitted to hospital. On interrogation, he turned out to be the fellow in the red cap. He was FAPLA's deputy commander in the area. He had been on his way to work when, in front of his own headquarters, he was shot at and rudely prevented from continuing his duties.

It seemed remarkable that, after the various noisy assaults and the morning's attack on the barracks, there were still people around in Sa da Bandeira who were unaware of the identity of the troops driving around in armoured cars, flying FNLA flags and yelling FNLA slogans. Maybe the FAPLA deputy commander had been out of town and had only arrived back that morning. If that was so, he had probably thought we were Cubans who had come to help them in their fight against the hated Boers.

9

Moçamedes

Brigadier Schoeman flew in from Rundu. He was particularly pleased at the remarkable rate of our advance since the commencement of the campaign two weeks previously. It was 'all systems go' and we were briefed about our next objective — which would be Moçamedes. Its capture would provide us with a viable seaport for logistical support.

A force similar to Zulu, Foxbat, had meanwhile been poking its head out of Nova Lisboa on the major highway to Luanda. It consisted mostly of UNITA troops with a squadron of South African armoured cars in support. Commandant Eddie Webb was the commander. He was a seasoned paratrooper and a friend who had done the Rhodesian SAS selection course with me ten years before. With him were some well-known characters such as Hollie Holtzhausen and Nic Visser, also paratroopers and friends of mine.

There would be two thrusts towards Luanda. Zulu would strike along the coast to open up the ports and Foxbat would head inland on the main route to the north. We were not sure how far north we were expected to go because nobody had told us. Some believed we were trying to capture as much of Angola as possible before 11 November, the official date of independence for Angola. This was to consolidate UNITA's position sufficiently for it to be a viable counter to the communist-supported MPLA. Others thought the intention was to capture the Benguela railway line to cut the export routes of troublesome neighbours like Zambia. Still others believed we would be heading straight for Luanda. The idea would be to put Dr Jonas Savimbi firmly in the Angolan saddle at the barrel of a gun — our gun.

My own FNLA troops asked similar questions but came up with somewhat different answers. They believed that FNLA had achieved all its objectives. Sometime or other Chipenda or Kambuta had told them the aim of the war was to take Sa da Bandeira. With the control of Sa da Bandeira in hand, the surrounding area would be turned into an FNLA bastion. The troops could be demobilised and everyone could settle down and make a good living in what would be a newly created FNLA state.

When it became apparent to my troops that as far as their white commanders were concerned the war was far from over, feelings of dissatisfaction and resentment swept the ranks. Now it seemed, they would be required to march again — this time maybe all the way to Luanda.

I assembled the battalion to explain to them why we could not stop — that we had to defeat FAPLA before there could be peace in Angola. And FAPLA was far from being defeated. They stood muttering in their ranks in their companies, a sullen mass of troops who only needed a small spark to start a mutiny. I had prudently warned a troop of armoured cars to stand by because I had no intention of sacrificing myself and my fellow South African soldiers to the blood lust of an unruly mob.

I spoke in English with Paul translating. It prompted an immediate uproar. Agitators began to shout and instigate trouble within the crowd. It was clear that things were beginning to get out of hand. I signalled the armoured cars to move in and take up positions, one at each corner of the parade ground with their 90mm guns trained inward. They rumbled into position and the shouting died to a murmur, then ceased altogether. They had learned exactly what a 90mm was capable of and they also guessed, correctly, that I would have no scruples about giving the order to open fire.

Soon it was deathly quiet. A stocky chap in the front rank started up again, shouting and shaking his fist and trying to inflame those around him. I lost my temper and stalked into the ranks. I grabbed him by his shirt, pulled him out and clapped him around his ears with a flat hand. Eventually he sank to his knees and begged me to stop. This triggered the welcome sounds of laughter by the crowd at his discomfort. It enabled me to regain control and get them settled down again. I resumed speaking and started to tell them what the war was about. This time I captured their attention. The four armoured cars had probably helped to concentrate their minds.

As I approached the climax of my speech — driving home the message that we were fighting for the survival of an Angola free from communism and imperialism and so on — an awful racket broke out to the rear of the back ranks.

An idiot of a tiffie had liberated a motorcycle from FAPLA and had been repairing it in the workshop. Having fixed it, he decided to take his machine for a trial spin on the parade square. He was apparently oblivious to the fact that a parade was in progress and had no appreciation of the importance of the occasion. I was furious. The whole future of Battle Group Bravo's role in *Operation Savannah* was hanging in the balance on my speech.

'Anton!' I bawled to one of my platoon leaders. 'Shoot that bugger's motor bike! Now!'

'Sir!'

Corporal Anton Retief moved into action with alacrity. He rushed out, cornered the motorcyclist and purposefully unslung his FN rifle. The tiffie scented danger and hurriedly abandoned his motorbike. He left it on its side with wheels spinning and engine roaring and he ran. He wanted to put as much distance between himself and the sergeant who had obviously gone mad.

Bang! Bang! Bang!

Anton fired three deliberate shots into the offending machine and the engine stopped. It was apparent to everyone there that the bike would never again pound the streets of Sa da Bandeira — or anywhere for that matter. Peering around the corner of a building, the shocked tiffie stared white-faced at the demise of his motorcycle. Their short-lived relationship had come to an abrupt and violent end.

A deathly hush settled over the troops. It was quite clear that the old man was exceedingly angry. With the 90mm guns turned inwards, it seemed likely that it would only be a matter of time before it was their turn. I finished my speech without further interruptions. It seems the troops had made up their minds. It would be safer going along with this crazy South African than thwarting him!

I realised that to avert further trouble it was essential I keep the troops busy. I also had to get rid of the elements who had been undermining my authority. These stirrers were mostly former FNLA *commandantes* who had lost their prestige after the South Africans had taken over and filled all the command slots.

ELP unwittingly came to my rescue. Major Aparicio had decided to put his grand scheme into motion. He would declare a free republic in the Huila Province with himself and his men forming the ruling junta. Some of my FNLA troops were understandably disturbed on hearing that Aparicio had been broadcasting on the local radio. In his broadcast he had announced the re-establishment of Portuguese rule in those parts of Angola liberated by the ELP with the assistance of Zulu Force. Until then, I had been unaware that a local radio station even existed.

I informed Corky that Aparicio was creating problems in Huila Province by claiming credit for Zulu Force's efforts. ELP, in fact, had not taken any part in the fighting and had stayed well away from areas where they might have been shot at.

Corky did not regard Aparicio as a major threat. Nevertheless, he distrusted him and admonished Aparicio about the contents of his radio broadcast. He made it clear that he should have made every effort to calm the people, not sow dissension by mustering support for himself and his organisation. Corky informed him that he had appointed Commandant Shylock Mulder as the acting mayor of the town. Henceforth all decisions relating to the disposal of loot and captured war booty would rest with him.

I gathered the *commandantes* together and explained that there was an imminent danger of FNLA losing control of Huila Province. I suggested they should form a political committee, wrest control of the radio station from Aparicio and start their own broadcasting service. They liked the idea and they moved out of the barracks into more luxurious quarters in town. After establishing themselves as a FNLA governing body, Aparicio and his crew abandoned their ideas of establishing a power base within southern Angola — let alone the liberation of Portugal — and they faded from the scene.

On Corky's instructions and to keep the troops busy, I dispatched Major Toon Slabbert with two troops of armoured cars and Captain Jack Dippenaar's company to Hoque on the main road to Nova Lisboa. They were told to clear the area of FAPLA. They found no evidence of FAPLA until they reached Hoque where they ran into a well-prepared ambush. Jack said later that he had never seen troops dismount as rapidly as his did. They slid from the mountain of kit stacked in the back of the trucks and hit the deck at the run.

There was a fierce fight that the armoured cars joined with their machine guns. They were too close to the enemy positions, however, to bring their main armaments to bear. Jack's troops finally overran FAPLA's positions and cleared the town. Jack suffered a few casualties, but in comparison FAPLA's were very heavy. It proved to be a most satisfying action. They arrived back at our garrison late that evening, full of war stories and ready for their nightly beer, pãos and cheese in our comfortable officers' club.

Lieutenant Connie van Wyk was sent to Vila de Arriaga and I went with him. It was down the escarpment to the west on the old road to Moçamedes. We passed through spectacular scenery as the dirt road wound steeply down the side of a rugged mountain range similar to the Drakensberg in South Africa, but not quite as high. The rainy season had commenced and streams had filled and were beginning to tumble down the mountains into thickly vegetated foothills below. Farther west towards the Atlantic coast the landscape became flatter and progressively drier.

We found only a few railway officials at Vila de Arriaga which was a neat little village at the bottom of the pass. There was no sign of FAPLA so we returned to Sa da Bandeira. I sent Sergeant Costa Marão's company back to João de Almeida. He was to tackle FAPLA gangs that we had either bypassed or who had reformed. They were threatening our lines of communication. Costa's men remained in the area for a week and accounted for approximately 150 FAPLA.

We had captured two Soviet-supplied 82mm B10 recoilless guns and mounted them on Land-Rovers The B10 was very useful in an anti-tank or anti-personnel role. We also managed to extract six paratroopers from Corky. He had been given a whole platoon of them but had kept them for protection of his headquarters. I split the six paratroopers into two teams of three for each B10. Under Connie's direction they were taught to fire these guns effectively. This gave me a viable anti-tank capability within Battle Group Bravo apart from the 90mm armoured cars which were not an integral part of our force.

Finally we were ordered to advance on Moçamedes.

Delville Linford, accompanied by Zulu Headquarters, moved on the new tarred road down the escarpment. Battle Group Bravo advanced via Vila de Arriaga rapidly because we had travelled the route before. Beyond Vila de Arriaga we passed through one narrow defile after another. They were flanked by hills close to the road and provided a series of ideal ambush positions. We cut the telegraph line every few kilometres as a precaution to prevent the enemy getting an early warning of our approach.

The terrain began to flatten out and it was then that we ran into FAPLA resistance. A small patrol had set up a delaying position, probably when they saw the head of the column appear from the mouth of the valley to the east. They clearly had no idea of our strength because they ended up being pulverised by the advance patrol of armoured cars, Oupa van Dyk's mortars and an infantry platoon. We killed five including a female — the first female FAPLA soldier we had seen. The rest vanished into the bush.

This skirmish was memorable only because of the slow reaction of Sergeant Mecchie van der Merwe's platoon when we hit the contact. Mecchie, so-called because he used to be an aircraft mechanic, was taken to task by me and told that in the future his platoon would lead the advance until I was satisfied that their reactions had been honed to my satisfaction.

Leading the advance of a column is not the healthiest job. Consequently, Mecchie's platoon sharpened considerably from sheer necessity. They looked at me expectantly for a favourable reaction after each contact, but I hardened my heart and kept them at it until long after we had taken Moçamedes. It was only then that I relented and moved them to the rear. Each time we struck a contact the replacement platoon acted with commendable alacrity without the need for prompting. It appeared that the lesson I had taught Mecchie and his men had spread throughout the battle group.

The winding road and our caution meant that we arrived late at Caraculo— the centre of karakul farming in Angola. We rejoined the main road there and discovered from locals that Delville had already passed through en route to Moçamedes. The local terrain is similar to the South African Karoo, but is closer to the coast. This arid strip of desert is a continuation of the Namib Desert to the south. We drove westwards in the gathering gloom into pure desert until we came across Corky's headquarters. He told us to pull off the road.

Delville had run into a strong FAPLA position up ahead and a fierce battle was raging. Tracers streamed across the night sky, there were the flashes of explosions and the deep crump of mortar bombs. We could see the odd vehicle silhouetted against the skyline on top of a sand dune. The battle had a World War-II Western Desert atmosphere about it. With a touch of imagination one could almost visualise the British Eighth Army and the German Afrika Korps slugging it out among the dunes.

We laagered in long lines of vehicles as our Springbok predecessors had once done in the Western Desert. We set our defences, then brewed tea and cooked food on make-shift stoves made from petrol cans half-filled with sand and doused with petrol, as they had once done. With the accompaniment of tracers, flares and crumping mortar shells in the background, the Western Desert picture was complete — right down to the chill that set in once darkness had fallen.

We awoke the following morning to survey a desolate landscape. The fighting had long since stopped and the dunes where FAPLA had attempted to stop Delville lay ahead.

Battle Group Bravo was tasked to pass through Delville's Bushmen and lead the advance on Moçamedes. Corky had accurate air photographs of this major seaport that would assist me in the planning of the forthcoming assault. It was a mystery to me where Corky got his air photos. They were always procured on time and available for planning the next attack.

Moçamedes had a similar layout to Pereira de Eça but it was bigger. I planned an attack by two companies, one east of the main road and the other to the west. A rifle section supported by an armoured car would be provided for each street that ran parallel to the main road. The cross streets would be used as coordination lines.

Jack Dippenaar's company would move first, clear the approaches to the town and secure a start line for the final assault. He would have the 81mm mortars and Oupa's three-inch mortars on call for fire support. Oupa's mortars, as usual, would move in bounds so as to stay within range. The machine guns would leapfrog along the eastern flank, giving support where it was required and cutting off any attempt by FAPLA to escape into the desert. I would control the assault line and rate of advance from the centre of the two companies.

After this we would clear the old airfield to the east and the new airfield to the southeast. Connie van Wyk would take his company to Porto Alexandre, a fishing harbour down the coast, and secure it.

Corky produced a guide for me. A local Portuguese man had appeared at his headquarters the previous evening and volunteered. His name was Martins (pronounced Martiens).

Corky had given an ultimatum to a Portuguese parachute unit based in Moçamedes to leave if they did not want to get involved in the battle. A small Portuguese military liaison team had come to his headquarters the previous day to assure him of their neutrality. The Portuguese paratroopers were a good bunch who had been soured by the inexplicable capitulation by the Army to Marxist demands from factions within the armed forces. Those still in town were flown to Luanda with Corky's permission.

There was also a Portuguese Navy frigate in the harbour. Corky feared intervention by the ship's personnel in favour of MPLA, so he instructed the naval officer accompanying the team to ensure the ship was out of harbour by first light and this was done. The navy was notoriously riddled with communists, so Corky was quite right in insisting that they either leave voluntarily or face being thrown out.

We moved ahead and took over the advance from Delville, passing the signs of the previous night's battle. Wrecked and burnt-out vehicles cluttered the road while some still-smouldering bodies, called 'smokies' by Delville, were lying here and there. Delville had also seized a lot of equipment including another 122mm rocket launcher mounted on a brand-new Unimog.

As we approached a dense forest — the only vegetation in the area — we came under small-arms fire. From the sand dunes we moved into a jungle situation, clearing the enemy in next to no time with our infantry. Mecchie van der Merwe, in the lead, went into action like greased lightning. After crossing a combined road/railway bridge over a dry river bed, we entered the port city proper.

Jack swept the approaches and two companies formed up on the first lateral road, each rifle section with an armoured car in attendance. The long line of infantry followed by the armoured cars moved forward in copybook style. There was no sign of life anywhere. The residents remained indoors, no doubt apprehensive that FNLA would launch a looting, killing and raping spree on them. It must have come as a pleasant surprise to the locals to see troops from a liberation movement carrying out a sweep under strict control and acting with the well-disciplined restraint of professional soldiers.

In the town itself we came up against no resistance, but we encountered a strong pocket on the southern side as we left the built-up area. A sharp firefight developed between Jack's company plus the armoured cars and FAPLA who had dug in around their headquarters. The contact lasted for about 30 minutes before the FAPLA remnants scampered off in the direction of the airport.

A large quantity of equipment and stores was seized at their headquarters. There were numerous weapons there including fine hunting rifles, ammunition and rations.

There was also a large quantity of expensive brandy, whisky and liqueurs. The booze was placed under strict guard but Jack, in a moment of mental aberration, ordered that it be loaded into a SAAF C130 for shipping back to Rundu for our later consumption. It was a bad mistake. Needless to say, it was the last we saw of our Napoleon brandy and Glenfiddich whisky. Jack should have known better than to accept the offer of an air force pilot to transport those luxuries and delicacies to a place of safety. With liquor like that, who could say where it would be safe?

Jack continued to the old airport where, after a short skirmish, his company killed or captured the remaining FAPLA in the area. Connie faced no resistance when he moved his company into the dockyard area. He found a veritable treasure trove. There were dozens of new tipper trucks, about 400 new pick-up vans, dozens of tractors and bulldozers and various other kinds of equipment that filled several warehouses. Many of the vehicles and the earthmoving equipment had been destined for Zambia but, because the war broke out, it never got there.

Connie continued to Porto Alexandre and took it without resistance. He was back at Moçamedes by late the same evening.

With Moçamedes secured, I took Martins to the only decent hotel in town. By then people were out in the streets in huge crowds. We passed through one joyful throng after another. They cheered wildly when they recognised Martins. He could not restrain himself either and returned the cheers with his hands clasped above his head like a conquering hero, alternating the gesture with the FNLA sign.

'Martins! Martins! Martins!' the multitude screamed.

A simple trip to a hotel had become a triumphant procession. Crowds fell in behind us and trotted to keep up with my Land Cruiser. I dropped Martins off at the hotel. He was mobbed by a back-slapping, kissing and hugging crowd. I thought he would probably be appointed the next mayor of Moçamedes.

Moçamedes was a clean and attractive place, especially the esplanade which was overlooked by the old fort that was used as a jail and also as the headquarters of the Prefecture. I found the Angolan police unconcernedly going about their business. I made my acquaintance with the Chief of Police and after coffee we parted on friendly terms.

The harbour at Moçamedes is a natural and very large one. There were general cargo jetties on the south side and skirting the bay on the north side stood recently constructed iron ore jetties capable of handling the largest ore carriers. Beyond the main dock area were fish and crayfish factories. Deep-sea trawlers, which kept the factories supplied, were moored offshore. With its railway line stretching as far inland as Serpa Pinto, this was an important port that could complement our logistical system admirably.

Junior, meanwhile, had managed to trace his mother and younger brother and he brought them to our laager. Like a real professional, he conducted Little Junior — who was only four years old and a miniature edition of his elder brother — around and showed him the armoured cars explaining how their impressive guns worked. They wandered hand-in-hand through the parked armoured cars and the adulation Little Junior held for his big brother was obvious in his eyes. I arranged for Junior's return to his mother — to his disgust because he had ambitions of becoming a real fighting soldier. His mother was loaded with a bountiful supply of rations and blankets. That was the last I saw of Junior. I heard later that his father was released from Moçamedes Prison shortly afterwards.

*   *   *

Brigadier Schoeman arrived at Moçamedes' old airport in fine fettle. The war was becoming a pushover and the advance far more rapid than he had ever expected. The brigadier accompanied Zulu Headquarters on an inspection of the Portuguese paratroopers' quarters. They had left the place in a frightful mess, with human excrement on tables, chairs and beds. The paratroopers had clearly made a statement that could not be misunderstood by those taking over the old Portuguese colony.

They had also abandoned a large quantity of Portuguese Army ration packs which we gathered up with gratitude. Most men preferred them to the South African rat packs, although the question was purely academic as we were getting no ration packs whatsoever at the time.

I sent for Sergeant Costa Marão and briefed him regarding his Charlie company. It would remain behind as an occupying force to ferret out any pockets of FAPLA resistance that might still remain in the area. The city folk were strictly pro-FNLA by this time, but probably only because we appeared to be the winning side. In Africa it is customary to back the strongest side or the winners with absolute enthusiasm — it is better for one's health.

Costa Marão and Silva Sierro, with their experience as DGS officers and an intimate knowledge of both Portuguese nationals and African Angolans, secured the area soon after we returned to Sa da Bandeira. FAPLA stragglers were rounded up and handed over to the new local authority, the control of which switched to UNITA a few days later. UNITA had become adept at following in the wake of Zulu and picking up anything going. What they did with the FAPLA prisoners was anybody's guess.

10

Regrouping

Back in Sa da Bandeira we discovered another FNLA force. It was commanded by Major Frank Bestbier and was ensconced in a block of flats south of our artillery barracks. It comprised two companies that had been formed and trained at Serpa Pinto by Frank and a staff of other South Africans. I was surprised to learn of its existence. I must have passed through Serpa Pinto while Frank was busy knocking them into shape without hearing of them.

Chipenda had his headquarters in Serpa Pinto, so Frank had seen him frequently. He was full of information regarding our mutual boss' drinking and womanising habits which, by all accounts, were of monumental proportions. He was also a great orator and motivator and could sway his audience with little effort. In other words, he was a typical example of Africa-style politicians — great at arousing the bloodlust of mobs but short on producing results.

Colonel Corky van Heerden decided that Frank's two companies would be amalgamated to form part of Battle Group Bravo and Frank would become my second-in-command. His companies, commanded by Captain Grobbie Grobbelaar and Major Jock Harris, were absorbed as Charlie and Delta companies respectively. Sergeant Costa Marão's Charlie company, still in Moçamedes at the time, became an independent unit.

The two new companies looked good and appeared to be well trained. There was a smattering of Zaïre-trained FNLA commandos amongst them who wore distinguishing red scarves to show that they were graduates of Zaïre's Commando School. Prominent in their number was *Commandante* Geraldo, Frank's right-hand man when liaising with the black soldiers. Frank also wore a red scarf and looked quite natty in his Commando School camouflage uniform. I was also happy to see some men from my old unit, 1-Reconnaissance Commando, amongst the platoon commanders.

Major Nic Visser, my original choice as second-in-command, had been sent by the brigadier to assist UNITA at Nova Lisboa. I would have appreciated Nic's well developed organising abilities, to say nothing of his unique sense of humour. Frank, as it happened, also turned out to be a star in the field of organising, so in the end it was only Nic's humour and personal friendship that I missed. Nic and I had come through much together in 1-Parachute Battalion and later when he was my second-in-command at 1-Reconnaissance Commando.

The day after our return to Sa da Bandeira, I was sitting on the back verandah of the main building boiling water in a fire bucket over a small fire. Suddenly someone approached and greeted me arrogantly.

'*Bom dia*' (Good day).

I looked up to see a splendidly dressed individual in crackling new camouflage fatigues, shiny new boots, a red scarf and a length of red mountain rope with two interlocking karabiners around his fat stomach. There was gold braid on his shoulders and he wore a peaked cap and sunglasses. Slightly behind him was a second well dressed character, only a little less gaudily adorned, who was carrying the first officer's briefcase. The first man was obviously of high rank and judging by the scarf and the mountain rope, was also a graduate of the Commando School in Zaïre.

Fortunately Paul was waiting for his tea close by. While he was useless at the preparation of food or even coffee, he saw no shame in having his commanding officer do it for him. Paul stepped forward and acted as interpreter.

'I want to speak to the FNLA commander', the splendid one said brusquely.

'I am the FNLA commander', I retorted. 'Who are you?'

'I am General (I forget his name), the newly appointed governor of Huila Province. I want to speak to the black FNLA commander. I don't want to speak to you.'

'There is no black FNLA commander. I am the commander of this battalion so you will have to speak to me.'

'In that case I will speak to the company commanders.'

'You cannot speak to the company commanders alone, but I am willing to call them so that you can address all of us together.'

I sent Paul to fetch the company commanders. I continued to brew my tea and offered some to the general from my fire-blackened bucket. He declined, rather impolitely I thought.

Without moving he rocked on his heels and let his eyes roam over the parade ground, the barracks, the Eland armoured cars and the stacks of captured weapons and equipment.

My company commanders eventually arrived; he was clearly shocked.

' What has happened to the *commandantes*? Why do you only have white officers?'

'I sacked the *commandantes* because they were bloody useless. Anyway, the troops didn't like them', I replied.

'Can I address the troops then?'

'No, if you have anything to say, say it to me. I will convey it to them.'

'In that case, I am wasting my time. Good day.'

He stalked out indignantly, followed by the minion with his briefcase.

I could not be certain, but because of the near-mutiny which I had to cope with earlier, I suspected that he was making another bid for the loyalty and services of the FNLA troops. I had come to regard them as my troops. I had replaced their FNLA *commandantes* with South Africans because they did not have the stomach or the training for a good scrap. The general, I believed, wanted a strong military unit under his personal command to uphold his political authority in the province by force. He came to the barracks unannounced in the obvious expectation that his grand entrance would throw us off-balance. This ploy, had it succeeded, would have given him the chance to address the troops without us understanding a word he was saying.

Later that evening we were briefed by Corky.

With Battle Group Bravo in the lead, we resumed the advance the next morning.

I never discovered whether Corky knew anything about the general in the fancy dress uniform. For myself, I did not deem it important enough to inform Zulu Headquarters. For the moment the general had moved offstage. He would resurface much later in the campaign in somewhat humbler circumstances.

11

Catengue

I was pleased to get away from Sa da Bandeira. Its undercurrents of political manoeuvring and hidden agendas had begun to impact negatively on our operational readiness. On our last day there UNITA had appeared and entered the scheme of things. It left the city seething in a cauldron of intrigue and political uncertainty.

I was ordered to leave Major Jock Harris and his Delta company for use by Colonel Corky van Heerden's successor as commander of the peacekeeping troops in the city. This reduced my strength to three rifle companies and the mortar and machine-gun platoons. The anti-tank platoon, excluding the two B10s, died a quiet death as most of its members elected to remain in Sa da Bandeira. It appeared they found politics more to their liking than fighting — especially as we were beginning to come up against Cubans.

Captain Jack Dippenaar detoured the column to Hoque where he had previously skirmished with FAPLA. There was no sign of them now. According to Major Dries van Coller and our advance patrol FAPLA was at the next town. On reaching it, the leading armoured car troop deployed and shelled those areas of town thought likely to be harbouring the enemy. Jack shook his troops out into two assault platoons. Keeping one in reserve, he used the other to enter town along the main road, clearing houses as they went. They met no resistance. A civilian was slightly wounded by a 90mm armoured car shell as he ran in panic from the service station to seek cover in the bush. Our doctor stitched up his injuries and we sent him home in reasonably good shape.

We spent the night in the town and next morning Delville's Battle Group Alpha took over the lead. While the Bushmen advanced steadily up the road, my troops relaxed on the shady stoeps of houses, glad to get shelter from the scorching sun while they awaited my order to board the vehicles. For some reason or other Corky decided to take a drive down the main street. He was decidedly unimpressed with Battle Group Bravo who appeared to be lounging around in lazy indolence and not taking the least notice of the appearance of their brigade commander. Corky found me at the town's entrance.

'Your troops have no discipline', Corky said angrily.

This put me on the defensive. I was the only one allowed to describe my troops as useless and ill-disciplined.

'I cannot accept that. They are better disciplined than the white troops and the Bushmen', I said.

I conveniently forgot about the near mutiny of a few days ago.

'Why do you call them ill-disciplined?'

'They refuse to respect me. They don't even get to their feet when I appear. I have even experienced problems getting into your camp. They treat their brigade commander with total disrespect.'

'Corky, I don't believe it. They always come to attention and salute when they see a senior officer.'

'Well let's drive through town. You'll see how they're lounging about. They're so idle they don't even bother to brush the flies off their faces.'

Corky and I drove down the main street. Everywhere we went soldiers jumped smartly to attention and saluted while grinning from ear to ear.

Corky remained furious.

'Teach your troops to pay their respects to me — not just to you and your officers. Tell them who I am, dammit! You've probably never even told them that I'm the senior commander in this road-show of comedians.'

Later that morning a man strolled up to make our acquaintance. To my surprise he introduced himself as a Mr Visser and addressed us in perfect although somewhat outmoded Afrikaans. I pretended not to understand but he had no intention of falling for that. He told me bluntly that all the whites in my force were South Africans. He could recognise a South African, particularly an Afrikaner South African, a mile off. He was a descendent of the Dorsland Trekkers. A Boer, he said, will recognise another Boer anywhere in the world.

He said that FAPLA had pulled out the previous day. They were waiting in ambush at a bridge up the road. We had evidently arrived in the nick of time for him because FAPLA had been about to close his café which was the only one in town. Major Dries van Coller, the intelligence officer, took him over from me.

We mounted our vehicles and set off after Delville.

Meanwhile, Delville had reached a bridge, but he was uncertain if it was the bridge that Visser had spoken about. It was dominated by high ground beyond the river where it seemed likely that FAPLA had dug in. Recent signs of digging were apparent. The probable positions looked tremendously strong, although there were no signs of FAPLA. This did not mean much because they were skilled at concealing both themselves and their crew-served weapons.

Delville decided to send troops to outflank the enemy. They would cross the river by a ford farther downstream and attack the FAPLA positions from the rear. The rest of us could do nothing so we halted the advance and waited for Delville to resolve the situation.

The hours ticked by but the troops Delville had detached did not reappear on the opposite bank. Finally, Corky could contain his patience no longer. He moved the armoured cars into firing positions on a hill overlooking the bridge and ordered them to blast the suspected enemy positions. The bombardment lasted for about ten minutes, but there was no reaction from the enemy.

Corky and Major Dries van Coller led the advance on foot, covered by armoured cars which followed. No fire was drawn and there were no signs of life. An engineer, protected by an infantry patrol, was sent to inspect the bridge. Demolition charges were found but they had been poorly laid. Even if the enemy had tried to detonate them, the ringmain system would have malfunctioned.

It was assumed the FAPLA troops had fled their trenches as soon as Delville's lead armoured car poked its 90mm gun over the horizon.

Our Zulu Force reputation for surprisingly fast movement and unexpected violent action had preceded us. I think many a FAPLA commander had his work cut out to keep his men in position when word got around that we were on the way. Most of the commanders, though, probably did not try too hard themselves as they were also not keen to oppose what had become an irresistible advance.

Corky ordered me to take the lead to allow Delville time to extricate his battalion from the difficult terrain some of his units had got themselves into while trying his outflanking manoeuvre.

We advanced rapidly and laagered for the evening at a farm just short of Catengue. En route we had bought some goats from a farmer. It was certainly a change to indulge in the good old South African custom of braaivleis (barbecue) — even if it was only goat meat.

Delville caught us up long after dark. He was thoroughly fed up with rivers, swamps, the terrain in general and some members of his Portuguese leader element in particular.

I sent out a security patrol comprising a troop of armoured cars, a platoon of infantry and the two B10s manned by my paratroopers. Just before last light a FAPLA patrol came sneaking up the road, probably to probe our position and strength. They bumped my security patrol about a kilometre up the road towards Catengue and there was a brisk firefight. We were laagered on high ground overlooking the scene of action and we watched the fight develop as interested spectators. But the entertainment stopped all too soon and we returned to our braaivleis.

FAPLA scampered back towards Catengue. It seemed they had suffered no casualties and nor had we. I deemed it prudent to redeploy the security patrol farther forward towards the enemy in case they decided to attack us again with a stronger force.

At first light we kicked off the advance with Connie's company in the lead. We were expecting a full-blooded fight in Catengue itself as the centre was strategically important to both sides. It straddles the main road from Benguela to Nova Lisboa in the east and the one to Sa da Bandeira in the south. The latter road forms a T-junction with the Benguela/Nova Lisboa road. Catengue is also an important station on the Benguela railway line. Taking the town would place us behind the right flank of the FAPLA forces that were facing UNITA over to the east. We would also be straddling their lateral communication lines between Benguela and Nova Lisboa.

We approached the town cautiously from the south. The mortars were deployed in well selected base-plate positions and the armoured cars were as far forward as possible so they could bring their firepower to bear the moment the enemy showed themselves.

Connie's company was stretched out in extended line and ready to clear the town.

There was an eerie silence over the whole place and nothing happened.

A sedan car suddenly appeared from the direction of Nova Lisboa. An armoured car opened fire and brought it to a fiery standstill. On closer inspection it seemed the dead occupants were senior officers from FRELIMO — the Mozambican resistance movement. It appeared they were in the field with FAPLA as observers. The war was becoming more internationalised almost by the day. Unfortunately for them, their 'observing' came to an abrupt and violent end at Catengue. We were pleased about our catch as their obviously high ranks made up for their lack of numbers.

Connie moved through town and pronounced it cleared of FAPLA. We had no idea where they had gone. In fact, the town was empty as its civilian inhabitants had also fled. It was the first town we had found that was emptied of civilians and this seemed ominous. I routinely informed Corky that the place had been cleared. He moved and established his headquarters under a huge baobab tree on the bank of a dry stream.

There was a sudden explosive thump and a strange cloud of dust rising to the west. It was followed by the sigh of a missile passing overhead. It exploded behind us with a tremendous bang and an impressive column of black smoke. It was a 122mm rocket — the Soviet Katyusha or Red Eye — as it became known to us later in the campaign.

It seemed odd to me that only a single rocket had been fired at us and not a barrage. I decided to send Jack Dippenaar's company along the main road to Benguela for about five kilometres in the direction of firing. He would clear the hills and approaches to the west. Connie van Wyk was sent on a similar errand out on the road to Nova Lisboa. They were ordered to take up blocking positions to protect both us and Zulu Headquarters. This would allow Corky and his staff to continue their planning of the war without the interruption of more rockets.

Toon Slabbert and I sat under Zulu Headquarter's baobab, cups of tea in hand, and contemplated our higher command in action. Corky, Willie, Dries and the rest were making a sand model for a briefing session.

Suddenly all hell broke loose in the direction of Jack's deployment. Toon and I looked at each other and decided that Jack should be able to handle whatever was going on while we finished our tea.

The crescendo of battle increased alarmingly, however, and seemed to be coming in our direction. This could only mean that Jack was returning in a hurry. We gulped down our near scalding tea and set out for the battle scene — Toon in his armoured car and I in what suddenly seemed to be a very vulnerable open Land Cruiser.

I came across some members of Jack's company on the western outskirts of town. They were trying to rapidly put some distance between themselves and FAPLA. Most kept running and refused to stop and talk. It was probable that in their panic they did not even recognise me, their own commander. I rallied a few with difficulty and turned them back towards the enemy.

Jack, with what was left of his company plus a troop of armoured cars, were four or five kilometres up the road. The problem was that just out of town, was straddled with incoming artillery fire and shells were continually mushrooming on the tar. To get to Jack we would have no option but to run this gauntlet.

With Paul in the passenger seat I charged my Land Cruiser at top speed into the mushrooming clouds in imitation of the Charge of the Light Brigade. Shells were bursting all around us. The noise was tremendous and I was told later that at one point my vehicle disappeared completely in the cloud of debris of a near miss. Jack, in fact, sent an eyewitness report to Corky that I had been killed by an enemy mortar shell. Unfortunately, he forgot to report his error to Zulu HQ who later in the day discovered me alive and well in Jack's company position. So for quite some time Corky remained erroneously under the impression that I would be unavailable to help him out of awkward situations in the future.

We caught up with the armoured cars. They were positioned behind a crest and pounding away at FAPLA about 800 metres up the road. I parked the Land Cruiser in a cutting and clambered up to the buttoned-up armoured cars. In the cutting below and slightly behind us were the four 81mm mortars. They were firing at a very rapid rate, but wildly. One mortar had a cook-off, caused by an overheated barrel, and a bomb landed about 200 metres in front of us. The mortars were also under enemy fire. Almost simultaneous to the cook-off, the discarded secondary charges caught fire and flared up with intense flame and smoke. The mortar crews scattered in all directions.

For a brief moment I thought I had lost my 81mm mortars, but once the smoke cleared I saw they were still there. The mortar men returned and apprehensively continued to drop bombs down the voracious throats of their weapons. There was no fire direction, however, and the shots were scattering widely over the FAPLA positions.

Oupa van Dyk and his three-inch mortar teams were chomping at the bit but I could not bring them into play as they did not have enough range to reach the FAPLA trenches. I could only deploy them in depth behind the 81mms, mainly as a secure base for fire support in the event FAPLA managed to launch an infantry attack on our positions and force us back to the outskirts of town.

There was a low rise about halfway to the FAPLA defensive system ahead of the armoured cars. Farther back was the river and a bridge. Just beyond that was FAPLA's main position. I could not see any trenches but my vision was obscured by backblast and the smoke of war as they laid into us with 75mm and B10 recoilless guns. Just in front of the crest were several heavy machine guns that were creating a curtain of fire through which an advance would be suicidal.

At last we had found the bridge that Mr Visser had told us about!

There was a continuous crackle of automatic fire at the foot of the FAPLA hill. This concerned me as I had been under the impression that Jack and his men were still engaged in an eyeball-to-eyeball confrontation with FAPLA along the west bank of the river. I was upset with the armoured cars which, I believed, had left Jack's company in a very precarious position when retiring to seek shelter from the recoilless guns.

I banged on the troop leader's hatch. I was angry and worried about the safety — perhaps even the survival — of Bravo Company.

'Why did you abandon Captain Jack Dippenaar and his men when you ran for cover? You should have brought them back with you or stayed and fought it out with them.'

The troop leader opened his hatch only enough for him to talk through. He obviously had no desire to be clobbered by flying shrapnel.

'But, sir, they did come back with us', he replied indignantly.

'Where are their lorries then?'

'They abandoned them just short of the bridge.'

The troop leader also began to get worried. If Jack and his company were not around, where were they? Had they retreated back to town and left the armoured cars on their own without infantry support? He eyed me somewhat dubiously, possibly weighing me up as the only infantryman still around who could protect the cars against a close-in attack by a thoroughly aroused FAPLA.

The enemy mortar fire was intensifying. Occasionally a salvo of four or five Red Eye rockets arrived to add to the cacophony. We discovered later that the enemy had deployed fifteen 82mm mortars and a battery of vehicle-mounted Red Eye launchers.

Our own 81mm mortars had begun shooting at the base of the FAPLA positions from where the light automatic fire was emanating. They did little to significantly reduce the volume of fire and it was not long before their commander reported that they had run out of ammunition. I had noticed the absence of a mobile fire controller who should have been directing their fire to make it more effective. It was the mortar group commander's job to sit where I was and bring accurate fire onto the enemy targets — in particular his crew-served weapons. Most of the ammunition fired had been wasted. All they had done was add to the general din of battle. Somewhat disgusted, I allowed the mortar commander to withdraw his battery from the action.

I suddenly caught sight of Jack Dippenaar through the thick bush. He was slightly to the right of the armoured cars. I made my way over to the remnants of his company — not more than 40 or 50 men. Fortunately, some of those whom I had turned back at the edge of town were dribbling back from the rear. The company slowly started to grow back to a reasonable size.

Jack had a few serious casualties and several lightly wounded men. He had no idea how many had been killed or were missing. Nel was bleeding from a shrapnel wound in his nose which made him sound as if he was suffering from a severe attack of adenoids.

Jack told me that he had dismounted from the transports in front of the bridge. His troops had spread out in an extended line ready to cross the dry river bed when FAPLA opened up with heavy automatic fire at short range from the other side. His advance had faltered, broken down and turned into an uncontrolled retreat. Jack was still having a hell of a job keeping his men in their present positions. The company seemed very jittery, but at least they were obeying Jack's command to stay where they were without scampering to the rear. I had no doubt that only the smallest spark would have caused them to resume their headlong flight to safety —— perhaps out of the war altogether.

There was no doubt we were facing the best organised and heaviest FAPLA position to date. If we did not win, it was doubtful that Battle Group Bravo would ever fight again. The situation called for a tangible sign that their commander was unconcerned, although I was not at all confident that Jack's Bravo company, in the state they were in, could stop FAPLA before Corky's HQ was overrun.

I decided that bit of play-acting was called for. I collected firewood, started a fire in the company position and began to brew tea. When they saw me enjoying my tea, the troops began to smile. It seemed obvious I intended to stay for a while. The old man was not contemplating a hasty retreat. In that case, the situation could not be too bad. Gradually the company started to fight back.

I decided I needed a boost to our combat power. I got on the radio to Zulu Headquarters and requested the services of a full 81mm mortar platoon that had arrived from Sa da Bandeira that morning. I also wanted my machine-gun platoon moved up to the crest of the hill where we were sitting to give us more firepower. Grobbie Grobbelaar's Charlie company also had to be readied to move in case I required them. Zulu, needless to say, were relieved that I was still around to pester them.

The machine-gun platoon included a low-bed truck on which eight Vickers guns were mounted. The drill was to turn the truck broadside on to the enemy, then engage with devastating destructive power. The continuous stream of lead flattened everything in its path with a weight of fire rarely equalled by the armoured cars. No FAPLA forces could stand up to such a death-dealing deluge of fire.

Vickers machine guns can fire prolonged bursts. I think, perhaps, that Fingers Kruger had somewhat overtrained his men in some ways. Their idea of a long burst was to run a belt of 250 rounds through the gun without a pause. The next burst would be the next belt after the gun had been reloaded. With 12 machine guns, including four in the Land-Rovers, hammering away with bursts of 250 rounds, the effect was awesome.

Toon Slabbert brought up two more armoured car troops. With the Vickers machine guns, we began to look quite respectable. FAPLA, if they still intended to push us out of Catengue, had lost the initiative by not pressing forward with their attack.

A young officer carrying a radio set and his mortar platoon sergeant appeared at my command post. I had shifted it to higher ground to the left of the cutting. He introduced himself as Lieutenant Aucamp, said he was the new mortar platoon leader and asked where he should establish his base-plate positions. His sergeant, Jack Greef, would later become a highly decorated Recce operator. He and his mortar team had only arrived from South Africa earlier that morning. I was impressed because shells were falling all around our command post, yet he remained unconcerned. It was a remarkable performance for a young subaltern, as it must surely have been the first time in his military career that he had been under fire. With the intensity of fire around us, it was hardly a painless introduction to war.

After discussions I decided to deploy his platoon along with the three-inch mortars about 1 000 metres to the rear. He and Sergeant Jack Greef then proceeded to discuss his fire plan with me. This was a refreshing change, considering that the previous mortar commander had forgotten all about fire plans. I felt that the first job was to tackle the crew-served weapons on the crest of the FAPLA hill and put them out of action with concentrated mortar fire. Following that, we could next tackle the FAPLA position at the foot of the hill.

Aucamp listened for a while, then respectfully suggested he be allowed first to use his mortars in a counter-bombardment role, considering the enemy were plastering us with their own mortars. After that he could go for other targets I had suggested. In other words, he was suggesting with respect that my fire plan was not particularly clever. The platoon leader's confidence astonished me. To use mortars in a counter-bombardment role, one needed equipment like the Cymboline (a radar device used to plot positions of enemy mortars and guns) to get an accurate range and bearing to the enemy mortar positions. Consequently, heavy artillery, which we did not possess, is used in a counter-bombardment role — not mortars.

'How would you manage that?' I asked.

'Well, sir, I can hear each mortar tube when it fires. I'll take a bearing on the sound of the first one, press my stopwatch, wait for the first shell burst from the salvo, press the watch again, get the time of flight, adjust it roughly against the speed of sound at this altitude, look at my 81mm mortar range tables opposite the adjusted time of flight and get a rough range. I'll then convert the information to bearing and range for my own base-plate positions. Then I'll play my mortars up and down 400 metres either side of the calculated enemy base-plates.'

This young officer had calmly worked out a rough and ready counter-bombardment system while he was busily ducking heavy enemy mortar, B10 and rocket fire — to say nothing of the continual streams of incoming lead from 12.7mm and 14.5mm machine guns.

'Jump to it', I said with enthusiasm.

We were taking quite a few casualties. It was also not very pleasant being plastered by enemy shells while sitting helplessly in the open on a rocky hill where digging in was an impossibility.

Lieutenant Aucamp made his calculations and it was not long before all eight of his 81mm mortars were barking back at the enemy's 82mms. He played his mortar fire up and down and the enemy fire slackened, then stopped as the mortar crews packed it in and ran to the rear to get out of range. They opened up again some time later but could not reach us from their new positions. This left us with their recoilless guns, heavy machine guns and a few Red Eyes to contend with. The Red Eyes were far less accurate than the mortars and, as we soon found out, far less destructive.

Corky and Willie Kotze, a gunner of some repute, had watched Aucamp's unorthodox application of mortar fire from a command post well to the rear. Being out of touch with the battle they were shocked to see Aucamp plastering a position that they thought was some distance to the enemy's rear.

In front of me, three paratroopers were sitting almost in the open with their B10. They fired at each and every flash on the FAPLA side and even silenced some of their crew-served weapons. From the crest of our hill my machine-gun platoon went into action against the FAPLA at the foot of the hill. Soon the sustained fire of 12 Vickers machine guns, sweeping from side to side across the FAPLA position, forced their automatic weapons to shut up.

The armoured cars were doing their thing by belting the crest of the FAPLA hill with their 90mm guns. They were particularly targeting the highest point by the road cutting. They were, however, running out of ammunition and had to withdraw, troop by troop, to replenish. This was the first time that our cars had to replenish during an action and my black troops had no idea of the appropriate drill. So when the first troop — the one that had given Jack his initial support — moved to the rear with guns traversed towards the enemy, Jack's company thought it was time to withdraw so they were not left behind. Jack and I had our jobs cut out to get his troops back into position.

Things were beginning to look up. Zulu Headquarters was safe and the time had come to drive FAPLA from their positions. I requested Corky to have Delville's Battle Group Alpha make a left flanking attack while we supported them with fire from the next crest which was about 400 metres to our front.

Corky had a counter-proposal. Delville Linford would march his battle group around FAPLA's right flank and adopt an ambush position some kilometres behind them. Meanwhile, Battle Group Bravo would drive FAPLA off the crest and, hopefully, straight into Delville's killing ground. I was a bit dubious at first, but after consulting the map, I saw there was a lot of merit in Corky's plan.

I ordered Charlie company to come up on our right and shifted Bravo company to the left of the cutting. I shouted for Jack to attend an order group at my hastily established command post. He ran towards the rear to get behind the crest before he crossed the road. The company, to a man, jumped up and followed him.

Jack cursed and kicked them back to their positions, eventually convincing them that he was not leaving them in the lurch but merely going to have a few words with the commander. They slunk slowly back to their positions and shamefacedly continued to return FAPLA fire.

An order group was held with Toon Slabbert, the two rifle company commanders, the two mortar platoon leaders, the machine-gun platoon leader, Frank Bestbier — my second-in-command and my support company commander, Captain James Hills. We were still under heavy fire but I had a good view from my position. So we stayed where we were, albeit uncomfortably exposed to the shell bursts that were straddling my command post.

The plan was to launch a two-phased attack that would culminate in us taking the dominating high ground beyond the river. The armoured cars would support us at close quarters while the mortars and machine guns shelled and sprayed the FAPLA slope beyond the first crest. After taking the intermediate crest in a first-phase infantry assault, we would pause and wait for the armoured cars, the Vickers platoon and the three-inch mortar platoon to reduce the range by leapfrogging to new firing positions. We would then go for the final objective, the FAPLA hill, in a second-phase infantry assault. All the armoured cars and support weapons, including the antiquated three-inchers which by then would have relocated to positions within range of the objective, would bring down devastating fire in support of the final attack. Oupa van Dyk's eyes lit up — until then he had missed out on the action because his mortars lacked range.

With our Vickers machine guns, two mortar platoons, three armoured car troops and one B10 — the other was with Connie van Wyk — I believed we could swamp FAPLA's main defensive position with a concentration of firepower not yet seen in the campaign.

Unfortunately, I had treated the continuous light automatic fire from the base of the hill with some disrespect. I figured that the infantry would easily be able to overcome on their own what I believed was a minor irritation.

Major Frank Bestbier and Captain James Hills joined me at the command post. James would coordinate all support fire and the redeployment and leapfrogging of the various support weapon groups. Frank, as my second-in-command, would take over from me if I was hit or be ready to dash to any critical part of the battlefield where he might be required. My headquarters would move on or near the Catengue/Benguela tar road, which was the axis of attack.

Those in the command group would remain where we were at first until the intermediate objective had been captured. We would then move forward with the armoured cars as they redeployed to the first crest. Then we would form up in a position roughly between the two assault companies for the remainder of the attack. As the Bravo command group, we would leave our vehicles at the phase one objective and continue on foot until the final objective. I confess that I had visions of a wandering FAPLA stray hijacking my abandoned Land Cruiser while I was engaged in other things.

The intermediate position was taken without resistance from FAPLA and the support weapons were redeployed according to plan. The infantry caught their breath and plucked up courage for the nasty final assault. This kicked off on schedule but Grobbie's Charlie company on the right was soon lagging behind because of the thick bush. Jack was making good progress on the left and I had to restrain him to allow others to catch up.

Bravo's command group, walking on the road, was at the receiving end of small-arms fire from the rear. My mind went back to a previous time north of Evale when the old Charlie company had brought Zulu Headquarters under fire.

'Grobbie, tell your depth platoon to stop shooting. They're shooting us in the back on the road', I called to him on the radio.

Grobbie came back a short while later and informed me that his depth platoon had not been shooting. It could only be FAPLA. I was perplexed and frankly I disbelieved him. In the thick bush to my right there was firing and a lot of angry shouting as we approached the river and the base of the high ground beyond. We passed Jack's abandoned trucks, but apart from flat tyres, they appeared to be in good order.

Again we came under accurate small-arms fire. This time I sent James to tell Grobbie that his troops were clobbering us and remind them that we were not FAPLA. Five minutes later James returned with the news that Grobbie was having a tough time breaching a FAPLA trench line in front of him that we in the command group could not see because of the thick bush.

One of Grobbie's black soldiers burst through the bush on our right, ran up to me and said in broken English: 'I look for the hand grenade. There are a lot of FAPLA in the hole.'

I handed him a grenade, having a sudden vision of a deep hole filled with FAPLA soldiers into which he would toss it. In reality, though, he had come up against FAPLA's main defensive system and rightly thought a grenade would be handy. Unfortunately, he had underestimated the effects of a single grenade on a long and well-prepared double line of trenches. Despite this, Charlie company finally fought its way through the trench line and went on to take the rest of their objective.

Jack, meanwhile had come up against no enemy troops whatsoever as his company swarmed over the dominating high ground to the left.

On our way up the hill my command group came across several recoilless guns and heavy machine guns, with Cuban crews sprawled dead behind them. Some crew-served weapons in good order had been abandoned. So was the command post where the Cuban commander had even left his maps and other useful documents when he hastily escaped to the rear. We found the terminal ends and electrical firing device for a demolition ringmain with leads that ran down to the bridge. Fortunately, the leads had been cut, probably by a 90mm shell.

I ordered Frank to consolidate our position with the two rifle companies, move up the mortars, machine guns and armoured cars and take up an all-round defensive position. Meanwhile, I would report to Zulu Headquarters and swop my Land Cruiser for a short-wheelbase Land-Rover we had captured in Moçamedes. My Land Cruiser had collected some splinters in the radiator and water pump when I drove through a shell burst earlier and it was overheating. Many FAPLA were still skulking around in the thick bush and to reach the vehicle, Paul and I took a rather hairy walk back to our first phase objective.

Colonel Corky van Heerden and Commandant Willie Kotze had earlier come forward to my first command post, but I had already vacated it. They wanted to see if I required assistance and whether Corky should take command of the situation and commit the total forces at his disposal. He had been concerned about the heavy enemy fire, the apparent unwillingness of the black troops to advance under fire and about my Land Cruiser being hit. When I appeared in one piece, I told a rather relieved Corky that everything was in hand. Somewhat prematurely as it turned out, I also told him that FAPLA had been driven off.

I was discussing the battle with Corky when renewed fighting broke out on the FAPLA hill to the west that we had just taken. Frank was engaged in another punch-up with FAPLA. I failed to raise him on the radio, so Paul and I rushed forward in my new vehicle. I could hear our three-inch mortars and some automatic fire but I did not hear FAPLA's weapons responding.

I found Frank Bestbier trying to persuade Grobbie's Charlie company to enter the thick bush and mount an assault against FAPLA. It appeared that FAPLA were still ensconced in or had reoccupied the part of their trench system that lay between us and Zulu Headquarters. For a while everything went well. The enemy fire petered out and finally stopped. Toon and I began to relax in the former Cuban command post. Charlie company returned, struggling and crashing through the bush. They were out of ammunition so Frank replenished them from Bravo company's stocks. Jack had not required ammunition for the final assault so he had plenty to spare.

While Toon and I studied the captured Cuban maps and Frank got on with his interrupted consolidation, there was a fresh bout of automatic fire at close quarters — in fact it was almost on top of us. We ducked into a shallow ditch as fire swept over us. FAPLA had launched a counter-attack in force from their trench system. We were cut off. I was never particularly fond of higher command headquarters, but to have the enemy forcibly separate me from mine was just not good enough.

I returned fire with my rifle at the enemy who seemed to be no more than a dozen paces away in thick bush cover. Toon was unarmed — he did not even have a pistol — and his armoured car was parked in the cutting just below us where the intervening ground was being swept by automatic fire. He was reduced to the normal condition of an infantryman in battle — hugging the bottom of a ditch while the enemy tried its best to get at him with a variety of shells, bullets and the rest. If that failed, they might even fall back on using the good old bayonet.

'Commandant, lend me your rifle', he pleaded.

'Why?'

'Because they're shooting at us and I have no weapon.'

'You must be bloody mad. This is my rifle', I retorted half in anger and half in amusement. There was no way I was going to hand my trusty weapon to an unarmed armoured corps man, particularly when the enemy was only a few paces away.

Frank launched another assault with the support of the three-inch mortars in a general downhill direction. Eventually they succeeded in pushing the enemy away from our general area and we could raise our heads. The assault, however, soon ran out of steam. The troops were tired and it was getting late. We had to consolidate before last light because the last thing I needed was a confused fight in thick bush after dark.

A crestfallen Charlie company returned. Frank told me he had run out on ideas of how to get FAPLA off the hill.

I approached Toon, by now thankfully back in his armoured car, to discuss the use of his cars in support of another assault. Toon shook his head and said the armoured cars would be unable to move or shoot in thick bush, especially when the light began to fade.

Fingers Kruger looked at me hopefully.

'Frank, use Fingers and his machine guns. You can use all four as light machine guns to give close support while Grobbie's Charlie company has another crack at FAPLA.'

Fingers beamed and started getting his machine guns ready. They would be removed from the Land-Rovers together with their tripods and the crews would carry them forward during the assault. On their tripods they would produce heavy sustained fire at short range in support of the infantry as they cleared out pockets of FAPLA. The mortars could not be used for fire support because they would pose a danger to our own forces. The thick bush had effectively cut the fighting distance between us and the enemy to no more than ten paces.

The assault went in again. I could hear the fighting move farther and farther downhill, then north along the foot of the hill until it finally died down in the distance.

The sustained bursts of the Vickers machine guns had proved too much for FAPLA.

The tired but happy troops staggered from the bush as the light faded. The sweating crews of the Vickers humped their guns proudly on their backs. The fighting finally ceased at about 18:00. The battle had lasted from 09:00 until approximately 18:00 without a let-up. It had been a very long day for all of us but an even longer one for FAPLA. They had been thoroughly beaten and were wearily escaping through thick bush in the general direction of Benguela. But they still had to get past Delville Linford and his Bushmen who were waiting for them in ambush.

We believed that many FAPLA had not been accounted for and they might be wandering aimlessly around in the general vicinity, so we routinely established an all-round defensive system. I posted a security patrol — comprising an infantry platoon, armoured cars and the B10 — about one kilometre down the road towards Benguela.

The B10, as it turned out, never left with the rest. Some time after they were supposed to move out, two of its paratrooper crewmen reported that the third member had refused to go and had disappeared. The Parachute Battalion was my parent unit, so it was disquieting that a soldier belonging to it could behave in such a way. It was pointless to look for him in the dark, so I decided to deal with the matter the next morning.

In the late afternoon Delville and his unit had engaged in a glorious turkey shoot as the retreating FAPLA, many of them Cubans from command elements, blundered into his well-laid ambush position to FAPLA's rear. Vehicles and trucks were left ablaze as the beaten enemy fled towards Benguela on foot or in vehicles. They were a disorganised mob and all control had broken down.

That night, after the fighting on his front had died down, a FAPLA soldier approached Delville and asked for assistance for himself and some of his FAPLA comrades. They were in obvious distress and had been abandoned by their officers. They were also totally lost. The soldier probably mistook Delville for a Cuban and the fact that he spoke reasonable Portuguese probably reinforced the mistake. A rendezvous and time were arranged when the soldier and his mates would be met. But it appeared the enemy soldier had second thoughts because he never showed up.

The next morning we cleared the battlefield, collecting 75mm and B10 guns and some 12.7mm heavy machine guns. We inspected the FAPLA trench system which zigzagged in two lines and stretched north of the road for almost a kilometre. It was only then that we realised we had been up against much more than a battle group. Signs pointed to it being a full-blown regimental task force. We marvelled at our temerity in attacking what amounted to a brigade with our two under-strength rifle companies — even if we were supported by three armoured car troops, mortars and machine guns. In the final analysis, we considered ourselves lucky that we pulled it off.

In their final assault on the objective, Charlie company broke through a front of not more than 200 metres in the very thick bush. They were unaware that when they reached the top of the hill most of the FAPLA were still intact behind them. FAPLA soon re-occupied the cleared trenches and this accounted for the heavy fire my command group had been getting from the rear. It also explained the determined FAPLA counter-attacks that occurred while Frank was consolidating our final objective.

I thanked the good Lord that I had not been captured or shot while I passed some FAPLA units close to me as they reformed and regrouped. The first occasion had been when I returned on foot to my Land Cruiser. The second was when I drove back to the final objective in my replacement Land-Rover. Added to this was my miraculous escape from almost certain death during that morning's mortar shelling. I had much to be thankful for. Imagine the political fallout if I had been captured! No doubt they would have put me on show in Luanda for the benefit of the world press; and what about the consternation at home when it was discovered that our hot pursuit operation against SWAPO insurgents was now en route to Benguela?

Major Dries van Coller was like a puppy with seven tails when he got his hands on the captured documents, particularly a map. The documents confirmed that we had been facing a regiment-sized unit, probably 1 000 men or more, plus their support weapons and crews. The map showed Zulu Force's advance to date and projections into the future. Their intelligence was absolutely correct, so Dries told me. I, of course, had no pre-knowledge of what our intended plans were for the rest of the campaign.

A blond, crestfallen young paratrooper — the missing crewman from the B10 — reported to me. I was in a quandary and also angry because it was a clear case of cowardice in the face of the enemy. I also remembered seeing the same young man sitting in the open behind the sights of the B10 the previous day. He had been the Number One on the gun and had calmly plastered the enemy crew-served weapons while mortar shells, rockets and other projectiles exploded all around. It must have been a long day for him. It was his first time in action and his coming of age as a combat soldier had been marked by a baptism of extreme violence.

'Sir, I'm sorry I ran away. I was scared', he admitted, his face colouring.

'Where did you go?'

'I slept under a bush in the laager.'

'Paratroopers don't run away. Why did you? Aren't you proud you're a paratrooper?'

'I know, sir. I'm sorry. It won't happen again. Please give me another chance.'

I decided to give him a second and last chance and he left to rejoin his crew. How he squared his behaviour with them I have no idea, but I subsequently saw him in action, seemingly cool, calm and unflinching while under fire. He was determined not to fail again and he never did. I am glad I gave him another chance. I kept the incident between myself and the other two members of his crew.

12

Cubal

Brigadier Dawie Schoeman flew to Catengue the day after the battle. He was as chirpy as ever and urged us to speed up the advance. Replenishment ammunition was flown in by Dakota as Bravo and Charlie companies had depleted theirs in the previous day's fighting.

Corky decided that Delville and I should both head for Benguela, but before that we should close up as we were currently about 30km apart in ideal ambush country. We would jointly clear any pockets of resistance that stood between us. The road ahead was narrowly confined between two lines of heavily vegetated hills. It was with some trepidation that the leading armoured car troop and infantry platoon led the advance. In fact, they led very slowly indeed, moving at not more than five kph and I became somewhat impatient after the first hour or so.

I was convinced there were no substantial bodies of 'Injuns' left in 'them thar hills.' Somewhat recklessly perhaps, I decided to ignore the threatening defiles and speed up the column's pace by leading from the front in my freshly repaired Land Cruiser. Unbeknown to me, Delville had decided the same thing at his end so both battle groups were approaching head-on at quite a clip.

Swinging around a bend in a narrow ravine, I was confronted by a camouflaged Land-Rover heading for me at some speed. For a brief moment I thought FAPLA had decided to have another go at us. Then I recognised Delville, rigged out in his own particular concept of what a commander should wear when off to war. He was deeply tanned and wearing a sleeveless brown T-shirt, a camouflage fatigue cap without a peak and displaying a large FINA petrol badge on the front, beads strung around his neck and camouflage trousers. His boots had probably been issued to him when he was a recruit some 25 years earlier.

We were happy to see each other and caught up with the news of our respective fights of the previous day. Delville, understandably, was pretty chuffed about his highly successful ambush. I was probably a little envious. A soldier is rarely presented with the chance to spring a really good ambush. My destiny seemed to demand that I was always the one ambushed rather than the ambusher.

We turned about and I led both battle groups back to Catengue. While en route Corky called me on the radio and said Battle Group Bravo should immediately proceed to Cubal and take it before nightfall. I was not particularly enamoured with the prospect of travelling some 90km between three in the afternoon and last light, then securing a large town before supper. I considered it physically impossible and I advised Corky accordingly on my return to Catengue. I asked him to postpone the operation until the following morning. After much argument, he relented. This also gave Battle Groups Bravo and Charlie a day of rest after the heavy fighting. It also gave me time to visit Lieutenant Connie van Wyk and his Alpha company. They had adopted a blocking position 10km east of Catengue.

The troops were spread out on the uphill side of a long stretch of road which descended towards a lone granite koppie. The road disappeared around the foot of the koppie and crossed a long, wide plain to the east of their deployment. To my surprise, the troops were not dug in, behind cover or even camouflaged. They were lounging around carelessly, talking to their buddies as if they did not have a care in the world. Next to the road and in good firing positions that covered the approaches were two armoured cars and a B10 recoilless gun manned by a team of paratroopers. Connie proudly informed me that this was his killing group.

To the left of the road, above a sheer drop to the bottom of a ravine, four or five naked FAPLA prisoners were digging graves. The graves were a continuation of a long line of 30 or so mounds that were obviously freshly filled graves. It was surely the most unusual cemetery in Angola.

Connie had a small patrol concealed at the bottom of the slope that kept a lookout for approaching vehicles. When enemy vehicles were sighted, they used visual signals to let Connie know what was happening. It seemed that the FAPLA garrison at Nova Lisboa had still not tumbled to the unpleasant truth that we were sitting astride their lateral communications line to Benguela.

Military vehicles, mostly moving singly, were sighted frequently. Once the vehicle labouring up the slope had been identified as belonging to FAPLA, either an armoured car or the B10 would move into position and open fire when it was on a part of the road that could not be seen from the base of the hill. The other would act as backup. The men closest to the shot-up vehicle would remove the bodies and capture those not killed. The wrecked vehicle would be shoved over the edge of the ravine where it would be well out of sight. The enemy dead would be delivered to the burial party which was reinforced by the latest prisoners and the bodies would be consigned to the freshly dug graves. Prisoners were passed back to Catengue to keep Major Dries van Coller busy when they were no longer required as grave diggers.

Civilians were apprehended, evacuated to Catengue and temporarily detained. Many angrily insisted they be allowed to continue their journey to Benguela. This, of course, could not be allowed until Connie's ambush had been lifted.

On my return to Catengue Corky gave me final orders concerning the following day's attack on Cubal. I decided to take Connie's Alpha company and Grobbie's Charlie company with me, leaving Jack's Bravo company at Catengue to lick its wounds and act as a reserve if one was needed.

The next morning we moved out towards Cubal, picking up Connie and his company from their ambush position en route. By then Connie could proudly boast of having accounted for well over 40 FAPLA dead in his ambush.

*   *   *

The first town en route to Cubal was a small one called Caimbambo. According to Dries, a resident garrison of approximately 40 FAPLA was based in barracks on the eastern side of town. I decided to use a platoon from Grobbie's Charlie company and a troop of armoured cars. They would charge through town and overpower the garrison with a sudden and violent coup de main. I had no wish to waste time as it was still a long way to Cubal which, according to Dries, was strongly held by FAPLA.

Ten kilometres before Caimbambo we came on a ten-ton Mercedes truck loaded with harvested coffee beans and escorted by two policemen. One was Caimbambo's Chief of Police, a friendly individual who had long since given up trying to figure out who his political bosses were. I wondered whether anyone was paying him, considering he had remained at his post long after his Portuguese paymasters had left. Perhaps he had nothing else to do anyway. He confirmed our information about the FAPLA garrison at Caimbambo and we sent him on his way to Benguela where he no doubt got his cut for escorting a lorry-load of valuable coffee beans through an unsettled part of Angola.

At last Caimbambo came into view. As the road descended into the valley we could see buildings clustered at the foot of a high bush-clad hill north of the road. Beyond that the road levelled out on a fertile plain that was mostly planted with lucerne.

I halted the main body of the column when its head was almost level with the first houses in the village to our left. I waved the troop of armoured cars and the infantry platoon forward.

Caimbambo was somewhat like Hanover in South Africa's Cape Province (now in Northern Cape Province). There was a strong resemblance between the Karoo-type houses found there and those in Caimbambo. In both, the houses were about 100 metres off the road. Many of the houses had stoeps that faced south towards the road — also a carbon copy of Hanover.

When I was beyond admiring the scenery I suddenly noticed that the stoeps of those houses were crammed with FAPLA soldiers. They were joyfully waving at us. Two men detached themselves from the enemy and ran towards Toon in his armoured car that had stopped just ahead of me.

'*Kamerad commandante*! *Kamerad commandante*!', they shouted, grinning from ear to ear while attempting to clamber on Toon's vehicle.

No one in the column looked less like a Cuban than the red-headed, red-bearded monster named Toon. He retained his presence of mind, perhaps wanting to play a joke, and without hesitation referred them to me.

'I'm not the bloody commandant. There he is in the Land Cruiser', he shouted in English and pointed at me.

The two happily rushed over to me. The one in the lead grabbed me by the shoulder and gave me a slobbering kiss on each cheek.

I recovered from my surprise and finding the FAPLA fellow was not particularly kissable, I grabbed my rifle, pushed the muzzle into his midriff and triggered.

There was an empty click.

It was a misfire.

Somewhat put out, I retained my composure and demanded that he give me his AK47. He meekly handed it over. After that I did not have the heart to shoot either him or his companion so I took them prisoner.

I have never before seen expressions change from exaltation to confusion to sheer fright in such a short time. The two obediently squatted on their haunches by my vehicle without saying a word. They looked as if they were about to throw up and were no doubt expecting the worst.

Meanwhile, the rest of the mob were still waving happily. They just didn't understand what had happened to them. I also had difficulty getting Toon to understand that I wanted his leading cars to open fire.

'Open fire, they're FAPLAs,' I yelled, indicating the crowded stoeps.

'What did you say?' Toon shouted back. He was cupping his ear so he could hear above the noise of his running engine.

'Shoot those bloody FAPLAs.'

'Huh?'

'Dammit Toon, look at the stoeps. Shoot those flipping FAPLAs.'

'What's that?'

Taking matters into my own hands, I raised my captured AK47 and raked the waving crowd.

Toon clicked. He ducked down, his turret traversed and moments later his guns blazed away at the rapidly disappearing enemy. We plastered the place with machine-gun fire while Oupa used his three-inch mortars on their escape routes to good effect.

Connie's Alpha company cleared the town. I followed slowly in my Land Cruiser with Toon's armoured car tagging along just behind my right shoulder.

Meanwhile, a fierce battle had erupted on the far side of town during which almost the entire resident garrison was killed by the advance patrol. Those FAPLAs who were able to were trying to escape to the hills to the north with Connie's men in hot pursuit. Oupa's group ceased firing as the enemy troops got beyond his support range.

One prisoner turned out to be the commander. He and his companion had been en route to Benguela and had arrived only minutes before us. The policeman who had confirmed our information about the garrison had been unaware of the pending arrivals when he met us. It was fortunate for him, otherwise he would have had some serious explaining to do later on.

The FAPLA commander kindly offered to assist us with target indications and pinpointed the most likely spots his escaping troops were heading for. Amazingly, he became quite enthusiastic when the mortars and armoured cars started hitting in the right places. Such was his loyalty towards his troops and the standard of leadership in the FAPLA army. His companion, to his credit, took a dim view both of the proceedings and of his erstwhile commander.

As the fighting progressed from south to north through the town, a young Portuguese girl ran straight from the post office to my Land Cruiser. She was the prettiest example of womanhood we had seen in months. Speaking in Portuguese, she asked for permission to go to her home which was near the railway station, since the fighting had moved on. She and her station-master father had been trapped in the post office when the firing broke out. She wanted to get home as quickly as possible. I gave permission and Toon gallantly offered himself and his armoured car to escort her home.

Meanwhile, unbeknown to me, some of Connie's vehicles had become stuck in the dry river bed that ran through the town's centre. I was concerned that some of the escaping FAPLA might make for Cubal and give the garrison an early warning of our approach. The minutes ticked by but there was no sign of Alpha company. I became agitated. The firing had long since ceased and I was raring to go and surprise the Cubal garrison.

I eventually made my way to the river. I found Connie unconcernedly examining some captured equipment while his troops were ineffectively trying to get the lorries out of the sand. I blew my top. Connie jumped to it, hurt by the old man's sudden anger, and his company was soon back on the road again.

En route to Cubal we halted briefly to clear a railway siding that turned out to be a minor FAPLA outpost.

We reached a position six or seven kilometres from Cubal from where we had a reasonable view of the target. My senior FAPLA prisoner, still with me in my Land Cruiser, said the garrison was probably about 50 strong. Their headquarters was situated in a particularly distinct building at the southern entrance to the town. The bridge to the south was unprotected. I moved to a slight knoll next to the road and carefully examined Cubal through borrowed binoculars. For the first time in the campaign, I decided to follow the battle drills as prescribed in the Infantry School and Army College textbooks. I had already given a warning order. It would be a two-company attack and the necessary steps were under way to group the armoured cars and infantry.

My company commanders, Toon Slabbert and his troop leaders and the mortar and machine-gun platoon leaders were sitting in cover just behind the knoll waiting for me to arrive at a plan and brief them. I gave them their orders. I hoped they were impressed with my new-found professionalism.

Alpha company would attack the left side of the long and narrow town, moving from south to north. The main road through the centre of town was their right-hand boundary. Their left-hand boundary would be the outskirts of the town to the west.

Charlie company would tackle the remainder of the town east of the main road including the railway station. The companies would each have two troops of armoured cars in support.

The start line would be at the southern edge of town. To get there, both companies with their armoured cars would have to rush across the bridge with Alpha company in the lead. They would then turn left off the main tar road to Nova Lisboa into a street skirting the southern edge of town. A section of infantry and an armoured car would be dropped off at the beginning of each street. They would wait for my command before starting clearing operations which would be achieved street by street working from south to north.

En route to his target, Connie would use his leading troop of armoured cars to shoot up FAPLA's headquarters. The house concerned stood alone but it commanded the entrance to the main street. Fingers Kruger and his machine guns would charge along the road to Nova Lisboa and deploy as a cut-off force to the north-east and rake the northern exits of town if I needed him to. Oupa van Dyk would deploy his mortars just across the bridge next to the road and provide support fire on call.

I thought the plan was excellent. I had arrived at it after going through all the required drills. I gave myself a mental pat on the back. There were no questions and the commanders moved off to pass on orders to their troops. We were due to kick off in 30 minutes.

The column had halted out of sight of Cubal some distance to the rear. I could see no movement or life on the surrounding farms which were covered as far as the eye could see with acre after acre of sisal.

It was about 15:00 and it was hot. Many of the men were preparing last-minute brew-ups to keep down the rising apprehension. Paul, as usual, could not find any firewood. So, as usual, I literally had to lead him to each stick. He was quite useless in the victualling department. We rearranged our order of march and moved off. I hoped to cover the six or seven kilometres to Cubal at speed in the hope that FAPLA would not have time to react by manning the bridge or blowing it.

The bridge was undefended. We crossed it in style, swung left and dropped off the assault troops. Connie shot up the FAPLA HQ which collapsed with a tremendous roar in a cloud of smoke and dust.

I gave the word and the companies moved forward textbook style to sweep the town. The armoured cars followed closely behind. Moments later we were confronted by a turnout of the local population, cheering and clapping as the sweep developed into a triumphal procession. I was fuming. There was not a FAPLA in sight despite my efforts to do it right for a change. We reached the far end of town without a shot being fired.

Suddenly, though, a flurry of small-arms fire broke out at the mortar base-plate positions by the bridge. I tried but could not raise Oupa, so I decided to drive across. The fighting had died down by the time I arrived.

Oupa was grinning from ear to ear. His men had clobbered about 30 FAPLA who had crossed the bridge from south to north in our wake. It appeared they were returning from a mission in the area of the sisal farms to the southeast.

FAPLA bodies were strewn around on the grass. So much for my careful plan. The only people who had seen any close-quarter combat were the mortar men. Their weapons were not designed for that sort of thing, so FAPLA had certainly not played the game.

This left a possibility that some pockets of FAPLA might be found along a dirt road that ran through the middle of sisal plantations to the southeast. I dispatched a troop of armoured cars and an infantry platoon on a reconnaissance/fighting patrol to check the road for about 15km and flush out any FAPLA who might still be around.

I was unaware of it but Oupa and Fingers, having got their bloodlust up, were following the patrol with a small one of their own. One of the officers had asked permission for this, but I had flatly refused. Oupa and Fingers had used their silver tongues to persuade this officer to ignore my decision. This resulted in them each taking a Land-Rover armed with twin Vickers machine guns and leaving town to to catch up with the patrol.

It was almost dusk and the battle group was preparing a night laager south of the town. A tremendous firefight broke out across the bridge by some farm buildings. We could see our armoured cars from the returning patrol plastering an area east of the buildings with their 90mm guns. Long bursts of tracer fire were streaming towards them. I got the impression that the cars were squaring up to a sizeable FAPLA force.

Oupa and Fingers were nowhere in sight. I was angry because I needed them urgently. The platoon accompanying the armoured cars was also rather tardy in moving into the attack. It would be dark in about 30 minutes and I wanted the scene wrapped up by last light. I could get little sense out of the troop commander or the platoon leader, so I decided to personally investigate the situation.

I reached the contact area and saw flames leap skywards from what I assumed was the FAPLA position. I deployed the infantry in an extended line and bullied them forward from my Land Cruiser. The armoured cars, meanwhile, gave covering fire with their machine guns. I suddenly noticed a familiar shape at the centre of the intense conflagration ahead. It looked suspiciously like a Vickers machine gun on the back of a burning Land-Rover.

My heart dropped. We had made a ghastly mistake, unless FAPLA had also acquired Vickers machine guns. I ordered the cars to cease fire and drove forward alone, hoping against hope that my suspicions were unfounded.

Unfortunately it was not to be. A blood-spattered Fingers Kruger, one arm badly shot up, staggered from a small copse. Oupa van Dyk lay face down in a ditch, bleeding from serious back wounds. Two black machine-gunners had been killed, some were wounded and several others were missing. Both Land-Rovers and their guns were in flames and total write-offs.

Fingers said they had tried to catch up with the patrol but had taken the wrong turning at the first fork in the dirt road, moving east instead of southeast. They drove for several kilometres but finding nothing, decided to turn back. The other patrol had also turned around and was returning to the area where the road forked.

The two groups had thus approached each other and, as fate would have it, reached the area of the fork almost simultaneously. Oupa and Fingers had seen the armoured cars in the dusk, identified them as FAPLA and promptly went into action. The patrol, of course, rapidly deployed and returned fire heavily and accurately, as vouched for by Oupa.

'Hell sir, the Boers can shoot! I never ever want to be at the receiving end of Boer fire again!'

Both paid a heavy price for their foolishness.

*   *   *

So our Cubal adventure ended on a sad note. I lost two of my best soldiers. Oupa and Fingers were evacuated the following day. The mortar and machine-gun platoons were never the same again. The troops were thoroughly disheartened at losing two men for whom they had the greatest love and respect. And I, to say the least, was thoroughly cheesed off with the officer who had disobeyed instructions.

Two replacement support platoon leaders arrived shortly afterwards, but they were not nearly as competent as Oupa and Fingers. Nor were they able to establish any sort of rapport with the troops. I finally decided to disband both support platoons and absorb them into the rifle companies.

13

Benguela

We returned to Catengue the next morning. Jack Dippenaar and his Bravo company had just returned from Caimbambo, having cleared the area after the previous day's scrap with FAPLA. Catengue was deserted, apart from Jack and his men. Delville Linford and Battle Group Alpha, Zulu Headquarters and the complete logistical system had moved to Benguela. Jack told us we had to follow on behind.

Jack was also the conveyor of bad news. Major Nic Visser had been killed in an aircraft accident the previous day. I also knew the other two killed — Piet Uys, the pilot and Des Harmse, an old colleague from Oudtshoorn. Nic's death touched me deeply. He had been my second-in-command at 1-Reconnaissance Commando and was more a friend than a colleague. His tremendous sense of humour and fun was legend throughout the SADF. He would be sorely missed.

While the column snaked through the valleys and defiles on its way to the coast, Toon Slabbert pulled abreast of my Land Cruiser in his Land-Rover and handed me a beer. The weather was really hot so I drank it gratefully as we drove abreast, reminiscing about the past. My Land Cruiser was a left-hand drive and Toon's Land-Rover a right-hand drive, so it worked well.

We passed the site of Delville's successful ambush a couple of days before. Burnt-out trucks and cars were scattered everywhere. There were no signs that Zulu Headquarters and Battle Group Alpha had passed that way but it did not concern us. It was pleasant relaxing for a while without worrying about possible unpleasant surprises like FAPLA ambushes that might be mounted from the hills on either side.

We passed through the final line of hills via a twisting and narrow defile where we found an extensive unoccupied trench system. We emerged on the coastal plain just south of Benguela. Somewhere ahead we heard the distant thump of guns and rockets. It seemed that Delville had run into a fair-sized fight.

Toon and I stopped our reminiscing and began to feel a little apprehensive. Suddenly, ahead of us on a long and straight stretch of tarred road, we made out a short rotund figure standing next to a short-wheelbase Land-Rover. It was Corky van Heerden. We had caught up with Zulu Headquarters.

Corky halted my column by putting his hand up like a traffic cop. He looked worried. Delville had picked up trouble at the airport just south of Benguela. We could clearly hear the almost continuous reports of heavy guns and could see the odd column of smoke on the far side of the plain ahead.

Meanwhile, there was a report that FAPLA had been abducting Portuguese families from Baia Farta just down the coast from Benguela and putting them aboard deep-sea trawlers in the harbour. Corky told me to go to Baia Farta and rescue the hostages. The balance of Battle Group Bravo was to concentrate at the old FAPLA garrison a few kilometres down the road where Delville, by then, had kicked FAPLA out of the place.

I detailed an armoured car troop and an infantry platoon and together with Toon, I headed for Baia Farta. Major Frank Bestbier took command of those going to the concentration area.

My group turned left off the main Benguela road and sped across a plain dotted with barren flat-topped hills towards the ocean to the west. The plain reminded me of the South African Karoo — the same barrenness with small shrubs, dongas and flat-topped hills. It was also very hot.

Not far from Baia Farta we came across a Mercedes Benz travelling towards Benguela. The driver was a local white Portuguese. He assured us that there was no truth in the abduction rumour. He told us, though, that FAPLA had a small garrison housed in a building in the town centre. He volunteered to act as guide.

We continued the advance with the Mercedes Benz tucked into the column just behind my Land Cruiser. We entered Baia Farta from the north-east. It was a surprisingly large town with the main street flanked by double-storeyed buildings and shops. There was not a soul to be seen either on the streets or in the buildings. The dockyard was to our right, where we could see masts of vessels and a jungle of intricate rigging above the roofs of stores and other buildings. Piles of junk were on the quay-side.

It was imperative we first clear FAPLA before taking a closer look at the docks. Under the guidance of our Portuguese friend, we finally got to the FAPLA garrison. It was the most unprepossessing garrison building we had seen in the war so far. Effectively it was no more than an ordinary looking four or five-bedroom house. There was no barbed wire, no machine-gun nests and no imposing fortifications made from sandbags or concrete. I questioned my Portuguese friend with scepticism. He insisted it was the garrison building and was adamant that we would find FAPLAs inside. In fact, he said, they were probably looking through the windows at us right then and would open fire at any moment.

I looked at the peaceful scene in front of me with disbelief, but decided that discretion was the better part of valour. We would do a proper clearing job on the premises. The problem was that, although we had fought our way through a number of towns, we had had little chance to practise house-clearing before. We had done a few in Pereira de Eça but that was very much an ad hoc affair. I had lacked the time to train my troops properly in this most difficult combat skill. Nevertheless, this was a golden opportunity. I would make the most of it to teach at least this infantry platoon about the skills of house-clearing. I would lead the operation and at the same time instruct and demonstrate in realistic circumstances how professionals tackled such a risky business.

We parked a 90mm armoured car at each corner of the house to ensure no one escaped. The infantry platoon dismounted and I briefly explained what I was about to do. They nodded and smiled. Obviously they thought it would be fun.

I rushed through the front door closely followed by the platoon leader and two other soldiers. We found ourselves in a passage. I suddenly realised that my Portuguese guide had also followed us. It was too late to chase him out as the house-clearing party was committed. The first door to the right was closed. There were no hand grenades in Battle Group Bravo. Grenades were an essential requirement for house clearing, but since we didn't have any we had to rely solely on our rifles.

I had trained hard for many years in the army to become a reasonably proficient infantryman. I believed I knew about house-clearing. I had also seen a few war films starring guys like John Wayne. To my mind such movie stars gave a far better idea of how a house should be cleared than the army ever did.

I kicked the door open and stormed in with my rifle at my hip ready to blast FAPLA into oblivion. The room was empty. I moved up the passage to the next room on the left. Somewhere in the house I was bound to come across FAPLA. The next door was shut and locked. I took a mighty kick at it. It nearly broke my leg but made no impression on the door.

The Portuguese was pointing at the door and mumbling something about 'Kameraden'. I took this as confirmation that some FAPLA were hiding inside. All I needed to do was force open the door, charge inside and empty my magazine at the terrified enemy. John Wayne had shown me the way. I stood back and with great determination charged at the door, shoulder first. I bounced off like a rag doll and fell flat on my backside. The demonstration was becoming embarrassing. I started to lose my cool, particularly when I noticed surreptitious smirks on the faces of my 'students'.

'Kameraden!' the Portuguese shouted frantically pointing at the door.

'Yes I know, dammit. I'll get them out one way or another', I responded.

I tried another John Wayne trick and emptied my magazine in an attempt to shoot off the lock.

'Kameraden! Kameraden! Not shiessen!', the Portuguese shouted showing he was proficient in German as well as English.

I was about to launch another assault on the door when I saw the handle slowly turning — which was indeed strange. The door opened a crack and a frightened black face peered out at me. The face broke into a broad smile and its owner threw the door wide open. It was one of my own men.

Some of the troops had decided to ignore my demonstration and had commenced their own version of house-clearing from the other side. Needless to say, I felt a damned fool but I tried to keep my composure — which was not easy in front of my opposition house-clearing party. Still, at least they had seen the way that the great John Wayne did it.

The house was empty. We moved to the docks to check the hostage rumour. We boarded several deep-sea trawlers — well-appointed ships they were too — to discover that the crews had prudently moved their own families on board so they could make a quick getaway if things got rough. They had seen our arrival and did not know who we were. They were about to cast off when we appeared and allayed their fears.

My Portuguese guide presented us with a bag of coal as a parting gesture. Perhaps the gift expressed what he thought of my house-clearing demonstration — or maybe coal was scarce in Baia Farta which made it a valuable present. Whatever the case, I accepted with thanks and left town as quickly as possible. The episode did not represent a high point in my military career.

*   *   *

We arrived at the concentration area as the sun was setting. Frank had moved Battle Group Bravo into a defensive circle, more or less following the embankments of the old garrison. Zulu Headquarters had been pitched on an open spot away from the buildings but sheltered by the embankment. The Cubans had used the quarters and they were in a filthy mess. They had no idea of the basics of hygiene and were much worse even than FAPLA. They defecated both within and outside the barracks, in other buildings and on top of the embankments. The place was in a disgusting state. Corky was unable to use any of the buildings as his headquarters because of the filth which was also compounded by fleas.

Night was closing in fast. To the north Red Eye rockets were mushrooming between us and the airport. There was also a lot of machine-gun and rifle fire. Delville was obviously having a hard time.

I found a spot in the garrison slightly less filthy than the rest of the place. I parked my Land Cruiser and went off to report to Zulu Headquarters.

There was no doubt that Benguela would be a tough nut to crack. It was a large city with some multi-storeyed buildings. It was surrounded by sprawling shanty towns. Delville was brought under the heavy rocket fire of BM21 Stalin Organs situated on high ground to the north and small-arms and mortar fire from the city itself. This prevented him from clearing the airport which was between him and the city. What was more, his troops were pinned down behind the terminal buildings.

Corky visited the airport the next morning to familiarise himself with the area so he could plan our next step. In a conference later we discussed various possible means of attack. An outflanking envelopment from the east would be in full view of the FAPLA mortar observation posts and the long distance rocket batteries which had been harassing us all day. Corky proposed a direct assault on the city using both battle groups. Delville and I expressed strong reservations. We thought it was not feasible because a city the size of Benguela could swallow up both battle groups. It would inevitably develop into the most horrible and costly form of warfare — street fighting — and this with troops untrained for it. It was also packed with civilians and many of them would get hurt or killed. Corky eventually opted for a limited attack on the outskirts of the city where it bordered on the airport. This would serve to quell the direct fire being brought down on us. It would also create space and allow us to regain the initiative and launch follow-up actions.

After further long discussions we decided that the best solution would be to outflank the city farther to the east and seize the dominating high ground to the north. That would cut off FAPLA's escape route and put us tactically on the most critical terrain. FAPLA would be compelled to stage a break-out and this would set up a lovely 'turkey shoot' for us. Alternatively, they could surrender. But more likely, they would discard their weapons and uniforms and blend with the local population. An outflanking movement would also neutralise FAPLA's rocket batteries and spare the lives of civilians.

I would send a patrol to reconnoitre a route to the east and a way to cross the river that ran into the sea just south of the critical terrain feature.

When the evening conference had finished, Corky produced and opened a bottle of Smirnoff Vodka. It was one of a few that had been supplied from Rundu and he had evidently saved it for a special occasion. Delville, as usual, was complaining about his Portuguese platoon leaders but nobody took any notice. The Smirnoff gradually made our surroundings and the awful prevailing smell a little more acceptable. I soon turned in, in spite of Red Eyes landing from time to time throughout the night around the barracks.

My mixed infantry-armoured car patrol left early the next morning to seek a passage around the eastern flank. It was to no avail. There was no suitable river crossing. The rainy season had started and the river was in spate as water flooded into it from its tributaries up country.

The shooting picked up towards daybreak and barrages of rockets began to land between us and the airport. Delville moved out with his men.

The Smirnoff had worn off. In the cold light of dawn I was repulsed by the general situation in the enemy camp where I had spent the night. Human excrement was everywhere and I felt as if I was infested with fleas. I decided I would prefer to take my chances at the airport with Delville. I set out to follow him and waved a grave goodbye to Corky as I passed his headquarters.

I kept the terminal building between myself and the FAPLA positions in the city which made it possible for me to drive right up to Delville's headquarters without enemy interference. I found him on the top floor open balcony where he had a bird's eye view of the town. The rocket positions on the high ground beyond the river were also visible. The problem was that he had nothing that would reach the Stalin Organs — not even his 81mm mortars with their range of 5 000 metres could deal with them.

His Bushmen were lying in cover in positions around the airfield and were hammering away at some city buildings across a stretch of open ground. Armoured cars were deployed around the airfield and adding to the general din with their 90mm guns.

An unmarked Dakota appeared above the city on course for the airport. For a moment everyone stopped shooting and watched it. Then FAPLA and Bushmen alike opened up at the Dak in earnest. But their aim was not too good and it flew on unscathed. We still had not identified it, so Delville ordered his troops to cease fire. It was clear that the aircraft was going to land anyway. If it was FAPLA's, we would capture it on the ground. If it was ours, it would not be good politics to shoot it down. It landed and taxied routinely to the dispersal area behind the terminal building. It turned out to be one of ours. We recognised the crew as it came to a halt. They had no idea that they were landing in the middle of an intense battle.

The firing picked up again. Incoming enemy rockets and mortars began to land all over the airfield. Some exploded uncomfortably close to the Dak.

The pilot sat waiting for a ground crew to appear and offload his cargo. No one came because everyone was busy with the fighting. The pilot must have realised that we were battling to secure the airfield, what with the amount of hostile metal flying around. That's when he and his crew decided they had better get on with it and unload the aircraft themselves — and quickly! Ammunition boxes were unceremoniously thrown from the rear cargo door. Never was an aircraft offloaded at such speed. Within minutes the pilot started up, swung the aircraft around, gunned the engines and took off straight across the rough veld ignoring all runways and taxiways. Keeping low to avoid ground fire, the Dak soon disappeared over the horizon to the south.

Meanwhile, Delville and I took a second look at the air photographs of Benguela. It was imperative we take the high ground north of the town. An outflanking movement to the east of Benguela was impossible because of the flooded river. The only way across it was to use the bridge just north of the city's main centre — but that was directly under the eyes of FAPLA. So to take the high ground, we would first have to clear the part of Benguela north of the airfield. With that in our hands, the 81mm mortars could be deployed within range of the rocket batteries. We had, partially at least, returned to Corky's first solution. Understandably, he was annoyed that Delville and I had decided to go for a scaled-down version of his plan, considering our vehement objections of the night before.

While Delville and I planned the assault, FAPLA did everything it could to wipe Delville's command post — which was also his OP — off the face of the earth with accurate rocket fire. He positioned Staff Sergeant Piet Lubbe — his RSM — to look out for incoming rockets while we studied the air photographs.

'Here it comes!' he would shout every so often in warning.

'Here comes another pot of crap!' Delville would invariably reply.

We would take cover, wait for the explosion, and carry on with our planning.

Finally FAPLA decided to let go with a major broadside of rockets.

'Here it comes. A whole lot of them!' Piet warned.

'Here comes a big pot of crap!' Delville shouted sardonically.

We took cover as best we could, but we were in one of the most vulnerable OPs I have ever come across.

Rockets exploded in various sections of the building. The place shook violently. We were covered in dust and smoke, but unharmed.

When the dust and smoke blew away, spent rocket motors could be seen sticking out of the ground in front of and behind the terminal building. They looked like the Army's well-known 'urinal lilies'.

The plan was that I would clear the shantytown north of the airport with two of my companies while Delville gave fire support. When this was done Delville's Bushmen would leapfrog through and clear the rest of the town towards the bridge while the mortars were redeployed forward to get them within range of the Stalin organs. The final assault to take the high ground to the north would be done by Delville.

Frank Bestbier brought up two of my companies and Toon Slabbert's armoured cars. I joined them and we made ready to attack from east to west across Delville's front. Jack Dippenaar's Bravo company was on the left and Connie van Wyk's Alpha company on the right.

Corky joined Delville at his command post from where they had an excellent view of my companies as they moved through the outskirts of Benguela. Everything was looking good. My troops were moving well, with the armoured cars a short step behind to provide immediate close support where necessary.

But there was no resistance. FAPLA had fled as soon as we started deploying.

I decided to clear the whole of Benguela without waiting for Delville's Bushmen. Jack's company was tasked to clear the southern approaches and the town centre, then cross the river and make for the high ground to the north. The job of Connie's company was to clear the eastern side of Benguela as far as the river.

The streets began to fill with people. When Jack arrived at the city centre, the streets were thronged with wildly cheering city folk. He was almost bogged down by the crowds and found it difficult to continue with his clearing actions. He asked my permission to fire over the heads of the throng to disperse them. This would clear his way to the bridge and to the high ground beyond.

I was flabbergasted and quickly kiboshed the idea. I instructed him instead to stop clearing the city centre and drive through in a victorious procession, accepting the flowers, beers and cheers. When he had finally shaken off the crowds, he was to make haste for the high ground to the north.

I made my own way to the city centre. It was in uproar. People stretched out their hands to touch the liberators while others ran next to the vehicles jabbering away in Portuguese. The troops beamed from ear to ear, grinning at the girls in particular.

Connie had cleared his area with more decorum than Jack. I instructed him to pull in for the night to a cemetery that was on high ground and surrounded by thick stone walls. It was a strong position but the troops were somewhat apprehensive about spending the night with Benguela's dead.

When Jack reached the high ground to the north, the birds had flown. They had, however, left some equipment, rockets and empty boxes behind. They were probably heading for Lobito.

That night I slept behind Delville's command post. There was no way anybody would get me back into that stinking ex-Cuban garrison for my last night in Benguela. I would rather take my chances with the odd FAPLA who might still be running around the airport or city.

14

Marking time

We were supposed to leave at 08:00 the next morning but two hours before our departure, Charlie Spiller, our 'loggie'/engineer, discovered an abandoned restaurant just south of the airport turnoff. It was stocked with the sort of goodies that we had not seen for ages. In its freezers were huge crayfish, fillet steaks and sausages. In the fridges were all the makings for salads and, more importantly, bottles of white and red wine. Delaying our departure did not concern me much as Delville was leading the advance. So Battle Group Bravo got stuck into the most fantastic breakfast of crayfish followed by perfectly grilled steaks washed down with wine and topped off with strong Angolan coffee. We discovered thousands of packets of cigars, probably for issue to the Cuban troops. Replete with all the good fare and with some of us smoking fat cigars, we leisurely strolled back to our vehicles ready to get back to tackling the rapidly retreating Cubans and FAPLAs. The war had finally gained a civilised note.

It was about 09:00 when I finally got the show back on the road. I went ahead to check out FAPLA's rocket positions of the previous day. There were still a few abandoned 122mm rocket projectiles and many empty boxes lying around, but no signs of any worthwhile war loot.

Beyond the crest of the high ground was a small church with the priest still in residence. He was the first priest we had seen up till then. There were also some respectable-looking houses which probably belonged to Benguela's upper classes.

When Battle Group Bravo caught me up, Toon Slabbert joined me in the passenger seat of the Land Cruiser. I led the column through kilometre after kilometre of sugar cane fields. It was under irrigation as rainfall along the coastal area was low. To our left was the blue Atlantic Ocean with miles of deserted beaches and a promise of tourism in the future. We crossed a fiercely flowing river that was disgorging into the sea a chocolate-brown flood coloured by eroding top soil. Next to the road ran the famous Benguela railway — although it actually starts in Lobito and not in Benguela.

Rumour had it that FAPLA had taken up a position halfway to Lobito on prominent high ground that dominated all approaches from the south. It was said to be just beyond one of the flooding rivers, but this was Delville's problem and not ours. Toon and I were at peace with the world, having fed well for the first time since the campaign started.

We stopped at the southern outskirts of Lobito and came to a halt stop just behind Battle Group Alpha. There was no shooting and no angry-looking armoured cars in firing positions. Instead we were greeted by truckloads of jubilant civilians who had come from the city. My men took this as a signal to display large FNLA banners from every lorry. There was much banter and shouting between the troops and the povos. People were laughing and singing and there was a general air of conviviality.

However, I could smell disciplinary troubles with my troops and decided to drive straight through Lobito and keep going for at least 30km — even if it meant a fight with FAPLA to secure a camping site. The fleshpots of Lobito would probably be just too much for my troops and I somehow doubted that I would see many of them again once I had let them loose in the city.

We passed the airport on our left and entered the city proper. The streets were thronged with wildly cheering crowds and I had difficulty in negotiating a way through. Hands were held out to be shaken. People laughed, danced and sang. One chap ran after us and deposited his girlfriend on my Land Cruiser.

'She's yours', he shouted in English.

I managed to make her understand that we were heading far to the north of Lobito. I suggested that she had better get off unless she wanted to go to war with us. Fortunately or unfortunately, depending on the viewpoint, she jumped off after a block or two.

We passed MPLA's headquarters. That morning, without prompting, a mob had attacked the place and driven the organisation from the city, killing a large number in the process. The multi-storeyed building was a mess of shattered glass and splintered wood. Broken furniture, paper and files littered the street. Attempts had been made to set the place on fire and burn it to the ground. These attempts had been largely unsuccessful although the occasional fire was still smouldering. Several bodies were sprawled on the pavement, but it was difficult to tell if they were locals or MPLA.

We turned right at the harbour and followed the road out of town. It wound up to the top of the escarpment, then swung north with the road parallel to the sea on the left.

The rejoicing among the troops soon diminished as Lobito and its fleshpots fell away behind us. En route I passed Delville and his Battle Group Alpha who had come to the same conclusion as I had. We continued for another 12km, then turned off into an abandoned farm where we made camp for the night.

There was no sign of FAPLA, but the local population told us that they had driven north in a great hurry earlier that morning. Some had come to grief in a mountain pass where landslides had sent some of their vehicles to the bottom of a ravine. I sent a patrol of infantry and armoured cars out in that direction, but they returned without making contact or seeing any signs of the enemy. I despatched Sergeant Danny Roxo and a platoon back to Lobito to secure the dockyard area and the fuel storage tanks. We were banking on captured fuel to sustain our farther northward advance.

The next morning Toon and I drove back to the airport at Lobito, where Corky had established Zulu Headquarters, to report to him and get further instructions. Corky said we would be marking time until the powers-that-be decided whether we should advance to Angola's capital, Luanda, or whether we should be satisfied with what we had already taken and consolidate our position. We had most of the country in our grip and certainly the most important part, including the Benguela railway line. The FNLA, it was said, had also made conquests in the northern provinces adjacent to Zaïre. It was not long to 11 November when Angola would become officially independent. Did we hold enough territory?

I returned to our laagering area to find a highly irate Danny Roxo waiting for me. He had returned with his platoon from the fuel tanks in Lobito harbour. He had been thoroughly beaten up. His platoon had been followed into Lobito by a group of UNITA troops commanded by a fellow called 'Lumumba'. A war name like that meant only one thing — he was not a friend of FNLA nor of the South Africans.

Lumumba peremptorily ordered Danny to vacate the dockyard. Danny rightly objected, saying he only took orders from his commander. Lumumba would have to discuss the matter with me. He replied that he would only speak to me if he needed to buy a pocket of potatoes. Danny lost his temper and obviously made some unflattering remarks about UNITA. Lumumba retaliated by ordering his troops to beat up Danny and the few men with him.

I saw red at this calculated insult from a pipsqueak UNITA commander whose organisation thus far had contributed nothing of note to the war effort. After our differences of opinion at Cuangar, Cuvelai and Artur de Paiva, I was more than just a little prejudiced against our UNITA allies. With an escort of two armoured cars I set out to locate this Lumumba character. I stopped at Delville's position to tell him of my intentions, only to discover that he was already en route to sort out another UNITA leader, a Dr Valentino. UNITA elements under Valentino's command had assaulted one of Delville's platoons, also in the dockyard area.

I made my way to the former Portuguese garrison, an old fort on top of the escarpment that overlooked Lobito Harbour. En route one of my armoured cars got stuck in a ditch and the crew of the second armoured car decided to stop and recover it. This left me alone to face down UNITA, who were garrisoned in the fort. On arrival I found that the fort was being looted by UNITA troops. I did not have Paul with me to interpret, so I tried to make myself understood in English. I was angry and this made me reckless. I roughly grabbed a likely-looking UNITA troopie by the shoulder and spun him around.

'Where is that scumbag Lumumba? I want him.'

My armoured cars were nowhere in sight and 20 or 30 troops had begun to press in around me.

'I don't know, boss. He's not here. Maybe he's at the radio station', a wide-eyed UNITA fellow said in Afrikaans.

'You're a SWAPO bastard because only SWAPOs can speak Afrikaans!'

'No boss, I'm UNITA, not SWAPO', he protested.

There was much ill-tempered mumbling amongst the UNITA troops so I hurriedly withdrew, having decided that discretion was the order of the day. I found the armoured car still stuck in the ditch at the bottom of the hill and the other one trying to pull it out. This did not improve my temper because without the armoured cars in support, I might have been killed up there. I ordered them to follow me as soon as they had dug themselves out.

I went to the radio station expecting to find some senior UNITA officers. The man in charge turned out to be a white Portuguese with several white assistants. They were adamant that Dr Valentino was extremely bad news for Lobito. Lobito had been under UNITA control some months before and Valentino had been the governor there. His method of spreading UNITA's political word had been to lock up dissenters and torture them until they changed their minds along with their allegiance. It was apparent that Lobito was not a UNITA stronghold. To judge by the spontaneous and joyous display that had greeted our arrival in the city, it mostly supported FNLA. The last the radio station crew had seen of Valentino was when he had escaped the city by ship when FAPLA had arrived to occupy it. If he was truly back, they would be very unhappy about it.

My quarrel was with Lumumba and not Valentino. They suggested that the two would probably be found together. Valentino was expected at about 21:00 as he was scheduled to broadcast to the people of Lobito at that time. I decided to wait there for him.

21:00 came and went with no sign of Lumumba or Valentino. The armoured cars had rejoined me. I was not prepared to wait any longer and decided to look for them in town. The radio station crew had said that the two had mentioned earlier that they intended to dine at the only hotel still operating in Lobito. I went there but was told they had left for the airport.

My little column stormed to the airport which was where Zulu Headquarters was situated. All was quiet at the terminal building but I went from floor to floor. Eventually I found Corky deep in conversation with the two UNITA gentlemen concerned in the baggage area.

I was ready to blow a gasket by then, having waited for hours around Lobito for Lumumba to turn up. I cocked my rifle.

'Which one of you slimebags is Lumumba?' I demanded angrily.

Corky was flabbergasted and caught off-balance.

'Why do you want to know?' he demanded.

'Because when I find out I'm going to shoot him.'

Valentino, who spoke perfect English, went grey in the face and started to stutter. 'It must be a mistake.'

He was the fat one with the glasses. Slightly behind him was a dumb-looking individual who obviously had no comprehension of what was going on. He had to be Lumumba, so I turned my rifle on him.

'Stop, you bloody fool. You're wrecking my whole diplomatic effort', shouted Corky as he moved between Lumumba and myself. 'Get out. Now I'll have to start all over again.' The little man was understandably very angry.

'But this bastard assaulted my troops at the dockyard.'

'We'll discuss it later. Get out.'

I left still the hell in but a senior officer's order had to be obeyed.

As I was leaving, Delville stormed in.

'Where's that idiot Valentino? I want to kill him.'

He had also been all over Lobito looking for Valentino, so the same performance was repeated, but with different actors. Poor old Corky was having a rough time with his battle group commanders.

The next morning, Delville, Toon, Frank and I returned to Zulu Headquarters. The high brass were arriving to discuss future operations. Zulu Force's upper hierarchy looked somewhat disreputable, having grown rather untidy beards. Delville looked particularly outlandish in his strange garb. I was the only smooth-shaven one amongst them. I have hated beards all my life.

A group of armoured cars had arrived from inland. It was Commandant Eddie Webb, the commander of Battle Group Foxbat, and his staff which included his second-in-command, Major Hollie Holtzhausen. The 'Eighth Army' and 'First Army' were meeting after months of campaigning. The 'Eighth Army' looked and felt somewhat superior, what with their air of devil-may-care, an assortment of looted vehicles and our novel modes of dress. No doubt the 'First Army' also felt superior when noticing our lack of military bearing and conformity. They looked far smarter and more militarily correct in their olive-green fatigues and pristine armoured cars.

Eddie demonstrated his M79 grenade launcher. It was the first time most of those there had seen one. I had fired the weapon on numerous occasions in America and had even obtained my expert classification. It was an effective weapon that threw 40mm high-explosive rounds up to a range of 200m. Eddie was using it as his personal weapon. Hollie was his usual perfectionist self and as always was thoroughly enjoying the war. Foxbat had pushed north from Nova Lisboa and cleared the road between Lobito and Alto Hama. This made lateral communications between Foxbat and Zulu possible.

A C160 transport aircraft appeared in the circuit and we adjourned to the airport building to watch it land. It was bringing in the top brass from the south, including our boss, Brigadier Dawie Schoeman. More importantly, it also carried the first load of beer flown in to the troops. Until then we had been relying on the occasional case brought in by the ammunition Dakota. Despite this, I was certain that Toon had some sort of secret arrangement. He always appeared to have a copious supply of Castle beer, while Delville and I did without.

Toon and I spotted the beer cases when the ramp at the back dropped. To us it was manna from heaven. We promptly forgot about the top brass and made for the beer. There must have been at least a hundred cases. We claimed a bottle each and sat on the aircraft's ramp and drank thirstily. It was Angolan beer fresh from the Sa da Bandeira brewery. Commandant Boy du Toit, a friend and a sort of military governor at Sa da Bandeira, had got his priorities right. One of the first things he had done was to get the brewery back in operation. We blessed good old Boy. The brass were unimpressed as they watched Toon and I putting away lagers one after the other. They wanted to get on with the indaba. But unlike us, they had not been deprived of beer for too long.

Finally we made our way to the conference area. The new faces were Colonel Johan van der Spuy, Commandant Toutjies Venter, Major Coen Upton and Captain Smoky Bouwer. Coen Upton had come to join Delville as second-in-command. Smoky Bouwer brought a troop of 25-pounder guns. FAPLA was going to have a rough time with our new firepower. The guns had been off-loaded at Benguela and were on their way to us. Toutjies Venter had come to polish off a few bottles of whisky that Coen had brought along and also to look at gunnery problems — strictly in that order. Johan van der Spuy was the new commander of 1-Military Area and he was on an orientation trip.

Brigadier Schoeman was pleased with the progress so far. We discussed further operations in a relaxed atmosphere. It was decided to push up the coast as far as Porto Amboine in the north and then turn east and head for Gabela and Quibale. Battle Group Foxbat would be thrusting up the centre towards Quibale and we would link up with them there. It had become evident, although it was unsaid, that we were on our way to Luanda.

Fresh troops were being deployed from South Africa. The campaign had begun to look like a South African invasion of Angola, rather than an exercise to assist UNITA and FNLA. A new battle group, X-ray, was in the process of being formed. X-ray would clear the railway line east from Luso, a large railway town in UNITA's hands. Another force, Battle Group Yankee, would move north-east of Foxbat and make for the Quanza River bridge at Malanje. Lobito had become the logistics base where ships from the south would bring in whatever was required for the military build-up. The war effort was escalating — not diminishing, as some of us had thought. It certainly did not look at all as if we would be leaving Angola by 11 November.

Lobito was Angola's major seaport. It was firmly tied to the Benguela railway which had not operated since before the days of *Operation Savannah* because much of it had been controlled by UNITA. Without the railway line, Lobito had no real importance except to serve the immediate hinterland that included the central highlands.

Lobito had been the major holiday resort for central and southern Angola. The central part was the agricultural heartland of Angola. In the days before they were forced to flee, it contained the largest concentration of well-to-do Portuguese settlers. Lobito had been renowned for its nightlife with its nightclubs, strip clubs, pubs, restaurants, carnivals and vibrant social scene. There were secluded beaches and sailing and boating in the natural harbour.

After the indaba with the brass, Delville, Toon and I borrowed Corky's black Mercedes and went for dinner at the hotel where I had sought Lumumba the previous evening. Under Delville's directions — he had been to Lobito before and could speak Portuguese — we had a good dinner in spite of the fact that war had brought austerity to the town. For tired warriors, though, it was entertainment fit for a king. By the end of it, we had forgotten all about Lumumba and Valentino.

The next day we decided to explore the coast farther to the north. We discovered a small seaside resort and packed off the troops to swim and lie around the beach. Beer from the previous day's consignment helped with rest and relaxation.

The resort was owned by a Portuguese family who were waiting for better days. We expected to be charged an entrance fee but the owner waived it, figuring, perhaps, that the better days had arrived. The water was crystal clear and teeming with fish. We were only sorry we didn't have scuba gear because there were some interesting reefs offshore. Just visible to the south at the end of a long curve of sandy beach was a small fishing village.

We had seen little of Lobito's seafront, so Toon and I decided to do some exploring. We set off down the bluff which sheltered the natural harbour from the Atlantic rollers. The road was flanked by houses, gardens and parks all the way to the point of the bluff. To our right was the tranquil water of the harbour with a few ships alongside and one or two anchored out in the roads. They seemed quite unconcerned about the war.

It was the same with the engine drivers. Many were the times that our column of armoured cars and troop-carrying vehicles passed a train on the line parallel to the road on which we were advancing. A battle might be raging in Sa da Bandeira, Moçamedes, Benguela, Lobito or wherever, but the trains came and went routinely, sticking to their timetables. We would wave to the drivers and they would cheerfully wave back. It never occurred to us to stop a train and find out about conditions farther down the line.

We sat on the seawall at the point of the bluff and admired the magnificent scenery. Palm trees lined the shore and secluded beaches were enclosed within parallel walls to prevent erosion of the narrow bluff.

On a nearby beach two sexy young bikini-clad girls, one a brunette and the other a redhead, were splashing about in the shallows. They spotted the two strange characters sipping beer on the seawall and walked over to make our acquaintance.

The redhead asked why we were in Angola, who we were and where we came from. I got in quickly before Toon could answer.

'My name is Gardiner and I come from Rhodesia. My friend is a Dutchman from Holland, name of Kerneels Koekemoer. Unfortunately he cannot speak English but I'll translate if you want me to.'

The red-haired girl glanced at Toon. He could not speak for fear of compromising my ad lib cover story. He was not happy.

'Jan, *bliksem*!' was all he could say.

I discussed the war with the redhead who, it turned out, belonged to UNITA.

After a while I decided that Toon should be brought up to date.

'Excuse me, but I would like to translate for my friend', I said.

'Toon, look at the figure and that bellybutton. Don't you think she's gorgeous?'

She was standing with her bellybutton more or less at eye level.

'You know, you're a real bastard. I'll never go anywhere with you again. You know just how to spoil a man's day', Toon replied in Afrikaans to keep up the appearance being a Hollander.

'My friend says he agrees with your impressions of the war and the political situation. Frankly, though, his concept of what is happening in Angola is a little hazy. He fights for money, you see.'

She looked at Toon disapprovingly. He was getting even redder than his normal beetroot colour, not with embarrassment but with frustration.

In the end we gave the girls a couple of cans of beer and they resumed their tanning positions under the palms. Toon stared regretfully after them.

It was time to move out and we were pleased to get under way again. The lull had allowed FAPLA to put distance between us and them and to prepare a hot reception for our advance. They had dug in on the far side of Angola's flooded rivers and blown up strategic bridges. We still had no bridging equipment with which to cross them. And where were the paratroopers we needed to seize crossing points? We were expecting to run into well organised defensive systems which might prove impossible to crack. That four-day break, although welcome for resting the troops, could turn out to be the biggest mistake we had made in the whole campaign. Having lost the initiative, Catengue and Benguela-type battles would no longer be possible.

Our own war leaders had either foolishly or deliberately given FAPLA a welcome respite.

15

Nova Redondo

And so it happened.

Delville's Bushmen ran into a nasty situation as Battle Group Bravo's tail-end Charlie was pulling out of Lobito.

A large river breaks out of a very narrow gorge onto a plain before it empties its muddy waters into the Atlantic about 20km south of Nova Redondo. To the south and north of this plain the escarpment forms a vertical barrier with the pounding sea breaking at its base. The plain, which is about five to eight kilometres wide, indents five kilometres into this line of cliffs. The cliff face has been eroded over thousands of years by the rushing water of the river.

Delville had entered the plain from the south and by a coup de main had seized the only bridge over the fast-flowing river. The Cubans had scrambled to blow the bridge before he could reach it but they had been foiled by the speed of his advance. His leading armoured cars, rushing for the northern edge of the plain, ran into an ambush while trying to negotiate the winding road to the top of the escarpment. Two armoured cars were lost and the rest pulled back under heavy fire.

The mortar platoon moved into action quickly to produce covering fire so that Battle Group Alpha's leading elements could withdraw. Unavoidably, this brought them within clear sight of a well dug in and concealed enemy position. The result was an accurate and effective counter-bombardment on Battle Group Alpha's base-plate positions. The platoon was rendered hors de combat and suffered about 18 casualties, one of them fatal. Lieutenant Aucamp, the mortar platoon leader who had come to notice at Catengue, again distinguished himself — despite being wounded — by carrying several of his wounded companions into cover while under heavy mortar fire. He was assisted by Alpha's RSM and engineering commander, Staff Sergeant Piet Lubbe. Both were subsequently awarded the *Honoris Crux* for exceptional bravery under fire.

Meanwhile, we had passed Major Jock Harris' company which, without my knowledge, had been sent from Sa da Bandeira to Lobito. They were holding a T-junction on the main road to Nova Lisboa at the Nova Redondo turn-off. His company had refused to move farther north. The men felt that they had entered a 'foreign' country for which they had no affinity nor any obligation to shed their blood to enhance Chipenda's chances of becoming president. Such feelings were running through the rest of Battle Group Bravo too. Although there was no question of another mutiny in the offing, I decided to preempt any act of sudden disobedience by getting Chipenda to come and inspire them. I had arranged to rendezvous with him at an airstrip 10km south of where Delville had been ambushed.

When he arrived I felt inclined to ignore him and push on to where I could assist Delville and his Bushmen. This was not to be, however. We pulled in at the airfield just as the last Dakotas with Battle Group Alpha's casualties aboard took off and climbed before turning south to head for South West Africa.

The SAAF Dakota with Chipenda aboard landed shortly afterwards.

Chipenda, with a beaming, well-fed face and dressed as usual in a floral shirt and slacks, got out and gave the troops the FNLA thumbs-up sign. A roar of approval came from the Battle Group Bravo troops.

'FNLA O yea! FNLA O yea! Chipenda O yea!'

The FNLA guerrilla leader and former FAPLA military commander launched into an impassioned speech.

Diaz, a former Portuguese soldier, translated for the benefit of Frank Bestbier and myself. He told the troops about a communist serpent that had to be killed before Angola could be free. He said that until now we had been attacking its tail but the head was in Luanda where we would have to finally grind the creature into the dust.

'FNLA, O yea!' he shouted at the end of his speech.

The troops answered him with exultant cheers.

Chipenda began boarding the Dakota for his return flight to Serpa Pinto and his ex-governor's palace, his whisky and his girls. Then the parade suddenly disintegrated. He was harassed from all sides by excited troops who were not entirely satisfied with his explanation as to why the war had to be fought in 'foreign' territory. Polite enquiries turned into shouts — then into downright insults, judging by the fists that were shaken in his face. Chipenda, an astute survivor, backed off, smiling and waving.

Everyone, including me, was perplexed by developments. Within minutes a manageable if reluctant body of troops had changed into a howling, belligerent mob.

Chipenda's Dakota lifted off and turned east towards Serpa Pinto. Around me an angry and gesticulating mob of troops shouted at each other and at their erstwhile *commandantes*.

The white South Africans were left as interested but worried spectators.

To the north, 25-pounder artillery pieces were booming away at FAPLA positions. I was well aware that Delville could have done with our help but there was nothing I could do since I had a rapidly disintegrating unit on my hands.

'Mount!' I bawled out.

It was the only order I could think of.

Fortunately the call was taken up, first by my South African company commanders and platoon leaders, then by the ex-*commandante* platoon sergeants. Without a further flicker of resistance the troops gathered weapons and kit and climbed onto their transports. They knew that we were about to drive towards the sound of the guns in 'foreign' territory, but suddenly this did not seem to matter.

From being an undisciplined mob they had been transformed into a well-disciplined battalion in a matter of a few short weeks. It appeared they had only been venting their pent up anger at Chipenda and his comrades and not against us. Chipenda's visit and speech had finally purged them of their last vestiges of loyalty to Angola's opportunistic politicians. From that moment on, their white South African officers had their allegiance. Now they were South African soldiers fighting for whatever objectives the South Africans decided on. I never heard any further discussion about the whys and wherefors of the war. When Chipenda's name was mentioned, it was with derision by some and sadness by others. Doggedly, stoically, they carried out the orders we gave them.

*   *   *

As we moved north we picked up a frightened FAPLA cadre who had also started to make his way north as best he could. Eventually thirst and hunger got the better of him and he headed for the main road and surrendered to our column. He said that many disorientated and beaten FAPLA troops, survivors of the heavy fighting in

Benguela and the rapid evacuation of Lobito, were moving north. We tightened our security in case some of them regained their courage and tried to spring an ambush on us.

I halted my battalion just south of the fighting and went to Delville's command post which was on a knoll overlooking the plain. Less than a kilometre ahead was the bridge he had taken. The river was a raging torrent. Boulders, testimony to a failed demolition, still lay in the roadway. The Cubans had tried unsuccessfully to undercut an adjacent cliff face to induce a rock fall on the bridge's southern approaches.

Captain Smoky Bouwer, the artillery commander, was with Delville and Corky in his command post. He was as excited as a lad on his first date at the chance to use his beloved guns. Delville was another old gunner and he also relished the opportunity of shelling the enemy. It was the first time those 25-pounders had been fired in anger since World War-II. So the 'old' and the 'young' gunners smiled happily as the troop of four guns delivered lethal airbursts, scattering red-hot steel shrapnel on the unprotected heads and bodies of the FAPLA troops cowering in their shallow open trenches.

In turn, FAPLA's shells were marching up and down and near the beach to our left. They apparently suspected that Delville's Bushmen were trying to execute a left flanking movement.

I wanted to join the battle and I suggested to Corky that I move my troops through the broken terrain to the right, cross the river and fall on FAPLA's left flank with a violent and, hopefully, well-executed night attack. He just looked at me without saying a word. His lack of enthusiasm was explained when I finally clapped eyes on the river which I had not properly seen until then. It was a raging mass of brown water constrained between the cliffs of a rugged gorge about 80 metres deep and with sheer vertical sides. The bridge could not be used because it was continually under fire and out in the open. It would form a lethal bottle-neck for advancing troops.

Eventually FAPLA's shelling began to die down and it finally stopped. Careful probes by armoured car patrols established that FAPLA had vacated the high ground to the north of the plain. They also found clear evidence that our airbursts had produced a large number of FAPLA casualties. The tar road and adjacent areas were littered with shrapnel. There were craters in the tar and the surface was marked with bloodstains and a scatter of bloody bandages. It was apparent that death and destruction had reigned supreme there.

The sun was going down so Battle Group Alpha consolidated its positions. We would take the lead the next morning for the push through a stretch of hilly country to Nova Redondo. Major Dries van Coller said that FAPLA was occupying strong positions, particularly on a high dominating feature to the west of the main road. They had fifteen 82mm mortars and some Stalin Organs at their disposal. This was in addition to B10s and other recoilless guns, RPG7 hand-held rocket launchers, 60mm mortars, heavy machine guns, light machine guns, and the inimitable AK47s given to all their troops as a general issue.

I was not of a mind to rush things. I decided to start my attack from a line behind Delville's FLOT (forward line of own troops). This meant that my attack would move in with troops and armoured cars deployed over a front of some five kilometres.

Smoky's artillery was at my disposal. I planned to have the guns and mortars on call, the primary target being the dominating feature west of the road. We had only a few details of FAPLA's deployments, which explained the 'on call' artillery and mortar fire.

The next morning at first light we kicked off with a company to the left and another to the right of the road. The armoured cars followed the infantry, moving from firing position to firing position. Smoky and I sat on a knob of a hill from where we viewed an infantry battalion in 'attack mode' in accordance with army battle drills. I felt rather like Wellington at Waterloo. This was the first time that I had seen my own attacks from a distance. It looked very impressive. A well-drilled and well-armed infantry assault formation was moving in a thin line through the shrubs and bush on either side of the tarred road, well spread out and acting like professionals. Following them were the equally well-deployed troops of the reserve company. Armoured cars moved smoothly, leap-frogging from position to position, their 90mm guns pointing menacingly at what we presumed was FAPLA's defensive position.

I was sipping a mug of coffee, lost in admiration at the warlike tableau at my feet, when Corky turned up. I proudly swept my arm over the scene below.

'That is how it should be done', I exclaimed.

'We are wasting time', he said.

Corky was unimpressed. He wanted me to speed up the advance.

'With all those FAPLAs and Cubans sitting on the hill over there?' I said. 'No way. Delville got a bloody nose yesterday and I've no intention of getting one today. Besides, I'm doing it according to the book, probably for the first time in my life, and it looks good to me. Maybe the book works after all.'

I was adamant. The process would not be stopped or changed until we had cleared the FAPLA positions in classical style. Corky remained quiet.

In fact, there was a deathly silence all around. The hill opposite seemed particularly peaceful as my infantry climbed steadily up the slopes and headed for the summit.

Smoky was eagerly watching for the slightest sign of enemy action so that he could let loose his guns to play their deadly airbursts over the skyline and beyond.

But there was nothing and the infantry slowly disappeared from sight.

'I said you could have moved faster.'

Corky had no need to say anything more as he made his way back to his vehicle.

I climbed into my Land Cruiser and sped forward to where my troops had disappeared, cursing Dries van Coller all the way. If FAPLA had been there, it would certainly have made for a beautiful scrap. I was almost disappointed that we had missed out after all the preparations we had made to ensure success.

So it was back to playing Rommel instead of Montgomery, hitting the enemy when we made contact with him instead of going through tortuous preparations for deliberate assaults.

I caught up with Connie van Wyk's Alpha company. I told him he should rush his men, with two troops of armoured cars in support, through the centre of Nova Redondo. He would bypass any FAPLA ensconced in buildings facing the road. His task was to take the high ground beyond with a coup de main and cut off the enemy's chance of withdrawal to the north. Jack and his company would follow in the wake of his advance and clear the town.

Smoky would remain with me and use his artillery to engage any targets of opportunity on the high ground that might interfere with Connie's advance. My command post was on a high hill on which there was a prominent radio mast. Again I had a beautiful view of the battlefield.

Nova Redondo was one of the most picturesque towns on the Angolan coast. Most of it was laid out along a palm-fringed beach on our left and the main road leading north that crossed a raging river to our right. Across the river were fields under irrigation that stretched for two or three kilometres. Beyond that, the main road turned abruptly right and wound its way up a steep incline to the top of the escarpment.

The road was clogged with fleeing FAPLA traffic. There was a gleam in Smoky's eye. He started to play a deadly tune with his artillery, firing airbursts over the fleeing enemy traffic. How nice it was to make war from a distance instead of close-up, as had been our lot until Smoky and his guns arrived. Some vehicles were on fire and others were wrecked and abandoned. Little figures were running on the road and others were scampering through the bushes. Soon the road out of Nova Redondo was deserted.

Meanwhile, Connie's men were doubling through the town, meeting only wildly cheering schoolchildren and their teachers. They faced no resistance whatsoever. It seemed to be a repeat of the Lobito scenario.

Frank Bestbier joined me at my OP, which left me free to advance and join Connie as he advanced on the high ground to the north. As I left, a Stalin Organ opened up from the south. The first rockets bracketed the position I had just vacated. Frank was up there collecting rockets meant for me. He was not amused, primarily because I had selected an OP that was obvious to even the dimmest of FAPLA commanders. The prominent radio mast made an ideal target marker for the enemy gunners.

I soon caught up with Connie's leading armoured cars. We continued Rommel-fashion like Delville had done the day before, and tackled the steep road to the top of the hill.

We ran into an ambush at the first cutting. There was an almighty bang as a small suicide group let fly with an RPG7 rocket at the leading armoured car. It missed. This was followed by an even louder bang as one of our 90mm guns returned fire. I valiantly dismounted from my vehicle and took some men to clear the position. We found two strangely intact but very dead FAPLAs with their RPG7. They had probably been killed by the blast when the 90mm shell landed just in front of them. We emptied their pockets of escudos so that we could buy freshly baked paos at the next village.

I returned to my Land Cruiser and found it had a flat tyre. To my disgust, the spare was also flat. This left me sitting helplessly in a cutting that was overlooked by menacing high ground beyond. With some anxiety I summoned Frank from his now vulnerable OP to bring me his own spare wheel. He turned up laughing unsympathetically at my predicament. We changed the wheel and I rejoined the leading troops.

We had a short and sharp engagement at the top of the escarpment. Connie's infantry cleared the thick bush on both sides of the road in professional style. We found several dead FAPLA and a wounded female soldier. She put up a great struggle as we tried to evacuate her. Wounded or not, it was clear she was expecting to be company-raped by Battle Group Bravo's troops. We also found many items of camouflage uniform, some covered in blood. It appeared that many of the enemy had hastily tried to discard all evidence that they were members of FAPLA, no doubt to avoid the merciless apartheid Boers committed to killing them out of hand. We had encountered this behaviour before. It created problems for us as many of the cadres just merged with the local population.

*   *   *

Jack Dippenaar's Bravo company cleared the town. He informed me that he had found the ideal place for our headquarters. Leaving Connie to consolidate on the high ground, I made my way to Jack's company via the cotton mill below where Corky was establishing his HQ. Jack had selected an elegant building in Nova Redondo as Battle Group Bravo's HQ. Above a well-designed ground floor were two separate flats on either side of a roof garden that was tastefully decorated with potted palms, shrubs and flowers. To the rear of the building was a paved driveway flanked by luxurious tropical gardens. In a corner of the main house was a tower with a small room at the top from which the town, the hills to the north and the fishing fleet anchored in the bay could be viewed.

The scenery was superb. An old Catholic church was diagonally across from us and a long curved beach fringed with palm trees was directly below. The Atlantic Ocean broke in long white rollers along the sandy crescent of the bay. A short wooden jetty reached out towards the fishing fleet. The first fishermen were already making their way towards us, laden with freshly caught crayfish for sale. This was going to be paradise.

I inspected the house with Frank. Judging by the signs of a rather panicky departure, it had only just been vacated. It was furnished with English antiques — or so our medical doctor said. He was an antiques expert of some renown from Cape Town.

Before long an elderly and angry Portuguese couple mounted the stairs to the roof garden. I was cleaning my rifle after the morning's excitement. Paul said they were complaining about us illegally occupying the premises. They continually referred to the 'law of the land' and insisted it would come down on us for breaking and entering. They persisted and shook their fingers at me. Paul scarcely got the opportunity to translate. In the end I lost my patience.

'I am the law in this place now, so get out!' I snapped.

I finished assembling my rifle and went through the drill of sliding the working parts backwards and forwards to ensure their smooth functioning. The effect was electrifying. The couple almost fell over each other in their haste to escape the madman who, it seemed, was preparing to shoot them out of hand. They rushed down the stairs and into the street. Good riddance, I thought. There was no harm in them spreading the word that the new occupants of the Pink House, as we called it, were a little crazy.

It transpired later that the former occupant had been the Portuguese governor of Nova Redondo Province. He also owned the fishing fleet in the bay, two cotton farms and several cacao farms inland. He was happy to change sides when FAPLA took over Nova Redondo after the Portuguese departed. He was a multi-millionaire and if protecting his investments meant serving under a Marxist government, then so be it. He no doubt thought that his day of reckoning had come when my troops, under the banner of FNLA, had suddenly and violently appeared on the scene. He probably also remembered that the local inhabitants were mostly FNLA supporters. He vacated his house in such a hurry that he scarcely had time to pack a suitcase.

His personal servant arrived and started cleaning up the place as if nothing had changed. He even took over our washing. Soon we were wearing crackling-fresh camouflage uniforms, nicely starched and ironed. The old boy was quite ancient but very amiable. I am sure he had no inkling of what the fuss, or the war, was all about.

Frank found some splendid and unmarked sets of medals in the ex-governor's office that had clearly never been presented. They all had striking ribbons. There were eleven sets of three medals. I invited Delville and his headquarters to dine at my 'palace'.

During the evening I solemnly presented each officer, including myself with the 'Angolan Freedom Medal', the 'Catengue Star' and the 'Angolan Campaign Medal'.

Brigadier Schoeman was coming to my posh residence the next morning to brief us. I told my visitors to wear their medals for the briefing.

The brigadier and Colonel Corky van Heerden were clearly perplexed when they inspected the throng of well-decorated officers across the table from them. The medals clinked in a satisfying manner whenever we moved. It would have made a wonderful picture for the newspapers back in South Africa — particularly if Toon Slabbert had shaved off his unkempt red beard which did not go at all well with our crisp and freshly ironed camouflage fatigues. Image the headline: 'South African mercenaries decorated deep inside Angola.'

'Where did you get those gongs?' Brigadier Schoeman asked bluntly.

'Chipenda was here early this morning and he held an impromptu medal parade.'

'How come I didn't know about it?' Corky asked. He viewed the display on our chests with obvious envy.

'It happened so quickly that I had no time to inform you. He left straight after the parade.'

'What are the medals for?' the brigadier asked.

I explained the purported significance of each. The ribbons looked like the real thing — as if they had been struck for a world war.

We continued with the briefing, the gist being that we had to find a way to cross the Queve River to the north, either along the coast towards Porto Amboine or from Gionda towards Gabela. On the map the terrain looked formidable with the widest river we had yet encountered — a significant obstacle — and rugged mountains inland. The rainy season had commenced in earnest and the going in the valleys inland would be muddy and soft. The armoured cars in particular would be greatly handicapped. They would be confined to the roads and would have to brave numerous defiles with no hope whatsoever of deploying into the soggy bush to escape the attention of FAPLA's B10s and RPG7s.

We had tea and cake to round off the briefing. It was better than the usual army dishwater and dog biscuits. Corky and the brigadier took the opportunity to closely examine our medals. The joke was on them. The ex-governor probably had a connection with local second-league soccer and it appeared that Nova Redondo had won the cup for three years in a row. Every year medals with different coloured ribbons were struck for the team members.

We spent the rest of the day preparing for our respective advances to the north — my group towards Porto Amboine and Delville's towards Gabela. The preparations also allowed time for several dips in the Atlantic Ocean and some lazing about on the beaches while soaking up the hot sun.

Jack Dippenaar, meanwhile, had moved Bravo company to the high ground that dominated a crossroads some ten kilometres north-east of Nova Redondo. The purpose was to block a FAPLA advance from either Gabela or Porto Amboine. Connie van Wyk and Alpha company were still spread out on high ground just to the north of the Nova Redondo plain. This blocked an approach along the coast and particularly along the beach below the cliffs. Grobbie Grobbelaar and Charlie company were in reserve at the cotton mill, protecting the Brigade Headquarters and the airfield.

I moved out at about 08:00 the next morning for an assault-crossing of the Queve River. I wanted to take Porto Amboine before the day was out. If the bridge had been blown, though, I had no bridging equipment with which to cross. It was rumoured that the existing bridge in the vicinity of the Queve River's mouth had been blown the night after we arrived in Nova Redondo.

We left in great order. The battle group was impressively strung out for at least ten kilometres along the road to the north. Smoky Bouwer's four 25-pounders and their gun tractors were bouncing around somewhere to the rear. Smoky in his Land-Rover was right behind my Land Cruiser. It was a beautiful morning, fresh and cool, as it had rained the previous night. We were in light-hearted spirits as we barrelled along a good tarred road on the top of the escarpment heading towards the Queve River estuary.

The country was flat along the narrow strip of coast. The Queve River was to our right, curving westwards towards the sea south of Porto Amboine. The hills rose in tiers to the east beyond the river, rising to become rugged mountains towards Gabela. Over the lip of the escarpment to the left we could see the blue Atlantic Ocean. A narrow beach, which was not visible to us, was wedged between the cliff face of the escarpment and the surf line. Cotton fields rolled over the horizon to the north. The rainy season had only just begun on the coastal plain and the veld beside the road was still dressed in its tawny dry season colours. The sparse bush provided little cover and the battle group stood out like a sore thumb. Nevertheless, we blithely cruised along expecting fun and games in the north.

Just south of the flood plain where the Queve River made a final westerly home run for the sea, I decided to stop the whole column and send a troop of armoured cars and a platoon of infantry to probe carefully towards the bridge. I accompanied them as I wanted to see for myself whether the bridge had been blown or not.

The road passed through a neck between two pimples on the landscape — the only two hills south of the river — and onto a flood plain about five kilometres wide before the bridge. The bridge was in the shadow of hulking cliffs with the river's main channel at the base. The cliffs stretched all along our front and were so high they masked potential FAPLA positions on top from inquisitive eyes.

The river, like the others, was in spate. We crept along the top of a causeway flanked by extensive swamps and reed beds. This made deployment off-road for the armoured cars and troop-carriers impossible. The latter were particularly vulnerable. There was no way that the troop carriers could escape if they were caught on the narrow causeway by FAPLA's defensive fire. It would become a death trap for men perched on the top of loads of kit. I halted Corporal Anton Retief's infantry platoon and continued in my Land Cruiser with an escort of armoured cars.

We saw some FAPLA soldiers in the swamp to our left. They were probably forward patrols that had been deployed to detect a night approach. We opened fire on them from the causeway and they disappeared into the reeds. We got close to where the bridge should have been, but it was gone. The rumours were true — the bridge had been destroyed.

Our shots signalled the opening of proceedings. The swamps on both sides of the causeway began to sprout gigantic mushrooms of dirty water, mud and smoke as FAPLA's shells began to fall. Fortunately, none of them landed on the road. Unable to go farther, we turned the armoured cars around on the narrow tar road and returned in a somewhat leisurely fashion towards the pimples. FAPLA was shepherding us away from Porto Amboine in no uncertain manner with their rockets and mortar bombs.

As I crossed the saddle between the pimples I saw that my battle group was spread out, almost in plan form, on both sides of the road as it gently descended from the highest point of the plain to the south. The descent started at the horizon about ten kilometres away and levelled out just north of the pimples. From the top of the cliffs, much higher than we were, FAPLA had a marvellous view. They could count every armoured car, troop-carrier and gun, plotting their positions so they could shoot them up at leisure.

The vehicles were strung out up and down the road. The men had dismounted. Some were brewing tea and taking no notice of the shell bursts that had begun to bracket them. We were getting rather blasé about this war.

Our advance to Porto Amboine and all points north had been effectively stopped. This was not because of a lack of aggression on our part, but because we could not bridge the flooded Queve River or cross its swamps. However, we were not about to meekly turn south again. That would be a disgrace. Until then we had fought with great success, not only against an escalating FAPLA resistance, but also against the dust, sand, flies and mud of Angola. Whatever happened, we would not bow out with a whimper. We would depart in style in our own time, slamming the door as we went. A defiant parting gesture was called for and I sent for Smoky Bouwer.

With Corporal Anton Retief's platoon as local protection, we ascended the eastern pimple and established an OP from which Smoky could direct his guns. The surface was slippery and muddy and a sticky mess soon built up on the soles of our boots. Once at the top, we spotted five Stalin Organ positions that were firing at us in turn. In the main, they seemed to be directing their rockets at the pimple on which we were standing. They were also targeting our command vehicles which we had left at the saddle. My Land Cruiser collected some more shrapnel just after Paul and I dismounted. Frank's and Smoky's drivers were pinned down in a ditch next to their vehicles throughout the engagement.

Smoky ranged his guns which were deployed in full view of the enemy to the east of the road. His first ranging shot crossed the path of a clearly visible incoming rocket. The flaming motor displayed the characteristic red flare that gave it the nickname of 'Red Eye'.

'Here she comes!' I shouted.

We all ducked into the mud. The rocket exploded in a shower of mud and smoke about 50 metres to our left.

'Repeat!' ordered Smoky, who had lost sight of his first shot as he ducked into cover. 'Shot!' from the guns, followed by the time of flight.

Smoky stood with his binoculars clamped firmly to his eyes, looking for the tell-tale mushrooming of a 25-pounder shell as it landed. Something appeared to be wrong with his binoculars because he kept fiddling with the eye-pieces.

'Here she comes!' I shouted again.

There was a repeat performance by the command group who got even muddier.

The rocket fell short and Smoky again missed the drop of his shell.

'Repeat!' called Smoky.

'Shot!' came from the guns. 'Time of flight so-and-so seconds.'

'Here she comes!' from me and we all ducked into the mud again.

In between, Smoky continued fiddling with his binoculars.

'Did anyone see my shot?' he asked hopefully.

None of us had.

Finally Smoky spotted a ranging shot. Judging by the column of mud, it had fallen in the water just short of the cliffs. Having found his range, he marched his shots on to the first Stalin Organ position and plastered it with airbursts.

He also discovered why he had experienced so much difficulty locating the ranging shots through his binoculars. The lenses were caked in mud. Every time he had ducked, the binoculars dangling around his neck had dipped into the sticky mud of the pimple we were standing on.

After Smoky had systematically destroyed three of the Stalin Organs, the remaining two positions decided that our command group must be immune to their rocket fire. We gathered from the sounds of rockets passing overhead that they were directing their fire at more lucrative targets. Our death dealing 25-pounders were deployed in the open and within easy range. Looking back over our shoulders, we saw rocket bursts flowering on the muddy plain as they landed around our gun positions. This forced the 25-pounder crews to pack up hurriedly and withdraw over the skyline to the south. It got them out of sight and range of the Stalin Organs, but it also put the enemy beyond the range of their own guns.

This signalled the end of our attempts to cross the Queve River. We could do nothing more, so we readied to withdraw to Nova Redondo. I formed up the column facing south and they pulled out sedately without displaying unseemly haste. The command group brought up the rear in good old British Army tradition. The rockets followed us for a while, but in a somewhat desultory fashion.

We suffered no casualties. The only damage was to the final drive of an armoured car and the drilling of a few extra holes in my Land Cruiser. Intelligence sources reported that Smoky's airbursts had created havoc in the FAPLA positions. Many of the wounded had been evacuated for treatment in the hospital at Porto Amboine. A lot of others had been killed.

There is no question that we got the better of the enemy as far as casualties and damage to morale was concerned. We left with frustration and only because our lack of engineering support had made a river crossing impossible.

During the return trip I dispatched an infantry platoon supported by a troop of armoured cars to check whether a bridge that crossed the Queve River between Nova Redondo and Gabela had been destroyed. Sources had reported that this was the case, but none of our probing patrols had actually checked it.

The bridge spanned a narrow gorge on the Queve River and was overlooked on the Gabela side by high buttresses and cliff faces. On our side, the road descended through a deep and narrow cutting for about a kilometre and the approach road to the bridge was long and straight. Fortunately, FAPLA had not yet occupied positions on the buttresses opposite. If they had, the armoured cars would have been sitting ducks as they approached the bridge hemmed in by the vertical walls of the cutting. FAPLA would, in fact, occupy those positions in force later, which would cause some anxious and exciting moments for Delville Linford and his Bushmen.

In the event, all this was purely academic because the bridge had been blown. The raging torrent at this spot made it even more difficult to cross than it was farther downstream towards the mouth.

We returned to Nova Redondo and reported to Corky. With the blowing of the bridges, stalemate had become a real possibility.

Delville and Battle Group Alpha disappeared into the mountains to the east in search of alternative routes north. We heard nothing of them for two days. Corky by then had almost given them up for lost. I flung out two patrols, each comprising a platoon of infantry and a troop of armoured cars, in an effort to make contact. My troops also, however, vanished as mysteriously as Delville and his Battle Group Alpha. It seemed to us that maybe a FAPLA monster was chewing them up somewhere beyond the mountain passes to our right.

Everything hinged on Delville's probe to the east — assuming that he and his column had not vanished forever. Fortunately though, three days later Delville reappeared from the fog-shrouded and rugged mountains, his vehicles covered in mud and accompanied by my two patrols. They had run into the torrential rain of the inland rainy season. In Angola the rains are much heavier inland than in the coastal plains which remain relatively dry throughout the year. It seemed to Delville the farther inland he went, the more sympathetic to FAPLA the population became.

I decided that a light patrol should follow the Queve River east into the mountains to seek an alternate crossing site. With myself and Frank Bestbier in the lead in our Land Cruisers, the patrol comprising infantry and a troop of armoured cars set out. We left in bright sunshine and followed a reasonable dirt road that entered the hills about ten kilometres to the east. The road soon became a muddy track and we moved in under the damp grey blanket of cloud that permanently clothed the higher mountains at that time of year. Rain began to fall and Frank and I in our open vehicles were soon soaked to the skin. The armoured cars merely closed down, so the crews remained snug and dry.

We passed several villages where the inhabitants stared at us with hostility. We were obviously unwelcome. The spontaneous relief and joy on the faces of the Nova Redondo inhabitants when we liberated their town was lacking here. There were two possible reasons. Either there was complete support for MPLA — which I somehow doubted — or a large number of FAPLA had discarded their uniforms during our attack on Nova Redondo and were hiding out among the population in the mountains. If this was so, the locals would be kept in line by the use of intimidation. Betrayal would have meant death.

I preferred my latter theory. In my experience of Africa, I have found that the rural populations are generally indifferent to the competing ideologies of various political parties. In the hope of avoiding confrontation the people will side with whoever is in armed control at a particular moment. We were just a patrol passing through. It would be bad for their health if they welcomed armed strangers or offered them guidance while FAPLA cadres were watching their every move.

We were very aware that bands of armed FAPLA troops dressed in civvies were still moving around the mountains. They were extremely dangerous as they were impossible to identify. The mountains provided perfect ambush country and were ideal for laying mines in bottle-necks along the tracks. The pouring rain favoured the mine-laying option as all signs and spoors would be washed away. Because the local FAPLA no longer had any transport, all vehicles using the roads or tracks could be safely attacked because they would almost certainly be FNLA. We wound our way through the mountains as if we were driving on eggs. We all had that characteristic tight feeling in our backsides, expecting a 'cracker' to pop off at any moment.

The country was lush, with dripping thick bush and tall trees screening the mountainsides and ravines. Every once in a while we broke into small valleys and discovered well laid out cacao plantations and beautiful coffee farms. We finally reached the Queve River winding its way through the wet mountains. Finding a possible crossing site, we dismounted and struggled on foot through the swamp to get a closer look at the main stream.

I found what I thought was a likely ford where troops could cross on foot. One look at the faces of my accompanying patrol, however, showed that I was alone in holding this opinion. I decided nevertheless to cross over and check the terrain on the other side. I informed my patrol accordingly. They looked at the raging waters in horror and then at me in barely concealed disbelief. They were adamant that they would not cross that river under any circumstances, not even if I threatened to shoot them.

Despite this, the bare bones of a plan began to form in my mind. We could operate on the far side as guerrillas on foot and ambush FAPLA's communication lines between Gabela and Porto Amboine. Eventually we could infiltrate sufficient troops to take Porto Amboine.

The lines of communication to the north of the river consisted of a tarred road and a narrow gauge railway line. Both tortuously wound their separate ways through mountain passes, which made them ideal targets for small infantry groups.

I decided to sell this plan to Corky.

First, though, I had to overcome the reluctance of my troops to cross the wild river which would stay in spate until the rainy season ended. Despite the absence of engineering support, maybe we could design a method of crossing by utilising locally available materials — perhaps some sort of easily concealed pontoon or a suspension foot bridge that could be lowered when not in use.

We headed downstream by vehicle, following the river bank to where our outdated map indicated there was a drift of sorts. We emerged from the misty mountains into the wonderfully warm sunshine lower down and soon dried out. The cacao and coffee farms gradually gave way to cotton and citrus as we headed towards the plains. With the aid of friendly locals we located the drift on a large citrus estate. But it became obvious that it would be impossible for vehicles to cross at that time of the year. Huge waves of brown water tumbled and foamed over the deeply submerged crossing.

The road wound along the southern bank of the river and joined the main road where the bridge spanning the narrow gorge between Gabela and Nova Redondo had been destroyed. I intended returning to Nova Redondo along the main road which was shorter and easier, but the friendly locals warned us against it just in time. That very morning a mixed detachment of FAPLA and Cubans had taken up strong defensive positions in the crags to the north of the river, possibly as a result of our previous day's probe. They must have thought we had obtained bridging equipment from South Africa.

It would have been suicidal to have taken that route. It would have put us under fire for several kilometres on our approach to the T-junction, followed by devastating, enfiladed fire on our backs as we returned along the steep-sided cutting to the top of the plateau.

In all likelihood the patrol would have been wiped out.

Instead, we turned around and plunged back into the dank mists and the incessant rain of the mountains. The threat of mines and ambushes would be more serious this time. Any guerrilla worth his salt would ensure that we got a hot reception if we were stupid enough to return along the same route. But unfortunately it was the only one available.

We ran the gauntlet of our own fears and the hostile staring eyes of the bedraggled population as we drove through their wet and miserable villages. We fully expected a hot reception around every corner — or at least a landmine detonating under the wheels of one of our vehicles. But nothing happened. We emerged from the mountains sighing with relief and returned safely to Nova Redondo.

I discussed my ideas with Corky and he thought they had merit.

He told me that in the near future either my or Delville's battle group would be moving inland to Cela on the central front. Whoever remained, he promised, would carry on along the lines I had suggested.

I hoped I would stay and that Delville would go to Cela.

This was not to be, however, and a few days later I got my marching orders. Corky and his headquarters would accompany us to Cela. Delville gladly moved into the Pink House and his troops took over the high ground to the north.

Delville's company would become an independent one. Although Nova Redondo had ostensibly become a backwater with the main thrust for Luanda shifting to the central front, he could develop and control the war on his own front without undue interference from higher headquarters. An independent command is the ambition of all true soldiers. While wishing Delville luck, I envied him.

16

Cela

Battle Group Bravo left Nova Redondo together with most of Major Toon Slabbert's armoured car squadron. The rest of the armoured cars remained behind with Delville Linford.

Shortly afterwards another FNLA battalion joined Delville. It was commanded by *Commandante* Kioto and was destined to become the second half of Battle Group Bravo after the termination of *Operation Savannah*. They did some good work while with Delville.

Kioto was quite a character. He ruled his men with an iron fist and exhibited no fear in battle. On one occasion he summoned a special parade and executed two of his men because they had deserted their trenches on the high ground north of Nova Redondo. He ordered them buried in the trenches they had deserted. He then calmly informed his troops that they would never again leave their positions to gallivant in town while the others were sticking it out in the cold and wet of the rainy season!

Our column moved south towards the Lobito/Nova Lisboa road before swinging east and climbing through the hills to the highlands of central Angola. The coastal bush gave way to more luxuriant vegetation, tall trees and intensively-cultivated fields and meadows. The weather deteriorated progressively as we moved inland, becoming distinctly drizzly and cool as we reached high ground. The dramatic fall in temperature was unexpected, considering that we were deep in the tropics.

The population density also increased. We passed through several medium-sized towns and eventually stopped for the night at a largish centre called Alto Hama. By then the rain was pelting down. We reconnoitred the town before nightfall to find dry quarters for the troops. We were fortunate enough to discover a large fruit packing shed into which the battalion fitted comfortably. There were plenty of wooden fruit boxes to burn for warmth and to dry out our wet clothes.

Toon and I moved into a small room on the first floor of an abandoned hotel. Zulu HQ took up the lounge and diningroom on the ground floor. That night we dined by candlelight with them.

Later, Toon, Dries van Coller and I adjourned to our room where we tackled a demijohn of wine that Dries had somehow managed to lay his hands on. He also sang rather well and his voice, accompanied by the less accomplished efforts of Toon and myself, resonated through the dark corridors of the empty hotel where a tired Zulu bunch were trying to get their heads down. They were not amused and Dries got it in the neck from Corky the next morning.

We headed north en route to Cela and crossed the north-west flowing Queve River by a bridge that had been miraculously left intact. Cela was the headquarters of Battle Group Foxbat which Zulu Headquarters took under its wing. With Battle Group Bravo and Toon's squadron already under command, this recovered the strength we had before Delville's Battle Group Alpha was detached at Nova Redondo.

Changes had taken place at Foxbat. Commandant Eddie Webb had been replaced

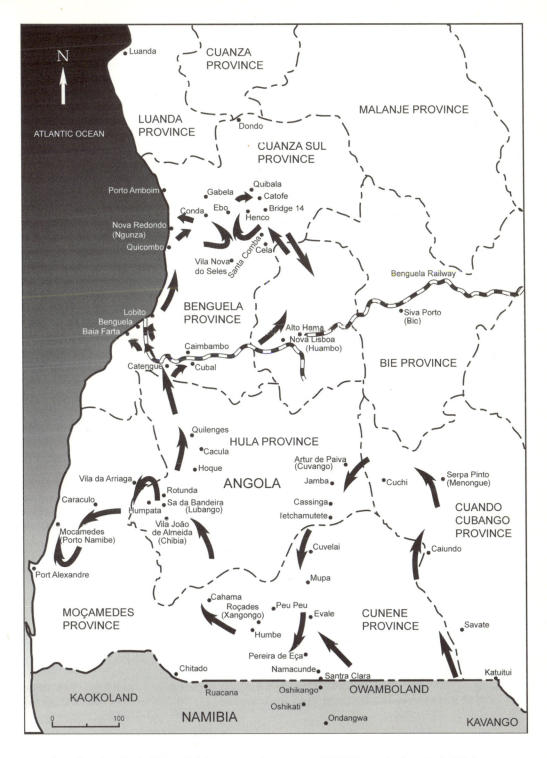

1   Map showing Task Force Zulu's opposed advance of 3 000km into Angola in 33 days.

by Commandant George Kruys. Major Hollie Holtzhausen, Eddie's second-in-command, was also returning to South Africa.

Cela had a good airfield into which C130s and C160s flew in supplies on a daily basis. In the past few weeks the war had begun to assume a distinctly South African flavour. It struck me immediately that most troops around Cela Headquarters were white, although a sizeable force of UNITA, of dubious quality but backed by armoured cars, was deployed on high ground to the north of Santa Comba. Santa Comba was about ten kilometres north of Cela and the main town in the area.

Colonel Blackie Swart, who had not yet arrived, had been designated to take over the command of Zulu from Corky. Corky was going home. In the meantime, in his stead, Colonel Skalkie Schalkwyk, the SSO Operations, had been running the war in the sector. He made no secret that he was glad to see us. I gained the impression that he regarded us as something akin to the US Cavalry, arriving in the nick of time to prevent a full-scale massacre by the Indians.

While taking a roundabout route to Gabela to the north-west, George Kruys had run into fierce resistance. His battle group had been ambushed while it was crossing a minor river near Ebo and he had lost several armoured cars and a large number of infantry.

FAPLA had concentrated on high ground immediately north of the crossing. They followed up their successes by trying to cut off George's withdrawal. If they had succeeded, there would have been nothing to prevent them from overrunning Cela. Until our arrival, there were no troops in Cela to check a determined attack into what had become a gaping left flank.

Yet, despite Battle Group Bravo's timely arrival, Skalkie was still worried. Radio communications between himself and George were abysmal, so he had no idea of the progress FAPLA had made in its effort to cut George off from Cela. For all anyone knew, they could have been arriving at any minute.

Skalkie and his staff had established themselves in an abandoned monastery. They had a spacious operations room with a myriad of well-displayed maps on the walls. He had unsurpassed communication facilities with higher headquarters, even if contact with the men in the field was poor. The monastery boasted a proper mess, decent rooms to sleep in and a well equipped hospital with Tony Dippenaar — the Surgeon of Cela — in charge. It even had a well-equipped light workshop troop.

To have packed up and vacated Cela in a hurry would have been impossible. With the panic that was fast developing, I thanked the heavens we in Zulu Force had learnt early on to remain fully mobile. All we had to do was climb into our vehicles, start them up and head in whatever direction our superiors decreed.

Corky and Skalkie conferred and ordered my battle group to take up an intermediate position on the high ground to the east to cover George's withdrawal. We would also hold up FAPLA's advance if they were following up on Foxbat's withdrawal.

Without delay we headed north past Santa Comba and turned west just behind the high ground occupied by UNITA. We took up position facing west in the direction from which we expected George to appear.

We were a short distance from a fork in the road. The northernmost branch leading from the fork had been dubbed the Blue Route. It was the most direct way to Gabela. The other road was known as the Green Route and it was along this that George was deployed.

From what I could see, of the broken and hilly terrain, although the Blue Route provided the most direct way to Gabela, it was less suitable for an advance than the Green Route.

I despatched outlying patrols, each comprising a troop of armoured cars and a platoon of infantry, along both routes for about ten kilometres where they would take up positions. Their task was to act as early warning against a FAPLA advance. They would delay FAPLA for as long as possible to enable us to leap-frog back to our main delaying position. For all I knew, George might have already been overrun, so we needed to act promptly before a drunk-with-victory FAPLA crowd began to knock violently on our front door. I deployed the companies as effectively as possible under the early-warning cover of the outlying patrols. By this time I had integrated the armoured cars, the three-inch mortars and the Vickers machine guns and their crews into the rifle companies.

We had just finished digging in when the first movement on the Green Route to the west was spotted. It was Battle Group Foxbat's 25-pounders withdrawing at a blistering pace. They passed us without pause, followed by the armoured cars and what remained of the infantry.

The infantry stopped within our lines. It was only then that I realised that they were my two old companies — Charlie under Costa Marão that we had left behind in Moçamedes and Major Jock Harris' Delta that I had last seen when en route to Lobito. Delta was now run by Sergeant Silva Sierro. They were all in a bloody mess and there were an awful lot of wounded in their trucks. Silva had taken command of what remained of both companies. I found Costa in one of the trucks, looking dreadful. He had been seriously wounded in both legs and would be out of the war for good.

George Kruys turned up and stopped briefly, obviously glad to see some new faces. He intended to establish his headquarters in an old pig farm farther south. I took the remains of the old Charlie and Delta companies back under my command and sat down with Silva to discuss their future. He filled me in on the recent bloody history of Charlie company. It made my heart bleed for them but it also made me terribly angry.

They had crossed the river ahead of the armoured cars and spread out to continue their advance, unaware that the high ground to their left was teeming with FAPLA, probably with Cubans in support.

The moment Charlie was in the open and beyond the point of no return, FAPLA opened up with a murderous hail of automatic, mortar and shellfire. Within moments, the whole company including the company commander had been cut down. Fortunately for Silva, his Delta Company had not yet crossed the river, which enabled him to cover the withdrawal of what was left of Charlie Company.

Charlie's casualties were between 80 and 90 killed or wounded. Most of the wounded were unable to escape and were killed in cold blood on the spot by the enemy. Costa escaped only by crawling several painful kilometres to safety.

While this was going on, the armoured cars had been coping with their own problems. They had come under accurate anti-tank fire and while trying to manoeuvre their way out of disaster, many had bogged down in the mud. They were in a shooting gallery and something like seven armoured cars were knocked out.

I was shocked to get my companies back in such a state. I had not even known that Jock Harris had been relieved and had gone home. I amalgamated the remnants of Charlie into Delta company and confirmed Silva as its company commander. I withdrew them to an abandoned cheese factory some distance to the south for rest, recuperation and reorganisation. For the moment they would act as our reserve.

Meanwhile, we waited for FAPLA but they did not show up. It appears the aggression they had displayed in their defence of Ebo had evaporated and their enthusiasm for the 'advance to contact' phase of warfare had disappeared.

We remained in position for the night. By morning though, Zulu Headquarters, in typical South African Army style decided to reorganise the whole show. Toon Slabbert and his armoured cars and Connie van Wyk and his Alpha Company were sent to join George Kruys. So a combat group that had been welded together perfectly through the exigencies of many battles was broken up into segments and attached and cross-attached to other units to form new organisations — the elements of which were strangers to each other.

My troops were battle-weary. We had fought little in the preceding two weeks, but before that we had frequently engaged in up to five contacts a day — each day bringing its own quota of fear and danger. The human nervous system can only stand so much and if the stress remains constant over an extended period, it eventually cracks. The danger lies in driving men beyond the psychological point of no return, which can cause irreparable damage. Dispersing my companies to all points of the compass made matters worse. They were now under new commanders who had little empathy or respect for them. They regarded them as just another bunch of incompetent Angolans.

*　　　*　　　*

George was ordered to advance towards Gabela along the Blue Route.

I was to take over two of George's badly shaken armoured car troops and move to an intermediate position to the south. We also had to man a combat outpost line on high ground five kilometres south of what became known as Bridge 14. It would achieve lasting fame in South African military history some weeks later. Bridge 14 was on the direct route to Quibale and Luanda in the north. I had to find out if it had been destroyed by the enemy.

We took up new positions in the mud and driving rain. Even as we were doing so, 122mm rockets were from time to time coming over from the vicinity of Catofé, just north of Bridge 14. I remember visiting Delta company at their rear area cheese factory. While I was speaking to Silva, rockets began bursting around us on the plain.

UNITA troops were abandoning their positions to the right of my own combat line and streaming past us, heading for the rear in a mad panic. They had a habit of withdrawing the moment the enemy artillery opened up and returning later when FAPLA's bombardments lessened. My troops, on the other hand, appeared to be oblivious to the rockets and none of them even bothered to dig in. They merely stared at the escaping UNITA with lack-lustre eyes, not even passing their normal cutting comments about UNITA's fighting capabilities. This, to me, was a sure sign of battle fatigue.

Deeply perturbed, I conferred with my company commanders. They confirmed my suspicions. While the troops could go on almost indefinitely, their fighting was becoming less and less effective. If the time came to assault a strong FAPLA position, I believed my battle group would probably have suffered numerous casualties through sheer indifference and blunted reflexes.

In spite of the heavy fighting, we had experienced very few desertions during the campaign. Frankly, I had expected many more. It would have been easy for the black troops to discard their uniforms and disappear into the local population. At Cela a few white Portuguese troops and, I am sad to say, one white South African soldier deserted and headed south for the SWA border. The South African was not from my unit, but had become loosely and accidentally attached to Delta company during the Ebo fiasco.

The black troops bore their lot stoically. This made it all the more necessary to petition higher authority to get them moved back to a rest area. They had proved their loyalty under adverse conditions and both they and their company and platoon commanders deserved my loyalty in return. The sickness rate had also increased, another sure sign of battle fatigue. Many went down with malaria. The first white platoon leaders to be evacuated were Sergeants Anton Retief and Nel. Nel had been with me from the start at M'pupa.

Then Captain Jack Dippenaar got malaria and was also airlifted out. Good old

Jack—quick and unafraid in battle — but always way ahead of his radio operator who often took cover with the set. He would stare perplexedly at it as a stream of swearwords issued forth as I tried to get Jack to answer me. I said goodbye to Jack with a heavy heart and handed his Bravo Company over to James Hills.

Corky did not remain in command of the reconstituted Zulu Headquarters for long. He spent a week handing over to Colonel Blackie Swart and returned to South Africa.

Before leaving, Corky invited Toon, myself and some of the old hands to a party. It was a subdued affair because there were only a few members of Corky's headquarters left. Commandant Willie Kotze had left long before to take over command of Battle Group X-Ray, which was currently pushing east along the Benguela railway line. Major Dries van Coller was still around as were some Portuguese members of his staff. All the rest had gone home. But we still managed to polish off a goodly quantity of beers and whisky.

Where Corky had got the booze from was a mystery — we hardly ever saw the stuff. I had heard, though, that a C160 with a cargo of beer had somehow disappeared while on its way to Cela. Whisky had begun to trickle through and was supposed to be issued to officers at the rate of one bottle per week. I personally never got a single bottle. We often had to make do with an Angolan whisky called, believe it or not, 'Shell Whiskey'. Whatever it was, it certainly tasted more like petrol than scotch whisky. Perhaps the 'distillery' filled their bottles at Luanda's petrol refinery.

In true South African fashion, the party was also a 'braai', (barbecue), which in our eyes was the only way to cook meat anyway. Everyone there enjoyed getting out of the incessant rain and into more relaxed company. We soon began to reminisce and, of course, compared our splendid dash up the west coast to the somewhat more cautious advance of Battle Group Foxbat up the centre. Conceited as we were about our soldierly achievements and being slightly inebriated, we concluded that we were indeed the most intrepid, battle wise and aggressive fighting troops in Angola. The rest could profit from our experiences and they would do well to listen to our wise words on the subject of war.

Towards the end the party became a bit maudlin. I decided that our intrepid commander could not leave Zulu Force without a suitable gesture from our side. I consequently fished out my medals — the 'Catengue Star', the 'Angolan Freedom Medal' and the 'Angolan Campaign Medal' — and ceremonially pinned them on Corky's broad chest. To complete the ceremony, I kissed him continental style on both cheeks and shook his hand in congratulation. We were, after all, fighting among people steeped in Portuguese tradition.

Corky was a proud man. I fancied that I saw a slight mistiness in his eyes, but it might have been caused by the whisky aggravated by smoke from the fire. Apparently he made a speech, but I cannot remember. When he left it was with three medals clanking on his chest — like a member in good standing of Nova Redondo's second-league soccer team. Maybe those medals will one day become collectors' items in view of the circumstances in which they were 'won'. Knowing him as well as I do, I am sure Corky will still have his medals. I am, of course, minus mine. But I could not have given them to a more deserving officer. He kept the show together — which was not easy with awkward customers like Linford and Breytenbach under his command. Corky was without doubt the driving force behind us.

Zulu Force advanced something like 90km a day against an enemy which occasionally did manage to get its act together. The reason FAPLA failed to stop us was not because of our fire superiority — a debatable point in any case — but because they were invariably caught off-balance by the speed of our advance. They never had time to dig in or prepare and organise sufficiently before we suddenly appeared and kicked them out of their new positions. Usually, too, they left all their 'toys' behind.

After he had taken over, Blackie Swart and I were driving through my delaying position when I noticed a rusty-looking Vickers machine gun deployed next to a telegraph pole. It was sited in an isolated and obvious position for a Vickers — in fact, an idiotic position. I chewed out the Vickers platoon leader — the one who had replaced Fingers Kruger — about the positioning and especially about the state of the gun.

He had shown little interest in his platoon until then. He started ranting about the uselessness of the black troops. I blew my top. The troops he described as useless had been going through a very rough time when he was a mere beginner in the battlefields of Angola. The platoon had always been sharp under the guiding hands of Fingers. I respected their fighting ability and the fighting abilities of my black troops in general.

I pointed this out but the platoon leader stubbornly and insolently persisted in putting the blame on 'those stupid kaffirs'.

I told him bluntly that I considered him to be the most useless platoon leader in Angola and relieved him of his command forthwith.

This man had destroyed the high morale of my Vickers platoon. Resulting from this, it became necessary for me to permanently break up the platoon and attach sections of it to each company. In the absence of a suitable platoon leader, it was the only sensible move I could make.

*   *   *

I gave the task of reconnoitring Bridge 14 to Sergeant Danny Roxo and his platoon along with four armoured cars in support. He had to work as far as a feature known as 'Top Hat'. He would ascertain whether the bridge had been blown, whether FAPLA was dug in on the far side and whether it would be possible to cross by vehicle or on foot.

Top Hat was a high hill west of the main road to Luanda. The road followed around the foot of Top Hat before it crossed the river at Bridge 14. The lower slopes of the hill masked the bridge from the view of our combat outpost line.

Danny and his patrol moved out that morning. I arrived at the outpost line later in the day and was in time to hear a tremendous scrap developing around the bottom slopes of Top Hat. Danny was clearly in trouble. I had visions of his platoon and the armoured cars being cut to pieces.

I suddenly saw two armoured cars racing back at top speed from the bridge. It seemed my worst fears were confirmed when I gathered from the radio of the troop leader (who was still sitting snugly in his car on the outpost line), that Danny had been attacked by a large FAPLA force. Even worse, Danny and his infantry were being abandoned in the face of the enemy by the rapidly retreating armoured cars.

I then realised that only two cars, instead of the whole troop of four, had gone with Danny. The troop leader, still jittery from his experiences at Ebo, had hung back and sent just his troop sergeant and another car to deal with a situation he regarded as too unhealthy for himself.

I dashed to my Land Cruiser and drove towards the retreating armoured cars to stop them. I intended to turn them around so that we could get Danny and his men out of trouble.

They stopped next to me but the car commanders refused to go back. They cited heavy FAPLA anti-tank fire from Top Hat which they feared would knock them out. The troop sergeant pointed out to me that even where we were, 122mm rockets were impacting and exploding all around us. It was true that we were under heavy fire, but it was from mortars and not rockets. Mortar fire was a lot more dangerous than rockets but I did not enlighten him on this point. He was already far too skittish for my liking. Fortunately Danny and his crew suddenly appeared, saving the need for me to employ harsher methods to force the troop sergeant back to Top Hat. Danny and his men rode the armoured cars for the last few kilometres to the safety of the outpost line, braving a belt of mortar fire in the process.

These armoured cars, it must be mentioned, did not belong to Major Toon Slabbert's squadron. They were newcomers to the joys and excitement of Angola. The loss of seven cars at Ebo must have played havoc with their nerves.

Danny told a remarkable story. When he arrived at Top Hat he decided to leave his men and the supporting armoured cars and go ahead on foot to reconnoitre the bridge on his own. Unbeknown to him, however, he passed through a strong FAPLA position on the slopes and all eyes were on him as he made his solitary way. When the bridge came into view he saw that it had been blown. He also saw three Cubans on the far side of the river. They were standing by what appeared to be a 14.5mm anti-aircraft gun. He promptly shot two of them.

All hell broke loose and a medley of weapons opened up at him from the far side. He had no option but to beat a hasty retreat along the same route that he had come on. This led him into view of the FAPLA unit deployed on Top Hat's lower slopes. Seeing a little man zig-zagging past them, they opened fire. Somehow, though, things did not work out quite the way they had planned.

Danny told me the story in his own, inimitable broken English.

'Coronel, I run and I go tat, tat, tat, tat . . . and I run and I go tat, tat, tat, tat . . . and I run and I go tat, tat, tat, tat . . . and suddenly the shooting, it stops. No more FAPLA!'

He smiled from ear to ear and only claimed he had shot the two Cubans. He did not claim any FAPLA.

Meanwhile, though, while Danny had been on his way to the bridge, FAPLA had captured two of Danny's men who had left the platoon to round up some cattle they had seen in the distance. The men were kept separately at Catofé as prisoners, one by the Cubans and the other by FAPLA. Both of them escaped and returned to our lines in the next two days.

When being debriefed they said that Danny had shot 11 of the enemy — two Cubans and nine FAPLA. He had bagged the nine FAPLA during his dash to safety through the ambush at Top Hat. He was evidently the talk of the town at Catofé.

I recommended Danny for the *Honoris Crux* and it was approved. He was the first Portuguese from their former colonies serving in the South African Army to receive this decoration. Although the chunky Danny had once been an infamous elephant poacher in Mozambique, he later ran his own group of Flechas with whom he successfully tracked down and killed many terrorists. He became a terror to FRELIMO in the far northern Mozambique provinces of Nyassa and Cabo Delgado.

The situation had become a stalemate. At Cela, because of the terrain and the mud which restricted the movement of the armoured cars off the main roads, we found ourselves in a plodding war. The Quanza River, the biggest river in Angola, still lay between us and Luanda. It was wide, rain-swollen and flowing furiously. The bridge over it had been blown and a major engineering effort would be needed to cross it. But we had no bridging equipment.

Brigadier Schoeman and I discussed the stalemate. He believed we should work some flexibility into the situation. He ordered me to form a force to operate on foot guerrilla-fashion, off-road in thick bush, mountains and mud behind enemy lines. We would blow up selected bridges on the enemy's lateral communication line between Gabela and Quibale, ambush their convoys and attack their gun lines and headquarter areas. The men, I thought, could be drawn from Lieutenant Johan Blaauw's under-strength parachute company, plus some Reconnaissance Commando teams already deployed in Angola and selected black soldiers from my own unit. I managed to get one patrol started on a mission — unsuccessfully as it turned out — but the idea never got off the ground. When I left Angola it died completely.

From time to time I visited George Kruys on the Blue Route to get acquainted with the terrain and to see how Connie and his Alpha Company were shaping. 140mm guns had been brought up. They had a longer range than the 25-pounders so we could at last tackle the Stalin Organs. George, however, was coming under sporadic fire from FAPLA guns which the 140mm still could not reach.

On one visit I found Foxbat on a muddy track near a coffee plantation. Connie's Alpha company was engaged in establishing a bridgehead on the far side of a fast-flowing stream. Connie had just picked his way through an unmarked minefield and was fortunate to still be alive, having come close to setting off at least one mine with his Land-Rover.   'The troops are tired', he said somewhat hesitantly. 'They'll keep on fighting until we tell them to stop but it's unfair to drive them so hard.'

I looked at them crouching in the mud where they had dug in to escape enemy artillery fire. FAPLA was using airburst for the first time.

'The troops have asked for three weeks leave, then they'll be happy to come back and chase FAPLA right out of Angola', Connie continued.

I had already mentioned to Brigadier Schoeman that my troops were tired and that they should be withdrawn for rest and recuperation. He had agreed to the whites being replaced but not the blacks, because he had no black replacements. I decided that was not on and that we would stay in the front line, blacks, whites and all. I informed the brigadier accordingly.

Shortly afterwards a group of young white and inexperienced second lieutenants arrived from the Infantry School as replacements for my older and experienced platoon leaders. I refused to accept them, except where an existing platoon leader was evacuated for reasons of sickness or wounds.

Those South African Battle Group Bravo commanders and platoon leaders still remaining had in any case refused to budge. They were determined to stay with their troops until the end, come hell or high water. For me this was the most emotional and heart-warming experience of the war.

The black troops looked to us, their leaders, not only to lead them in battle but also to look after their welfare. They were Angolan FNLA and not even remotely South African, but their own leader, Daniel Chipenda, had left them in the lurch. It seems he had sniffed the wind and spotted the danger signs — that the South Africans were probably about to withdraw from Angola — so he had flown off to Portugal. This left the white South Africans with the obligation of carrying the can.

We had come to know our troops and respect their fighting ability over the months we had spent with them. They had done our bidding without fail, completely trusting our integrity as commanders. It would be a dastardly thing indeed to leave them facing the enemy in the mud at Cela while we disappeared back to South Africa and basked in the sun on some holiday beach before the next round of army life.

That we refused to do.

Brigadier Schoeman brought me a signal from the General Officer Commanding operations in Angola. It informed me personally that the Chief of the Army had ordered me to return to South Africa immediately.

I asked the brigadier to pretend that he could not locate me and he agreed.

Toon Slabbert and his squadron were also pulled from the line and replaced by a fresh armoured car squadron. We held a farewell party for him that was somewhat less inhibited than the one for Corky. Toon was always rather basic in his general outlook and as a parting gesture he gave me a case of South African beer because I was the only commander who had not lost an armoured car in action. A case of decent beer was such a scarce commodity it was like gold. We reminisced somewhat raucously, drank and generally made a nuisance of ourselves with our sleeping neighbours. The tone and character of the party were not improved by the presence of some well-known chopper pilots!

The next morning a bleary-eyed Toon strapped his 60mm Eland armoured car to his huge frame and with a laugh and some rude parting comments, signalled his squadron to head for South West Africa. They left as smoothly as always, looking impressively smart with their antennas whipping in the breeze.

During *Operation Savannah* Toon had evacuated only one armoured car back to South Africa for repairs, although several were shot out by the enemy. The rest had been repaired in the field by his own light workshop troop which, theoretically anyway, was beyond its capability.

In my mind's eye I can still see them at Catengue, their 90mm guns cracking away at FAPLA in a cauldron of smoke, flames and fury; and at Benguela in little knots on the airfield under rocket, anti-tank and mortar fire. Wherever they were, they were invariably shooting and manoeuvring towards the enemy, leading the advance with my infantry, deploying at lightning speed and returning fire the moment we hit an enemy position.

I remember the bearded laughing faces of the troop leaders when we sat down to a hasty meal of bread, cheese and beer in the officers' mess in Sa da Bandeira. I remember that Toon's squadron never left my infantry in the lurch. They were always up front with them and supporting them in style whenever and wherever they were required. They were committed to my platoons and they believed my troops were the most professional infantry in Angola. For their part, my troops just loved the armoured cars — especially the devastating bang of the 90mm main gun.

I handed the battalion over to Major Frank Bestbier for the time being while I tried to get the guerrilla concept off the ground. Even Paul, my interpreter/batman, had decided to abscond. When I arrived at the rather filthy and rickety farm cottage where I was staying, there was no coffee or supper waiting. Paul, it seems, had packed his gear and left without telling anybody where he was going. When I dropped in at Frank's headquarters the following day, however, I found Paul there as large as life.

'Paul couldn't take you any longer', Frank said grinning from ear to ear. 'He's decided to come and serve as my batman'.

Frank already had a batman, but now he had two and I had none. I suppose I had been hard on Paul, especially during the heat of battle when I had the bad habit of getting downright sarcastic. Anyway, I left him in peace and thankfully moved in with the Recces. Their food was better and the company more congenial. They were all old troops of mine. I never saw Paul again.

While waiting for the powers-that-be to make up their minds about rest and recuperation for my troops, we moved around the countryside looking at what had once been productive farming land. The Portuguese authorities had settled farmers from metropolitan Portugal on farms in much the same way as the Israeli kibbutz system. Small villages with pretty cottages were established, with the surrounding land and fields belonging to the farmers living in the village. The breeding of cattle and dairy farming were very attractive because of the rich pastures. Some of the largest cheese factories in Angola were located in the area. Thousands of abandoned cattle — carefully bred Herefords, Brahmans, Siementhalers and Friesians — roamed the plains. They were not the tough breeds of Africa that could survive with little attention and many succumbed to tick-born diseases.

Santa Comba was the largest town in the area. It was well laid out with wide, tree-lined streets, attractive houses and a huge church that had fallen into disrepair. There were numerous indications that FAPLA and the Cubans had deliberately fouled the church before it was 'liberated' by Battle Group Foxbat. There was a stud farm with about 20 Arab stallions still in their stables and many mares and foals grazed in the adjacent paddocks. The owner had fled to Portugal leaving his stock and all his possessions to the mercy of the fighting factions.

When the South African forces eventually retired from the area, the Cubans moved in and stripped the cheese factories, grabbed the breeding stock from among the herds of cattle and horses and canned the rest of the beef for export to Cuba. Both UNITA and ourselves had also drawn on the abandoned cattle as a food source, but we had never destroyed whole herds. We certainly never touched the breeding stock, especially the prize bulls and stallions, as we hoped the Portuguese owners would one day return to their farms.

Meantime we still had no idea whether the river at Bridge 14 was fordable. Danny, after all, had not been given much chance to investigate. I decided to send a patrol with one of my platoon leaders, a recce corporal called Diedies Diederichs. He was told to establish his patrol on the crest of Top Hat from where they could observe the bridge and Catofé. The problem was that Top Hat was occupied by FAPLA. Nevertheless, I believed that Diedies was quite capable of carrying out such a difficult and dangerous task.

They made for Top Hat in a roundabout way. Diedies and an asthmatic black soldier finally established themselves in an OP on the northern slope above the bridge. They were virtually surrounded by FAPLA. Diedies stayed for a few days while reporting back to Frank Bestbier at his headquarters. It was not long before he reported the interesting news that hundreds of FAPLA were wading shoulder-deep across the blown bridge towards Top Hat. This showed the river was fordable and that Top Hat could be effectively defended by FAPLA. It also made future river crossings by our forces problematic. George Kruys and Blackie Swart were already planning an assault on Bridge 14 and the Catofé area beyond. The occupation of Top Hat was of vital importance. Whoever controlled Top Hat would control the crossing at Bridge 14.

FAPLA had to be thrown off Top Hat. Diedies was on the spot so he was given the task of doing it with the assistance of the 140mm guns. However, as he had no experience of directing artillery fire he was given an abbreviated course over the radio on target identification and fire control procedures. Then he calmly set about his allotted task from his OP right in the middle of FAPLA forces.

He brought the ranging shots onto the bridge area and then gleefully tried 'firing for effect', using airburst. The results astonished him. Troops wading across the submerged bridge were caught bunched up in the open. They had no overhead cover and literally hundreds were slaughtered.

Diedies followed up by giving the BM21s at Catofé a devastating pasting. When he finally arrived back, he demanded to see a 140mm gun at close quarters. He had never seen one before and was suitably impressed by the sheer size of the monster. He watched the guns being loaded and fired at a distant target. To him it was sheer magic.

FAPLA fell back in disorder. It was a rout that required an immediate follow-up, but unfortunately our own available forces comprised only Diedies and his one rather sickly black soldier, so it was out of the question. We needn't have worried. FAPLA vacated Top Hat anyway — without prompting.

Diedies was awarded the *Honoris Crux* for his exploits. So with Danny Roxo, Top Hat produced two well-deserved decorations for 1-Reconnaissance Commando. The Recces earned another four *Honoris Crux* decorations during the *Operation Savannah* campaign. The men involved were Lieutenant Connie van Wyk, Sergeant Costa Marão at Ebo, Staff Sergeant Kenaas Conradie and posthumously, Sergeant Wannies Wannenburg.

The following week Commandant George Kruys and Battle Group Foxbat seized Top Hat after an unopposed night assault. That night engineers worked feverishly to construct a bridge of locally available materials, using what was left of Bridge 14 as a foundation. While doing so they had to withstand very heavy enemy artillery, mortar and rocket fire.

The next morning at first light, George opened up with his own artillery on targets in the nearby hills. Under this cover, his infantry and armoured cars crossed the river. They caused havoc amongst the enemy forces who were mostly Cubans. The South Africans took Catofé, killed hundreds of the enemy and destroyed a large haul of weapons and equipment. Quibale was within their grasp when the order came through to stop their advance. If nothing else, George could look back on Bridge 14 with satisfaction. The mauling his battle group took at Ebo had been avenged.

Simultaneous with George's opening moves on Bridge 14 and Catofé, I was told by Zulu HQ that my troops had been granted leave. We could withdraw south to our old stomping grounds around M'pupa, Serpa Pinto and Cuito Cuanavale. Lieutenant Connie van Wyk and his company were brought back under my command. I gave up my attempts to fight a guerrilla war and resumed command of Battle Group Bravo for the withdrawal.

Fresh FNLA troops moved into the Cela area. Weapons and ammunition were taken from us and given to them. They were formed into platoons and placed under the command of the white platoon leaders fresh from Infantry School who had originally been scheduled to relieve my own platoon leaders.

We were left with a minimum of weapons to protect ourselves during our withdrawal. Following Chipenda's premature departure for Portugal, fighting had broken out between UNITA and FNLA to the south. So we could expect some resistance from UNITA during our move, especially at roadblocks and in towns under their control.

On 11 December 1975, a month after independence, we said goodbye to the mud and rain of Cela. Red, white and yellow FNLA flags festooned the trucks as we drove towards the SWA border at Katuitui where we had originally crossed into Angola. The troops were in a boisterous and happy mood and seemingly oblivious to the pelting rain and the dangers posed by UNITA. Nova Lisboa, by then a prominent UNITA stronghold, was given a wide berth and we headed for Serpa Pinto, historically an FNLA town. We arrived there in the afternoon of the next day. The first batch of troops were allowed to go to their homes in Serpa Pinto and surrounding areas as far as Cuito Cuanavale.

The driver of a flatbed truck with 'Novel', the name of a construction firm, painted on its side, approached me and asked if it would be okay for him to resume working with his firm in Serpa Pinto. I then discovered for the first time that he was a civilian who had been press-ganged into service by FNLA together with the truck he happened to be driving. He had been used to convey troops to M'pupa for training. There I had commandeered both him and his truck and he had accompanied us throughout the campaign. His truck had become one of my main firepower bases, mounting eight Vickers machine guns in a row. It had often swung fights in our favour.

The fact that he and his truck had come through unscathed was a miracle. He frequently had to deploy under fire well to the front so the gunners could deliver devastating machine-gun fire on FAPLA positions. I just let him go. What his employer had to say to the errant driver when he appeared out of the blue after so many months absence, I shall never know. It seems unlikely that they would believe his exciting war stories about life as a driver for Battle Group Bravo's machine-gun platoon.

We moved fast to get as close to the border as possible before nightfall. Foolishly, I raced ahead of the main body in my Land Cruiser. I unexpectedly ran into a hostile UNITA roadblock at the Okavango River bridge at Caiundo. A UNITA soldier swaggered over, the muzzle of his G3 rifle pointing straight at me. Other troops turned out from the embankment below to have a look at the white officer in his Land Cruiser. I was wearing my FNLA cap badge so it was easy to see where my loyalties lay.

The Battle Group Bravo column was maybe 15 minutes behind me, but a lot could happen in 15 minutes. A UNITA soldier arrogantly shouted something unintelligible in Portuguese. I lost my temper and jumped from the Land Cruiser. I wrenched the G3 away from him and hurled it down the embankment. I then singlehandedly demolished the roadblock, kicking over the 44-gallon drums and tossing the barrier pole at the open-mouthed UNITA below the embankment. The soldier who had incurred my wrath scrambled down the embankment to the safety of his friends. He must have thought that I had gone berserk.

I climbed back in my vehicle and drove off fuming, hoping that they would pick a quarrel with the rest of my troops when they arrived. Nowadays my behaviour would probably qualify as a classic example of road rage!

We left Angola and the *Operation Savannah* campaign much as we had started. The opening action was the demolition of the UNITA roadblock at Artur de Paiva and the closing scene was my frenzied destruction of another UNITA roadblock at Caiundo.

The rest of my troops were dropped off at Cuangar and Calai. I promised them I would return in three weeks when retraining would commence. Once completed we would return to the business of fighting the war which, in our opinion, could not be won without us.

Relaxed and with a drink in my hand at the bar in Rundu, I began an eloquent discourse on the pleasures of commanding troops in battle — troops which one had trained to one's own high standards. (To be fair, MPLA and the Cubans had conducted most of my troops' training long before I had even arrived on the scene.) A battle command is not something that happens very often to a soldier nowadays as wars are not easy to come by. I was full of praise for my black FNLA troops and explained how my combat teams had been honed to a fine edge — exactly as we had been taught on numerous courses. I expanded on the beauty of seeing one's guns, armoured cars and infantry deploying against the enemy with practised ease .

I pointed out that the scruffy, undisciplined and ill-trained FNLA battalion that I had found at M'pupa had learned their war crafts gradually as enemy resistance had stiffened. And how towards the end they had fought with skill and discipline against an enemy that was always stronger in numbers and firepower. It was a battalion, I said, that had truly been 'forged in battle'. This was later adopted as the unit's motto.

I was undoubtedly blowing my own trumpet, perhaps a bit loudly. A friend at the bar, a very senior medical officer, concluded from my behaviour that like my troops, I was suffering from battle fatigue. He deduced, wrongly, from my war stories that I was reckless and addicted to battle. He saw clear indications that I had become an adrenaline junkie and that all was not well with me on the top floor. Now it would be called post-traumatic stress. In World War-I it was called shell shock. The doctor told me to report to a rest centre that he had established on the peaceful and beautiful south bank of the Okavango River where my stress would be 'defused' in pleasant surroundings.

I hurriedly finished my drink and left the club. I went to my room and packed my kit for my return to South Africa. Once there I intended to take my family for a holiday by the sea. I had to get out of Rundu before a medic clapped me into a 'rest centre' — probably just a glorified mental home.

I was not mad, dammit, I just had an overweening pride in my scruffy Battle Group Bravo.

17

Operation Savannah
Thoughts in retrospect

Operation Savannah was a brilliant operation in most tactical respects, but strategically it failed miserably. This was due solely to the crumbling resolve of the South African politicians, particularly Prime Minister John Vorster, towards the end of the campaign. I believe he was ill-advised by certain cabinet ministers and BOSS General Hendrik van den Berg. However in my opinion the then Minister of Defence, P W Botha, was not involved.

They undoubtedly used the withdrawal of American support for the operation as an excuse to back off when victory was within our grasp. Many people to this day are convinced that American military and diplomatic aid held the key to our success in Angola. But this, as some of my American friends might say — is a lot of baloney, particularly when looked at from a military perspective.

In truth, American aid was not that extensive. They certainly poured war material and money into the corrupt hands of Holden Roberto. And they lived to regret it when Roberto, with CIA advice, deployed an undisciplined mob of mercenaries commanded by a psychopath and ordered them to advance on Luanda. They quickly lost the offensive to unimpressive Cuban/FAPLA forces. They killed civilians and murdered their own troops. Some of the leaders were captured by FAPLA and put on trial. One or two were executed as war criminals — which is exactly what they were.

The South African forces deployed in Angola had built up sufficient momentum before 11 November 1975. They were scattering FAPLA ahead of them like chaff — especially our Zulu group.

We had hit FAPLA hard from Pereira de Eça early on, quickly following up and sometimes getting ahead of them — as happened at Sa da Bandeira. FAPLA was not allowed the slightest breathing space to regroup, reorganise or prepare proper defences. Of critical importance was the fact that they never had sufficient time to destroy any of the numerous bridges until they were driven north of Nova Redondo. Angola's raging rivers during the rainy season are formidable barriers to any military force. Virtually all the rivers rise in the central highlands and flow to all points of the compass — which guarantees that river obstacles are encountered whatever the direction of advance.

Then 11 November came. The impression I got on the ground was that South Africa had made no plans subsequently for any actions beyond this date. Everything we achieved was based on ad hoc planning at the highest levels. As far as I am aware, there was no overall strategic aim, let alone a plan, for *Operation Savannah*. Nobody can win a war stumbling along from day to day, just seeing what the new day will bring.

The politicians, in their questionable wisdom, decided to halt the SADF steamroller just before 11 November while they made up their minds about their next move. Militarily speaking, this proved fatal.

It was the responsibility of the South African General Staff to point this out firmly and urgently to the dithering politicians. But maybe the generals belonged to the same school of ditherers. The successes achieved on the field of battle by the South African-supported black troops surprised them to an extent where they began to doubt their own wisdom in starting the war. Perhaps they decided, like General Joubert at Ladysmith during the Anglo-Boer War, that it was tempting fate to grab a greater share of the spoils of war than they already had.

When making our drive north along the coast, we would have captured the bridge south of Porto Amboine intact if we had continued the fight instead of pausing and suntanning on the beach for four days. We would have outflanked the Gabela and Quibale positions and joined in a race with FAPLA to cross the Quanza River at Dondo. We would also have been neck-and-neck with the Cubans to get to Luanda harbour first. The Cubans were expecting us and had started preparations to board specially designated ships and sail back to Havana.

We needed no further assistance from the Americans or anybody else.

Our forced pause of four days gave FAPLA plus their Cuban and Soviet mentors sufficient time to rig all river crossing sites for demolition and prepare formidable defences on the dominating high ground.

When we continued our advance we came up against the insoluble problem of having no means to cross rivers. There were no combat engineer units deployed anywhere in Angola. A solitary engineer was attached to me and he was without the tools and equipment of his trade. So he became my logistics officer instead of commanding the engineering capacity that should have been with Battle Group Bravo from the outset. Delville Linford's Battle Group Alpha also had just a single unequipped engineer — who was appointed as RSM for the unit.

The silliest aspect of the whole fiasco was that bridging equipment was available in the South African Army's engineering establishments at Bethlehem and Kroonstad. Yet we saw none of this equipment until the final stages of the SADF's withdrawal from Angola when a pontoon ferry was established on the Okavango River opposite Rundu. We could have done with it in the interior.

In 1975 the Corps of Engineers of the South African Defence Force was the direct successor of the Corps deployed so successfully in World War-II. South African engineers became justly renowned for their barrier crossing feats in North Africa — of minefields in particular — and for their taming of the rain-swollen torrents in Italy during the advance of the 5th and 8th Allied Armies. Some of the bridges they built remained in use for many years after the war. At least one still is in use. They repaired roads, constructed new ones and repaired tunnels destroyed by the Germans.

Yet here in Angola, where communications were particularly tenuous and prone to interruption from the violence of nature — to say nothing of the enemy — we were provided with no field engineering support. What on earth were the generals and their staff establishments thinking of when they planned the *Operation Savannah* campaign in the safety of their headquarters in Pretoria?

Was *Operation Savannah* the product of a proper analysis of all factors — terrain, weather and enemy capabilities — or was it just the ad hoc chucking together of ideas over beers in some army pub?

Millions of rands had been spent on training paratroopers for the South African Army. By 1975 we had 1-Parachute Battalion with at least two rifle companies plus 2 and 3-Parachute Battalions with four or five Citizen Force companies attached. They had been trained to a very high standard and were ready for operational deployment. We also had 1-Reconnaissance Commando with their highly honed specialist skills.

None of these organisations were effectively used during *Operation Savannah*. Although there were several half-hearted attempts to deploy them against the enemy, they were not used in the roles for which they had been trained.

If my memory serves me correctly, the general staff sent two paratrooper companies to Angola after Sa da Bandeira had been taken. One was split up into its constituent platoons and posted out to Zulu Headquarters. Some were detached to Battle Groups Alpha, Bravo, Foxbat and X-Ray but the rest were used for protecting the headquarters of the formations they served.

To their shame and more pointedly, to the shame of the general or generals who made this stupid decision these highly trained and motivated paratroopers — shock troops in the real sense of the phrase — were used as nothing more than armed guards. The few paratroopers I managed to get my hands on for Battle Group Bravo rendered a highly professional service on the battlefield. I certainly would not have dreamt of using them as armed sentries trailing behind me to safeguard my valuable person.

One under-strength parachute company commanded by Lieutenant Johan Blaauw successfully operated behind enemy lines north of Cela. This resulted from initiatives taken on the ground, by me amongst others, far away from the out-of-touch generals in Rundu and Pretoria. They performed excellent service for which Captain Blaauw was decorated with the *Honoris Crux*. There were, however, far too few of them to have a decisive influence on even a local battle.

If the paratroopers had been grouped into a battalion of four rifle companies and one support company drawn from all three battalions, we would have had a formidable force available with which we could have swung many a combat situation in our favour.

Let us examine a few scenarios.

Zulu's rapid advance north along the western coastal route had turned the enemy's withdrawal into a rout. But we needed blocking forces to deploy well behind the enemy's helter-skelter rush to the rear. Their task would have been to decimate those FAPLA and Cuban elements that had managed to escape. Because of the inadequate road and railway network, it was almost always impossible to outflank the retreating enemy or get behind them. When the rains came we were restricted to the few macadam roads on which Battle Groups X-Ray, Foxbat, Bravo, Alpha and others were advancing north and east.

If paratroopers had been available, they could have been parachuted in to establish ambushes or blocks and ensure that the enemy was wiped out. Delville managed to establish such an ambush/block during the ferocious battle at Catengue. This was only possible, however, because, unusually, there was a track that took him around FAPLA's right flank. Later, in other battles, these circumstances did not exist and important elements of FAPLA escaped to reorganise and re-equip to fight another day. As mentioned, the paratroopers available as blocking forces were not used in this role.

Because of off-road restrictions brought about by the weather, the importance of defiles as potential delaying or ambush positions became even more critical. A road-bound column advancing to contact a retreating enemy is vulnerable to ambush unless it rapidly gains control over bottle-necks such as defiles and passes. Dropping paratroopers ahead could have secured those danger spots.

Where a bridge had been destroyed, there was little point in capturing the crossing point because we could not utilise it without bridging equipment. Once again paratroopers could have been dropped ahead to secure the position. If the bridge had been blown they could have held the crossing point until engineers with bridging equipment caught up with them.

Let us look at a pertinent example of how this technique might have been employed.

Even before taking Nova Redondo, we knew that FAPLA intended withdrawing behind the Queve River. If Colonel Corky van Heerden had had a parachute battalion at his disposal on the day we took the town, he could have dropped the paratroopers on to the high ground controlling the Queve estuary and the bridge. The next morning, at the latest, I could have followed up with Battle Group Bravo, crossed the Queve River in style, joined up with the paratroopers and entered Porto Amboine before FAPLA gathered their wits. After that, either Delville or myself or both of us could have rushed through the open flank into FAPLA's defensive positions on the Gabela-Quibale line. We would have rolled them up in short order. In addition, the paratroopers occupying the bridge and the high ground would have interdicted FAPLA's escape route from Nova Redondo and stopped them in their tracks. In all probability, FAPLA forces in that area would have been wiped out. Porto Amboine itself would have been left more or less defenceless.

Following the defeat of FAPLA on the Gabela-Quibale line, a further paratrooper deployment at or close to the bridge over the Quanza River would also have secured that crossing, trapping those FAPLA and Cuban remnants deployed south of Dondo and the river.

The limiting factor, in the eyes of some hide-bound desk warriors, was the availability of aircraft. But this is a fallacy. C130s and C160s were used extensively to fly in our logistics, leaving no capacity for transporting paratroopers. We used SAFAIR stretched CL100s for transporting freight and passengers to 1 Military Area in Rundu. They could have been harnessed for logistical support in Angola, which would have freed the C130s and C160s for paratrooping. There was ample airfield capacity available in Pereira de Eça, Sa da Bandeira, Moçamedes, Benguela, Lobito, Nova Redondo, Cela, Silva Porto, Luso, Nova Lisboa and even Serpa Pinto.

There was no enemy air threat. Reportedly there were Soviet MiG19s still crated on the dockside in Luanda, but that is where they remained for virtually the whole *Operation Savannah* campaign. In any case, we had combat air support aplenty. We had Canberra and Buccaneer bombers available to soften up target areas ahead of the paratroop deployments. Impalas could probably have been deployed well forward from airfields such as Lobito, Benguela and Nova Lisboa for close air strike support. We had Puma helicopters for providing tactical mobility within the established paratrooper airheads (defensive perimeters). Paratroopers could also have deployed and redeployed in an airmobile role instead of by parachute.

The options were endless. We were hamstrung by unimaginative generals, however, who braked *Operation Savannah* when it should have kept moving. Brigadier Dawie Schoeman was probably removed for being too bold and daring. He was certainly the most able senior officer around.

What about the Recces? Opportunities abounded for them if they had been handled by a combat commander with intelligence and imagination. Their training made them the ideal organisation to use to undermine the enemy's psychological equilibrium in accordance with Liddell Hart's Theory of the Indirect Approach. They were trained to raid headquarter installations, logistical installations, airfields and so on. Imagine the consternation, particularly amongst the Cubans, but also with the MPLA leadership, if Recce frogmen had sunk Fidel Castro's specially designated evacuation ships in Luanda harbour. And what about raiding and destroying the oil refinery there? Or targeting the enemy's top command structure? The MPLA leader, Agostino Neto, his top military brass and high-ranking Cuban liaison teams would have been legitimate targets.

At the battlefronts, the Recces could have deployed small teams deep into enemy territory and provided us with hot intelligence. They could also have brought down artillery and air strikes on targets of particular importance, such as formation headquarters, artillery positions, troop concentrations an d so on. Corporal Diedies Diederichs, an inexperienced Recce hand at the time, did just that at Top Hat.

Without American help, we could have defeated MPLA and the Cubans and installed Jonas Savimbi in Luanda. Following that — but only then — it would have been imperative for South African forces to disengage smartly to avoid the country from becoming embroiled in a civil war. This would probably have assumed uncontrollable dimensions with UNITA on the one hand and FNLA and MPLA on the other. Eventually, though, without the benefit of Cuban and Soviet logistical and manpower assistance, they, along with the FNLA, would have been forced by Savimbi to enter some sort of alliance.

Indirectly, the SADF would have caused SWAPO, our real enemy, to collapse and stay out of the picture for probably decades to come. This would have given South Africa sufficient time to bring SWA/Namibia to a satisfactory state of independence in which Sam Nujoma and SWAPO would probably not have featured.

Namibia would have been better off economically and politically. The Republic of South Africa, after soundly defeating the Cubans and communism in Africa, would have gained stature in Africa and the rest of the world. It was something that not even South Africa's bitterest enemies could have ignored. Even Savimbi would have been forced to take favourable cognisance of his former ally's interests in a newly-liberated Angola. After all, South Africa could always turn and support FNLA in removing UNITA from power if it suddenly felt the need to clip Savimbi's wings.

If *Operation Savannah* had been allowed to run its course through to Luanda, South Africa would have become the unassailable power in southern African. History will judge I am convinced, that our political and military leaders did not have the nerve to see this through. They blinked when victory was within their grasp.

18

Legio patria nostra

By the time I arrived back at the Rundu-based headquarters controlling the ongoing war in Angola and northern South West Africa, Angola had slipped into chaos. I had been cut off from developments in the north except for government-inspired half truths issued in press releases and reported in the newspapers. It was certainly not the fault of the press, for they — unlike the overseas press which was having a heyday with stories about South Africa's intervention — were only allowed to print what they were told.

Not a single South African reporter was seen by me during our advance north. I saw an overseas TV cameraman shooting without hindrance seemingly unlimited film of us entering Lobito. This was when the South African media were being briefed that our forces were engaged only in 'hot pursuit operations' slightly north of the South West African border.

At the SADF's main base at Grootfontein in northern SWA, which was as far as the military milk run could fly me, I found myself in a typical military administration, logistics and concentration centre. It was a world of chaos, far removed from the reality of war.

It was pelting with rain which appeared to have been coming down for days on end. The normally dusty transit camp had been transformed into a mud bath by the wheels of incoming and outgoing armoured cars and logistics vehicles. Typically, nobody had the slightest idea of what was happening at the battlefront.

There was a cluster of tents with a military police signboard at the entrance. I slopped through the mud to where a sign cryptically ordered me, as a new arrival, to 'Report Here'. An arrow directed me into the damp canvas interior of a tent.

A burly military policeman directed me to another tent to 'clear in' — the army opposite of 'clearing out'. A disinterested NCO from the Personnel Service Corps handed me forms to complete. My immediate problem was that I had not 'cleared out' when I had left on what amounted to unofficial leave in December. Worse still for the bureaucratic mind, I had failed to 'clear in' before I started to train Battle Group Bravo at M'pupa before *Operation Savannah* became a reality.

We had fought for months without being bothered by the tangle of army red tape. But now the administration and logistics guys had caught up with us and they soon made up for lost time. I had to complete forms as a new arrival. I invented my own authority, spinning a yarn about losing my travel voucher, otherwise I would have been packed off back to South Africa on the first available flight. If I had told them I was returning from unofficial leave, it would have caused me never-ending complications.

I was directed to the officers' quarters, a long low bungalow surrounded by mud. It was a long way from the officers only ablution block. Mud caked the floors and even some of the beds. The stuff was everywhere. There were several bedraggled and mud-splattered senior officers in the quarters who were in transit between Pretoria and Rundu.

I was welcomed raucously and shown an empty bed. I knew my bungalow mates well. Most were inveterate snorers, which is something I cannot stand. I also knew that my sleep would be disturbed by the light going on and off all night. The place was also plagued by millions of mosquitoes.

Upon realising this, I moved my kit to the laundry at the end of the distant ablution block. I would be more comfortable there despite the cold and hard concrete floor. For supper we were served the treat of warmed up tinned peas, tinned green beans, tinned mystery balls and, horror of horrors, large dollops of cold smashed spuds. An over-sweetened cup of cold coffee finished off this gourmet feast.

Yet, compared to the troops who were quartered in tents across the mud to the south, we were living in luxury. I watched with sympathy as the miserable poncho-clad troopies, boots caked with mud, squelched their way through the morass, dixies and mugs clattering as they made their way to wherever they were supposed to have supper. Unfortunately for them, their food was no different from ours.

The next morning, after a wet night beneath a leaking roof, I tried to persuade the military police to take me through to Rundu where, I insisted, my services were urgently required. This failed to impress anyone and I was told to wait until the following day when a military police patrol was going that way. Instead, I sought help from my gracelessly discarded friends of the previous night. One, a general officer, was heading for Rundu and he offered me a lift. I arrived in style and General André van Deventer welcomed me with open arms.

I soon found out why. My FNLA troops had faithfully followed orders and returned from leave — or most of them had — on the date appointed by me, a week before I got back myself. They had become a problem for Commandant 'Pale' Kotze based in Calai across the river from Rundu where he had been placed in charge of refugees. Of course my men insisted they were not refugees but soldiers reporting back for duty from leave. They were thus entitled to the same consideration as other South African soldiers.

Pale knew nothing about this. He flattened a few with his more than capable fists when they began throwing their weight around and intimidating other refugees. This established his bona fides, so good order and military discipline was restored. He was even able to use some of my men to help with administration of what could be described as a refugee headache of gargantuan dimensions.

A few of my men had waited at M'pupa, but others had gone to Cuangar where, unfortunately, they had fallen under the spell of Chuangari, a local FNLA commander.

Angola was fast sinking into chaos. The South Africans were still facing a combined FAPLA-Cuban force, but fighting was at a minimum. MPLA was aware we were withdrawing, so there was no need to spill blood unnecessarily — particularly their own. They kept their distance. The rate of our withdrawal was determined by the speed at which we could dismantle and evacuate our, by then, extensive logistical bases within Angola.

Battle Group Bravo had already, in effect, withdrawn. I was concerned with finding a future role for them. It did not take a military genius to forecast an escalation in guerrilla incursions by SWAPO, particularly into Owamboland, as soon as the last South African had shaken the mud of Angola off his boots.

To my mind it was obvious that my men, as Angolans, should be deployed against SWAPO on the Angolan side of the border. We would operate as small, highly mobile and well-trained teams. We would become guerrillas ourselves and hunt down and destroy SWAPO's guerrilla gangs in their highly organised rear base areas where they believed they were safe.

My men were as delighted to see me as I was to see them. My first priority was to get them back under military control. I recommended, with General van Deventer's approval, that we should return to M'pupa and embark on a retraining programme.

Pale Kotze was ecstatic when I mentioned that I was moving my troops to M'pupa. He was so pleased that he even offered transport and drivers to expedite the move. My own transport left over from *Operation Savannah* had dissipated in various directions while I was away. I managed to root around and salvage only a few of our lorries.

Fortunately, the rains in southern Angola were late that season, so the rudimentary dirt and gravel tracks were still usable, even if only by four-wheel-drive vehicles. When the rains come in the Cuando Cubango, even the best 4x4s bog down in the soggy *omurambas* and flood plains which are usually impossible to circumvent.

The move to M'pupa was conducted at night to protect us from the prying eyes of SWAPO. They might have tried to create an international incident if they gained concrete evidence that we were providing shelter and military training to former FNLA soldiers who were still Angolan citizens.

Gradually, more troops began to collect at M'pupa, many bringing their families with them. They had accurately read the signs. We were not about to abandon their families to the untender mercies of the Cubans and FAPLA.

Commandant Flip du Preez — our liaison officer with UNITA and FNLA when it still existed as a liberation movement — helped tremendously in the relocations by spreading the word through his old FNLA contacts.

I learned through him that sporadic fighting had broken out between leaderless FNLA gangs roaming in the bush and the better organised UNITA forces. In fact, many of my troops had to fight their way through UNITA units to get to M'pupa and the other assembly areas. A tremendous battle between FNLA and UNITA had taken place at Serpa Pinto. It was clear the latter were intent on pushing the former completely out of Cuando Cubango Province. The action merely escalated a legacy of hostility between Battle Group Bravo soldiers and UNITA that persisted for many years.

With Daniel Chipenda gone there was nobody around who could lead FNLA against UNITA. Worse still for FNLA, the South Africans had switched their major support to UNITA which was under the firm control of Jonas Savimbi. It had retained its cohesion as a military force. Savimbi was also a very charismatic leader. The upshot was that many FNLA troops who had not been part of Battle Group Bravo, together with their families, began to swell its ranks. M'pupa was soon almost bursting at the seams and every day the logistical nightmare worsened.

At first I was alone, so I had no option but to use the former FNLA *commandantes* to assist me in controlling the rapidly expanding crowd. Fortunately, Danny Roxo, Silva Sierro and Robbie Ribeiro returned from wherever they been on leave. I put Robbie and Silva at M'pupa but kept Danny at Calai to help Pale sort out the clamouring refugees.

At M'pupa I selected recruits from the new arrivals and passed on the rejects to the Calai refugee camp. There was strong resistance from the headquarters at Rundu to this dumping but I ignored them. They had passed the buck to me in the first place and it was no concern of mine if they ended up being stuck with my discards.

When addressing the crowd at M'pupa, I made it clear that I was only interested in troops willing to fight, and that it would involve hard training and much physical danger later on. If this worried them, they should opt to become refugees at Calai where the South Africans would feed, house and look after their welfare. At Calai they would not be expected to face the uncertainties and dangers of battle.

Naturally, it was not quite as simple as that. They were already genuine refugees or displaced persons — although this seemed to be an inadequate description of the desperately hungry and helpless men, women and children at M'pupa. They had limited choices. The men could either become soldiers — with a future of some sort

— or continue as refugees with very little to look forward to.

Those with a spark of ambition enlisted while those who had been bludgeoned by fate into a state of fatalistic submission took the refugee option. This, at times, was an animal-like existence. Their energies were mostly directed at getting to the front of the ration queue, usually at the expense of others in the same boat.

Some unscrupulous elements elected to remain refugees because they saw opportunities to get rich on the misery of others. In the refugee camps, earthly possessions were inadequately distributed amongst the populace. In a very short time, most of those belongings were concentrated in the hands of a few racketeers who set up shops and engaged in all manner of sharp and exploitive practices. Many eventually became sufficiently wealthy to break out of the refugee cycle. They set up businesses in Rundu, Ondangwa, Grootfontein and even Windhoek. Some became millionaires, despite having left Angola as refugees with only the clothes on their backs and a few worthless escudos in their pockets.

There were also highly qualified individuals amongst the refugees who could set themselves up in South Africa, Portugal or Brazil where they could continue their old occupations. Such people were easily absorbed.

It was not the same for the majority of the ill-educated and unqualified blacks and mulattos. South Africa did not want them, nor did Portugal. Portugal was still in the throes of a socialist revolution with its phoney euphoria and barrages of high-minded slogans that demanded equality for all. These revolutionaries piously insisted that all refugees should return to the newly achieved socialist Utopia that was Angola. Portuguese communists from the new regime advised them against remaining in the shadow of fascist South Africa. Despite this, they were strangely reluctant to assimilate black Angolan refugees into the predominantly white communities of metropolitan Portugal.

It would be absurd to pretend that most of the eligible refugees wanted to join Battle Group Bravo because they were intent on continuing the war against Marxism. A few did because of their hatred for MPLA, but they comprised a small minority. I had no illusions about the others. They were opting for a future with us because it offered a life with a modicum of security. Their only other alternative was to return to Angola and throw themselves on the uncertain mercy of their former enemies or to continue as stateless refugees. Most of them had enjoyed only a subsistence lifestyle in the Angolan bush, and as long as they were left alone to get on with their own daily struggle for survival, they could not care less who ruled in Luanda. Unfortunately, the civil war had drawn the whole population of Angola into the vortex of a violent struggle that few of them could avoid or understand.

Consequently, I approached the task of creating an efficient combat unit from an unorthodox angle. To suggest to Angolan recruits that they would be fighting for South Africa would have been preposterous. In any case, most of them had no idea what South Africa was about and had only heard of it for the first time after *Operation Savannah* was launched. There was only one feasible cause I could get them to fight for — the unit. It had to become all important — a living, breathing, fighting, reasoning, loving, hating creature into which all of us, white and black, had to sink our individualism, ambitions, loyalty, energy, talents and expertise. Only in that way would we become a fighting machine par excellence.

It was the way of the French Foreign Legion. Battle Group Bravo would effectively become the new 'tribe' for our displaced Angolans who variously owed allegiance to at least seven different tribes. The unit would give them a new identity, a new direction and a sense of stability, safety and community. Tribal and racial loyalties would be replaced by a single allegiance to the unit.

This meant, of course, that whites entering the unit also had to change their outlook. I demanded from them a total and unselfish commitment, particularly towards the black troops. If they could not or would not give me that, they had to go. There was no place for career-orientated individuals wanting to use the unit only as a stepping stone on their way up. As long as they were with us, they had to concentrate all their energies and loyalties on serving the unit. I expected them first and foremost to be members of Battle Group Bravo and only after that members of the South African Army. Like the legionnaires of the French Foreign Legion who accept that Legio patria nostra — the Legion is our country — so Battle Group Bravo would be our country.

Undoubtedly the vast majority of South African army officers did not agree with this philosophy, but that did not bother me. What was important was that my black troops and most of my white leader group supported the concept. I provided higher headquarters with scant detail of what I was doing in the certain knowledge that my philosophy would be misunderstood. Only time would prove or disprove it.

The commander of Battle Group Bravo (and later 32-Battalion) was always potentially the weakest link. If he did not wholeheartedly believe in the concept, the unit would soon wind down to become less effective than a normal infantry unit. Because of its Irish stew-type structure, it would become less combat efficient than an infantry unit composed of white national servicemen. I believed it was essential that future battalion commanders should be selected from officers who had extensive previous service with the unit. It was also crucial that a successful commander knew his black soldiers intimately in times of war, in the training field and at home in the barracks or married quarters.

I was fortunate in having had the opportunity to observe my men from the outside during the *Operation Savannah* campaign while they still owed allegiance to FNLA. Initially at least, I was not tied closely to their personal well-being so I could keep my distance from their daily life patterns and problems. This changed when Daniel Chipenda and his cronies became so involved in satisfying their own selfish needs that they forgot about their troops. I then became Chipenda's replacement. Neither the blacks troops nor I had any choice. I was the only one around and we had to accept each other whether we liked it or not.

A thorny issue was immediately apparent. How would we handle the introduction of armed black soldiers into the South African Army? Traditionally there had never been black fighting troops in the South African Defence Force. To be blunt, in 1976 it was very difficult to sell such a concept to the political hierarchy of the day.

Most of us tended to exploit the cynical stance that it was more expedient to have foreign blacks killed in battle than to send young white South African National Servicemen home in body bags. Like the Israelis who also have a small population, we white South Africans were obsessed with keeping battle casualties among our young men to a minimum. It followed then that if a military operation — even if it was deemed vital — was likely to lead to casualty figures unacceptable to the public, in all probability it would be called off.

Having a unit like Battle Group Bravo available to take the fall was an attractive proposition. Its casualties would have a minimum effect on the homes and hearths in white South Africa. Bravo personnel could be used in places and in situations where other units — with the exception of the Reconnaissance Regiments — would never be sent. So the establishment of the unit became a politically attractive proposition for almost everyone, especially those in the higher command echelons.

Those of us in Battle Group Bravo, however, never regarded our black soldiers as cannon fodder. Far from it. My successors and I always insisted that we, the white leadership, should always be in the forefront of battle, facing the enemy shoulder-to-shoulder with our black comrades. That we did so was proved by the lopsided casualty rate amongst the white leadership. It was always far higher than in other units of the SADF. There was no race, tribal or national distinction. We fought as members of Battle Group Bravo. We mucked in equally from top to bottom. Our very lives depended on our mutual support in combat situations.

In exchange for being given a home — or rather a new tribe — the soldiers knew they would be required to fight and go on fighting until they were wounded, killed or became physically unfit or too old to continue. The black and white soldiers of Battle Group Bravo, and later 32-Battalion, would indeed live by the sword.

Far too frequently they also died by the sword.

Their roll of honour became by far the longest of any South African unit. In fact, I believe it was longer than the rolls of all other infantry units combined.

Having established my philosophy as to how the Unit would be run, I started training them for the new shape that the war on the Angolan border had begun to assume. Elements intent on contaminating my troops with alien ideas, particularly relating to continued allegiance to FNLA, were ruthlessly weeded out. This resulted in many former FNLA *commandantes*, notably the political commissar types, being summarily dismissed. I deliberately began a campaign to undermine Daniel Chipenda's position, stressing his desertion to Europe when we were still locked in combat with FAPLA and the Cubans. Contact between my soldiers and FNLA cadres in the refugee camp was also stopped. This occasionally led to friction between Flip du Preez and myself. FNLA sometimes approached him to ask for access to the unit, but I always flatly refused.

The general opinion throughout the army at the time was that Battle Group Bravo's existence was of a temporary nature — that we were acting as caretakers only until the FNLA problem had been resolved. I vehemently disagreed and told everybody, including my black troops, quite bluntly that FNLA's days were over.

Kambuta, the FNLA's secretary-general, was the main culprit. The only viable FNLA formation still in the field was under my command. Through the incompetence of the FNLA command structure, FNLA had disappeared elsewhere as a military factor after its ignominious defeat by both FAPLA and UNITA. Kambuta saw Battle Group Bravo as his last chance to re-establish FNLA as a major role-player in the Angolan civil war. The vast majority of our soldiers, however, could no longer stomach the hypocrisy of the Angolan political leaders. Nor did they want to be part of the dreadful chaos of a three-cornered fratricidal fight to the death.

So Battle Group Bravo had changed its loyalties. Soon it would be cheerfully fighting South Africa's war and not a war of liberation designed to bring freedom to a Marxist-dominated Angola.

Meanwhile, on the war front, the South Africans were still slowly withdrawing south along Angola's west coast through Sa da Bandeira and down the centre through Nova Lisboa and Serpa Pinto. Farther east, Jonas Savimbi and UNITA were withdrawing east along the Benguela railway line and south towards Gago Coutinho from the region of the Cazombo bight.

Under cover of the withdrawal of South African forces, particularly in the west, refugees were streaming towards the South West African border. *Commandante* Kioto's FNLA unit that had fought under Delville Lindford's command had been disarmed by the South Africans and was amongst those refugees. They and the others ended up at Chitado, north of the Cunene River and about 30km west of Ruacana Falls. This escalated General van Deventer's already extensive refugee problem. I was despatched to gather intelligence from the new arrivals and recruit any that I found suitable.

Commandant Hank Badenhorst had been placed in charge of the Chitado refugees. He was based in a large house and was under constant pressure from the milling horde. People demanded attention, proffering papers and travel documents, even fistfuls of worthless escudos — anything just as long as they could get out of Angola.

While watching I heard lusty singing and the rhythmic sound of a body of men approaching at the double. A small, energetic and sinewy black man heading a column of troops, all stripped to the waist, came to a halt on the open ground facing Hank's house. They turned right and stood at ease, sweating and panting while their commander harangued them. It was Kioto. He dismissed them and they ran to their tents. Kioto obviously still had his men under control.

Hank introduced us. It was the first time I had met Kioto. He was confident, extremely fit and as hard as nails, both mentally and physically. He grinned from ear to ear when he heard who I was.

He said he had fought his way south through swarms of rampaging UNITA bands from Nova Redondo to Sa da Bandeira. At Sa da Bandeira he had fought alongside South African forces. He afterwards took control of Sa da Bandeira but soon found himself engaged in combat with UNITA troops who tried to force him from the city. This was despite the fact that their common enemy, FAPLA, was advancing from the north to take on both organisations.

Savimbi had turned against the FNLA instead of making common cause with it, presumably because it had refused to amalgamate with his organisation. This underlined the depth of the animosity that existed between the two organisations. It remains my opinion, after many years of experience with FNLA and UNITA, that Savimbi — a convinced socialist — found it easier to relate to the Marxist MPLA than to the capitalist-inspired organisation of Holden Roberto.

Their fight in Sa da Bandeira had gone well for Kioto until the South Africans decided to disarm them and send them packing to the south.

I was doubly impressed at the way Kioto had kept his men together as a fighting body, even after being disarmed by his South African comrades-in-arms. Kioto and his men proved to be excellent acquisitions for Battle Group Bravo.

I learned from him that Hank had locked up a former Portuguese paratrooper on the suspicion that he had killed someone during a quarrel over a woman. The complaint had been laid by some politically inclined refugees with longstanding grudges from the colonial days against white Portuguese paratroopers. By all accounts the paratrooper was a good soldier.

Hank claimed he had kept him in custody purely as a protective measure and not with a view to charging him. So, on my advice, he brought him up on orders. The paratrooper appeared unimpressive. He was flabby, wore glasses and slouched. I told him through an interpreter that he was free to go. He looked at me in astonishment, gulped like a fish and slipped to the floor in a dead faint. We revived him and after reassuring him that he was truly free to go, he left, almost skipping with joy at his unexpected release.

Hank ran in almost immediately afterwards to say that we had released the wrong man. This fellow had been held on suspicion that he was an MPLA agent. His appearance certainly suggested that he was no paratrooper. The real paratrooper was still in jail. He turned out to be a better proposition and elected to join us. He became a valued member of Battle Group Bravo.

Unfortunately, the man released in error could not be rearrested without it harming the credibility of the Defence Force. So he remained with the refugees, many of them openly unenthusiastic about having to live with his dubious company.

Unexpectedly, another former acquaintance surfaced in Chitado. It was the FNLA general who had strutted around so arrogantly in Sa da Bandeira and who had almost caused a mutiny among my men. He was a different man at Chitado. I found him amongst the refugees, inconspicuous and nondescript, wearing a filthy white shirt, tattered pants and battered shoes without laces. I only remembered him because he reminded me about our auspicious meeting at the artillery barracks. I felt sorry for him so I offered him a job as storeman, considering him useless as infantry material in spite of his 'commando' qualifications. He accepted with alacrity but it was not long before I had to fire him for stealing shirts from the store and selling them on the black market in Rundu.

The reforming of Battle Group Bravo was cloaked in secrecy. M'pupa provided the ideal base as it was sufficiently remote to rule out the possibility of snooping from any quarter, especially the media.

I commenced another weeding-out programme and reduced the vast horde to a more manageable 1 800 men, women and children. The rest were despatched to Calai to join the refugees in the great tented town that had sprung up under Commandant Pale Kotze's cynically disapproving eye. Needless to say, Pale did not exactly brim over with joy when I unexpectedly offloaded another bunch of fugitive refugees on him.

Bravo Group's logistics were problematic, in fact virtually non-existent. Firstly there was the terrain which made M'pupa virtually inaccessible to wheeled vehicles during the rainy season. The rains came down with a vengeance as soon as my men were ensconced there and the direct road to Rundu was cut. Secondly, there was a serious shortage of personal equipment and weapons. Thirdly, for food we had to manage with the skimpy ration scale that had been set for refugees. Finally, I had no logistics personnel to execute my flimsy logistical plan.

I was generally suffering from a serious lack of leadership personnel, especially at lower levels. There were only my three Portuguese NCOs from *Operation Savannah* and myself. I began to hunt around for junior leaders and sent signals to Army Headquarters detailing our predicament in dramatic detail.

I approached General van Deventer and Colonel Johan van der Spuy, the sector's local commander. He sent me Des Burman— a lanky young second lieutenant who had been posted to the border by Natal Command only because he had nagged them until they succumbed. Burman was originally intended for the Bushmen Battalion, but because the paperwork had not caught up with his physical movement, Commandant Delville Linford had uncharacteristically declined to take him on. If he had known at the time what a potential star Burman was, I am sure he would have had second thoughts. Des duly reported in the casual manner that was natural to him and which only he could assume without facing the danger of a superior officer sorting him out.

Major Venter, another new arrival, together with Des and the Portuguese NCOs began retraining the companies in earnest. We had finally been issued with sufficient rifles and ammunition for our needs, but little else. For personal kit we had to make do with old khaki overalls and 1940s-vintage webbing. It seemed that the darkest corners of the quartermaster's stores in South Africa had been explored and cleared of everything that had been gathering dust, damp and rat droppings over the years.

The troops were soon decked out in baggy and far too large overalls, boots of the old ABR and F pattern that curled at the toes, skewed webbing belts and ammunition pouches. All of it had originally been manufactured for the brawny and large physiques of Springbok soldiers in the Western Desert during World War-II, not for slightly built black Angolans.

We struggled with a housing problem. M'pupa was a former Portuguese marine base — a *quartel* or barracks — but the buildings were soon bulging to overflowing with wives and droves of children. Those lacking accommodation had to scavenge for whatever materials they could find to provide at least rudimentary protection against the incessant rain. Beneath these threadbare tarpaulins, rusted corrugated iron sheets and precarious grass roofs, there was almost as much mud and water inside as outside.

Young children began to die of malaria, pneumonia and other diseases. I located a black Angolan who called himself a doctor on the strength of his three or four years experience as a medic at a military Portuguese hospital. In spite of his lack of formal training, he performed wonders with the drugs and medicines we managed to secure via refugee channels at Calai. His assistant was a remarkable lady, a mulatto nursing sister whose Portuguese husband had deserted her and their two young children and run off to Portugal when the situation had turned sour. She was destitute when she arrived at M'pupa. We took her under our wing and she soon proved her worth. She was better trained in medical matters than the 'doctor' but in the chauvinistic Angolan world, her qualifications counted for little.

We also had a transport problem. We had to rely on a few broken-down civilian lorries left over from *Operation Savannah*, augmented by a couple of crotchety military Bedfords and several captured Soviet Gaz trucks.

Commandant Flip du Preez told me that a FNLA company was at Vila Nova da Armada on the banks of the Cuito River, 180km or so north of M'pupa. He asked me if I could use them and I decided to investigate the situation personally.

One rainy day I set off north along the west bank of the Cuito River, going through various little towns and villages until I reached Vila Nova. It had been built as a marine base by the Portuguese navy, which accounted for its naval-sounding name. Marines based there had patrolled the Cuito River as far north as Cuito Cuanavale and south to the marine detachment at M'pupa. They had used specially designed gunboats to interdict FAPLA's routes that led from its bases in Zambia into Angola's interior.

The Cuito is one of Africa's wildest rivers. The east bank was completely depopulated at the time. Thick tropical savannah fringed its flood plain in an almost unbroken green wall as far south as Dirico on the South West Africa border. The west bank was dotted with tiny villages inhabited by primitive people barely able to scratch an existence from the poor sandy soil. The occasional maize patch and muhango field was found below the highwater mark of the flood plain which varies from about five to eight kilometres in width. The exceptionally clear water of the main stream meanders in broad loops across an extensive belt of grass and reeds. It is fringed by numerous lagoons and tributaries. Flat grassy islands barely rise above the swampy surface. In those days thousands of red lechwes found sanctuary there. Hippos snorted in the pools and lagoons. Lurking crocodiles sometimes took careless villagers when they went to fetch water or wash their clothes in the river. Elephants and other big game abounded. It was magnificent, wild and unspoilt country.

A FNLA flag fluttered limply from a pole in front of a substantial red brick building which had been well constructed by the Portuguese. There were a number of brick-built bungalows of typical military design, a large workshop, messes and kitchens. A large water tower loomed over the barracks next to a well-prepared gravel runway. The water pump worked and, as I later discovered, so did the electricity.

Suspicious looking individuals in ragged uniforms gathered around my vehicle as I stopped in front of the offices. My arrival was unexpected and communications were complicated by the language barrier. I finally got through to them that I had thoughts of incorporating them into Battle Group Bravo. Fortunately, they had heard of us as our fame had spread far and wide by then. They escorted me in silence while I conducted a brief inspection of the barracks. From the high ground above the base I spotted a small port installation on the river. I made my way down to have a closer look.

There were some interesting looking patrol boats tied up at the jetty. My long dormant naval blood began to pump a bit faster. I had visions of commanding a gunboat squadron in the heart of tropical Africa.

My daydreaming was rudely interrupted by loud yells as a man bounded towards me. I found myself clasped in the enthusiastic embrace of a smelly soldier named Zaïre, whom I had given up for lost after he failed to report back for duty after leave. He had a youngster of about 12 with him whom I had not met. Zaïre told me they were en route to M'pupa, having arrived at Vila Nova da Armada from Cuito Cuanavale only the day before.

The two of them comprised the entire FNLA garrison at Cuito Cuanavale when

UNITA attacked with several hundred troops, intending to drive them out. They fought back for a day, but eventually decided the odds were insufficiently favourable to merit continuing the fight. They slipped away and made for Vila Nova where they found that the largely unarmed FNLA force in occupation had been cowed by a UNITA detachment. Zaïre took charge, however, and they succeeded in ejecting UNITA from the base.

I inspected the gunboats and liked what I saw. One, powered by two Volvo marine diesel engines, had two cabins on the lower deck, a proper bridge with a small cabin, a gun deck without a gun — the Portuguese had removed it — a loading ramp and sufficient space in a well-deck to embark a Unimog.

The second was a landing barge. It had a well-deck capable of taking 70 fully equipped troops, a three ton truck or two Unimogs. It was powered by two 80hp outboard engines controlled from the bridge.

A third, much longer vessel was drawn up on a slipway. But it was without an engine so I omitted it from my scheme of things. My idea was to base a company at Vila Nova and run supplies to them in the gunboats from M'pupa. This would dispense with the need to use four-wheeled transport over tracks that the rains had rendered virtually impassable.

I placed Zaïre in command of Vila Nova da Armada and the resident FNLA group. I saw Brigadier Schoeman at Rundu and asked him to request some boat crews from the navy, but he refused. Eventually, though, I managed to scrape some crews together from the South African Engineers. With Staff Sergeant Spiller, they set off to retrieve the boats. Some 2-Recce Commando operators, meanwhile, had been deployed to Vila Nova and they had already repaired and serviced the boats.

Shortly afterwards the boats pulled off from the jetty and began their first long voyage down river to M'pupa. As they steered from the moorings into the current, a few headless torsos, skin bleached a sickly pink by the water, bobbed grotesquely up to the surface behind them. They were the grisly remains of UNITA soldiers that Zaïre had dealt with on his arrival there. The bodies had been trapped beneath the bilges of the boats for about two weeks. The pump for the base's drinking water supply was only a few hundred metres downstream, so we were concerned about the effect of the rotting corpses on the quality of the water.

The engineers pulled into M'pupa two days later and took on the first load of stores for the return trip. They could not operate on the river south of M'pupa because of the M'pupa Falls and a long stretch of rapids below that. The return trip against the current took two and a half days.

I think the engineers had the most enjoyable job of us all. They were National Servicemen doing their border stints, which was not something that many conscripts looked forward to. But this time they were spending their duty idyllically, viewing game from the decks of slow-moving river craft in a part of Africa so remote that few had ever been there. It was an adventure that many tourists would have paid a fortune to experience. Nor were the engineers hassled by raucously shouting corporals, parade grounds, inspections, guard duties and other factors that make life miserable in a military base area.

Meanwhile, Commandants Flip du Preez and Johan van der Spuy had persuaded me to deploy troops as far north as possible in the Cuando Cubango to keep SWAPO away from the Okavango border area. I needed little encouragement. I believed we had to fight SWAPO to earn our keep. I was also set on making Battle Group Bravo indispensable to justify its continued existence in the operational area as a fighting unit.

My first move was to garrison Vila Nova da Armada with a fully trained company under the command of Sergeant Danny Roxo with Sergeants Silva Sierro and Robbie Ribeiro to assist him.

I decided to investigate the reported presence of FNLA troops at Mavinga and Luengue. Flip du Preez found a Cherokee aircraft — part of our *Operation Savannah* war spoils — and got Lopez, a former Portuguese Air Force pilot, to fly it. Flip assured me that the plane and its pilot were both in tip-top condition. So Lopez flew both of us to Luengue — once a private safari camp — where a detachment of ragged looking FNLA met us. I checked the accommodation and decided it was suitable for placing another company there. I would base a further platoon farther north at Mavinga. I was surprised to hear that my old acquaintance, Oginga Odinga or Double O, was the FNLA commander at Mavinga.

Operation Savannah, meanwhile, was grinding through to finality. Several combat groups were still deployed to the north covering the South African withdrawal. Combat Group Piper had taken up defensive positions at Caiundo on the western bank of the Okavango River. It was commanded by Commandant Dan Lamprecht, a former Recce officer who had served with me. But north of Rundu along the Cuito River no forces were available to stop an enemy advance. Neither were there any to stop the enemy advancing via Mavinga and south to Mucusso.

It was in this vast vacuum that my troops would come into their own and do their bit to keep SWAPO away from the border area. Savimbi and his UNITA were somewhere to the north, concentrating in Moxico Province and in the northern parts of the Cuando Cubango. It was an area that would later become 'Free Angola' — UNITA's so-called piece of liberated heaven.

We began to take up forward defensive positions on a vast chess board and waited for FAPLA, SWAPO and UNITA to begin moving their own pieces.

At long last I got the first of my promised platoon and company commanders. Commandant Sybie van der Spuy, commander of 2-Reconnaissance Commando, and nine of his men stepped off a C-130 transport one day in late January. I divided them into two groups. The first, under Sergeant Major Willy Ward, went to Vila Nova to take over from Danny Roxo whom I shifted to the former Portuguese base at Baixo Longa about 100km farther north. The other group, with Sybie in command, went to Cuangar to locate and take control of any FAPLA who might be there. After that they went 80km north of the Katuitui border post to Savate on the Okavango River. They were to take charge of any FNLA elements and look for some Battle Group Bravo men who it was believed had reported there. They were thought to be under the command of Geraldo, a former *commandante* of mine from *Operation Savannah* days.

My headquarters complement had also been strengthened. My intelligence officer until then had been Major Chuck Chambers from the Cape Town Highlanders. He was replaced by another Cape Town Highlander, Major Pat Tate. Pat originally came for three months but volunteered to stay longer. He even brought his family for a visit. Later he joined the Permanent Force on a short service contract.

RSM Pep van Zyl, a legendary figure, arrived towards the end of 1976. Pep was certainly no oil painting. He was built like a tank, had the moustache of a walrus and the voice of a concrete mixer. I have seen men shake in their boots when his cold blue eyes bored into them. I had felt the lack of a real fire-and-brimstone RSM type and Pep filled the gap admirably. With a vehicle and a free hand to move around the widely spread unit, he quickly made his iron presence felt.

I managed to get hold of a small corrugated iron building which I used as a signals centre, orderly room and operations room. I also managed to pry some signallers out of Task Force 101 HQ. To solve our vehicle problem though, we had no option but to rely on the risky expedient of 'liberating' our requirements from other units. We began by snaffling unattended vehicles wherever we found them. This process was accelerated after I gave Pep orders to liberate as many newly arrived Unimogs from 16-Maintenance Unit's transport pool at Grootfontein as he could.

Nothing daunted, Pep rounded up drivers and early one morning set off for the

SADF's main base at Grootfontein. He reported back with 14 trucks! This gave the process of obtaining coveted military equipment a totally new dimension and boosted our reputation as champion liberators. We immediately moved the trucks to the safety of Angola where they were beyond the reach of probing military police. Conveniently for us, for security reasons such areas were deemed to be no-go zones for base wallahs such as the feared red caps. Not surprisingly, enquiries by an irate 16-Maintenance Unit and the military police drew a complete blank.

From time to time we continued to add Unimogs to our fleet. If a careless driver left his vehicle to sleep, eat or drink and was foolish enough to leave the keys dangling from the ignition, it would be gone by the time he returned. Keys, in fact, were unnecessary because a Unimog could be started with a screwdriver or a nail file.

In due course we even managed to acquire a 10-ton military truck and a Caterpillar D-8 bulldozer. We liberated a river tug from Cuangar and later added some barges to our fleet. The tug was moored in mid-stream with a cargo barge in tow. At Rundu we found a passenger barge fitted with two cabins, separate heads, a shower and a galley. It accommodated eight passengers. I later moved the whole lot downstream when I established our new Woodpecker Base in the Western Caprivi.

Major Ken Greeff reported for duty unexpectedly. He was small, slight and blond. He was also fitted with a pair of outsized ears which promptly got him christened 'Wing Nuts' — a name he has retained ever since. He became my logistics officer and took over from Major Fanie Walters, a Citizen Force officer who was returning to South Africa. Ken Greeff, without a doubt, was the best logistics officer in the operational area.

Fanie Walters, a great character, is a doctor in entomology and was — perhaps still is — a professor at Stellenbosch University. He used to regale us with hairy stories about his efforts to upset the life cycle of some species of moth or butterfly. He maintained that he had attempted to transplant the brain of an insect at flying stage into the brain box of one at the creeping stage — it might have been the other way around. It seems that the attempts of the creature to fly or crawl or spin or whatever was something to behold. This learned scientist became happily ensconced amongst a bunch of uncouth and non-academic soldiers. He also arranged for tinned bully beef, old condemned bell tents, blankets and suchlike to be delivered to the various bases. He juggled and performed miracles to get the supply line operating. His was a tough job considering the extremely difficult circumstances, our isolation and the almost non-existent transport and drivers.

A paratrooper friend of mine, Sergeant Major Piet Slade, who had left the army and rejoined after second thoughts, arrived at Rundu with his wife. His Christian name is actually Eugene but because he could scarcely speak Afrikaans when he joined the paratroopers and since Eugene was not considered the right sort of moniker for a rough and tough paratrooper, he was re-christened Piet — which he has remained to this day.

Other officers arrived but they did not stay long before they were moved on elsewhere. They included Lieutenant Peter Rose, Major Venter and several officers from Commando or Citizen Force units who were posted to the border to do operational stints. Some liked it so much that they returned for seconds — or even joined the Permanent Force.

Another key man who came our way was Major 'Peanuts' Collins who got his name probably because he was put in charge of the unit's rations. He was Wing Nuts Greeff's right-hand man.

A friend, Colonel Carl van Rooyen, was the Senior Staff Officer Operations at Task Force 101 headquarters, which was moved from Rundu to Grootfontein after the tail end of *Operation Savannah*. We had joined the army together, were commissioned together, resigned from it on the same date and became employees of Consolidated

Diamond Mines at Oranjemund at the same time. After that our paths diverged until we both rejoined the service.

There was Lieutenant Mike Malone, a tall stringy fellow who at one time served as the South African Consul-General in Luanda and later as ambassador to one of the Scandinavian countries. He arrived to do his Citizen Force stint as my intelligence officer. He overstayed — to the annoyance of the head of Foreign Affairs, Dr Brand Fourie. This led to a fight with his bosses at the ministry and he eventually ended up becoming a member of the Permanent Force.

The brunt of the fighting, however, fell on the shoulders of young and newly commissioned second lieutenants and newly striped corporals — all fresh from the Infantry School — and on the somewhat more experienced shoulders of Reconnaissance Commando operators, paratroopers and selected soldiers from South African infantry units.

It can be said without contradiction that 32-Battalion could claim direct descent from South Africa's Special Forces — in the shape of 1 and 2-Reconnaissance Commandos — and their unlikely alliance with Chipenda's FNLA forces during and just after *Operation Savannah*. What 1-Recce started during *Operation Savannah* in 1975 was continued by both Recce units during the opening months of 1976. As a former Recce myself and as the first OC of 32-Battalion, I feel that the Battalion and Special Forces should have been affiliated. For a long time, as a matter of fact, General Fritz Loots, then General Officer Commanding Special Forces, looked after both the Recces and Battle Group Bravo — at least until 1977 when I was press ganged into attending a command and staff duties course.

19

Learning to be guerrillas

When Commandant Sybie van der Spuy and his 2-Recces arrived at Savate it was to find a leaderless FNLA mob under the loose control of Geraldo and his mate — a certain *Commandante* Fantome. This bunch was more intent on exploiting the trickle of refugees moving south and the local population than playing a positive role in fighting FAPLA.

Sybie was faced with a subtle struggle to be seen as the boss, with himself on the one hand and Geraldo and Fantome on the other. He resolved the problem by providing the FNLA troops with rations at just the right moment — an area where Geraldo and Fantome could not compete.

By that stage most FNLA were in a state of near starvation, which to some extent explains their exploitation of the locals and refugees. Angola was gripped in a struggle for survival and under the jungle law conditions that prevailed, only the fittest would survive. This says little for the highflown idealism of the communists in the Portuguese forces who, by their coup, liberated the oppressed Angolans from Portuguese colonialism — then recklessly replacing it with the anarchy and tribal violence of pre-colonial days.

It was impossible to get the authorities to send food into southern Angola to feed displaced refugees. South Africa had enough problems coping with those inside South West Africa or hovering just across its borders — people for whom she was directly responsible. But Sybie located a large quantity of mealie meal condemned for human consumption — probably because of weevils — that was readily available. Without seeking authority he had it flown by SAAF Dakota to the Savate airstrip. His actions, of course, were contrary to current Air Force policy, so it took a little twisting of the arms of the air crew, which fortunately were somewhat rubbery.

With a guaranteed food supply, the Savate FNLA switched loyalties to the South Africans, which left Geraldo and Fantome out in the cold. To rid himself of their disruptive influences, Sybie had them taken to Cuangar where they soon got involved in black market activities along with the local FNLA commander, Chuangari.

Sybie established and trained three complete rifle companies and placed them under the command of three of his men. Sybie and Staff Sergeant Mike Tippett were the battalion headquarters. The companies were equipped with a bewildering variety of weapons that included 30 calibre Brownings, PPSHs, AK47s, G-3s and a few FNs. It would have made a firearm collector's heart jump for joy. However, ammunition supplies became a logistical nightmare that resulted in a sorry display of firepower. There were only a few machine guns, some unserviceable 3,5 inch rocket launchers for use against armour and no medium mortars whatsoever. On the other hand, they were equipped with a reasonable supply of explosives and mines.

It became obvious to me that a confrontation between Sybie's battalion and FAPLA would prove disastrous. The answer was to confine Sybie's men to delaying tactics by deploying them as guerrillas. They would plant mines, lay ambushes and engage in hit-and-run attacks designed to disrupt enemy supply lines to the north. The farther FAPLA advanced to the south, the more tenuous their supply lines would become.

The Okavango River to the east of Savate, with lots of bush and empty space beyond, formed an ideal barrier from behind which to launch guerrilla attacks. I ordered Sybie to base his training on guerrilla tactics and get ready to move east across the river when FAPLA's expected advance on Caiundo materialised.

Sybie was also engaged in attempts to exercise control over the refugees fleeing south. It was a trickle at first, but then became a stream and finally a flood. His main concern centred on protecting the defenceless refugees, most of them Portuguese settlers who had been abandoned and left to their fate by the Portuguese government. They were being subjected to injury and exploitation by the FNLA and by an antagonistic local population. Sybie also had to prevent the infiltration of SWAPO gangs who might be using the refugees as a convenient Trojan horse.

He also tried to build up an intelligence picture of the situation, both up and down the river, by questioning the local tribes-people. Little was forthcoming, though, and the people were generally sullen and professed ignorance. They regarded the South Africans with scarcely concealed animosity. When the use of their *makoros* — dugout canoes — was requested for crossing the Okavango River, they refused point-blank. Before the arrival of the South Africans, FNLAs in the area had taken what they wanted from the locals without recompense, including their women if they felt the need. The reputation of the South Africans had also suffered badly at the expert hands of the communist-trained political commissars of SWAPO, UNITA and MPLA. So it was understandable that they regarded the resident FNLA's new white commanders with trepidation.

One of Sybie's first actions was to install the disciplinary code — agreed by the former FNLA soldiers of Battle Group Bravo — as an instrument by which troops in Angola not subject to South African military law could be disciplined. The latest batch at Savate listened politely to Sybie as he explained the dos and don'ts of the code, obviously not believing the South Africans would actually apply it. After all, their own commanders had never used a disciplinary code — for none existed — and the commanders were the most undisciplined of the lot.

Just after this lecture, an FNLA soldier felt the need for a woman, so he went to a nearby village, looked around to see who he fancied, then selected a 13-year-old girl. To ensure compliance, he threatened to blow up the village with a hand grenade if anyone objected. He took the girl to a hut, stayed the night and raped her three times. That was the final straw for the locals. They descended on Sybie en masse and demanded that something be done about the rapist and the poor behaviour of the FNLA in general.

Sybie constituted a court on the lines of a South African court of law, but with a jury composed of FNLA soldiers. The evidence was heard in open court while the villagers looked on. After a fair trial the culprit was found guilty, and according to tribal custom he was made to recompense the family and the girl for the loss of her virginity. Sybie could have invoked the death penalty in accordance with our own jungle justice code, but this would have meant that everyone would have lost, including the girl and her family.

The positive effect on the FNLA was instantaneous and they quickly fell into line. As far as I know, not a single Battle Group Bravo soldier was subsequently found guilty of rape. The population began to cooperate once word got around and they began to take their own problems and quarrels to Sybie for adjudication. With such trust established, they also became his eyes and his ears. Information began to flow in about FAPLA's movements to the north and of the activities of dissidents among the local povo.

Sybie and his men were flooded with gifts of scrawny chickens and offers to lend sometimes leaky and precarious *makoros* for crossing rivers. He reciprocated by providing them with the most desirable commodity of all — pure salt — something they had rarely seen, let alone tasted, since the departure of the Portuguese.

FAPLA, in the meantime, had captured Serpa Pinto and were cautiously advancing south towards Caiundo on the west bank of the Okavango River. Combat Group Piper was still deployed at Caiundo with the task of delaying FAPLA's advance, but Task Force 101 HQ decided to withdraw them. I was also ordered to get my troops, including my newly acquired rifle companies at Savate, out of the way.

Sybie's battalion was stripped of non-combatants and those considered useless. They were moved south to the refugee camp at Katuitui. There were others who had decided that the life of a disciplined soldier was not for them and they also moved on. Others, fanatical FNLA supporters to the end, were issued with PPSHs and dispersed into the bush to act against FAPLA independently.

Those remaining, the best of the bunch, followed the South Africans across the Okavango River. After considerable drama — during which some men drowned when their homemade ferry capsized — the battalion settled in on the east bank and in the area beyond. It was proposed they would hit FAPLA in the flanks and rear with lightning guerrilla raids, ambushes and mines as their expected advance southwards laid bare the enemy's logistical jugular vein.

Mike Tippett, who had become something of a roving ambassador on the west bank, resumed his task of cultivating the goodwill of tribal villagers on the east bank. In the process he developed a discerning palate for a foul concoction of local brew. It was probably the same poison we had come across the previous year when the *Operation Savannah* campaign kicked off from more or less the same location.

Sergeant Major Harry Botha mined the runway at Savate and planted more mines on the north-south road after Combat Group Piper had passed by en route to Katuitui.

FAPLA, however, were slow in continuing their advance south, so I eventually decided to withdraw Sybie's troops to our newly established base at Woodpecker and move Sybie to Rundu as my second-in-command. It appeared that for the moment FAPLA was stuck at Caiundo.

I asked for permission to demolish the Okavango River bridge some eight kilometres north of Katuitui to hinder any future attempts by FAPLA to penetrate to Cuangar and beyond to gain domination of the north bank of the river. Downstream from Katuitui the Okavango River forms the international boundary between SWA/Namibia and Angola. We were concerned that SWAPO would use FAPLA as a screen behind which they could move into the Cuangar area. From there it would be easy for them to infiltrate western Kavango, particularly the Mpungu Vlei district which had long been a hotbed of SWAPO sympathisers.

Permission was denied, but there was more than one way to skin a cat. I had left Harry Botha, some Recce operators and selected members of Battle Group Bravo in the Savate area. I told Harry to blow up the bridge and signal that he had heard explosions in the direction of Katuitui. I received his signal as arranged and told Task Force 101 HQ in Grootfontein about the mystery bangs and said I was investigating. The next morning Harry signalled that a reconnaissance had revealed the bridge had been dropped into the river. According to locals, UNITA was responsible. I passed this hot information to Grootfontein and to this day I have had no comeback.

Things had become lively on the Vila Nova da Armada front. Sergeants Danny Roxo, Silva Sierro and Robbie Ribeiro and their men were still at Baixo Longa on the Longa River. It was a six hour trip by Unimog over an abominable track to get there. Sergeant Major Willy Ward had begun to train the local FNLA at Vila Nova. A confrontation developed between him and Zaïre — whom I had left temporarily in charge — but this was soon sorted out.

To supply Savate with the absolute minimum of logistics was a problem. But to supply Vila Nova while the boats were being repaired and brought into service was a nightmare as the only existing track had become impassable because of the rains. I almost went on my knees to the Air Force and begged for a Dakota to run supplies there. They agreed reluctantly, but the Dakota run to Vila Nova soon became a regular feature. The pilots, in fact, became so infatuated with the place that they would have liked to night-stop there, but Air Force HQ at Rundu refused to allow it. MiG fighters put in an occasional appearance, but fortunately never when a Dakota was sitting vulnerably on the airstrip.

Willy Ward and his leaders trained their men as best they could with the limited material available. Like Sybie's unit, his also had an amazing assortment of small arms and ammunition but nothing that could provide an effective counterpunch to FAPLA's conventional forces. So he was also directed to act as a guerrilla force and to train his men accordingly.

Baixo Longa became an extension of Willy's command because we had problems communicating with Danny from our headquarters in Rundu. Willy and his men visited Danny regularly, using an old and clapped-out Unimog called Betsy to move rations and ammunition forward. It was the only vehicle Willy had, but Danny had no wheels at all.

I was constantly concerned that Willy or Danny or both of them would tie themselves to their comfortable bases. I reminded them repeatedly, almost nagging like an old woman, to emphasise the point that they should redeploy into the bush before FAPLA could hit them. Willy always patiently reassured me he had everything under control. I always experienced problems keeping my troops away from the malignant magnetism of towns, no matter how broken down and forlorn such places might have appeared to us westerners.

I flew to Baixo Longa in the Cherokee to see how Danny was shaping. Everything seemed all right, although I was again put out to discover that he had based his troops in the middle of town instead of in the bush outside, contrary to my orders. Baixo Longa town was in a hollow and I regarded it as indefensible.

On returning to Rundu I received a garbled report that Baixo Longa was under FAPLA attack. I could not raise Danny on the radio, so I ordered Willy to investigate and deploy troops forward between Vila Nova and Baixo Longa to act as a backstop for Danny.

Just before this Commandant Flip du Preez had brought a Frenchman to see me. He was second-in-command to the mercenary leader, Colonel Bob Denard, and was anxiously enquiring the whereabouts of certain French mercenaries who were serving with UNITA. He had lost touch with them some time before.

A few weeks previously Lopez had flown Flip and myself in the Cherokee to meet Jonas Savimbi at Gago Coutinho, a former Portuguese military strong point on which UNITA was falling back. Flip, as the SADF liaison officer, wanted to discuss and clear up problems relating to UNITA's future activities.

During discussions Savimbi and I had agreed on the spheres of influence of Battle Group Bravo in the Cuando Cubango and on an operational boundary between ourselves and UNITA. I naturally informed him of our various deployments, including the one at Baixo Longa. The last thing either of us wanted was a confrontation between our forces — or so I believed. Savimbi said nothing but somewhat reluctantly undertook to keep his men north of an imaginary line from Baixo Longa to Mavinga.

I noticed that a number of French mercenaries were hanging around Savimbi's HQ and the local UNITA girls, who were far more presentable than the poxy camp followers that followed in FNLA's wake.

I told Denard's man that I had seen his mercenaries. In reply he implored me to locate and make contact with them. I refused because I had no wish to clash unnecessarily with UNITA. In any case, the situation north of Mavinga and Baixo

Longa was obscure and I had little knowledge of the current whereabouts of UNITA. FAPLA, according to unreliable intelligence, was still holed up in Cuito Cuanavale.

When news of the attack on Danny came in, I naturally assumed that FAPLA had resumed its march south. From a mess of garbled messages I constructed a jigsaw picture of an overwhelming enemy force with armoured cars in support.

Willy raced forward with as many troops as he could pack into Betsy. While engaged in deploying his men south of Baixo Longa, Sergeant Sierro and some FNLA appeared from the bush on foot. They reported that Danny's company had been driven from Baixo Longa and had scattered into the bush — where I believed they should have been in the first place.

Willy, Sergeant Jan van der Merwe, Sergeant Brian Walls and some black troops got back in Betsy and advanced cautiously to locate Danny who was clearly in need of urgent military assistance. Suddenly, as they crested the top of a rise, they were confronted by the 60mm gun of a Panhard armoured car that was straddling the track.

The troops, wisely, hurriedly bailed out of Betsy and took cover in the bush. Fortunately, nobody was manning the Panhard's turret and its three white crewmen were engaged in trying to sort out a fuel stoppage problem in the rear engine compartment.

Willy dashed forward without hesitation and menaced the startled men with his AK47. They were at his mercy because they had foolishly left their personal weapons in the vehicle.

'You are my prisoners!' Willy shouted.

'Who are you?' one asked in broken English.

'A South African . . . I'm taking you in . . . get off and no nonsense . . . you are surrounded!'

They reluctantly clambered down from the back of the vehicle. On interrogation two turned out to be French and the other a Portuguese. They said they were the advance patrol of a UNITA force that had just attacked Danny at Baixo Longa. Having captured it, they were heading for Vila Nova da Armada to attack that as well.

Willy kept his wits and his temper. He ordered the car commander to contact UNITA's main body by radio and to tell the commander that they and their armoured car had been captured. He told him to say they were surrounded by troops of Battle Group Bravo so the others should come forward and surrender otherwise they would be fired on.

The UNITA column edged sheepishly into view. They surrendered to the South Africans while a handful of Battle Group Bravo soldiers stayed out of sight in the bush. The prisoners, 70 UNITA soldiers and 13 French mercenaries, reluctantly threw their weapons in a pile at Willy's feet. There was a dangerous moment when a Frenchman expressed doubts that they were surrounded. At Willy's command, a dozen black troops — the only ones there — appeared from cover and gesticulated menacingly with their rifles. This was enough to convince the UNITA men and their French allies.

Captured war materiel comprised an armoured car, four or five Land-Rovers mounted with 12,7mm heavy machine guns or 106mm anti-tank guns, some Unimogs and similar vehicles, 82mm mortars, light machine guns, Entac missiles, RPG-7 hand-held rocket launchers, four Soviet SAM-7 ground-to-air missiles — the first we had seen — AK47s, G3s, R1s and Savimbi's luxurious Citroen sedan that was loaded on a truck. Willy shipped the Citroen south, but as we all should have anticipated, it disappeared somewhere en route. A year or so later I saw a senior officer driving around Pretoria in a Citroen that looked suspiciously similar to Savimbi's former staff car.

In one glorious hit Willy Ward had resolved his transport and heavy weapons problems. The prisoners were escorted back to Vila Nova and Danny's troops who had dispersed into the bush were located.

In retrospect it seems to me that Savimbi, who was being driven out of Gago Coutinho by FAPLA, decided that despite our agreement, he would attack and drive Battle Group Bravo from Baixo Longa and Vila Nova. That would allow him to establish a new headquarters at the latter which was close to a logistical support base being established for him in South West Africa by Military Intelligence. It seems he had no wish to share the Cuando Cubango with Battle Group Bravo, which to him still represented FNLA. The force he had assembled was a potent one, far superior to ours in firepower. He must have scraped together everything he could muster for an enterprise he felt certain could not fail — especially as it was being spearheaded by Bob Denard's ex-French Foreign Legionaries.

For us the situation at Vila Nova was hilarious, but it was undoubtedly less so for Savimbi. The UNITA prisoners were locked up in several bungalows. I told Willy to let them move around freely, seeing that they were our supposed allies. Willy said, however, that he could not do so as the UNITA prisoners had locked themselves in. They were apparently scared stiff of our black troops who were glaring menacingly at them through the windows.

The French wandered about disconsolately, in spite of having put away a bottle or two of their own wine which they shared with Willy and his men to toast the international comradeship of paratroopers. Quite correctly, they felt they had badly lost face in their game of wits with the South Africans. They all wore the green berets and badges of French Foreign Legion paratroopers, which meant they considered themselves the most formidable fighters in the world. They had never even heard of the South African Recces who had taken them for such a ride.

I flew in the next day to collect them, which resolved Bob Denard's problems. One of them, however, the son of a French general, had been killed by Danny during the fighting at Baixo Longa. He had been buried there by his comrades.

I redeployed Willy and his troops to Baixo Longa and arranged for the UNITA prisoners to be moved by boat downstream to M'pupa. Many elected to sign on with Battle Group Bravo, including their commander, Major Fonseca dos Santos. He became my workshop commander with the rank of sergeant and turned out to be one of the best armourers I have ever come across.

Some ladies of the night, camp followers with the captured UNITA column, were also absorbed by the unit. Most of them continued to ply their trade in the only profession they knew.

We kept the heavy weapons, the AK47s and the vehicles, including the armoured car. We only returned the PPSHs, the Stens and other assorted junk. Savimbi was furious. I had a major set-to with Flip du Preez about our retention of Savimbi's best combat kit. To my mind, though, he had got his just desserts because of his treacherous attack on us at Baixo Longa.

Immediately after this episode more ominous moves were reported from the Cuito Cuanavale region. It appeared that a full scale advance by FAPLA was at last getting under way from there. I flew to Baixo Longa to confer with Willy who had re-occupied the place. I urged him once again to clear out of the barracks and take up a position in the bush beyond. As usual, he assured me he had everything under control.

I was scarcely back at Rundu when the fun and games started. It seemed my lot to be the harbinger of bad experiences at Baixo Longa. Each time I visited, it was followed by trouble.

Willy and Sergeant Jan van der Merwe heard vehicle movement to the north of a demolished bridge. Willy and a handful of blacks manned a RPG-7, a B10 anti-tank gun and a machine gun in the immediate vicinity of the bridge, while Jan and his men positioned themselves farther back in a support position with several 82mm mortars.

They could scarcely believe their ears when they heard the growling approach of a tank beyond the crest of the high ground east of the bridge. Suddenly the armoured monstrosity of a Soviet-built tank, four Soviet-supplied BRDM armoured cars, a second tank and trucked infantry hove into view. Willy promptly knocked out the leading tank with three RPG-7 rockets. The second withdrew hastily and adopted a hull-down position beyond the high ground about 1 000 metres away. It began plastering Willy's position with high explosive shells.

A Battle Group Bravo soldier, quaintly called Guinea Bissau, emptied a machine-gun belt into the back of a truck packed with Cubans, killing dozens of them. The BRDMs, which are amphibious, crossed the river and attempted a flanking attack on Willy's position. Things were getting too hot for comfort. His recently captured ex-UNITA Suzuki Jeep was shot out by the second tank, so he and his men began to run back to the mortar baseplate positions where Jan was tackling the BRDMs with mortar fire. As luck would have it, a bomb dropped straight through a BRDM's open hatch and the car spectacularly exploded in a shower of flying slivers of steel and other debris.

Once back at Jan's position, Willy ordered all the mortars except one to withdraw. He and a black soldier fought a rearguard action with the remaining tube. When the time came to clear out, the soldier began to manhandle the mortar baseplate towards the Land-Rover which had been left as a getaway vehicle. Unfortunately, a bomb exploded next to him and neatly amputated both his hands.

Willy slung the wounded man over his shoulder and ran for the Land-Rover. The starter motor churned but the engine refused to fire. The FAPLA armoured cars were drawing closer, which forced Willy to abandon the vehicle. He again picked up the profusely bleeding man and amazingly ran the four kilometres to Baixo Longa, hotly hunted by fire from the remaining tank, the armoured cars and some mortars.

Sergeant Major Willy Ward was awarded the *Honoris Crux*, silver class, for this action.

At Baixo Longa preparations were made to beat off the expected FAPLA attack, but it failed to materialise. I believe FAPLA was so taken aback by the spirited resistance and their losses at the hands of a combat outpost of Battle Group Bravo troops that it made them reluctant to tangle with the main body. Of course they were not to know that the main body was non-existent.

Deciding again that it was unprofitable to defend towns, I ordered Willy to vacate the place and concentrate on delaying FAPLA's advance south with mines and ambushes.

Task Force 101 Headquarters then ordered me to move my troops from our main base at M'pupa. So Willy got a somewhat changed mission. He was to delay FAPLA's advance to give us sufficient time to move Battle Group Bravo lock, stock and barrel to a newly reconnoitred location on the Okavango River.

I appointed an unexpected arrival, Major Charlie Hochapfel, as the base commander and Piet Slade as Base Sergeant Major. Charlie, an infantryman, was renowned throughout the army as an inveterate organiser. His new position at Woodpecker enabled him to indulge his organising abilities to his heart's content. He had the ability to create something out of nothing, which was, in any case, the way we normally resolved our problems and satisfied our needs.

Charlie Hochapfel did not know it, but the black troops had called the base) after him. He thought it had been named Woodpecker (Pica Pau in Portuguese) after the red-headed woodpeckers that abounded at the base. Charlie was a stocky, sharp-featured fellow with quick, energetic movements. He had fair hair, blue eyes and fair skin which, because of blazing Caprivi sun, was always red. This, combined with his sharp nose, apparently reminded the troops of that particular bird.

Willy began planting mines between Baixo Longa and Vila Nova da Armada, booby-trapping the barracks, mining the airfield and planting mines on the road from Vila Nova to Rito, the next town downstream. Information subsequently came in regarding tanks and vehicles being blown up between Baixo Longa and Vila Nova and about mines detonating within the latter base.

At M'pupa, meanwhile, we began to load the troops and their families into trucks for the exodus. Charlie, with the assistance of Lieutenants Peter Rose and Des Burman and operators from 2-Reconnaissance Commando, was hurriedly preparing Woodpecker for occupation. Chaos reigned supreme because of the chronic lack of logistical support. There were insufficient tents and a general lack of shelter. Women and children were uncomfortably exposed to the almost constant rain. Everything was wet and millions of mosquitos began making their presence felt.

People began to die. The death toll increased rapidly, especially amongst the children. Medical facilities were hopelessly inadequate and the medical personnel could do little but fight a rearguard action against the malarial onslaught. Indents and requests followed by frank pleas for help made no impact on the granite edifice of the army's, and especially Sector 20's logistical machine.

We were not a legally constituted unit of the SADF. We had no war establishment tables, so we were not due the normal logistical support — the right of every unit in the army's order of battle.

We were, in effect, a bloody nuisance. That, as far as Sector 20 at Rundu was concerned, was the bottom line. The lives of Jan Breytenbach's 'kaffirs', as they called them, counted for very little, whether they were in or out of contact with the enemy.

Fortunately, Ken Greeff knew how to improvise. Liberating equipment and supplies from other units was, as usual, the only way to satisfy our requirements. On my orders and under Ken's direction, we raided transport parks, broke into armouries, pimlico stores, engineers' stores and any other store we came across. In this way we ended up with most of the basic equipment we needed. But we were still short of tents, blankets and rations, especially for the families of soldiers.

To overcome the ration problem, we had no option but to hunt game for the pot — as much as I disliked doing it. As well as providing me with a partial solution, this also put the noses of Sector 20 HQ out of joint. They were, after all, directly responsible for our logistical support. I sent an official signal to Woodpecker and copied it to Sector 20 at Rundu for information. It granted Major Charles Hochapfel permission to hunt buffalo inside an official game reserve, being the only way to stave off the starvation that was threatening my troops and their families. This prompted an indignant uproar and protests from the sector commander. Despite this, trucks loaded with mealie meal and other rations were soon running between Rundu and Woodpecker.

Fortunately, the Staff Officer 1 Logistics at Sector 20 HQ was an accomplice of ours and he did his best to alleviate our desperate situation by sidestepping his boss whenever he could.

I sent another tear-jerking signal to Army Headquarters just before Easter. It told of the sorry plight of my people and explained how they were crouching in misery without blankets beneath dripping and inadequate tarpaulins on the wet, cold and malaria-infested flood plains of the Okavango River. The inference was that this was happening while in South Africa happy, laughing, healthy and warm citizens were peacefully departing for their coastal holidays, unaware or indifferent to the plight of the soldiers who had made it possible for them to do so.

Before Good Friday a DC4 load of warm blankets from Red Cross supplies was flown in for distribution in the unit. Just for once, somebody at headquarters had reacted rapidly to Battle Group Bravo's plight. Woodpecker gradually took shape. The doctors began advancing instead of retreating in the face of the dreaded malaria parasite enemy.

Small operations north of the border continued after our withdrawal from Angola. West of Cuangar and up the Chissombo omuramba a FAPLA radio station was pinpointed. Sybie van der Spuy's 2-Recces backed by Bravo troops were despatched to destroy it. They achieved their objective, discovering in the process the beautiful little town of Bando. Tanks appeared unexpectedly and attempted to intervene, prompting Sybie to stage a precipitous withdrawal.

Xamavera was a village on the Cuito River to the east of Rundu. This and another unnamed village not far south of it on the north bank of the Okavango River were reported to be harbouring SWAPO elements. They were raided and several SWAPOs in the unnamed village were captured. Others at Xamavera were shot.

I sent a reconnaissance probe to our old training base at M'pupa. It found that FAPLA had still not penetrated that far south, indicating that Task Force HQ's orders to vacate it had been somewhat premature.

*   *   *

Major-General Constand Viljoen, GOC Task Force 101, launched *Operation Cobra* to clear out SWAPO elements that had infiltrated into northern Owamboland in the wake of South Africa's retreat from Angola. They caught exactly nothing in their nets.

Masses of infantry were called up from South Africa. Huge convoys headed north. Supply bases, bursting at the seams, were set up in the operational area to provide everything from hot showers to ample issues of daily ration packs. The Southern Cross Fund even sent beer and cookies plus lots of other goodies such as 'I was there' plaques and imitation Swiss army knives.

Battalions of infantry moved backwards and forwards through the bush in long sweep lines south of the cutline, like General Kitchener's troops during the Anglo-Boer War. It was the biggest deployment of South African troops since World War-II. But this huge force did not get a single kill.

Meanwhile 'Jan's Kaffirs', as they still derisively liked to call our troops, were operating eight widely dispersed platoons north of the cutline without support and were bringing in kills daily. In spite of the fact that we did not have even a single LMG or M79 grenade launcher to boost our fire power. No wonder that the general and his staff at Task Force 101 insinuated that we were cooking the books.

The lack of success of *Operation Cobra* stemmed from a basic misconception — that one needs a sledgehammer to swat a fly. Another reason, of course, was that those running it did not understand the philosophy of guerrilla war — the somewhat modified concept of the indirect approach. They did not understand that SWAPO had to be kept off balance by maintaining intolerable pressure on them until they were driven to psychological and therefore military collapse.

Battle Group Bravo was tasked to move into an area north of Beacon 28 on the border cutline. Our mission was to destroy suspected SWAPO bases in *chana* Hangadima and to drive SWAPO cadres south into Owamboland where other South African forces would be poised and ready to deal with them. We would adopt the pose of FAPLA troops engaged in clearing UNITA forces from that part of Cunene Province. UNITA and SWAPO, for all practical purposes, were still allied and working together in Cunene Province. Both organisations drew the bulk of their recruits from the Kwanyama tribe.

I placed three companies under Sybie's command. They were equipped with Gun Unimogs mounting double-barrelled water-cooled 50 calibre Browning machine guns, 106mm anti-tank guns and mortars. The vehicles were liberally adorned with MPLA graffiti and slogans to disguise their identity. They departed in great secrecy by a roundabout route for the Angolan border. They headed for a position north of *chana* Hangadima where they turned south and approached it from the north as if they were FAPLA forces.

SWAPO, unfortunately, had monitored their movement and a short skirmish resulted. Not surprisingly, when they swept through Hangadima no trace of the enemy was found. They laagered south of the major *kimbo* (kraal) for the night.

During the night they were attacked by a large SWAPO force which was driven off after a tremendous display of our newly acquired firepower. The number of enemy casualties resulting from this enormous expenditure of ammunition is unknown, but pools of blood, blood-soaked bandages and items of bloodied clothing were found in a sweep the next morning. SWAPO, as usual, had removed their casualties, including the dead, from the field of battle.

Intelligence had correctly suggested that SWAPO was in the area, but they had pinpointed the wrong *chana*. The enemy had been at *chana* Mamuandi, eight kilometres to the north-east. It would prove to be a tough nut for Battle Group Bravo to crack in a later operation.

After this operation Sybie and his 2-Recce men returned to South Africa. From then on I had to rely almost entirely on junior leaders fresh from Infantry School. They eventually became totally integrated into the unit because they did not have mother units in South Africa to return to. Most of the others who served with the unit spent short detached periods with us before they returned to their mother units. It was these youngsters, together with the black platoon sergeants, who would become the backbone of the unit.

It became apparent that FAPLA had failed to venture farther south than Rito. Flip du Preez heard through UNITA channels that they had also withdrawn to Cuito Cuanavale from the Vila Nova da Armada area. He also heard that a UNITA force operating in the Baixo Longa area was desperately short of supplies. In consultation with Flip and Colonel Johan van der Spuy, who was still concerned about a SWAPO presence on the Kavango border, I decided to send a company to secure the area as far north as Baixo Longa and to establish contact with UNITA. Another company would be sent up river from Katuitui to just south of Caiundo, as the expected FAPLA advance along this route had not materialised.

A third company would be sent to Luengue via Coutado do Mucusso to probe as far as Mavinga and establish a presence there. Sergeants Roxo, Sierro and Ribeiro, in the meantime, had been inserted by air into Luengue where they took control of the resident FNLA. To a small extent they were provisioned by air using Lopez's Cherokee. Mostly, though, they had to rely on local resources including whatever rickety transport they could lay their hands on.

After that Danny Roxo went to Mavinga to take charge of the FNLA there who were commanded by Oginga Odinga or Double 0 as he was known. They established a working relationship but shortly afterwards Double 0 treacherously led Danny and some of his men into an ambush. Some were killed in action, but most casualties were Double 0's men. He escaped to Cuito Cuanavale where he rejoined FAPLA. Having formerly worked for the Portuguese DGS and now the South Africans had probably proved to be more than he could stomach.

FAPLA occupied Mavinga shortly afterwards and Danny began a campaign of harassing them with long-range mortar fire. It seemed that this and the vulnerability of their long supply lines from Cuito Cuanavale made the situation too hot for them and they withdrew to Cunjamba in the north-west.

Peter Miles, a second lieutenant and a platoon commander, was senior to the battle-wise Danny Roxo. So when he arrived at Luengue he took command of the FNLA and Battle Group Bravo forces there. With Danny as his capable mentor, Peter took his forces north to Mavinga. He cleared the town and left Danny behind to look after things while he secured the area as far north as Cunjamba.

However, without Danny to guide him at Cunjamba, he foolishly lowered his guard. The situation seemed peaceful and the villagers appeared to be blissfully unaware that a war was in progress. They laughingly reassured him that the last time rifles had been fired in the neighbourhood was when a Portuguese safari operator, Simoes, had taken some rich American clients to his hunting concession to shoot elephant, lion and buffalo.

Peter sent patrols into the town and across the river. On their return they reported that they had seen the tracks of heavy vehicles with wide tyres. The locals expressed ignorance and were seemingly mystified when these were pointed out.

Peter established a base for the night and slept peacefully, ignoring the signs of a strong enemy presence that was just about screaming at him. The next morning he took eight of his troops for protection and drove a Unimog to the river to perform his morning ablutions.

They ran straight into a vicious firefight at the bridge. The place was swarming with FAPLA's BTRs and BRDMs. Peter's Unimog was shot out and he was cut off from the main group. Thoroughly alarmed at the sudden eruption of such a solid contact, they concluded that Peter and his men had either been killed or captured.

The next in command was a senior black NCO. He decided the company would stay where it was and fight back. Soon, though, they were surrounded by an overwhelming FAPLA force which seemed determined to wipe them out.

I was in the radio room at Rundu apprehensively listening to the battle over the radio. Cunjamba is about 320km north of Rundu as the crow flies. The Air Force had no assets in Rundu or anywhere else within range to aid them. Helicopters were no good because it would have been suicidal to land and unload troops there. Besides, they also lacked effective range.

I ordered the black sergeant to forget about Peter — he was probably dead or captured anyway — and to concentrate his forces to break through the encircling FAPLA. He was then to head for Mavinga.

My plan worked perfectly, but in the process they had to abandon two or three Unimogs. It was a great loss to us, particularly to RSM Pep van Zyl. He had been to a lot of trouble getting his hands on those Moggies and now they were being recklessly whittled away by a greenhorn subaltern. And as all subbies found out sooner rather than later, it was unwise to mess around with an RSM of the calibre of Pep van Zyl!

I despatched Danny and his men towards Cunjamba to assist Peter's company with their breakout and to cover their withdrawal. He eventually reported that indications were that Peter and at least some of his men had escaped. This was contradicted shortly afterwards by a report that suggested Peter had been captured. FAPLA, I speculated, would probably fly him straight to Luanda for a show trial.

I knew that the government viewed the probable capture of a white South African with the gravest concern. The army would probably look on it with alarm bordering on panic. We expected FAPLA to begin crowing immediately and start to make propaganda capital out of it. Strangely enough, though, we did not pick up anything on radio intercepts about Peter's capture, despite the fight itself being reported in detail. According to FAPLA's reports it had been a violent scrap in which they had suffered many casualties. In view of this I decided to keep quiet about Peter's disappearance for a maximum of three days. I did not relish the thought of the panic and censure that would otherwise descend on us in all its fury from higher headquarters.

It was with the utmost relief to me personally and to the unit when two days later Danny reported that Peter and most of his men had reappeared from the bush. They were unhurt and in high spirits, having walked unaided all the way from Cunjamba.

We had lost two or three men killed and about eight missing. I sent Lieutenant Barry Roper to Mavinga to replenish the company and bring back Peter. Barry, armed to the teeth with pistols, grenades and knives as was his custom, left Woodpecker with a convoy of seven Unimogs.

The road from the border to Coutado do Mucusso, Luengue and Mavinga was, and probably still is, the most atrocious in Africa. The trucks had to battle through deep soft sand almost the whole way. The only firm stretches were in a few areas where the road crossed the *omurambas*. During the summer rains the *omurambas* become sumps of deep black muck that can suck a truck in up to its door sills and keep it trapped until it can be dug out at the end of the rainy season.

Throughout those years Unimogs proved to be the best vehicles for those appalling conditions, although they were small for bulk supply transport. Barry ground his convoy slowly north, labouring in four-wheel drive the whole way and with differentials locked for long stretches. It took him a week to get to Mavinga, where he offloaded the supplies. On his return trip he transported part of the company to Luengue. Danny remained at Mavinga to keep his ear to the ground so he could give us early warning if FAPLA resumed its advance south.

During this trip, Barry accidentally ran over and killed a black soldier. He buried him without ceremony, out in the middle of nowhere. After a contact, when operating on foot far away from a support base, it was our policy to bury our dead where they fell. When a body could be returned to base by vehicle, however, we always did so to give the deceased a proper military funeral in our rapidly expanding cemetery at Woodpecker base. We had a responsibility to the men's families as well. Consequently, I was furious when Barry reported on his arrival back at Woodpecker that he had buried the soldier somewhere between Luengue and Mavinga. I promptly sent him back on another long and energy-sapping journey to exhume and bring back the decomposing body.

After a rocket from me and a very serious talking to by the RSM, I sent Lieutenant Peter Miles on leave. I despatched a newly arrived major — who shall remain nameless — to Luengue to take over Peter's company. He settled in and made himself comfortable, evidently doing little or nothing to improve defences or to dominate the area with aggressive patrolling.

Fortunately, Danny retained his system of patrolling the area north towards Cunjamba. His platoon suddenly came under pressure at Mavinga from what appeared to be a large FAPLA force advancing south. Its objective was unknown. South of Mavinga the Cuando Cubango is an empty space, roamed in those days by thousands of elephant, buffalo, zebra, sable antelope, giraffe and all the other major species of African game. It was, in short, a paradise on earth where I could happily have lived out the rest of my days, far from so-called civilisation. It had no military significance until Savimbi established his headquarters at Jamba. After that, of course, it became a magnet for FAPLA advances.

FAPLA had begun moving on a broad front down the Cuito and Okavango Rivers. Danny pulled his platoon back to Luengue and alerted the major. Task Force HQ ordered us to avoid pitched battles and withdraw all Battle Group Bravo forces to South West Africa.

I ordered the major to mine the road between Mavinga and Luengue and the airfield at Luengue. After that he was to move his company south to Woodpecker Base. The mining was soon completed and the company began its trek to Coutado do Mucusso. Unknown to the major, though, FAPLA had slipped a strong force in behind him, probably by helicopter, between Luengue and Coutado do Mucusso. Danny's patrols and the locals had spotted helicopters operating in the area with increasing frequency.

The convoy, almost unavoidably, ran into a well-placed FAPLA ambush. An RPG-7 rocket was fired at the lead Unimog driven by Robbie Ribeiro's brother. It was loaded with about two tons of plastic explosive and went off with a tremendous bang. The shockwave and a gigantic flash took out the two vehicles behind, atomised Robbie's brother and flattened the whole ambush area — including, I believe, the ambushers who had probably adopted firing positions only a few metres from the road. The scarring of the surrounding bush is visible to this day.

The major, who was travelling towards the rear of the convoy, panicked and fled south through the thick bush, leaving the leaderless survivors of his company to shift for themselves.

Danny took charge, brought order out of the chaos and re-established control over the survivors who had not fled. They came out of the bush at the Okavango River many days later. About 20 or 30 had run off into the bush during the action. They wandered around, lost and leaderless. Most of them were eventually found. The last of them, one of my best sergeants, was discovered in a kraal on the Okavango River, almost dying from thirst and hunger and looking like a skin-covered skeleton. He had struggled on alone for two weeks with a badly wounded arm. I hardly recognised him, for he was normally an unusually well muscled man of great physical strength. He smiled on seeing me and gave an assurance that after he had eaten something and his wounds had been seen to, he would be ready for the next battle.

I listened with disquiet when Danny reported the major's lack of combat leadership. He expressed his disgust at the events that had led to the company being dispersed in the bush. He insisted that an immediate counter-attack would have saved the day and some lives if the major had only kept the company under firm control. I was furious, particularly as some of my men were still unaccounted for. They were probably wandering about in the hostile bush, in agony from wounds and being hunted down by FAPLA's follow-up patrols.

I grabbed the major, a husky man, barely restraining myself from physically assaulting him. Instead, I delivered a tirade that I hoped would sink into his thick skull. He seemed to flinch, but in retrospect it was probably only a shock reaction to my order that he should return towards Luengue and search for those still missing. In addition he was to destroy the bridge at Dirico, an obvious objective for a FAPLA column moving south along the Cuito River. If the bridge was allowed to remain intact, the enemy might get to the rear of the company and cut their return route.

The major departed with what remained of his company to carry out my orders. However, instead of travelling in proper formation as a mutually supporting fighting force, he strung a column out over many kilometres. He ordered Danny, Silva Sierro and Robbie Ribeiro to range far ahead in a Wolf — a mine-resistant Unimog — and blow up the bridge. The rest of the company followed far behind with the major, as usual, bringing up the safe and distant rear in his command vehicle.

On the north bank of the Okavango River near Macunde, the Wolf detonated a heavily boosted tank mine. The explosion threw it in the air. It crashed down on its side crushing the bodies and breaking the limbs of the occupants. There was some firing from the side of the road, but this was quickly suppressed by Robbie and two or three others who had been flung clear.

Silva Sierro's skull was crushed like an eggshell, although he was still alive but unconscious. Danny Roxo was pinned to the ground by the damaged vehicle. He was dying from severe internal injuries, but was still conscious. The survivors tried desperately to lift the vehicle off him, but it was far too heavy.

They dragged Silva into the shade. Robbie told the uninjured to protect the casualties. He could not call the company for assistance because the radio was damaged, so he ran back down the road to intercept the approaching company. He found the major still gallantly guarding the rear of the column and reported what had happened. The major listened to Robbie's report then, unbelievably, ordered the column to turn about and withdraw to Woodpecker to get assistance.

This miserable coward deserted Danny and the others — leaving them to choke in their own blood, racked by pain, mercilessly flayed by the sun and pestered by flies — to save his own miserable skin.

Danny Roxo, in keeping with his dauntless character, made the best of the situation. He lit a cigarette and calmly smoked it until it was finished. Then he died — still pinned under the Wolf. He had not complained nor uttered a single groan or moan, although the pain must have been excruciating.

Before he came to us, Danny had been a living legend amongst the Portuguese Security Forces in Mozambique. It was a legend that grew rapidly in the South African Special Forces. He died because a craven coward lacked the guts to lead from the front and put the welfare of his men first. Ironically, he belonged to one of the best army units and had been a top rugby player for Griquas.

When this tragedy took place I was away dealing with another crisis farther up the Okavango River. Charlie Hochapfel reported it to me by radio when the yellow bellied major returned to base. I ordered Charlie to immediately lay on a helicopter and have Danny, Silva and the others casevaced at all costs.

Back at the wrecked Wolf, a Soviet-supplied Antonov aircraft appeared overhead and its crew began rolling bombs from the lowered tailgate. They exploded haphazardly all over the place, but fortunately the Wolf was not hit. The pilot of the casevac chopper, however, refused to fly across the river and land by the contact position while the Antonov was still around. He waited for it to depart, then landed some distance away on the far side of the river. He remained there while Charlie struggled to negotiate several kilometres of swamp and reeds on foot to evacuate the wounded. He had to cross and re-cross the river several times in a commandeered *makoro* before he could complete his task.

Meanwhile, Charlie's Land-Rover arrived from the base with reinforcements. Charlie placed Silva in the back of the vehicle and did everything possible to save him. They had crossed the swamp and the river, but the last stretch across a bumpy ploughed field to get to the helicopter finally finished off the gallant Silva. Charlie was disgusted and he swore at the pilot. As a measure of his contempt Charlie sent him packing back to Rundu with his helicopter empty. The rest of the wounded, who fortunately were not grievously injured, together with Danny Roxo's and Silva Sierro's bodies, were returned to Woodpecker by road. If it had been me I would have done the same as Charlie.

But Battle Group Bravo's black week was not yet over. The wounded were scheduled for evacuation from Woodpecker to Rundu the next day. Robbie Ribeiro, the last survivor of my Portuguese-speaking Recce operators, was driving a Land-Rover with four of the injured men in the back. A white national serviceman returning to South Africa after the completion of his border stint was in the passenger seat.

The dirt road between Bagani and Rundu had always been appalling, especially in the dry season when convoys churned up the powdery surface in billowing clouds of dust. Robbie saw a long convoy of 10-ton trucks from 16-Maintenance Unit approaching him from the front on its way to the Eastern Caprivi. He drove cautiously and kept well to the left, as the billowing dust lowered visibility to almost zero.

For some reason the driver of the second vehicle in the convoy decided his leader was not making sufficient speed. Contrary to convoy discipline, he recklessly swung out towards the right side of the road to overtake the lead vehicle. He was blinded by dust and the inevitable happened. He crashed his huge Magirus Deutz transporter head-on into Robbie's Land-Rover, flattening it and killing everyone on board. I believe the subsequent inquest was doctored by the Sector HQ which allowed the criminally liable driver to get off scot-free.

In spite of previous unsuccessful attempts, Commandant Flip du Preez insisted that we again try to contact the UNITA forces said to be floating around in the bush somewhere between Baixo Longa and Cuito Cuanavale. I sent a company-size probe, commanded by Major Fourie of the Walvis Bay Commando, north up the Cuito and Longa Rivers. Accompanying him was a temporary sergeant and a namesake of his, Herman Fourie.

They passed the deserted base at M'pupa and turned slightly left at Rito to give

Willy Ward's heavily mined flood plain hugging road to Vila Nova a wide berth. They followed a crude track crushed out of the thick bush by FAPLA tanks as far as Baixo Longa.

The probe made contact with UNITA at Baixo Longa, but it was of the wrong sort and developed into a major firefight. Battle Group Bravo was definitely at fault. Unfortunately my ex-FNLA troops still regarded UNITA as the enemy, even though it had officially been declared a friend. So it became a splendid opportunity to level old scores.

A second attempt to talk to UNITA was made but the results were the same. Flip was not impressed and neither, I imagine, was Jonas Savimbi. Fortunately, I had a solution at my headquarters in the form of the lanky Lieutenant Mike Malone. He was fluent in Portuguese, knowledgeable about the Cuando Cubango where he had often hunted in the old days and had the valuable skills of a career diplomat. He was the ideal choice to smooth the ruffled feathers of the thoroughly incensed UNITA.

For the next attempt at making contact, Mike was unceremoniously put in the leading Unimog on his own. It was a typically no-nonsense mission thought up by diplomatically dumb military officers. Simply put, the instruction was: 'Drive in front till you see the whites of their eyes, shake their hands and tell them we want to be pals from now on.'

Mike set off with the company following some distance behind. If things went wrong, only he would be taken out by crossfire or by a vengeful and suspicious UNITA. He drove until he was suddenly confronted by a small and wiry man standing in the road with his hands raised in a gesture of surrender. Speaking in Portuguese he told Mike that UNITA was desperate to make friendly contact. Would Battle Group Bravo please stop the shooting!

The little guy was Epelanca, the local commander. The next few days became an exercise in bridge building. Eventually and with some reluctance, the black soldiers of Battle Group Bravo accompanying Mike accepted that they would henceforth have to live with the UNITA people — even if they didn't like them.

Mike brought Commander Epelanca and Johnny Katale — who had the distinction of belonging to both SWAPO and UNITA — down to Rito. Flip du Preez, myself and a UNITA liaison officer were flown in. We had an indaba at which I made reluctant peace with Johnny. We were old adversaries. Just before *Operation Savannah* I had been closing in to kill him, but our advance into Angola had put paid to that.

Mike remained with UNITA to continue his task of reconciliation and Flip and I returned to Rundu. It seems a pity that Military Intelligence had not snapped up Mike Malone at the beginning of 1976 when it first engaged in liaison with UNITA. He would have been worth far more than his weight in gold.

With peace between Johnny and myself restored, Battle Group Bravo undertook to supply Epelanca's group with rations and ammunition. I gave Johnny a HF radio set so we could maintain communications. After that we conducted operations against FAPLA and SWAPO in the Cuando Cubango on a cooperative basis. Johnny refused to speak to anybody but me. He had apparently developed a strong liking for his erstwhile hunter.

'Hello, Carpenter, this is Johnny . . . do you read me?'

'Johnny, this is Carpenter . . . I read you five-five. Can I help you . . . over?'

'This is Johnny . . .I just wanted to ask how you are . . . over.'

'This is Carpenter . . . I am fine. . . out.'

In the meantime the two Fouries took a patrol in a single Unimog to Cuito Cuanavale to administer a pasting to FAPLA. They travelled north without detection, set up mortars on the outskirts of town and dropped bombs into a packed transport park of tanks, BRDMs, BTRs and trucks. They also bombed some Soviet-supplied MiG17 jet fighters on the airfield.

It was fun while it lasted, but having kicked over a hornet's nest they were in no position to handle the dire consequences. FAPLA figured it was time to crush Battle Group Bravo's impertinence and launched an immediate counter-attack. The tiny patrol found itself locked in mortal combat with a fully-fledged mechanised brigade.

They left in a hurry, but not quickly enough. The sergeant in charge of the mortars, one of my best black NCOs, was killed.

The patrol sped south in their solitary Unimog with tanks and armoured vehicles roaring angrily after it in hot pursuit. From time to time MiG17s appeared overhead and thundered down, harassing them with rockets and machine-gun fire, forcing them to jump clear of the Moggie and scamper for cover. Major Fourie was unlucky enough to break his ankle when bailing out the first time, so after that he was confined to the Unimog and could not join the others when they ducked outside to take cover from the strafing. Fortunately the pilots' marksmanship was abysmal, so the patrol got back to Baixo Longa unscathed.

On their return the Battle Group Bravo troops and UNITA forces combined to establish a defensive position. I despatched Charlie Hochapfel north to take over from Major Fourie who had to be evacuated because of his injury. Charlie, though, got lost and blundered around in the bush for several days. When he finally arrived, he was just in time to be at the receiving end of an air attack.

MiG strike jets dived down in pairs, rocketing and strafing the town and the defensive positions which, very wisely, had been vacated. Charlie's position was well back in the forest where he had a grandstand view of FAPLA's abortive attempts to flatten his group. An Antonov also lumbered overhead and huge bombs were rolled from its rear. They exploded with thunderous crumps in an impressive display to the front of our positions. FAPLA's artillery and 122mm rocket launchers joined in and battered the town, but the missiles also fell short of Charlie's company. By then Battle Group Bravo had learned the hard way that the bush was always safer than any town, no matter how strong one's defensive positions were.

Word finally came through from Task Force HQ that we should break contact with FAPLA on all fronts. Major Brian Reagan took over command of the group from Charlie who returned to his post as camp commandant at Woodpecker.

The combined force of Battle Group Bravo and UNITA withdrew slowly to Vila Nova da Armada. While there they managed the amazing feat of shooting down a Dornier spotter aircraft with AK47 fire. It plunged into the swamps of the Cuito River with its crew still aboard and sank from sight. With their airborne eyes gone and our ground fire becoming increasingly accurate, the enemy's strike aircraft decided to pull out of the battle and look for easier pickings farther south.

While patrolling in that area and looking out for targets of opportunity, the MiGs surprised Lieutenant Barry Roper who was travelling north in a Bedford truck stolen from the transport park of 16-Maintenance Unit. Barry and his co-driver baled out and took cover while the enemy jets took several unsuccessful turns in trying to convert the truck into a fiery wreck.

When the aircraft left, presumably to refuel and get more ammunition, Barry decided that further movement by truck was dangerous. It would only serve to attract more unwelcome attention from FAPLA. He decided to abandon the vehicle, but realised he had to do something to stop it from falling into enemy hands. So the pair dug a huge hole in the sand and buried it. The wheels were removed and buried in a separate hole. They booby-trapped their handiwork and set off back to Woodpecker on foot. Unfortunately they forgot to accurately plot their hidden treasure and nobody has been able to find it since.

Many years later, in 1988, I was interviewed by a police detective-inspector who was enquiring after the whereabouts of a Bedford truck that he had reason to believe had been stolen by my unit from Grootfontein in 1976. I said truthfully that I had no idea where it was. Hopefully, by now the case has been closed.

Meanwhile, Brian Reagan and his men continued their withdrawal south along the Cuito River. They crossed the still intact bridge at Dirico, and although harassed by MiGs from time to time, they made it safely back to Woodpecker.

From Katuitui I had moved a company up river to the area of Chimbueta, about 40km south of Caiundo. They were tasked to keep an eye on FAPLA at Caiundo through active patrolling. If they saw that FAPLA was attempting a move south, they were to engage in general delaying tactics, fighting as guerrillas.

The local populace, however, had other ideas. Working in cahoots with the black Battle Group Bravo troops, the company commander was told that a SWAPO group, ensconced at a large base to the east of the Okavango River, was terrorising them. The reported position of their base was somewhat suspect. If the report was correct, they had made a complete break from their usual behaviour. Normally, SWAPO's bases were situated behind FAPLA's protective screen. In this case, rivers intervened between them and their protectors — which would have placed them out on a limb and far from combat support. Logistical support via FAPLA forces at Caiundo would also have been difficult.

Despite these doubts SWAPO was still our prime enemy and an opportunity to attack them could not be passed up. I gave the necessary permission. The company slipped across the Okavango River at night using *makoros* that the local povo willingly supplied. They launched their attack at dawn. The company commander jubilantly claimed some 80 or 90 enemy kills. Each kill claimed, however, had to be substantiated by a captured weapon. Eventually, a Unimog loaded with rusty G3 rifles was deposited at Battle Group Bravo's headquarters in Rundu.

The penny suddenly dropped. UNITA at that time was generally armed with G3 and R1 rifles, while SWAPO and FAPLA were always equipped with AK47s. It seemed that Battle Group Bravo had tangled with a rather substantial UNITA force.

An investigation established that the local tribes people were being terrorised by a 200 strong UNITA group resident in the area. They were commanded by an old acquaintance of mine — Dr Valentino, the one-time tyrant of Lobito — who was still up to his old tricks. The locals and my black soldiers had drawn up a scheme to pretend that Valentino and his gang were SWAPO, so they could be eliminated. We swallowed the story hook, line and sinker.

Personally I had few regrets, remembering the way we had been treated at Lobito by Valentino and his sidekick, Lumumba. Valentino, though, was lucky. He managed to escape and presumably carried on with his scheming. Eventually Savimbi personally clipped his wings the African way — and simply did away with him. It was a pity that his old mate Lumumba was not around at the time.

Because of distances involved and the laborious logistical procedures we had to put in place to supply by road platoons deployed deep inside Angola to the west of Chimbueta, from time to time we reverted to parachute drops. The platoon, however, was operating in uncomfortable proximity to SWAPO strongholds on the western side of the Okavango River. This made them a fair target.

Bags of salt were included on every resupply mission and this more than anything else helped us to win the hearts and minds of the local population. For a village to get a whole bag of salt was something akin to being a major jackpot winner in a sweepstake.

Air supply drops, inevitably, attracted undesirable attention. One night, after a DZ (drop zone) had been prepared and the signal fires lit as markers for the incoming Dakota, the DZ party was jumped by a strong SWAPO force. A furious fight developed, with tracers zinging back and forth, while the Dakota unknowingly headed for an unexpectedly hot reception.

At Rundu we chewed our finger nails to the quick. We were unable to contact the

Dakota on the HF frequency because it had already gone over to VHF to contact the DZ party. Fortunately though, the pilot came back on HF for an unscheduled call shortly before they arrived overhead the DZ. This gave us the chance to turn it around before it blundered into a raging firefight at an uncomfortably low level.

The troops on the ground, meanwhile, were fighting to regain control of the DZ because we could not afford to have air-dropped supplies falling into SWAPO's hands. Eventually they managed to drive SWAPO off, the Dakota returned and the air drop was resumed.

A few nights later the same Dakota on another resupply run was harassed by a MiG fighter and chased all the way from Caiundo to just short of Grootfontein in SWA. The MiG clearly possessed an intercept capability for it to have remained with the Dakota the whole way to Grootfontein. It could presumably have shot the Dak down at any time and why it failed to do so remains a mystery. The aircrews were game to continue the supply runs, but we called them off for a time because Dakotas were hardly a match for jet fighters.

Major Ken Greeff was the prime mover behind our air supply efforts. It was through him, for the first time in the history of the SADF, that steps were taken to establish an air-drop capability on a large enough scale to supply sizeable ground forces continuously with the wherewithal to conduct extended operations behind enemy lines for lengthy periods.

Ken's namesake, Lieutenant Willie Greeff, eventually took command of the company at Chimbueta. Another attached officer, Major Swanie Swanepoel, went to Savate with a white radio operator and some troops. FNLA had once again reformed there this time under the command of the crafty Chuangari who had moved there from Cuangar.

Swanie's task was similar to that of Sybie van der Spuy's before him. He set about training the FNLA cadres and established a degree of control over what was little more than an undisciplined rabble. The airfield could not be used because it had still not been cleared since Sergeant Major Harry Botha mined it all those months before. For the same reason we could not utilise the road north of Savate. To avoid mines we had no option but to bundu-bash through virgin bush, which was somewhat detrimental to the bodywork of our long-suffering Unimogs.

After the two Fouries opened their Pandora's box at Cuito Cuanavale, I told Swanie and Willie Greeff that a FAPLA advance would doubtless soon materialise on their front. I instructed Willie Greeff to despatch a patrol north to Caiundo to check on FAPLA's preparations, then move south and join up with Swanie at Savate. Swanie would lead the combined force back to Woodpecker in accordance with the orders from Task Force HQ. Willie's patrol returned in a hurry. They were brimming with stories of a massive enemy buildup at Caiundo. They reported that there were at least 20 tanks, numerous BRDMs, BTRs, trucks, artillery pieces and even four helicopters at the airstrip.

While Willie was engaged in debriefing the patrol in his forest hide on high ground overlooking the Savate-Caiundo road, a FAPLA tank fitted with mine detecting apparatus on its front, appeared in view. It rolled on south past the hide. Willie hastily assembled his men and they set off on foot in a southerly direction, their heavy kit piled in their only Unimog. They managed to stay abreast of the FAPLA advance on a parallel line of retreat. Unfortunately, hard as he tried, he was unable to raise Swanie on the radio to warn him.

Swanie, meanwhile, had assembled his FNLA troops and their camp-followers in the forest west of Savate. He had arranged to rendezvous with Willie Greeff in the town and set off with a protective element of four or five men. Inexcusably though, he left his signaller and the radio behind, which explains why Willie could not contact him.

While waiting in a house for Willie to appear, Swanie heard rumblings at the northern end of town. Unsuspecting, and assuming it was Willie's Unimog, he stood up and looked expectantly through a window, intending to wave and attract Willie's attention. Instead he found himself staring at a T54 tank as it crawled slowly past. It was acting in support of a FAPLA infantry section operating on foot, but there were plenty of other armoured fighting vehicles around.

They hastily left the house through the back door and crawled into a bushy thicket from where they watched as FAPLA mounted a perfunctory sweep through the houses. At the same time Swanie's National Serviceman radio operator in the nearby forest was viewing the proceedings with consternation. He contacted me and reported that his major had been captured. On questioning him I soon ascertained that the capture was not confirmed. The signaller could only be sure that Savate was swarming with tanks, armoured cars and guns. He had made what he thought was a logical deduction. To his mind, nobody — not even Major Swanie — could escape a concentration of force like that.

Just in case the signaller was correct in his assumptions, I ordered him to lead everybody else back to the cutline on foot. Despite his youth and inexperience, he accomplished the assignment and got everyone back to the safety of South West Africa.

Swanie and his bodyguard waited impatiently for nightfall. When darkness came, they slipped out of town, but failed to locate the FNLA company which had already departed under its young white leader.

Swanie crossed to the east bank of the river, keeping it as a barrier between himself and FAPLA. For the next few days he remained abreast of the FAPLA forces, noting their composition and strength. Unfortunately though, he was unable to report any of these vital details back to me because he lacked a radio.

There was another bout of nail chewing at Battle Group Bravo's HQ.

Where was Swanie?

Had he been captured?

Was he dead or just lost in the Angolan bush?

I once more decided to wait three days before reporting him missing. It was a repeat of the Peter Miles situation.

Willie Greeff and his men crossed the cutline with FAPLA close on their heels. They adopted a position on high ground overlooking the cutline at Katuitui immediately to their north. They were faced by the tanks, BRDMs, BTRs and artillery of a FAPLA brigade heavily stiffened with Cuban soldiers.

A routine South African cutline patrol appeared. They mistakenly identified the FAPLA brigade as Battle Group Bravo and crossed into Angola to make friendly contact. It could easily have turned into an ugly scene, but it appears that the Cubans had orders not to interfere with the South Africans. They merely wanted to occupy the Cuando Cubango and destroy all remnants of UNITA and FNLA that they found there. So, fortunately for the patrol, they refrained from starting a scrap and the troops managed to get back across the border.

Willie Greeff and his men in their position overlooking the scene of confrontation, not surprisingly misinterpreted the incident. They reported to Battle Group Bravo's HQ that FAPLA forces had captured some South Africans. This information was routinely monitored by Sector 20 Headquarters.

I ordered Willie to immediately get himself and his FNLA out of the path of the FAPLA forces. He was to move south for about five kilometres, then swing east towards Nkurenkuru, staying out of sight of the river. I was convinced that FAPLA was after FNLA and not South African forces — and Battle Group Bravo was still basically FNLA.

I was relieved to get news that Swanie and his bodyguard had crossed the border at Katuitui. They were all well, although hungry and footsore. This did not stop me from reprimanding Swanie for going on an extended exploration trip in the bush without a radio.

I received an order to report to Sector 20 Headquarters forthwith. When I arrived, Commandant Hans Moller somewhat off-handedly informed me that FAPLA was engaged in mounting an invasion of South West Africa through Katuitui. I was ordered to rush to Nkurenkuru, grab everybody and everything I could lay my hands on and delay FAPLA's advance until viable forces could be concentrated to repulse the invasion.

Very apprehensively, I must admit, I rushed off in my Land-Rover to do battle with the tanks and armoured vehicles of the FAPLA brigade that Willie had reported. He was checking back with me by radio every 15 minutes, as I had ordered.

At Nkurenkuru, a small fortified base on the river bank opposite Cuangar, I mustered a Commando platoon of part-time soldiers who were performing duty there. They were armed with FN rifles and had a single 81mm mortar. They were somewhat taken aback when I told them grimly that a FAPLA armoured brigade was fighting its way from Katuitui to Rundu and that we were going to stop them. This ridiculous situation became even more ludicrous when I worked out a fire plan for their solitary mortar. Meantime I asked Hans Moller to send me every piece of armour he had available. He rounded up four armoured cars at Rundu and despatched them to me.

While this was going on, Willie had swung eastwards and I religiously plotted his quarter-hourly locstats as they came in. At the same time I was getting regular locstats of the enemy from Sector 20 HQ. It became apparent that they were close on Willie's heels. I emphasised the danger he was facing and instructed him to head for Nkurenkuru as fast as he could.

There, with the Commando platoon of part-time soldiers — some of them on the elderly side — we would together make a glorious last stand and save South West Africa from the invaders.

I contacted Major Brian Reagan and told him to get himself and his anti-tank weapons from his position south of Vila Nova to Nkurenkuru asap. He travelled as fast as he could and when he arrived at Cuangar was hastily ferried across the water. He reported to me with a single RPG7 hand-held rocket launcher. After looking at the weapon dubiously, I briefed him on the situation and ordered him to establish an anti-tank ambush five kilometres up the road towards Katuitui.

He looked at me, then back at his handful of men, in frank disbelief. He left to carry out his task shaking his head at the mysterious ways in which the army moved.

I later found out that the anticipated invasion had caused great consternation in South Africa. The only way to effectively bring considerable force to bear at short notice, it was concluded, was to commit the SAAF's British-built Buccaneer jet bombers. They had the range and the weapons that could at least blunt FAPLA's advance. So the Buccaneers were rolled from their hangars at Waterkloof near Pretoria. They were hurriedly bombed up, their guns were loaded and they were frantically refuelled so a first strike could be launched before nightfall.

I then noticed something peculiar. Each time Willie reported his locstat to me, Sector 20 HQ came back within moments with the identical position for the FAPLA brigade.

'Willie, can you see any FAPLA tanks following you?' I asked.

'Negative', Willie replied.

'Can you hear any FAPLA tanks or vehicles?'

'Negative.'

So that was it!

I asked Rundu where they were getting the information to plot FAPLA's locstat.

'Wait one', replied Hans Moller.

He soon came back.

'The Intelligence Officer says he is monitoring your company's intercepts when it

1. Instructors' Unimog —
M'pupa, Aug 1975.

ortar platoon under
ing on old World War-II
e inch mortars. Platoon
mander, Sgt 'Oupa'
Dyk, in front of mortars
t) — M'pupa, Aug 1975.

3. Commandant Delville Linford,
commander of Battle Group Alpha,
Aug 1975.

4. UNITA control point attempts to halt Battle Group Bravo. Pointing distinguished UNITA fro FNLA (thumbs up) and MPLA (V sign) — Artur Paiva, Oct 1975.

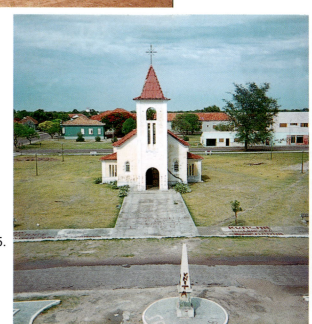

5. Little Cathedral — Pereira de Eça, Oct 1975.

6. Sgt Oupa van Dyk's mo stonking road running sout from the former Portugues Artillery Barracks at Sa da Bandeira — Oct 1975.

19. FNLA leader, Daniel Chipenda, attempts to motivate Bravo Group's FNLA troops north of Lobito. Capt Jack Oppenaar second from right with back to camera and AK47 slung over right shoulder — Oct 1975.

20. Bravo Group's HQ in the 'Pink House' at Novo Redondo — Oct 1975.

21. FAPLA ammunition truck shot out on road to Lobo — October 1975.

22. After lifting mines contrived from enemy shells from a small bridge on the Blue Route to Gabela, Lt Connie van Wyk effects repairs — Oct 1975.

23. G2 140mm artillery pieces sent to Angola by the SADF to combat the enemy's B21 Stalin Organ multiple rocket launcher — Oct 1975.

24. Tony Dippenaar, 'The Surgeon of Cela', at work — Oct 1975.

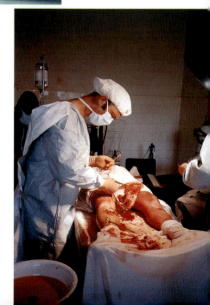

Lt Connie van Wyk's
bush east of
tengue. FAPLA
soners dig graves for
of their less fortunate
mrades — Oct 1975.

14. (L to R) Lt Connie
van Wyk, Sgt Mechie
van der Merwe,
Unknown, Chris
Hillebrandt. Knocked
out FAPLA vehicle
burns in the back-
ground — Oct 1975.

Infantry with armoured
rs in support clear Cubal
Oct 1975.

16. Crowds welcome Battle Group Bravo on i arrival at Lobito. Note FNLA banner and Vickers machine guns – Oct 1975.

17. Battle Group Bravo enters Lobito led by Maj Toon Slabbert's Eland armoured cars — Oct 1975.

18. Lt Connie van Wyk front of FAPLA's HQ in Lobito after its capture. Sgt Robbie Ribeiro is wearing the cowboy ha — Oct 1975.

Paratroopers with Battle
[Gro]up Bravo familiarising
[the]mselves with a captured
[2]0 — Sa da Bandeira, Oct
[19]75.

8. Aircraft shot up during
the attack on Sa da
Bandeira Airport — Oct
1975.

[T]aking on the defiles from
[Sá] de Arriaga to Moçamedes.
[Aut]hor's Land Cruiser is
[imm]ediately in front of this
[veh]icle, fourth from the front of
[the] column — Oct 1975.

10. A FAPLA delaying position clobbered while en route to Moçamedes from Vila de Ariaga. Sgt Mechie van der Merwe's infantry platoon in the background — Oct 1975.

11. Capt Jack Dipenaar's Bravo Company clearing the old airport at Moçamedes — Oct 1975.

12. Lt Connie van Wyk's Alpha Company leaves to secure Porto Alexandre. Note the motley assortment of vehicles — Oct 1975.

37. (Above) Author on operations with Sgt Maj Tony Vieira's platoon north of Beacon 28 in Angola — 1976

38. (Left) After the fight. Troopie of Sgt Maj Tony Vieira's platoon searches body of dead SWAPO guerrilla — 1976.

39. (Below) Recce Wing operators in the Stagger Inn after an operation . (L ro R) Leon Myburgh, Eeben Barlow, Peter Williams and Connie Riekert. Note Peter's Afro wig for disguise purposes.

40. (Left) Capt Eeben Barlow's Recce Wing group. Note the preponderance of machine guns for increased fire power.

41. Butterfly operation. Helicopter deploying fireforce.

42. (Left) Donkeys utilised for logistical purposes — *Operation Forte*.

31. (Above) UNITA forces at the 906km peg on the Benguela Railway. Jonas Savimbi with his hand out and his foot on 906 — 1976.

32. (Left) Bravo Group finally reestablish contact with UNITA. Epelanca (far left) and his men discuss future arrangements with the SADF liaison officer, Commandant Flip du Preez (right) — 1976

33. (Right) UNITA group before they were reequipped by the SADF. Note the variety of weapons, even including a shotgun — 1976.

34. (Left) The troop lines at Buffalo Base before the barracks were constructed — 1976

35. (Right) The Omauni operational base south of Beacons 24 to 35. A flourishing herd of beef cattle was kept at the base and Bushmen, shown in the picture, were hired to look after them. Sgt Maj Piet Nortje is just above the left hand Bushman.

36. (Left) Omauni's pub the Winged Stagger. The milestone was liberated from Ondjiva during *Operation Protea*.

25 & 26. Gunboat of the Porlu-guese Marines abandoned at Vila Nova D'Armada and taken over by Sgt-Maj Willy Ward. (Above) Shown on a supply run to M'pupa. (Left) Alongside at Vila Nova. Willy Ward is on the bridge and Sgt Brian Walls is next to the crane. The rest were from the Engineer Corps who crewed the boat.

27. Sgt Maj Willy Ward's FNLA company at Vila Nova D'Armada. Morning PT.

28. (Left) Sgt Maj Willy Ward and 12 black soldiers captured 13 ex-French Foreign Legion mercenaries and 70 UNITA troops with all their equipment including an armoured car, when they attacked Vila Nova D'Armada. Those with arms are Bravo Group soldiers and the rest are UNITA prisoners. Note the 106mm anti-tank guns etc mounted on the Land-Rovers — 1976.

29. (Right — L to R) Sgt Danny Roxo, Sgt Robbie Ribeiro, Sgt Brian Walls, Cpl Jan van der Merwe and Sgt Sierro. With captured Land-Rover and 106mm anti-tank gun — 1976.

30. (Left) Commandant Sybie van der Spuy's company, posing as FAPLA, on a deep penetration operation within southern Angola — 1976

43. (Right) Some of the FAPLA trucks captured at Savate. Savate can be seen in the background — May 1980.

44. (Left) Soviet-supplied assault bridge captured at Savate — May 1980.

45. (Right) Captured SWAPO under interrogation — *Operation Protea*, August 1981.

46. (Left) Rifle company formed up for kit inspection at Buffalo Base.

47. (Below) March past of 32-Battalion with company banners leading. Capt 'Buttons' Heyns right — Buffalo Base.

48. (Below) Commanders of 32-Battalion. (L to R) (Author) Col Jan Breytenbach, DVR, SD, SM, Brig Gert Nel, SM, Maj-Gen Georg Meiring, SM (Commander SWA Territorial Force), Col Deon Ferreira, Col Eddie Viljoen, HC, SM — Buffalo Base.

reports back to you.'

We then realised it was only a ghost FAPLA brigade that was chasing Willie so relentlessly.

Brian Reagan displayed open relief when I called him back and explained the position. So did the Commandos when I stood them down.

*   *   *

So in October 1976 *Operation Savannah* finally ended for Battle Group Bravo. For the time being there would be no more fighting with FAPLA. Farther west our campaign against SWAPO was already in full swing. After this it would be concentrated in an area north of Owamboland, which would form the focal point of our operations for the remainder of 1976.

FAPLA had succeeded, at least temporarily, in occupying most of Angola and had pushed the last remaining South African forces back into South West Africa.

Our final FAPLA casualty for the year was one of their brigade commanders. His command vehicle detonated a mine that we had planted on the outskirts of Cuangar. To our satisfaction he was blown up while we stood watching on the south bank of the river.

To the west, a weary Jonas Savimbi, a thin Dr Valentino, an aggressive General Chewalle and a few others walked into the arms of a not particularly friendly Bravo Group soldiers patrolling the cutline. The UNITA people had walked, sometimes run, hundreds of kilometres while FAPLA had chased them virtually the whole way. They were almost on their last legs when we found them.

Commandant Flip du Preez took charge and Major Brian Reagan and a handful of my instructors were detached to retrain the few troops that UNITA had left. They were mostly from Epelanca's group and had escaped south to what I was told was Savimbi's secret base in south-east Angola.

When I visited Brian and his men a few weeks later, the 'secret' Angolan base turned out to be the horseshoe lagoon south of the Recce's base at Fort Doppies in the western Caprivi.

20

Guerrilla tactics pay off

Sir Basil Liddell Hart wrote a book called *The Indirect Approach*. It was studied by the likes of German general officers such as Rommel and Guderian who based much of their blitzkrieg strategy on what he had to say about the mechanised lightning strike.

The objective of a blitzkrieg was to totally disrupt enemy forces through deep and concentrated *schwerpunkt* penetrations to capture strategically important targets in the soft tissue well behind the fortified crust of the defending enemy forces. The idea was not to attempt to destroy the enemy in well constructed and tactically situated forward defences but to get deep behind them, cut them off from their supplies and communication infrastructure and disrupt their command and control systems, particularly at the highest levels. The enemy would then become fatally unbalanced, both physically and psychologically. The whole tightly organised structure should theoretically then collapse into chaos.

We saw these results of blitzkrieg in practice on both the German western and eastern fronts during World War-II. Hundreds of thousands of French troops, still well-equipped but fatally demoralised, surrendered en masse in the west and millions of Soviet troops laid down their arms in the east. Whole armies, totally disrupted, capitulated with hardly a shot being fired. Significantly, both the French and Soviet general staffs lost virtually all control over their fighting formations within days of the launch of blitzkrieg.

Of course, when Hitler started to meddle in the conduct of the war, the fruits of Guderian's blitzkrieg withered away in the vast expanses of the Russian steppe and against the inexhaustible industrial power of the Allies — the United States in particular. On a far smaller scale, guerrilla warfare is a different expression of the indirect approach. It is an offensive designed to get the enemy, especially its command structures, off balance physically as well as psychologically.

The SWAPO forces facing Battle Group Bravo — as it was then — and 32-Battalion — as it later became — were far too numerous and well equipped to be tackled head on. Guerrilla warfare provided the only way to wrest the initiative from them. We had to out-guerrilla the SWAPO guerrillas. We had to get them off balance and keep them on the wrong foot until they began to collapse psychologically and subsequently also militarily.

SWAPO began to use the so-called shallow areas 150 to 200km inside Angola. In these areas it established its forward front headquarters and operational bases. Separate headquarters were established for its Eastern, Central and Western fronts.

Dense bush around SWAPO bases provided a friendly and protective environment within which their cadres could safely hide from the interference of South African Security Forces, particularly the South African Air Force. The local population in the heavily forested fringes around the *chanas* close to the bases was forcibly mustered to supply SWAPO with food, water, intelligence and early warning of an approaching enemy. Recruiting was also carried out amongst their number.

It was Battle Group Bravo's intention to turn the southern Angolan bush into a menacing, hostile environment for SWAPO. We also wanted to sever the links between the locals and SWAPO's satellites clustered near their villages.

Our objective was to psychologically undermine SWAPO's command structure. To achieve this we needed to deploy a wide spectrum of psychologically significant tactics. These ranged from setting ambushes at the widely scattered waterholes, footpaths and kraals that helped to provide SWAPO with sustenance; ground attacks and air strikes on their bases; the eventual use of Rhodesian Army-style fireforces when it was finally authorised; and the planting of mines at choke points.

There was also our own version of pseudo operations (as used in Rhodesia by the Selous Scouts) which we used against SWAPO gangs — particularly their contact men within SWA. Fortuitously, we had a great variety of tribesmen in the unit who originated from the areas we operated in, so they could be effectively used in pseudo roles.

We adopted an unusual device to compensate for our lack of men and to substantially increase our combat presence on the ground. We called it an 'automatic ambush.'

Having determined SWAPO's patterns of movement, it was relatively easy to lay ambushes on at least some of the tracks that led south towards Owamboland or north into Angola or on those that laterally connected various SWAPO bases and FAPLA concentrations. The footpath network was far too extensive to interdict with sufficient conventional ambushes to make even a reasonable dent in SWAPO's lines of communication.

The automatic ambush was a deadly device that admirably filled this gap in our combat power. It was perfected by a friend of mine who worked for the CSIR (Council for Scientific and Industrial Research) in Pretoria. It comprised a number of claymore mines, usually four or five, set up so they would spray a killing ground with deadly shrapnel when a wire was tripped by the lead scout in an enemy patrol. It was initially developed by the Americans in the Vietnam war, but its killing capacity was vastly improved by my friend.

At first, using the Vietnam model, kills achieved were disappointingly low — perhaps three kills in a patrol of 20 or 30 guerrillas. My friend then discovered that setting the claymores up in line so they squarely faced the killing ground caused their shockwaves to bounce off one another, creating dead spots (so to speak) where no shrapnel flew.

He changed the positioning of individual claymores and angled them so that the shockwaves generated overlapped sequentially. This eliminated dead spots and covered the whole killing ground with a storm of lethal shrapnel. This was achieved by slanting the face of each mine at between 30° and 45° degrees to the near perimeter of the killing ground. They were also tilted slightly backwards to prevent the lower portion of the shock wave from being tripped by the soil surface and initiating a kind of rolling action that led to the shock wave becoming attenuated before much damage was done.

A claymore is not buried but is set up on a stand above the surface to one or other side of the selected killing ground. The face of the device is packed with pre-cut shrapnel with an explosive layer behind it to drive the shrapnel horizontally into the target area. A line of multiple claymores will, of course, extend the slaughter area, depending on the size of the expected enemy patrol.

Claymores are detonated either with a thin and well concealed tripwire stretched across a footpath or they are command detonated. Tripwire detonated mines, unfortunately, were liable to extract a toll of the local population or their livestock. Consequently, we preferred to command detonate from a safe distance by means of an electrical wire and firing device. This ensured that the victims were SWAPO guerrillas and not civilians — or even one of our own patrols.

Only a two-man team was needed to fire the mines. Sometimes we used more men so that a follow-up could be launched to clean the killing ground immediately after the claymores had been fired and to hunt down injured survivors who had escaped.

In the first contact after our automatic ambush had been perfected, a patrol of about 20 SWAPO walked into a carefully selected killing ground. When most were exposed and vulnerable to the five mines used, the system was command initiated. Eighteen of the 20-man patrol were scythed down by shrapnel and killed. Two escaped but they were probably badly injured.

Our two operators booby-trapped some of the bodies by placing doctored grenades beneath the corpses with the pins pulled. The grenades had their fuses cut sufficiently short to ensure an almost instantaneous explosion. The men also planted anti-personnel mines along the footpath to delay and play havoc with follow-up patrols that SWAPO would surely send to investigate.

Sure enough, a follow-up patrol arrived. A soldier rolled over the body of a dead comrade and exploded a grenade. The blast lifted him off his feet and he returned to earth a few paces away on top of a buried anti-personnel mine. A second blast boosted his gory remains into a tree just above the pathway where an investigating patrol from the nearby platoon found him. SWAPO's follow-up patrol abandoned the mission in panic and fled back to their base in disorder.

We learnt from radio intercepts that our psychological assault, using a wide spectrum of guerrilla techniques to undermine SWAPO's perseverance and stoicism, was beginning to bear fruit. Unnerved, they clamoured to be withdrawn from their so-called Eastern Front and the forward operational bases associated with it. In due course their eastern front became far less active and eventually it was closed down. SWAPO henceforth concentrated their guerrilla base areas on the western and central fronts where, at the time, no Security Forces were operating against them.

But at Task Force 101 and at Sector 10 the penny did not drop. They frankly disbelieved our kill rate, sent in every day via contact reports and sitreps. The rest of the deployed troops within Owambo got no kills from one day to the next.

In due course our successes, particularly in this area, forced SWAPO to spend much of its efforts securing its own backyard, albeit unsuccessfully. It no longer had the time or resources to infiltrate South West Africa from its Eastern Front. Incursions into eastern Owamboland and the western parts of Kavango came to a halt.

If Task Force 101 and Sector 10 HQ had expanded the pseudo concept into areas west of Beacon 25 as far as or beyond Ruacana, the war against SWAPO would have acquired a more positive dimension very early on. They did not, however. Instead of maintaining Battle Group Bravo's pressure against SWAPO north of the Angolan border, they scaled it down — admittedly in response to political pressure. SWAPO was given the opportunity to regain its composure and balance allowing the organisation to regroup and regain the initiative.

SWAPO operatives, of course, learned from their mistakes. Our enforced inactivity gave them the breathing space to redeploy their forward bases into less vulnerable areas. We began to find large SWAPO base establishments tucked under the skirts of fortified FAPLA garrison towns and bases held by reinforced FAPLA brigades.

A new type of war was in the offing. To attack SWAPO it often became necessary to attack FAPLA first. Counter-guerrilla war would eventually escalate into full-blown conventional warfare. This in turn sent our nervous Department of Foreign Affairs scurrying back and forth, usually between Lusaka and Pretoria, in frantic efforts to stabilise the situation. The result was that SWAPO and FAPLA were given the time to regain their equilibrium. It destroyed the fruits of our successful campaigns directed specifically at destabilising their military capacity to wage war.

By October 1976 FAPLA forces, with a tremendous superiority in firepower, were occupying most of the Okavango River line from Cuangar to Mucusso. The maintenance of large and viable garrisons at the end of long and tenuous supply lines was not easy. UNITA, when it again took the field, began to interdict them, causing the garrisons to wither on the vine. FAPLA was forced to evacuate some forward bases within a few months of occupying them. Its forward deployments, however, influenced Battle Group Bravo's future location and led to a name change which, at first, we resisted.

Woodpecker base was about 30km from FAPLA's garrison at Mucusso. This raised fears that FAPLA might attempt a pre-emptive strike against us. To their minds, Battle Group Bravo was not South African but synonymous with Chipenda's FNLA and thus a legitimate target that the outside world would approve.

So we were ordered to shift, yet again, to somewhere out of FAPLA's reach. I was told to seek a new location away from the Okavango River. I was reluctant to move because, in spite of high rainfall, the sandy soil of the Western Caprivi leaves it without perennial water pans or streams, except for the Quando River in the east and the Okavango River in the west. The sources of those rivers are deep inside Angola.

The Quando River region was unacceptable because of security problems, remembering that Battle Group Bravo's existence was still being kept under the wraps of strict secrecy.

I reluctantly investigated a few possibilities, but because of a shortage of water none was acceptable. Finally, to keep Pretoria happy, I moved Battle Group Bravo's fighting element from Woodpecker to a place eight kilometres upstream on the Okavango River. I left the non-combatants at Woodpecker, which afterwards became known as the *Kimbo*. The move actually brought us closer to FAPLA forces at Mucusso, so we dug in and prepared defences just in case they were rude or foolish enough to mount an attack against us across an international border.

The new operational encampment was called 'Buffalo Base'. This, perhaps, led to outsiders nicknaming our fighting men the 'Buffalo Soldiers'.

Most importantly, as far as I was concerned, we still had the beautiful and tranquil Okavango River at our feet.

Task Force 101 HQ staff in far away Grootfontein were pleased at the move because they assumed it had put us out of FAPLA's reach. By the time they discovered we were actually closer than before, the danger had passed. So we stayed on and in time developed Buffalo Base into a showpiece. It was nevertheless shown only to a select few because of the secrecy surrounding our operations.

For the welfare and morale of a unit more or less continuously in combat, it is important that its home base be in pleasant surroundings — somewhere the men could think of as home and regard with pride and affection. Buffalo Base, as developed by myself and subsequent commanding officers, became such a place.

Amenities were primitive in the beginning. The officers'/NCOs' mess was constructed of reeds with a tarpaulin roof. In the pub, whites and blacks rubbed shoulders at sundowner time. It did not look like much, but the atmosphere there was terrific.

A passenger barge was moored a short distance downstream — one of the craft liberated from Cuangar — and provided sleeping accommodation for important guests. The setting was romantic, with the broad Okavango River sliding peacefully beneath the hull on its way to the famous inland delta and swamps in Botswana. Hippos snorted and grunted nearby and elephants trumpeted on the bank when they came down to drink and splash in the shallows. Some years later the barge broke free from its moorings and drifted downstream into Botswana where it was salvaged at Shakawe by a safari company and used as tourist accommodation.

Junior leaders were responsible for building their own accommodation, which they did with commendable ingenuity. They became known as 'sparrow nests' because of their reed and canvas construction. They were occasionally the focus of unwelcome attention by hippos and elephants. One such sparrow nest was destroyed when Herby, a resident irascible bull hippo, chased Harry, the unit's dog, through the narrow doorway and brought the whole lot down around him.

This incident persuaded Staff Sergeant FL Smit to build his nest in the boughs of a huge tree where it was safe from hippos and clear of the searching trunks of inquisitive elephants. It was laborious work because first a platform had to be made, then all material needed for the construction had to be hoisted up by rope. FL had just finished his nest when Commandant Gert Nel, who had just taken over as acting unit commander, decided that it had to go. It was too far removed from the others — and besides FL had not asked permission before he built his nest in a tree like a real sparrow. It was also true that the structure was somewhat untidy and not neat and military-like. FL objected strenuously to its destruction and continued to occupy his nest in disregard of authority. Gert refused to tolerate this and ordered the tree felled. A power saw was deployed and quickly did the job. FL's pride and joy was smashed into matchwood while he looked on in sorrow, not daring to protest.

At the same time as it changed location to Buffalo Base, Battle Group Bravo was ordered to change its name. Radio Luanda had mounted a propaganda campaign against Bravo and its 'FNLA mercenaries'. They called them *Les Affreux* — The Terrible Ones — a derogatory term originally applied to white mercenary forces in the Congo in the 1960s. The broadcasts maintained that Bravo was manned by treacherous Angolans recruited by a notorious American mercenary named Colonel Carpenter (who, in fact, was me).

Commandant Delville Linford's Bushman Battalion at Omega Base in the Caprivi got similar treatment at the hands of MPLA.

The time was ripe for changes to our image.

Delville and I reluctantly decided on new designations. Battle Group Alpha would become 31-Battalion and Battle Group Bravo would henceforth be known as 32-Battalion.

Both units were renowned for their combat efficiency and for being perpetual thorns in FAPLA's flesh. We were proud that the enemy was so discomfited about the threat we posed that it had launched a special propaganda campaign to discredit us.

32-Battalion would eventually become an even greater and more terrifying menace to FAPLA and SWAPO than Battle Group Bravo had been.

Later, during 1976, the Chief of the Army, General Magnus Malan, visited Buffalo Base. I confronted him with the thorny issue regarding the future 32-Battalion's black troops. They were not, after all, white South Africans but black Angolans. There were no black combat troops in the South African Army because it was unacceptable to the ruling National Party's political constituency. 31-Battalion, being comprised of Bushmen, posed no threat to South Africa's policy of white supremacy, so it did not fall into the same category.

I briefed the general on the unit's history, its achievements and on the ongoing cross-border deployments into Angola that were keeping SWAPO away from South West Africa. I pointed out that if they and their families had to return to Angola one day, it would be a highly dangerous exercise as both FAPLA and UNITA would be gunning for them.

'What are we going to do with the unit if South Africa ever decides to leave South West Africa?' I asked.

'What do you suggest?' the general asked.

'We should enrol them in the South African Army', I answered. 'As Angolans they would be the ideal troops to infiltrate deep into SWAPO and FAPLA territory — a no-go area for our regular South African forces'.

The implication was that as part of the army they would accompany the rest of it to

South Africa if the SADF should withdraw from a newly independent Namibia. A discussion followed about how this could be achieved without raising the hackles of the National Party with its policy of apartheid, since nothing like it had been done before. It meant absorbing a foreign legion, which is what they were — and a black one at that — into our virtually lily-white armed forces. The discussion ended with the general giving me an unequivocal undertaking that 32-Battalion, as a unit, would be absorbed and become an integral part of the South African Army. I asked him if I could inform the troops accordingly and he replied in the affirmative.

The next day I called a battalion parade to announce the general's decision. I wanted to remove any fears of an uncertain future from their minds. The troops were ecstatic. At last they had a permanent home. With the assistance of a special team commanded by Commodore van Achterberg from the Chief of Staff Personnel, the usual paperwork to enrol them in the South African Army was completed. This officially transformed the unit into 32-Battalion, a name they had been using for a while. A process was urgently set in motion to house and equip the battalion's soldiers to a reasonable standard which, because of financial constraints, was still below that of other army units.

In 1977 I attended a Command and Staff course and my second-in-command, Commandant Gert Nel, acted as commander. During my absence Prime Minister John Vorster, Minister of Defence PW Botha and General Magnus Malan visited the unit. Gert wisely confronted Vorster, telling him that General Malan had already approved the amalgamation of 32-Battalion into the SADF. Vorster and Botha both agreed with Malan's decision. PW Botha, after he became State President, repeated the promise.

*   *   *

In the west and to the north of Owamboland within Angola, 32-Battalion platoons were deployed independently to operate against SWAPO. The situation gradually began to change in favour of the Security Forces.

An operational philosophy had been developed to cope with the extensive SWAPO deployments and supporting infrastructures in place in the south of Cunene Province. During *Operation Savannah*, SWAPO forces deployed just north of the cutline had gone to ground. They had been closely associated with UNITA which gave them material support in the way of rations and, most importantly, adequate areas for guerrilla bases from where they could mount incursions into Owamboland. It will be remembered that UNITA and SWAPO units operating in Cunene Province had the same tribal affiliations. Their support, in the main, came from the warlike Kwanyamas. Blood, as they say, is thicker than water. The policies of both organisations were Marxist, which was another reason for their friendship.

Things changed after *Operation Savannah*, however, when SWAPO sought support from the MPLA and turned against its erstwhile UNITA friends. It will also be appreciated that UNITA's newest ally was South Africa, which placed their old alliance under impossible pressure. There were many armed confrontations between the two organisations and UNITA became the recipient of several serious hidings.

After the South African withdrawal and with the new alliance with FAPLA giving it military protection, SWAPO was well placed to build up its forces just across the Owamboland border in Angola. In Portuguese days its cadres had no option but to trek thousands of energy-sapping kilometres from Zambia through Portuguese controlled areas across the breadth of Angola to get to jump-off positions in the south of Cunene Province. Negotiating obstacles like that made it difficult for them to pose a serious military threat to South West Africa.

After the precipitate departure of the Portuguese and the wind-down of *Operation*

Savannah, though, the bush to the north of the cutline was soon swarming with SWAPO insurgents. It was estimated that in the shallow area north of Beacons 22 to 34, there were some 52 SWAPO forward operational bases.

Task Force 101 decided that action had to be taken to reduce SWAPO's presence in Owamboland. More battalions were brought from South Africa to boost the Security Forces already deployed. They were to be used to track down and kill large numbers of insurgents. It followed, however, that there was little purpose in eliminating the enemy on the SWA side if no attempt was made to turn off the tap in Angola.

Our job was to track SWAPO down and destroy its safe bases in Angola, beginning with the shallow areas. There were, however, serious international political implications. With the controversial *Operation Savannah* having just been put to bed, it would have been folly for substantial numbers of South African forces to cross openly into Angola to thump SWAPO. The national and international outcry would have been deafening.

It was only at that stage that the SADF woke up to the valuable contribution that 32-Battalion could make. From being a bloody nuisance and an unsatisfactory tool for solving the chronic refugee problem, 32-Battalion became virtually overnight Task Force 101's solution. The brown-eyed Angolan darkies had suddenly become the blue-eyed boys.

We could cross the border without raising an outcry because we had an advantage that no other South African forces possessed — except for the Recces for different reasons. Our troops were black Angolans. They could fade into the landscape without anyone thinking anything was amiss. If they were captured, who could say they were South Africans — particularly if it was denied.

We lacked firepower, however. We only had AK47s, a few magnificent 7.62mm FN GPMGs or MAGs (general purpose machine guns or medium automatic guns) and a few 30-calibre Brownings that we had snaffled from other units. SWAPO, on the other hand, had a profusion of RPD light machine guns, PKM machine guns, RPG-7 hand-held rocket launchers, 60mm and 82mm mortars, 122mm Stalin Organs with multiple rocket tubes, 14.5mm anti-aircraft guns, 12.7mm heavy machine guns, plus B10 and 75mm anti-tank guns.

We soon discovered that the stopping power of the much vaunted AK47 was mediocre. We joked that it was not its killing power but the sheer weight of lead that brought the enemy down. Insurgents often escaped into thick cover, despite being peppered with bullet holes, which made it difficult to find the body to claim a kill. Fortunately, we were permitted to replace our captured AK47s with R1 rifles. The R1 is powerful enough to kill someone sheltering behind a substantial tree, or bring down a quarry at long range with a single well-placed shot.

To make good our firepower deficiencies, we retained all captured weapons. This was against standing orders which laid down that all captured equipment should be sent to Grootfontein. Keeping the stuff, however, allowed us to build up our arsenal — especially by the way of machine guns and RPG-7 rocket launchers. Despite this, we never matched SWAPO's superiority in firepower. This profoundly affected our tactics. We could not always expect to come off best in face-to-face confrontations with SWAPO forces, since they were invariably better armed than we were.

Another problem we faced was that we got virtually no support from Sector 10 under whose control fighting within Owamboland and north of the border in Angola fell. No helicopters were made available to us, not even for casevacs, let alone for logistical or gunship support. The Air Force was forbidden to operate north of the border after *Operation Savannah*. Neither could we call for assistance from conventional ground forces like armoured cars or infantry because the South African Army was also restricted to Owamboland.

The truth was that we were on our own.

Our internal logistical support was barely adequate at best and at worst, non-existent. Heroic efforts were made to keep platoons deployed in Angola well supplied, but getting ground transport through to them was always a battle. We had insufficient troops to swamp SWAPO's guerrilla bases and a shortage of junior leaders, particularly platoon and company commanders, to lead the troops we had.

It was this that led us to adopt guerrilla tactics which called for a small but exceptionally well-led and well-trained force.

Our task, as we saw it, was to harass and wear SWAPO down, destroy its infrastructure and terrify its troops. In their own home base areas we needed to disperse them into small groups which would slow their advance into South West Africa. We had to get them off balance, take away the initiative and act as the spoiler in their attempts to overrun Owamboland. Whether Task Force 101 saw it in the same light is debatable.

My friendship with Colonel Carl van Rooyen prompted him to divert many promising officers who reported to Task Force 101 Headquarters to 32-Battalion. He was acutely aware of our desperate needs. Although he never said as much to me personally, I believe he was also unobtrusively trying to upgrade our somewhat slack and unorthodox administration — a feature of 32-Battalion's HQ. His concern accounted for many unexpected arrivals at our humble headquarters.

Sergeant Major Carl Roza joined us and took over what we grandly termed our 'personnel office' — which was no office at all but a shared desk. Soldiers without records who had been floating around for ages were finally brought on strength. Men no longer died without somebody officially knowing about it. The unit, for the first time, was properly mustered into sections, platoons and companies. Best of all, the men got their first pay — a princely ten rand a month, plus back pay. They thought they were in heaven — until the next month's pay day.

Major Eddie Viljoen, then the commander of Rustenburg Commando, arrived from Grootfontein. Carl had given him the express mission of sorting out Battle Group Bravo's administration. I looked him up and down and heard from his own lips Carl's desires, or rather forlorn hopes. Then I crammed Eddie into the hot and cramped operations room which he shared with the intelligence officer, the ops logistics officer, their staffs, a bunch of signallers, Sergeant Major Roza and very occasionally, myself.

Within a few days order had been created where none had existed before. Maps were updated, logs were properly kept and, best of all, Carl was getting all important sitreps (situation reports) promptly and regularly at Task Force 101 HQ.

We would fight on foot rather than from vehicles, because a vital element in a guerrilla's armour is the exploitation of surprise. Without the element of surprise 32-Battalion would likely be slaughtered, an awful truth we had to face on more than one occasion.

First we needed an operational base closer to Owamboland than Rundu, which was too far to the east. From Rundu we could not exercise proper control or provide combat backup by way of reserves and adequate logistical support. The distances were too great.

I wangled the base at Omauni, just east of the Owambo-Kavango border, from Sector 10 HQ. From there we would conduct operations in the area north of Beacons 24 to 35. At the time, Omauni was garrisoned by a commando company from Namaqualand and a troop of mounted infantry.

Eddie Viljoen pestered me to deploy him on operations. I held out for a long time because he was a star in the operations room. His chance came with our takeover of Omauni — I had nobody else available who could take charge of the new operational commitments. So reluctantly, I let him go to Omauni from where he commanded operations in Owambo and in Angola north of the Owamboland cutline — the boundary with the Cunene province of Angola — an area under the total domination of SWAPO. This left me free to busy myself with operations against FAPLA in Cuando Cubango Province.

After that Eddie served mostly in an operational capacity. He left the unit for a short while to become properly educated as a soldier at our senior training institution. Then he had to go through the mill by serving as a commando group commander — a procedure conceived by some bright senior officers in Pretoria who considered it a mental aberration for a soldier to actually like facing lead, sleeping rough and eating bully beef.

He eventually returned and became 32-Battalion's most effective and best known commanding officer. In later years people rarely spoke of 32-Battalion without mentioning Colonel Eddie Viljoen — as he later became — in the same breath.

The word having been given, Eddie made ready to occupy the base the moment the commandos and horse soldiers pulled out and before Sector 10 could change its mind. He wanted to be on the spot to stop the outgoing tenants from removing vital base equipment like generators, deep freezers, refrigerators and so on, as well as operational hardware like radios — maybe even crew-served weapons such as machine guns and mortars. I told Eddie to treat the exercise as a means of substantially adding to our equipment inventory. He succeeded beyond all expectations. The mounted infantry even left some of their horses behind for those of us who indulged in equestrian activities.

Eddie Viljoen stamped his personality on Omauni in more ways than one. New arrivals in the operational area, freshly posted to 32-Battalion from South Africa, were always ambushed on their first trip there by road. In those days the road beyond Mpungu Vlei was a mere sand track, ideal for laying a terrifying ambush with mines, claymores and whatever other goodies were available to create ear-shattering bangs. Sometimes the victim would be faced with a super-boosted mine that exploded in clouds of dust, smoke and flames virtually beneath the vehicle and with sufficient force to preempt an immediate heart attack.

The shock was invariably aggravated tenfold when the newcomer was suddenly confronted by a mob of camouflage-clad black troops wielding AK47s, all laughing uproariously at his terror and discomfiture. It normally took a while before the victim realised he had been on the receiving end of an elaborate prank and that his last day at the hands of SWAPO or FAPLA had not yet arrived.

Eddie did not restrict his practical jokes only to 32-Battalion. Sometimes he caught out others, often officers more senior than he was. This often resulted in the discomfort of 32-Battalion's OC who had to field the comeback.

On one occasion a group of senior Air Force officers visiting Omauni saw a black soldier screaming abjectly in terror as he was being roped to a tree. The officers watched in amazement and disbelief as a section of troops marched out and formed up in extended line with rifles at the ready.

'Fire!' an NCO bawled.

Shots rang out, the screaming ceased abruptly and the soldier slumped apparently lifeless within the coils of rope that bound his blood-soaked body to the tree.

The officers could scarcely believe the evidence of their eyes as the drama unfolded in front of them. Sure, they had heard about the iron discipline in 32-Battalion, but this was beyond the pale. While the 'execution' was going on Eddie Viljoen chatted nonchalantly to them about the state of the airstrip only 100 metres away from the scene. He did not even pause when the shots rang out.

'Major', an officer interrupted Eddie shakily, 'what's going on?'

He pointed to an open Land-Rover into which the blood-smeared body was being unceremoniously dumped by the 'executioners'.

'Oh, that', Eddie answered nonchalantly. 'It's just a troopie we had to execute.'

'Yes, but how can you shoot a man just like that? What's he done that's so terrible?'

'He's a bloody thief, that's what he is', snapped Eddie. 'In accordance with our disciplinary code, thieves are shot after being found guilty.'

'But what did he steal that merited a sentence of death?'

'He pinched a chicken from the pantry', Eddie replied blandly.

The senior officers suddenly found an urgent need to cut short their visit. They walked hurriedly to their twin-engine Aztec. It was obvious they doubted Eddie's sanity and had no wish to spend further time in his company.

A few days later the Aztec returned unexpectedly, this time with an angry Major-General Ian Gleeson aboard. He confronted Eddie.

'Where is your mass grave?' he asked bluntly.

Eddie was caught off guard. He genuinely had no idea what the general was talking about.

'What mass grave, sir?'

'Don't pretend you don't know. The one in which you toss the bodies of the men you execute. I can smell it from here.'

The wind was blowing from the rubbish pits beyond the buttressed embankment and there was indeed a faint smell of decay hanging in the air. Eddie suddenly clicked as to what the general was on about. He hurriedly explained that the episode was an elaborate hoax staged for the amusement of himself and his men.

'I'll only believe it if you produce the troopie, hale and hearty . . . right here and now', the general ordered.

This put Eddie in a tight spot. By coincidence, that same soldier had been killed in a contact the day before. It was a joke that took a lot of explaining before the general was finally satisfied.

Major *Oom* (Uncle) Hannes, a wine farmer from Boland in the Cape, was a rough diamond if ever there was one. He was also in charge of Omauni for a time and in spite of his advancing years, he was forever threatening to head north into Angola to sort out SWAPO. Oom Hannes donated a couple of stud bulls to improve our expanding herd of beef cattle at Omauni.

The story goes that after I had left 32-Battalion, Oom Hannes attended a formal military function in Rundu at which the then Minister of Defence, PW Botha, was the guest of honour. He knew the minister personally, but as a relatively lowly member of one of the dozen or so South African fighting units at the border, he was allotted a chair well below the salt — probably at one of those detached tables deep in the shadows where juniors were expected to maintain a low profile and behave themselves. This, however, did not bother Oom Hannes. He simply picked up his chair and humped it over to the Minister's table where he squeezed himself in at PW's right hand. He then lectured PW in forthright farmer fashion, no holds barred, on how the war should be fought — much to the consternation of the phalanx of almost purple-faced generals, brigadiers and colonels. After airing his views, he coolly picked up his chair and lugged it back to his proper place among the military minnows.

Commandant Jan Martins, OC of Fouriesburg Commando, was another who left his Free State farm and headed north to become the commander of Omauni. He returned for several more spells. Major Koos Verster, too, served more than his allotted time at Omauni while his wife kept the home fires burning.

The rifle platoons deployed in Angola from Omauni varied between six and seven in number with two or three more in base as a reserve. Sometimes we mustered as many as ten platoons on deployment, particularly after operations in the Cuando Cubango came to an end.

Generally, the operational area of a platoon was ten kilometres wide from east to west between two cutline beacons, and extended as far north into Angola as they could penetrate on foot. A one kilometre wide strip known as the Yati, just south of the cutline, was included in those areas of operation. This gave the platoons a buffer of home territory where they could be replenished, cache equipment they could not carry and, theoretically, fall back into the comforting arms of backup troops when superior SWAPO forces were chasing them.

The Yati strip was a depopulated no-go area cleared of bush within which the Security Forces could engage SWAPO without the danger of civilians being caught in the crossfire. It was easier also, in the absence of civilian tracks, to pick up SWAPO spoor there. But the spoor of locals often confused trackers, especially when, as sometimes happened, civilian traffic was deliberately used as a counter-tracking measure.

The sandy soil made tracking easy, but conversely it made counter-tracking extremely difficult. To survive, we needed skills and cool heads not often found in city-bred youngsters. The 32-Battalion platoons invariably operated in areas where they were heavily outnumbered by resident SWAPO gangs. This gave them two problems — how to survive and how to achieve enough kills to make the effort cost-effective.

To achieve enemy kills — which, of course, is the objective of war — under these circumstances meant adopting the more subtle attitude of a stalker, rather than the bludgeoning approach of a mechanised army. Familiarity with the terrain at least on par with the SWAPO groups was vital. The painstaking gathering of local tactical information through careful patrolling and patient observation-post work was another important aspect.

Interrogating the local population north of the border, amongst whom SWAPO lived, almost certainly meant compromising one's own presence and location. Although extremely risky, there was sometimes no option. This often resulted in a violent punch-up with superior SWAPO forces — unless the platoon leader got in first by mounting a rapid attack to exploit hot information just gained.

The black troops of 32-Battalion fitted into this style of warfare as if born to it. Many were experienced guerrillas anyway, having operated against Portuguese forces, sometimes as far back as 1961.

The white platoon leaders, though, had to undergo a complete change of military outlook. They had to accept that they would be operating in a hostile environment with the hands of everybody, from SWAPO guerrillas to the local population, turned against them. They learned to cope with severe extremes of temperature — soul-scorching heat by day and bitter cold at night — thick bush, mopane flies, lack of water, and poor food with little of it for sometimes three months at a time. It was hard becoming accustomed to the idea that the nearest military assistance was several hundred kilometres away. There was also the sobering fact that neither they nor their men could expect prompt evacuation or even reasonable medical support if they were wounded. Worst of all was the constant tension under which they operated both by day and by night. It stretched nerves to breaking point for months on end. A violent contact with SWAPO came almost as a relief.

I ensured that the black platoon sergeants allocated to these platoons were the best in the unit. I drummed into the fledgling second lieutenants and corporals, whom we made temporary sergeants, that they must rely completely on their black NCOs. Consequently, if there was a clash of personalities, it was the platoon leader and not the black platoon sergeant who found himself replaced. In most cases, though, the two became a formidable team. Interpersonal relationships between the platoon leaders, the platoon sergeants and the men in the platoons were often so good that the transfer of a platoon leader sparked a near mutiny.

It was here, I believe, that the unit's unique bonding began to form. It matured into an abstract, almost spiritual concept of camaraderie never before seen in the SADF.

Platoons were welded into tough and formidable teams. Each man fitted perfectly into his own specific slot. Everyone supported everybody else. Weaknesses were ironed out and strong points were made unassailable. Steely bonds were forged under operational conditions.

Some platoon leaders eventually became company commanders, able to effectively plough back the experience they had gained in the field. Lieutenant Des Burman, who probably attained the most kills amongst the platoon leaders, was one of them. He served in the unit for several years before leaving for pastures greener although, no doubt, not nearly as rewarding.

Another was Lieutenant Gerhard Keulder, killed in action in Angola. There had been a close relationship between Gerhard and his platoon. They carried his body for days on end all the way back to the cutline while engaged in a running fight with SWAPO. They refused to abandon their leader in a hastily dug hole deep inside Angola. It was not his country, the platoon said. They would bury him in his own country come hell or high water— and they did. It was a sign of their devotion to him.

Sergeant Rademeyer was another much-loved platoon leader. He was wounded in the stomach during an attack and went down in agony, unable to continue leading the assault. His troops, ignoring the intense SWAPO fire, bunched around him in an exposed group, loudly lamenting the sergeant's misfortune. Rademeyer summoned up sufficient strength to berate his troops for not continuing the assault. So they did, furiously attacking the superior enemy force and putting them to flight. They also carried him all the way back to the cutline.

There were others, like Lieutenant John Taylor — a knife fighter par excellence — and Lieutenant Daan de la Rey who many years later lost both his arms in a training accident. There was Sergeant 'Blue' Kelly and Staff Sergeant Mike Rogers — both Australians, Lieutenant Griesel, Lieutenant Piet Botes — an aggressive paratrooper, Lieutenant Koos Sadle, Captain Jumbo Lotter, Lieutenant Groenewald, Sergeant Major Tony Vieira, Petrus Johannes 'Piet Boer' van Zyl — a farmer from Dundee in Natal, Sam Heap — son of a good friend, and many more.

Lieutenant Herman Fourie started off as a temporary sergeant but was summarily commissioned on the battlefield by me, to the consternation of the personnel section of the South African Army. It took a lot of angry signals and many years of resentful paper manoeuvring to sort out the administration of that promotion.

There was a minority who were not so good.

A Sergeant Major in neatly pressed uniform, shiny boots, and with a soldier-like bearing that would have been the envy of RSM Britten — the legendary RSM of Britain's Brigade of Guards — arrived at the unit. He halted in front of me, his back ramrod straight. His boots crashed to attention and he gave an impeccable salute. His pace stick was tucked firmly beneath his left armpit and his fingers pointed straight along the head with his left thumb clamped on the inside in regulation manner. He barked out that he was reporting for duty as RSM. Unfortunately for him, I already had one — the best in the army, in fact — but I thought the new fellow could be utilised to iron out the generally unsoldierlike bearing of the Omauni detachment in particular.

We wore a great variety of fatigues, combat boots and forage hats. The headgear probably represented half the armies and uniformed terrorist organisations in the world. Salutes varied from the boy scout two finger variety to fond little waves, usually accompanied by friendly inane smiles. Yes, the unit could definitely be sharpened up. I sent the new RSM to Omauni to assist its base commander in instilling some military discipline. He quickly contrived to be sent on operations because that was why, according to him, he had come to the border in the first place.

Two or three weeks later he was found by Commandant Jan Martins, the base commander, reclining on a stretcher beneath a shady tree. He made his troops carry him around on the stretcher, wearing only his underpants and surrounded by the luxuries of life normally found only in the home base at which he had been so reluctant to serve. He had remained static for at least a week, sending off new and continuously shifting locstats (present location coordinates) to his base in Omauni, creating the impression that he was energetically patrolling the area of SWAPO-infested Angola allotted to him.

Within 24 hours he was aboard a C130 transport on his way back to South Africa, indignant at his summary dismissal and the highly unorthodox way that he, as a senior warrant officer, had been treated. There was no way I was going to waste my time and that of others on a preliminary investigation leading, perhaps, to a court martial.

The normal procedure when despatching a platoon on patrol was to take them by vehicle and deposit them in the Yati strip at the southern end of their allotted sector. They were fully equipped for at least two weeks. They would wait for the vehicles to leave, then move away as fast as possible from the drop-off point, backtracking carefully as they went, to escape detection by SWAPO. They would establish a cache, sometimes in the Yati strip or just across the border in Angola, bury the bulk of their supplies and protect the site with anti-personnel mines which they would carefully plot. It was a fixed drill that those who laid the mines were the ones who lifted them when they returned to a cache for resupply.

To avoid the establishment of a routine that might be noted by the enemy, caches were shifted to different locations after a resupply. Counter-tracking in the vicinity of caches was insisted upon and carefully carried out to prevent SWAPO from lifting supplies for their own use or adding their own mines to our devil's garden. The platoons moved stealthily, usually at night, avoiding foot paths and the notice of the locals, into areas where SWAPO was believed to have bases.

The waterless terrain made the finding of SWAPO bases fairly easy because it confined them to obvious locations. The sandy ground was overgrown with thick bush and often very thick scrub, with a few *chanas* scattered around the area. A *chana* is a shallow, saucer shaped indentation, sometimes of considerable size, with a black turf surface and a thick grass cover. Water is usually found within or at the edges of *chanas*, sometimes in wells or in small open pans. The *chanas* are the focal points of subsistence agriculture and often supported a whole string of Kwanyama villages as well as adjacent SWAPO bases.

Locals were employed by SWAPO as their eyes and ears. Their task was to report all suspicious signs, movements or strange spoor to the local SWAPO commander. They usually communicated by sending fast-running youngsters, known as mujibas, to the nearest SWAPO base. I soon learnt that when one spotted a lad disappearing at speed into the bush, he would invariably return with a force of the local SWAPO.

When a platoon moved into an area, it established a hide and sent out small patrols to carry out a surreptitious reconnaissance. The best place to look for SWAPO spoor was at the waterholes. The locals, of course, used the holes for domestic and stock farming purposes. When checking for signs of SWAPO it was vital that the patrols eliminate signs of their own presence. They used tricks like going barefoot, wearing SWAPO-style boots if they had any and using cattle to obliterate their spoor. In the rainy season, frequent storms washed away spoor and other signs of a patrol's presence. Sometimes they laid up near waterholes and laid ambushes. They might watch for many days on end without going near the waterholes, because that would have betrayed their presence to sharp-eyed locals — especially the youngsters.

SWAPO tended to congregate in the local kraals. Sometimes a fresh spoor was picked up that led our patrols straight to them. Kraals were high on the list of places kept under observation. They frequently became the focal points around which anti-SWAPO operations were launched. SWAPO, of course, also had to move, but in Angola they were far less concerned about hiding their spoor than we were. They regarded Angola as their own well-secured stamping ground where they could move about freely. We were the intruders and not them. Sometimes their movements between bases and their routes in and out of Angola created wide and well-used tracks through the bush — liberally endorsed with the chevron patterned spoor of SWAPO boots. In the circumstances, the platoon had the choice of following the tracks or backtracking to where it started at a SWAPO base. Despite this, they had to exercise extreme care, as they invariably had to deal with SWAPO's early-warning posts. Alternatively, they could mine or ambush the track in relative safety.

In the early days a contact generally led to enemy groups in neighbouring bases deploying to locate and attack the offending platoons. This often resulted in skirmishes and running fights that lasted for days. The platoons mostly got the upper hand, although sometimes their survival was balanced on a knife edge. There were times when platoons were down to their last few rounds before a neighbouring formation came to their rescue. It was for this reason that platoons on deployment always maintained lateral communications with each other. When a contact was sprung, as indicated by a sudden outbreak of rifle, machine-gun and mortar fire, the flanking units always maintained a radio watch so they could go to their neighbour's assistance if the situation turned sour. This drill saved many platoons from being wiped out by superior SWAPO forces.

The guerrilla war developed into a battle of wits between 32-Battalion platoon leaders and SWAPO detachment commanders. Our young platoon leaders, however, almost always managed to outwit the supposedly battle-hardened and veteran SWAPO guerrilla commanders who had literally grown up in the bush. They had also received many years of intensive training at the hands of their Soviet, East German and Cuban instructors.

No matter how hard they tried, SWAPO never found a way to combat the havoc caused by our platoons. They tried to move in larger bodies for greater protection, but this only presented us with bigger targets. They even attempted to counter-attack on horseback, which certainly took us by surprise. Horses, however, present a larger target than a foot soldier, so sadly the horses bore the brunt of our return fire. They tried splitting their men into smaller patrols in the hope of escaping attention, but this made them even more vulnerable and we simply overwhelmed them.

Eventually, but only much later, SWAPO adopted the only other policy left. That was to operate in battalion-sized formations, but this made them succulent targets for our own semi-conventional forces. This particularly applied to a new concept known as 'butterfly operations'. It was introduced to the counter-insurgency war after on-the-job experiments by 32-Battalion plus gunship and Puma pilots.

SWAPO were in trouble, so they withdrew northwards. This took them away from the shallow areas north of the cutline, making it difficult for them to infiltrate Owamboland which is what the fighting was all about. It also meant they had to hump all their equipment on their backs through the hot and dry bush for greater distances than before.

As SWAPO withdrew we followed them, enlarging the area of Angola under SADF control. This created an even deeper gauntlet that they had to run to reach and infiltrate SWA and within which 32-Battalion had more freedom of movement and many more opportunities to maul them. This in turn gave the Security Forces within Owamboland more time to concentrate resources on picking them up before they could disappear among the locals.

Yet only the areas north of Beacons 25 to 35 were the focus of our operations. SWAPO could still infiltrate central Owamboland to the west with relative impunity. The terrain there was more open, which theoretically gave other units operating there a better chance to pick up enemy groups. The central Owamboland tribes were also less supportive of SWAPO than the Kwanyamas farther east.

We were very thin on the ground even when we began to operate between Beacons 25 and 35. We were still deploying troops against FAPLA in the east, especially in the Cuando Cubango, in an effort to create a breathing space for UNITA. There were no men to spare to increase our presence either westwards or deeper into Angola's

Cunene Province.

With hindsight, Delville Linford's Bushmen of 31-Battalion should have been deployed north of the cutline, perhaps between Beacons 23 and 35, allowing us to move farther west to cover the sector east from Ruacana Falls to Beacon 23. I had, in fact, carried out a recce by chopper over the area west of Ruacana and south of the Cunene to select a forward base for just such an eventuality, but nothing came of it.

Unfortunately, our more conventional Security Forces did not, at first, rise to the challenge. When some years later the police Koevoet counter-insurgency organisation appeared on the scene, everything changed. Within SWA Koevoet efficiently hunted down infiltrating SWAPO terrorists so that very few of them got as far south as the white farming belt; while in Angola 32-Battalion was dominating vast tracts of Angola formerly under SWAPO control. It was the ideal recipe for combatting SWAPO gangs both north and south of the border.

With the launching of such unorthodox operations, successes became almost embarrassingly easy. Successive conventionally-minded commanders of Sector 10, however, lacked the perception to latch on to this philosophy. Acrimonious recriminations designed to minimise Koevoet's successes finally caused co-operation between the South African Police and the Army to collapse. This was particularly during the time of a certain army brigadier nicknamed 'Brigadier' Danger. He turned out to be far more dangerous to our Security Forces than he was to the enemy.

There was much bloodletting as 32-Battalion and SWAPO hammered away at each other in almost daily contacts deep in the Angolan bush. Fortunately for us, most of the blood spilled was SWAPO's. To paraphrase General George Patton: 'Why should you die for your cause if you can let some other bastard die for his?'

Well, a lot of SWAPO died for their cause.

Lieutenant Des Burman led his platoon into a suspected SWAPO area in the Omalapapa area north of Beacon 28 where he found spoor leading to a kraal. Soon three or four SWAPO were seen to approach and enter it. They did not reappear.

Des deployed some of his platoon under Sergeant Eduardo into the *muhango* and mealies by the narrow entrance to the kraal and moved in from the rear with the rest. An Owambo kraal is surrounded by a dense stockade within which there is a maze of enclosures with living areas, cattle pens, cooking areas and so on. They carefully removed poles at the rear, slipped inside and moved from enclosure to enclosure.

Des noticed smoke rising above the cooking area and he heard voices. He peeked through a gap and saw a group of SWAPO and locals dining from a communal pot and engaging in friendly conversation. He pushed down some poles and unceremoniously burst in. The diners took to their heels and fled, joined by others elsewhere in the kraal. One SWAPO was in bed with a woman. A soldier grabbed the terrorist's own AK47 and unsportingly shot him at a most inappropriate moment.

Shots pursued the cadres as they bolted for the exit, trampling each other in an effort to escape from the fiends in pursuit. They were greeted outside by Sergeant Eduardo and his men who cut them down as they popped through the narrow entrance. By the end of the contact, eight SWAPO were dead and others were badly wounded. Only a few managed to escape.

We experienced many problems operating in enemy-dominated areas that were far from combat service support forces. Platoons were re-supplied by Unimog from Omauni on a fortnightly basis. This often placed convoys in dangerous situations, for supplies had to be dropped at positions near the cutline that were within easy reach of SWAPO reaction forces. The cutline and the Yati up to its southern boundary were both cleared of bush, so they made ideal killing grounds not only for us but also for SWAPO lying in ambush. The mining of both areas was also not difficult for SWAPO.

The border road, affectionately known as Oom Willie se pad (Uncle Willie's road), which ran east to west between five and ten kilometres south of the cutline, was mined regularly. It became so bad that driving a vehicle along it was tantamount to committing suicide. It became the longest, densest and narrowest minefield in that part of Africa. Some members of the Security Forces refused to learn from the mistakes of others and used the road with reckless abandonment. This resulted in proliferating burnt-out wrecks of Hippo mine-protected vehicles every few kilometres between Nkongo and Eenhana. Reaching the deployment areas from Omauni meant avoiding Oom Willie se pad like the plague. The alternative involved long stretches of bundu-bashing through thick bush from the point where convoys bisected the north-south cutline between Owamboland and the Kavango.

The stalwart Unimogs took the bush in their stride, although their good looks got extensively dented. Rearview mirrors were torn off, rear flaps fell off, fenders and mudguards were crumpled and battery mountings were ripped away, but the bush failed to tame them mechanically. We removed the doors as an aid to a fast exit in the case of ambush, despite knowing that this substantially weakened the cab if the vehicle ran over a mine. But in spite of massive punishment, the Moggies kept going day and night for weeks, months and sometimes even years on end. Eventually, though, mines got most of them and some men died in the process.

After obtaining the services of a Dakota based at Rundu for re-supplies into the shallow areas, a regular night supply dropping programme was commenced. The aircraft dropped supplies at marked DZs from east to west for each platoon in succession. This was all right, except that it took the platoons at least a day to round up their supplies. Some were lost on almost every drop. Sometimes, during the rains, airdrop sorties had to be aborted, meaning that platoons had to go without supplies — including ammunition, which could prove fatal in SWAPO-controlled territory. The main problem was that it took time for an aircrew to get into the swing of things. When they got to know the drill, it was certain they would be replaced by green crews straight from South Africa who had to be trained from scratch. Nevertheless, this was when Ken Greeff laid the foundation of a doctrine for the resupply of large forces in the field by parachute at night. It was a doctrine I expanded on later when I was faced with getting 44-Parachute Brigade off the ground.

Air supply problems, especially the uncertainties of having aircraft available, eventually led us to fall back on our faithful Unimogs. They again began to crawl through the thick bush on ration runs. Lieutenant Barry Roper became synonymous with those convoys. Loaded down as he was with knives and pistols, the Recces called him 'the masked soup bone'.

Barry mostly kept to tracking through the bush, but he became complacent. One day on a return trip to Omauni when he was just past Nkongo, he reasoned that the worst was behind him and decided to take the short cut by turning on to Oom Willie se pad. The convoy had only travelled a few hundred metres when his own Unimog hit a mine. Fortunately for him, only the detonator went off with a smallish bang and the main charge failed to ignite. It nevertheless frightened the hell out of Barry and after that he took to the bush as if he had forgotten that roads even existed.

One convoy leader, the son of an army friend of mine, was not as careful as Barry. He and his driver decided to take Oom Willie se pad just short of Elundu. They hit a mine and both were killed. It seems to be a national trait of South Africans not to learn from the mistakes of others.

The mines south of the border were planted either by SWAPO gangs operating within Owamboland or by sympathising locals working under the direction of a combat SWAPO contact man. The locals, generally speaking, were warned of the location of SWAPO mines to prevent them falling victim to them.

I hit on a solution to protect our convoys and to cut out the tedious days of bundu-bashing that was ruining our Moggies. I told convoy leaders to begin using Oom Willie se pad again, but they were first to pick up the local SWAPO contact man from the village nearest to where they entered the road. As they passed each suspect village en route, they were to drop and replace him with the next local contact man. We well knew the identities of the contact men, but had insufficient evidence for successful prosecutions. Understandably, the contact men complained bitterly about this violation of their human rights. But they made absolutely sure to point out mines and ensure that they and their unwanted companions were not blown sky high. The brass at Sector 10, as might be expected, were not amused. They claimed we were seriously undermining the 'Hearts and Minds campaign' they were conducting. Of course none of them ever had to drive on Oom Willie se pad. If they went to Omauni, they always flew there by chopper.

After that interference, it was back to the bush for the long-suffering Moggies.

Eddie Viljoen, Commandant Jan Martins and Major Koos Verster often used ration runs as opportunities to visit platoons and check on their combat effectiveness and morale. This was necessary because some platoon leaders had the habit of going on until they literally dropped from physical and emotional exhaustion. Deployments usually lasted for six weeks but at times, because of operational requirements, they were extended far beyond that. Sometimes our men were in the bush for three months or more without a break. They were most likely having almost daily contacts with SWAPO, which put them under constant physical and mental pressure. I always kept a weather eye open to ensure we were not driving a platoon leader and his men beyond the breaking point. Doing that would render them useless for further operations for a long time to come.

Because of evacuations through sickness, injury and wounds, the strength of one platoon was reduced to 17 men. They were flown out from deep inside Angola after more than three months deployment. They were examined by a doctor. Their morale was high, but they were all suffering from scurvy — which said little for the dry rations we were getting at the time. This led to the design of new ration packs after a period of experimentation during which the right mix was arrived at — It was formulated especially for 32-Battalion on extended operations.

Meanwhile, the war was heating up. Contacts became more frequent and fiercer as SWAPO tried desperately and unsuccessfully to drive our platoons from Angola.

Lieutenant Des Burman took his platoon north towards *chana* Namixe and *chana* Bau in the combat-hot Omalapapa area. While carefully approaching Namixe from the south, he spotted an open water hole or *cashimba* which had good cover around it. Des put his men in ambush positions, taking care that no telltale tracks were left in the vicinity. Everybody dug in, an elementary but essential precaution.

The *cashimba* was in frequent use by the locals. A few arrived and wandered around apparently looking for signs of a Security Force presence. Then some herd boys arrived, driving cattle before them. The adults despatched one of the boys on an errand.

Shortly afterwards three SWAPO insurgents appeared and made themselves at home in the shade of a tree directly opposite the platoon's ambush position. Des was about to spring his ambush when another six turned up and joined the others. Three were carrying machine guns, which were much coveted by 32-Battalion. They settled down to enjoy the peace and quiet of the picturesque water hole, but the tranquillity of their afternoon was shattered by a burst of machine-gun fire from Des' platoon.

What Des had not realised was that many more SWAPO were in the bush nearby. They immediately supported their comrades, using intensive machine-gun fire, RPG-7 rockets and AK47s on fully automatic. They fired RPG7 rockets into the trees above the platoon's position, producing highly effective air bursts. There were several casualties as men collected red-hot shrapnel in their heads and upper bodies.

But Des' men gave as good as they got.

Fernando was in his element with his 30 calibre Browning. He poured long bursts of automatic fire into the strongly reinforced enemy who had taken up firing positions opposite the platoon. Gabriel on the 60mm mortar played a useful role by dropping high explosive bombs into the SWAPO positions, doing more than most to put the platoon on the winning side.

Des was pinned down by a lone machine gunner. He killed the man with his folding butt FN by shooting him right through the tree that he was using as cover. Afterwards, Des examined the body and found that one bullet after another had ploughed through the tree and through his erstwhile opponent, tearing him into a pulp of flesh and bone. This again proved the superiority of the FN over the AK47.

Des had difficulty in restraining his troops from rushing into a headlong attack before the moment was ripe. Soon, however, SWAPO's fire slackened. The platoon attacked, rushing forward in short dashes, mutually supporting each other with rifle fire. They went through the enemy positions like a dose of salts, shooting those who had not escaped. Sixteen bodies were counted and their weapons and equipment collected. There was no time to bury the dead, so they were left for the villagers or the vultures to dispose of. The frenetic pace of behind-the-lines activity in SWAPO territory allowed little time for consideration of the enemy dead.

We also had a seriously wounded own casualty needing evacuation, but policy still did not allow choppers to cross the cutline under any circumstances. This time, though, after much pressure, HQ relented and despatched a chopper to collect the wounded man and the captured equipment. As usual, we retained the weapons.

It became apparent to the planning staff at Omauni and Eenhana that SWAPO was entrenched in the Omalapapa area in strength. They immediately ordered that an attempt should be made to dislodge the enemy by a strong 32-Battalion force deployed on a search-and-destroy mission.

Commandant Jan Martins at Omauni ordered the platoon flanking Des' to join up with him. The combined force was to sweep the area in a manner that was completely contrary to their usual guerrilla tactics.

Des had already fired flares to attract the casevac helicopter and he sent up more to effect a rendezvous with his neighbouring platoon. This sacrificed the element of surprise as the flares would obviously pinpoint his location. He was short of ammunition because of the previous contact. SWAPO, of course, was sore as hell because of the mauling the Buffalo Soldiers had dished out to them. They put together a strong force with which to teach the persistent spoilers a final lesson.

Des was waiting in his original ambush position when three SWAPO columns, each led by a European-looking commander, appeared in view. They approached the old contact area somewhat casually, obviously believing the platoon had long since left for the south. They were surprised by sudden bursts of machine-gun fire from Des' platoon and they ducked into cover. A tremendous firefight developed. SWAPO's small arms and RPG-7 fire was soon supplemented by 82mm mortars and Des began to pick up shrapnel casualties.

Des ran from trench to trench personally re-supplying ammunition to his troops. They were soon reduced to using the weapons and ammunition captured in the previous contact. Sergeant Eduardo called Omauni by radio and asked for gunship support. His English was limited and because of the intensity of the firefight — which SWAPO appeared to be winning — he was unable to provide a detailed sitrep. This created a state of depression in the operations room and it was assumed that Des had been taken out.

Yet, in spite of their precarious position, the men's spirit was magnificent. Des had difficulty preventing them from charging forward into the deadly fire that SWAPO was putting down. Four did just that when Des was not looking and were promptly knocked down by a shell burst. They all got up, however, despite one being badly wounded, and made it back to their trenches. Another black rifleman was seriously wounded in the chest. Although bits of his left lung were adhering to his shirt and his left arm was out of action, he gamely continued to fire at the enemy from a standing position behind a tree the butt of his R1 rifle clamped beneath his right armpit.

Fortunately, the other platoon appeared just as they got down to their last rounds. The newcomers launched an unexpectedly fierce flanking attack on the SWAPO positions and drove them off.

Omauni could not persuade HQ Eenhana to release the helicopter to casevac Des' eight or so wounded. They felt the enemy situation on the ground posed too much of a threat for the choppers. Consequently, all the wounded had to be carried back to the cutline which they only reached in the evening. The helicopters came and evacuated the casualties from there. This once again gave away the platoon's position and, as a consequence, SWAPO spent the night moving in heavy weapons.

The next morning Des again came under fire, this time from 122mm Stalin Organ rockets supplemented by 82mm mortars. It was the first time since *Operation Savannah* that 32-Battalion had come under 122m rocket fire.

Just for a change the platoon happened to be on the right side of the border, so Eenhana despatched a Puma helicopter with an 81mm mortar group under Major Dave Mentz. They returned fire, bringing a heavy and accurate bombardment down on the enemy and forced them to withdraw.

Des used the rest of the day to replenish and reorganise his platoon. Next day he moved back to the same location to lay another ambush in the hope that SWAPO would return to recover their dead and their abandoned equipment. The smell of death was abominable. In addition to the SWAPO dead there were also the carcases of cattle killed in the crossfire and they had putrefied in the sweltering heat. The men stuck it out but they must have been spotted by locals who arrived at the water hole and left in a hurry. It resulted in a light shower of 82mm mortar bombs which stopped as suddenly as it had started.

Des, thoroughly aroused, followed up and swept his platoon towards the suspected positions of the 82mm base-plates. The SWAPO still around must have decided that enough was enough. They fired parting shots and decamped to the north, pulling out of a substantial base area that had been made untenable by the 32-Battalion guerrillas. One small platoon of less than 30 men had inflicted defeat on a 300-strong enemy force.

It was decided to clear the local population from the shallow areas north of the cutline. It had become clear that they were supporting SWAPO and providing them with food and information. The platoons rounded them up with their cattle and set them on the road to the north. The vacated kraals were burned down so that SWAPO could not use them. Soon a 10 to 15 kilometre swathe north of the border was totally depopulated.

The support given to SWAPO by locals south of the border varied from area to area. I believe that when we began to operate north of the cutline, most of the Owambos in eastern Owamboland, particularly the Kwanyamas, were firmly on SWAPO's side. Satisfactory co-operation from the locals was rare and when it existed it had to be dealt with carefully. This changed to some extent when the Hearts and Minds campaign began to take effect, but we never fully weaned them from supporting SWAPO.

Lieutenant John Taylor was operating in Owamboland in an area just south of the Yati. He had built up a good relationship with a local chief who passed him hot information on SWAPO. On the strength of this, John laid an ambush for a SWAPO gang suspected to be arriving from Angola. The chief suggested he place himself and his small patrol in a particular place in the thick scrub next to the most likely footpath. He followed the advice. As ambush commander, John would spring the trap if SWAPO came his way.

Unbeknown to the chief, John also mounted ambushes elsewhere, including one at a particular watering point which, as luck would have it, SWAPO stumbled into. After a sharp firefight, SWAPO broke contact and ran, inadvertently selecting the path leading to where John and his men waited in ambush.

When they were in the killing ground, John stood up to shoot an insurgent only an arms length away. His weapon misfired. The enemy swung his rifle to bring it to bear and John closed and grappled with him. He threw him to the ground, grabbed the bayonet from his opponent's own belt and stabbed him to death.

The rest of the ambushers had opened up with rifle fire. The body count was an eye-opener. Amongst the dead was the RPD machine gunner, complete with weapon. He turned out to be the trusted chief who had provided John with the hot information. He had obviously been setting John up for an unexpected attack, probably into his rear. Only John's clever use of other ambushes had torpedoed the treachery.

In that sort of warfare a sixth sense was needed to winkle out the enemy, but it usually took years of bush fighting to develop that talent. Sometimes it was only a small sign that indicated a situation might be unusual or suspicious. The less experienced, perhaps, would fail to notice the sign, often to their cost.

My brother Cloete, a photo-journalist with the Johannesburg *Sunday Times*, arrived on my doorstep and asked permission to take action shots and write a story about the border war. I consented on the conditions that he did not publish the unit's name and that he placed the story somewhere in Owamboland rather than Angola.

This provided me with a welcome opportunity to see how my platoons were coping and to get a clearer picture of the conditions under which they were operating. As the battalion commander I could no longer lead platoons. My task was to remain abreast of problems facing the men on the ground and to evaluate the effectiveness of our tactics and training.

We joined Sergeant Major Tony Vieira's platoon at Omauni and went off to Beacon 28 where a set-to with SWAPO was almost guaranteed. There is a point on the Angolan side where the southern edge of a *chana* fronts on the cutline. I spotted the spoor of bare feet and the tracks of a dog that led south across the border. It was SWAPO's practice to send locals across the border to pinpoint the positions of the Security Forces before venturing across themselves. Dogs played an important role in such missions. While running about combing the bush as dogs do, they would sniff out Security Force ambush positions, no matter how carefully they were concealed.

I told Tony to backtrack the spoor into Angola to see where the local had originated. We followed it to the upper end of the *chana*. Tony manned an observation post and watched a kraal 200 metres away while the rest of us hid in the thick bush nearby. Tony soon spotted seven SWAPO in discussion with locals beneath a lone tree north of the village.

Tony formed his platoon into extended line in the bush fringing the *chana*. When we reached the end of the cover, we dropped down on our stomachs and began to leopard-crawl across the open grassy plain, intending to get as close as possible before opening fire. Not even the locals working in the fields noticed our approach and surprise was complete. Tony stood up and opened fire when we were less than 100 metres away.

Four managed to return fire and escape, but the other three went down beneath the hail of bullets. A fourth body was later found a kilometre away. Its upper torso was riddled with shots. No single shot had been mortal, but he had eventually succumbed to wounds and died alone in the bush.

21

Living by the sword

The first steps were taken to have all black troops properly enrolled in the South African Army. A dedicated team arrived from Pretoria to attend to this and we took the opportunity to embark on a final sifting to remove those unsuitable — in particular those who were unable to put aside their loyalties to FNLA. From this time on, 32-Battalion became an integral part of the South African Defence Force. It also signalled substantial pay increases — to the joy of the men and their wives who were suddenly in a position to indulge their appetites for the minor luxuries of life.

In Buffalo Base, sales in our rudimentary little shop took off. It was manned by the UNITA girls we had captured at Vila Nova da Armada and later freed. Major Charlie Hochapfel found himself with a trunk of money under his bed — the only place it could be kept in reasonable safety. It was a continual worry of his that somebody would rob him at gunpoint. Sergeant Major Roza allayed those fears by opening a bank account in Rundu.

Army Headquarters sent Commandant Gert Nel to become my second-in-command. I think they were forced to send a staff course-qualified officer to establish a proper army system of administration to replace the bush-expedient one that had taken root. This was a system developed by officers who were not only reluctant to follow the book — they refused even to read it.

With Gert in the operations room matters began to function smoothly — to the utter amazement of those convinced that the army way never worked. There were a few hiccups, usually between Sector 20 and the unit's headquarters, but Gert quickly sorted them out. It was not long before he was regularly storming into Sector 20 HQ, just like I had done, thumping tables and giving those who cared to listen — including the Sector Commander — a piece of his mind.

Gert's lack of diplomacy, my indifference to most levels of higher command and our still rather unorthodox approach to army routine — in spite of Gert's efforts — did little to endear 32-Battalion to Sector 20 HQ. The Air Force regarded this relationship with barely concealed mirth, for they were having clashes of their own with Sector 20 HQ.

It was decided we needed a logistics and operational base closer than Omauni to the platoons deployed in the west. Major Eddie Viljoen had only recently signed on in the Permanent Force and outside of 32-Battalion he was virtually unknown. He persuaded Sector 10 HQ in Oshakati to let us take over an important operational base known as Charlie November. It was to be used as a forward support base, being close to the western side of our area of operations between Beacons 25 and 35. Platoons could be re-supplied from it and a reserve force could be held there within striking distance to assist our westernmost three or four platoons.

Eddie was sent with a company to take over the base from the major in command. At the time it housed a 5-South African Infantry rifle company and it was fully equipped with machine guns, mortars, radios, the lot. Eddie's company, by contrast, were like paupers with nothing but their personal weapons and the clothes they stood up in.

As with Omauni when we took that over, Charlie November was lavishly equipped with refrigerators, deep freezers, generators and the latest in field kitchens. Noting this, Eddie set about convincing the major he was relieving that when handing over an operational base within a war zone, the procedure should be handled in accordance with the accepted battle drills known as 'relief in the line.' This meant that all machine guns and crew-served weapons should remain in bunkers and laid on their defensive fire tasks; radios should remain in the signal centre tuned in to the upper and lower command nets; support facilities like vehicle workshops, kitchens and the sick bay should be handed over fully equipped.

Nothing was to be removed by those being relieved except for their personal weapons and equipment. The major was impressed by Eddie's superior knowledge of such matters and went along happily with official procedures. So once again 32-Battalion scored nicely.

Sector 10 HQ staff in Oshakati were furious. They pointed out that Eddie's handbook, Battle Handling of the South African Infantry Battalion, applied to North Africa during World War-II. Things had changed and that no longer applied. We nevertheless stubbornly hung on to everything that Eddie had snaffled. We simply ignored Sector 10 HQ. Their increasingly hysterical signals demanding immediate compliance ripe with threats, provided huge hilarity to the staff of 32-Battalion HQ squashed into their tiny oven of a building. It had become a symbol of defiance of authority in the operational area.

Eventually I was cornered by the Sector 10 Commander, Brigadier Bischoff, in his HQ in Oshakati. He angrily demanded that I return everything from Charlie November to the stores immediately. I tried the old 'relief in the line' trick but Brigadier Bischoff, a gunner, refused to buy that. Somewhat disparagingly he reminded me that as a former instructor on staff duties, I had chosen the wrong man to try to fool with such an obvious ploy.

I eventually compromised by agreeing to hand over everything to the next company to relieve us at Charlie November. Brigadier Bischoff grudgingly relented. When the time came, though, we only handed over the kitchen stove, the generator, an immovable refrigerator and an empty LAD vehicle stripped of all its tools and appliances. The rest? I have no idea what happened to that.

Water was a problem at Charlie November. It had to be fetched from an *omuramba* three or four kilometres to the east where there was a waterhole for livestock and a point equipped with a pump to provide water for human consumption.

The first day a platoon went for water they noticed a previously identified SWAPO contact man viewing the proceedings from a chair in the shade some distance away. Our men were experienced veterans by then. Noting the unusual interest of this individual, they decided to prod for mines.

It was as well they did, for a mine was discovered close by the water point — to the obvious disgust of the contact man. The previous company in occupation of Charlie November had already lost vehicles at that waterhole — also within spitting distance of a known and obviously delighted SWAPO supporter. It was clearly the same man who took up his position at the times we collected water.

The scenario was repeated two or three times, but by then mines had begun to appear on the road leading to the water point. This meant our men had to painstakingly and laboriously prod an ever increasing area every time they went to refill their water cart.

It was clear I could not allow this to continue. Sooner or later men and vehicles would be lost, to the satisfaction of the SWAPO contact man. I got six or seven of the unit's Kwanyamas together, kitted them out as SWAPO guerrillas and sent them into Angola.

A few nights later they crossed back into South West Africa and made for the contact man's substantial house in a kraal close to the water point. They knocked on his door.

He opened it and they shook hands in a comradely fashion. They entered and sat down. It was all smiles and bonhomie as they cheerfully regarded their victim. They informed him that SWAPO's Eastern Front commander, His Excellency Munanganga, wanted to see him to bring him up to date with local information. The front commander, they told him, was planning to attack Charlie November and wipe out the hated Buffalo Soldiers. Would he please go with them to the Eastern Front HQ?

Yes, he certainly would. The contact man was in his seventh heaven as he threw some kit together and readied to accompany his newly acquired friends to the HQ.

I never really found out what happened to him. Neither did I try. Sometimes it is best to let sleeping dogs lie. Suddenly, though, the *omuramba*, formerly a hotbed of SWAPO intrigue, became tame and co-operative.

No SWAPO mines were laid in that area again.

The success in conning the SWAPO contact man motivated me to again try my hand at pseudo operations — or special operations as we called them — shortly afterwards.

Many 32-Battalion soldiers were Owambos — Kwanyamas to be precise — who originated from the Angolan side of the cutline. For training purposes we established a base in a remote area of the Western Caprivi. We began to train a selected number of men on SWAPO's methods and procedures so that genuine resident groups and the local population would accept them as SWAPO guerrillas. The knowledge of our activities was restricted to a few people on a need-to-know basis.

The special operations concept had the blessing of the new General Officer Commanding Task Force 101, Major-General Ian Gleeson, because little hot intelligence was forthcoming about SWAPO. The intelligence the Security Forces were getting was mostly outdated, so it rarely led to successful contacts. Fresh information would clearly result in an increase in successful contacts. If that intelligence could be gained directly from the insurgent gangs themselves, so much the better.

SWAPO groups generally kept on the move after infiltrating Owamboland and rarely settled into secret operational bases. This meant the Security Forces were almost always one step behind them.

I sent Captain John Wooley to oversee the building of the new special operations base. He displayed an unsuspected artistic flair in its design. Such places normally comprised tents surrounded by high earth embankments with pillboxes or bunkers at the corners. There was no shade because, according to the rule book, the area had to be cleared of trees. So almost all fortified bases in the sectors, except for the Recce's Fort Doppies and our own Buffalo Base, baked unmercifully under the hot tropical sun.

John's base was different in other ways too. The entrance was an archway built of weathered logs topped by a bleached pair of buffalo horns. The horns were the first thing visitors saw when arriving by helicopter. Beyond was a wide sandy street with wooden houses and other buildings of various sizes, most with verandas, and wild-west-style hitching rails on both sides of the street.

On entering 'town' the first building on the left was the blacksmith's forge. After that came boarding houses, a doctor's sick bay and a dispensary. There was no mess, but there was a saloon. There was also a sheriff's office and jail, a drugstore where the necessities for life in the bush could be bought and a hotel with a restaurant that served a disguised but tasty version of army rations.

Most visiting staff officers disapproved. It became known as Dodge City, a name that stuck even after all traces of John's original wild-west town had disappeared. John apparently fancied himself as the Wyatt Earp of the Caprivi.

Our Intelligence Officer, Captain Gert Brits, with Lieutenant Des Burman and Zaïre were tasked to train the operators. Zaïre, of course, had been a guerrilla for more years than he cared to remember. He was the expert, having been trained in the Soviet Union, North Korea and Algeria. He was the ideal instructor to run our 'dark phase' of training.

The first team trained was deployed in the Opapela Dam area south-west of Nkongo and instructed to locate the resident SWAPO gang. They looped back into Owamboland from Angola, posing as a new group on its way to Tsumeb to commit terrorist attacks against the white farming community. They were dressed, armed and equipped to look the part and had been briefed with the available information regarding SWAPO's latest deployments in southern Angola.

A control group — again Gert, Des and Zaïre — followed in their wake but separate from the pseudo SWAPO gang so as not to compromise them. A regular rendezvous with the pseudos kept the control team abreast of developments relating to SWAPO sightings, attitude towards them and support given them by the locals, plus anything else that might lead to a successful contact. The next leg of the operation was planned at my tactical headquarters at the Ondangwa Air Force Base where the information gained was converted into action.

A platoon of paratroopers with Puma helicopters and Alouette gunships stood by as a fireforce at Ondangwa. They could be deployed rapidly to hit and destroy any SWAPO targets located. The men of the fireforce, including the pilots, were unaware of the source of the information they would be acting on. Committing them involved delicate timing and planning. We had to ensure that nothing was done that might compromise the identity of our pseudo operators — even to those on our own side. We also had to take precautions to ensure the pseudos were not wiped out in error by our own fireforce. And to guard against creating a situation where SWAPO gangs became suspicious and reacted against them. Our pseudo guerrillas were putting their necks on the block in more ways than one.

The operators located a SWAPO gang that had murdered a local chief and abducted his daughter. They made contact and arranged a meeting with the gang leader through the SWAPO contact man. A date, time and place were agreed for the real SWAPO gang and the bogus one to meet. Naturally, only the real SWAPO gang would keep the rendezvous. It would be their appointment with death as the fireforce helicopters and the paratroopers swooped in on them. We were hoping to eliminate the entire gang which would help to maintain the security of our pseudo operators.

The pseudos could also be used as cut-off groups to track and run down SWAPOs attempting to escape back to their bases in Angola. It was important that we manipulate the contact between the enemy and the pseudos in such a manner that, if any of the former successfully escaped from a contact, our pseudos' covers would not be broken and they would still retain their credibility. The operation demanded delicate handling and we had to restrain our ambitions as we ventured into untrodden territory.

I personally kept General Gleeson at Task Force 101 informed on the progress of the operation as things developed, stage by stage. He was delighted that we had located and were continuously monitoring a gang within South West Africa. It was the first time this had been achieved. It consequently came as a shock and a terrible let-down when I was summarily ordered by Army Headquarters in far away Pretoria to terminate the operation. We were told to immediately break contact with the gang we were setting up for the kill.

It was impossible for our men to merely walk away and disappear without raising SWAPO's suspicions. So I ordered Gert Brits to instruct them to say that they were returning to Angola because they doubted the loyalty of the resident terrorist gangs. Zaïre personally took on this almost impossible task, putting his life on the line in the process. Not being an Owambo, he did not fit into the normal SWAPO pattern. In fact, as a Bakongo from northern Angola, he stuck out like a sore thumb. The pseudos, however, were too inexperienced to be entrusted with such a delicate task.

Zaïre appeared at the rendezvous with his group. He began to harangue the real

SWAPO like a true political commissar, using Portuguese which most SWAPO understood. He worked himself up to such a pitch that the SWAPO leader became truly alarmed about his future in the organisation.

He forced the gang leader to apologise for his lack of enterprise in launching operations against the hated Boers, and for lazing about drinking beer and chasing women while others were dying for the revolution. He attacked their loyalty, bluntly saying he had information that some of them had betrayed his men to the Boers, so for their own safety he had decided to return with them to Angola. He intended to report the gang's appalling lack of enthusiasm and their suspect loyalty to the area commander, Munanganga.

As luck would have it, two Pumas overflew the rendezvous at that very moment. Zaïre looked up, obviously taken aback.

'There, look at them!' he shouted in an apparent panic. 'I told you there are traitors among you. The Boers have come to kill us!'

He terminated the meeting and dashed for the cover of the bush. The SWAPO gang, who were dressed in civilian clothes, also bomb-shelled and scattered in all directions.

The locals later rounded up cattle and walked behind Zaïre and his men to obliterate their tracks as they 'fled' northwards.

That was the end of our only attempt at this kind of operation. The outcome was galling to say the least, because success had been virtually guaranteed.

I subsequently discovered that we had inadvertently jumped the gun regarding pseudo operations. General Loots, the commander of Special Forces, already had some Recces training with the elite Selous Scouts of Rhodesia with a view to setting up South Africa's own dedicated pseudo guerrilla organisation. When this organisation materialised, it became known as 5-Reconnaissance Commando, later 5-Reconnaissance Regiment as it expanded in line with demands for its services. We had not been in contact with either the Selous Scouts or 5-Recce with regard to pseudo operations. The fact that our approach to training pseudo guerrillas was similar to theirs was purely coincidental.

Nevertheless, it rankles to this day that General Loots had robbed me of a successful conclusion to a well set up pseudo operation. To crown it all, many of the role players, particularly my Kwanyamas and, of all people, Zaïre, ended up serving with 5-Recce.

22

My goodbye to 32-Battalion

Towards the end of 1976 the time came for me to say goodbye to 32-Battalion. Someone at Army Headquarters had been trying for many years to get me on a Staff and Command Duties course. I had always managed to wriggle out of it. My nemesis finally arrived in the shape of the Chief of the SADF, General Magnus Malan, who personally ordered me to attend the course. No excuses, no matter how relevant they were in my opinion, were acceptable. I was given no choice.

Commandant Gert Nel took over, firstly as acting commander and later as commander. A new era of operations arrived with him.

SWAPO had developed large bases farther back in Angola. From there they had been providing logistical support and rapid reaction forces to aid their forward bases in the shallow area in the event they came under pressure from 32-Battalion's roving guerrilla platoons. The rocket and mortar fire, which had become a feature of SWAPO's counter-attacks against us, originated from the rapid deployment of batteries from those rear bases. They were also thought to house the headquarters of various command levels. Eheki, for instance, was the headquarters of SWAPO's eastern front Commander, Munanganga, while Cassinga was the site of PLAN's overall headquarters. SWAPO called its guerrilla army PLAN (People's Liberation Army of Namibia) but we used the more common term SWAPO. The rear bases also housed large concentrations of SWAPO fighters in transit to or from forward operational bases.

From the middle of 1977, a series of semi-conventional attacks was launched against SWAPO's major command bases. This forced them to gradually shift farther north. Eventually they were pushed almost entirely out of the Cunene Province east of the Cunene River. But despite this, they remained a viable guerrilla force. They were not the terror-stricken collapsed structure that, to a large extent, we had turned them into after launching our platoons against their Eastern Front in 1976 and early 1977.

They developed a new strategy of sheltering behind the protective skirts of FAPLA. FAPLA occupied all the major towns in Cunene Province and had heavily fortified some of them, particularly those close to the SWA border. SWAPO concentrations as well as its headquarters were deployed in close proximity to these positions. These deployments progressed even further until eventually SWAPO's logistical and other support functions were integrated with FAPLA's. The latter even provided SWAPO with retaliatory fire support by way of rocket, mortar and artillery batteries when the South Africans attacked SWAPO concentrations.

Nevertheless, during the ups and downs characteristic of the last half of the 70s, 32-Battalion's task remained the same. It was to chase SWAPO from the eastern Cunene Province and anywhere else necessary.

The first major operation planned to achieve this objective involved attacks on Eheki and Namuidi. Eheki still contained SWAPO's Eastern Area HQ under Munanganga's command and was the deepest inside Angola. Intelligence and rumours regarding its whereabouts — believed to be somewhere north of the Eenhana Base — drifted in during August and September 1977. It was finally pinpointed by SAAF Canberras flying photographic missions at *chana* Eheki, 25km north of Beacon 25.5 .

The assault was codenamed *Operation Kropduif* (pigeon). D-day was set for 27 October 1977. Forces involved were three rifle companies and an 81mm mortar group from 32-Battalion and about 90 Special Forces operators from 1- and 2-Reconnaissance Commandos.

Major Eddie Viljoen commanded the 32-Battalion rifle companies while Major Hennie Blaauw was in charge of the Special Forces. At the tactical headquarters at Eenhana, Major-General Ian Gleesson, GOC Task Force 101, was in overall command of the operation. He was assisted by Gert Nel, OC 32-Battalion (newly promoted to colonel), Commandant Sybie van der Spuy, OC 2-Reconnaissance Commando and Commandant Joe Verster from 1-Reconnaissance Commando. General Loots, GOC Special Forces, was in attendance as an observer. There was also a MAOT (Mobile Air Operations Team) to control air support and 'Drop Short' Tobie was there to take charge of the artillery. It was certainly an overweight command structure to control so few troops on the ground.

The plan called for 32-Battalion to approach Eheki stealthily from the south. The Special Forces group would be para dropped at night about 15km north-west of the target. They would approach on foot during the hours of darkness. The combined forces would then deliver a nutcracker attack at first light the next morning.

As a paratrooper I well know that para drops, especially at night, have the uncomfortable and almost invariable tendency to go wrong.

32-Battalion's approach march was carried out as planned — except that they bumped into SWAPO's advanced early warning post at *chana* Namuidi. This lost them the element of surprise. An attack under Major Eddie Viljoen's command was launched by three 32-Battalion companies with mortars and artillery in support.

During the attack, SWAPO's return mortar fire landed accurately on the leading companies. Unfortunately, it was also backed up by drop-shorts from our own artillery that caused heavy casualties and set back the momentum of the advance. Shrapnel from an air burst badly wounded Eddie in the neck and head. Despite his wounds he inspired his men, reassuring and reforming them and courageously running forward under enemy fire to drag the wounded back into cover. The attack went ahead as planned and was reasonably successful.

Eddie Viljoen was awarded the *Honoris Crux* for bravery.

There were other brave men around with that rare capacity to laugh in desperate situations and be able to cheer up and restore the morale of those around them. One such man was Lieutenant Piet Botes, a rough and tough paratrooper who was in command of a rifle company. Fearless in battle, he had been badly wounded by shrapnel. His mouth and lips had been slashed into fleshy ribbons and some of his teeth were missing. Bleeding profusely and pinned down by SWAPO fire, he turned to the wounded Eddie Viljoen and spluttered through his blood:

'Major, if this is how SWAPO pull a man's teeth, then I refuse to have them put in fillings.'

But they soldiered on until by the early hours of D-day they were four or five kilometres south of Eheki.

Deploying such a large force did not go unnoticed by SWAPO. It was not as easy to hide the advance of three rifle companies with guns and mortars as it was to hide a single guerrilla platoon. The new dispensation was appalled at the old for having allowed small weak platoons to be deployed in the face of SWAPO. They favoured throwing whole battalions at them. They did not understand that in the thick Angolan bush there was more safety in maintaining the secrecy of small groups than in the deployment of larger ones. Our low casualty rate should have proved that conclusively.

A superior force of SWAPO mounted a violent attack against 32-Battalion. It was repulsed simply by the Battalion stubbornly refusing to withdraw. SWAPO was thoroughly aroused and from then until first light the attackers were subjected to an intense bombardment by B10s, 122mm rockets and 82mm mortars.

The Special Forces group, meanwhile, had been dropped in the wrong location. They were too far from their objective to close with the enemy before first light. So the final attack had to be delayed to allow Major Blaauw and his men to get in position.

The enemy picture on the ground was unclear. A well entrenched position south-east of *chana* Eheke had been pinpointed by the Canberras' aerial photography, but more extensive positions at the *chana*'s north-eastern tip had remained unnoticed.

SWAPO had moved support weapons, including mortars and 14.5mm anti-aircraft guns, to just south of the base from where they had heavily engaged 32-Battalion. Hennie Blaauw took bearings on the thumps as the mortar shells left the tubes and concluded, logically but mistakenly, that these indicated the likely direction to the SWAPO base.

Dawn came and went without an attack by the Security Forces. Only by about 15:00 both 32-Battalion and the Special Forces, by now out of water, were finally ready to launch their long delayed joint offensive. The Battalion went in as planned against the south-eastern base, driving SWAPO from their positions towards the northern base.

Farther north, Special Forces were locked in desperate combat with the occupants of the hitherto unsuspected north-eastern base. SWAPO troops were ready and waiting with 14.5mm anti-aircraft guns for an expected follow-up by 32-Battalion from the south. The enemy swung their guns to face west as the unexpected attack by Special Forces swept past them. Only Lieutenant Kokkie du Toit's stick made physical contact with the trench system there.

Firing from the flank into the fatally exposed Recce operators, SWAPO virtually wiped out Kokkie's stick.

SWAPO counter-attacked the balance of the Recce operators and a desperate situation developed. The vastly superior enemy forces threatened to overrun them. They stood their ground, however, meting out more punishment than they were getting. Special Forces operators, it must be remembered, are carefully selected and trained to fight like wildcats, especially when cornered and facing fearful odds. In desperate circumstances they are unsurpassed.

By sunset SWAPO's resistance started to slacken and they began to withdraw. It was estimated that the Recces had killed at least 52 of the enemy. Shortly after sunset both 32-Battalion and the Special Forces were ordered to return to South West Africa because of political repercussions in the distant south, so there was no time for an accurate body count. Our forces were back over the cutline by 07:00 the next morning.

The losses, regrettably, were not one-sided. Seven Recces were killed, all veterans. Amongst them were some who had been involved with me in the formation of the unit in 1970-1971. They were all friends and comrades, but the losses I felt most were Sergeant Major FC van Zyl, one of four of us who had dreamed of forming a South African Special Forces unit while we were operating far behind the enemy lines in remote Biafra many years before; Corporal Fingers Kruger who had commanded and magnificently fought Battle Group Bravo's Vickers machine-gun platoon during *Operation Savannah*; and Sergeant Bernado Mindonambunga, a tall, sinewy and fierce man, my best black sergeant in 32-Battalion — he always reminded me of Shaka Zulu. There were others too, like Staff Sergeant Neville Clack and Sergeant Major Les Greyling from 2-Recce. They were all sorely missed.

Eheki conclusively proved one point. 32-Battalion, even when deployed in battalion strength, was too lightly armed to take on prepared SWAPO bases protected by batteries of 82mm mortars, B10s, 122mm rocket launchers and, most terrifying of all for me, 14.5mm and 23mm anti-aircraft guns deployed in a ground role. It also proved to me that the planners of the Eheke operation had no concept of the value of guerrilla forces or of the shrewd use of the indirect approach as a tool in conducting war.

From lessons learned during this operation, it became clear that if Task Force 101 wished to continue with the use of 32-Battalion in a semi-conventional role, it was vital that it be supported by artillery, ground attack aircraft and close-in overhead fire from Alouette helicopter gunships.

The Eheki attack rang in the era of the sledgehammer for 32-Battalion. After that, far larger forces were used to attack the big SWAPO bases that had become much tougher nuts to crack. SWAPO, at first, had used temporary bases protected by rudimentary slit trenches. But as the war escalated and their situation became more precarious, they began to dig deeper trenches and encircle their bases with extensive all-round defensive systems. These systems were lavishly provided with roofed bunkers to serve as cover during preliminary bombardments. The major bases could call on elaborate defensive fire support from 82mm mortars, 122mm single-tube-launched rockets, 12.7mm and 23mm anti-aircraft guns used in a ground role and later, the longer range BM21 Stalin Organs that fired salvoes of 122mm rockets.

SWAPO had changed from a purely guerrilla army to a semi-conventional one. This was a direct result of our own semi-conventional attacks on them. To beat off our assaults SWAPO had been forced to concentrate its forces and dig in extensively. The better prepared its positions were, the stronger the forces required to overrun them. The stronger we got, the more the combat power needed by SWAPO to beat off our attacks and the better it had to prepare its positions.

It was an escalating arms race with a vengeance.

32-Battalion, regrettably in the opinion of some of us, followed suit. I believe it is more difficult to infiltrate a guerrilla base area with a large body of troops than with the platoon-sized forces we used in 1976. A platoon, however, could not have hoped to mount a successful conventional attack against a well-fortified base. We allowed Eheki to become such a base by default, through suspending our own guerrilla operations against SWAPO which effectively returned the initiative to them.

The platoons should have continued to mercilessly harass SWAPO at bases like Eheki. Our ongoing guerrilla activities should never have ceased. Continually bleeding the enemy with casualties would have sapped their ability to launch incursions into South West Africa, lost them the initiative and forced them to go on the defensive. In turn this would have undermined their equilibrium to a point where they would have been forced to vacate their bases, no matter how well defended they were.

If our platoons had been in the area they could have brought in up-to-date intelligence on the Eheki base. They would have prevented SWAPO from deploying effective early warning outposts by wiping them out or pushing them back to the base. Behind our guerrilla screen, a main attack force could then have got close to Eheki without being detected. During the assault on the complex our platoons should have been deployed in ambush positions on pre-identified escape routes to the north. They would have taken a heavy toll of the enemy who attempted to escape.

The best option was to deploy 32-Battalion in the role it knew best, which was harassing and wearing SWAPO down with guerrilla tactics and softening them up militarily and psychologically until they became ripe for the plucking by semi-conventional forces. The Eheki operation should have been followed up immediately by the re-insertion of guerrilla platoons — they should never have been withdrawn in the first place — but this never happened.

Intelligence gathering proved to be a problem. When operating in platoon-strength units, gathering intelligence relating to SWAPO's locations — and sometimes even their deployments — was relatively simple. A platoon could sneak in using counter-tracking techniques and get out again without SWAPO even being aware of it. Even if they were, it was usually too late for them to do anything about it.

It was different when company and battalion-sized forces were used because they could not be concealed from SWAPO's outlying security patrols. This meant that SWAPO invariably received an early warning of their presence, and often their exact locations. So while SWAPO knew where the South African forces were, the opposite did not apply.

Extensive use was made of air photography, but because of technical problems and delays associated with the taking and interpreting of photographs, the material provided was often out of date. There were times, too, when the interpretations were incorrect. The SWAPO base at the north-eastern corner of Eheki that was not picked up by the interpreters is a good example. This failure resulted in the Security Forces — particularly the Recces — unnecessarily losing lives.

32-Battalion experimented with the tactic of placing an advance patrol well ahead of the main body with the mission of deliberately bumping the enemy and drawing their first fire. They would then flee to the rear in simulated panic in the hope that SWAPO would be tempted to pursue them. The main body, meanwhile, would deploy into an ambush position to kill the enemy as they came charging back in pursuit of the bait.

Typically, Lieutenant Piet Botes volunteered to be the bait when the concept was first tried out in the field. The results, however, were somewhat questionable. SWAPO was usually aware when large forces were around and they were too wily to be drawn. The experiment ended up with Piet and his men playing an elaborate sort of Russian roulette — advance, get shot at, run away, advance, get shot at, run away, and so on. It became inevitable that if this questionable game continued, somebody sooner or later would get bored and end up as a casualty.

It was then decided to select and train officers, NCOs and men for a reconnaissance wing with the specific mission of locating and reconnoitring SWAPO bases, including operational, logistical and training establishments. They were also to find secure and concealed routes that could be used to lead in strike forces, usually at night, for the launching of surprise attacks at first light. It was important that they confirm whether a particular SWAPO base, usually pinpointed by aerial photography, was still 'alive' before an attack was launched. Finding a base empty after an adrenalin-pumping approach march of many long, hot and thirsty kilometres through thick bush was a major let-down. It left a feeling of angry resentment, with the blame for such lemons being invariably laid on the shoulders of 'those idiots at headquarters'— often wrongly, it must be said.

'I discovered the colour of adrenalin the other day', someone remarked. 'It's brown!'

Lieutenant Piet Botes selected and trained personnel when the Recce Wing was formed at Omauni. An Australian, Sergeant Major 'Blue' Kelly, joined the unit at the end of 1977 and because of his experience with Special Forces, he was detailed to train the unit's own Recce teams.

Training was based on Special Forces's methods, with the emphasis on small team work. A team comprised anything from three to five men. They wore SWAPO kit. The leader, usually a white, carefully blackened his face with a cream known throughout the army as 'black is beautiful' (an invention of Dr Vernon Joynt). They were trained in counter-tracking techniques, in all types of small arms used by the unit and the enemy, demolitions, signals, advanced medical aid, bushcraft, bush survival, navigation, minor tactics, forward control of air strikes, mortar and artillery fire control and the handling of small boats. They were all parachute qualified.

Captain Willem Rätte, a veteran of the Rhodesian SAS, afterwards built on the foundation laid by Blue and became renowned for his efficiency and meticulous attention to detail as a scout leader. He adopted the alarming habit of reconnoitring SWAPO bases at the closest possible range — at times going right in and almost rubbing shoulders with the occupants — so as to accurately plot each trench and weapon position.

Some years later when I was in command of 44-Parachute Brigade, I was on my way north into Angola with the Pathfinder Company of the Brigade. Willem and the two members of his patrol, all looking like veteran SWAPO fighters, requested a lift in my sabre vehicles and asked to be dropped at a particular point. To ensure absolute accuracy, Willem had me drive from one *chana* to the next, backwards and forwards from checkpoint to checkpoint, until he was absolutely certain of his location. To my exasperation, he refused to take my word for it.

That night his team started to walk towards a suspected SWAPO base. Before first light they found a hide and laid up for the day, continuing once darkness fell. Eventually they located the base and walked into it. Around them SWAPOs were busily packing up and vacating their positions. Willem and his men coolly helped to take down the 14.5mm anti-aircraft guns and manhandle them to alternative positions outside the base.

They were expecting a raid, so they were setting up the guns in an ambush position to shoot down the troop-carrying Puma helicopters when they arrived to attack the group. It dismayed Willem to discover that the enemy had accurate information of an attack by Security Forces. He slipped away and contacted the tactical headquarters by radio. It was only then he discovered that no such raid had, in fact, been planned.

I was returning with my paratroopers from what had turned out to be an abortive ambush of a FAPLA supply convoy when we were diverted to attack Willem's SWAPO base. A 32-Battalion company was also called in. The attack was successful and we captured the 14.5mm anti-aircraft guns that SWAPO abandoned after their planned flak trap came to nought.

*   *   *

In 1977-1978 Sector 20 vacated their ramshackle HQ complex on the edge of the Rundu airfield and moved to a brand new complex that had been constructed for them farther on. It was complete with airconditioning and other luxuries which, until then, had been unheard of in the operational area.

It was planned to demolish their old headquarters, but after some behind-the-scenes manoeuvring, Colonel Gert Nel was allowed to take them over for 32-Battalion. He developed and improved the facilities — which were palatial compared to what he had been used to. Eventually there was a proper operations room, a signals centre, a personnel administration section and a logistics section with stores, offices and other facilities. The unit started to resemble a proper infantry outfit instead of a ragtag mob of buccaneers cobbled together by expediency and with headquarters in a crowded matchbox-sized shack.

RSM Pep van Zyl built a combination diningroom, tearoom and kitchen under thatch, which became the envy of the Rundu military base. Later a pub, named after *Operation Forte*, was added where members and ex-members could hang up their own suitably inscribed glass-bottomed silver or pewter beer mugs. Tradition demanded that when a 32-Battalion warrior died, the bottom of his mug was ceremonially smashed while a final toast was drunk by his comrades. The mug was hung up in the bar, never to be drunk from again.

Gert Nel got involved in the development of Buffalo Base and the *Kimbo*. The engineers tried to provide semi-sunken accommodation, but they had to abandon the idea when the buildings began to sink in the soft sand. Some even disappeared below the surface because of the lack of proper foundations. Plans were also afoot to build accommodation for the companies a kilometre north of Buffalo Base, virtually on the river's edge. It was a several years before this materialised, however, and until then the troops had to stay in leaky tents.

Living quarters for visitors were established on the site of the old pub, buildings for the headquarters were erected, mobile homes were brought In to house the married white base personnel, a proper workshop was established, quartermaster stores were erected and a well equipped and well stocked small hospital was built. Best of all, a delightful pub, reeking of atmosphere, was built in a magnificent setting that overlooked the Okavango flood plain, the main stream of the river and the forested west bank on the far side. The old reed and tarpaulin officers' and NCOs' mess was replaced by splendid new premises. Major Gideon Rossouw, a well-known artist, had brought canvas and brushes with him when he took over as base commander. Gideon contributed immensely to its construction. The club was perversely named 'Tretchi's Mess' after our resident artist, although his canvases bore no resemblance to those of Tretchikoff, the famous Russian/South African artist.

The combined officers' and NCO's mess became, naturally, the centre of the unit's social life.

At the *Kimbo*, proper wooden houses with ablution facilities were constructed for the married black families as well as a small sick bay where doctors could attend to their needs. The existing shop was expanded, completely reconstructed and incorporated in the SADFI chain of stores — the SADF's supermarkets for frontline troops in the field and in military bases at home. The most important development was the building of the Pica Pau Primary School. Initially, schooling was provided up to Standard 5, but eventually it was upgraded to include a high school with education to matriculation level.

Under Gert Nel's command, the training wing staff expanded their commitments to train black section leaders, mortar crews, drivers, signallers, medics and other personnel to turn the platoons into multi-capacity organisations capable of carrying out any task required of infantrymen under operational conditions.

They also conducted retraining. It was a 32-Battalion principle that a man's training never stopped, no matter how well qualified or experienced he might be. There were always mistakes to be rectified and new techniques — the result of operational experience — to be learned.

*   *   *

Operation Reindeer was launched on 4 May 1978. SWAPO's main base at Cassinga was flattened during an airborne assault operation — of which I was privileged to be the commander — by a composite battalion from 44-Parachute Brigade. The body count was at least 608 SWAPO killed on that day, with the figure rising to over 1 000 when others succumbed from their wounds.

The Cassinga operation created worldwide uproar. SWAPO maintained that the base was a refugee camp. The 'refugees', however, were the best armed and best trained I have ever come across. They were equipped with AK47s, RPD machine guns, 14.5mm and 12.7mm anti-aircraft guns and even 82mm mortars. Cassinga, in fact, was PLAN's main training and logistical base and its army commander's forward operational headquarters. The fighting was intense, often eyeball to eyeball, in well constructed trench systems.

Farther south, Commandant Frank Bestbier, formerly second-in-command of Battle Group Bravo during *Operation Savannah*, levelled SWAPO's Vietnam base with a mechanised column, killing another 250 of the enemy and capturing a large number of prisoners.

Following this, 32-Battalion launched three rifle companies across the cutline to mop up SWAPO's forward operational bases which had been cut off from supplies and reinforcements once their Cassinga main base had fallen. Colonel Gert Nel established his tactical headquarters at Eenhana and Major Eddie Viljoen led the rifle companies into Angola on foot and to *chana* Namuidi. SWAPO had evacuated it, however, so they continued on to Eheki. Again the bird had flown so helicopters were brought in to fly them to other bases, hopefully before SWAPO got the chance to escape. With some troops working on foot and others in troop-carrying Puma helicopters, the Battalion swept through SWAPO bases north of Beacons 26-30 — *chana* Omepapa, *chana* Henhombe, *chana* Chinoti, *chana* Mamuandi and others.

There were some chance contacts where a few SWAPO were killed, but in most instances the bases had been abandoned. They were littered with hastily discarded equipment. Word had obviously gotten through, possibly by radio, that Cassinga and Vietnam had been attacked and destroyed and that the forward bases should be vacated before the South Africans arrived to sort them out.

Maybe 32-Battalion's attack should have been first, in tandem with Bestbier's on Vietnam. After that the airborne assault on Cassinga could have gone in. In retrospect, one realises that SWAPO had believed it highly unlikely that Cassinga would be attacked. Consequently, if the forward bases had been assaulted first, they would have been packed with SWAPO's operational guerrilla fighters. Those who escaped would have made their way back to Cassinga, which would have provided 44-Parachute Brigade with an even fatter target a few days later. If the guerrilla platoons had still been operating, those SWAPO who escaped to the north would have been in for a torrid time, whatever the sequence of attacks.

SWAPO, however, was thoroughly beaten. It withdrew, leaving its former guerrilla base areas in a vacuum that we failed to fill by dominating them with our own forces. There was a general relaxation on the part of the South Africans with no follow through to maintain the initiative. We should have kept SWAPO off balance by repeatedly hitting their troops as they tried to slink back.

This would have been the time to reinsert 32-Battalion platoons into Angola to thwart and frustrate SWAPO's attempts to reorganise and reoccupy its former base areas. The platoons should also have been tasked to track down the small gangs of disorientated leaderless guerrillas who had no idea what they should do next.

Sector 20 HQ, SWA/Namibia Territorial Force HQ, Army HQ and SADF HQ failed to maintain the initiative — such an important ingredient in a strategy to fight and win a war. They cringed in their psychological trenches, aghast at the storm of condemnation that was being directed at South Africa by the international community. The remarkable successes achieved at Cassinga and Vietnam proved too much for them. There would never be an encore to Cassinga., The powers-that-be did not have the guts to do it.

We entered another of those self-defeating exercises known as 'maintaining a low profile.' Meanwhile, SWAPO regrouped, reorganised, retrained and redeployed into their forward base areas with support for their rear areas stronger than ever. This time, though, they moved their elaborately defended positions even closer to the protection of FAPLA's major bases.

Once again we had lost the initiative.

Note: 44 Parachute brigade was still on the drawing board during *Operation Reindeer.* I use its designation, however, to identify the paratroopers involved as all of them were grouped into a parachute brigade within weeks after the termination of Reindeer.

23

Jacks of all trades . . .

In January 1979 Colonel Deon Ferreira took over the command of 32-Battalion from Colonel Gert Nel. He was briefed on his new command by Lieutenant-General Constand Viljoen, by then Chief of the Army, who told him to strike a happy medium somewhere between Gert Nel's and Jan Breytenbach's styles of doing things. He was to ensure he fought the unit effectively and administered it properly and did not neglect one aspect in favour of the other.

Deon Ferreira was the first commander to be brought in from outside the unit. This meant he had to overcome a certain amount of suspicion before he was accepted as someone who could be served loyally. The black troops of 32-Battalion did not accept strangers easily. They wanted leaders who had proved themselves under combat conditions. This decided Deon to give his primary attention to the operational side while Commandant Eddie Viljoen, to his disgust, was detailed to look after administration.

Deon was fortunate to have Eddie as his second-in-command. He was an experienced officer who knew the ropes and was accepted by the unit. It also cleared the decks for Deon to imprint his own personality on 32-Battalion's operations.

Deon's four years as Commander can be characterised by operational innovations that made 32-Battalion more effective in battle and gave it a broader range of techniques with which to hammer the enemy. This constant changing of tactics bewildered the opposition to such an extent that they never found a workable answer.

The old style guerrilla platoons were reintroduced, but they were also used as motorised infantry and equipped with heavy support weapons. Strong company-sized search and destroy combat teams, airmobile assault troops and fireforces, as well as infantry elements, were deployed. If the wide range of tasks performed by the Recce Wing under Willem Rätte are added — from small team reconnaissance missions to ambushes deep inside Angola   the Battalion had definitely become Jacks of all trades.

The unit's flexibility made it popular with the Sector 10 and Task Force 101 commanders because it could be used for virtually any kind of operation in Angola. This resulted in it becoming the prime strike force of Task Force 101 — or as it later became, the SWA/Namibia Territorial Force.

However, the Battalion's versatility, which was a logical consequence of continuous external operations, did not allow it to achieve the same degree of success within Owamboland as other units that were better organised and trained for internal counter-insurgency operations. In particular I would single out Koevoet, the police counter-insurgency unit, as outstanding in the internal counter-insurgency field. They were constantly maligned in the press and elsewhere (undoubtedly because of their successes) but they became the scourge of SWAPO within Owamboland and other border areas.

101-Battalion of the SWA/Namibia Territorial Force later adopted Koevoet's tactics and achieved similar, although not as many successes. Certain journalists claimed they had witnessed widespread brutal excesses by Koevoet, but to this day they have remained strangely reluctant to produce concrete evidence to substantiate their accusations.

'I saw women being raped, old men beaten up, suspects summarily executed and then buried in shallow graves. These psychopaths indulged in all sorts of atrocities. I was filled with disgust and horror'.

This was the regular tune some reporters played in the media about Koevoet.

But where did it all happen? Who were the victims? When did it occur? Where is the evidence? The whole situation around Koevoet — to me anyway — smells of deception and disinformation.

The subject of atrocities also crops up in relation to 32-Battalion's operations. In Deon Ferreira's time a white deserter named Edwards — a British subject who later joined the ANC — fled to Britain and claimed that 32-Battalion troops had slaughtered civilians and committed atrocities in Angola. He alleged that eliminating SWAPO's supporters was official South African policy. The overseas media and some newspapers in South Africa soaked up every word.

From time to time other similar allegations were made against the unit, including the malignant falsehoods from Edwards, but they were all investigated by qualified independent commissions from outside the ranks of the armed forces and found to be without substance. Not that it bothered the self-righteous media. Some journalists persisted in backing proven liars like Edwards while pursuing barely camouflaged political agendas. It was part of the crusade to discredit the apartheid government.

The truth was that the soldiers of 32-Battalion continually defeated SWAPO on the battlefield. So, characteristically, its allies pulled out the communist propaganda cards and smeared the SADF with false accusations of atrocities. This was in the hope that it would be forced to withdraw from operations in the face of national and international revulsion. A similar scenario cropped up after 32-Battalion's withdrawal to South Africa and its subsequent deployment into ANC-dominated black townships.

I can state categorically that any commanding officer would have known if atrocities were committed. Guilty secrets of that nature cannot be successfully hidden or covered up. More importantly, neither I nor my successors would have wanted a coverup. We would have quickly brought the culprits to trial. The unique disciplinary code of 32-Battalion specifically catered for acts of intimidation and exploitation of the local population by its members.

It is true we depopulated large areas of Angola north of the cutline. But this was carried out in a controlled manner to remove potential and real assistance to SWAPO gangs. It was an act of war. It must be remembered that SWAPO's intention was to infiltrate South West Africa on missions of murder. In fact, although they may not have seen it that way, we probably saved the lives of many locals by moving them away from where they could be caught in the crossfire. SWAPO habitually, often deliberately, based themselves in or near kraals and made them the focal points of battle — and contacts took place almost on a daily basis.

Whenever I crossed into Angola, whether it was with the Recces, 32-Battalion or the paratroopers, I was struck by the absence of fear displayed by the locals towards South African forces. Certainly, they hardly lined the streets to welcome us with flowers and bottles of wine, but they went about their business as usual. I never saw civilians evacuating town and taking to the bush from fear of us. In fact, it was more normal for them to wave to us, even if it was only somewhat tentatively. They appeared to regard the goings on between the South Africans on one side and FAPLA and SWAPO on the other only with interested curiosity. They clearly regarded it as none of their business.

There were times when we fought SWAPO and FAPLA over the same piece of ground for months, even years, yet the population remained as friendly as ever. Although dangerous for them to do so, many civilians expressed satisfaction at the hidings we gave FAPLA and SWAPO.

We never poisoned wells, no matter what was claimed, for there would have been no military advantage in doing so. Water is scarce in southern Angola, especially during winter, and it would have curtailed our own guerrilla operations if we had been unable to make use of wells.

Mines were planted by both sides. Each will claim that their mines were intended only for the discomfort of the opposing armed forces. In Owamboland, where SWAPO planted mines indiscriminately, there was extensive use of motor transport by the local population, whether private cars, buses or taxis. Consequently, many were killed or maimed when vehicles detonated mines. SWAPO almost never planted mines at or close to military bases. They were also aware of the remarkable effectiveness of our mine-protected vehicles. So members of the Security Force were rarely seriously injured or killed in mine blasts.

In Angola, where we planted mines, there was virtually no private transport. The locals simply could not afford it. When the occasional private vehicle was owned by a local, it was soon confiscated by FAPLA or by SWAPO. This made certain that all the victims of our mines belonged to one of those organisations. We never planted mines indiscriminately and when we suspected civilian vehicles were using a track or a road, we left it well alone.

At Deon Ferreira's request, the shallow area under 32-Battalion's control north of the cutline was extended west to include the area between Ruacana and Beacon 36.

Two Alouette helicopter gunships fitted with deadly 20mm cannons were allocated to the Battalion for fire support. Casevac by chopper was also guaranteed. From time to time, even troop deployments were handled by the rugged and versatile Pumas. Until then, except on rare occasions, helicopters had not been allowed to cross the cutline into Angola. This allocation of air support gave the unit extra flexibility and bite.

During 1979 and 1980, after SWAPO had begun to re-establish themselves, Deon launched company operations against the eastern, western and central SWAPO detachments, moving from area to area in a random pattern designed to keep the enemy guessing.

Willem Rätte and the Recce Wing fitted well into the new operational concept. Their task was to locate SWAPO bases and reconnoitre infiltration routes with small recce teams. On completing their task they would guide in one or maybe two companies who would march on foot to be in position for a dawn attack. Well before first light, the stopper or cut-off groups would be in position and the assault troops would be formed up and ready to go.

At H-hour the gunships would arrive overhead and begin to circle the base. SWAPO would respond by firing on them with RPG7s, SAM7s and 14.5mm anti-aircraft guns. When the troops moved forward, the gunships engaged running targets, killing or pinning them down until the infantry assault line could get there and annihilate them. The choppers, being immediately available overhead, could soon deal with any tough pockets of resistance. They were also able to assist the whole or parts of the assault line if it came under enemy pressure.

Ground to air communications were excellent. It was not long before the ground forces and the gunships became formidable cohesive teams. The chopper crews in the air and the 32-Battalion infantrymen sweating it out on the ground soon discovered that they got on just as well on the battlefield as they did in the pub.

Deon often flew in a gunship to act as controller, especially in the early stages, but it did not take long before the regular chopper pilots picked up the skills of controlling ground troops when a controller was not sitting next to them. They also became as familiar with the characteristics and capabilities of SWAPO's weapon systems as the troops on the ground. Most were already well aware of the capability of SWAPO's anti-aircraft systems.

Major Neall Ellis was probably the most outstanding gunship pilot of the war. He was excellent at controlling ground fighting from the air, realigning assault lines, plugging gaps by redirecting stopper groups — even organising the picking up and redeployment of troops by the Pumas which were invariably in attendance.

The gunships collected their share of shrapnel and bullets and the aircrews were sometimes killed or wounded by ground fire. Field expedient repairs were frequently carried out on the ground within the contact area. For example, even soap — an old-fashioned remedy for leaking petrol tanks — was sometimes used to seal the punctured fuel tanks of choppers.

In August 1980 Deon's tactical headquarters asked Neall Ellis to go to the assistance of a company that was in hot pursuit of a SWAPO group 20km south-east of Xangongo. He and his number two scrambled and were soon in the area. They flew on ahead of the company and spotted a SWAPO base. To their alarm, it was equipped with 14.5mm anti-aircraft guns and SAM7 missile launchers. It was too late to turn around, so they had no option but to fly straight through the gauntlet of fire. The chopper was hit somewhere behind the cockpit, but this did not deter them and they decided to have another look. They turned about and flew back over the base, collecting a second dose of anti-aircraft fire in the process.

Captain Bakkies Smit, the number two, warned that the chopper was on fire. The normal pilot action in the case of an onboard fire is to land immediately. Neall, though, had no wish to land in a SWAPO base. His flight engineer said the situation was desperate but not terminal and said he should fly on. Having little choice anyway, he continued, but landed not far beyond the SWAPO base. They worked frantically to extinguish the fire while some interested SWAPO cadres looked on as spectators. They were clearly wondering whether or not they should sortie out from their base and capture a South African helicopter gunship complete with crew.

Fortunately, the 32-Battalion company on the ground, still well short of the SWAPO base, had called Ombulantu to ask for troop reinforcements and a resupply of fuel. Two Pumas were already on the way. They arrived overhead Neall's chopper and put down two loads of troops straight into a contact situation. They were only just in time to save him and his crew from a SWAPO prison camp or possible death. In the end the base was successfully attacked and Neall got his bullet-riddled chopper back across the border.

At last the Battalion was allowed to send its own selection group to the Infantry School to recruit officers and NCOs from the junior leader groups. They did not have things their own way, though, because they had to compete with other elite units like 1-Parachute Battalion. By then the exploits of 32-Battalion in combat had become so well known that many youngsters spoiling for a fight with SWAPO put a posting to 32-Battalion above the glamorous attractions offered by the paratroopers.

It was an era of young officers and NCOs often in trouble for their social escapades off the battlefield, but never for a lack of professionalism while facing the enemy. Names that spring to mind are Lieutenant Eric Rabe, probably the smallest officer in the SADF; his friend Lieutenant Duppie du Plessis, maybe the second smallest; Captains Tony Nienaber, Jim Ross, Sam Heap and Jan Hougaard; Lieutenants Peter Williams and Eeben Barlow; Sergeants Dave Hodgson, Alex Hayes, Piet Brink, Kevin Sydow; and many others.

Some who had already served with the unit returned. Sergeant Major Koos 'Crocodile' Kruger went to the SANAE base in the Antarctic after service with 32-Battalion. The experience of sitting on the world's largest block of ice soon drove him back to seek the heat of the Caprivi. His nickname had come about when he and a large crocodile played a game of tug-o'-war using Koos' leg as a rope. Koos, displaying an unsportingly thorough knowledge of the reptiles, reached down its throat, forced open the throat flap and drowned the croc.

The selection of junior leaders at the Infantry School was purely tentative. The real selection began after their arrival at Novo de Marco, 32-Battalion's training base. The concept of the selection course, depending on the incumbent unit commander, changed from time to time. It varied from a rough four-day slog through swamp, bush and sand followed by a theoretical phase, to only an expanded version of the theoretical course.

Whatever the procedure followed, the final selection was made in the field while the applicant was in command of troops. The troops did the final selection. To pass, the aspirant platoon leader or platoon sergeant had to pass their critical scrutiny whilst under fire. If he did not shape up, he was taken off operations and posted to another unit.

Lieutenant Duppie du Plessis was one who passed the critical eyes of Alpha Company's 2-platoon. The company commander, Captain Tony Nienaber, was a veteran bush fighter. The company was on deployment in a hot area close to Mulemba, about 60km east of Ondjiva. They were moving on foot to achieve surprise. Tony established a temporary base for the company and despatched two platoons in opposite directions on a search and destroy mission. A platoon was kept in reserve and for base protection. This was the classic pattern used by the British during the Malayan emergency in the 1950s. If a company managed to establish itself in an insurgent-dominated terrain without the latter's knowledge, it invariably produced results.

The unblooded Duppie and his platoon set off in a northerly direction to look for SWAPO. He was scarcely clear of the base when he bumped a three-man SWAPO reconnaissance patrol. Shooting broke out with bullets flying all over the place. The troops, however, were keener to see their new platoon leader's reaction than they were to kill SWAPOs. The contact, nevertheless, ended satisfactorily and Duppie passed the acid test. The only casualty was the radio operator who was wounded. He was dropped off at the company base and the platoon resumed its patrol.

Some nine kilometres farther on they heard the unmistakable noises of a running contact. Duppie deployed his troops into an immediate ambush position on the edge of a kraal and designated an old *muhango* field in front as the killing ground. The sounds of combat drew near and eventually some SWAPOs burst through the bush into the killing ground. The platoon opened fire and killed eight, including a female. She was the first woman we had seen in uniform that far south, although some were killed at Cassinga and during *Operation Protea*. Duppie freed three reluctant recruits who had been abducted in Owamboland and taken to Angola for training as SWAPO fighters.

While returning to the company's temporary base the patrol bumped another SWAPO patrol and a third contact erupted, this time without kills.

So Duppie underwent the test of being under fire three times in one day, watched by the critical eyes of his platoon. He passed with flying colours and was accepted. He eventually became one of the Battalion's most successful operators.

32-Battalion, for some reason or other, always rotated back to Savate. It was as if the place had a fatal attraction for the unit. Colonel Flip du Preez asked the Battalion to attack and destroy the FAPLA garrison there on behalf of UNITA.

UNITA had considered attacking Savate itself, but decided the garrison was far too strong for them. So they schemed to involve the South Africans, whom they knew wanted to get rid of the garrison in order to get easier access to the SWAPO bases they were protecting.

Caxito, the UNITA intelligence officer at the briefing, eventually became the general officer in control of all UNITA intelligence. He was a slippery character. I got to know him well later when we had dealings in the late 1980s. He was so adept at manipulating intelligence to serve UNITA's purposes that his bait was almost always taken. For him, truth and accuracy were of minor concern. He probably presented correct scenarios to UNITA's general staff, but the ones he gave to his South African allies rarely, if ever, reflected the situation on the ground.

His motives went deeper than that. By presenting an invented enemy presence where none should be and by making them disappear when they were still deployed, he often exerted a subtle but decisive influence on the planning of SADF operations in areas that UNITA claimed as liberated areas. The Recces, in particular, suffered many frustrating experiences as a result of those ploys. Caxito, in common with intelligence officers in other organisations, was not so much beavering away to get a true picture of the enemy, but was manipulating intelligence with considerable skill.

Deon Ferreira, spoiling for a scrap, jumped at the opportunity and promised assistance. The Battalion would adopt the guise of UNITA for the operation. Control of Savate was vital to UNITA because the enemy garrison there was interfering with its supply lines. The lines ran north-west of the town and up as far as some *omurambas* in the north of Cunene Province where UNITA was deployed. The Savate garrison, consequently, was well positioned to cut off UNITA units in the Cunene Province from South African supplies in the Okavango.

The planning for the attack on Savate was based on intelligence presented by Caxito which, as usual, fell far short of the truth. UNITA had enough patrols on the ground to be able to judge the correct enemy picture, and without doubt they knew the correct dispositions and strengths of the FAPLA units. Caxito manipulated the intelligence to persuade the South Africans that the FAPLA garrison there comprised only a single battalion. They could easily, he persuaded them, handle opposition like that.

What Caxito omitted to tell Deon was that the FAPLA garrison greatly surpassed them in combat power. It comprised three battalions and the brigade headquarters. He ignored the presence of the brigade headquarters and said the other two battalions were located up-river and too far from Savate to provide support. So Deon could safely ignore them as a factor in his planning.

While I would not accuse Caxito of wanting 32-Battalion wiped out, I believe he wanted to get the South Africans committed to a battle that they could only be extricated from with the greatest of difficulty. UNITA knew only too well that we would pour in enough reserves to save our own men from annihilation or to push the assault through if it became bogged down. They also knew that if they had told Deon he would be facing a complete FAPLA brigade, he would probably have refused to assist. So it was essential that UNITA present a rosy picture to persuade the South Africans to commit 32-Battalion.

The operation unfolded in a way that was directly attributable to Caxito's colouring of the intelligence picture. Fortunately, Deon was himself on the ground and in command of the operation. If it were not for his quick thinking and aggressiveness, the assault might have become a bloody disaster.

Deon grouped three rifle companies and a mortar platoon for the attack and used the Recce Wing to confirm the enemy picture. Eddie Viljoen was in a Bosbok reconnaissance aircraft to advise Deon on his own and the enemy's dispositions. The thick bush, however, made ground observation virtually impossible.

On the night of 19 May 1980 Willem Rätte went into Savate to conduct a final confirmatory reconnaissance. He immediately detected that something was wrong with the enemy picture as painted by Caxito. Instead of the 300 or so FAPLA troops dug in around the place as expected, the area was crawling with soldiers. It was impossible to complete a detailed reconnaissance in one night — and the Battalion's attack was scheduled to kick off at first light.

The decision was Deon's — should he go ahead or not?

Finally, because Willem's report lacked specifics and no extra troops had been picked up on air photographs — and ultimately because of the firm assurances Caxito had given him — Deon gave the order to go ahead.

The mortar platoon took up base-plate positions south of Savate and opened fire. This provoked a violent counter-bombardment. It certainly did not auger well for the infantry, but the attack went in with two rifle companies on foot who launched themselves at the enemy with their usual élan and aggressiveness. A platoon from the third company under Sam Heap took on a complete FAPLA battalion. Inevitably their attack bogged down, as did the other platoons as they came up against superior FAPLA forces. The company's third platoon had been retained as a reserve.

The enemy's defensive fire was intensive and the unit had no heavy support weapons except for mortars with which to dampen down FAPLA's superior firepower. The only solution was to stick it out and slog forward in the hope that FAPLA's nerve would crack.

Deon's small command group was in the thick of the firefight and it was soon pinned down. His intelligence officer was killed next to him. Eventually, though, the enemy's fire began to slacken and its resistance began to show some cracks.

To Deon's amazement, it became apparent that the FAPLA commander was about to order his brigade to break contact and leave Savate in the hands of 32-Battalion.

Deon quickly brought up his Buffels — he only had four of them — and hurriedly organised a small pursuit force. Eddie Viljoen spotted a long convoy of FAPLA vehicles moving north at speed away from the battlefield. Twenty-four infantrymen were divided up into six men per Buffel and they set off in pursuit of the enemy convoy which was disappearing in a cloud of dust in the direction of Caiundo.

The chase was on and Deon led the pursuit personally. The excitement mounted and like cavalry on the rampage, the Buffels broke away from each other and began hunting down groups of enemy vehicles and soldiers.

Tally-ho! It was like a fox hunt.

They snapped at FAPLA's heels and poured intensive fire into the madly fleeing trucks. The frightened occupants clung on helplessly for dear life as they careened through the bush, desperately trying to escape the Buffalo soldiers.

Deon took his Buffel around a flank and managed to get ahead of the fleeing column. He skidded to a halt and by blocking the way of the lead vehicle, brought the entire column to a screeching halt.

RSM Ueckermann shot the driver of the lead vehicle out of his seat with an R1 rifle. Completely panic-stricken FAPLA soldiers leaped from their vehicles by the hundreds and scattered into the bush, the reed beds of the flood plain and into the river itself.

Eddie Viljoen aloft in his Bosbok spotter directed the Buffels so they could intercept enemy parties in vehicles or on foot as they tried to break out of the trap.

The enemy's organisation had disintegrated.

By the end of the day 32-Battalion had captured at least 39 FAPLA trucks, a few buses and smaller vehicles and great piles of arms and ammunition. The FAPLA brigade had not only lost all its equipment, but it had ceased to exist.

Captured booty that could not be taken away, including a mobile assault bridge, was destroyed on the spot. UNITA moved in to carry out their part of the action — which was to grab as much of the spoils of war as possible.

The Battalion had not escaped unscathed. It had lost 16 men killed in action and many more wounded. It was the highest casualty count the unit had ever suffered in any contact.

Hundreds of FAPLA soldiers had fallen victim to the guns and mortars of the Battalion. Some had drowned while attempting to cross the river and others had been taken by crocodiles.

Captured documents proved that Savate had been occupied by an enemy force of

1060 men and not Caxito's 300.

After this, the troops of 32-Battalion troops looked on Deon with the respect due to a true warrior and leader. He had passed all the tests and more with flying colours.

The French Foreign Legion celebrates Cameroon Day which commemorates an incident when a small force of legionnaires was wiped out to the last man after they had stubbornly resisted an overwhelming force of Mexicans. South African paratroopers would celebrate Cassinga Day — recognised in Western military circles as the most successful airborne assault since World War-II — until the passing of the old political order in 1994. 32-Battalion would celebrate their own Savate Day.

UNITA, of course, claimed Savate as their victory. 32-Battalion was not permitted to add 'Savate' to its battle honours because it had stood in as a surrogate for UNITA which had not possessed the military competence to take Savate on its own.

*   *   *

Major Neall Ellis, with his extensive helicopter gunship experience, helped the unit develop a concept known as Butterfly Operations. Two Alouette gunships would fly into an area of Angola thought to be occupied by SWAPO. They would hop like butterflies from *chana* to *chana*, spotting enemy bases or trying to draw fire from any that might be there. Meanwhile, troop-carrying Pumas with sticks of troops aboard would be standing by on the ground only a few minutes flying time away, ready to scramble when a SWAPO presence was detected.

On locating SWAPO, the gunships would fly just out of range of their anti-aircraft guns, giving the impression they were having difficulty pinpointing the usually well camouflaged defensive positions. They made sure, though, that they stayed close enough to keep them under discreet observation until the Pumas arrived. The gunships would then move in and engage the enemy with their 20mm cannons.

If SWAPO's resistance broke and they started to flee, the gunship flight leader would order a Puma to put down stopper groups on their line of retreat and cut them off. A second Puma would drop an assault group to follow up the retreating enemy and drive them into the arms of the stopper groups.

If SWAPO elected to stay and fight, the contact would develop into a slogging match. The moment cut-off groups were in position behind SWAPO, a strong assault force would launch the main attack with gunship and perhaps mortar support. There were seldom more than two Pumas available, so troops would be ferried from the forward concentration area to the battle site in a series of short hops. Those who had already landed would keep the enemy pinned down with the aid of the gunships until sufficient combat power had arrived to launch an assault.

The Butterfly technique was first used successfully in 1980 in an operation against *chana* Umbi, 30km north of Beacon 28. Six Alouette gunships, eight Puma troop carriers and several 32-Battalion rifle companies broken into separate fireforces were deployed. Every night the helicopters withdrew to Eenhana for reasons of safety.

Kicking off the operation, the entire fireforce was deployed to attack the suspect *chana*. It turned out to be a lemon as the base had been vacated long before.

This failure gave Neall the opportunity to try out his newly developed Butterfly technique. It worked like a charm. He dispatched two gunships from Umbi to look for SWAPO. From the air they noticed several well-worn footpaths converging near a distant *chana*, which indicated the possibility of a SWAPO base. When they got closer, they spotted huts and some defensive systems beneath the shelter of trees. The choppers broke away, circled the base at a safe distance and called for the Pumas which were five to six minutes flying time away.

When the Pumas arrived overhead the gunships moved in and opened fire. The insurgents began to run in one direction like sheep. This made it easy for Neall to order the deployment of the fireforce sticks in exactly the right positions to cut off the enemy's escape routes. Forty SWAPOs were killed without loss to the Security Forces.

Similar sorties were mounted in the next few days. The toll of SWAPO kills mounted to about 90.

In 1981 an area Butterfly-type operation was launched to locate and destroy SWAPO bases east of Ondjiva. Deon Ferreira was in command. An Israeli Army officer was at his tactical HQ to observe how the South Africans went about their business. Deon wanted to locate the headquarters of SWAPO's eastern detachment with, hopefully, its commander still at home.

Captains Heinz Katzke and Rassie Erasmus, a gunship pair, set off from Eenhana and headed for a suspect area to locate a suitable landing zone for the troop-carrying Pumas. They found one to the south. When the Pumas landed, though, they came under fire from SWAPO positions to the north. The gunships had left the area, but immediately returned and went to their aid, drawing a tremendous volume of anti-aircraft fire from what was obviously a huge SWAPO base. Heinz and Rassie hurriedly climbed away to the north until they were out of range. The Pumas, meanwhile, unloaded their troops so they could keep SWAPO busy until reinforcements arrived. They also cleared the area as quickly as possible so they could fetch and ferry more troops into what was rapidly becoming an escalating contact situation.

Ferrying the 32-Battalion forces forward took time. Meanwhile SWAPO attempted to escape in vehicles travelling in the direction of Ondjiva. Two Alouette gunships, however, engaged and destroyed most of them. They achieved this while under intense anti-aircraft fire from the FAPLA garrison dug in at Ondjiva.

At 15:30 the ground forces were ready to commence their assault. The main force was dropped south of the base and a cut-off group about 14km away between the base and Ondjiva. By the end of the attack 56 SWAPO dead had been counted. A mass of equipment, including three 14.5mm anti-aircraft guns, was captured. It was suspected that Munanganga, SWAPO's Eastern Area commander, had made good his escape.

The six gunships involved flew back in formation towards Eenhana almost skimming the treetops. Their crews were looking forward to a few cold beers to celebrate a hard day's work well done.

Heinz was drawing on a freshly lit cigarette when he glanced down through the clear perspex between his feet. He happened to see the faces of some SWAPO insurgents staring up at him in alarm. He swore later that he had seen the proverbial whites of their eyes.

He turned hard to port, bringing the cannon manned by his flight engineer to bear. The engineer opened fire and hammered an explosive tattoo. The bush below erupted with SWAPO trying desperately to escape. The other choppers turned about and joined the fray. It became little more than a duck shoot. For ten minutes they darted and wove, at times almost colliding with each other as they chased groups of the enemy.

At one stage Heinz's gunner had some SWAPO pinned down beneath the shelter of a huge baobab tree. When he fired, they dodged to the opposite side, keeping the huge trunk between themselves and the shells. Eventually, deciding they were getting nowhere fast, Heinz called in a second chopper and between them they covered both sides of the tree. A few short bursts wiped out all the insurgents.

Heinz , with some alarm, noticed that a chopper was on the ground with the rotor blades stationary. Its two crewmen were outside the aircraft and engaged in a furious close-quarter firefight with their personal AK47s. He knew they had to be Major Arthur Walker — the only recipient of two gold class *Honoris Crux* decorations — and Soutie (Englishman) his number two, probably the most famous — or was it infamous — of all chopper flight engineers.

While Heinz and the others concentrated on shooting down insurgents from the air and keeping them at bay, Arthur and Soutie enthusiastically cleared up the contact area on foot. When the action was over the two of them gathered up 30 AK47s representing 30 confirmed SWAPO kills. There were probably many more, but darkness was falling and it was too late to deploy ground troops to carry out a sweep.

In due course Arthur Walker found himself on the carpet for taking on SWAPO like a trooper on the ground, instead of doing it from above like a good airman should.

Normally, FAPLA did not interfere when 32-Battalion conducted anti-SWAPO operations in the vicinity of Ondjiva. Their firing on gunships that day was unusual. As a consequence, Deon Ferreira wrote a letter to the FAPLA brigade commander, Major Alfonso Maria. He thanked him for his co-operation in the past but warned him not to interfere with his anti-SWAPO operations in future. Major Maria, it seemed, took the warning seriously because after that, whenever 32-Battalion was operating against SWAPO near Ondjiva, his FAPLA brigade refused to assist their SWAPO comrades.

This was not, however, the situation farther west at Xangongo where the FAPLA commander was more aggressive. He constantly interfered with 32-Battalion's anti-SWAPO operations in his area.

Not long after the Ondjiva episode, an operation was launched against a SWAPO base near Xangongo. Deon trooped three companies in by Puma to Cuamato, some 30 to 40km north of the border. Gunships were based south of the cutline at Ombulantu while the Pumas flew in daily from Ondangwa — the main SAAF air base in Sector 10. It was intended to establish a tactical headquarters at Cuamato for the operation and also a HAA (helicopter administrative area) which would be an advanced logistical base where they could refuel and be ready to support the ground troops when they attacked.

Major Johan Blaauw and a company of paratroopers from 1-Parachute Battalion was also deployed. To add to the cosmopolitan flavour there was a handful of French, American, British, Rhodesian and even Soviet paratroopers from 44-Parachute Brigade's Pathfinder Company that was attached to Deon to gain battlefield experience in a combat environment peculiar to South Africa's own bush war.

Deon deployed some troops in advanced positions on the road to Xangongo as security patrols. In the late afternoon the Alouette gunships commanded by Heinz Katzke and two Pumas commanded by Commandant Hap Potgieter flew in for a briefing by Deon. Security patrols in the north, meanwhile, had picked up suspicious signs of movement not far from their position. They reported it to the tactical headquarters. Three gunships were scrambled to investigate and they almost immediately ran into a terrific curtain of anti-aircraft fire. Simultaneously, the troops on the ground were raked by heavy ground fire which they returned as best they could.

It suddenly became horribly obvious to Deon that he had sited his tactical headquarters, in all innocence, on the outskirts of a large SWAPO base. The paratroopers probed forward and even entered the enemy trenches, but they were soon thrown out by SWAPO's vastly superior numbers. Two paratroopers died of their wounds because the helicopters could not get in through the heavy fire to casevac them. Streams of tracer were wildly crisscrossing the landing zone.

The imminent onset of darkness forced Deon to call off the attack until the next day. That night SWAPO continued to mortar and machine-gun suspected South African targets at Cuamato. Meanwhile, a plan to clear SWAPO away from their immediate doorstep was being hammered out by 32-Battalion's tactical headquarters.

The gunships returned at daybreak and 32-Battalion's mortars began softening up the target. The Battalion's troops advanced with the paratroopers and they re-entered SWAPO's extensive trench system. This time they systematically and aggressively cleared the trenches, despite still being heavily outnumbered. The gunships circled and gave fire support, picking off insurgents trying to get away. The base was cleared and in the hands of the Security Forces by 16:00.

SWAPO lost 96 men killed. Much equipment was captured, including 14.5mm anti-aircraft guns. Several vehicles were destroyed.

This victory enabled Deon to focus his attention on his primary task — which was the eradication of the SWAPO base near Xangongo. He concentrated his troops at Cuamato in preparation for the next phase. He also vacated the extensively entrenched SWAPO base they had just captured.

While this was going on, a security patrol located between the SWAPO base and Cuamato, reported that vehicles were approaching their patrol position. Nothing could be done about it at that time and the Battalion waited for daylight. When the gunships returned the next morning they were asked, while still airborne, to pick up the security patrol and return it to Cuamato. Heinz and his number two carried out this mission while the other gunships carried on to land at Cuamato.

As they approached the captured and supposedly vacated SWAPO base, streams of 23mm anti-aircraft fire ripped into the sky around them. They banked hurriedly taking evasive action, ducked low and raced back for Cuamato.

The base had been re-occupied during the night — not by SWAPO, but by a strong force of FAPLA. Evidently the brigade commander at Xangongo had felt a little tetchy about giving up ground to the South Africans, so he had intervened with a reaction force.

After regrouping, the six gunships took off to attack the base with their 20mm cannons. However, they were kept at bay by FAPLA's 23mm anti-aircraft guns which put out a barrage far too intense for them.

Impala ground attack jets were called in, but after carrying out some high level attacks, they also pronounced the target was too tough a nut for them.

The gunships returned for another attack. To get more range they resorted to flying their choppers tilted hard over to starboard and lobbed their 20mm cannon shells to port at a high trajectory. This gesture of frustrated defiance had no observable effect on the enemy.

While all this was going on, Deon prepared to launch ground troops to recapture the base for the second time. But Sector 10 HQ, to his chagrin, thought better of it and called off the operation. Deon hated walking away from a job before it was completed, but he was given no option. It appeared that the FAPLA commander at Xangongo was a far more formidable opponent than his Ondjiva counterpart.

Colonel Deon Ferreira's revenge would come later.

24

. . . and masters of war

Colonel Flip du Preez, on behalf of UNITA, asked for 32-Battalion and Recce support in driving the FAPLA garrisons from Cuangar, Calai, Dirico and Mucusso. They were all within easy reach of South West Africa across the Okavango River. They had been suffering from serious supply shortages as UNITA had been planting mines and laying occasional ambushes on their long and tenuous supply routes north, as well as subjecting the towns to frequent stand-off bombardments. From a South African point of view, it would be easy for SWAPO to infiltrate the Okavango area from there at any time it suited them — provided FAPLA protection was available. So Deon Ferreira agreed to the request.

The first move was a UNITA attack on Cuangar, for which 32-Battalion provided mortar support. The thoroughly demoralised and almost starving FAPLA soldiers didn't even put up a fight, but scattered into the bush. At Calai, 32-Battalion and the Recces, with mortar support, literally chased FAPLA out of town. Farther inland UNITA easily overran another of their so-called strong points. After such setbacks FAPLA deemed it prudent to withdraw the rest of their river line garrisons without a fight.

*   *   *

FAPLA's aggression against South African forces crossing into Angola on hot pursuit operations, or when making pre-emptive strikes against SWAPO, had escalated. Until *Operation Protea* was launched, South African forces had refrained from taking on FAPLA except on the rare occasions when they tried to interfere with anti-SWAPO operations, like at Cassinga.

32-Battalion, of course, had engaged in a number of scraps with FAPLA at the tail end of *Operation Savannah* when lending clandestine support to UNITA or when executing operations on its behalf. Such operations were always conducted with troops disguised as UNITA forces. FAPLA remained under the impression, probably even to this day, that its severe beating at Savate was at the hands of UNITA. I am happy to correct the position. The enemy situation in the Cunene Province, however, changed to such a marked extent that an open military confrontation between South African forces and SWAPO and their FAPLA protectors became inevitable.

FAPLA began to fortify strong points or forts in southern Cunene Province from which its soldiers could sally forth to assist SWAPO whenever they were attacked by the South Africans. This provided SWAPO with a secure haven for its bases and headquarters. The Cuamato incident, when the FAPLA brigade at Xangongo came to the assistance of SWAPO with direct military intervention, was a typical example. FAPLA, from its forts, was also able to provide substantial indirect artillery support to SWAPO guerrillas within range when they came under pressure from ground attacks. FAPLA's extensive and excellent anti-aircraft systems prevented the SAAF from plastering SWAPO bases.

Cahama was fortified to such a degree that all efforts by the South Africans to dislodge its FAPLA garrison failed. Fortunately, it was of minor tactical or strategic significance as it had little influence on SWAPO's deployments. Xangongo and Ondjiva, however, were different propositions. Those heavily fortified positions each contained FAPLA brigades that gave close succour to SWAPO guerrillas. With their guerrilla base area secure from disruptive attacks, especially by 32-Battalion, it gave them the cover to launch operations into SWA with impunity.

So while the South Africans were intercepting gangs on the ground with limited success, they had lost the ability to turn off the taps at source. To deal with the SWAPO threat — which was escalating almost by the day with new recruitment and a massive injection of sophisticated Soviet Bloc armament — the SADF was faced with no option but to square up to SWAPO's protector.

Operation Protea was launched firstly against Xangongo and then against Ondjiva, using two independent mini brigades. The limited air strike capability available prevented simultaneous attacks on both targets. The intention was to deploy north towards Cuvelai to seek and destroy SWAPO bases in that region once FAPLA's screen to the south had been destroyed.

32-Battalion's first task was to capture Xangongo. From there they would bypass Ondjiva, where fighting would probably still be in progress, and slip around FAPLA's northern flank to find and destroy SWAPO bases to the east of the north-south road from Cassinga to Ondjiva.

The Battalion was part of a brigade commanded by Colonel Joep Joubert. It also included a mechanised battle group under Commandant Dippies Dippenaar. After the Xangongo attack, an independent mechanised battle group under Commandant Roeland de Vries would come under Joep's command. 32-Battalion would be detached from Joep to carry out the second part of its mission under Colonel Vos Benade's command. Virtually overnight 32-Battalion was transformed into a motorised battle group with its infantry mounted in lightly armoured mine-protected Buffels. For extra muscle, a squadron of Eland 90 armoured cars, a battery of 120mm mortars and a battery of 140mm G2 guns were added.

32-Battalion was retrained as a conventional motorised infantry force at Otjivelo in southern Owamboland. There they learned the intricacies involved in timing manoeuvre plans, usually in phases, in accordance with detailed fire plans. The fire plans included support fire from the artillery and SAAF strike fighters. They had to become experts at fighting in trenches and bunker systems, in taking out strong points like 23mm anti-aircraft guns used in a ground role, in dealing with obstacles like barbed wire and, far worse, minefields. During previous fighting the Battalion had, of course, come across trenches, bunkers and the like, but never on such a large and intricate scale as they would have to face at Xangongo.

The senior leaders had to learn to control and coordinate an assault internally between companies and externally with flanking units. They were also taught how to clandestinely move large motorised forces through trackless and featureless bush so as to arrive intact at the right place and time to kick off the assault at H-hour — the time a co-ordinated attack is launched by the main body of a force.

Xangongo was heavily defended by extensive and complex trench systems and bunkers arranged in concentric half circles that protected the town to the south and east. The western side of town was covered by the wide Cunene River. There was only a single crossing point — a long concrete bridge. It was overlooked from high ground by the old Portuguese fort that FAPLA had extensively fortified. The bulk of their anti-aircraft guns had been dug into the trench and bunker systems. It had a well surfaced gravel air strip.

We were uncertain about the northern approach. From information available it appeared that this sector, where SWAPO's area HQ was believed to be, was less heavily fortified. This was the decisive factor that led Deon Ferreira to launch Captain Tony Nienaber's company from the north at the Xangongo fort and the high ground on which it sat. The assault was designed to gain control over this tactically dominating feature right inside FAPLA's defensive system. Once there he could control access to the bridge, cut off FAPLA's escape route to Cahama and prevent reinforcements from reaching the beleaguered FAPLA garrison from the west.

Captain Jan Hougaard's company would be launched against the strong eastern defensive systems, a hard nut to crack as it meant infantry storming it frontally on foot. Effective artillery fire support would be the telling factor in this sector.

Commandant Dippies Dippenaar would attack the southern and south-eastern defensive system and the airstrip. The defences there, although less extensive, were spread over a wider area in interlocking pockets. A Soviet adviser group was based in the town, which made it likely they could expect a more professional approach to the imminent battle than would usually be forthcoming from FAPLA.

32-Battalion, along with the whole force from Otjivelo, moved through Owamboland to a harbour area just north of Okankolo and close to the cutline. Major Willem Rätte's task was to navigate the Battalion to its start lines north and east of Xangongo. The Buffalo Soldiers set off in pitch darkness at 04:00. Willem in a Buffel led the way across the cutline. A following vehicle in the convoy detonated a landmine, but the march continued with hardly a pause.

I was fortunate to be attached to 32-Battalion together with 44-Parachute Brigade's pathfinder company, commanded by Captain Rooies Velthuizen. I was the brigade commander but I just went along for the ride. There was an excellent chance of a good punch-up with FAPLA and SWAPO and I didn't want to miss it. My 'official' excuse was that the pathfinder company comprised foreign volunteers from all over the world and I needed to assess their capabilities under fire.

My open Sabre Land Cruiser, heavily armed with twin 50 calibre Brownings, was at the tail end of the column where I breathed in the thick choking dust churned up by the vehicles of my old battalion.

The bush was dense and the sand was deep. It was September 1981 and there had been no rain to firm the going. We were soon running behind time, our progress retarded by the Buffels that could not make the same speed through sand as the Ratel armoured cars of Dippies' battle group. This resulted in a postponement of the attack from 08:00 to 12:00.

We drew level with Xangongo and the air strikes went in. Steeply diving F1 Mirages were met by intensive anti-aircraft fire that rose in greenish streams of tracer from the fort area. It was an impressive and disconcerting display of firepower. I knew, as did everybody else, that the same guns would soon be directing their tracers directly at us across open ground that would suddenly appear to be devoid of cover.

The smoke and flames from the air strikes marked the exact location of Xangongo. Deon formed up his battalion. I was with the northern company assault force. The company commander, the irrepressible Tony Nienaber, was an old hand at bush warfare.

Commandant Eddie Viljoen was personally coordinating the attacks by both companies. He went with Jan Hougaard's, while Deon positioned himself with Tony's. There was some confusion at Jan's start line when some of Dippies' force got mixed up with his, but this was sorted out.

The attack went in at midday.

The artillery's guns and mortars began to accurately drop shells on their objectives. On the high ground by the fort a tank was ablaze. It was belching the black smoke and the very red flames of burning diesel fuel. The smoke of fires and explosions generated by the bombardment hung over the town in a boiling cloud. The anti-aircraft guns sited centrally at the fort were knocked out and ceased firing, but a 23mm gun deployed on the eastern approaches by the airfield came into operation in its dreaded ground role.

Tony's company made excellent progress from the north, facing virtually no resistance. While Lieutenant Duppie du Plessis and his platoon were clearing bunkers they came on some FAPLA in hiding. Before anyone could embark on anything bloodthirsty, one of them rushed at the platoon with a case of beer and proceeded to distribute it amongst the astonished soldiers.

To the south, though, Dippies had picked up problems. 32-Battalion's attack was temporarily halted so that Joep Joubert could sort out a situation that threatened to bring them into the arcs of fire of Dippies' lagging battle group.

Jan dismounted his troops from the Buffels and put them on foot into the trench systems to clear out FAPLA in hand-to-hand combat. Unfortunately, for infantrymen there is no other way to clear trench and bunker systems. If resistance is tough, every metre has to be painfully fought over with grenades and rifles, killing those who fight back and winkling out the less aggressive ones who lie low in underground shelters. In this case, resistance was relatively light. They progressed well until they were level with the main road leading into town. Jan halted the attack to allow Dippies' force on the left to catch up. A twin-barrelled 23mm anti-aircraft gun opened fire in a ground role. It was impossible for the company to continue its advance until that was dealt with. Air strikes were called for and were put in, but to no avail. When the dust cleared the gun crew merely popped up from their dugouts and continued firing. Even the base-plate positions of the mortars, three kilometres to the rear, began to take casualties.

Eventually Jan ordered Crocodile Kruger, a platoon leader, to take out the gun with an infantry attack on foot while the rest of the company supported him with fire. Crocodile formed his platoon up for the assault, but before they could move out they were all floored by an air burst overhead. It turned out to be a shell fired by one of Dippies' big G2 guns. No one was killed, but about 15 were wounded and the platoon ceased to exist as a fighting unit. Dippies had begun a preliminary bombardment of his target area and a totally avoidable 'over' had caused the damage. Eddie Viljoen angrily asked Deon to call a halt to Dippies' artillery fire, then went forward to assist with the evacuation of casualties. After that, both companies moved forward without artillery support.

The Pathfinder Company of 44-Parachute Brigade probed forward to the tank that was brewing near the fort and discovered that FAPLA had gone. This allowed Tony's company to move in and occupy the terrain that dominated the FAPLA units opposing Jan's company. Many of the FAPLA, on seeing the imminent threat, took to their heels to avoid being cut off. The resistance on Jan's front crumbled and collapsed, speeding up their fight through the trench systems. The 23mm gun that had given them so much trouble was found abandoned and captured intact. Jan cleared the town below the fort and to the east and south of it. He then placed combat outposts on its eastern and southern approaches.

In the fort area, 32-Battalion captured a battery of brand new 20mm anti-aircraft guns and a large quantity of ammunition. It had been those guns that had been chiefly responsible for keeping the SAAF Mirages at arm's length.

In the south, Dippies' attack against cut-off FAPLA remnants unaccountably ran out of steam. He began to reorganise and regroup for another attempt later.

By the time Jan Hougaard reached what had been the Soviet military HQ, the sounds of battle had died down. The former occupants had escaped in their vehicles and sped off westwards towards Cahama the moment the attack began to unfold. Jan sat down on the front steps of the HQ and attempted to make radio contact with Deon Ferreira.

Suddenly shots cracked within the building. A dead FAPLA fell through a window and his body landed right next to Jan. Further shots reverberated within the confines of the building as Lieutenant Jim Savory's platoon started to clear the rooms. To Jan's surprise he discovered the place was still occupied by FAPLA. Jim's men cornered the final remnants in a bomb shelter adjacent to the house. In a display of unemotional efficiency they threw grenades into the shelters, waited for the explosions, then charged inside and fired short bursts into any shell-shocked body that still showed signs of resistance. When checking the headquarters later they found many refrigerators and deep freezers stuffed full of all sorts of goodies like hams, cheeses, sausages and so on. There was also a large stock of beer. It was a feast indeed for the hungry and thirsty troops.

Deon established his headquarters in the building that housed the joint operations set-up of FAPLA and its Soviet masters. A search revealed a map of the town's defensive systems. It was an elaborate and detailed series of 'hedgehog' type strong points of a kind developed by the Soviets to use against NATO forces if they had got it into their heads to launch an invasion of Warsaw Pact countries. In a typical and unimaginative fashion, the Soviets took the whole system without a single significant change and transplanted it to the African bush. The map indicated details of each trench and bunker, arcs of fire for every weapon, anti-aircraft deployments, positions of heavy weapons systems, the locations of brigade and subordinate HQs, and so on. The installation had one glaring weakness. It was orientated towards the south, east and north-east — with nothing covering the north from where Tony had launched his assault. We could not decipher the Russian writing on the map, but a reasonable deduction was that we had overrated the Soviets' military expertise as planners, together with their fighting skills.

Darkness set in. Security patrols and early warning patrols were posted. A dog-tired 32-Battalion settled down for the night. Sergeant Trevor Boucher, commanding an early warning patrol on the south-eastern edge of town, heard sounds of vehicle movements just after midnight. He called Jan Hougaard on the radio and reported the approach of unidentified troops from the south-east. Did he have any idea who they might be?

Jan told him to stand by while he checked with Deon.

Maybe it was Dippies' battle group moving towards 32-Battalion. Dippies had still not cleared his sector of the brigade's objective.

Deon believed it was more likely FAPLA trying to get away.

Joep Joubert could offer no explanation but said Trevor should open fire if he was in doubt.

The troop movement came closer to Trevor's position, but he still had no idea who they were. Eventually, though, they came close enough to identify. There were trucks, infantry on foot and last, although certainly not least, he heard tanks clattering along the tarred road.

It was FAPLA!

Trevor and his ten men huddled down in the captured trenches. He whispered a hoarse radio message to Jan. The enemy swarmed around and across the trenches. Amazingly, no one spotted the patrol that was literally crouching under their feet. They waited surreptitiously for the tanks to come past, then discovered they were not tanks but trucks with their tyres shot out. The racket had been caused by them driving on the wheel rims.

Jan Hougaard and Jim Savory were next in line along FAPLA's escape route and they deployed troops to intercept the approaching enemy. Shortly afterwards the first FAPLA trucks drew abreast. The occupants saw the 32-Battalion men but did not even raise their weapons.

'Hello, comrades', said one in Portuguese. 'We are happy to see you are still here'.

'Me too, comrades', Jan shouted and opened fire.

The others followed suit and riddled the cabs of the trucks with slugs.

For a moment the enemy, not realising what was going on, were sitting ducks. Then panic set in. Soldiers jumped from their vehicles and fled towards the bridge. A few tried to run the gauntlet in their trucks, but most of them came to flaming grief. Streams of tracer fire pierced the night sky seemingly from every direction, which heightened the chaos.

A Soviet Gaz truck mounted with a twin-barrelled 14.5mm gun bounced to a standstill by Deon's headquarters. The occupants had adopted firing positions behind the garden wall. The Gaz's gunner opened fire and blasted away up and down the street. A black soldier of 202-Battalion sleeping in the rear of a Buffel awakened with a start at the sudden crescendo. He blinked at the sight of the enemy vehicle no more than 20 metres away. Scarcely believing his good luck, he cocked the Buffel's mounted machine gun and opened up. He emptied the belt with short and vicious bursts.

The truck caught fire and some of its occupants turned into flaming human torches. A FAPLA soldier escaped the flames and tried to merge with the shadows. The sharp-eyed 202-Battalion soldier spotted him and killed him with a last long burst. It was the first time that intrepid soldier had been in contact with the enemy.

During the early hours of the morning, Dippies made another attempt to take his allocated part of the objective. He put down a heavy artillery barrage that lasted for 30 minutes. Finally his infantry mounted in their Ratels moved forward, only to discover that the enemy had absconded long before. It was they who had blundered into Jan's company during the night.

It was not until 09:00 that Jan and his men rounded up the final stragglers from the enemy's breakout attempt. Many FAPLA bodies were found during the next few days, some in the most unexpected places. They were buried by Roeland De Vries' mechanised unit which took over from Deon's battle group.

To the east, Commandant Chris Serfontein and his mini brigade, including three companies from 32-Battalion commanded by Commandant James Hills, were engaged in an attack on Ondjiva. North of Ondjiva, James sent the companies on foot to sweep the area east of town for SWAPO bases.

They also took up stopper positions to cut off any FAPLAs or SWAPOs who attempted to escape in that direction. Shortly afterwards, Major Tinus van Staden, commanding one of the companies, sighted a long convoy of trucks, BRDMs and tanks bolting from Ondjiva in his direction.

He called for an air strike and with commendable promptness the convoy was attacked by Mirage and Impala jets. Burning tanks and trucks were scattered all over the area. The FAPLA troops bailed out and escaped into the bush. When Tinus moved forward to sweep the area and annihilate any remaining resistance, darkness was falling. To his surprise they found the bodies of some Soviet advisers in and around the wrecked enemy transport.

As they were continuing their sweep, a pistol shot was fired at them from a kraal. They returned the fire, then attacked and overran the kraal. They discovered the bodies of two Soviet lieutenant-colonels and two Russian women. A Soviet soldier, Sergeant Major Nikolai Pestretsov, was unhurt and hysterically clinging to the corpse of his wife. He was taken prisoner and evacuated to Pretoria. He was later exchanged for Sapper van der Mescht, a South African POW in FAPLA's hands.

It was said there were children with the Soviet party who had run away from the fighting. Our troops searched the area for days, but to no avail. The local kraals were the only places where water could be found. Without it they could not have survived in the bush for more than three or four days. Eventually it became pointless to continue the search.

It is difficult to believe the Soviets could have been so callous and unfeeling, or were they just plain stupid to have allowed the families of military advisers to live in such a dangerous operational area.

Deon took his battle group to complete the second part of his mission — which was to find and attack SWAPO bases east of the road leading to Mupa. Information was that SWAPO's overall military headquarters, their so called PLAN HQ, was about 20km to the east. The battle group moved at speed towards Mupa, side-stepping Ngiva to the south-east. When they reached Mupa, intelligence assured them the target was still active and occupied by SWAPO. With meticulous navigation, Willem Rätte guided the battle group in pitch darkness through 21km of thick bush to a point two kilometres west of the target — precisely where they were supposed to be.

The next morning, Colonel Dick Lord, formerly of the British Royal Naval Fleet Air Arm and a top gun pilot, took his F1 Mirages in to soften up the target. They arrived overhead at the right moment, asked for smoke indicators, then pounded the target area with bombs and rockets. When they departed, the artillery took over and dropped shells accurately in the centre of the target area. Clouds of dust and smoke curled above the tree tops. Oddly enough, though, there was no return fire.

Deon ordered a cease-fire and the rifle companies moved forward on foot to sweep the area. They found an extensive complex with trenches and bunkers encircling it in a strong defensive embrace. Not a single SWAPO was around. The base had been vacated at least three months before. So much for up-to-date intelligence from higher headquarters!

Operation Protea resulted in the removal of FAPLA's protective screen from SWAPO, which forced them to retire to bases deep in the Angolan bush. FAPLA made a few half-hearted attempts to recapture Xangongo and Ondjiva but they were easily repulsed.

During *Operation Protea* the Recces demolished the bridge at Xangongo. This made any attempt by FAPLA to attack the town from Cahama, west of the Cunene River, an extremely difficult operation. They could, however, still move down the east bank of the Cunene River from the north, despite UNITA having assured us that they had the area under control.

*   *   *

In December 1981 Deon was ordered to deploy 32-Battalion troops along the Cunene River line and sweep both its banks from Calueque to beyond Peu-Peu north of Xangongo. He was to destroy any SWAPO bases found. He established his tactical headquarters at Peu-Peu and sent Jan Hougaard's company to sweep north from Calueque to Humbe and then to a crossing point at Peu-Peu. Another company was tasked to operate east of the river.

Jan's company worked its way north, getting a number of contacts by the use of Butterfly techniques. They killed a lot of badly trained FAPLA auxiliaries but found no SWAPO bases. They laid up for the night south of the Humbe-Xangongo tarred road and moved up early the next morning to cross it. Some local women saw them and left in a hurry, which was a sure sign a contact was in the offing. Sure enough, shortly after crossing the road, they walked into a FAPLA ambush. There was a violent firefight during which Sergeant Trevor Boucher was hit in the knee. The enemy broke contact and retreated hastily towards Cahama.

After crossing the river at Peu-Peu, Jan took control of the other 32-Battalion companies which were working the main road from Cahama to Humbe. He was passed information that FAPLA was intending to dispatch a force from the north via Peu-Peu and another via the Cahama to Humbe road. The intention was to attack and reoccupy Xangongo. The latter force, if it came, would have to cross the river higher up or, if they wanted to cross at or near Xangongo, make use of bridging equipment or ferries.

Jan's tactical HQ at Peu-Peu was comfortably established in tranquil and pleasant surroundings. Helicopters were on the ground with a large dump of fuel drums for resupply stacked by the landing zone. Tents had been pitched to house the HQ staff and the air crews.

Their tranquillity was disrupted a few days after arriving when they heard the drone of vehicles about three kilometres away to the north. It was coming from an area that was supposed to be 'firmly under the control' of UNITA. There were definitely no South African forces operating in that area, so it could only be FAPLA. A patrol returned in a hurry and caused immediate consternation. A large FAPLA force was advancing towards Peu-Peu and was about to intrude on the idyllic surrounds of Jan's bushveld camp.

The peaceful atmosphere at the Tac HQ erupted into frantic chaos. The helicopters had to take off and the tents, generators and other paraphernalia had to be packed and loaded onto the trucks. The only available forces to stop or delay the enemy was Jan's rifle company and a few mortars. He promptly ordered the mortars to open fire at the FAPLA column, knowing it would cause them to pause and consider their next move. Meanwhile they continued to dismantle the headquarters heaving everything haphazardly into the transport.

The mortaring strategy worked and gained them a breathing space. Jan asked for an air strike and Impala jets were scrambled at the Ondangwa Air Base. They soon screamed down, rocketing and strafing the enemy column. The first flight was replaced by another and then by another. Soon there was little left of the enemy column except smoking, burning and twisted metal. Fifty wrecked vehicles were later counted. The Impala boys never believed in half measures

The FAPLA soldiers who survived the holocaust retreated on foot, either to Cahama or to the north from where they had come. Their attack on Xangongo had been stopped in its tracks. Jan and his men unpacked their kit and resumed their peaceful existence on the banks of the beautiful Cunene River.

An advance on Xangongo from Cahama was repulsed in similar fashion.

*　　　*　　　*

After three months of continuous operations in Angola in the area north of Ruacana, 32-Battalion was taken out and trooped back to Buffalo Base for rest and recuperation. While this was in progress, Captain Jan Hougaard, then commanding the Tac HQ at Ruacana, was asked to support a 5-Recce reconnaissance mission.

He scratched together little more than a platoon of infantry from several companies, flew to Marienfluss in Kaokoland and made contact with José, a black Angolan who was the Recce team leader. He was deploying his team of black operators into Angola to conduct a reconnaissance of a suspected SWAPO base in the Cambeno Valley north of the Cunene River and believed to be close to Iona.

Major Neall Ellis flew in with two Alouette gunships to join the two Pumas that had flown in the 32-Battalion platoon. It was a scratch outfit and geared only to go to the Recce's assistance if required. There was no question of them getting involved in a major punch-up. The operation was, as Neall put it, 'just a jolly.'

Ten Recces, dressed in SWAPO kit, were dropped by Puma east of the point where the southbound road entered the mountains in which the Cambeno Valley was thought to be situated. They reached the road after walking throughout the night and confirmed it was in regular use, probably by SWAPO supply vehicles. They planted a mine as a surprise packet.

They went into concealment on a hill about a kilometre away and settled down to see what happened. Shortly afterwards two SWAPO trucks trundled up the road from the south. One detonated the mine, but there appeared to be no casualties. Its passengers clambered aboard the other vehicle and they continued on their way.

José and his men remained in their grandstand position, keenly awaiting developments. During the afternoon a patrol of 28 SWAPO insurgents appeared through the heat haze to the south. Once at the wrecked truck, they spread out and began checking for spoor. It did not take them long to find it and they began tracking the Recces towards their hide. The operators viewed this development with alarm and reported the situation to Marienfluss by radio.

SWAPO reached the hill and surrounded it, cutting off any possibility of escape. The ever resourceful José stood up and revealed himself. He identified his team as SWAPO fighters and beckoned the SWAPO leader to approach them. The man rather stupidly did so and came within a few metres of José. An argument developed as to who was the genuine SWAPO. José accused the other group of being UNITAs, intent on finding the SWAPO base. The SWAPO leader said that José and his men were Boers and accused them of planting the landmine. In the end the Recce leader gave up his persuasive attempts and shot the SWAPO leader dead. Then the fighting began in earnest. The Recces were heavily outnumbered and surrounded.

Neall scrambled his two gunships and the 32-Battalion platoon climbed aboard the troop-carrying Pumas which also took off. The gunships were soon in position They circled the hill and put the enemy, who were only a few metres from the Recce positions, under 20mm cannon fire. The Pumas landed two sticks of troops which formed up and mounted an attack on SWAPO's rear.

The fighting petered out as the Special Forces operators and 32-Battalion soldiers began to get the better of the enemy. They swept through the contact area, took six wounded SWAPO as prisoners and found another 21 dead. It was assumed the 28th man had survived and made good his escape.

More troops and helicopters were flown into Marienfluss. Eventually there were four gunships, five Pumas and slightly more than two infantry platoons plus a section of two 81mm mortars for ground support.

The captives were separated and intensively interrogated. They were individually instructed to construct sand models of the base. The various models were compared to ensure that critical details had not been falsified. Eventually, a master sand model was made and utilised for briefing purposes. David, a captured SWAPO originating from the Caprivi, was thoroughly disillusioned with SWAPO, so he volunteered to assist the Security Forces. The base, they were told, contained about 200 to 250 SWAPO.

That afternoon four gunships and five troop-carrying Pumas took off for an attack on the base. They flew into a rain storm. The weather clamped down and the visibility in the mountains dropped to virtually zero. The assault force turned about and returned to Marienfluss. Putting troops down without the gunships available to give fire support would have been suicidal. The operation was postponed until the next morning.

By then the top command structure at Sector 10 HQ at Oshakati was convinced that SWAPO had withdrawn from the base. Jan Hougaard as a precautionary measure, however, had deployed two stopper teams in the area of José's contact. They reported that there had been no movement north from the SWAPO base, so the enemy was most likely still there. It was assumed they were unaware of 32-Battalion's deployments and its intentions.

The next morning, 13 March 1982, the attack force flew out. Jan was in command of the ground troops. Neall Ellis commanded the gunships and he would control the ground deployment from the air. Major Polla Kruger was in command of the Pumas.

Neall's gunships overflew the base and noticed that SWAPO's bivouac shelters were exposed and drying in the sun following the previous day's downpour. The enemy were congregated in a relatively small area and it was estimated that there were about

300 of them. Cover was sparse and the thorny scrub was dry so the cover it provided against air observation was inadequate.

Four Pumas landed simultaneously and dropped the assault teams. Another deployed a mortar team to a hilltop from where it would provide support fire. The gunships began to pump 20mm high explosive shells into the crowded base.

After dropping the troops, the Pumas flew north to pick up the stopper groups previously deployed about 20km north of the base. They were brought back to redeploy on escape routes leading from the valley. Before Sergeant Fanus 'Nella' Nel's stick could get to their stopper position, they were dropped literally straight into a close quarter firefight with SWAPO.

The Pumas offloaded fuel at a mini HAA established about five kilometres south of the base where Neall's Alouette gunships could refuel. They had insufficient endurance to fly back and forth to Marienfluss and still have enough time over the target to give the ground troops adequate fire support.

Four SAM7s were fired from the base at the gunships, but no hits were scored. There was also a deadly profusion of RPG7 rockets bursting in puffs above the contact area. When the gunships engaged the base, the enemy started to scatter.

When the stopper groups got into position, they found themselves bottled up in a narrow valley enclosed by steep hills on all sides. The 40-strong assault group advanced with difficulty over the broken terrain. They were constantly under fire, causing them to lose direction and cohesion. Neall in his gunship up above, however, did a grand job by keeping them in line. It was virtually impossible for Jan to do it at ground level.

Every so often gunships peeled off in pairs to refuel. Neall tried to keep at least a pair of them overhead and in the fight at all times, but he could not always manage it. There were moments too when real crisis situations developed and he needed all four of them on station.

The terrain was broken into hollows, little valleys, rocky outcrops and even cliff faces, so as the assault line advanced, the ground battle developed into a series of isolated firefights. Progress was slow and the small pockets of SWAPO they encountered fought back fiercely. The fight started at 08:00 and there were no signs of a let-up by the time the sun had climbed to its zenith. Heat and thirst had a debilitating effect on the combatants on both sides as the battle turned into a long and drawn out slogging match.

There were barely 60 soldiers of 32-Battalion, including the stopper groups, pitted against 300 or more SWAPO. The weighing in of the gunships, however, made a tremendous difference to the balance of combat power. But only the infantrymen could get down and fight in the hollows and crevices where the enemy had taken cover from the relentless 20mm cannons of the gunships.

Later in the day, as the assault line fought slowly forward, SWAPO's fire increased to cover several of them trying to break out. The stopper groups under Sergeants Nel and Peter Burley inflicted a heavy toll on those trying to escape. The deep valley had turned into a cauldron of fire.

At one stage, when Neall had all four gunships on the ground for refuelling, SWAPO began to shell the assault group with 82mm mortars which, with additional small arms fire, pinned them down. The stopper groups were stuck behind cover and unable to move either forward or back to lend assistance to the assault group. Consequently, the assault troops had to seek shelter behind the limited cover available and return fire as best they could.

Sector 10 HQ at Oshakati chose this most inopportune moment to demand a sitrep. They were unable to raise Jan Hougaard because communications from the depths of the valley to the outside world had packed up. Neall in his gunship replied instead, telling them what he knew, but Sector 10 insisted on speaking personally to the ground commander. They didn't seem to realise that Jan was not just lying about in leisurely fashion on the rocks cultivating a tan. He was critically engaged in a violent scrap that could go either way. And at that particular moment he was pinned down under a hail of fire.

Bowing with great reluctance to superior authority, Jan and Lieutenant Duppie du Plessis, accompanied by their guide David the SWAPO prisoner, attempted to re-establish communications with the persistent HQ. In the process they unavoidably dropped several hundred metres behind the assault line.

A SWAPO group had managed to filter between the assault line and Jan's command group and they launched a sudden attack. Within moments they were only a few metres away and threatening to overrun the command group. Jan and Duppie fought back for their lives. So did David, who fired at his recent comrades with an AK47 he had grabbed off a dead insurgent. Under direct assault, pinned down by mortars and with the gunships on the ground refuelling, the command group's fate tottered in the balance.

And Sector 10 were tapping their fingers and waiting for an immediate report.

Nella's six-man stopper group were the only ones not pinned down and Jan ordered them to come to his assistance — despite them being 800 metres away. They set off but immediately bumped a group of 38 SWAPO. Undeterred in the face of a desperate situation, Nella bawled 'charge!' and ran straight at the enemy. He was shot and died almost instantly.

The confusion and the distraction caused by his act of bravery, however, gave the rest of his stick the chance to take cover and return fire. Not knowing that he was dead, they discussed the next move. Whatever they did, they had no intention of leaving Nella among the enemy. Sergeant Kingutu suggested to the quaintly named Sergeant Dracula that they retrieve their leader, who lay directly in the line of fire in front of SWAPO's positions.

The ground in front of the stopper group was being raked with small arms and PKM machine-gun fire. Four of them returned fire as best they could while the two sergeants leaped to their feet and charged forward. They reached Nella, confirmed he was dead and started to crawl back, dragging his body with them. SWAPO tried their best to kill them with a heavy curtain of fire. They struggled from rock to rock taking pot-shots as they went, while their comrades also vainly tried to suppress SWAPO's fire.

Finally, getting tired of crawling, they stood up. Sergeant Kingutu slung Nella's body over his shoulders and the two made a dash for it, pausing occasionally to return fire. Eventually they dropped behind cover with the rest of the stick, totally exhausted. Miraculously, they both escaped without a scratch.

A gunship arrived overhead and began hammering at the enemy. The six soldiers, worked up into violent fury over the death of their sergeant, stood up and charged madly at the enemy who outnumbered them and outclassed them in firepower. With the gunship's support they overran the SWAPO positions and killed about 15 of them.

Nella's death had been avenged.

Sergeants Dracula and Kingutu were both awarded the *Honoris Crux*. The decoration was awarded posthumously to Sergeant Fanus Nel.

Meanwhile, the command group of Jan Hougaard, Duppie du Plessis and David had also been rescued by a gunship. It was not all plain sailing either. Jan told the pilot by radio that he would mark his position with a white phosphorus grenade. He told the pilot to shoot just beyond the grenade smoke into the enemy who still had them pinned down. Duppie lobbed the grenade — one of the nastiest in anyone's armoury because of its incendiary characteristics and its capacity to cause the most terrible burns. Unfortunately, it hit a rock and bounced back into the centre of the command group. They were trapped. They could not move because SWAPO's fire was crackling continuously only a few centimetres over their heads. So they waited helplessly for it to detonate — for the phosphorous to explode in fiery streaks and sticky blobs that would burn agonisingly deep into their living flesh and bone.

It duly detonated but instead of white phosphorous, it belched out thick clouds of yellow smoke. By accident and the grace of God, Duppie had mistakenly lobbed a coloured smoke grenade. The smoke bellowed out and completely enveloped them. The gunship began firing all around the thick yellow cloud and drove the enemy back.

It was a grinding uphill battle and there was no let up as the day wore on.

Sergeants Stewart and Joao were both shot in the head and killed.

An interesting situation developed at the mortar position on the hilltop. While providing fire support, a SWAPO group attempted to overrun them. Some of the crew grabbed their AK47s and saw the enemy off at close quarters, while the rest carried on firing their mortars at enemy deployments.

Back at Oshakati, Sector 10 Headquarters was still insisting that it wanted speak to Jan and right away. They refused to accept Neall's explanation that things were still a little busy and that several hundred SWAPO had already been killed.

In desperation Neall landed his chopper close to Jan's command group to confer with him, but he first took the opportunity to 'swing the tube', as urinating is known in army slang. He had been stuck in his chopper for a long time and felt as if his bladder was about to burst. At that very awkward moment SWAPO brought Neall's Alouette under fire. An RPG7 rocket projectile exploded in a tree just above his head and caused him to dive wetly into cover.

The shooting gradually died down, but the men were so mentally and physically exhausted that they were incapable of properly consolidating the objective. Most of them had run out of ammunition and had re-supplied themselves in the field from SWAPO casualties. Every 81mm mortar bomb had been expended.

Some of the Pumas were still at the HAA because their fuel was insufficient to get them back to Marienfluss. It was also impossible for the little force to continue without replenishment. But the choppers could not fly without fuel, so a withdrawal by that means was out of the question. All they could do was rest for the night and keep their fingers crossed in the hope that a reorganised SWAPO force would not launch a counter-attack during the night.

Jan was flown to the tactical headquarters at Marienfluss, making it on the last smell of an oil rag. He reported back to a still nagging Oshakati by radio, leaving Duppie to reorganise the troops and arrange security patrols. The troops soon regained their spirits and settled down for the night. They were occasionally disturbed by lost SWAPO guerrillas stumbling into their temporary base, but otherwise the night passed peacefully.

The next morning Father Christmas arrived overhead with two C130s for a sleigh, having flown from Pretoria overnight and dropped fuel and ammunition at the mini HAA. After resupply the troops were able to continue with consolidation and exploitation. On sweeping the area, they discovered to their astonishment just how extensive the base was. There were countless tons of ammunition, weapons, mines and explosives. A stock of Zodiac boats indicated that they had intended crossing the Cunene River to establish themselves in Kaokoland. Prisoners also confirmed this. Interestingly too, they came across mealie meal stocks supplied by the UN High Commission for Refugees.

Sixty tons of ammunition, hundreds of weapons, mines and other supplies were flown out to Marienfluss. That was only a fraction of what was there. It was impossible to uplift everything, so the balance was blown up.

SWAPO lost 201 men killed, including a very senior commander. Many others were captured. The SWAPO troops had belonged to its elite Special Forces. Their elaborate plans for opening up a new front to terrorise Kaokoland and the farms beyond had been wrecked by the magnificent fighting spirit of 32-Battalion troops, Major Neall Ellis'

Alouette gunships and Major Polla Kruger's Pumas.

Neall was decorated with the *Honoris Crux* for his bravery while under constant heavy fire that day.

Retrospectively, the action became known as *Operation Super*.

There were several lessons arising from this extraordinary episode but I will touch on only three.

The first is that, even if outnumbered and outgunned in a critical situation, aggressiveness coupled with clear thinking and a calmness under fire will always carry the day. The aim must be to disrupt the enemy's equilibrium so that it loses cohesiveness and thus the initiative. Control of events on the battlefield must be taken out of the hands of the enemy commander. Once the enemy force is caught off balance, it must be kept that way. The most vulnerable points, especially those of command and control, must be sought out and hit with all the force available.

The second lesson is that the game will not be won without the finest teamwork. It took months, even years, of close co-operation between the choppers and 32-Battalion to weld them into a formidable team. Neall and Jan understood each other's methods and capabilities. They acted as equal partners in a battle-proven relationship. Teams such as this are built and developed to perfection only if commanders and men train and operate together for extended periods. A group that is thrown together on the spur of the moment will consist of strangers who do not understand each other. There will be little confidence or cohesion among them.

The third lesson is that the commander and his staff at Sector 10 HQ seriously prejudiced the operation at its most critical stage by demanding that Jan relinquish his hard-won control over the battle and move to his 'rear headquarters' at Marienfluss to provide a sitrep. This was despite Neall having given them a perfectly adequate report-back from his chopper. In the circumstances the Sector 10 commander, if he felt in the dark, should have climbed into a Bosbok reconnaissance aircraft and flown to the battle scene to check out the situation for himself while speaking to Jan on the VHF radio. His actions nearly ended in disaster for Jan and his command team after they came under attack.

Ultimately, in spite of the extremely strong resistance from SWAPO aided and abetted by the panic at Sector 10 headquarters, Jan Hougaard, Neall Ellis, Polla Kruger and their well-honed battle team managed to hand out a crushing defeat to SWAPO's Special Forces that day.

But it was a close run thing.

SWAPO never recovered the initiative on that front.

25

Recce Wing

The operations of 32-Battalion's Reconnaissance Wing were often so integrated into the wider operations of the Battalion and its sub-units that their contribution was sometimes overlooked. They also often worked in support of other units. There were times, though, when they operated independently, harassing SWAPO and FAPLA along their main communication lines or wherever they found them.

The Recce Wing should not be confused with the Reconnaissance Regiments of the Special Forces. The latter concentrated their activities on targets of strategic importance. They were not supposed to get involved in tactical operations in support of other units. That they often did, highlights a serious weakness in the organisation and training of the units they supported. The truth is that all combat units should be responsible for collecting tactical intelligence for themselves and for conducting fighting patrol operations within their spheres of responsibility. They might occasionally stray into other areas of interest, but this should only occur when operations are co-ordinated at the highest level.

32-Battalion 's Recce Wing was formed to satisfy the Battalion's need for fresh tactical information. It made a remarkable impact and caused people outside the unit to sit up and take notice. Consequently, it was not long before the Recce Wing began to get bids for its services. Suddenly the teams found themselves being controlled by people who had no idea of their capabilities and limitations and they were given tasks better suited to specially trained commando-type units. Some commanders planned completely unrealistic Captain Marvel missions. Others sent them on mundane excursions that could have been performed by normal infantry.

In one instance a battle group commander wanted to send a four-man team armed with RPG7s deep into enemy dominated areas to independently hunt down and destroy tanks. He was apparently unaware that tanks never operate singly, but in formations with large numbers of attached motorised infantry. For a four-man team to take on that lot — even if they managed to knock out a tank or two — was tantamount to suicide.

A unit commander should be conversant with the capabilities and weak points of any reconnaissance elements he intends to use. The recce commander's advice should always be sought and never overruled — unless the unit commander personally has extensive experience of that kind of operation.

There were teething problems in the beginning. The Recce Wing's first contact in April 1979 nearly turned out to be their last. It was touch and go as to whether they would be wiped out before they even got off the ground.

A newly trained team of white and black soldiers was sent to reconnoitre *chanas* Namixe and Henhombe for signs of a SWAPO base. They flew in by helicopter to south of the cutline and then walked in to Namixe. Piet Nortje, later to become the Battalion's RSM, was one of three whites in this patrol.

There were no signs of an enemy presence at Namixe, so they set off north to

Henhombe, following a footpath. This was not the right way to go about it. The object is to always remain invisible in enemy territory. Tracks must be avoided at all costs. It should have come as no surprise when they blundered into six SWAPOs just south of Henhombe. There was a firefight and the surprised SWAPOs scattered, but the team had been compromised. They went to a lying-up position south-west of Henhombe from where they spotted a 12-strong SWAPO group trying to cut their spoor.

Appreciating that they were targets, the team determined to have a final stab at the enemy before withdrawing. They decided to lay an ambush for their pursuers at the only waterhole north-east of Henhombe. SWAPO, however, had the same idea and concluded correctly that the team had to use that waterhole if they remained in the area.

The team reached their ambush position a mere five minutes before SWAPO. A tremendous firefight broke out and although heavily outnumbered, the team reckoned that attack was the best means of defence. Their impromptu assault resulted in a black soldier being wounded then finished off by a direct hit from an RPG7 rocket. The team valiantly got his body out in spite of the bullets flying around. They hastily withdrew to the south-east, dragging the body of their comrade with them. SWAPO stayed hotly on their heels during the running firefight. Eventually they had no option but to abandon the body.

They were also getting short of ammunition and decided on a final ambush to frighten off the enemy. They would use up the ammunition that remained and bombshell in all directions. Each would make his own way home independently.

They had just adopted their ambush positions when five SWAPO guerrillas appeared from the bush on their flank and paused about 15 paces from the Recce Wing machine gunner. They stood for a moment discussing the progress of the follow-up and plans to deploy more cadres to catch the intruders.

The machine gunner, virtually out of ammunition, took the initiative. He pulled the pin of his only remaining white phosphorous grenade and tossed it amongst the enemy. It exploded and splattered them with blobs of deadly phosphorus. They began a frantic jig as they desperately tried to scrape the burning phos from their bodies with their bare hands. This only made matters worse and spread the clinging hellfire to new areas. They smouldered, burned and writhed in agony as the team escaped towards the south-east. Before SWAPO could rally their follow-up forces, Puma troop carriers dropped down, picked up the team and flew them to safety.

This is where Willem Rätte, our navigator, first came into the picture. On arriving at 32-Battalion he took command of the Recce Wing. Willem was well known for being unorthodox and eccentric. He even looked it and wore glasses that contributed to a general professorial air of studious introspection. When planning operations he was oblivious to everything around him. After deciding on a course of action, he would follow it through to the exclusion of everything else — even the informed opinion of well-intentioned fellow officers.

Reconnaissance tasks are hardly ever spectacular. To be successful a team has to be effectively invisible, carrying out its task without being detected by the enemy and withdrawing without leaving signs that it had ever been there. Fireworks are not a characteristic of a successful reconnaissance — they are a sign that the team has failed in its mission.

The Recce Wing became renowned for its outstanding navigational abilities in featureless terrain. The countryside where it operated is predominantly flat and covered in thick bush which gets even thicker towards the north and east. Everywhere looks the same. One *chana* can hardly be distinguished from another and each *omuramba* seems like a mirror image of the next. Even the rivers are confusing. There is high ground in the areas around Tetchamutete, Cuvelai and Mupa. West of the

Cunene River the land is broken and hilly. It eventually changes until it is as arid, inaccessible and mountainous as Kaokoland south of the river.

Mostly, though, 32-Battalion operated in the flat and tropical savannah plains of southern and south-eastern Angola. The terrain demanded meticulous compass navigation and accurate measurement of distance, assisted occasionally by rare fixes obtained from the few features that could be used as reference points.

Willem became the master of this type of navigation. Of course, there was no such thing as GPS at the time. His teams extensively reconnoitred the Xangongo and Ondjiva target areas on foot before *Operation Protea* and, as has already been seen, he accurately navigated the combat group to their start lines. Later, during Operations Meebos, Askari and Forte, his teams again provided accurate information regarding SWAPO and FAPLA deployments and movements. When required, they acted as guides. They were rarely detected by the enemy, so they didn't make too many headlines.

The FAPLA garrisons in Xangongo and Ondjiva received their supplies via a good tarred road leading from Lubango and running through Cahama and Humbe. It crossed the Cunene River at Xangongo then continued through Mongua to Ondjiva where it ended. It was relatively free from interference by the South Africans and UNITA. There was another route from the north which went through Cubango (formerly Artur de Paiva), or alternatively Jamba, then south through Cassinga, Cuvelai, Mupa and on to Ondjiva. This route, however, was continually subjected to interdiction by UNITA and 32-Battalion which both operated in that area for extended periods.

During ongoing operations, Sector 10 HQ ordered the interdiction of both supply lines. The best results were achieved by Impala strike aircraft based at Ondangwa. They struck convoys and even single vehicles on both routes, often assisted by Willem's forward observation posts on the ground. This forced FAPLA to start moving their convoys at night, which in turn led to the Impalas inflicting heavy losses on convoys that were easy to spot because of their blazing headlights. They then tried moving on moonlit nights only, but the Impalas found this was even more to their liking as it saved them the hassle of using illuminating rockets. Finally, the only option they were left with was to move at night without lights.

That is where the Recce Wing came into its own. It mounted night ambushes using elaborate semi-automatic ambushes with previously rigged mines and claymores that could be attended by a minimum number of operators. They were usually deployed by Puma helicopters to predetermined drop-off points some distance from the targets. They would walk several kilometres to the road, lay the ambush, spring it, and sweep the killing ground. From there they would depart for a pickup point at speed, then rendezvous with the Pumas before first light. That was the theory at least, but more often than not hitches occurred that resulted in some hairy moments — often in the shape of a FAPLA rapid reaction force that tried to destroy them before they could reach safety.

In one ambush a fiercely burning fuel bowser rolled directly towards Willem's team and bounced to a halt amongst them. Their position suddenly changed from gleeful satisfaction at their success to an anguished rush to escape before the tanker exploded and showered them with blazing fuel.

The flames illuminated them and the enemy zeroed in. A truck-mounted 14.5mm machine gun began pumping streams of tracer at them whilst attempting to cut off their escape. Success had been replaced by the almost certain prospect of annihilation. Burdened with casualties, they withdrew for the pickup point, chased by mortar and 14.5mm machine-gun fire. They eventually managed to get out of range and to the pickup point where the ever faithful Pumas were waiting for them.

Cahama was a heavily fortified town. Although we never succeeded in neutralising the enemy brigade based there, we conducted numerous operations against SWAPO's bases and FAPLA's supply lines in the area. From time to time Special Forces also operated successfully there and so did the Pathfinder company of 44 Parachute Brigade. They attacked a combined artillery and anti-aircraft regiment and captured their equipment, including a BM21 multiple rocket battery and a battery of 23mm anti-aircraft guns virtually on Cahama's doorstep. The area, in fact, became the happy hunting ground for all kinds of specialist forces.

Consequently it came as no surprise when Deon Ferreira ordered Lieutenant Eeben Barlow to lay a vehicle ambush between Cahama and Chicusse. The team was flown in by helicopter and dropped before darkness fell at what, unbeknown to them, was the wrong position. They began their approach to the predetermined ambush position halfway between Cahama and Chicusse. However, instead of giving the lion's tail a good jerk as intended, the wrong drop meant they were heading straight for its jaws.

After dark they closed in on what they thought was the ambush site and stopped at a nearby lying up position. Eeben and a black team member, a former FAPLA sergeant, made for the road to investigate. They almost stumbled over a dug-in 82mm mortar and a control point. Eeben decided to shift the position of his ambush site.

Still believing they had been dropped at more or less the right place, Eeben took the team north of the mortar pit which, without realising it, took them closer to the lion's fangs. Reconnoitring the road, they found another mortar pit. Time was running out, so they decided to lay their ambush between the two enemy mortar positions which were about 300 metres apart.

They waited for the right moment, even leaving alone a long convoy of trucks packed to capacity with troops that thundered past. They heard a single truck approaching, which was a target more suited to their limited firepower. Sergeants Clifford and Smith hurriedly laid the previously prepared mines while Eeben and Kevin Sydow prepared the ringmain to command-detonate them.

The FAPLA vehicle, a Soviet-manufactured Ural 6X6, drove into the killing ground. Eeben detonated the mines. There was a massive explosion and the truck burst into flames. It careered down the road for about 50 metres before coming to a grinding halt with its bonnet crunched against a tree.

The killing group leapt to their feet, doubled over and shot five survivors who were still dazed by shock and the numbing blast. Others inside the blazing vehicle were already dead. Sergeant Clifford dashed through the dense smoke and to his absolute shock found himself confronted by an enemy tank which promptly fired a shot in his general direction. Clifford charged back through the smoke, his eyes as big as saucers.

'Holy smoke', he shouted, 'they've got tanks!'

Their ambush had been laid at the entrance to the Cahama base. Eeben later recalled having noticed the driver flick his lights just before the mines detonated. This was obviously a signal to the control point of which the tank was a component.

It was evident that an angry enemy was about to react. They hurriedly retreated eastwards for their pickup point, tracked by thunderous salvoes of 122mm rockets and 120mm and 82mm mortar bombs.

The enemy mounted a strong follow-up at daylight. Unfortunately, the pickup by the Pumas had been postponed for an hour which gave FAPLA ample time to catch up. When the Pumas finally did arrive, the team was under heavy and direct enemy fire and they could not land for fear of being shot up. They returned to base and left the team to try to break contact with FAPLA so they could make another attempt to extract them. This proved to be impossible as the hunted were on foot and the hunters were pressing hard in armoured vehicles.

A flight of Impala strike jets was committed. They pounded the FAPLA force with rockets and guns and destroyed many vehicles. This provided enough respite for the Pumas to land and extract the team.

Interceptions of FAPLA's radio communications determined the damage inflicted by this cheeky ambush. Apart from the truck being mined and burnt out, certain intriguing but unidentified equipment 'from the UK' was destroyed, eight soldiers were killed, seven badly wounded and another four were missing.

*   *   *

There were times when circumstances demanded instant offensive action by Recce groups. Insurgent gangs were constantly on the move between temporary base and temporary base. Waiting for the launch of a properly planned operation against a freshly detected 'live' base invariably resulted in 'lemons' when reaction forces arrived to attack it. The planning, organisation and grouping took far too long and made the process cumbersome. The best way to achieve positive results was by utilising fireforces with dedicated Pumas and Alouette gunships on immediate standby a short reaction time away. It allowed an on-the-spot command and control system that could react immediately and independently of Sector 10's apron strings.

For reasons not understood by paratroopers, the fireforce concept was unpopular with virtually all sector commanders. The brass preferred the time-consuming and hidebound drills structured around staff teams working 08:00 to 17:00 within a sophisticated operations room set-up. Consequently, reaction forces were almost always under the direct command of an officer who was light years away in a totally different environment.

When 32-Battalion began to provide its own fireforces and launched its own immediate follow-ups, the Recce Wing's hot information was acted on with commendable speed.

During *Operation Meebos* after *Operation Protea* in July 1982, 32-Battalion companies were deployed to find and destroy SWAPO bases in the area south and east of Cuvelai. Cuvelai was firmly in the hands of a FAPLA brigade at the time and SWAPO was based as close by as possible.

Willem Rätte's Recce teams were deployed in search roles while Neall Ellis and his gunships were there to support Puma-borne 32-Battalion troops boosted by a company from 1-Parachute Battalion. The first attack on a SWAPO base was abortive because of bad planning at the Sector 10's Tactical HQ, by then situated at Ondjiva. While its staff beavered away planning parachute drops, mechanised attacks and all sorts of other destructive things, they overlooked the basic fact that the massive movements of South African forces would serve to give the game away. It also gave SWAPO ample time to vacate its base in a leisurely fashion. Apart from that, the long drawn-out planning and deployment cycle was counter-productive and an enormous amount of money was wasted.

In fairness to Sector 10, though, their tactical headquarters in Ondjiva was run by senior officers from South Africa on three monthly rotation cycles. Frankly, they lacked the feel for bush war, unlike officers based permanently in the bush who had the experience and intimate knowledge that could be gained only by fighting an unorthodox enemy in a bush environment over a long period.

Willem Rätte determined the location of another SWAPO base and confirmed it was 'live'. Ondjiva's Tac HQ began to laboriously put together a sledgehammer to swat the SWAPO fly. Fortunately, Neall Ellis — the most experienced SWAPO fighter in headquarters at the time, put his foot down and demanded control of the operation. He got his way and Willem's information was acted on before SWAPO became aware they had been targeted.

Mirages went in and completed an air strike. They were immediately followed by Neall and his gunships. The SWAPO gunners, however, had cunningly held their fire while the Mirages were dusting up the base and the choppers were met by a barrage of anti-aircraft fire.

The gunships covered the Pumas while they dropped the 32-Battalion stopper groups, then went to deal with the 14.5mm guns. The Pumas executed a rapid turn around and returned with Lieutenant Eric Rabe's 32-Battalion company and Jeb Swart's paratroopers. They attacked from the east while the stopper group covered escape routes to the west. Between 70 and 80 SWAPO guerrillas were killed and a lot of equipment was captured.

*   *   *

Deon Ferreira briefed Eeben Barlow to reconnoitre a dirt track that was believed to run between the Cahama-Humbe main road in the south and Mulondo on the Cunene River in the north. It was suspected that, if it existed, the track was being used by SWAPO. The team, travelling in two Buffels, deployed to an area about 20km east of Cahama. They were unable to find a north-south track to Mulondo, but located a shorter one that joined the main road to the south close to their location. Many patrol leaders would have reported a negative result and returned to base. Eeben, however, was naturally aggressive and he decided to stick around to see what turned up.

They established a hide in the bush off the road. Shortly afterwards they heard a vehicle approaching along the dirt track. Deciding against laying a hasty ambush, they prepared to attack it on foot. When the truck appeared from around a bend, they charged it frontally and blazed away at the cab and engine compartment with machine guns, rifles and M79s. It rumbled to a halt and they finished it off with further bursts of fire, killing four FAPLA soldiers. A fifth was wounded and hiding in the long grass. He was shot and killed by José as he raised his pistol to shoot Eeben who had not realised he was there. One member of the team was wounded.

The truck was carrying a cargo of radio equipment and some SAM-7 missile launchers complete with missiles. The team withdrew to a suitable landing zone. That night, under difficult conditions with almost zero visibility, a Puma flew in and lifted out the wounded operator and the captured equipment.

At dawn Deon gave Eeben clearance to lay an ambush on the main road to the south. Suddenly, though, they heard the sounds of vehicles starting up nearby and correctly assumed a sizeable FAPLA force was preparing to track them down. Eeben concluded that the enemy was angry about the loss of its vehicle and its precious cargo and he deemed it prudent that they should get away fast. As they moved out in the Buffels they heard the sounds of vehicles following them. They had grown a tail that would be difficult to shake off and they knew it would be impossible to outrun the pursuers on foot if they abandoned their transport. The only other option was to ambush them.

The FAPLA vehicles in pursuit also decided to call a halt. Eeben and his men waited in ambush but nothing materialised from the direction of the pursuit. Suddenly a tribesman appeared coming from the opposite direction and walked straight into their killing ground. They grabbed him and found a note from the local SWAPO gang addressed to the nearby FAPLA garrison. This was obviously where the follow-up group originated. The note told a sorry tale. The SWAPO group had been out of food for a long time and were starving. Would FAPLA rescue and replenish them? The tribesman had instructions to guide FAPLA to SWAPO's temporary base.

Eeben's team had a FAPLA force snapping at their heels while a starving SWAPO force en route to infiltrate South West Africa was to their front. They decided to ignore FAPLA for the moment and turn their thoughts to the SWAPO group. Using the tribesman as a guide, they set off in their Buffels for the SWAPO base. Cocking their ears to the wind they confirmed that FAPLA was once more in pursuit several kilometres behind them.

About three kilometres from the SWAPO base they left the Buffels with the drivers and continued on foot. On the bank of a dried-up sandy river they spotted five SWAPO insurgents washing their clothes at a waterhole about 50 paces away. Several tribes people were nearby to the left. In trees 50 metres beyond the waterhole was the temporary base.

Eeben deployed his men in extended line and they slowly advanced. The faces and hands of the white team members had been blackened with Black is Beautiful and they were all wearing SWAPO camouflage, so they looked like any other SWAPO. The odds of about 100 to eight against were hardly favourable, but they had the element of surprise and enormous firepower for so small a party. Five of them had light machine guns and two had M79 grenade launchers as well as AK47s. But it was still eight against 100!

The washermen scarcely looked up. When they were four or five paces away the team opened fire and killed all five. They charged into the base with guns blazing. Men died and others bombshelled madly into the bush. The base was littered with abandoned equipment.

The drivers of the Buffels heard the firing and drove up to join them. They reported rather nervously that the FAPLA pursuit force had almost caught up. So they cut short the base clearing instantly and headed for the safety of Xangongo. FAPLA did not pursue them, presumably because they became involved in sorting out SWAPO's problem at the base,.

On reaching Xangongo the team discovered that Deon Ferreira had gone to Rundu, leaving the tactical headquarters under the command of Chris Clay, an American. He suggested rather off-handedly that they make their own way back across the Cunene River. This was easier said than done because the only bridge had been blown during *Operation Protea*. However, Eeben, a stalwart from the Engineers Corps, was not in the least put out. They found enough lengths of steel and billets of wood lying around to build their own bridge. Some time later the two Buffels picked their way gingerly across the rather flimsy structure and made their way home to Omauni for a good few beers in the pub there.

Just after this, the Recce Wing was removed from 32-Battalion to become the nucleus of the newly formed South West African Special Forces Commando. In the event, the commando failed to get off the ground because of leadership problems and a decline in professionalism. Willem Rätte stayed on to give the new concept a fair trial. But he was not the commander so he had little influence on the training and the conduct of operations. The unit was eventually disbanded.

The removal of the Recce Wing was a severe loss to 32-Battalion as it took away its capacity for gathering its own tactical intelligence. The loss was felt all the more keenly because it had just started to work closely with UNITA. This left no alternative but to rely on the intelligence of that suspect organisation. UNITA, which as we have seen, was adept at manipulating information to suit its own needs. For these reasons, when Eddie Viljoen took command of the Battalion, he took steps to reconstitute the unit's Recce Wing, this time under the command of Major Peter Waugh. It did excellent work, particularly through the later operations around Cuito Cuanavale. It was during the last of these that the Recce Wing reached its peak of perfection.

It is unfortunate, however, that excellent men of the first Recce Wing — particularly Willem Rätte, Kevin Sydow, Peter Williams and Eeben Barlow — with their invaluable skills and experience were lost to 32-Battalion. It was also a loss to the South African Army because these men afterwards either left the service or were posted to positions where combat experience played no part in the advancement of one's career. As a matter of fact, in some circles in the hierarchy combat experience was often regarded as a handicap — especially if it was coupled with service in an outlandish organisation like the Recce Wing of 32-Battalion.

26

'This is my guerrilla battalion' . . . General Viljoen

At an official parade ceremony on 31 December 1982, Colonel Eddie Viljoen took over command of 32-Battalion from Colonel Deon Ferreira. During Eddie's period of command, the unit would be acknowledged as the best infantry fighting unit in the South African Army. General Geldenhuys, at the unit's presentation of colours parade, said that no other unit since World War-II had achieved as much on the battlefield as 32-Battalion during the fleeting years of its existence. It became the first unit to receive its colours in an operational area.

While in command, Eddie was responsible for the erection of a memorial to commemorate those who had fallen while fighting in the ranks of the Battalion. It took the form of a huge leadwood log with one highly polished surface on which hundreds of small plaques, each engraved with the name of a fallen comrade, were mounted,.

Under Eddie, unofficial traditions became official. It became official policy, for instance, that, before confirmation, new platoon or company commanders had to pass a baptism of fire with the troops they were to command.

Another tradition related to the coveted camouflage beret and black and white stable belt that could be worn only by those who had passed the stringent tests of a 32-Battalion warrior. It was a privilege not extended to personnel on temporary attachments.

In early 1983 Eddie sought permission to move the unit's tactical headquarters from Ondjiva in southern Angola. It was swamped by a suffocating environment of unnecessary restrictions and the debilitating influence of rigidly correct staff officers that emanated like poison gas from Sector 10's Tac HQ next door. The rotation of often inexperienced senior officers to the Tac HQ on three-monthly cycles caused unnecessary strain with the Battalion. Reasonably, Eddie wanted the freedom to manoeuvre without a budding Napoleon looking over his shoulder.

Brigadier Joep Joubert, the new battle-experienced and flexible Sector 10 commander, readily agreed. Joep was a tremendous improvement on the previous sector commander.

Major Willem Rätte and some Recce Wing teams were sent to reconnoitre the Ionde area, halfway between Ondjiva and Caiundo, for suitability. The area was controlled by UNITA, so it was alright for the establishment of a secure logistical base from which operations to the north could be supported. Ionde was found to be ideal for the Battalion's purposes. It even had a runway which, when cleared of mines, was used to bring in Dakotas from Ondangwa, Rundu, Omega Base and elsewhere. This simplified the logistical problems associated with deep penetration operations.

32-Battalion took occupation of Ionde in June 1983. Major Boela Niemann, the unit's second-in-command, took four rifle companies with support weapons there. His instructions were to develop it and conduct area operations in the region to consolidate the Battalion's position. This base subsequently became known as Fort Boela.

Willem Rätte and his teams were working in conjunction with UNITA guides, reconnoitring possible routes which could be used clandestinely without arousing the suspicion of SWAPO and FAPLA. The local UNITA, in the main, originated from the Kwanyama and related tribes, so they had a tribal affiliation with SWAPO whom they had actively supported until after *Operation Savannah*. Then SWAPO had treacherously turned against them and caused the slaughter of many UNITAs.

The Kwanyamas are a fractious lot with a tendency to go their own way. UNITA's one-time leader in Cunene Province, Dr. Vakulakuta Kashaka, was a Kwanyama. Neither he nor his men took kindly to Dr Jonas Savimbi and his UNITA hierarchy at their Jamba headquarters in the Cuando Cubango. (This was not the same Jamba as the FAPLA strong point in the Huila province). Chewalle, Savimbi's best general and the overall commander of the UNITA army, was also a Kwanyama.

It seems that a plot was developed among the Kwanyama top structure to take over UNITA's leadership, but they were found out. Dr Kashaka 'disappeared' and General Chewalle was reduced to the ranks for being a 'whisky guzzler' and a 'womaniser'. He also conveniently 'disappeared' a short while later. This fiasco resulted in the Jamba lot treating their Cunene brothers-in-arms as second class citizens. They were kept badly equipped, improperly trained and short of supplies — in fact, they had the appearance of a rag-tag bunch of scavengers. They were keen to fight, however, which was more than could be said for most of UNITA's forces.

In return for the local UNITA's assistance to 32-Battalion, Eddie Viljoen, within his limited capabilities, fed, clothed and armed them. He also trained the cadres working with the Battalion. To Savimbi's consternation, this ended up with them wanting to join the unit. They did, and what excellent recruits they were.

So at last 32-Battalion was on friendly terms with UNITA, even if it was with those that harboured the incipient germs of revolt against Savimbi and his cronies. Savimbi, of course, was not amused.

*   *   *

By early 1983 it became apparent that SWAPO, after its ejection from the Xangongo and Ondjiva areas, had returned to its old haunts east of the Mupa-Cassinga road to take advantage of the protection provided by the FAPLA brigade at Cuvelai. While SWAPO bases in that area were periodically attacked, South African forces could not maintain control there in the manner they could farther south, because of the threat posed by FAPLA's Cuvelai garrison.

SWAPO used to move down from Cubango or Jamba (in Huila Province) through Cassinga and on to Cuvelai. They began their infiltrations into South West Africa on foot from there. In December 1983 South African forces were given the green light to attack and occupy Cuvelai. At the same time they were to launch a diversionary attack on Cahama to the west. The code name was *Operation Askari*.

32-Battalion's task was to penetrate deep into Angola, attack and destroy SWAPO bases west of the Cubango River, south of the Bale River and in the Cassinga-Tetchamutete area as far north as Indungo. They were also to prevent FAPLA reinforcements in the north from reaching Cuvelai and to act as a blocking force to intercept FAPLA forces retreating from Cuvelai.

Operation Askari kicked off with 32-Battalion lunging deep into Angola from its forward operational and logistical base at Ionde. Eddie Viljoen took three rifle companies with mortars and machine guns mounted on vehicles and established a forward base west of the Cubango River and south of the Bale River. He recalled Willem Rätte's Recce teams and redeployed them to locate SWAPO bases. The first one detected was on the Bale River. This was successfully destroyed with SWAPO taking a large number of casualties.

Three large SWAPO bases in the Micolongonjo area were pinpointed by a Recce

Wing team led by Lieutenant Peter Williams. The Recces were, however, spotted by the enemy who chased them for a day and a half before they were snatched to safety by a Puma. More bases were found at Cassimba, west of Cassinga and in the Indungo area.

On 16 December a series of attacks was launched against the bases that had been located. SWAPO had not expected the Battalion to operate so deep inside Angola and surprise was complete. The targets were destroyed, causing SWAPO a large number of casualties with virtually none on the side of the Battalion.

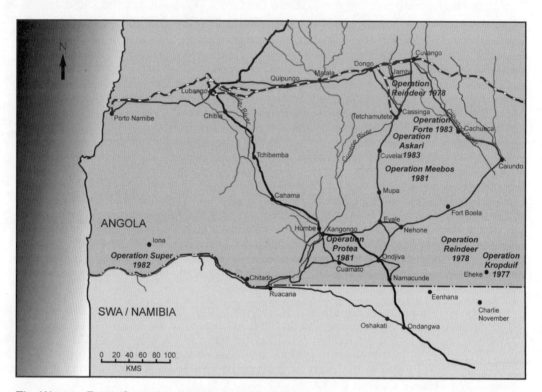

The Western Front: Operations in Angola 1977-1983.

By the end of this phase, the area south of the Bale River between the Cassinga-Cuvelai road in the west and the Cubango River in the east had been cleared of SWAPO bases. This put paid to SWAPO's planned infiltrations of SWA by their so-called Typhoon units. So no serious incursions of Owamboland, via this route, took place during 1984.

The attack on Cuvelai by other forces to eject FAPLA was about to go in. Eddie Viljoen assembled his dispersed companies and moved south to establish a blocking position on both sides of the road between Tetchamutete and Cuvelai. They were readied to cut escape routes to the north.

Tetchamutete straddles the road between Cuvelai and Cassinga. It is a mining centre and in Portuguese days, high grade iron ore was mined and exported through the port of Moçamedes (now Porto Namibe). The mines had not been operational since the commencement of the 'civil war'. The town, including the mine compound, was still intact and occupied by the local population. Information suggested it was garrisoned by between 300 and 400 FAPLA troops. A high hill, the most critical terrain in the area which was known as the 'hill of iron' overlooked the town to the east. The hill dominates seemingly never-ending flat, trackless and featureless bush that stretched from the town in a full 360° to a distant hazy horizon. It did not take a military genius to work out that FAPLA had centralised and heavily fortified the hill's defences in case of attack.

As the opening move of the operation Eddie sent a company to mine the road well south of FAPLA's presumed defensive positions at Tetchamutete. He wanted to discourage the garrison from interfering with his intended blocking position farther south. The company made a night approach and were surprised to spot a FAPLA forward control post where none had been expected. The sighting, unfortunately, was mutual and a FAPLA sentry opened fire. The rifle company immediately went into assault mode and charged through the control post into what they later discovered were the enemy's main defensive positions.

Without stopping to gather their wits, the FAPLA garrison to a man took to their heels and fled into the night, leaving behind all their equipment. Within ten minutes of the first shots being fired, the company found itself in possession of the town's main defensive positions and consequently Tetchamutete itself.

The next morning Eddie took stock of the captured equipment. It included many vehicles, a battery of 14.5mm and 23mm anti-aircraft guns, mortars and B10s. It was obvious that intelligence had positioned the enemy's main defences wrongly. FAPLA, incredibly, had established them on a slight rise to the south, completely ignoring the tactical importance of the 'hill of iron'.

Eddie had no intention of repeating that mistake. He moved some of the captured guns to the summit of the feature which gave the gunners excellent fields of fire through 360°. He expected FAPLA would try to recapture the town and in any battle, the possession of the hill would prove critical. Having found himself in unexpected possession of the town, he was better placed to carry out his primary mission of blocking FAPLA forces escaping from the south.

Feeling very pleased with himself, he signalled Joep Joubert.

'Juliet, Juliet, this is Echo Victor. We have taken Tetchamutete, over.'

There was a long silence, then Joep came up.

'Echo Victor, this is Juliet . . . er . . . er . . . Juliet, now who the hell told you to take Tetchamutete?'

This was followed by another long, almost reflective silence.

'But now that you are there you had better stay, over', he said

Brigadier Joep Joubert always had difficulty remembering his callsign — his initials JJ or 'Juliet Juliet.' He used to come on the air and say: 'Juliet . . .', then release the pressure switch and ask somebody: 'What are my initials again?' The interruption would be followed by the second 'Juliet' after one of his staff had reminded him that his surname was Joubert.

Cuvelai was attacked through well-laid minefields and captured by a strong battle group after severe and prolonged fighting. FAPLA'S remnants were driven off to the north. They did not, at first, realise that Tetchamutete, which was supposed to be their backstop, had been captured by 32-Battalion. It was not long before the first waves of FAPLA, tired of the fighting at Cuvelai, arrived looking forward to the shelter of Tetchamutete. They were careless and obviously feeling safe and thankful that they had escaped with their lives.

A strong convoy of troop-carrying trucks and BTRs led by three tanks approached the two-company blocking position south of town. 32-Battalion opened fire with the captured 23mm guns and everything else they had. FAPLA was completely surprised, so their reaction was uncoordinated. They returned fire but their shooting was chaotically wild and it got them nowhere. The accurately placed fire from the Battalion, however, cut swathes through their ranks. It was a merciless butchering that they could not withstand for long and their resistance melted away. Terror-stricken survivors fled into the bush, abandoning their tanks and a large number of vehicles.

The 32-Battalion troops were Angolans and spoke Portuguese. They were armed with AK47s and were dressed in camouflage fatigues instead of the usual SADF browns. As a trickle of FAPLA troops advanced on the road block they raised their arms in greeting, mistaking the 32-Battalion troops manning it for their own.

Two early arrivals were a FAPLA lieutenant and a sergeant who reached the southern road block and began to regale the Battalion's troops with tales of their depressing experiences at Cuvelai. The troops listened, not bothering to conceal their mirth. The lieutenant, understandably, became annoyed at their insubordination and demanded to see their commander.

Tickled pink at the unexpected chance of having some fun, two soldiers escorted the still armed FAPLA men to Eddie's headquarters located in a horizontal mine tunnel. Eddie had started his working life as a miner, so he felt quite at home in such surroundings. The two FAPLAs walked into his command post and complained bitterly about the unbecoming hilarity that had greeted their tale of woe.

Sergeant Major Crocodile Kruger, a fluent Portuguese speaker, acted as interpreter and politely invited them to sit down. Food and coffee was produced and they dug in like trenchermen, enlightening Eddie and Crocodile between mouthfuls about the sorry state of affairs at Cuvelai. They explained how the Boers had attacked them with artillery, strike aircraft and armoured cars and said how desperate the fight had been. The lieutenant expressed gratitude that they were back safe and sound with their own people.

Eddie and Crocodile, although obviously white, were dirty and bearded. It was clear the arrivals did not think such kind Samaritans were South African. Curiosity, however, led the lieutenant to tentatively question them.

'I suppose you are Cubans?'

'No', said Crocodile, shaking his head. 'Have another guess.'

'Ah, then you are Russians?'

'No, still not right.'

'Then you must be East Germans', the lieutenant said finally.

'No!' bawled Crocodile at the startled FAPLAs, who had no idea that they were already prisoners of war. He thrust his terrifying whiskered face at the lieutenant. His fierce blue eyes held his prey captive.

'We are not Cubans, Russians nor East Germans . . . we are Boers!'

The two were stunned with shock. They watched limply as Crocodile took their rifles. The recriminations began immediately. The hysterical sergeant shrieked at the officer: 'I told you something was wrong. But no, you knew better. You said they are our people. Now look . . . because of your stupidity we will probably be killed'.

Eddie packed FAPLA prisoners like sardines into every available Puma helicopter that came his way and despatched them to Joep Joubert.

Eventually Joep had had enough and he called Eddie on the radio.

'Echo Victor . . . this is Juliet . . . er . . .wait . . . Juliet . . . over.'

'Juliet Juliet, this is Echo Victor . . . . go.'

'Echo Victor, this is Juliet, Juliet. Stop sending me these prisoners . . . what the hell must I do with them? . . . You keep them . . . over.'

Eddie also had nowhere to billet the scores of prisoners he had netted. He took the only other course possible. He relieved them of their weapons and equipment and pointed them on the road north that led to communist-controlled Angola. Understandably perhaps, many refused to leave saying that if they went north they would be shot by their own people. Whether this was true or not is difficult to say, but many of them volunteered to join 32-Battalion. The Battalion's recruiting sources were restricted and its strength was constantly whittled away through the casualties it suffered. Consequently, whether they were from FAPLA, UNITA or any other Angolan source, volunteers were always welcome.

FAPLA eventually realised, probably through feed-back from released prisoners, that Tetchamutete had been taken by 32-Battalion. They must have concluded that this would make attempts to retain, let alone recapture Cuvelai, a futile exercise. As a consequence, those FAPLA forces still in contact with South African forces at Cuvelai were ordered to abandon their defences and pull out. Simultaneously, a brigade was ordered to advance from the north to retake Tetchamutete to assist the withdrawal of its sister brigade.

Eddie had deployed a strong force at Cassinga to the north. It was equipped with 81mm mortars and captured 23mm anti-aircraft guns for use in a ground role to stop an enemy advance. FAPLA's advanced patrols made contact with this force and were almost annihilated. The main body of the brigade stopped in its tracks and withdrew. They had no wish to face up to the South Africans — especially those Terrible Ones on top of the iron mountain. It was best to leave them alone and let the Cuvelai brigade stew in its own juice.

By the end of *Operation Askari* the South Africans were in control of Cunene Province east of the Cunene River and as far north as Cassinga. Tetchamutete and Cassinga had been unexpected and thus unplanned gains. In February 1984 the Battalion was ordered to withdraw from Tetchamutete to Cuvelai. The four to five thousand-strong black population there were unhappy to see them go. While occupying the town the unit had treated them with respect and consideration. They had provided medical aid and had distributed captured FAPLA stores amongst the needy. The citizens bewailed the prospect of indiscriminate exploitation, even terrorisation, that awaited them when FAPLA and SWAPO returned.

The operation confirmed several truths. Firstly, the unit was superbly trained, led and equipped to conduct battalion-sized guerrilla-style penetrations deep into enemy dominated areas. With the Recce Wing to act as their eyes and ears, they could invariably achieve surprise — the hallmark of successful guerrillas. They were the SADF's own Chindits and should have been deployed in that role later. For a short while that did happen, but the narrow-mindedness of commanders and staff at the higher levels reasserted itself and squandered the brilliant opportunities that were available to fatally disrupt the FAPLA/SWAPO war machine.

During *Operation Askari*, most of the Battalion's white leader elements were volunteer Citizen Force officers and NCOs who had formerly served with the unit. They were called up from civvy street to fill the slots created by the departure of National Service leaders who completed their two years' service in December 1983. In spite of them having stepped straight from civvies back into camouflage, their leadership qualities had remained as good as ever — perhaps even better.

*   *   *

The MPLA had learned well from its Soviet masters. Negotiations with the South Africans, via diplomatic channels, soon got under way in Lusaka, Zambia. The MPLA succeeded in regaining the lost territory that had formed the base area from which SWAPO's guerrilla incursions into Owamboland had been mounted.

What 32-Battalion and the other SADF fighting components had gained through sweat, blood and hardship was returned to a communist regime at the stroke of a diplomatic pen. The SADF vacated and FAPLA re-occupied its bases at Xangongo and Ondjiva.

The process resulting from the Lusaka Accord was based on wishful thinking by our Foreign Affairs people and misplaced trust in the integrity of the SWAPO/FAPLA leadership. Because of this and with the connivance of FAPLA, SWAPO got back its former bases on the border. All we got back was square one.

Most of the officers and men of 32-Battalion could have correctly predicted the outcome even before the JMC (Joint Monitoring Commission) was launched. After years of fighting SWAPO and FAPLA, we knew our adversaries better than anybody else. Scant attention, however, was paid to the viewpoints and opinions of our senior commanders. We were not privy to the bigger picture, according to them.

A condition set for the South African withdrawal — viewed with derision by 32-Battalion — was that SWAPO cadres would not be allowed to return to their former base areas, either alone or by being integrated with FAPLA forces. To police this and other conditions set by the negotiators and to monitor FAPLA's return to the Cunene Province, the JMC composed of FAPLA and South African military elements was established.

32-Battalion provided three companies to work with three FAPLA companies to police this unworkable condition. Only fools could have believed that SWAPO would keep its distance from the South West African border. After all, invading that country for the purpose of taking political control there was its raison d'être.

The first JMC meeting was held at Cuvelai on 23-24 February 1984, where 32-Battalion was joined by its very suspicious FAPLA counterparts. There seemed to be no ill will on the part of the Buffalo Soldiers, however. Their recent victories on the field of battle had given them a feeling of magnanimity towards their thoroughly subdued FAPLA colleagues.

Comparisons were unavoidable. While the 32-Battalion troops were neatly dressed in browns, well disciplined and competent, the FAPLA soldiers slouched, were ill disciplined and scruffy. Generally they either neglected or refused to perform tasks allocated to them by their officers and NCOs.

The troops of 32-Battalion were soon calling the shots during the combined patrols, while the FAPLA elements followed meekly in their wake. There were several occasions when the Battalion's soldiers cunningly led their FAPLA counterparts into combined operations against SWAPO cadres infiltrating under the protection of FAPLA.

In one or two notable ambushes FAPLA soldiers became as enthusiastic as 32-Battalion about killing SWAPOs who had strayed into the killing ground. It was not long either before FAPLA soldiers began to enquire about career opportunities with 32-Battalion. This was not well received by senior FAPLA officers at JMC Headquarters.

The Lusaka Accord and the JMC's abortive efforts to keep SWAPO out of Cunene Province had no effect on diminishing the war in SWA once FAPLA was re-established in its old fortresses. They dug themselves in deeper and even more securely than before. They laid extensive minefields and prepared devastating fire plans. They had learnt their lesson along with their mentors, the Soviets, the Cubans and the East Germans.

The episode proved that we on the other hand, had learnt nothing from our own experience, let alone from history. We still did not appreciate that a defeated enemy must never be allowed the chance to recover, regroup, re-equip, reorganise, retrain and rebuild the morale broken under the strain of battle. Our generals and political leaders seemed not to understand that a defeated enemy must always be pressed, remorselessly and without letting up, until his resolve to carry on fighting collapses.

South Africa's Foreign Affairs Department and Foreign Minister Pik Botha should not have handed the initiative back on a plate to FAPLA and SWAPO. After all, what on earth was the SADF doing on the border in the first place if it was not there to combat and defeat communism?

*   *   *

It was decided to launch a clandestine anti-SWAPO operation in FAPLA-controlled areas that were occupied by 32-Battalion during *Operation Askari*. It went under the code name of *Operation Forte*. The plan was to determine whether SWAPO was re-establishing itself and to stop it if it was. For reasons of political expediency and particularly to keep the Department of Foreign Affairs out of the picture, the Battalion essentially operated as a UNITA force. This meant a minimum of air support for casualty evacuation and the flying in of only the most crucial supplies. For sustained medical cover the Battalion would have to depend on its own internal medical resources augmented by doctors from the Recce Regiments. For basic supplies it had to rely on a long and tenuous overland route by bundu-bashing vehicles.

The first exercise was to re-issue the unit with equipment in line with UNITA's. Fortunately, UNITA's Cunene Province guerrillas — as opposed to the well turned out regular and semi-regular troops who adopted heroic poses for newspaper photographs at Savimbi's rear base at Jamba — wore anything from football jerseys to World War-II surplus uniforms. Major Jan Hougaard was sent to raid the Quartermaster's stores in Pretoria for 1939-1945 equipment. He returned with a mountain of the stuff.

Jan and Major Johan Schutte were ordered to develop a nutritious alternative to the standard South African ration pack. They came up with a thick polony-type sausage that contained a concentrated witch's brew of soya beans, flour, vitamins and sauces added for flavour. Its purpose was to augment the dry mealie meal rations carried by the troops. It had to provide them with adequate sustenance for weeks, maybe even months. Something, however, went wrong between the design and manufacture. It had the characteristics of a time bomb. On reaching a certain temperature generated by the blazing Angolan sun, it exploded messily in rucksacks. It also had a vile taste. Jan Hougaard and Johan Schutte were very unpopular, to say the least. Finally they were hoisted by their own petard when Eddie Viljoen insisted they come to his forward operational base . . . and eat and live on the stuff.

The Battalion moved secretly across the cutline into Angola, somewhere west of Katuitui. It was planned to pick up UNITA guides to take them farther north, but they somehow missed each other. This resulted in them approaching a UNITA base from a direction different to that which the occupants expected.

UNITA never really trusted 32-Battalion and vice versa, which created problems for Sergeant Major Piet Nortje, in command of the advance party. The upshot was that he and his men spent some hairy moments as prisoners in the hands of several heavily armed and trigger-happy UNITA guards. Things were eventually sorted out amicably. The force, guided by a UNITA colonel, went up river to Tandaue and established a forward logistical support base under the command of Major van der Vyver.

A few days later they drove across country through thick bush, crossed the Caiundo-Ondjiva road and continued to a base that UNITA had prepared west of Cachueca and away from the Cubango River. Cachueca was a former Portuguese administrative post. The bush was thick enough to create a trap if FAPLA cornered them. It made a a viable defensive plan almost impossible. Eddie decided to select his own base away to the east on the Cubango River and informed the UNITA colonel accordingly. The colonel raised strenuous, almost hysterical objections, but the trucks were reloaded and the unit bundu-bashed its way to where Eddie wanted to go. Despite UNITA's objections, they dug in and prepared a comfortable base for a long stay.

It became a textbook example of what a major guerrilla base should be. It had an oven for baking bread, a clinic with a small operating theatre, an operations room and headquarters, accommodation and messes — all in shacks made from poles, reeds and grass. Camouflage precautions were excellent and they had to be, for FAPLA aircraft flew regularly up and down the Cubango River in an attempt to locate UNITA bases.

They located a disused airstrip that dated back to Portuguese days. It had been heavily mined, but the mines were lifted and it was made ready to take Dakotas. It could not be used during daylight hours for obvious reasons. It was then camouflaged with layers of branches. Every night fires marking the runway were lit and the supply aircraft came in.

Reconnaissance patrols were despatched towards the Bale River and west towards Tetchamutete. They were tasked to locate SWAPO bases and logistical installations and determine the infiltration routes they were using to get into SWA. There was a major punch-up between a 32-Battalion patrol and a strong FAPLA one that mistook them for UNITA. FAPLA fled after taking heavy casualties. Fresh signs of a substantial SWAPO presence were detected. They were back in force in northern Cunene Province, despite the clauses spelt out on a piece of paper in Lusaka. They were using the route to Ondjiva past FAPLA-occupied Cuvelai. It said little for the Lusaka Accord and the effectiveness of the JMC. It also indicated the gullibility of the Department of Foreign Affairs.

Patrols were also sent north of the Cubango River as far as Cuchi, but no signs of SWAPO were found there. However, a patrol found a SWAPO logistical and transit base on the Bambi River. Golf company, under Major Mike Bastin, moved overnight to launch an attack. The assault went in at first light. The base and its facilities were destroyed and several SWAPOs were killed.

The Battalion also got a bloody nose in this encounter, mainly due to the overeagerness of a company commander. He ordered a short cut through a known dangerous area heavily infested with SWAPO concentrations that had not been pinpointed. They walked straight into a strongly defended SWAPO base. During the firefight the company pulled back to regain control and reorganise themselves for a proper assault. Unfortunately, they formed up in the middle of a defensive fire task by SWAPO mortars. Mortar bombs rained down and caused numerous casualties. The attack still went in against tremendous odds. After a desperately fierce scrap they dislodged SWAPO, but paid a heavy price.

There were five dead and many with serious wounds. Counted amongst the dead was Lieutenant David Light, formerly of the British Army. SWAPO tried to drag David's body away. In spite of his surname he was a solidly built and heavy man with the physique of a rugby forward. The men of his platoon charged and drove off the enemy. This once more illustrates the bond that existed between the soldiers and their leaders, even though in this case David had only been with the unit a few months.

They went through a nightmare withdrawal. SWAPO mounted a follow-up. There were numerous running contacts, but each time the enemy was bloodily seen off with heavy losses. No helicopter casevacs could be called for because of the clandestine nature of the operation, so the wounded, the dying and the dead had to be carried by an under-strength rifle company while they fought an almost continuous rearguard action.

Sergeant Major Piet Nortje arranged for vehicles to come forward to Bale to collect the seriously wounded and the dead. It was the closest he could get by road. Finally the exhausted company, having finally shaken off SWAPO, arrived at the rendezvous. The wounded black soldiers and the dead, including David Light, were put aboard the trucks and unavoidably bounced over rough terrain through the bush to the airstrip at Cachueca. The wounded, by then, had been carried on foot for two days and thrown around in the back of a truck for the best part of another. It was not surprising that some of them died en route despite the sterling efforts of the company doctor. The tally of dead climbed until it finally reached 15.

That night a Dakota flew in to evacuate the dead and the wounded. The flight crew were unaware of their identities because of elaborate plans to keep them in the dark. Landing instructions were relayed using a system of code words indicating the runway was safe to land on. No one spoke English or Afrikaans. The features of Eddie Viljoen, who was exceptionally well-known, had been rendered unrecognisable by a thick beard daubed with 'Black is Beautiful.' The other whites meeting the Dakota were also blackened up and in the dark the crew took them for UNITA, which was the intention.

The problem with casevacs by vehicle was that bush tracks leading to the numerous abandoned landing strips both up and down the river had become hazardous because both UNITA and FAPLA had indiscriminately mined them. The alternative was to use the river. In theory this was fine, but in practice it also carried hazards.

A company operating up the Cubango River had Klepper kayaks to use for the evacuation of the wounded or the sick. In theory casualties would be canoed downstream with a doctor for every two craft. Two occupants, one per kayak, would be patients or, in army language, 'non-effectives.'

The company was operating upstream at maximum range when Lieutenant Martin Geldenhuys, son of General Jannie Geldenhuys, and a black sergeant became very ill and required immediate evacuation. The Kleppers were assembled and readied to take the patients downstream that night, as had been planned for such an eventuality.

At the last moment a slightly eccentric Lebanese sergeant, an inveterate collector of snakes, asked the paddlers to take a rucksack of the reptiles back to Cachueca.

They pulled away from the bank and began to paddle. At first the going was good. They did not realise, however, that there were violent rapids downstream. Shooting rapids in kayaks by daylight can be terrifying enough, but to find oneself unexpectedly sucked into them in pitch darkness is petrifying and a recipe for disaster.

When those violent rapids took charge, they could only hope they would not be smashed to pulp against the rocks as they cannoned from one to the next like snooker balls. The inevitable happened and the Kleppers overturned and were smashed by the raging waters. The occupants, including the two very sick men, struggled for their lives to get ashore. Their rifles, food, medicines and the radio sank to the bottom. What remained of the kayaks had disappeared downstream along with the snakes — to the later disgust of their Lebanese owner.

After much buffeting in the turbulent white waters, the men were finally dumped in a calmer pool below the rapids. Bruised, battered and very wet but thankful to be alive, they dragged themselves ashore. All they had left were the clothes they stood up in and their World War-II-style haversacks. With the radio gone they could not call for assistance, so they could do nothing but painfully bundu-bash their way to Cachueca, avoiding the river bank because of the danger of mines.

Their boots eventually gave in, which forced them to bind their feet with tree bark to protect them against thorns, sharp twigs and branches. At the end of a nightmare march they finally staggered into Cachueca. Their clothes were falling off their backs and their feet were cut to ribbons. They were starving and on their last legs.

The Battalion lived under austere conditions during *Operation Forte*. But this was only to be expected when they were operating as a guerrilla force for up to six months — another similarity with Chindit operations in Burma during World War-II.

Rations for the companies were perpetual hassles because of resupply difficulties. Everything a man required for a six-week patrol had to be humped on his back. This problem was partially alleviated by the use of pack donkeys captured from SWAPO, but there were never enough to go around. At times the men tottered on the brink of starvation. Some lost up to 14kg in weight in a single patrol — a dangerous amount if one remembers that the men were lean and fit and without an excess ounce of fat when they started.

After being foodless for several days one company shot a leopard. They skinned it and cooked every edible part. The troops filed past and each of them was served with a portion of meat, bone, gristle and tripe. The head was boiled into soup, of which each man got two or three spoonfuls which they savoured like connoisseurs. They recalled it later as a meal fit for kings — so much so that in later years I caught some of the same men staring with unhealthy intent at my own tame leopard which had become my somewhat unpredictable companion at the SADF's guerrilla training base at Fort St Michel on the Quando River in the Caprivi.

Towards the end of *Operation Forte*, a company was sent from Cachueca to Sequendiva near Mulondo on the Cu nene River to escort 500 UNITA women and children across FAPLA-controlled territory to a UNITA base south of Cachueca. Getting to Sequendiva was no problem, but returning to Cachueca was another story because of the slow-moving column of women, their children, cattle, goats, donkeys, dogs, chickens and other livestock. It was an exercise they managed with skill and without having a single contact with FAPLA, to the thankful delight of the UNITA men who had been worried about the fate of their families.

The operation improved relations between 32-Battalion and UNITA to a large extent. It also helped that at about this time their original colonel in command, who had been sour and uncooperative, had stepped on a mine and written himself off. His replacement, Colonel Jaoul a Kwanyama, got on so well with the unit that it provided instructors to train his men. UNITA's combat efficiency, which until then had been indifferent, improved by leaps and bounds.

Operation Forte ended after six months. The unit withdrew to Buffalo Base with neither FAPLA nor SWAPO being any the wiser that it was *Les Affreux* and not UNITA who had been behind their lines, causing them so much grief. South Africa's Department of Foreign Affairs also remained blissfully unaware of what was going on north of the border.

*   *   *

During 1984 it became apparent that UNITA could no longer prevent FAPLA from launching a conventional offensive into the heartland of its guerrilla base areas. This was primarily because UNITA had prematurely abandoned its second phase of intensive guerrilla war in favour of the final phase of mobile warfare that involved the use of semi-conventional and conventional battalions. This action was foolishly precipitate because it had not achieved its vital objective of tying down FAPLA and Cuban forces throughout Angola by persistent guerrilla operations. If this had happened, the enemy would have had insufficient combat power to destroy UNITA's carefully husbanded semi-conventional forces. It was only then that UNITA would have been in a position to release its regular and semi-regular battalions to attack immobilised and strategically isolated targets and mop up the enemy. Its forces would have simply overwhelmed the opposition with vastly superior combat power concentrated in secret and released like an unexpected thunderclap.

In fact, the unpalatable situation was that FAPLA, even without Fidel Castro's help, had more than enough combat power to take on and destroy UNITA's regular forces. So eventually it became the South African Army's lot to go to UNITA's assistance and save its skin on several occasions.

32-Battalion, more than any other unit, would be used in this frustrating role. It was more experienced than others in the Angolan war theatre and its use caused the least disruption on the national and international political fronts. There would, however, be a need for it to face up to conventional FAPLA brigades. This dictated the necessity to restructure and expand its capability to wage conventional war.

An armoured car squadron, a battery of MRLs (multiple rocket launchers) — the 127mm Valkyrie — a battery of 120mm mortars and a troop of anti-aircraft guns were added to the Battalion's establishment. Its support company's combat power and flexibility were strengthened by an anti-tank capability with 106mm recoilless guns and Milan anti-tank missiles. Its mortar and heavy machine-gun capabilities were expanded by the addition of extra 81mm mortars and 50 calibre Browning machine guns.

This revamp demanded that the Battalion be intensively retrained, from the commander to the riflemen in the platoons. Their days of operating deep behind enemy lines in the footsteps of the famous Chindits, sadly and foolishly were over. As guerrillas they had no equal anywhere in the world. Now they were destined to surpass the best in the field of conventional war. A final attempt would be made, during *Operation Hooper*, to re-activate the old guerrilla warfare philosophy. The inflexibility of the SADF's top command structure, however, would extinguish this sudden flicker of military common sense. They lacked the insight to appreciate that there was ample space in Angola for 32-Battalion to penetrate deep behind enemy lines as an unconventional unit and cause chaos and havoc among FAPLA's forces. They did not appreciate that wrecking FAPLA's equilibrium would lead directly to its final destruction.

32-Battalion would no longer be 'my guerrilla battalion' as General Constand Viljoen had once claimed it to be when he was commander of Task Force 101 in 1976-1977.

27

32-Battalion to the rescue

During the second half of 1985 FAPLA decided to penetrate deep into UNITA's guerrilla base areas to capture large tracts of Angola that UNITA had long considered as liberated areas. FAPLA's build-up was detected long before an advance materialised. It appeared the main assault would be launched towards Mavinga from Cuito Cuanavale and continue to UNITA's major logistical installations and maybe as far as Jamba, Jonas Savimbi's bush capital.

It was evident to bush-wise South African soldiers from the beginning that UNITA would be incapable of stopping the FAPLA forces. It wasted South African money and resources on the training and deployment of regular battalions while neglecting to step up the scope and intensity of its guerilla war. This was the reason why defeat stared them in the face.

This fatal flow enabled FAPLA to concentrate its ample forces at leisure and without serious interference at the places and at the times that best suited its operational plan. The comparatively few regular battalions that UNITA possessed in relation to the enemy were inadequately trained and lacked the equipment to deal with an advance by FAPLA's mechanised forces. For UNITA to build up forces that could handle everything that FAPLA might throw at it was totally impractical at that stage of the guerrilla war. Savimbi wasted South Africa's support in war materiel, training expertise and combat support which should have been used to expand and improve his guerrilla detachments. Unfortunately the Special Tasks officers from the Chief of Staff Intelligence (CSI) who were advising and liaising with Savimbi had no concept of guerrilla war either — especially at the higher levels. Most of the instructors doing the actual training knew that they were tackling the problem wrongly and spoke out, but the chief liaison and training officers slapped them down.

The biggest surprise to UNITA when the advance materialised was that FAPLA had sufficient forces to advance on two widely separated fronts, each with enough combat power to give it a decisive advantage. UNITA's intelligence officer, Caxito, made a major contribution by providing incorrect estimates of the general situation —he was playing on Jonas Savimbi's inflated opinion of himself as the master of guerrilla war on the African continent. If any of his generals had the temerity to point out weak aspects of Savimbi's war strategy, it was regarded as an unforgivable insult. Such temerity was usually rewarded with a bullet in the back of the head. The know-alls in CSI's Special Tasks Division were clearly awed by Savimbi's charismatic presence and they dared not contradict his strategy.

The rout started when FAPLA unexpectedly advanced from the north into the Cazombo Bight and derisively scattered the small UNITA units that faced them. Savimbi predictably took the bait and concentrated all his reserves on that front, which drastically thinned out his forces in the Mavinga-Cuito Cuanavale sector. This placed the strategic initiative firmly in FAPLA's hands. Savimbi and his military high command had already been defeated on the battlefield of wits by the opening move. UNITA was now exposed to a lightning thrust that would bring the campaign to a quick and successful conclusion with little cost to FAPLA.

The moment UNITA's forces in the north were firmly tied down in a diversionary battle, FAPLA began its main effort — an advance by four brigades from Cuito Cuanavale towards Mavinga. They scattered UNITA's only regular battalion deployed on the east bank of the Cuito River and began a two-pronged attack along different routes. This placed UNITA in a precarious position as most of its forces had already been lured north. There was no way they could be brought back over 1 000km of almost impassable tracks in time to stop FAPLA from taking Mavinga and its strategic airfield.

In desperation Savimbi turned to South Africa for help. 28-Squadron SAAF was tasked to airlift UNITA troops south from the Cazombo Bight to the Mavinga sector as fast as it could turn its aircraft around. C130 and C160 workhorses flew every night for many weeks, their holds crammed with UNITA troops who were disgorged and immediately rushed forward to do battle with the advancing FAPLA columns. UNITA, however, could not stop FAPLA which had captured the high ground on the Cuito River's east bank and established a bridgehead that UNITA had no hope of dislodging.

FAPLA's 8- and 13-Brigades were advancing along the old Portuguese road from Cuito Cuanavale via Cunjamba to Mavinga, while their 17- and 25-Brigades were moving down the Cunzumbia River to the Lomba River where they planned to swing east towards Mavinga. Again UNITA tried to stop them but in spite of limited successes which slowed them down a little, they could not disrupt FAPLA's momentum. It seemed likely that Mavinga would fall to FAPLA unless the South Africans intervened.

*   *   *

Eddie Viljoen flew to Jamba to meet Savimbi and discuss the contribution that 32-Battalion could make. Most of all, the clearly embarrassed Savimbi wanted artillery and strike aircraft.

32-Battalion was flown to Mavinga at night in 28-Squadron's C130s. Eddie deployed his support company with mortars, a troop of Valkyrie 127mm multiple rocket launchers and three rifle companies to provide local protection. The South Africans called the exercise *Operation Wallpaper*. The Battalion's role was restricted to the Mavinga area with the mission to stop FAPLA's advance and prevent them from capturing the Mavinga airfield.

Mavinga was a ruined village of no consequence, but it had a splendid gravel surfaced runway. Possession of this by the enemy would have placed Savimbi's Jamba base in range of FAPLA's strike jets. It would have also provided them with an excellent secure base from which to launch a further advance into the southern depths of the Cuando Cubango. So it was essential that Mavinga be held, otherwise UNITA would be flushed down the drain.

FAPLA's 8- and 13-Brigades advanced with little difficulty, eventually reaching a position just north of the Lomba River and 20km due north of Mavinga. Eddie Viljoen, with the Battalion's resurrected Recce Wing commanded by Major Peter Waugh, deployed teams with UNITA guides to keep all four FAPLA brigades under close surveillance.

Using the Recce Wing's information and their accurate target indications, the right moment for a devastating reaction was chosen. The MRLs launched shattering ripples of rockets into 8 and 13-Brigades and inflicted heavy losses with air bursts. FAPLA's advance along that route ground to a bloody halt. They turned west and moved along the north bank of the Lomba River to rendezvous with 17 and 25-Brigades. Usually unreliable UNITA sources suggested FAPLA was being attacked all the way. At one stage UNITA claimed that it had surrounded the opposing force and were about to annihilate them — a threat that remained a flight of Caxito's imagination. The truth was that the FAPLA brigades joined up without any problems.

By concentrating their four brigades, though, it became FAPLA's turn to play into somebody else's hands — this time the South Africans. The combination of four brigades was a perfect target for 32-Battalion's multiple rocket launchers commanded by Commandant Jakkals Cilliers and later also for the Impala strike jets based at Rundu under the ground control of Colonel Dick Lord.

FAPLA was being re-supplied by helicopters from Cuito Cuanavale. Eddie Viljoen arranged for a Recce patrol to take up station on high ground that overlooked the town. When FAPLA's choppers took off they reported it to Eddie who relayed it to Dick Lord. Dick had worked out a plan to shoot them down. Keeping in touch with Eddie, he waited patiently until it was reported that the choppers had left the brigades and were on their return trip to Cuito Cuanavale. He then launched his Impalas.

The enemy choppers were operating in formation, the flight leader behaving like a worried mother hen shepherding along her less experienced charges. The jets screamed in at low level, attacked the helpless formation from the rear and picked them off one by one with rockets.

The chopper's flight leader suddenly found he was alone — the sole survivor. He knew with a fatalism born of despair that his time had come. Messages were intercepted during the attack indicating the sad acceptance of his fate. Even we hardened warriors found them quite moving. Then, except for the crackling of static, the radio fell silent. The helicopter flight had been reduced to a trail of blazing wreckage scattered over many kilometres of remote bushveld. The Impalas accounted for six helicopters in two days. More were destroyed on the ground by artillery fire directed into the brigade areas. The final tally was 11 choppers destroyed.

The enemy resumed its advance on Mavinga, harassed by somewhat feeble UNITA attacks and more effective South African artillery fire. Then they paused 12km north-west of the town, probably for a final regrouping before launching their attack. The huge concentration of troops and equipment presented an irresistible target. It was as if FAPLA had laid bare its chest and invited an assassin to strike with a dagger. The dagger came in the form of artillery and Impala air strikes.

The Valkyrie multiple rocket launchers went into action and put in ripple after ripple of air bursts above the heads of the massed FAPLA troops and cut them down by the hundreds. Later we discovered that FAPLA had given the Valkyries the apt nickname of *shindungus* — a small but exceptionally hot chilli. The 120mm mortars contributed to the slaughter but being incapable of firing air bursts, the results were less spectacular.

That night four Impalas struck with 120kg fragmentation bombs, but they failed to explode because the armourer had left the switches on safe. Unperturbed, Dick soon had them bombed up and back in the air. This time there was no mistake. The bombs exploded in the centre of the already bleeding and bruised FAPLA brigades.

Having taken serious punishment, they decided to return to Cuito Cuanavale which was still within easy striking range of Mavinga. FAPLA abandoned the battlefield and left it strewn with hundreds of burnt-out vehicles, heaps of discarded equipment and hundreds of dead. FAPLA's 17 and 25-Brigades had been virtually annihilated. The carnage was horrible to see.

It was, however, an excellent propaganda coup for Savimbi who quickly arranged for the press corps to be flown in. Numerous photographs of UNITA troops in heroic poses standing by the fire-blackened wreckage of trucks, BRDMs and helicopters appeared in the media. They waved their AK47s at the cameras to show a sceptical world that UNITA had once again scored a great victory over FAPLA.

Probably because they were so busy with the press, UNITA failed to follow up the thoroughly routed enemy in its demoralised retreat and annihilate the remnants. They

(Right) A UNITA
portable short
wheel base Land-
Rover armed with
23mm anti-aircraft
gun. Part of a group
of five, two with
106mm anti-tank
guns and three with
23mms to defend
them. 50 were
supplied by the CIA.

(Right) Crossing a river
on Operation Alpha
Centauri, 1985

51. (Left) Author and 'friend' on the Quando
River before deployment to Cuito Cuanavale
for *Operation Alpha Centauri*, 1985.

52. (Left) Preparation for *Operation Modular*. 32-Battalion's anti-tank platoon's firepower is increased by the addition of 106mm anti-tank guns (in photo)and Milan anti-tank guided missiles — 1987.

53. (Right) Preparation for *Operation Modular*. Experimenting with Milan anti-tank missiles. Mounted on a tripod so as to be clear of long grass — 1987.

54. (Left) Preparation for *Operation Modular*. 127mm Valkyrie multiple rocket launchers mounted on Buffels congregate, 1987.

5. (Right) Ratel armoured cars going into the attack on the Lomba River — *Operation Modular*, 1987.

6. (Above) This missile Ratel knocked out three T55 tanks. One is brewing to the right on the flood plain — *Operation Modular*, 1987.

7. (Right) Maj Hannes Nortmann (left) and Capt Mac McCallum, later KIA, examine knocked out Soviet-supplied T55 tank on the Lomba River flood plain — *Operation Modular*, 1987.

58. (Left) Another knocked out T55.

59. (Right) And another knocked out T55.

60. Left) A 32-Battalion Support Company's 81mm mortar in ambu position — *Operation Modular*, 1987.

(Right) Commandant Les [—]dman borrowed [the] idea from [Op]eration Savan[na]h. A Vickers [wa]gon — three [Vic]kers machine [gu]ns mounted on a [truc]k — *Operation* [Mo]*dular*, 1987.

62. (Left) A South African Engineer-built bridge over the Lomba River. A Ratel armoured car crosses to follow up — *Operation Modular*, 1987.

(Right) South [Afri]can G6 155mm self[-prop]elled gun in 32-[Batt]alion's echelon [area]. Because of the [ene]my's air supremacy [it mov]ed only at night and [afte]rwards moved at [leas]t 100km to avoid [bein]g pinpointed — [Op]*eration Modular*, [198]7.

64. (Left) Comma[...]
vehicle of Comba[...]
Group Bravo. (Sit[...]
Major Doep du
Plessis, (centre)
'Doc' and Sgt Ma[...]
Mike Rogers —
Operation Modula[...]
1987.

65. (Right) 81mm mortar
Unimog crossing river —
Operation Modular, 1987.

66. (Left) 32-Battalion OP
on high ground north of
the Calueque Dam
watching for an antici-
pated Cuban advance on[...]
Ruacana — 1988.

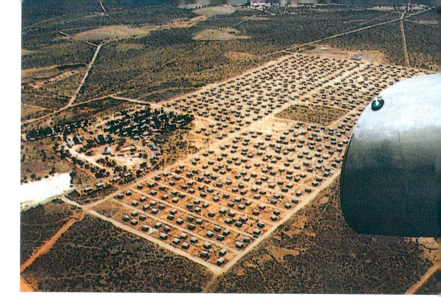

67. (Right) Pomfret from the air. The mine dumps containing the deadly asbestos fibres can be seen all around the base.

68. (Left) Death of an elite Regiment. 32-Battalion forms up on parade at Pomfret prior to disbandment.

. (Right) Two dignant ex-lieut 32- platoon command- s. Gert Kruger (lt) arched on 32-Bn's sbandment parade, dressed the parade Portuguese and rangued the review- officer. Dr Botties thma (rt) with the pieces of silver that Willie Snyman tried give Pres FW de erk.

70. (Above) The colours of 32-Battalion showing its battle honours.

71. (Left) Troops tending the war cemetery at Buffalo Base where the majority of 32-Battalion's honoured dead lay buried. It is neglected now and the jungle is reclaiming its own.

72. (Right) The leadwood tree stump showing 32-Battalion's Roll of Honour at Buffalo Base. It was later moved to Pomfret.

escaped without further harassment and re-crossed the Cuito River. A brigade-strength formation had sufficient time to dig in on the east bank and hold the bridgehead for the development of future anti-UNITA operations. FAPLA's first priority was to lick its wounds, re-equip, reorganise and retrain in readiness for round two.

Again the initiative had been allowed to slip from our hands. But Savimbi's reputation was not only intact — it had been enhanced to where he was considered to be the embodiment of UNITA. Louis XVI once made the unforgettable statement: 'I am the State.' It cost him his head. Now Savimbi was allowing his sycophants to claim 'Savimbi is UNITA.' He eventually became an outcast in Africa and little more than a murderous bandit leader who, like a common criminal fleeing the long arm of the law was eventually gunned down in Moxico Province. Like the Royal Louis Savimbi paid for his self-inflicted ego with his life.

Despite Savimbi's posturing, the FAPLA offensive was a very close-run thing for UNITA. Only 32-Battalion had stood between it and certain annihilation.

The Battalion suffered one fatal casualty, the irreplaceable Major Jan van der Vyver who inadvertently walked into the propellor of a C130 transport aircraft while it was unloading supplies at Mavinga. He was one of the best logistical officers to have served with the Battalion. Just before his death he had been awarded the Southern Cross Medal for devotion to duty and superb efficiency.

FAPLA's defeat at the hands of the South African Forces gave UNITA a pause in which to take stock of the overall situation and alter its military strategy to regain its lost initiative. The obvious answer was to broaden the guerrilla war and intensify it countrywide as rapidly as possible, abandoning the futile efforts to step up its conventional warfare capability. The latter amounted to an arms race against a super power — the Soviet Union — which they did not have much hope of winning. Nor could they win while Cuba continued to provide training teams, planning staff and even combat formations. UNITA, however, for whatever reason decided not to scale down its conventional forces or to upgrade its under-manned and ill-equipped guerrilla forces. Instead, it saw a golden opportunity to modernise its regular battalions.

It must be kept in mind that at the time UNITA was still getting a lot of bad advice from singularly inept South African officers from CSI's Special Tasks. When Savimbi put in a bid to equip a fully fledged UNITA mechanised unit — Ratels, armoured cars, guns and all — the Director-General of Special Tasks did not even grasp the stupidity of the request and actively supported him. He had clearly learned nothing from the latest fiasco. How a sophisticated armoured unit could be maintained and kept in fighting condition almost indefinitely in the remote African bush, especially when handled by a bunch of ill-trained officers and men, had apparently not occurred to that general officer. Fortunately nothing came of the request, so in some quarter or other reason must have prevailed.

FAPLA's 13-Brigade based in Cuito Cuanavale and 25-Brigade which had dug in on a wide front along the eastern bank of the Cuito River, were rapidly being brought back up to strength. They were re-equipped by huge convoys from Menongue, invariably escorted by strong detachments drawn from 8-Brigade. UNITA had three semi-regular grossly under strength battalions of 230 men each operating from the north against those supply lines. Not surprisingly they scarcely made a dent in FAPLA's efforts to rebuild its shattered brigades.

The South Africans, operating intermittently, also interfered with the build-up. From time to time Special Forces were deployed against the Menongue-Cuito Cuanavale supply line, but they did little lasting damage. To keep this line cut, it would have been necessary for UNITA's guerrilla forces to have dominated the area continually. They could not do so because they were the Cinderellas in Savimbi's order of battle.

32-Battalion sent a troop of Valkyrie MRLs escorted by a company of infantry to fire ripples at Menongue. After a tedious journey via Cuangar which involved crossing the

Chissombo, Luatuta, Quatir and Queve Rivers, they finally reached their firing position south of Menongue. They fired one ripple which evidently hit the target, then hurriedly withdrew when it was wrongly assumed that a strong FAPLA follow-up was developing. On the return journey they detoured to Baixo Longa and gave this much fought-over place three ripples of rockets for luck. It was an unwelcome interlude for the well dug-in FAPLA who had been a thorn in the side of UNITA for years. After this the Battalion withdrew to Buffalo Base.

Another 32-Battalion MRL troop moved east of the Cuito River and, more aggressively, fired rocket ripples into FAPLA positions. But these were only harassing attacks in spite of the satisfaction they gave to the gunners.

Nothing particularly effective was done either by UNITA or the South Africans to stop FAPLA's build-up. The South Africans obviously had to be circumspect when deploying forces in support of UNITA in Angola, particularly when done on a large scale. It could easily have escalated the war and drawn them into a vortex from which they might not have been able to extricate themselves. The fact was that it should have been UNITA's task to put FAPLA on the defensive by the widening use of guerrilla tactics, but they failed by default.

32-Battalion began an extensive retraining programme with their organic infantry and their newly allocated armoured cars, artillery and anti-aircraft weapons. They used an area north of Dirico in Angola as a training ground. It was time well spent and allowed them to absorb the huge influx of heavy support weapons and combat arms into their system. Rifle companies, more used to guerrilla operations and hit-and-run raids, were integrated into really hard-hitting combined arms combat teams.

*   *   *

It seems that UNITA began entertaining ambitions to capture Cuito Cuanavale in early 1986. It obviously wanted to remove FAPLA's threat aimed at Mavinga before the latter completed its build-up for a new offensive — or so we believed at the time.

32-Battalion had been tasked to conduct preliminary planning and training to attack Cuito Cuanavale with only limited assistance from UNITA. Colonel Eddie Viljoen and his staff produced a feasible plan.

The plan was kicked around by the hierarchy, revamped, refined and rehearsed, but in the end the operation was called off. It was decided that UNITA should be left to do whatever it wished about Cuito Cuanavale. By then the place had become a festering sore. The plan was later partially adopted by UNITA when it tried to take the town with itself playing the major role.

Savimbi began to press the SADF for combat support elements. He started obliquely by promoting an attack on Masseca about 80km north-west of Cuito Cuanavale. Masseca controlled one of the bridges on the Menongue-Cuito Cuanavale tar road. This action appeared to fall well within the scope of classical guerrilla warfare, so in a spirit of misguided co-operation, the South Africans loosened their grip on a troop of 32-Battalion's Valkyrie MRLs.

I was involved with UNITA at the time and it became my misfortune to provide specialist assistance for this abortive operation. After traversing many appallingly bad roads and bundu-bashing through at least 500km of bush to approach Masseca from the north, it was found that Savimbi had summarily snatched away the MRLs and sent them to Mavinga. This left his main assault force of 230 semi-conventional troops to conduct the surprise night attack on Masseca with no credible fire support. And Masseca was defended by a full FAPLA battalion.

I refused to commit my two advisor teams to the attack after we had been shorn of the most vital part of our combat power, including a formidable squadron of 5-Recce sabres. On my insistence the attack was aborted before we reached the start line.

I was peremptorily ordered to fly to Mavinga by helicopter for discussions with the Special Tasks SLO (Senior Liaison Officer) attached to Savimbi. It was a long flight because we were far behind enemy lines. The dark interior of the Puma and the black featureless terrain below matched my dark mood and smouldering temper perfectly. By the time we landed I couldn't wait to give the SLO a piece of my mind. I found him, a colonel in the South African Army Staff Corps, clambering around in the cargo space of a just-landed C130. He saw me bearing down on him in the dimly lit interior of the plane.

'Hallo Jan!' he smiled and advanced on me with outstretched hand.

I ignored it and tore into him.

'What the hell are you trying to do — kill us or something?'

Alarmed at my failing sense of humour, he stuttered: 'Nobody wants to kill you. I don't know what you mean.'

I could hardly believe that a full colonel, once the commander of an infantry battalion, could be so abysmally stupid.

'Now look here, *boet*. I thought you knew that the requisite combat power is allocated to a commander to carry out a specific operation with at least a reasonable chance of success. That combat power is never ever taken away or significantly reduced until the job is done. As a staff qualified officer you should know that. First you took away Renato's promised sabre support and then you informed me innocently by radio — and only after I had nagged you for two days — that the MRLs were still here at Mavinga 500km from the target. We were supposed to have gone in last night, but I refused to let Renato go ahead. And why must Bert Sachse get himself killed through your stupidity anyway?' I added maliciously.

Renato was the UNITA brigadier in command of the Masseca operation and whose troops had to attack and take FAPLA's defensive positions at the bridge. After that, Commandant Bert Sachse and his team were to blow the bridge. Obviously there was no way I was going to even consider continuing an operation that had become a kamikaze mission.

'And then you had the temerity to insist we continue with the job after you and Savimbi had emasculated our effort.'

The senior liaison officer began to duck and dive.

'You know the old man', he replied lamely. 'It was his way of getting his hands on South African combat assets so that he can go for the big one, Cuito Cuanavale.' He continued brightly: 'He wants you to help with the planning'.

He appeared to be suggesting that being a consultant to the great Savimbi was a singular honour.

This elaborate deception plan, now finally exposed, did not go down too well with us. Duncan Riegaardt and his 5-Recce sabres were so disgusted that they headed south for Fort Doppies without even saying goodbye to Savimbi. They were no longer willing to contribute to what had become a farcical situation. Besides, they had better things to do in other parts of the war theatre.

At least I finally had the measure of our senior liaison officer at the court of King Savimbi. Unlike the Recces, though, we had nothing better to do elsewhere, so we foolishly convinced ourselves that the Cuito Cuanavale operation would be an experience no soldier in his right mind would want to miss.

Savimbi's real intention all along, as had been so airily confirmed by the SLO, was to attack Cuito Cuanavale with his conventional forces supported by South African artillery. He had obviously reasoned that once he got hold of an MRL troop, it would attract the rest of the rocket battery and maybe even the 155mm G5 gun battery with its range of 50 odd kilometres. His assumption was correct. By the time we returned from the aborted Masseca operation, Savimbi officially had the support of all of 32-

Battalion's artillery. Eddie Viljoen was moving his guns and MRLs, with three rifle companies to protect them, to Mavinga. He had already deployed Major Peter Waugh's Recce Wing teams to reconnoitre gun positions, observation posts for the forward observation officers, headquarters areas, routes into those localities, and a host of other associated tasks.

Colonel Koos 'Bom' (short for Bomb) Laubscher arrived from Pretoria to take control of the artillery while Eddie Viljoen was appointed the overall commander of all South African forces involved in the operation.

My colleagues and I were the South African counterparts of the Soviet officers with FAPLA across the river. Savimbi and his tame liaison officer persisted in calling us liaison officers too — a nomenclature I refused to accept. Our job was to advise. Whether they took any notice of our advice was up to them.

I deployed two adviser teams, one per UNITA brigade. Our plan required a UNITA brigade to attack FAPLA's 25-Brigade positions on the east bank of the Cuito River with the support of 32-Battalion's artillery. Its purpose was to draw off any 13-Brigade tanks within the town on D-day minus one. The brigade was also tasked to break through and capture the bridge at Cuito Cuanavale after the town itself had been taken by a second UNITA brigade.

The main attack, which would be the attack on the town, would be launched from the south by the second brigade after it had crossed the Cuito River to the south. The anti-tank weapons and mortars that could not be moved across the flimsy pontoon bridge we intended constructing downstream would be taken across the main bridge after its capture by the first brigade at first light on D-day. The weapons would then rejoin their own formation. By then, hopefully, most of the town would be in UNITA's hands. The final assault on the airfield and against strong points on the western edge of town would be conducted by both brigades.

Bom, Eddie and I worked out a fire plan to suit the scheme of manoeuvre. Everything was ready to go, except that UNITA was running a long time behind its movement schedule.

Brigadier Renato, whom I was advising, was commanding the brigade that was crossing the river to launch the main assault. He was a fine soldier and one of the best trained and most experienced general officers UNITA had. He was, however, faced with the problem of working with troops who were not his own and who were untrained for the task ahead. The engineers, for example, did not have the slightest idea of how to cross a river or construct a pontoon bridge. Of the more than 40 assault boats we had mustered, all but 11 were lost that night because the engineers had neglected to properly secure them. They just drifted off downstream. It was a humiliating indictment of the standard of training UNITA had received from CSI's Special Tasks. No doubt some happy black fishermen along the Cuito River are using our expensive and sophisticated rubber ducks to this day, instead of their Iron Age *makoros* made from hollowed out logs.

After numerous stops and starts the second UNITA brigade began to cross the river and 32-Battalion's artillery began plastering FAPLA's 25-Brigade on the eastern bank. It was a whittled down unit comprising little more than a single battalion and the brigade headquarters. It was deployed to block an attack on the bridge but its position was not particularly strong. The brigade's only other battalion had been deployed so far north that a timely intervention by it to stop the attack on the eastern bridgehead was impossible.

The problem was that the UNITA brigade was commanded by Brigadier Numa — Savimbi's brother-in-law and UNITA's most inexperienced field commander. Yet despite this, they came close to overrunning the badly over-extended 25-Brigade. Victory was within their grasp and they were about to clear FAPLA from the rear of their battalion positions. However, the brigadier — who had stationed himself 20km to the rear and well clear of the battlefield — ordered an immediate withdrawal. His rationale was that his troops had to collect their newly arrived rations. This so-called administrative withdrawal soon turned into a general retreat that took them all the way back to their earlier concentration area.

Brigadier Renato's brigade, meanwhile, could not get up to its start lines, despite Colonels Laubscher and Viljoen pounding the hell out of Cuito Cuanavale's strong points with G5 155mm guns and MRLs. The place was ablaze, but it made no difference because the UNITA attack did not materialise. With Brigadier Numa having already abandoned his diversionary attack, the operation was postponed for 24 hours.

Jonas Savimbi, as the overall commander, ordered that Brigadier Renato put in a daylight assault, without the benefit of artillery preparation, against the full strength of the FAPLA 13-Brigade that was ensconced in extensive trench-works inside the town.

The artillery could not fire by day because enemy fighter aircraft were constantly patrolling overhead in an effort to spot the firing positions of the batteries. So Savimbi abandoned the plan to divide FAPLA's forces as originally intended. Instead, he ordered Renato to take on the enemy's full might without a diversionary attack and without the tremendous fire support from 32-Battalion's artillery. If it had gone ahead, Renato's brigade would probably have been slaughtered and my team along with it. It said little for the military competence of Jonas Savimbi.

Fortunately, it took time for Renato to reorganise his troops. Whilst he was doing so, Savimbi left for Jamba to placate the press which had been mustered there in strength and readied to fly by helicopter into Cuito Cuanavale the moment it had been secured.

Although Savimbi was in sole command of the operation, he had left without deputising anyone to take his place. Renato tried to contact Savimbi's Tac HQ on his rear link to ask for clarification and instructions, but there was no answer.

I tried to raise the South African senior liaison officer with Savimbi through my own channels, but it was to no avail. But after a lot of effort a voice came through that I recognised. It was General Georg Melring who was also trying to find Savimbi. He had walked into the deserted Tac HQ and heard me calling fruitlessly for someone to answer so he picked up the microphone. He could not, of course, enlighten me regarding Savimbi's whereabouts or what had happened to the senior liaison officer who was supposed to be the link between Savimbi and my adviser teams. This, at least, gave us the space to wait until darkness fell before launching an assault with artillery support.

The G5s and MRLs repeated the previous night's fire plan. This time Brigadier Renato's men actually succeeded in taking Cuito Cuanavale. Once in possession, they anxiously waited for Brigadier Numa's brigade to join hands with them from across the bridge. They waited in vain. Brigadier Numa, instead of producing an encore, had decided that discretion was the better part of valour and had hurriedly withdrawn his brigade to a position 20km farther back than the previous night.

FAPLA's 13-Brigade, with tanks in the lead, launched a counter-attack. If Numa's' men had been there they could have tied them down in battle on the wrong side of the river. In the event, Renato's brigade crumbled and was put to flight. Renato, usually a calm and civilised man, almost went berserk as he unsuccessfully attempted to stop his men from running away. Renato, his headquarters, myself and my adviser team had no option but to follow suit and make an undignified rush for the safety of the thick forest to the south. Fortunately, 13-Brigade's counter-attack fizzled out before it could make contact with the fleeing UNITA brigade.

I crossed the river with my team to initiate a new plan with Bom, Eddie and the senior UNITA officers commanding the battle in Savimbi's absence. After discussions it was decided to cancel Cuito Cuanavale as an objective — only the bridge between 25-Brigade and the town would be destroyed.

It was planned to send a South African demolition team, protected by UNITA commandos, to infiltrate around 25-Brigade's left flank to get to the bridge. The commandos would kick off by capturing the weak and isolated FAPLA post that controlled the eastern end of the bridge.

Renato's brigade would attack the high ground and the anti-aircraft guns that overlooked the bridge from the west. Once we had control of the bridge, the demolition team would move up to it, attach their previously prepared charges and blow it. They would vacate 25-Brigade's area before first light and return to our lines. 32-Battalion's G5 155mm guns and MRLs would execute a fire plan to support the preliminary attacks on both sides of the bridge, then fire on FAPLA's 13- and 25-Brigades to stop them from launching counter-attacks on the demolition party. UNITA's 120mm mortars were included in the fire plan, but they insisted on referring every fire correction to Jamba, 400km away. This ensured that its contribution was worse than useless.

The plan was simple and success was virtually guaranteed, except for one vital factor — UNITA's high command and its attached CSI training officer. They took part in the planning cycle and agreed to everything, but then changed their plan without telling us or even the South African demolition party that was due to be escorted by one of their 'crack' units. The reason for this was that this particularly inept South African Military Intelligence officer, who was also in charge of UNITA's training, advised UNITA's General Ben-Ben behind our backs that an attack on the weakly held control point on the east bank would be unnecessary. Effectively, this made it impossible for the demolition team to get to the bridge. In all probability the intelligence officer knew that the 'crack' commando, trained by him after all, would most likely flunk this important test of courage and ability. It seems he wanted to save face, even if it seriously jeopardised the demolition party's lives.

Eddie, Bom, Padre Middlemost and I took up position in an observation post north of the confluence of the Chambinga and Cuito rivers where we had a good view of the town and the bridge. We waited in the expectation of a gigantic explosion that would signal the end of the bridge. That would sever FAPLA's access to the Cuando Cubango east of the Cuito River and trap 25-Brigade on the wrong bank.

The artillery opened fire when Commandant Bert Sachse, leading the demolition party, told us that his team was in position to attack the bridge. He then discovered, to his dismay, that no UNITA attack was about to be launched against the eastern control point. It was only then that the commander of the highly regarded special commando told him that General Ben-Ben had ordered him not to attack it, but only to screen him and his team from FAPLA attacks by sticking as closely to them as possible. Despite this change of plan, Bert took his men towards the river, but they immediately came under heavy 23mm fire from the western bank. Those positions were supposed to have been attacked by Brigadier Renato's men, but that had not occurred either. Bert was left with no option but to get away as fast as he could.

Thus ended UNITA's attempt to capture Cuito Cuanavale. This exercise in futility was later grandly styled *Operation Alpha Centauri*. 32-Battalion's guns and multiple rocket launchers had fired almost continuously for three consecutive nights. They had caused considerable damage to FAPLA's defensive positions and equipment, including some newly erected radar installations, and had destroyed a large number of vehicles. Installations, of course, could easily be rebuilt as long as the Soviets continued to pour in an apparently endless stream of equipment to replace that which had been lost.

From our standpoint the exercise had been pointless. FAPLA was still firmly ensconced at the Cuito Cuanavale bridgehead and had begun to build up and concentrate its forces for round three. The exercise proved conclusively, yet again, that UNITA should never have become involved in conventional campaigns, but instead should have expanded its guerrilla warfare capability. It had persisted against all reason on the premise that its conventional forces could see FAPLA off, providing South Africa gave them artillery support from time to time.

When Savimbi deserted the battle to conduct his press conference — which turned out to be a blatant exercise in disinformation — he abandoned his brigade commanders and their brigades to stew in their own juice. He also cost South African tax-payers over R20 million in wasted artillery ammunition. It must again be emphasised that he had been aided and abetted by some operationally ignorant South African intelligence officers who should never have been allowed to leave their Pretoria offices to discuss strategy with this very overrated UNITA commander.

The scene was set for South African forces, including 32-Battalion, to become more heavily involved in Angola than ever before. It would lead to what would become the heaviest commitment of South African troops on foreign soil since World War-II.

28

'Enjoy this war – the peace will be worse!'
Operation Modular
1987

At the end of 1986 Colonel Eddie Viljoen handed over command of 32-Battalion to Colonel Jock Harris. Eddie would be a hard act to follow. He was a man who had over and over again proved himself to be a formidable warrior in battle and was loved and respected by his men.

The change of command marked a new era of the big battalions. 32-Battalion's transformation from a guerrilla-style unit to a quasi-mechanised battle group was almost complete. It would have more firepower than any other South African infantry unit, except for 4- and 61-South African Mechanised Infantry Battalions. The change was a direct result of the rapidly escalating threat to UNITA posed by the FAPLA brigades concentrated at Cuito Cuanavale.

FAPLA had recovered from the last fiasco. Its brigades had been lavishly refurbished with new Soviet equipment and brought up to strength with personnel replacements. Ominously, a swarm of tanks was being concentrated at Cuito Cuanavale. Even more ominous was the fact that the SAAF would be unable to provide adequate air support for future operations, for fear of whittling away resources required for guarding South Africans closer to home.

Without fear of contradiction, it can be said that the SAAF pilots outperformed their FAPLA and Cuban counterparts by a large margin. Aerial combat invariably ended with the downing of enemy fighters. It was, however, inevitable that wear and tear should take its toll amongst our aircraft. Furthermore, they were not as readily replaceable as FAPLA's because of the UN arms embargo.

There had been a general misconception about the strategic importance of the bridge at Cuito Cuanavale. It was regarded as the only access route to the area of the Cuando Cubango lying east of the Cuito River — the heart of UNITA's guerrilla base area. If UNITA had destroyed the bridge during *Operation Alpha Centauri*, FAPLA would probably have been incapable of adequately replacing it. By 1987, though, FAPLA had more than enough bridging material and Soviet-supplied ferries, making the bridge virtually redundant anyway. Despite this, 32-Battalion was ordered to prepare a plan to attack and destroy it.

Without air support, 32-Battalion would have to attack the bridge at night. The major difficulty was that it could only be taken by a frontal assault. The first tough nut to crack was the by then heavily entrenched and fortified bridgehead that UNITA's Brigadier Numa had failed to take in 1986 when the defenders were still very thin on the ground. Assuming this could be achieved, there would be more enemy brigades available in Cuito Cuanavale to launch counter-attacks. There was also the reality of the heavily fortified terrain on the west bank of the river that dominated the bridge.

All this meant that the Battalion had to storm the bridge and capture its entire length plus several hundred metres of built-up causeway on both sides of the river before it could secure the dominating terrain. Only then could the demolition charges be placed. What's more, the Battalion would have to hold out for several hours against counter-attacks of at least brigade strength.

The planners estimated that the Battalion could expect 300 Category 1 (serious) casualties, apart from those killed in action, and many more with minor wounds. This meant placing a heavy burden on the Battalion's slender medical and casualty evacuation capacity — apart from the horrific prospect of a third of the men being wiped out.

No commander worth his salt would agree to carry out an assault under such conditions unless the situation was truly desperate. The butcher's bill was too high, so the plan was dropped and other methods examined.

A valiant operation by Special Forces in August 1987 in support of *Operation Modular* succeeded in partially destroying the bridge. It did not, however, stop logistics sufficient for six FAPLA brigades from crossing the river via the damaged bridge and by ferries.

FAPLA finally started to cross the Cuito River at the beginning of July 1987. It established a secure base on high ground by the Chambinga River from which to launch its invasion of UNITA territory. Two weeks later four brigades advanced, following the courses of the Cunzumbia and Cuzizi rivers. One diverged towards Mavinga via the course of the Cunjamba River.

The SADF was rightly reluctant to deploy South African forces. There was a danger that it could be drawn into a prolonged war with FAPLA that would probably escalate beyond our capacity to cope with it. The State Security Council, however, ordered that something should be done to pull Savimbi's chestnuts out of the fire. It was decided to send 32-Battalion because it was less conspicuous than other South African units. The Battalion went with its attached armoured car squadron and artillery. Two rifle companies were detached from 101-Battalion to boost its infantry strength.

And so the first steps were taken towards an armed confrontation. Because of its fatally flawed incremental nature, though, it would lead to a stalemate — an unsatisfactory situation.

The FAPLA brigades of 1987 were vastly different propositions from those of 1985. Their combat power had been augmented with powerful tank formations. Each battalion had at least one tank company of ten T54/55 tanks. In addition, two so-called Tactical Groups, each with two tank companies and a mechanised infantry company, supported the advance on Mavinga. There was probably a total of 160 tanks amongst the four brigades. FAPLA had discovered from experience that UNITA never stood its ground when it was faced by tank attacks, even when the terrain favoured well-trained aggressive infantry armed with rocket launchers and anti-tank guns.

In most of the heavily bushed areas east of the Cuito River, anti-tank weapons could be gainfully deployed to sort out FAPLA's tanks. In fact, an experienced tanker would consider the use of tanks to lead an attack through thick bush to be suicidal. FAPLA felt the same way and tried to bypass dangerous areas like that by using the tree margins that fringed the open flood plains and by always advancing behind an infantry screen.

Separating FAPLA's infantry from its tanks called for the use of mortar and heavy machine-gun fire with weapons crewed by the kind of riflemen found in 32-Battalion and not with UNITA. When the infantry had been shooed away, their armour would become vulnerable to anti-tank weapons crewed by 32-Battalion troops.

UNITA's fear of tanks made it inevitable that 32-Battalion's armoured car squadron would play the major role in stopping FAPLA's advance. Major Hannes Nortmann was in command of this squadron which had been specially trained and equipped for an anti-tank role. He possessed the foresight to integrate black 32-Battalion riflemen into the squadron. They rode as infantry sections along with national service crewmen in the 90mm-gunned Ratel armoured cars. This gave them their own organic infantry protection. The squadron also had four missile-Ratels armed with a recently developed

South African anti-tank missile system known as the ZT-3 which had never been used in battle before.

Hannes noticed a wariness amongst the black riflemen when they first married up with the young white armoured car crews. In the eyes of the black veterans they were not yet proven in battle. A period of intensive training, however, welded the men into formidable teams. After the first battle, the white troopers in the armoured corps and the black riflemen could not be prised apart.

*   *   *

32-Battalion deployed to the Lomba River in August 1987 with orders to halt FAPLA's advance. A tactical headquarters was established in Mavinga to conduct what became known as *Operation Modular*.

Jan Hougaard, now a commandant, flew in to assist Colonel Jock Harris who was new to working with the highly unpredictable Jonas Savimbi and his UNITA forces. Jan had served in the unit for almost as long as Eddie Viljoen and he was familiar with UNITA's penchant for devious and frustrating schemes.

In early September Colonel Deon Ferreira, by then with SWATF (South West Africa/ Namibia Territorial Force) was sent to take overall command of the operation. 61-Mechanised Battalion had been added to the 32-Battalion deployment and the HQ was upgraded to become 20-South African Brigade Tac HQ. The one-step-too-late incremental increase in combat power was about to be demonstrated in all its futility.

UNITA, unsurprisingly, had failed to stop FAPLA's southward advance and many of its men had been crushed beneath the tracks of the rampaging tanks. In July 32-Battalion's Recce Wing teams had deployed north of the Lomba River to locate the FAPLA brigades and plot their advance. Staff Sergeant Piet Fourie's team operated along the Cunzumbia River, while Sergeant Mac da Trinidade and his team were responsible for the Cuzizi River axis. They followed FAPLA's armour the whole way on its route down to the Lomba River, reporting its every move to the Tac HQ at Mavinga.

By the clever use of artillery Jock Harris managed to slow FAPLA's advance to a crawl. As part of this action, Sergeant Piet Fourie was sent north to locate FAPLA's 16-Brigade on the Cunjamba River. He was given a small Land-Rover-type vehicle by UNITA, one of a large batch provided by the United States as military aid. For a while, at least, the team could dispense with foot-slogging. They soon found the enemy who were somewhat out on a limb to the east. He called for long range G5 artillery fire and an air strike which caused frightful slaughter amongst a brigade that had been relaxed and blissfully unaware that they had been under close observation by a scruffy patrol of Buffalo Soldiers. The brigade's advance came to an abrupt halt, which allowed more attention to be given to the enemy forces advancing along the Cuzizi and Cunzumbia rivers.

Piet Fourie took his team back up the Cunzumbia to scout for the enemy's 59-Brigade. Unexpectedly, they bumped a FAPLA patrol while conducting a close-in reconnaissance in the dark. For some reason the team's identity was not tumbled by the enemy. After exchanging a few pleasantries, the patrols went their separate ways.

At the time the South Africans, for some reason, were using artillery fire sparingly, so little was done to harass the brigade once it was located and positively identified.

To the west Mac da Trinidade's patrol, accompanied by Major Pierre Franken — the commander of 32-Battalion's Valkyrie 127mm MRL battery — moved parallel to the Cuzizi River to track FAPLA's advance along that axis. It was established that the brigades using this route were the 47th and the 59th. They located the 47th close to the source of the Cuzizi. Pierre, acting as fire controller, brought artillery fire down on them, but it proved ineffective. They got another chance the next night while following in the brigade's wake as it advanced southwards. The artillery found the centre of the formation. The enemy soldiers panicked and many just milled around screaming as shell splinters slashed down from air burst shells exploding over their heads. The brilliant white flashes of salvo after salvo lit up the scene of destruction. Most of the troops were shell-shocked by the devastating onslaught. Many of them died, watched by their tormentors who were controlling the long distance artillery from an observation post a mere stone's throw away.

Mac withdrew his team to the Lomba River source where UNITA was supposed to have deployed a battalion-sized ambush position designed to halt 47-Brigade's advance. They had not done so and the enemy rounded the source and swung east towards Mavinga. Mac's men, without the promised support, were spotted and fired on — which necessitated a rapid retreat to avoid capture. The enemy brigade advanced as far as the junction of the Lomba and Cuzizi rivers and dug in.

Mac and his team re-crossed to the north bank of the Lomba River. They established an OP on high ground overlooking the flood plain and 47-Brigade's positions directly south of them. For ten days and nights Pierre directed artillery fire, causing havoc amongst the enemy. They knew that someone was fire controlling for the artillery, but they could not work out the location of the OP.

The shelling did not stop the brigade, however, and in due course it resumed its advance down river towards Mavinga. Unlike the situation in 1986, the South African artillery fire on its own, while causing tremendous damage, was not the ultimate answer. Furthermore, 32-Battalion could not effectively challenge with artillery fire alone the swarms of tanks that led every FAPLA attack.

Commandant Robbie Hartslief, commanding 32-Battalion's support group, became the commander of a newly formed Battle Group Charlie. It comprised Franken's MRL battery, the anti-aircraft troop and Major Hannes Nortmann's anti-tank squadron of Ratel-90s and Ratel-ZT3s. This nucleus was augmented by two attached 101-Battalion rifle companies. The Owambo infantry of 101-Battalion, mounted in Casspir armoured personnel carriers, were excellent fighters.

Splitting up fully integrated battle groups to create ad hoc groups comprising bits and pieces from virtually every unit employed in a combat zone, was a strange custom that was probably unique to the South African Army. These ad hoc units were composed of strangers who had never trained together, let alone fought together.

It is a mystery why Robbie was not allocated rifle companies from his parent battalion. This would have given him a fully integrated unit of men used to each other's ways. There were enough 32-Battalion rifle companies engaged on unimportant tasks which could have provided the infantry necessary to flesh out Battle Group Charlie. The 101-Battalion companies could have taken over the tasks of the released 32-Battalion companies.

Hannes Nortmann's armoured cars were ordered to adopt a defensive position south of the Lomba River and east of its junction with the Cunzumbia. The Lomba, like all rivers in those parts, is narrow, deep and fast flowing. It runs between deeply cut banks with extensive marshy flood plains on both sides, often several kilometres wide. This swampy ground can almost swallow large vehicles, so it is virtually impossible to cross except at a few places where the ground is hard enough to support heavily loaded trucks. Such spots are difficult to identify. Even then the surface often has to be improved by using logs and sandbags.

At one such crossing point there was a long tongue of dry land extending south from a demolished wooden bridge and across the flood plain to the edge of the tree line at its southern rim. It was there that Hannes took up a position concealed in the tree line from where he could cover the spit of sand.

He was soon ordered to head downstream along the Lomba River to stop an expected crossing by FAPLA's 16-Brigade that was believed to be deployed farther east towards Mavinga. It was thought that the brigade had reached the Lomba after an encounter with Piet Fourie's patrol. But it turned out to be a wild goose chase. 16-Brigade was nowhere in sight when Hannes reached the crossing. While away from their previous position, however, FAPLA's 21-Brigade took the opportunity to slip a battalion across to occupy it. The force adopted a defensive position facing south, thus establishing a bridgehead for the planned crossing of the rest of the brigade.

Robbie instructed Hannes to return there and hurl the enemy back across the Lomba. Hannes, however, could only move at night as the lack of combat air support made movement by day impossible in the face of MiGs that were constantly prowling the skies in an effort to catch the South Africans in the open.

It was, as Hannes put it, a hairy prospect because armoured forces do not normally attack at night. In spite of his reservations, he headed back for the crossing point in the pitch darkness of an African night with two armoured car troops interspersed with Casspirs in extended line abreast formation. Progress was slow because of the inevitable control problems associated with an extended line, especially in thick bush in almost zero visibility.

Just before first light Hannes decided to laager for the day — a reversal of the usual drills as tanks and armoured cars normally laager at last light. Dispensing with the traditional laager square, they formed up in files with a defensive leg from east to west along the tree line edging the flood plain and a second north-south leg facing the suspected enemy deployment to the west. They completed an 'L' by tying in the right flank of the second leg with the left extremity of the first. While the west-facing leg was moving into position, they suddenly found themselves looking at FAPLA infantry at uncomfortably close quarters. It turned out that they were busily hunkering down in a laager position already occupied by the FAPLA battalion they were hunting. It was a severe shock to both parties.

The Buffalo Soldiers recovered first and brought FAPLA under heavy fire. But the enemy were not far behind and they began to rocket the armoured cars and Casspirs with RPG7s. They registered several hits at point-blank range but none exploded because the rockets need 15 metres of flying distance before they arm. This gives a good idea of how mixed up both sides were as they fought at very close quarters.

The remainder of Hannes' combat team joined the fray and the enemy was rudely evicted from its recently acquired premises with heavy losses. The several kilometre wide flood plain was soon dotted with groups of wildly fleeing FAPLA as they desperately tried to reach the safety of their friends on the far bank of the river. They were left brutally exposed by the first light of dawn on a flat and open killing ground, making them pathetically easy to shoot down. Machine-gun fire kicked up spurts of black mud at their feet and thudded into flesh and bone. Figures stumbled and fell. It was like shooting at falling plates on a rifle range.

Only a few made it back across the river. Several hundred were killed and their bodies sprawled obscenely on the mud flats or gently tumbled along the surface of the Lomba River. The rotting corpses later polluted 16-Brigade's drinking water downstream.

Across the river 21-Brigade heard the sounds of battle and guessed what was going on. They weighed in with heavy rocket and mortar fire and launched an armoured counter-attack to retake the bridgehead. They had developed what they believed was an effective battle drill. So after suffering a setback at the hands of UNITA, they immediately hurled their tanks at them in an aggressive response. UNITA's drill in the face of this kind of action was almost always to quit whatever they were doing and run to the rear.

FAPLA's mistake, however, lay in their assumption that they were facing UNITA. It was a reasonable error because they lacked a clear view of the dawn battle from across the river. Three T55 tanks lumbered across the ford and charged towards the combat team's positions, confidently expecting to flush them out and send them running.

Hannes had a problem. Only one of his ZT3 missile-Ratels was serviceable. So he had no option but to order the armoured cars to open fire with their 90mm guns using HEAT(high explosive anti-tank) shells. They registered hits but the range was too extreme for the shells to penetrate the thick armour. The tanks kept on coming with the shells exploding harmlessly on their steel hulls.

Hannes jumped into the only serviceable missile-Ratel and told the gunner to fire on the leading tank. The first two ZT3 missiles missed and flew over the top. The third struck the lead tank's track idler and it stopped. The fourth missile struck squarely and engulfed the stationary tank in a sheet of flames. It began to brew. The exuberant and over-excited gunner fired his fifth missile at the second tank, but it fell short. Hannes brought him back to earth in time-honoured soldier's fashion by swiping him on the side of his head. The sixth missile, maybe as a result, was a direct hit on the second tank and it was knocked out. The driver of the last tank lost his nerve, turned about and began to drive for safety. The seventh missile hit the weaker armour at the rear and knocked that tank out as well. The driver escaped through the hatch, but he was brought down by machine-gun fire.

FAPLA called in the MiGs. In a violent demonstration watched by an amused audience of South Africans, they devastated a large area of the bush, but missed the combat team's positions entirely. The crossing of the Lomba River by the Goliath-sized 21-Brigade had been stopped in its tracks by a David-sized combat team.

FAPLA's 47-Brigade was the next problem. The Ingwe stream, a small tributary of the Lomba, was west of where Hannes had beaten off 21-Brigade. Some 1 000 metres or so farther on in dense forest was a former UNITA logistics base. It was honeycombed with trenches, dug-in huts and bunkers. Tac HQ told Robbie Hartslief that information from UNITA suggested that some loose elements from FAPLA's 47-Brigade had penetrated the old base, possibly with a few PT76 amphibious tanks armed with outdated 76mm guns. They were no match for the 90mm guns of the Ratels and would he please go and see them off.

Robbie ordered Hannes' armoured car squadron to rejoin Battle Group Charlie. It had by this time been augmented by a troop of Ratel-90 armoured cars from the newly arrived 61-Mechanised Battalion. This was another of those strange spur-of-the-moment attachments and detachments the South Africans seemed to go for. Consequently, Hannes temporarily lost command of his combat team to become Robbie's second-in-command. In this capacity he took over 'A' echelon — comprising the recovery, ammunition, fuel and other back-up vehicles — while Robbie as the commander took direct control of the F (fighting) echelon.

On 13 September they sallied forth. When they reached the old UNITA base, Battle Group Charlie's right flank came into contact with FAPLA infantry. They quickly routed the enemy who again attempted to escape across the featureless flood plain to the north. The machine gunners on the 101-Battalion Casspirs mowed them down in droves.

While moving through the old trench systems in battle formation, three Ratels fell through the roofs of some deep and well-concealed bunkers and found themselves firmly stuck. It was at this difficult moment that infantry elements working their way through the base reported that tanks — real tanks and not the obsolete PT 76s — had been spotted. The intelligence from UNITA that had been fed to an unsuspecting Robbie was once again completely inaccurate. The Tac HQ, it seemed, had not learned that it was wise to treat UNITA's intelligence with circumspection — something we old-timers in the field had learned from bitter experience.

They could not locate the tanks immediately because the infantry callsigns that had reported their presence had used incorrect indication procedures. The base was large and like an untidy maze, so the axis on which the various sub-units were moving did not necessarily conform to the battle group's east-west axis of attack. Consequently, reports that tanks were 'in front, left, right, half left or half right' confused the issue to the extent that Robbie had absolutely no idea in which direction the threat lay.

Hannes was bringing up the rear with three Wit Hings (White Stallion) armoured recovery vehicles and ambulances. Glancing casually to his left, he was shocked to see an enemy T55 tank amongst some trees only 200 metres away. He hoped against hope that his small group of unprotected thin-skinned vehicles had not been seen. They were exposed and could be casually demolished by tank fire like ducks in a row. Hannes passed the enemy's position to Robbie who thanked him politely for the first accurate tank information of the day.

The T55, however, had spotted Hannes' group. It fired a shot but missed. Robbie almost simultaneously replied with an accurate round from his 90mm gun at short range. The tank began to brew, which saved Hannes and his non-fighting vehicles from certain destruction.

The fight took a turn for the worse when some 101-Battalion Casspirs charged past heading east. They claimed that tanks were following in hot pursuit. The three Ratel-90s, meanwhile, were still stuck in the bunkers. Five Cuban T54 tanks appeared from the dusty haze and careened through the base. Two passed one on each side and within a few metres of a trapped Ratel. Amazingly, they didn't even notice it or its very surprised crew who were desperately trying to dig out their car. Fortunately, the tanks were operating half blind with their hatches battened down for the expected battle. Cuban tank crews were invariably averse to exposing themselves to environments likely to be polluted by flying bullets and shrapnel.

Another Cuban T54, however, could scarcely avoid spotting a second Ratel that was stuck in a ditch right in front of it. What they did not see, though, was that a third Ratel was trying to recover it from the far side. The cripple was hooked to its rear by a tow-bar which the troopers were frantically trying to unhitch so they could either get into action or out of harm's way. The Cubans, believing their intended victim was trapped and helpless, seemed in no hurry to shoot it out. Perhaps they were savouring the idea of an easy kill with their 100mm gun at point-blank range.

Unfortunately for them, they left it too late to get in a fatal shot. They must have been shocked to see a second Ratel burst from behind the trapped one. Its 90mm gun swung menacingly towards them. A grim dance of death followed with the two armoured monsters, only 20 metres apart, chasing each other around in circles as the gunners tried to bring their guns to bear. The Ratel won the contest and fired the first shot. It struck home and the Cuban tank began to brew.

A 32-Battalion Ratel troop leader, Captain Mac Macallum, who had served in 32-Battalion for several years, was killed by a shot through the neck. His inexperienced young gunner tried to drive the Ratel out, but he ventured into the oozing muddy trap of the flood plain and bogged down. Enemy tanks began to crowd in on him. He had insufficient experience to be able to give his exact position to Robbie over the radio but reported that he was about to be shot out.

'Even if they get me', he said, 'please remember that I've already shot out one of theirs. I've already had my kill'.

Hearing on the command net what was happening, Hannes leaped down from his very vulnerable soft-skinned vehicle and rushed to Mac's assistance on foot. With a Wit Hings recovery vehicle driven by Staff Sergeant Riaan Rupping dogging his footsteps, he ran across the front of trenches still manned by FAPLA, trying desperately to locate the trapped Ratel. Mac was a special friend, which gave Hannes added impetus as he made his death-defying dash through the veld. The FAPLA infantrymen began targeting him as he ran, but he returned fire with short bursts from his R5 rifle to keep their heads down. He came upon another Ratel that was also stuck in a trench.

The crew directed him to Mac's Ratel, but announced that they were just about to get the hell out of there. They had picked up a radio signal from Robbie ordering them to withdraw as more enemy tanks were on the way. Hannes would not be side-tracked however, and almost immediately found Mac's Ratel. It was blazing like a furnace inside, but he leapt on the back to check if anyone was still alive. He was too late. The intense heat started to cook off the ammunition in a spectacular display of fireworks.

Hannes returned to the other Ratel that was still stuck in the trench, sprinting the last hundred metres past the FAPLA trenches, but found that the crew had abandoned it. Two FAPLA soldiers were looting the disabled vehicle. Thoroughly aroused, Hannes let fly with his rifle and scored a hit on one who had a sack of canned rations slung over his shoulder. The 5,56mm round, though, was stopped by a tin of army issue bully beef. While no recommendation for the stopping power of the R5 rifle, it was unqualified proof of the protection that army bully beef can provide against rifle fire. A FAPLA soldier appeared from a trench and tried to drill Hannes with his AK47. Fortunately, Hannes saw the movement from the corner of his eye and like a true gunslinger he floored the man with a long and instinctive burst fired from the hip.

He was really angry by then and in no mood to lose any more of his squadron's Ratels. He decided to recover them come hell or high water, using Riaan Rupping's recovery vehicle that was still dogging his heels like a St Bernard on a rescue mission. First, though, something had to be done about the intensifying fire that was being directed into his personal space. After a radio call for assistance, two Ratels appeared and suppressed the FAPLA fire with deadly bursts of 20mm machine-gun fire. They then withdrew on Robbie's orders, as other enemy tanks were getting too close for comfort. Hannes, in fact, could see dust being churned up by their tracks through the trees to the west.

He decided to go ahead with the recovery. He hooked the Wit Hings to the Ratel's rear and signalled Riaan to heave, but the armoured car wouldn't budge. They checked and found a large log jammed underneath it. Hannes decided to have another try with a kinetic tow rope. In feverish haste they hooked up, this time to the Ratel's front end. Hannes took the wheel. The recovery vehicle reared in the direction of the approaching tanks — five were clearly visible through the trees towards the flood plain. The kinetic tow rope stretched like a gigantic rubber band. The White Stallion charged until its massive weight was jerked to a sudden halt as the rope reached its limit of expansion. Then it contracted rapidly as it was designed to do and the Ratel was plucked from the hole like a ballistic missile from an underground silo. Riaan hurriedly dropped the tow and the two of them wheeled about and raced after their retreating mates before the tanks could cut them off. But the Ratel, to Hannes' dismay, took a violent dip into another unseen hole, having seemingly developed a liking for them, but fortunately its momentum carried it up the other side. Shortly afterwards they joined up with the others and regrouped.

In the action that followed, the battle group knocked out all the advancing tanks. It was discovered later that the 32-Battalion anti-tank squadron had lost only one Ratel. Four Buffalo Soldiers, including Captain Mac Macallum and his valiant national service gunner, were killed. Hannes Nortmann and Riaan Rupping were awarded the *Honoris Crux* for exceptional bravery in recovering the Ratel under extremely dangerous conditions.

After this Hannes resumed command of his combat team of Ratels and Infantry and continued his task of facing down FAPLA's 21-Brigade across the Lomba flood plain.

20-South African Brigade entered an intensive planning cycle. For the next few weeks the protagonists remained in their positions and sniped at each other with artillery. The advantage went mostly to the South Africans. The MRLs and the long range G5s played havoc with FAPLA, but the enemy's mortars, D30s and BM21 rockets had little effect on the combat teams.

A forward fire control team of FAPLA's 21-Brigade that was sited on high ground north of the Lomba River rendered admirable assistance in knocking themselves out. Hannes had an EW (electronic warfare) Casspir fitted with equipment for intercepting FAPLA's radio transmissions. One burning hot day he settled down in an attempt to fix the position of the enemy's forward fire controller. Taking him out would not only affect the accuracy of FAPLA's harassing shelling — it would also relieve the boredom of watching the enemy day in and day out with nothing exciting happening to stir up the adrenalin.

They fired a mortar salvo into the general area of where they believed the fire controller to be and monitored his transmissions.

'Enemy bombs falling 200 metres in front of us', the controller reported to his gun positions.

'Add 200 metres', ordered 32-Battalion's mobile fire controller.

'Fire!'

The next salvo dropped 200 metres farther on.

'Bombs are falling just to our right', the controller told the gun positions.

He had no idea that the Buffalo Soldiers were eavesdropping on his brigade's fire control net.

'100 metres more', ordered the MFC.

'Fire!'

'Bombs are falling among us!' the forward fire controller screamed. 'We are going to get out of here'.

The MFC dropped the range, having a fair idea of the fire controller's likely route from the OP back to their brigade.

'Fire!' he ordered.

'The bombs are falling behind us', yelled the panicky fire control party.

'Drop one hundred'.

'Fire!' ordered the MFC.

They kept a listening watch on the intercept frequency but heard not another squeak from the enemy's forward fire control team. They had all been accounted for. It is not often that enemy fire controllers effectively control one's own artillery.

An old friend, Captain Piet 'Piet Boer' van Zyl, reported for duty and took over 32-Battalion's Foxtrot company, formerly commanded by the late Captain Macallum.

For this veteran campaigner, the introduction to *Operation Modular* was an intensive artillery bombardment from the enemy just across the river while he was seated on the 'long drop' with his pants around his ankles. He dived for cover in the nearest trench, not caring whether his business was finished or not.

An indication of the bombardment's severity was that some men had to be dug from collapsed trenches afterwards.

Hannes intercepted a message that 21-Brigade was about to fire a 'secret weapon' at the South African positions. There had been much speculation that FAPLA would deploy poison gas if their situation became desperate. This was a credible assumption as they had already used it against UNITA.

The Brigade Tac HQ under the control of Deon Ferreira ordered Hannes to withdraw from his positions and move south to get out of the way. A Recce Wing patrol remained in the area to keep track of enemy movements. Shortly afterwards 21-Brigade commenced a massive bombardment of the vacated entrenchments. This was apparently a softening up in preparation for a full scale attack. It was vital that Hannes find out if FAPLA's 21-Brigade was about to be launched across the Lomba River to resume its delayed advance on Mavinga.

The Recce Wing patrol reported seeing an enemy reconnaissance patrol investigating their vacated positions. The patrol returned to their side of the river and the Recce Wing reported indications that FAPLA was concentrating and forming up ready for a final assault on the empty trenches. Hannes, nothing daunted, decided to sneak back and re-occupy his former positions, wait for FAPLA, then slaughter them on the conveniently provided killing grounds to their front. They made their way back as stealthily as possible.

UNITA had been mortaring the enemy ineffectively as they formed up. Hannes prudently used their impact strikes to disguise the ranging shots of Pierre Franken's MRLs. He waited impatiently, nerves taut as guitar strings, for FAPLA to move across the river. Eventually darkness closed in. The enemy had delayed the attack. It was picked up in radio intercepts that they had spotted movement in the trees beyond the flood plain and had guessed something was up.

Hannes could not wait any longer. At his bidding, Pierre ordered the MRLs to open fire. They threw everything they had at 21-Brigade's fatally concentrated attack formations deployed in their forming-up place north of the river. It became another killing ground even deadlier than the previous one on the flood plain.

Pierre's first ripple of 192 air burst rockets fired by the eight 24-barrelled Valkyrie MRLs exploded directly above the heads of the startled troops of 21-Brigade. Shrapnel sabred them down, killing and maiming men by the hundred. Some fragments even penetrated the engine covers of the tanks. They began smoking, then as the heat generated by the white-hot splinters overwhelmed their fuel systems, they caught fire.

Vehicles were shot out by the score. Amidst the fires and smoke, the burning vehicles, the quick and the dead, the 155mm G5s joined the fray and their huge shells crashed down right on target and piled on the agony for FAPLA. It was more than flesh and blood could stand and they panicked and broke. Survivors began to struggle north as best they could. The dead were sprawled obscenely around the battlefield and tons of burning and wrecked equipment were left to mark what had once been FAPLA's forming-up point.

47-Brigade had already suffered cruelly from Battle Group Charlie's unexpectedly tough resistance in UNITA's old logistics base area. They were also running out of fuel, ammunition and rations. To make matters worse, a forward observation officer named Pierre Franken was in a hide north of the Lomba River. He was giving them continual grief by directing the shooting out of everything that moved, either with the G5s or the MRLs and sometimes with both. The TAC HQ decided reasonably that 47-Brigade was ripe for a knockout blow.

61-Mechanised Battalion under Commandant Bok Smit set out to launch an attack from west to east against their positions. This meant swinging through trackless bush to the south of 47-Brigade to reach their forming-up place to the west. Due to faulty navigation and unexpected heavy going, though, the wide flanking attack bogged down before the battalion could reach their start line and launch an assault before dark. This forced them to call it off.

After reorganising, Bok decided to 'keep it simple stupid'. They moved to UNITA's old logistics base and ploughed west through the thick bush towards 47-Brigade. The enemy was unable to withdraw because of fuel shortages and were engaged in a re-supply from 59-Brigade. They had to remain in place until this was completed.

There was a mighty clash as Bok and his troops crashed into 47-Brigade's eastern flank. T54 and T55 tanks were matched against Ratel-90s. The Ratels had to gang up against the tanks because 90mm HEAT rounds would not penetrate the thick steel of the tanks at the longish ranges from the edge of the flood plain.

The dense bush to the south enveloped most of the battle group, so the main battle broke up into numerous individual duels fought at ranges of 20 metres or less. Young national servicemen of 19 or 20 years of age tested their mettle against the highly professional Cubans of Tactical Group One and, it must be said, the somewhat less professional FAPLA of 47-Brigade.

At times the battle was poised on a knife edge. Bok and his men, however, kept pushing forward, shooting out tanks and other armoured vehicles. From time to time they ran out of ammunition and had to withdraw to replenish, but they soon rejoined the noise and fury of the armoured clash. Slowly but surely they whittled down the enemy's tanks, especially those of the Cuban Tactical Group One.

Finally, unable to take the horrors and destruction of this gory battlefield any longer, the enemy broke and ran for the open flood plain. It was Pierre Franken's specially selected killing ground and this was the moment he had waited for. He signalled and unleashed the wholesale death that was already loaded into the breeches of the G5s and MRLs. The slaughter was awful as FAPLA tried to cross the river to reach the relative safety of 59-Brigade. Very few made it. Furthermore, the enemy was unable to recover a single item of major equipment from what had fast become a smoking and flaming cauldron.

SAAF Mirage attacking aircraft appeared overhead to signal that their agony was not over yet. Almost at will they dive-bombed, rocketed and strafed the tanks, BTRs, armoured cars and other vehicles and turned them into flaming wrecks. Eventually, all movement stopped within what had once been 47-Brigade's defensive perimeter.

FAPLA's forlorn hopes of bridging the Lomba River to escape to the north came to nought. They attempted to form an instant bridge by driving a tank into the deep but narrow stream. The first tank that tried to drive across slid off the rounded hull of its sacrificial mate and finished up on its side in the river. This blocked all further attempts to cross. They had been waiting in a long line and became easy meat for the Mirages which were eagerly waiting to pounce on them.

47-Brigade abandoned its expensive Soviet-supplied tanks and equipment on the wrong side of the Lomba. Its troops fleeing on foot were mercilessly mowed down in droves by Bok Smit's rampaging Ratels and Pierre Franken's artillery. 47-Brigade effectively ceased to exist.

Piet Boer was tasked to provide local protection for Jan Hougaard and a specialist team of technicians to clear, with UNITA's assistance, equipment that had been abandoned on the battlefield following 47-Brigade's destruction. UNITA was already there when they arrived and were reluctant to allow the South Africans to remove the more sophisticated stuff.

A UNITA colonel even forbade Piet and his company to wipe out a small pocket of FAPLA resistance skulking around the battlefield that was interfering with the recovery process. Piet took no notice and his men chased the remnants of 47-Brigade across the river where Pierre Franken was literally still calling the shots for the artillery.

Jan and the technicians discovered, to the amazement of attached air force personnel, that they had hit the jackpot. Staring them in the face was a Soviet SAM-8 anti-aircraft missile system. It was virtually intact and complete with firing system, radar control system, rocket transporter and other integral vehicles. Only the tyres of the firing system had been shot out. The enemy's panic must have been total to induce them to abandon such highly sensitive and prized equipment. The West had been trying to get its hands on the system for many years without success. It was thought to be the most sophisticated anti-aircraft system in the world.

Piet became an instant tank driver and hooked a captured T55 to the SAM-8, then set out for the cover of trees before enemy MiGs could appear overhead and destroy the jackpot. It was a laborious business, what with the firing system's shot-out wheels and the spoiling attempts of the UNITA colonel who was acting on the direct orders of Savimbi in Jamba. To speed things up, Piet high-handedly grabbed a group of reluctant UNITA soldiers and turned them into unqualified tank drivers — with hilarious results. Tanks and their tethered loot were soon careering in all directions except to the cover that would shelter them from air attacks.

They gradually sorted things out, in spite of intermittent bombing runs by the MiGs.

Leaving UNITA to recover the macho looking battle tanks — which the colonel seemed to think were the most valuable items to grab, they sneaked off the battlefield with the first prize of the SAM-8 system.

They struggled throughout the night, dragging the firing system on its wheel rims. They laid up at first light, but then the MiGs found them. They dropped parachute-retarded bombs that caused ear-shattering blasts. A second bombing run followed 20 minutes later. They hit nothing, but surely must have upset birds that were nesting with chicks at that time of the year.

The SAM-8 system finally arrived at Rundu.

Savimbi demanded the return of *his* captured SAM-8. He conveniently overlooked the fact that 61-Mechanised Battalion had done the capturing. The SAAF ignored him, for they had no intention whatsoever of relinquishing such a prize. Predictably, this caused Savimbi to throw a tantrum of monumental proportions — to the alarm of the attached Special Tasks liaison team. But not even the indignant intervention of this lot could budge the Air Force. The SAAF treated the UNITA hierarchy with a certain deference, never with obsequiousness and sometimes with just the right touch of disrespect to bring them back to earth with a sobering bump.

On 8 October Major Hannes Nortmann and his combat team — by then, believe it or not, attached to 61-Mechanised Battalion — accompanied this unit to the source of the Lomba River to attack a formation that comprised shell-shocked remnants of 47-Brigade and the more or less intact 25- and 59-Brigades.

FAPLA had received enough supplies as well as reinforcements from Menongue to rebuild its shattered battalions. The attack was abortive as the enemy had already begun a general withdrawal towards the watershed between the Cuzizi and Mianei rivers.

Consequently, Robbie Hartslief ordered Hannes to take his combat team on an independent mission to block a 10km gap between the two rivers. The terrain was covered in thick scrub and trees and there was barely 100 metres visibility. To cover a 10km gap with a small force like that was clearly impossible. So he was instructed to take up a defensive position on high ground north of the Mianei River's source. The enemy was believed to be only three kilometres north of that location.

He moved in on the 'high ground' during the night. This turned out to be a slight rise, an insignificant elevation marked on the map as a spot height. Nevertheless, by first light his combat team was comfortably deployed there.

Almost immediately his infantry came into contact with FAPLA infantry to their front. It transpired that they were only 700m away from the enemy's forward positions and not the three kilometres they had supposed. Skirmishes continued throughout the day until finally Robbie ordered both Hannes' and another combat team away to the north and out of touch with the enemy.

While Hannes was digesting the order, FAPLA launched an unexpected tank assault against his position. The Ratels hurriedly withdrew. Advancing enemy armour was brought under fire by the G5s and pounded to a standstill on the vacated spot height.

Recce Wing teams continued to follow up FAPLA's general retreat, acting as the eyes and ears of the South African forces. They were frequently accompanied by forward observation officers to direct the South African artillery fire. Sergeants Mac da Trinidade and Gilbert Evelett took their teams to Viposto between the Vimpulo and Hube Rivers and found the area overrun by troops of the retiring enemy brigades. It was suspected in South African General Staff circles that the FAPLA brigades were withdrawing to a safe base area south of the Chambinga River, there to reequip, reorganise and await reinforcements before they launched a second attempt to penetrate as far as Mavinga.

While they were drawing water from the Hube River Gilbert's team experienced an unexpected contact with the enemy. They withdrew in a hurry to the Mianei source and joined up with a resupply patrol under Commandant Les Rudman. Rudman had somehow collected a few young paratrooper roughriders from the Pathfinder Company who were roaming around in the enemy's rear and giving them all sorts of grief.

This small combined force was suddenly overtaken by an advancing FAPLA battalion. A desperate fight ensued before the enemy broke and fled. During the fight a young lieutenant paratrooper and 12 FAPLA were killed. Another FAPLA was captured and proved to be a valuable source of information.

At the same time Staff Sergeant Piet Fourie's team, with Captain Boshoff of the South African Artillery as a forward observation officer, was operating deep in the bush around the Mianei River area. They managed to close with a FAPLA deployment and, to their surprise, spotted two more SAM-8 anti-aircraft systems. It was too good a target to resist, so Captain Boshoff opened fire with his 120mm mortars and scored direct hits on both targets.

The team was hopelessly outnumbered, so they withdrew but returned without detection later in the day and gave the enemy another pasting. One mortar bomb landed within the SAM-8's missile dump and generated spectacular flames. The team was close enough to overhear the FAPLA commander screaming in a state of abject panic for his troops to put the fire out. The FAPLA missile crews rushed towards the burning dump, even though the fire was out of control. Having no idea what to do next, everyone began to huddle around the raging conflagration. They were probably deliberating on the pros and cons of a variety of action plans, but they were too close when the dump exploded with a thunderous roar. Intercepts confirmed that both SAM-8s plus 25 vehicles were destroyed, apart from 300 casualties.

In the wake of the FAPLA withdrawal from the Lomba River front, Raiding Force Delta was formed to harass 59-Brigade. Piet Boer and his Foxtrot company were part of it but the enemy was too far away for them to inflict any damage. A pleasant interlude resulted when they stumbled on a secluded lake. Having nothing better to do, they lazed around for a few days, tanning, swimming and eating ration packs until the brigade found out what they were up to and yanked them back into the war.

When 4-South African Infantry, a mechanised battalion, arrived on the scene, Foxtrot company was attached as its permanent infantry screen. They were responsible for scouting ahead on foot for its tank squadron, its Ratel-90 squadron and its own mechanised infantry mounted in Ratel-20s. As Piet reflected later, a bloody scrap with FAPLA became a near certainty for his company.

4-South African Infantry, now renamed Battle Group Charlie (not to be confused with Commandant Robbie Hartslief's Battle Group Charlie which had been renamed Battle Group Bravo!), was ordered to attack 16-Brigade at the Chambinga River source and destroy this formation before 9 November. It was then to exploit south as far as the Hube River and establish a barrier between the Chambinga and Hube Rivers. It was hoped that 21- and 59-Brigades, which were withdrawing to the safety of the Tumpo Triangle, would run up against this barrier and also be destroyed. Charlie would attack from north-east to south-west while 61-Mechanised Battalion (now Battle Group Alpha), would launch a feint from the south-east.

Four kilometres from target, Piet's Foxtrot company debussed and deployed as a screen 600m to the front. The mass of armour was out of sight and, incomprehensibly, in the thick bush behind them and out of range to give close support. Foxtrot Company soon bumped an outlying ambush of enemy tanks to their left front and not far from 16-Brigade's main defensive locality. It took some time for Piet to convince the sceptical commander of Battle Group Charlie that he should send a force to deal with the threat.

For the first time since World War-II South African tanks engaged enemy tanks in battle. They knocked out three of them and captured two, destroyed a BM21 Stalin Organ and captured another, destroyed trucks and captured much other equipment. There was no loss to own forces.

Battle Group Charlie was reorganising in a rather leisurely fashion when Foxtrot, still way out in front, hit the main defensive locality. All hell broke loose and FAPLA threw everything they had at Foxtrot, using small arms, mortars, tanks and the dreaded 23mm anti-aircraft guns in a ground capacity. Foxtrot could only press forward — hunkering down would have invited being pinned down out in the open with the consequent mounting of casualties. The Ratel-20s lagged behind, reluctant to close up with Foxtrot and give it close-in fire support.

Piet recalls drily that they really got mad at the Ratels that day.

Foxtrot's Buffalo Soldiers cleared the first line of trenches with small arms and grenades, but they got pinned down because the rest of the battle group failed to close up. A noisy action had also broken out in the rear as the two mechanised companies on the flanks became embroiled in beating off counter-attacks by enemy tanks.

Charlie was supposed to pass through Foxtrot and take the rest of the objective, but they had lost momentum. Piet Boer fumed with frustration.

The artillery, like Kipling's guns ('The guns, thank God, the guns!') rescued them. The forward observation officer shifted the 155mm G5 and G6 fire to take out the 23mm anti-aircraft guns that were pinning down Foxtrot.

The Ratel-20s finally arrived and added their fire more accurately. The mortars also became more effective. A respectable crescendo built up as the ranges to various targets were found. The tanks finally arrived to restore momentum to the attack.

With the dismounted mechanised infantry assisting alongside, Foxtrot began systematically clearing the trenches and bunkers, generously lobbing grenades to the ungrateful FAPLA recipients.

The tanks passed through and beyond the brigade's defensive locality then, for no discernable reason, they stopped — they failed to relentlessly push through towards the Hube River to close the gap so that FAPLA could not escape. Instead, they withdrew northwards to laager for the night and to resupply. Foxtrot and the other infantry companies were ordered to vacate the objectives they had just taken. This was in violation of all infantry battle drills. Piet Boer was disgusted. They moved back to their prior and by now very distant concentration area, vacating ground they had fought hard for and would probably have to fight for again the next morning.

The commander of Battle Group Charlie, for reasons best known to himself, had given 16-Brigade the opportunity to escape and lick its wounds. Worse still, he gave 16-, 59- and 21-Brigades a reasonable chance to reach the safety of the Tumpo Triangle instead of destroying them in a mini 'Falais pocket' farther south. (After the breakout from the Normandy beachheads in World War-II, large numbers of German formations were trapped in a pocket centred on the French city of Falais. Through a lack of aggressiveness the Allies failed to close the gap which allowed most of the German forces to escape. This probably led to the war in Europe being prolonged for another 10 months. Likewise, the Cuito Cuanavale campaign would probably have had a different outcome if the Battle Group Charlie commander had carried out his mission effectively as ordered.)

Deon Ferreira, understandably, was livid. He should have sacked the commander of 4-South African Infantry and replaced him with any one of an array of competent commanders who were eagerly awaiting an opportunity to cross swords with the enemy. In combat situations one cannot be lenient. The lives of men depend on the commander in actual charge of the battle. Ruthless action should always be taken to rectify failures anywhere along the line of command.

The next day Battle Group Charlie made a pathetic attempt to retake the ground it had already fought over. The action was called it off because, believe it or not, a man had an accidental discharge and shot himself in the stomach. An army does not avoid battle because it suffers a single casualty — especially through the injured party's own stupidity.

16-Brigade had in the meantime reorganised and taken up two covering/blocking positions south of the Chambinga River source and at the source of the Hube River. Ironically, it achieved what Charlie had failed to do the previous day, but for the opposite reason — which was to cover the gap between the Chambinga and Hube rivers. The brigade could now cover the withdrawal of the FAPLA brigades in the south against South African aggression all the way to the safety of the Tumpo Triangle.

With unwarranted generosity, the commander of Battle Group Charlie was given a second chance to redeem himself. On 11 November he was ordered to execute an attack from the south on two 16-Brigade strong points and take each in succession. They would move from their concentration area and pass to the rear of Battle Group Alpha in a rugby-style switch pass. Alpha would pass the ball to Charlie while feinting towards the southernmost objective from the east. This would send Charlie on a crashing end-run to trample over the same objective, then rush for the score line on the Chambinga River.

Unfortunately, the mad dash degenerated into a laborious crawl through thick bush. Piet Boer and his 32-Battalion company took turns with 4-South African Infantry to operate on foot as an infantry screen during the advance-to-contact phase. In between, they rested either in the Ratels or on the backs of tanks — a risky procedure as any combat-wise infantrymen from World War-II could have told them.

Meanwhile, the artillery gave FAPLA's northern strong point on the Chambinga River a good work-over to create the impression that it was first in the queue for a repeat attack by Charlie from its by-then vacated concentration area to the north-east. The artillery then switched to the southern strong point to assist Charlie in knifing through the FAPLA defences — this time, hopefully, with more speed and aggression and without stopping to mop up so that it could charge the stronger second objective in good old cavalry style.

The speed of the armoured formation moving through the dense bush was soon reduced to that of a slow moving herd of oxen. It soon attracted the unwelcome attention of MiGs that were lazily cruising the clear blue skies above.

The bombs began to fall. The MiG-21s and -23s circled like vultures over a kill, advertising Charlie's desperately slow crawl to close with 16-Brigade. Unfortunately, the battle group could not stop and conceal itself. It could only direct intensive although largely inaccurate and ineffective anti-aircraft and machine-gun fire at the MiGs in an effort to force them to release their bombs at high altitude. The plan must have worked because the armoured column survived unscathed.

The element of surprise, of course, was lost. FAPLA's ground forces only needed to watch the wheeling and diving of their jets to get a fix on Charlie's position. This gave 16-Brigade plenty of time to redeploy their forces. So not surprisingly, the first objective was empty and no longer a target.

Battle Group Charlie soldiered on north, fighting not only the unyielding bush but against time too. Foxtrot Company and 4-South African Infantry riflemen continued to rotate duties as a screen until the moment of contact, after which they would become 'bullet collectors'. The long haul and the almost intolerable nervous stress had an adverse effect on the men. They were aware that the enemy was expecting them and thanks to the MiGs, their position was no secret. Conversely, they had no idea where 16-Brigade was and when or if they would make contact. This uncertainty, more than anything else, ate into their nervous stamina.

Vehicle crews got down from the cramped and sweaty cabs and stretched luxuriously. Riflemen dismounted and looked for shade. Those who smoked fumbled in their pockets for a loose fag to give momentary relaxation to their highly strung nerves. Piet Boer, a non-smoker, stretched out on the hull of a tank and dozed.

Just beyond the limit of ground level observation, which was frustratingly restricted by thick vegetation, FAPLA observers snugly ensconced in tall trees watched incredulously as almost the entire battle group spread out on the ground. It was FAPLA's lucky day, for the area was in the centre of the killing ground they had covered with an integrated fire plan for their weapon systems.

Battle Group Charlie had not only found the FAPLA strong point — it had unknowingly blundered into it.

All hell broke loose. Charlie found itself under a storm of shrapnel from FAPLA's artillery and tanks as well as facing an almost solid horizontal sheet of heavy machine-gun fire and shells from the frightening 23mms.

Two of Piet's men on top of a tank were killed when a shell hit the turret. This brought the total of Foxtrot's casualties to three dead and several wounded since they were detached to Charlie and started to tangle with 16-Brigade. FAPLA tanks knocked out several Ratel-20s which brewed as their ammunition cooked off. Treetop snipers took out another seven riflemen. To increase anxiety, EW (electronic warfare) using electronic eavesdropping devices reported that 30 T54 and T55 tanks were concentrating in three separate groups in and around the strongpoint. This was three times the number of tanks that Battle Group Charlie had.

The squadron commander of the tanks reacted swiftly. He initiated a tank fire belt action whereby all the tanks fired salvo after salvo at a rapid rate straight ahead into the thick bush to suppress the enemy's direct fire that was scything through the killing ground. This created conditions where control over the battle group could be regained and action could be initiated to pin down and destroy 16-Brigade.

Piet Boer and a lieutenant, Tobias 'De Villiers' de Vos, got the men back on their feet. They linked up with the 4-South African Infantry riflemen and with the support of tanks and Ratel-20s, moved forward towards the near perimeter of the objective. The Ratels came under accurate RPG7 fire from infantry in trenches.

A clutch of T55 tanks appeared. A Ratel-20, firing bursts of armour-piercing bullets from its machine gun, amazingly shot out a tank. Mitton, the gunner, had coolly and deliberately aimed at the weak junction between the turret and the hull. The tank brewed and then burst into flames. Unfortunately though, another T55 hit Mitton's Ratel with its 100mm gun and the vehicle started to cook. The driver was killed outright and Mitton was fatally wounded. Unaware that his driver was dead, Mitton still had the presence of mind to elevate his gun to ensure that the driver would not be trapped in the burning hulk. Then he managed to get out through his own hatch. His buddies picked him up next to his Ratel, but he died of wounds later.

Battle Group Charlie's infantry, aggressively accompanied by tanks, swept through trenches that FAPLA had hurriedly abandoned. The tanks took the lead and rushed ahead. They were brought up short when one had part of its track and suspension blasted off in an unsuspected minefield. A Ratel also fell victim to a landmine and was finished off by a T55.

Foxtrot Company's infantry with Ratel-90s in support tried to outflank the minefield, but were frustrated by Pom-Zs and other anti-personnel mines. A Plofadder mine clearing device was sent in to blast a breach through the minefield. The equipment was still in an experimental stage and it failed to detonate mines automatically. It had to be hand-initiated by assault pioneers who had no option but to gingerly pick their way through this devil's garden before they could do so.

Most of the tanks managed to make their way either around or through the newly created breach in the minefield. The infantry were able to walk through in extended line because anti-tank mines require far more pressure than the weight of a man to detonate them. Sometimes it is preferable to be an infantryman rather than a tanker.

The tanks were drawn up north of the minefield but the attack was stopped by the Tac HQ. The generals decreed that no Olifant tank (a much upgraded British Centurion) should be allowed to fall into enemy hands — even if it meant calling off a mission. For a vacillating commander, like Battle Group Charlie's incumbent, an imperious order such as this was the excuse he needed not to press home an attack that was already rolling. The fact that this would allow the enemy all the time in the world to withdraw, reorganise, regroup and even launch a counter-attack if it wanted to, did not seem to concern the generals. There have been times when I have thought that the top brass must have learned their trade at different military establishments and in a different army to me.

An armoured recovery vehicle was sent to pull the disabled tank from the minefield. With FAPLA's support weapons still in position and covering the recovery area, it was a tricky operation. There was the real possibility of stepping on an anti-personnel mine — not to mention the ever present need to dodge flying scrap metal as you busied yourself hooking the lame duck to a recovery vehicle and pulling it out backwards. Straying to the left or right of the tank's tracks with the recovery vehicle added another dimension to the problem.

The recovery vehicle moved behind the cripple, but its crew remained firmly battened down. There was far too much unhealthy lead out there. Finally volunteers were called for to go and assist the crew. One of Piet Boer's platoon leaders, De Villiers de Vos, stepped forward.

The situation at the disabled tank and the recovery vehicle was chaotic. They were attracting everything the enemy could throw at them. The tiffies in the recovery vehicle were relieved to see the friendly face of De Villiers looking up at them in their high cab. One of them mustered all his courage and scrambled down. They managed to hook on the tank. Before it could be towed, though, it was necessary to shorten the damaged track and take it around the bogies that were still usable. But the track was jammed solid and it needed to be cut away with heavy cutting gear.

Ignoring FAPLA's bullets, the two scrambled up to the cab and fetched tools. Sorting it out was a difficult job at the best of times. Under heavy enemy fire, including exploding mortar bombs, it was almost impossible. Somehow they managed it. But when the recovery vehicle took the strain it could not budge the cripple from the soft sand. They had to call for a second armoured recovery vehicle to assist. When that still did not work, another tank was sent for.

Time dragged on while De Villiers and the tiffie fiddled with tow bars, shackles, pins and the rest to connect up this train of armoured monsters. They were still exposed to enemy incoming cracking past them, ricocheting off the steel hulls or exploding in the soft sand around them. When everything was ready, De Villiers carefully directed the procession out of the minefield. If a whole string of stranded tanks had ended up being lost to the enemy, it would not have done much good to the ulcers of the generals.

De Villiers de Vos was awarded the *Honoris Crux* for his bravery. And before the day was out, he would again volunteer for a mission impossible.

All this had caused the attack to mark time instead of it crashing through to the objective to catch the enemy on the hop and wipe them out. One could have coined the slogan: 'Save a tank and lose the war'. Eventually the momentum picked up again as tanks and infantry moved forward to clear the FAPLA position. Then before the objective had been cleared and consolidated, for some unaccountable reason the assault was stopped in its tracks and the battle group was ordered to withdraw.

The infantrymen were furious and some junior leaders refused to obey such a ridiculous order. Whoever gave it must have been a complete idiot. It was necessary to read the riot act to one young 4-South African Infantry corporal before he reluctantly agreed to withdraw his section from recently captured trenches.

South of the minefield Piet Boer gathered his company to take stock and reorganise. His platoon leaders, De Vos, Wessels, Human and Theron, found that a section of eight men was missing. Piet returned to the area now controlled by FAPLA and found seven of the missing troops. He returned and told the tank squadron commander that he was going back to search for the last man. It had been reported that he had been seen sprawled on his back in a FAPLA trench. He was either seriously wounded or dead.

The commander refused permission, having just become aware that Battle Group Charlie was pulling out. FAPLA's fire had picked up again and it was impossible to delay the withdrawal. Piet Boer was a captain and outranked, but he ignored the major's orders — he had no intention of leaving a buddy to the untender mercies of the enemy. It could be a fate worse than death. FAPLA would delight in getting its hands on one of the dreaded Buffalo soldiers.

It was a point of honour with the unit's officers that a 32-Battalion soldier, whether dead or alive, should not be abandoned to the enemy. There had been rare occasions when leaving a dead comrade behind had been unavoidable, but a wounded 'brother' — the troops in the Battalion addressed each other as *Irmao* or brother —had never been left to the mercy of an enemy or abandoned to his fate in the pitiless African veld.

De Villiers volunteered to accompany Piet back to the trench system that had been reoccupied by FAPLA. The two officers sprinted several hundred metres across the minefield, dashing in alternate bounds for the trench where the rifleman was reported to be. This was a drill known by 32-Battalion, the Recces and the Paratroopers as 'the buddy-buddy system'.

Piet and De Villiers were under heavy fire from FAPLA's re-occupied strong points. An involuntary spectator in a Ratel-20 squadron called the dash a highly dramatic display of real courage and concerned leadership. He watched as they launched their own counter-attack to snatch a buddy from under the noses of the enemy. Number one would jump up and dash forward ten metres or so before dropping and furiously returning fire. Number two then jumped up, dashed past number one for five or ten paces, went down and returned fire. Number one sprinted past him, and so on.

Piet and De Villiers made it to their badly wounded comrade unscathed. He had been shot in the back by a 14.5mm heavy machine gun. It was impossible for him to walk, let alone run. They pulled him from the trench, and still under fire, dragged him back the way they had come. While one handled the casualty, the other returned fire with his R4 carbine. They withdrew from firing position to firing position until they reached slightly safer territory. From there they shuffled painfully slowly across 200m of bullet-lashed open space until they reached a Ratel that had driven into the minefield to pick them up. The tanks, forced by events to reconsider, gave fire support from beyond the minefield. Miraculously the two officers were still unscathed.

Captain Petrus 'Piet Boer' van Zyl was decorated with the *Honoris Crux* for bravery. Lieutenant De Villiers de Vos had earned his earlier in the day. In another army he would surely have been awarded a higher decoration for two such outstanding acts of bravery within hours of each other. By any standard, it was sustained heroism of a remarkably high order in the face of a determined enemy.

The rescued soldier pulled through and made a full recovery. When Piet visited him in hospital he expressed his heartfelt thanks to Piet for placing his life in jeopardy by returning to rescue him from certain torture and death. This gratitude and, of course, the man's life meant more to Piet than any decoration.

Let me add a couple of my own observations about this day.

It appears to me that the commander of Battle Group Charlie and his higher commander considered the recovery of a disabled Olifant tank of such importance that they sacrificed the achievement of the mission for it. On the other hand, the extraction of a badly wounded 32-Battalion soldier from the clutches of FAPLA did not merit a delay in withdrawing from the battlefield. It seems that the black soldier was expendable. Fortunately for him, Piet and De Villiers thought otherwise and ignored orders. They believed he was more valuable than an Olifant tank.

Battle Group Alpha launched a belated attack from the east in an attempt to salvage something from the prevaricating efforts of Battle Group Charlie, but it was too late. 16-

Brigade had withdrawn in good order to a new position from where it could block the South Africans or cover FAPLA's withdrawal from the south. This was in spite of the brigade having lost about 300 men and 14 tanks — which is a good thrashing if one is into the numbers game. The bottom line was that Battle Group Charlie had failed in its mission to destroy 16-Brigade in its defensive locality and to block the escape of the FAPLA brigades.

The heavily outgunned and outnumbered Battle Group Bravo—just a rump of its former glory but still with two attached companies of 101-Battalion — and FAPLA's tank-equipped and resupplied 59-Brigade were circling each other warily in the heavily forested area of the Mianei River source. Bravo was tasked to prevent 59-Brigade's withdrawal until Battle Groups Alpha and Charlie were in position to launch a battle of destruction against 59-, 21- and 25-Brigades.

21-Brigade, however, launched a spoiling attack with its tanks and two battalions of infantry against Bravo, forcing the battle group to disengage from 59-Brigade. By the time Bravo was able to resume the initiative, 59-Brigade had withdrawn to safety north of the Chambinga River, using two adjacent fords across the Vimpulo River. There were no other fords. By the time they had rounded the source of the Hube River and continued on to Tumpo, neither Battle Group Charlie nor anyone else was around to stop them.

This left only FAPLA's 21-Brigade, a battalion from 25-Brigade and an independent battalion from 66-Brigade. These remnants of FAPLA's invading army could still be boxed in and trapped.

Battle Group Charlie was ordered to proceed at flank speed to seal off the newly discovered escape route via the fords on the Vimpulo River. With Battle Group Alpha, they were to attack and destroy the withdrawing FAPLA forces as they tried to cross. The Brigade Tac HQ ordered Charlie to concentrate near this crossing site. Piet Boer advised that the concentration point should be no farther than two kilometres away from the crossing.

Battle Group Charlie's commander, however, had not yet exhausted his capacity for snatching defeat from the jaws of victory. He thought it would be imprudent to get closer than six kilometres from the selected killing ground, which obviously had to be the Vimpulo River's swampy flood plain that led to the crossing. So they established their laager there and turned in for the night.

A thunderstorm allowed FAPLA's noisy tanks and other armoured vehicles to approach the fords without being heard by Battle Group Charlie six kilometres away. The enemy found the fords — left uncovered by Charlie — and slipped across while the South Africans slept.

A foot patrol of Piet's, deployed north of the Vimpulo River and the crossing point, were the only ones — despite the thunder claps and the roar of a typical African downpour — who heard the sounds of tank engines fading away to the north. No block had been established ahead of the escaping FAPLA forces to prevent them from reaching the safety of the Tumpo Triangle.

The violence of the weather was tame compared to the storm that broke in Brigade Tac HQ when Deon Ferreira discovered that the crossing site had remained uncovered throughout the night — and that FAPLA was escaping north of the Vimpulo towards the Hube River that was still astride their withdrawal route.

Deon peremptorily ordered Battle Group Charlie to rush at more than flank speed to an intercepting location west of the Hube source. It was to take up an ambush position in the tree line, engage FAPLA's flank and destroy it on the open flood plain. Battle Group Bravo, reinforced with Hannes Nortmann's anti-tank squadron, an infantry company from 101 Battalion and another from 61-Mechanised Battalion, would follow Charlie and act as a reserve.

On reaching the area at the confluence of the Hube and Chambinga rivers, FAPLA spent almost a whole day looking for a crossing through the extensive swamps. But a short cut to safety in the Tumpo Triangle did not exist. The only other option was to go the long way around by the Hube River, but this raised a strong possibility that the South Africans would at last intercept them. To avoid this they moved upstream at speed to the river's source to double around it before the South Africans got there.

Battle Group Charlie beat them to it all right, but unfortunately it arrived at the wrong place. It appears that Charlie's navigator, presumably the intelligence officer, was jinxed by unaccountable navigation errors throughout *Operation Modular*.

Then the battle group stumbled into an unexpected minefield in the darkness. Its presence should have confirmed that they were in the wrong place. They should have withdrawn, checked their navigation and headed for the correct location. Instead they called for two Plofadders to blast a breach through the minefield. This was in spite of them having orders to get to their ambush positions by stealth. To compound this folly, they continued their deployment using a series of illumination flares. This negated whatever might have remained of the element of surprise — so vital in an ambush situation.

Eventually, after much blundering, Charlie ended up facing west instead of north. This meant that, come morning, the opposing forces would clash head on, allowing FAPLA to deploy maximum combat power to their front. This was not a pleasant prospect for a small, outnumbered and outgunned battle group to find itself in.

At dawn Charlie's command cadre finally discovered that they were in the wrong place. So they started to move westwards, deployed in extended line abreast to be ready for an imminent shootout. Shortly afterwards a column of dust was seen approaching from the west along the Hube River flood plain and another from the south-west. The first was identified as 21-Brigade and the second turned out to be the independent battalion from 66-Brigade on a converging course with 21-Brigade.

Instead of Battle Group Charlie setting up an ambush situation where FAPLA's long and vulnerable flank would have been exposed and with an excellent killing ground behind them into which they could be driven, its commander had set himself up for a bruising meeting engagement — the worst possible scenario that anyone else would have avoided at all costs.

Contact was made long before Charlie reached the edge of the flood plain. Its infantry screen, including Piet Boer's Foxtrot company, drew enemy fire first. A confusing battle developed — which is the hallmark of any meeting engagement. Hannes Nortmann's 32-Battalion anti-tank squadron, which had been moved to Battle Group Charlie, was ordered to move his Ratels to the right flank to relieve pressure on Alpha Company. A shootout commenced and FAPLA vehicles and other equipment were destroyed. Hannes was then ordered to the left flank to stabilise the situation there. Away to the left, Commandant Robbie Hartslief, with his once more truncated Battle Group Bravo, also made contact with FAPLA tanks and infantry. Hannes found himself at the epicentre of this threatening storm.

Some FAPLA tanks that were still invisible to Hannes but were only a few metres away to the front of his Ratel 90s, disconcertingly began to mark their positions with smoke for their artillery to identify friend from foe. The smoke appeared just in time to warn Hannes. It enabled him to have a hot reception waiting as they suddenly burst from the bush. The Ratels knocked out three tanks and the rest broke off the engagement and escaped the way they had come. They fled through the centre of Robbie's command group, but because of the thick bush cover, he did not notice them.

Hannes spotted a stray tank but had a problem indicating its precise position to his Ratel-90s. His was a Ratel-20 which was incapable of taking on a thickly armoured, 100mm-gunned T55. He left the relative safety of his Ratel-20 amidst the shot and flying shells of battle, walked calmly to the nearest Ratel-90 and pointed out the T55 lurking in the bush. Its turret was already swivelling to bring its gun to bear on the

Ratel. The Ratel however, was quicker on the draw and moments later the T55 began to brew.

The battle developed into a general brawl over a wide area. South Africans, FAPLA and UNITA were mixed up in pockets of violent localised combat. Enemy T55s, BRDMs, BTRs, BM21s and soft-skinned vehicles were burning everywhere. FAPLA also took heavy personnel losses, including their brigade commander.

It came as a surprise and a welcome respite when FAPLA began to withdraw to the west to establish a dug-in defensive perimeter on the open flood plain. This presented a brilliant opportunity to wipe them out. Battle Group Charlie, however, was running low on fuel and ammunition. We have also seen that its commander was not a believer in exploiting unexpected battlefield successes.

He could have called his A1 echelon (vehicles with fuel and ammunition, on-wheels repair and recovery facilities, casevac and immediate medical aid facilities) to immediately replenish the armour while the F echelon (fighting echelon) stayed on the battlefield. He had the opportunity to finish off FAPLA before they had a chance to recover. Instead he deemed it more prudent to withdraw to the echelon rear area to re-bunker and re-ammunition at a more leisurely pace.

Bringing the A1 echelon forward to replenish an F echelon is the usual drill with mechanised and armoured units in combat situations. To break contact and withdraw to a rear location (it was 10km to the east) was an astonishing thing to do.

FAPLA must also have been amazed and relieved when they saw Battle Group Charlie withdrawing and disappearing towards the rear.

One officer, at least, objected. That was Major Hannes Nortmann who was engaged in a heavy close quarter punch-up with enemy tanks. A precipitate withdrawal in the face of the T55s would have been suicidal and he told the commander so. He said he needed the assistance of a mechanised infantry company because the 101-Battalion's Casspirs were extremely vulnerable to tank shellfire. Instead of providing support to break contact cleanly with FAPLA, the CO firmly ordered Hannes to head back to the echelon area. An incipient act of insubordination was nipped in the bud because FAPLA themselves turned tail and fled.

It was already 16:00. By the time replenishment was completed there would be insufficient daylight left for Battle Group Charlie to return to the battlefield, regain contact with the enemy and complete the job before darkness fell. The CO, oblivious to the consequences of his weird military behaviour, ordered the battle group to laager in his rear echelon area for the night. The battle would be resumed the next morning.

The Tac HQ was also partly responsible for Charlie's strange conduct. It surely must have had an updated locstat of the battle group's position. Despite this, nothing was done to redeploy it to where it could have intercepted 21-Brigade if the latter had tried to break out during the night — which was exactly what they did.

Strangely enough, commanders at all levels seemed surprised that FAPLA did not remain in position as they were supposed to. Instead, they used the cover of darkness to rescue their forces from the trap that Deon Ferreira had tried so hard to set.

Inevitably this finally resulted in FAPLA's potentially superior combat power being compressed into a strong defensive pocket within the Tumpo Triangle. The last opportunity to pin down and destroy 16- and 21-Brigades and elements of 66- and 59-Brigades east of the Cuito River had been frittered away. Subsequent efforts to redeem the situation proved to be a waste of time, lives and war materiel.

After this Hannes Nortmann and his squadron were withdrawn to Buffalo Base.

On 17 November Battle Group Alpha, with Battle Group Charlie's tank squadron under its command, was ordered to squeeze the remaining FAPLA elements from the corridor between the Hube and Chambinga Rivers and chase them across the Chambinga bridge towards the Tumpo Triangle. It was hoped that the Chambinga bridge would turn out to be a bottleneck that would cause a massive congestion of troops and equipment, providing a lucrative target for the artillery. With this objective in mind, forward observation officers were infiltrated into OPs on the Chambinga high ground overlooking the planned scene of slaughter. One was a gunnery officer, Lieutenant Breytenbach (no relation of mine), who would earn himself the unfortunate nickname of the 'Butcher of Chambinga' for his outstanding artillery fire control that day.

Battle Group Alpha set off to attack FAPLA's 21-Brigade and its Tactical Group Two which were withdrawing. It went fast and had begun to catch up with the enemy when our UNITA allies frustratingly called a halt claiming that they were about to blunder into a minefield. This created a delay of more than an hour while engineers checked the ground ahead, but no mines were found.

While this was going on, the FAPLA force continued its run and was approaching the Chambinga crossing. Alpha resumed its hot pursuit but was once more brought up short by another report from UNITA that the approaches to the crossing had also been heavily mined. This also turned out to be false. After another delay Alpha resumed its pursuit and finally caught up with the tail end of 21-Brigade. It knocked out two tanks and a few other vehicles and was just getting into its stride when UNITA called a halt by announcing that an air raid was imminent. Battle Group Alpha had no option but to break contact and seek shelter under the trees. The air raid, of course, failed to materialise.

Meanwhile, enemy tanks, vehicles, guns, other equipment and personnel were piling up in a chaotic mass just south of the crossing site. It was an area of not more than 800m by 500m and provided an ideal target for an air strike. A raid was called for, but for some unknown reason the Tac HQ failed to approve it. Perhaps FAPLA's phantom air attack had something to do with it. Instead, the gunners climbed in and sowed wholesale death among the enemy. Without a supporting air strike, though, it was not half as destructive as it could have been.

Battle Group Alpha called for a pause in the bombardment and charged, guns blazing, into the tight concentration of men and war machines that lay exposed on the open marshy approach to the bridge. It was a chance to completely wipe out 21-Brigade. The tanks and Ratels poured eagerly onto the flood plain.

When Alpha's intentions became clear to UNITA, they immediately announced that another enemy air strike was imminent. Without air support of its own, the battle group again had no option but to withdraw into the cover of the bush. If they had remained and been caught by enemy strike jets on the open expanse of the flood plain, the consequences might have been devastating.

Needless to say, the air strike once again failed to materialise.

Despite having suffered heavy losses from artillery fire, 21-Brigade and Tactical Group Two managed to withdraw across the river and get clear. This left them safe to lick their wounds before the next round with the South Africans.

It is anyone's guess what UNITA's motives were for feeding the South Africans false intelligence on four separate occasions that day. Maybe the reason could be found in the dark and convoluted mind of Jonas Savimbi. One can only speculate. He had a huge ego and was extremely protective of his often undeserved reputation as a brilliant field and guerrilla commander. Maybe if the South Africans had taken Cuito Cuanavale in a coup de main — having destroyed the major part of FAPLA's forces along the way — it would have been hailed as a South African triumph. UNITA, at best, was only capable of filling a minor supporting role. Perhaps Savimbi's giant ego could never have stood such a drastic deflation of his reputation, particularly with other African leaders.

The SADF, for political reasons, had always portrayed battlefield victories and FAPLA's disastrous losses to the world's media as the brilliant successes of General Savimbi and his UNITA army. This suited Savimbi's vanity and he probably even believed it. He noisily and frequently strutted his mastery of conventional war stuff at Jamba press conferences. The briefings were suitably embellished with carefully vetted photographs hot from the battlefield showing victorious UNITA troops brandishing rifles and adopting heroic poses on the burnt-out hulks of FAPLA's tanks. Savimbi's image as a warrior, consequently rose to dizzy heights on the strength of what were South African victories.

I think Savimbi's idea was to get the South Africans to bleed FAPLA dry to a point where they were so weakened that it would have been easy for UNITA, with suitable heroics, to administer the final coup de grace. This scenario would have allowed Savimbi to reap the honours of victory for himself, without even having to mention South Africa. That was why it was important for UNITA and not the South Africans to take Cuito Cuanavale.

It is conceivable, to my mind, that CSI's Special Tasks, by then an unashamed sycophant of Savimbi, had also urged the SADF to leave the town for UNITA to deal with. By then Cuito Cuanavale had achieved celebrity status in the eyes of the world's media.

I had personal experience of the divided loyalty of certain CSI officers. In the end, it caused major damage to my military career. I wrote an unflattering 'Top Secret' report to Special Tasks marked 'for certain eyes only' after the Cuito Cuanavale fiasco in 1986. It dealt bluntly with the shortcomings of Savimbi's and UNITA's military leadership. I considered it my responsibility, as the officer at the sharp end as it were, to inform the department that the R400 million of taxpayers' money they had coaxed from a tight defence budget was being squandered on Savimbi's amateurish attempts to make war.

A very senior member of Special Tasks on the liaison staff to Savimbi furnished him with an unabridged copy. This was a 'top secret' SADF document and doing so was highly irregular. This officer's action set in motion an escalating train of events.

As commander of the Guerrilla Training School in the Caprivi, it was my responsibility to train UNITA's officer corps. It was a tough school, but it had to be because guerrillas operate on foot and not in vehicles. A particularly slack, undisciplined and uncooperative group of UNITA officers was sent there for signals training. Problems began when they started to boycott muster parades. In an insulting response to my angry reaction, they truculently appeared on the weekly flag-hoisting parade in T-shirts, PT shorts and unlaced boots. I blew my top and gave them ten minutes to pack and vacate the school premises.

They walked north across the cut line into Angola and pitched up at Jamba some days later. It was said they were almost at the end of their tether. They were allegedly suffering from thirst and hunger. They also told nonsensical stories about having been relentlessly stalked by lions and leopards en route. While I concede that this was the African bush such animals had long before been wiped out by Savimbi for commercial gain. Furthermore, UNITA guerrillas were quite capable of walking great distances — 100km or more at a stretch — at forced march speed. Whatever we did at the training school, there had never been a requirement for me to get them fit. They were that already.

My immediate boss, the Director-General of Special Tasks, decided it was wrong that I should discipline this small group of malcontents in a SADF training base of which I was the appointed commander. For some obscure reason, the general regarded the Guerrilla School as part of Savimbi's UNITA forces. It most certainly was not that, for I trained guerrillas there from all manner of dissident movements in southern Africa. Nevertheless, he ordered me to attend a meeting in Rundu with him, his second-in-command, an air force brigadier and the CSI Special Tasks Senior Liaison Officer to Savimbi.

I had a good idea of the reception I could expect. I dressed in a well-ironed parachute smock complete with silver wings, my Recce operator's badge and my attack diving badge, plus my red beret, my red stable belt and glistening jump boots. In this splendid ensemble I set off to face the music. We normally dressed inconspicuously in nondescript and unmarked olive drab fatigues to present an appearance of low profile anonymity. So when I strolled into the sombre meeting in full uniform it took the wind out of their sails — especially since all three senior officers there were dressed casually in slacks and golf shirts.

I crashed to a halt and gave the general, an ex-schoolteacher, my best salute.

I agree it was a derisive gesture in the circumstances, for this kind of parade ground behaviour was out of character for me.

The general made it clear that he was thoroughly disgusted with my lack of respect for Dr Jonas Savimbi (his hero), and ordered me to immediately fly to Jamba with him and apologise for my intolerable behaviour.

A Puma was waiting outside ready to take off.

I refused point-blank and insisted, to the contrary, that Savimbi apologise for the appalling behaviour of his signals officers who had treated the South African flag and a senior SADF officer (myself) with contempt. I assured the general that I would welcome a court martial. A stalemate was inevitable.

The three officers departed in the helicopter without me. The general was in a huff, the SLO as pleased as punch that Breytenbach was deservedly heading for the rocks and the airman second-in-command secretly happy that I had refused to knuckle down to such an idiotic order. The general, needless to say, should have backed me instead of shooting me down.

The affair resulted in Savimbi ordering my transfer out of the Caprivi (South African territory) and threatening to break off all contact between UNITA and the SADF if the general failed to do so. It was no surprise to me that he fell eagerly into line.

My arrogant behaviour, coming on top of the leaked report that was highly critical of UNITA, and particularly of Savimbi's disgraceful conduct during *Operation Alpha Centauri*, was for him the last straw.

But then Admiral Dries Putter, the Chief of Staff Military Intelligence SADF, came to my rescue. He took exception to Savimbi assuming the powers and authority of a South African Army general officer and his arrogance in daring to order the transfer of a South African officer for his own ends as a punishment measure.

Putter flew to Jamba a week or so later and had a major row with Savimbi. He told him, quite rightly, that he would stop training UNITA cadres rather than allow him to interfere in SADF matters.

Nevertheless, CSI's Special Tasks, particularly its Director-General and the senior liaison officer with Savimbi, were from then on waiting balefully in the wings for the right moment to put the knife into me.

I gave them the opportunity shortly afterwards. I had been appointed as an unpaid conservator with the SWA/Namibian Conservation Department in anticipation of a second career after I left the army. It was in this capacity during 1987 that I discovered that certain very senior members of Special Tasks were highly involved in poaching and smuggling ivory and rhino horn on a gigantic scale. Such merchandise commanded high US dollar prices in the Far East. They were working in cahoots with Savimbi. It was a serious Mafia-style crime syndicate operating in the operational area under the cover of the uniform that I was immensely proud of.

Although very disturbed, I did not suspect that my own boss was involved, so I used the proper military channels to report what was going on to CSI Special Tasks as well as to the relevant nature conservation agencies in Windhoek.

I found myself at the epicentre of a tornado of epic proportions. I had not realised that I had uncovered the biggest smuggling racket of ivory, rhino horn and game products in the history of Africa. After opening such a can of worms, it was obvious (although not to me) that my immediate removal from the Caprivi was inevitable to prevent me from fingering those in the top structures of the SADF who were involved up to their necks.

I had already applied for early retirement from the SADF to take up the post of Park Warden of the Western Caprivi Game Park for which I had been accepted. This suited my wife and I because it would enable us to remain in the paradise that was the Caprivi. My application for early retirement was granted with alacrity, but my job offer with the SWA/Namibian Conservation Department was withdrawn almost simultaneously.

I discovered there had been a secret meeting in Windhoek at which CSI Special Tasks had pressured the Nature Conservation Department to withdraw my job offer for 'security reasons'. This effectively ensured that I was bundled out of the Caprivi virtually overnight. I had become a security risk in a highly sensitive area — the Guerrilla School. Yet I had started the school some six or seven years before almost single-handedly. I had drawn up the syllabus, the courses, the standard operational procedures and so on without input from above.

It became obvious that my continued presence in the Caprivi would cause serious problems for the Director-General of Special Tasks, the senior liaison officer to Savimbi, a host of senior SADF general officers and for Jonas Savimbi himself. I had inadvertently played right into their hands. In the end, with my resignation already approved, not even Admiral Dries Putter could save me.

When I realised what had happened, it decided me to thoroughly investigate the ivory and rhino horn smuggling racket. I was well known and respected in SWA/Namibia, which enabled me exploit various sources. They included the SWA/Namibia Police and a small army of informers that was used to get to the bottom of what was going on. My motivation was to prevent the slaughter of the African wild life I loved.

It resulted in the appointment of a judicial commission of enquiry under the chairmanship of Judge Kumleben of the Natal bench. He found that Special Tasks had been at the centre of a massive scam, using a front company called Frama Inter-trading to handle and dispose of ivory and rhino horn in lucrative international markets. In the main, Savimbi's poachers did the actual shooting on a mass scale with military weapons. They had virtually denuded the Cuando Cubango of elephants and had even wiped out the Chobiense black rhino sub-species. All this was done to benefit Savimbi's foreign bank accounts. It had been a deeply covert operation orchestrated by unsavoury elements of the SADF.

At the end, though, despite the findings of the Commission of Enquiry, the tumbrils did not rumble along the corridors of the SADF's headquarters in Pretoria and no one lost his head.

*   *   *

The true losers in the Cuito Cuanavale campaign were the South African formations and their troops who had fought heroically and magnificently without receiving the recognition they deserved. Other losers were the badly led and trained UNITA troops who did most of the cannon fodder fighting and dying on the ground, while the South African artillery and air force were trying hard to ease their lot with long distance combat support from way behind the lines.

The fighting for most of them became a question of personal survival on the battlefield. This explains their highly honed talent for executing lightning-fast withdrawals. It was extremely unusual to find a UNITA officer of senior rank at the firing line. Invariably they kept well away from zones that were characterised by angry flying lead.

Captain Piet Boer Van Zyl had been stood down from his operational deployment and had returned home to plant mealies at his farm in Dundee. Commandant Jan Hougaard had already returned to Buffalo Base. His new task was to train a battle group, or rather an inflated combat team, to disrupt FAPLA's supply line between Menongue and Cuito Cuanavale.

These movements accorded with the new vision of the General Staff. On 18 November 1987 they had gone into a brain storming huddle. They came up with three courses of action. The first was to withdraw South African forces to Rundu on the assumption that *Operation Modular* had ended. The second was to exploit all the way up to the Cuito River and drive FAPLA back across it to Cuito Cuanavale. The third was to cut off all FAPLA forces from their supplies by an attack from the west. This would make the destruction of FAPLA east of the Cuito River easier.

The third course of action was the best and the one the General Staff selected. It would deal FAPLA a devastating blow by wiping out all its brigades that were committed to the Cuito Cuanavale front. The plan was good until the usual political restrictions imposed by the South Africans, compounded by a host of emasculating reservations and debilitating operational imperatives demanded by Savimbi, were built in. The main flaw of the second course of action was that the focus of the continued offensive would remain restricted to the east of the Cuito River, instead of being shifted across it to the west. This would have cut FAPLA forces off from their secure rear base at Menongue and opened the way for them to be attacked and destroyed from the rear.

The course of action finally selected turned out to be a disguised combination of a partial second and a fully fledged third course of action — despite some unconvincing window dressing to make it appear otherwise. It is a matter for conjecture how it was possible for the generals — supposedly masters of war — to be so easily manoeuvred into abandoning the only course of action likely to work. Jonas Savimbi must indeed have been persuasive.

The immediate consequence of this committee-driven compromise was that *Operation Modular* could not be terminated. Preparation for a continuous offensive on the existing front meant that the Chambinga River and the dominating heights to the north of it had to be secured to provide a safe base for the next phase of the campaign.

On 25 November Battle Groups Charlie and Bravo launched an offensive from the source of the Chambinga, along an axis of attack towards 25- and 66-Brigades' defensive locality around the river crossing point. Both battle groups advanced along the southern slopes of the Chambinga high ground north of the flood plain.

Farther north, Battle Group Alpha made a feinting attack west towards the high ground north of the Cuatir River, then switched it south, then back to the west. The purpose was to clear the Chambinga high ground from east to west in tandem with Battle Groups Bravo and Charlie which were about five kilometres away on Alpha's southern flank. It also had to prevent a FAPLA counter-attack against the right flank of Charlie and Bravo.

Two of UNITA's regular battalions were to launch a coordinated attack on the bridge from the south-east and north-east, to induce FAPLA to withdraw into the waiting arms of the outflanking Bravo and Charlie. It was hoped that 25- and 66-Brigades would be destroyed, or at the least, suffer a severe mauling before they retreated into the Tumpo Triangle to the west.

Intelligence from UNITA, suspected to be manipulated, indicated that the tangle of bush and forest on the southern slopes of the Chambinga heights was so dense that a mechanised approach would be impossible. To no one's surprise UNITA was ignored. For a change, though, the information turned out to be correct — to the dismay of the battle group commanders.

Commandant Robbie Hartslief's Battle Group Bravo, advancing through the riverine forest with Battle Group Charlie's tanks, covered only 800 metres in four hours. They were caught up in an unyielding green wall of trees. It was the most effective anti-tank obstacle they had ever come across. The tankers battered away at it with ill-tempered frustration. Visibility, and thus the fighting range, had been reduced to zero. The tanks could not use their guns or coaxial machine gun, because the density of the trees made it impossible to traverse the turrets. Battle Group Bravo halted well short of its objective. The infantry on foot were also seriously delayed by the armour's snail's pace.

Robbie returned the tank squadron to Battle Group Charlie and recommenced his advance at a somewhat faster rate. But it was too late. When they reached their FUP (forming up place), insufficient daylight was left to launch an attack. The assault by UNITA had not materialised either. This resulted in FAPLA's two brigades escaping mostly intact while the South African forces were huffing and puffing through the thick bush.

After its failure to separate a sizeable portion of FAPLA's forces from their secure base area on the Tumpo, 20-South African Brigade could only consolidate its positions at the summit of the Chambinga heights. No hope remained of destroying FAPLA east of the Cuito River. Despite this, subsequent operations indicated that some generals and their staff officers laboured under the delusion that it was still possible.

Operation Modular had been successful in one respect. Enemy forces were withdrawing to Tumpo and Cuito Cuanavale after finally abandoning all hope of wresting Mavinga from Savimbi's grip. South African forces had stopped and inflicted savage losses on them. Apart from 47-Brigade, though, no other enemy formation had been destroyed, but they had all been badly mauled. They had lost about 90 tanks and other armoured fighting vehicles, a large number of soft-skinned vehicles, numerous artillery pieces, Stalin Organ MRLs and a mass of other equipment. They suffered about 4 000 casualties against negligible losses by the South Africans. UNITA, however, had taken punitively heavy casualties. A stalemate was almost inevitable.

The fact that three under-strength South African battle groups had fought against tremendous odds, seeing off FAPLA's brigades each time while inflicting massive destruction in war materiel and lives, was testimony to the aggressive spirit and superior combative qualities of the South African soldiers. This applied particularly to the junior leader element, both black and white. There were some exceptional commanders at middle level. Witness the professionalism of combat officers like Commandants Robbie Hartslief, Jan Hougaard and Bok Smit, Majors Hannes Nortmann and Tinus van Staden and Captain Piet 'Boer' Van Zyl. The artillery forward observation officers were proven to be outstanding and so were the majority of the battery commanders of the 155mm G5s, the Valkyrie multiple rocket launchers and the 120mm mortars.

It was a pity that the commander of Battle Group Charlie had not been made of sterner stuff. A better leader would not have allowed FAPLA to escape.

Towards the end of 1987 Colonel Jock Harris handed over command of 32-Battalion to Colonel Mucho Delport. Mucho found himself at the tail end of a war that was grinding to a stalemate on the Cuito Cuanavale front and at the beginning of a final flare-up on the Calueque-Ruacana front to the west.

After this, 32-Battalion's main operational exertions would be aimed at FAPLA and at Cuban and SWAPO targets in the west. There were some fresh companies in Buffalo Base that had not been blooded in the current operations. A bid was made for more rifle companies for deployment on the Cuito Cuanavale front and, as usual, 32-Battalion rose to the challenge.

29

Operation Hooper and so on

The name 'Operation Modular' was scrapped and it became Operation Hooper instead. Maybe it was thought that a name change would lead to some sort of revival which would restore the campaign's fortunes.

On 8 December 1987 Colonel Paul Fouche, with a reconstituted 20-South African Brigade HQ, moved out from Mavinga to replace Colonel Deon Ferreira and his old HQ to the east of the Chambinga source. This was part of a general change of personnel. 61-Mechanised Battalion (Battle Group Alpha) and 4-South African Infantry (Battle Group Charlie) were manned with replacements at all levels, including the commanders. A tank squadron from the Pretoria Regiment was attached to Battle Group Charlie and a second one to Battle Group Alpha. This gave the brigade two tank squadrons with a total of 24 tanks complete with spares to replace battle casualties and breakdowns.

The artillery batteries were not so fortunate. The personnel were replaced, but they retained the guns that had been in the thick of all the battles from the beginning of the campaign, except for the three G6 self-propelled 155mm guns which were withdrawn. The general wear and tear on the guns that remained and the absence of the G6s would have a serious adverse effect on 20-South African Brigade's combat power.

FAPLA was strengthening its bridgehead on the east bank of the Cuito River to prevent the South Africans or UNITA from breaking through — although the chance of the latter achieving this lay in the realms of fantasy. FAPLA's 25-Brigade's old positions, compared to the time in 1986 when UNITA Brigadier Numa had failed so miserably to take them, had been strengthened beyond recognition.

FAPLA's defensive system was based on three belts deployed in depth. One was centred on Cuito Cuanavale west of the Cuito river, the second ran through the Tumpo Triangle east of the Cuito River bridge and the third, an outer perimeter belt, encroached into the thickly forested western slopes of the Chambinga heights.

FAPLA's 13-Brigade and leading elements of 50-Cuban Division had arrived in Cuito Cuanavale to bolster the forces there. They were deployed as an in-depth defence, bringing an increased concentration of artillery between the town and the west bank of the Cuito River. The fresh artillery deployments were an alarming development that failed to get the priority attention it deserved from the South Africans. This mistake would cost them dearly when FAPLA's outer defences were contracted into the Tumpo Triangle. The joint Cuban/FAPLA forward command post (the equivalent of the South African Tac HQ) had been established just north of Cuito Cuanavale. Shortly afterwards the Cubans took complete control of this facility.

FAPLA 16- and 66-Brigades had been deployed into the Tumpo Triangle between the Dala and Tumpo Rivers with a frontage of about six kilometres and a depth of about four kilometres. 66-Brigade's task was to protect the Cuito River bridge and it was dug in on tactical terrain that controlled the approaches. 25-, 59- and 21-Brigades held the outer perimeter belt from south to north to cover a probable South African advance from the east.

Operation Hooper's mission was to destroy all FAPLA forces east of the Cuito River and in front of the Tumpo Triangle, or to force them across the river into Cuito Cuanavale which would, hopefully, become an untenable position. To achieve this, a series of attacks was launched to destroy or force back the outlying brigades.

On 2 January 1988 an attack on 21-Brigade at the northern extremity of the outer defensive belt between the Cuatir and Chambinga rivers was launched by UNITA with South African artillery in support. It failed and UNITA was quickly ejected from the few trenches it had managed to capture.

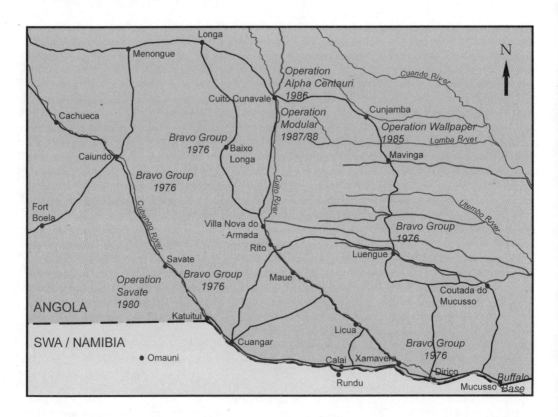

Operations on Angola's Eastern Front, 1976-1988. Note: Operation Modular became Hooper, then Packer and finally Displace.

The SAAF took on the task of destroying the bridge over the Cuito River to isolate the FAPLA bridgehead from Cuito Cuanavale itself. The importance of the bridge as a vulnerable feature in FAPLA's logistical system was still being overrated by the General Staff.

It appears that the General Staff had abandoned their original third course of action as the basis for destroying FAPLA forces on the Cuito Cuanavale front. They had narrowed their options to concentrating on FAPLA's formations east of the river, preferably by launching a battle of destruction against them. How to achieve this would occupy their minds for the next few months.

Buccaneer strike bombers escorted by Mirages flew several missions against the Cuito River bridge on separate days. These attacks introduced a South African-developed 'smart bomb'. The first two strikes failed because of technical problems, but the third was partially successful and the bridge was damaged. The bombing, coupled with a weakening of the bridge structure by previous artillery strikes, was enough for FAPLA to suspend the movement of heavy vehicles across it until it could be repaired. The Soviet-supplied ferries were still operating though, despite them frequently coming under heavy artillery fire. FAPLA's engineers got the bridge back into operation in time to reinforce their outer ring of brigades during and after a series of ground attacks that were launched against them.

On 13 January, after a Mirage strike and artillery bombardment to soften up the target, Battle Group Charlie under the command of Commandant Jan Malan, and supported by tank squadrons and a UNITA infantry battalion, launched an attack against FAPLA's 21-Brigade. Battle Group Alpha was deployed to cover Charlie's left flank and block any counter-attacks that might be launched from defensive localities in the south.

Despite delays caused by the weather and the terrain, the attack went in as planned. FAPLA's artillery, meanwhile, had been wasting considerable quantities of ammunition shelling a well planned dummy artillery position. Jan Malan's men aggressively attacked the enemy's trench system and FAPLA's infantry suffered heavy casualties from the guns of the tanks and Ratels. Enemy tanks and other armoured vehicles were shot out.

They penetrated the defensive system around 21-Brigade's HQ and destroyed several tanks of 16-Brigade that had got through as reinforcement. Unable to take the punishment, 21-Brigade cracked and ran, mostly into Battle Group Alpha on the left flank. They were mowed down in droves as they fled for the safety of the Tumpo Triangle to the south-west.

Battle Group Charlie continued to exploit well into the night, even using illumination to do so. Eventually it withdrew a short distance and resumed attacks at first light. It swung south-west and exploited up to the Dala River, killing many panicky FAPLA troops who had fled into the bush. It had punched a huge hole in FAPLA's defensive perimeter. 21-Brigade had cracked and its remnants were running helter-skelter into a thoroughly disorganised Cuito Cuanavale.

Eventually, though, Battle Group Charlie ran out of steam.

A fresh battle group was needed to take over and continue the attack. Commandant Liebenberg's Battle Group Alpha was the only formation available. It needed two fresh tank squadrons to give it sufficient punch to maintain the momentum and to take the bridge, with a coup de main if the opportunity presented itself, followed by the town, its logistical installations, the forward command post, the gun lines and the 13-Brigade positions.

But Alpha had no tanks, it had given its squadron to Battle Group Charlie for its assault — so because of the lack of tanks, the operation was called off and the South Africans handed over their captured objectives to UNITA and withdrew.

To put it bluntly, the brigade commander, Colonel Paul Fouche, had been given insufficient combat power to do the job. It was not that higher military authority was out of touch with what was happening. The Chief of the Army, Lieutenant-General Kat Liebenberg with his staff of brigadiers and colonels, and the GOC SWA Territorial Force, Major-General Meyer with his staff, had flown in and were sitting in 20-South African Brigade's Tac HQ keeping a close eye on the management of the battle.

It appears that the coffee-drinking generals in the Tac HQ had somehow lost sight of the most important principle of war — which demands that an adequate reserve should always be maintained to grasp unexpected opportunities when they present themselves.

During the attack Colonel Fouche had based himself close to the scene of action, probably to get away from the generals who were only too ready to advise, criticise and order him about while he was engaged in conducting a major and intensive battle. That he coped so well says much for his capabilities as a combat leader. Unfortunately, in the SADF it had become an accepted battle drill for the higher HQs — all the way up the line to the top — to deploy into the field when a battle was in the offing.

Fidel Castro was not to be outdone by the South African generals. After the disastrous performance of an Angolan brigade, he peremptorily informed Luanda that he was taking personal charge of the fighting around Cuito Cuanavale — from Havana in Cuba! He ordered FAPLA forces to withdraw into the small bridgehead on the Tumpo River and to pull back and redeploy its artillery on the west bank. In fact, despite this being an instruction from afar, this was an astute move.

FAPLA, however, took little notice of General Cintra Frias, their newly appointed Cuban field commander, and opted to retake 21-Brigade's lost positions. 8-Brigade, with new equipment, was sent across the river and tasked to chase out the UNITA occupying force. 21-Brigade would be reformed and redeployed on the northern extremity of the outer defensive ring. After some desultory resistance, UNITA withdrew and the reformed 21-Brigade strolled calmly back into their old trenches and bunkers.

This meant the South Africans had to repeat the whole process of evicting FAPLA from its outer perimeter. Commandants Liebenberg and Malan, commanders of Battle Groups Alpha and Charlie respectively, had both contracted hepatitis and had been replaced by Commandants Cassie Schoeman and Mike Muller.

Once more a gaggle of generals from Pretoria, each with his own set of guidelines and restrictions, descended on Colonel Paul Fouche to plan the next operation. One plan was that all FAPLA east of the Cuito River should be driven across it. This was clearly impossible because of the massive concentration of artillery fire now at FAPLA's disposal — thanks to Fidel Castro's foresight. FAPLA could swamp an ever narrowing front with gunfire and anticipate only a puny reaction from 20-South African Brigade because most of its guns were out action awaiting repairs and barrel replacements.

Paul Fouche returned to South Africa to form and train 82-Brigade. It would later replace 20-South African Brigade. He was relieved by Colonel Pat McLoughlin, widely known as Rooi (Red) Mac, an infantryman whose father was a respected gunner from World War-II. Mac senior used to claim in all seriousness that one gunner was worth ten infantrymen. It can only be hoped that Pat was not disinherited when he opted to become an infantryman!

The next attack, planned for 14 February, was a three-pronged affair. A strong UNITA force would move from east to west straight at the re-occupied 21-Brigade trenches and eject a much-weakened FAPLA force from their positions. On UNITA's left Battle Group Alpha, while aiming for high ground straight ahead — known as 61 koppie — would lever itself into the gap between 21-Brigade in the north and 59-Brigade in the south. From there it would dominate the battlefield in an arc spanning from 59-Brigade positions in the south, then west and north across 21-Brigade's position. Once in position it would be capable of reinforcing in any direction. It could also beat off counter-attacks and when required, could exploit to the northern edge of the Tumpo Triangle. Battle Group Charlie, meanwhile, would advance on Alpha's left with the mission of swinging south at the appropriate moment to attack 59-Brigade from north to south and drive it from its trenches.

At this critical time FAPLA's brigade commanders were absent from their brigades and attending a conference at FAPLA's forward command post at Nancova. They would not get back to their posts until after the rot had set in.

The usual fire plan was adopted as the three prongs moved to their start lines. 59-Brigade, in particular, was given a good pasting by the guns. UNITA easily broke through the brigade's flimsy combat outpost line and moved forward against weak resistance to claim its objective.

Battle Group Charlie swung south to the left rear of 59-Brigade and experienced only light resistance. When it reached the brigade command post area, however, it ran into stiff resistance backed up by T55 tanks. An exciting tank battle developed during which most of the enemy's tanks were destroyed. Battle Group Alpha took up station in the vicinity of 61 koppie, but it soon had to move to a new location west of 59-Brigade's defensive locality to intercept a counter-attack directed at Battle Group Charlie.

Confusion reigned supreme throughout FAPLA's command. This was aggravated when Cassie Schoeman of Battle Group Charlie ordered his electronic warfare Ratel to jam FAPLA's tank command net. The enemy tanks milled around, having no idea which way to go. Some strayed into the midst of Battle Group Alpha and became sitting ducks for the South African tanks and Ratel-90s.

59-Brigade finally cracked and abandoned its trenches en masse. The two South African battle groups continued with mopping up and exploitation until it became too dark to continue. During the night they were ordered to withdraw, which they did with their crippled vehicles in tow. By daylight they were on the eastern edge of the battlefield and positioned to clear up a few pockets of FAPLA bypassed the previous day.

FAPLA's forward command post was unable to locate its 21- and 59-Brigades. 59-Brigade had scattered across the Cuito River bridge and disorganised elements had evaporated into the thick bush west of the Cuito River. 21-Brigade had also dissolved and disappeared. Nobody knew where they were, least of all their brigade commanders. It was small wonder that the somewhat frayed patience of General Cintra Frias finally snapped. He ordered all FAPLA forces, except for 25- and 66-Brigades, to withdraw into Cuito Cuanavale. They were to maintain a small bridgehead in the Tumpo Triangle which, it was thought, would have its right flank firmly anchored against the Tumpo River and its swamps.

General Frias by then was firmly in command of all forces on the Cuito Cuanavale front.

The South Africans had again missed a golden opportunity to exploit an unexpected success because their forces were not organised to do so. It could not, of course, have been foreseen that the FAPLA brigade commanders would have been absent from their brigades at the most critical time, but that again proves the dictum that a reserve must always be at hand to be flung into battle — and that is why a formation commander should always position himself where he can read the battle and anticipate his next move which might well be decisive.

Cassie Schoeman's jamming of 59-Brigade's tank control net could, perhaps, have been expanded to include the FAPLA command net and the artillery fire control net. In any case, with chaos already reigning supreme in FAPLA at all command levels, its artillery had probably been neutralised for long enough to have made FAPLA's destruction a certainty. The guns, the only major obstacle preventing the South Africans from getting into Cuito Cuanavale, had unexpectedly collapsed. With night closing in it would have been difficult for FAPLA's guns to engage with even a minimum effect. A follow-on illuminated night attack on the Tumpo Triangle and Cuito Cuanavale was required.

General Frias, however, was given plenty of time to regain control. His obvious ability as a commander became apparent when he cunningly developed minefields that would canalise any future South African attacks against the Tumpo bridgehead into well-placed killing grounds. To do the killing he deployed artillery — masses of guns, BM21s, 23mms, 120mm mortars and even tanks — across the river behind the lip of its high western bank where the South African guns would have had problems pinpointing and taking them out.

The South Africans played into the hands of General Frias by concentrating FAPLA's widely dispersed combat power by driving all fleeing FAPLA remnants before them into the Tumpo Triangle. They should rather have cut them off and destroyed them piecemeal. Earlier in the campaign when the enemy was widely scattered, they could have brought overwhelming combat power to bear against any FAPLA brigade at a time and place of their own choosing. They did try, of course, but their efforts were ruined by the incompetence of the first commander of Battle Group Charlie.

In the end FAPLA's later granite-hard deployments would dictate military tactics and ensure a stalemate. Circumstances had changed and only a fool would force an attack on a hardened and contracted bridgehead covered by deep and extensive minefields. A head-on charge would have taken an attacking force into the deadliest storm of concentrated artillery fire ever seen in southern Africa. It was too late to do anything effective on the Tumpo sector.

The SADF, however, did have its fair share of fools in the rarified atmosphere at the top. What lured on the General Staff was that FAPLA forces were still obstinately dug in on the wrong side of the Cuito River. They should have just left them there, hemming them in with minefields or, even at that late stage, they could have switched the focus of the attack to the west of the river and taken Cuito Cuanavale from the rear. Instead it was decided that only more of the same would succeed.

It was planned to launch an attack against 25-Brigade. This, as it turned out, became the first of a series that later became known as Tumpo One, Two and Three.

The first went in on 25 February 1988. The attacking force consisted of 61-Mechanised Battalion, UNITA forces and Major Tinus van Staden's three 32-Battalion rifle companies and combat support elements. Tinus' troops and an accompanying UNITA battalion were to launch a night attack on a 25-Brigade battalion defensive position close to the source of the Tumpo River. Because of its shape, the defensive position was called the Scorpion's Sting. The slight rise on which it was deployed was given the identification of Hill 1208. Tinus' attack would precede that of 61-Mechanised Battalion. It would secure a foothold within the enemy's defensive perimeter from which 25-Brigade's trenches could be systematically cleared from south to north by a combined tank and mechanised infantry assault.

Tinus' force began its approach march from Viposto in the early hours of D minus one. They crossed the swampy Chambinga River at first light and laid up in the thick bush beyond. This put them behind the minefields that protected 25-Brigade's front. A FAPLA outpost that could interfere with and delay their attack on the Scorpion Sting lay on the approach route to their target. Tinus asked the accompanying UNITA battalion to take out this nuisance factor while en route to execute a scheduled diversionary attack farther west. Not unexpectedly UNITA refused, so Tinus called for an artillery strike instead.

32-Battalion used the cover of darkness to get to their forming-up place about three kilometres south of Hill 1208 where they slept until 03:00. Tinus shook his men out into extended line — a difficult exercise in thick forest — and they set off in the direction of the enemy on a compass heading.

When by Tinus' judgement they were on their start line, he asked the 120mm mortars for illumination rounds. To the obvious consternation of 25-Brigade they popped precisely over their position. They were suddenly in the centre of a circle of glaring white light. It appears their nerves could not take the strain of waiting helplessly for hordes of madmen to charge at them with spitting rifles and sharp bayonets. (Unfortunately General Constand Viljoen had already abolished bayonets when he became Chief of the Army). They broke and ran for the rear.

As Tinus' men slowly advanced under the glare of the flares, they could hear the enemy noisily vacating their positions. At first light the troops were still advancing across the exposed and open expanses of the Anhara (flood plain) Lipanda. The lack of cover prompted Tinus to order his troops to charge at the double. This was enthusiastically carried out and the last few hundred metres were covered in record time. Momentum carried them into the vacated trenches and beyond. A truck trying to escape was shot out by a staff sergeant armed with an RPG7 rocket launcher. It was the only shot fired during the assault.

FAPLA had deserted a splendidly constructed trench system. They found indisputable evidence of panic reaction. Boots, lots of clothing, piles of ammunition boxes, equipment packs, rations and so on had been abandoned. A serviceable BRDM was found dug into a well entrenched firing position.

Not long afterwards the trenches proved to be very useful. Tentatively at first, then with an increased concentration and improved accuracy, FAPLA's guns and BM21s began to shell and rocket the vacated 25-Brigade positions. 32-Battalion soon found itself under a continuous bombardment from guns firing from behind the rim of the prominently higher west bank of the Cuito River's flood plain. From north to south the western skyline flickered as FAPLA artillery hurled thousands of shells and rockets at them. Sixty guns plus BM21 MRLs concentrated their fire on Tinus and his 230 men. It must have been somewhat like a repetition of the Battle of Delville Wood in World War-I. The trench system had been so well-constructed, though, that they caused only a few shrapnel wounds.

61-Mechanised Battalion, in the meantime, had moved forward to launch its attack on the rest of 25-Brigade. They passed through a minefield that engineers had already breached, but were brought up short by another unsuspected one. General Frias had had sufficient time to prepare a few surprises. Four tanks lost their tracks. Exploding mines gave away the battle group's position to the enemy artillery. They soon found themselves on the receiving end of what was later described as the heaviest artillery bombardment of the war. Plofadder mine clearing devices were shot across the minefield to blast a breach, but they failed to explode.

The minefield had to be breached before they could get to grips with 25-Brigade. The assault pioneers moved forward to initiate the Plofadders manually from the far side. Those dauntless young national servicemen, under a veritable storm of exploding shells and shrapnel, achieved it with the aplomb of seasoned combat veterans. They were later decorated with Southern Cross medals for their bravery and calmness under fire.

It nevertheless still took 61-Mechanised Battalion more than five hours to get through the minefield. They finally joined up with 32-Battalion, only to have the UNITA troops riding on their tanks open fire on the 32-Battalion troops in the captured FAPLA trenches. Forbidden to shoot back, they resorted to shouting terrible insults at Savimbi's men. This served to increase the not-so-friendly fire. Finally, a yellow smoke bomb was hurled to signal that the occupants of the trenches were not the foes.

The yellow smoke, however, attracted the FAPLA gunners' attention. The tanks and their UNITA passengers were soon under artillery bombardment. Shock waves and a hail of shrapnel swept the unfortunate UNITA troops from the hulls of the tanks. 61-Mechanised Battalion was given permission to withdraw from this hellfire and its commander ordered Tinus to do likewise.

There was no way that 32-Battalion and 61-Mechanised Battalion, even with the addition of the three UNITA regular battalions forming part of the *Operation Hooper* force, could have remained in the captured positions in the face of FAPLA's overwhelming artillery superiority. It would have degenerated into a Flanders-style Western Front on a smaller scale.

The South African planners had not regarded FAPLA's artillery and its new deployment pattern as a critical factor. Neither had they fully appreciated the significance of the minefields. It was mines that initially delayed 61-Mechanised Battalion, caused it to lose momentum and made it impossible for it to press home a vigorous attack — even into an already-vacated trench system. It was FAPLA's guns and BM21s, though, that forced their withdrawal from the battlefield.

After nine hours of an intensive artillery barrage, 32-Battalion withdrew to Viposto. From there they moved to a concentration area for combined arms training with 61-Mechanised Battalion.

On 29 February, 61-Mechanised Battalion with a somewhat reduced tank component, two UNITA regular battalions and 32-Battalion launched a second attack against the Tumpo bridgehead. Tac HQ had learned from Tinus van Staden's unexpected successes. It was a night attack as it was believed that the cover of darkness would neutralise FAPLA's artillery significantly. It made FAPLA's target acquisition and fire control more difficult — hopefully impossible — because of the inability of their forward observation officers to get visuals on movements at night.

It was intended that Commandant Les Rudman would demonstrate with a strong and, more importantly, very noisy force to the south-east to distract FAPLA's attention from 61-Mechanised Battalion's stealthy movements from the north-east.

61-Mechanised Battalion's H-hour was continually extended because landmine clearing rollers had not been brought forward in time. Commandant Mike Muller had been suffering problems with his Olifant tanks and had been reduced to only seven. He was given some additional Ratel-90s to overcome the paucity, but they lacked the heavy punch of the tanks.

The attack commenced with Les Rudman's demonstration, which attracted attention and drew the enemy's fire.

By first light 61-Mechanised Battalion was closing with the enemy. It was behind schedule but had remained unobserved. The night attack had fallen away because of the delays, making it inevitable that the battalion would soon have to face the full fury of FAPLA's artillery.

32-Battalion and a regular UNITA battalion followed in the wake of the 61-Mechanised. They were ready to move through the forward screen of UNITA troops and clear the positions as soon as contact was made with 25-Brigade's main defensive locality.

FAPLA, however, suddenly realised that the real danger was approaching them from an unexpected direction and that it was not those making such a tremendous noise elsewhere. They opened fire on 61-Mechanised with 23mm anti-aircraft guns, anti-tank weapons, mortars, artillery and even some Sagger anti-tank missiles. By then the South Africans were at the near edge of a minefield and several tanks had detonated mines. FAPLA's artillery soon ranged in and began giving them a really torrid time. This forced the relatively meagre South African artillery to lift their close-fire support of the advancing troops and bring down counter-battery fire on FAPLA's guns. Consequently there was an increase in the intensity of fire on 61-Mechanised Battalion from both flanks and the front.

They were forced to withdraw a short distance to re-organise, but the exploding shells of the 23mm guns deployed in a ground role followed them. A further withdrawal was called for, but this developed into a general pull-out executed by several involuntary bounds. Further tanks had become unserviceable, which left the armour too depleted for the attack to continue. The action was called off.

Earlier SADF Chief, General Jannie Geldenhuys, had arrived at the Brigade's Tac HQ with three of his generals. Not to be outdone, Army Chief General Kat Liebenberg pitched up shortly afterwards with five of his generals. They were joined by Major-General Meyer, the commander of the SWA Territorial Force. During the attack, the generals and their staffs were comfortably although somewhat anxiously ensconced in the Tac HQ, giving unwarranted advice and even orders whenever they felt like it.

As Napoleon put it: 'There is only one thing worse than one bad general and that is two good generals.'

The generals finally decided to end *Operation Hooper* and replace it with the brand-new *Operation Packer*. 20-South African Brigade was closed down and Colonel Pat McLoughlin returned to South Africa with his brigade HQ.

Colonel Paul Fouche returned with the newly formed 82-Brigade and took over on 13 March 1988.

*   *   *

The new arrivals found the Chambinga front static.

It was planned to make another attempt — a truly misguided one — on the Tumpo Triangle using battle groups comprised mostly of Citizen Force regiments. 32-Battalion would also play a role. It became obvious towards the end of *Operation Packer* — even to the generals, but only when it was too late — that the Tumpo nut would never be cracked by employing the scandalously discredited World War-I strategy of using attrition as a battlefield tool. This was particularly true when the minuscule combat power released for the task is considered. For the first time, too, the SADF would lose major weapon systems to the enemy — three Olifant main battle tanks would be recovered by FAPLA after the South Africans had abandoned them in a minefield.

The fresh troops were formed into a main attack force that comprised two tank squadrons from Regiment President Steyn, an armoured car squadron from Regiment Mooi Rivier and a mechanised company from Regiment De La Rey. The President Steyn tank heavy battle group was commanded by Commandant Gerhard Louw from the School of Armour.

A secondary attack force was formed from Major Tinus van Staden's three 32-Battalion rifle companies and elements of Regiment *Groot* (Great) Karoo. The remainder of Groot Karoo, with some attachments, would be a deception force.

The balance of Regiment De La Rey, with attachments, formed a protection force for 82-Brigade's Tac HQ. Its service and combat support elements were deployed to the rear.

The interim role of 32-Battalion and elements of Regiment Groot Karoo was to dominate the western slopes of the Chambinga high ground through aggressive patrolling. They were to locate minefields and mount a demonstration against 25-Brigade's right flank while the main assault force punched a hole through the left rear of FAPLA's defences.

The attack by the main attack force was to go in on a westerly heading and hug the Dala River flood plain. They would turn 25-Brigade's left flank, swing south then south-east within the tree line of the Cuanavale and Cuito rivers and across 25 Brigade's rear. They would then make for 66-Brigade's defensive locality at the bridge. This, it was hoped, would drive a wedge between 25- and 66-Brigades. They were to scatter all FAPLA forces and drive the remnants at the bridgehead back across the Cuito River. They were also to capture the bridge and the critical terrain that controlled it. 4-Recce Regiment and UNITA's 5-Regular Battalion would move in and thoroughly destroy the bridge so that it would take a major engineering operation to rebuild it.

To maintain themselves in the face of the enemy for the several hours needed to prepare the bridge for demolition, Regiment President Steyn would have to rely heavily on artillery fire support which, to be effective, needed to be used mostly in a counter-battery role. Given FAPLA's vast superiority in artillery and its overkill in 23mm guns and tank fire assets, the drastically reduced artillery of 82-Brigade had little hope of matching — let alone cutting back — the inevitable deluge of fire that would be directed at Regiment President Steyn from the dominating terrain west of the river.

In retrospect, it seems remarkable that this stark reality did not occur to the SADF's General Staff. Maybe reservations were expressed by lower-ranking officers but were ignored with contempt. Oddly enough, a similar plan to launch 32-Battalion against much weaker FAPLA deployments a year earlier had been turned down because the butcher's bill was considered too high.

South African artillery support consisted of a battery of G5 155mm guns and a battery of G2 5.5 inch guns of World War-II vintage. This gave them 16 guns to subdue more than 60 FAPLA guns and MRLs (BM21s). Add to that an abundance of 120mm mortars — there was only a handful on the South African side — and batteries of the obnoxious 23mms for which 82-Brigade had no answer, plus dozens of tanks deployed in a direct fire support role on the west bank. The overall balance of combat power could only point to a disastrous outcome for Regiment President Steyn— unless a military genius could somehow pull off a miraculous feat of arms.

Generals Liebenberg and Meyer and their senior planners attached themselves to Colonel Paul Fouche and his brigade staff. They could now closely monitor the operation and influence the course of the battle should it, in their minds, become necessary to do so.

Late on 22 March Commandant Gerhard Louw and Regiment President Steyn left the concentration area and conducted a night approach march to get to the forward assembly area by early the next morning. At first light they moved out along the Dala River to flank 25-Brigade to their left. They turned south to climb out of the Dala valley and drove into a minefield — a so-called 'early warning minefield'. A tank lost a bogie and part of its track. Defective Plofadders and the availability of only one anti-tank-mine roller, together with the complicated recovery of the crippled tank, delayed the advance for two and a half hours. The moment they crested the rise of the Dala River's left bank they became visible to enemy forward observation officers. FAPLA opened up with every support weapon that could be brought to bear, engulfing with fire the advancing tanks and the UNITA infantry riding on their backs.

A cynical American infantry officer once remarked: 'The mission of the infantry is to close with and die with the enemy'. Well, the UNITA soldiers did a lot of dying that day, even before making contact with FAPLA. The 23mms swept the passengers from the tanks like chaff, while shrapnel from the artillery and mortar shells took a further toll.

Gerhard Louw experienced difficulty shaking his two tank squadrons out in an assault formation in extended line with squadrons abreast. They had just begun to advance when they ran into a second minefield. A tank rode over a boosted mine and its rear suspension and a track was blown off. This brought them to a halt in one of General Frias' minefields, sited to make a perfect killing ground. It was a registered artillery target and the full weight of FAPLA's defensive fire was brought down on the heads of Regiment President Steyn and the already bleeding UNITA.

The solitary roller tank moved forward to detonate a breach through the minefield, but the vehicle itself drove over a mine and was disabled. The Plofadders again failed to explode and had to be initiated at the far end — which meant the engineers again had to prod their way across the minefield to do so. In any case, the Plofadders could not breach the full width of the obstacle.

An armoured recovery vehicle was brought forward to recover the first tank blown up, but it was held in a firm grip by the soft sand and would not move, even after Gerhard hitched his own tank to the rear of the recovery vehicle. In the end, the crippled roller tank had to be hooked on to four other tanks and laboriously dragged backwards from the minefield.

The artillery bombardment again erupted while Gerhard was dashing around on foot directing the recovery of his tanks. It was a hazardous task because the minefield was literally a devil's garden liberally sown with anti-personnel mines as well as tank mines.

The attack was brought to a grinding and definite halt. Despite the mechanical mine-clearing devices having been expended or put out of action, they had not even breached the minefield.

The enemy's defensive fire was so intense that the battle area was blanketed in dust and smoke so dense that the tanks disappeared from view. Shells poured in and long bursts of 23mm fire rattled against the hulls of the tanks. Gerhard decided to withdraw as soon as he had extracted his tanks from the minefield. He could not allow them to fall into FAPLA's hands.

It was only a matter of time before casualties started to climb. Anti-tank weapons were already shooting at them from close range and enemy tanks had started to engage from longer ranges. There was no way to manoeuvre within a killing ground covered by a hurricane of shot and shell while hundreds of mines lurked ready to blow off tracks and suspensions — that would turn them into helpless hulks ready to be picked off at the enemy's leisure. At least a full squadron of tanks was stuck in the minefield like a dozen flies caught in the sticky mess of a flypaper.

Alpha Squadron withdrew a short distance to cover Bravo Squadron as its crews struggled to extricate themselves from the killing ground. The first cripple was abandoned amongst the mines as there was no means of recovering it. The painfully slow recovery of the roller tank — the heavy roller was like an anchor dragging through thick sand — resulted in that also being ditched. Gerhard requested permission to knock out both tanks with his tank guns. General Liebenberg refused, saying that both tanks could be recovered later. His confidence that they could be salvaged from the middle of an active and deadly killing ground was frankly ridiculous.

Just short of the first minefield on the return trip, another tank threw a track and was abandoned. Regiment President Steyn withdrew to its previous assembly area and plans were made to recover the three disabled tanks. FAPLA, for a change, was quicker off the mark. They occupied the vacated battlefield and mobilised their more effective recovery effort. They captured their first and only trophies of the war and got them back to Luanda.

It was a major propaganda coup, amplified by the complete silence on the part of the SADF. They acted, no doubt, on the advice of the singularly incompetent COMOPS (Communication Operations — propaganda) department. After Major-General Meyer's return to Windhoek he signalled a belated order that the tanks were to be destroyed. By then, of course, it was too late — FAPLA had them already.

The only good thing to come out of Tumpo Three was a series of gallantry awards. The *Honoris Crux* was awarded to Commandant Gerhard Louw for outstanding bravery.

In the main, his force came out of this futile experience intact and combat ready. The same cannot be said for the poor UNITA infantrymen who went into action riding on the tanks and Ratels. Their dead littered the battlefield in great numbers.

*　　　*　　　*

32-Battalion's feint from the south-east against 25-Brigade's right flank came to nought because Regiment President Steyn called off the main assault. The battalion was withdrawn to its assembly area before it made contact. The rifle companies, still under the command of Major Tinus van Staden, returned to Buffalo Base.

FAPLA meanwhile began to redeploy its forces and strengthen its bridgehead with elements from 50-Cuban Division. It also pushed forces west of the Cuito River to the south to block attacks by the South Africans against its supply lifeline between Cuito Cuanavale and Menongue. It reinforced the Tumpo Triangle with about 50 tanks and SAM systems. Strong outposts, including T62 tanks, were placed in blocking positions south-west of Cuito Cuanavale and west of the Cuito River — in addition to those forces already in place. No further opportunities would arise for the South Africans to destroy FAPLA on this front, whether such an operation was launched from east or west of the river. Numerous winning opportunities had been squandered by the SADF's High Command.

The only thing left was for the South Africans and UNITA to effectively consolidate their forward positions and hem FAPLA in so they could never again break out from the Tumpo Triangle and stage another invasion of Savimbi's territory.

It was time to pack up *Operation Packer*.

32-Battalion's role on the Cuito Cuanavale front diminished and finally ceased after South African and UNITA forces began to focus on keeping FAPLA corralled behind its bridgehead. To achieve this, they laid an extensive belt of mines for UNITA to deploy behind and gaze across at 25-Brigade while the brigade looked back at them. The preparation of such extensive defensive systems and the staring match that followed, required a code name. *Operation Packer* was changed to *Operation Displace*, an unfortunate name considering the circumstances.

30 April 1988, when the command switched from Colonel Fouche to Commandant Nel, marked the beginning of *Operation Displace*. Piet Nel, an illustrious paratrooper known in those circles as 'Piet Graspol', took command of a force that was named, wrongly, Combat Group 20. It should have been called Battle Group 20. It included Major Hannes Nortmann's anti-tank squadron from 32-Battalion, a motorised rifle company, two troops of engineers and a G5 155mm battery. UNITA provided three battalions to man the well dug-in defensive system designed to keep FAPLA at bay.

Piet Nel, a naturally aggressive soldier, decided to dominate the rear area, including the Chambinga heights, with foot and Ratel patrols. He also decided to dominate the no-man's land between UNITA and the Tumpo Triangle, a necessary condition for laying minefields in relative safety.

Hannes Nortmann, with an attached rifle platoon, was ordered to occupy 61 koppie, the slight rise between the old 21- and 59-Brigade positions that was well forward into no-man's land. His unit became Combat Team One. His missile Ratels were positioned on the koppie and two troops of Ratel-90s were used to dominate the forward area between the Dala and Cuatir rivers.

A company from 201 Bushman Battalion arrived on 12 May and Piet Nel deployed them west of the old 25-Brigade positions to dominate, through aggressive patrolling, the ground to their front up to the Cuanavale River. Piet's artillery fired many harassing salvoes at the bridge and into the Tumpo and Cuito Cuanavale areas. To spook FAPLA, he even used a captured T55 tank to drive around his area of responsibility. Ongoing deception operations were launched to mislead and alarm FAPLA's command structure. They were designed to keep the enemy in cover behind their ramparts so the South African engineers could carry out their part of the mission in relative safety. It was important that FAPLA did not discover how weak the combined UNITA-South African forces were until the minefields were in place.

The engineers laid their devil's gardens with a mixture of tank and personnel mines. Many of FAPLA mines had been lifted and these were used to improve the scope and the depth of minefields. Accidents are bound to happen when laying mines and this time was no exception. A few sappers trod on their own mines, including the commander who lost a foot. The engineers, nevertheless, did a splendid job.

On 13 June Hannes Nortmann, his missile troop and a rifle company were withdrawn to Buffalo Base. He was required to form a second anti-tank squadron that was needed for urgent deployment to Calueque in the far west. He left his two troops of Ratel-90s with Piet Nel. Piet's slowly unravelling Combat Group had started to become a rather thin-on-the-ground combat team. In July SWA Territorial Force in Windhoek sent him an incomprehensible order to the effect that he should prevent the capture of any South African soldiers or equipment by withdrawing to safer areas in the rear if it became necessary. Conversely, he was also told that his combat group should behave as if it was a major force that was about to resume the offensive against Cuito Cuanavale.

In the first week of August a final withdrawal from the Cuando Cubango began. It was completed by 27 August and *Operation Displace* ended.

30

Back behind the enemy lines

For a time, elements of 32-Battalion reverted to their old game of guerrilla warfare. To assist the final attacks on FAPLA's positions east of Cuito Cuanavale during operations *Modular* and *Hooper*, attempts were made to interrupt FAPLA's supply lines between Menongue and Cuito Cuanavale — a sort of compromise for not going the whole hog against this fatally vulnerable sector.

Commandant Jan Hougaard had formed a force made up of a rifle company, a MRL troop, the anti-tank squadron minus its missile vehicles, mortars, anti-aircraft weapons and other support elements. He also took along three Recce Wing teams because, as usual, Savimbi wanted the force escorted through his territory by UNITA guides. 32-Battalion had learnt the hard way that UNITA guides were as unreliable as their heavily doctored intelligence. Jan had no intention of being manipulated by Savimbi through these guides.

During December 1987 Jan moved his force to a position south of the tar road from Menongue to Cuito Cuanavale, FAPLA's main communication line. He deployed the Recce Wing teams with their attached forward observation officers at various places between the Quatir and Longa rivers. Their mission was to monitor FAPLA and Cuban convoys moving in strength under heavy escort towards Cuito Cuanavale. When a convoy was sighted, they passed the information to Jan who told Rundu who scrambled Mirages to attack them. The air strikes caused massive damage, destroying hundreds of vehicles that were left shattered and burnt out all along the length of this vulnerable supply corridor.

If Mirages were unavailable, Jan waited until the convoys were within range of his MRLs. He then struck them with ripples of rockets and wreaked large-scale damage. The problem was that his troops had to scamper south for about 100km to get out of reach of the brigade-sized revenge attacks that were launched after each bombardment. Returning to within range of the FAPLA supply corridor once a hue and cry had died down took time. But like a perniciously persistent gadfly, Jan did not give up.

FAPLA finally decided it had had enough of his impertinence and despatched a reinforced 8-Brigade to hunt him and his men down and destroy them. Seeing the tremendous odds that were being stacked against him, Jan hurriedly withdrew. He had accomplished his mission and broken new ground by developing a raiding philosophy acceptable to the SWA Territorial Force and the SADF.

He handed over command of his force to Commandant Flip Genis. Once FAPLA's 8-Brigade had returned to its base, Flip continued to harass FAPLA convoys with MRLs and later with 120mm mortars that replaced the somewhat less flexible MRLs. The reloading of rocket tubes was a tedious job that took too long, particularly in situations where plenty of targets of opportunity were the order of the day.

On 6 February Commandant Robbie Hartslief took over from Genis. He added two rifle companies and a fresh MRL battery commanded by Major Pierre Franken — FAPLA's nemesis on the Lomba River.

By 14 February 20-South African Brigade readied to launch attacks on 21- and 59-Brigades for the start of *Operation Hooper*. Robbie was tasked to interrupt the flow of FAPLA logistics to the Cuito Cuanavale front as a preliminary move. The success of the operation depended on an extensive deployment of reconnaissance patrols, a rapid response radio intercept capability, an excellent communication system and an immediate response capability from the Mirages and his own artillery. All these elements were at Robbie's disposal, with some restrictions designed to minimise the risks attached to deep penetration raids. The entire length of the Menongue-Cuito Cuanavale corridor was covered by OPs and recce patrols drawn from UNITA's Special Forces, 1- and 5-Recce Regiments and 32-Battalion's own Recce Wing.

Robbie's electronic warfare Ratel could provide him with hot intercepts. He could track the minute-by-minute movement of convoys and determine precisely when they would be at their most vulnerable — perhaps to an air strike when they were bunched up at a bottleneck, for instance.

Between 7 and 28 February enemy convoys were hit successfully on 16 occasions by SAAF Mirages, MRLs or both. The MRLs were particularly useful for striking at FAPLA convoys when they were outspanned for the night at known resting points en route. Mirages, used only by day, flew in on a precise track at low level to the plotted target. They pulled up over an exact ground point a short distance from target and tossed their bombs in parabolic arcs into the centre of enemy concentrations of fighting and soft-skinned vehicles. They rarely missed and inflicted devastating damage. Results were monitored and confirmed by Recces on the ground, so the figures can be regarded as accurate.

More than 400 tanks and soft-skinned vehicles were destroyed during this period. On one raid the Mirages left about 60 vehicles burning on one stretch of road.

I am almost certain that the Mirage pilots learned their bomb tossing technique from Colonel Dick Lord. It was a method of attack that had been honed to a fine art over many years by British Fleet Air Arm crews. It must have given Dick great satisfaction to see it all come together on the battlefields of southern Angola.

The SADF's General Staff decided that the assault of 14 February on 59- and 21-Brigades' defensive localities on the outer perimeter of the Tumpo bridgehead should be supported with a raid of some consequence.

They ordered that an attack be put in on Menongue airfield to neutralise it as a forward operational base for FAPLA's strike aircraft. Robbie Hartslief was ordered to take his Buffalo Raiders close to Menongue and unleash ripples of rockets into or above parked fighter jets and into the living quarters of the air and ground crews. The attack would be executed at night.

Robbie conducted a carefully planned approach march through territory nominally under MPLA influence and patrolled regularly by FAPLA. Attached engineers had to build a bridge at each river crossing. It took five days to reach the deployment area, which was ten kilometres from a concentration of FAPLA tanks.

At 22:30 Pierre fired a ripple of 96 rockets. They waited for enemy reaction but there was none as far as they could tell.

At 01:30 they fired a second ripple and left hurriedly for their secret base on the Gimbe River. They had to get well clear of Menongue before FAPLA could launch a tank-heavy search-and-destroy mission at first light.

The return journey took two days. From intelligence reports they were able to estimate the damage. It was disappointing. Seven Cuban and 37 Angolan air and ground crewmen were killed, but only a single MiG had been destroyed. The air base was back in operation by the early afternoon of the same day.

After that, the raider's Gimbe base area was subjected to three or four enemy air strikes a day in an enemy attempt to flush them from their well camouflaged hides. The enemy achieved no successes, but the raids called a halt to Robbie's movements and prevented him from attacking FAPLA convoys. This became the exclusive preserve of the Mirages which continued their attacks with much success.

On 19 February four Mirage F1AZs flew a mission against a FAPLA convoy assembled at the Quatir River bridge, 40km east of Menongue. Three Mirages performed their low level approach runs, pulled up, tossed their bombs, rolled off the top, dived to get out of the envelope of anti-aircraft missile systems and streaked back to the safety of SWA/Namibia at treetop level. During their dive to get away, they saw their number four performing his run-in below them.

Recces deployed in the area saw him pull up, toss his bomb and gain height as he completed his half loop. Suddenly smoke poured from the belly of the aircraft. It must have been hit by an anti-aircraft weapon of some sort. Moments later a black column of smoke rose above the trees, indicating that it had crashed.

Robbie Hartslief and his Buffalo Raiders away to the south also saw the column of smoke. Confirmation that a Mirage had been shot down came through from the Recces. It was followed by news that a Cuban Battalion was on its way to the crash site to investigate.

The Recces had not seen the pilot eject, but UNITA claimed they had seen a parachute coming down and a man clothed in green running through the forest to the south. The report was followed up, but nothing was found to substantiate it.

Pilots were meticulously briefed on escape and evasion procedures. If they came down south of the Menongue-Cuito Cuanavale road there was no need to run because it was UNITA-controlled territory. Pilots had detailed maps with the accurately plotted locations of 32-Battalion and Recce callsigns.

Robbie was concerned that the Cubans might find the maps in the downed aircraft. If they did, his position would become untenable and he would be forced to withdraw out of operational range of the FAPLA supply corridor.

A Recce team kept tabs on the approaching Cuban battalion strength column. It reached the wreck after nightfall and soldiers were seen searching the area with flashlights.

At Gimbe base Piere Franken's men carefully loaded rockets into the tubes of the MRLs. They had a chance to compensate for the disappointment of the Menongue show and to avenge the shooting down of the Mirage. The Buffalo Raiders were on first name terms with Mirage pilots whom they regarded as friends and comrades.

When the Recces indicated that most of the Cubans in the column were bunching around the burnt-out wreck of the fighter, Franken loosed off a ripple of 96 airburst rockets.

The night erupted in blinding explosive flashes. White-hot shrapnel tore into the unprotected flesh of several hundred of Castro's men. The Recces reported later that two trucks were needed to cart away the bodies. Intercepts confirmed that 143 Cuban and FAPLA soldiers had been killed and that many others had been wounded.

The pilot of the downed aircraft, Major Ed Every, was never found. It was presumed he was incinerated in his fiercely burning aircraft.

Robbie and his raiders could stay around no longer. Several brigade-size posses had set out to get them. FAPLA was nearby in considerable strength. Their secret HQ was a secret no more and had already been shelled by a M46 gun and BM21 rockets.

Robbie and his force were recalled to Buffalo Base. En route they passed west of FAPLA's garrison at Baixo Longa. They decided to make a farewell gesture to FAPLA in the Cuando Cubango. That night they sneaked the MRLs and the 120mm mortars to within eight kilometres of the base. A ripple of 96 rockets and 350 mortar bombs were delivered as a parting gift from *Les Affreux*.

Jan Hougaard and Robbie Hartslief believed that disruptions of FAPLA's supply corridor could only be a gesture and one of short duration at that. The Buffalo Raiders lacked the strength to maintain themselves in the area indefinitely in the face of FAPLA's overwhelmingly superior strength. There was absolutely no hope whatsoever of cutting the enemy's supply lines permanently. In the end their accomplishments amounted to little more than nuisance value to FAPLA. In spite of its frightful losses, enough supplies got through to the Cuito Cuanavale front to reequip and even reinforce its severely mauled brigades. It was impossible for the South African combat forces to chew them up faster than they could be re-supplied from the virtually inexhaustible dumps of Warsaw Pact stocks in Porto Namibe, and presumably, forward dumps at Lubango, Huambo and Menongue.

*   *   *

At the beginning of 1988, Major Duppie du Plessis with three 32-Battalion rifle companies and mortars in support, was despatched to the area east of Mupa with orders to conduct guerrilla operations against both SWAPO and FAPLA.

During the operations they shelled FAPLA positions at Mupa and at Missao de Mupa and successfully attacked several SWAPO bases. In one ambush, conducted by Staff Sergeant Scheepers, a vehicle loaded with enemy soldiers, including seven Cubans, was attacked and destroyed.

They brought the area back under SADF control, but only as long as Duppie du Plessis could stay. The moment his force vacated the area, SWAPO and its allies returned in force. They were also reinforced by an integrated SWAPO/Cuban regular battalion that was based either in Mupa or nearby.

31

The Western Front

Late in November 1987 Fidel Castro became seriously alarmed at the military situation in Angola. His socialist stronghold had come under serious threat from the hated white capitalists in the south. Castro had become disillusioned with the Soviets who were treacherously swaying towards some form of settlement with America. To his mind they were succumbing to the temptations of capitalism. Maybe Castro was thinking the long-term communist plan of getting the Cape sea route into communist hands was about to slip from his hands.

The international boundary between Namibia and Angola comprised hundreds of kilometres of barely discernable cutline that provided easy access to the heartland of the southern country. The obstacles presented by the formidable Cunene and Okavango rivers in the west and east were no real barriers to an invading army.

Owamboland was the territory in SWA/Namibia immediately across the cutline. It was well known that the majority of Owambos overtly or covertly supported SWAPO. With the SADF tied down in eastern Angola on the Cuito Cuanavale front, invading SWA/Namibia would be a walkover for the mixed SWAPO/Cuban battalions. There would be none of the backbreaking bundu-bashing associated with the Cuando Cubango because the sophisticated road systems on both sides of the Owambo/Angola cutline facilitated the rapid deployment of a large conventional army.

In 1975 Castro had regarded the deteriorating political situation in Angola as an opportunity to spread the communist revolution into south-western Africa. Now, 13 years later, the military situation on the ground had become so critical that his dream of a communist Utopia in southern Africa seemed to be slipping away. What stared him in the face, after the numerous hidings suffered by FAPLA on the Cuito Cuanavale front, was the possibility of a communist Angola being replaced by a capitalist-supported UNITA government. FAPLA was hovering on the brink of collapse and the military situation had to be stabilised — and quickly.

It was to stop this that Castro had rudely taken over the running of the war from FAPLA's incompetent generals. He began the deployment of his crack 50-Cuban Division into Angola and sent his best general, Ochoa Sanchez, to take direct charge of the war. The measures taken by the Cubans under the able command of General Cintra Frias to stabilise the situation on the Cuito River have been detailed already.

With a lack of foresight the South Africans had allowed the bulk of their available combat power to become tied down on the Cuito Cuanavale front. Strategically the South Africans should have regarded it as a secondary front. The bush war, after all, revolved principally around a Hearts and Minds campaign designed to shunt the loyalties of Owambos from SWAPO to non-communist parties that they expected would form a future government that was likely to be friendly towards South Africa. Until this was achieved, the SADF would have to hold the line to prevent SWAPO infiltrations into SWA/Namibia — something it had done very successfully until then.

Castro directed General Sanchez to divert elements of his 50-Division, particularly its tanks, to Cuito Cuanavale to bolster FAPLA's combat power there and to deploy several specialist units to provide rear area security. When 20-South African Brigade's advance was brought to a halt in front of the Tumpo Triangle, Castro decided he had sufficient forces in hand to deploy the bulk of 50-Division into brigade (regimental) strong points west of the Cunene River and east into Cunene Province north of the cutline. The strong points were established in a west to east loop beginning at TChibemba in the north-west, then running south-east to Cahama, east to Xangongo and Ondjiva, north to Cuvelai and Cassinga and ending at Jamba (again, not to be confused with Savimbi's Jamba HQ in the Cuando Cubango).

50-Division's combined regimental deployments were:

- Six rifle regiments, each between 1 500 and 2 000 men strong (i.e. brigade-sized formations). Each regiment comprised three battalions, most of them with a tank company.
- One tank regiment with three tank battalions (i.e. an armoured brigade).
- One artillery regiment with three artillery battalions (i.e.,an artillery brigade).
- One composite air-defence regiment (a brigade formation).
- Three composite Cuban and SWAPO battalions 600 strong under joint command.

In addition there were resident FAPLA brigades in Cahama, Xangongo, Ondjiva, Cuvelai and probably also in Cabomba and Jamba. Add to this a large number of SWAPO deployed in forward bases in their western, central and eastern fronts. FAPLA's deployments on the Cuito Cuanavale front were insignificant by comparison.

The Cuban 50-Division completed its deployments by late May 1988. This meant that the SWA Territorial Force's Sector 10 HQ, which was tasked with the security of Owamboland and Kaokoland, was suddenly faced with a major threat.

The South African Government and its military commanders viewed these alarming developments somewhat ambivalently, having concluded that Fidel Castro would not dare invade SWA/Namibia in the face of American and Western opinion. While this might have indeed been the case, it was not something that could be cast in stone.

It is the author's opinion that 50-Division's unexpected deployments towards the cutline caught the SADF's top structure off guard. They tried to make light of it for public consumption.

In a long and detailed discussion with the Sector 10 Commander, Brigadier Chris 'Swart Hand' (Black Hand) Serfontein, it became apparent he had been extremely worried — and rightly so. As the military commander, he had to examine the situation from the viewpoint of a combat soldier. If the worst happened, he had to be prepared not only to stop the Cubans but to give them a hiding as well. This could be relied on with a man like Chris who had already demonstrated his personal courage and command capabilities in a number of battles. He was certainly not prepared to succumb to an attack of wishful thinking however

Swart Hand had only four or five battalions available and they had been trained for counter-insurgency operations. They were lightly armed and were not trained or equipped to be pitched into battle against superbly equipped conventional regiments. He also had a couple of squadrons of obsolete Eland-90 armoured cars and, presumably, he could call on the police COIN unit Koevoet, equipped with Casspir infantry fighting vehicles, to carry out a suicide mission or two.

The Cuban squadrons of T62 and T55 tanks would probably have blasted the Eland-90s and the Casspirs into oblivion.

It is difficult to fathom the devious mind of a fanatic like Fidel Castro. He must have grasped the strategic significance of his force's deployments and would have known there were only scratch South African forces available to face them. He probably did it to intimidate the South Africans out of Angola and SWA/Namibia as a first option, but he might also have been ready to eject them out of northern SWA/Namibia if they tried to call his bluff. With a UN settlement in the offing, this would have placed SWAPO bases there under Cuban protection. Certainly the forces faced by Swart Hand were far too strong to suggest it was merely an empty threat.

The SADF's preoccupation with saving Savimbi had left its Owamboland flank wide open. A general of Sanchez's undoubted ability would have spotted this glaring weakness and informed Castro accordingly. What a brilliant opportunity presented itself for Castro to become the hero of the third world!

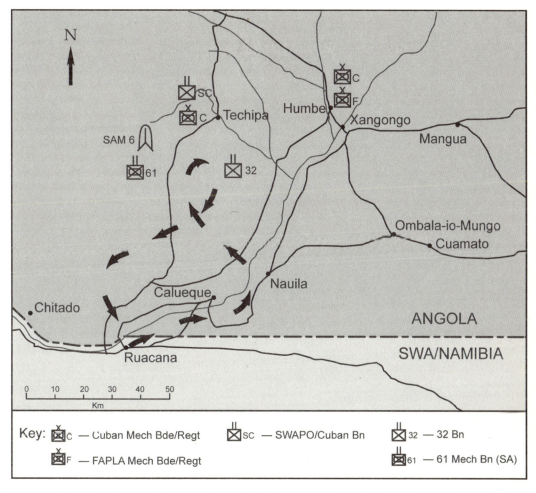

The Western Front: Deployments and clashes around Techipa and Calueque: May-June 1988.

Shock waves were felt in Washington. The level of Cuban military involvement, the dispositions of Cuban forces and Castro's unilateral assumption of personal command indicated to the Reagan administration that there was a real threat of Cuban expansionism in the region. The Cubans had to be removed from Angola and the volatile Castro reined in before events escalated out of control. To accomplish this, the Cuban sting had to be plucked from the FAPLA (MPLA) scorpion and the South

African fangs pulled from the UNITA snake. Both foreign forces would have to vacate Angola — according to Dr Chester Crocker, the academic appointed by Reagan to facilitate a solution.

The conditions were propitious. The MPLA was becoming heartily sick of the arrogant Cubans running the internal security situation as if Angola was an extension of Cuba. The South Africans were frustrated with a war that had no end in sight and was breaking their economy. The Soviets had already shot their bolt in Africa as well as in Afghanistan and would welcome any moves that got them out of the mess with their honour intact. Savimbi, as devious as ever, went along with Crocker's ideas because he believed that with the Cubans removed he could easily defeat FAPLA. What he overlooked was that his South African backing would also fall away. But he was arrogant enough to believe his own propaganda that the South Africans were merely an appendage of his UNITA army.

Predictably, a stingless scorpion and a fangless snake were still at it years later, trying to get the better of each other in a contest that seemed endless.

The Cubans found themselves isolated when even their Soviet 'friends' advised them to cooperate with Chester Crocker. So, no doubt with frustrated reluctance, Castro tore up his plans for an expansion of communism based on the rich resources of the southern African sub-continent.

Crocker's patient shuttle diplomacy, however, did not stop the war in its tracks. Castro was not the kind to throw in the towel without making a final statement to save his face and Cuba's honour.

*   *   *

At Techipa, 40 to 50km north-west of Calueque and close to the SWA/Namibia border, a Cuban regiment (brigade) had dug in and established a forward secure base from which it could threaten the Calueque Dam and hydro-electric scheme. This brigade had probably relocated from Cahama. Ominously, they were accompanied by a composite Cuban/SWAPO battalion, a battle indicator that suggested a possible invasion. A second Cuban brigade based at Xangongo began to make similar threatening gestures south and east of the Cunene River in the direction of Cuamato.

It is unknown if the Cuban regiment at Ondjiva had been tasked to move rapidly towards Oshikango, just south of the cutline, as part of a plan to advance on the SWA/Namibia border on a broad front. If this was the case, the SWA Territorial Force's Sector10 HQ would have had insufficient forces to prevent 50-Division from crossing in strength into Owamboland.

It would have taken only a day for enemy regiments farther back to form up in depth just behind the invading regiments to provide impetus for an attack. This would have accorded with the Soviet doctrine of backing up the leading formations with an equally strong second wave to maintain the momentum of the attack by passing through the first wave when it started to run out of steam.

With South African forces thin on the ground, additional forces were deployed to protect Calueque dam and prevent the Cubans from reaching Ruacana. Task Force Zulu was formed and Colonel Michau (known as Mucho) Delport was placed in command. Zulu comprised a 32-Battalion battle group, three rifle companies from 101-Battalion, 61-Mechanised Battalion, a battery of Valkyrie 127mm MRLs, a battery of G5 155mm guns, a troop of G2 guns and a 120mm mortar troop.

It took time, however, to bring this brigade-sized task force together from all points of the compass. As a holding measure, three 32-Battalion rifle companies and some Recce Wing teams under the command of Commandant Jan Hougaard were dispatched to interfere with the enemy buildup and gather information about their strength, deployments and intentions.

On 16 May Jan Hougaard was the first arrival at what became known as the Western Front. He quickly made Task Force Zulu's presence felt by taking the fight to the enemy in his usual aggressive fashion. He was ably encouraged by Brigadier Chris Serfontein under whose command he temporarily fell. Spoiling attacks by 32-Battalion threw a major spanner into the Cuban works and brought disarray to their plans to move two or maybe three regiments to the SWA/Namibia border.

Little intelligence was available so Jan set out to discover the Cuban intentions. He knew that Techipa was being activated but with what units and in what strength was unclear. So he deployed Recce Wing teams under Sergeants Piet Fourie, Mendes and Da Trinidade to gather intelligence.

*   *   *

In the first attempt Piet Fourie and his team were dropped in rugged mountains too far away to the south-west. To reach Techipa they had to move through open terrain occupied by a hostile population. They moved at night and by day laid up in clumps of bush to remain undetected. The Cubans had an interesting but alarming way of checking possible lying-up places. They simply drove their tanks backwards and forwards through likely looking clumps, flattening everything beneath their steel tracks — including, if they were lucky, a concealed Recce operator. That Recce might well end up as a 'bushman painting on the ground', to quote my parachute instructor when he was discussing the consequences of the malfunctioning of both the main and reserve chutes.

Having to dodge the enemy as well as the locals, it was not surprising that Piet and his team ran out of water and rations long before they could reach target. They were extracted by helicopter, re-rationed and reinserted into a less hostile area from where they could approach Techipa clandestinely.

Piet and his men were deployed by truck using a well-known ruse from Malayan days. They bailed out unobtrusively from a moving truck after dark. Lying up by day, they took four nights to get within seeing distance of the target.

From their hide in long grass, they spotted two FAPLA soldiers approaching from the rear. Commandant Jan Hougaard had asked for a prisoner to be brought in and here was an opportunity to satisfy that request. However, as any soldier will confirm, capturing a hostile enemy is a tricky job fraught with all kinds of unexpected possibilities.

The two FAPLAs almost stumbled over them. The four-man team materialised from underfoot and grabbed the two very startled enemy soldiers. One quickly regained his wits, broke loose and ran off towards Techipa. The other was interrogated, using 'field expedient' techniques, to get information as expeditiously as possible. Then, as a precautionary measure, they immediately began to move south to avoid the patrols that the enemy was bound to send out after them. This was confirmed shortly afterwards when the enemy began to shell the area they had vacated. Their prudence had not been misplaced.

Piet, however, had not finished. He wanted to find out what was going on inside the Techipa base. When darkness fell he and another team member traced the course of a dry river bed that bisected the place. The prisoner was petrified and it was clear he had no intention of making an escape attempt. Instead he eagerly cooperated. They penetrated to the centre of the defensive locality and got within hearing distance of some newly arrived Cuban soldiers. After eavesdropping for several hours, they exfiltrated in time to be clear of the base before first light. Piet spoke Portuguese so he understood enough Spanish to gain useful items of intelligence.

They laid up for the day on the edge of a large *chana*. Piet checked in with Tac HQ and passed a sitrep, proudly announcing that they were returning with a prisoner for interrogation by experts. Astonishingly, a very senior officer at Task Force Zulu HQ — which had deployed by then — ordered him to release the captive. Piet was thunderstruck. They had risked their lives to get the prisoner and obtain intelligence about the Cuban deployments in the Techipa area. Now some idiot of a senior officer was nonchalantly ordering them to get rid of the most promising source of information they were likely to get their hands on. Letting him go would also compromise all their reconnaissance activities in the vicinity of Techipa.

An acrimonious debate followed between Piet — who was not the sort of operator who suffered fools gladly, irrespective of rank — and the very senior officer responsible for the inexplicable decision.

In the end Piet was peremptorily ordered to do as he was told. Regretfully he waved goodbye to a thoroughly bemused prisoner who understood the ways of the South Africans almost as little as Piet did. Jan Hougaard, it appears, had been temporarily sidelined while the newly constituted Zulu HQ moved in and took charge. He was probably just as furious as Piet when he heard about the release.

The team moved south gathering information as they went. They discovered numerous tank and vehicle tracks along with the spoor of infantry patrols. This indicated that the enemy was undertaking aggressive patrolling towards Calueque with large mixed units of infantry and tanks.

They found a sizeable Cuban combat outpost at a waterhole. During the night they crept up close and listened to conversations in Spanish. After withdrawing they reported their discovery by radio to Zulu Tac HQ. Zulu, however, insisted their information was wrong as no other sources had reported enemy deployments so far south. This response, as far as Piet was concerned, negated the whole purpose of the patrol. Thoroughly disgusted and disillusioned with Tac HQ he asked for extraction. A helicopter soon arrived and lifted them out. Headquarters remained blithely unconcerned that they had lost the eyes and ears of an experienced patrol which had been closely monitoring the enemy.

Fortunately, officers like Jan Hougaard had sufficient combat experience and military professionalism to study the reports of the Recce teams, the deployed 32-Battalion companies and radio intercepts and arrive at the right conclusions.

*　　　*　　　*

Jan Hougaard deployed 32-Battalion's Echo Company, commanded by Major Mike Devenish, to an area 10 or 15km short of Techipa. Two more 32-Battalion companies were to work around the flanks of the Cuban deployments at Techipa with the easternmost one also paying particular attention to Xangongo. They were instructed to attack the enemy's rear and its supply lines and take prisoners for interrogation purposes. The identities and composition of the Cuban/FAPLA formations were extremely vague. In addition they were to harass and attack small enemy patrols and outposts to delay an enemy advance south. Finally, they were to hold the fort until the cavalry, in the shape of 61-Mechanised Battalion, could ride to the rescue.

Mike Devenish loaded his company plus two mortars into two Unimogs — it must have been a hell of a squeeze — then set out on the Techipa Road. He took up an ambush position on a road that ran south-east from Techipa to Calueque. It passed between two Cuban outposts 15km south of their main defensive locality. He deployed his mortars two kilometres behind his ambush position. His plan was to lob mortar bombs at both outposts to provoke a relief column into rushing to the rescue from Techipa. The idea was to attack the relief column as it reached the killing ground of their ambush position.

Mike was about to order the mortars to open fire when they spotted five Cubans moving towards them sweeping the road for mines. Machine guns opened fire and cut them down. As with every military plan, well laid or not, rapid changes had to be made to compensate for unexpected developments.

FAPLA infantry escorting the Cuban sappers suddenly appeared and there was a need to deal with them expeditiously.

'Advanca! Advanca!' Mike shouted.

In typical 32-Battalion fashion the company mounted a banzai charge accompanied by enthusiastic bloodcurdling yells.

FAPLA would not have stood a chance but they were saved by the engine noises of armoured vehicles starting up nearby. Four BRDM armoured cars thundered from the bush and opened fire on the company. Mike concluded that they had overstayed their welcome and ordered a hasty retreat. The mortars would cover their rapid but organised withdrawal as platoon leap-frogged platoon, until they got to the Unimogs. Fortunately, the Cuban commander of a BRDM was killed by a well-placed rifle shot and this prompted the armoured cars to withdraw to reorganise.

The enemy's withdrawal, however, was accompanied by the unmistakable sounds of tank engines starting nearby. Mike had unknowingly laid his ambush close to another combat outpost that nobody was aware of. And it had tanks in it.

The company had no weapons capable of stopping or even delaying tanks, so there was no option but to change from contact drills to a straightforward sprint. Mike gave the order and the company doubled to the waiting Unimogs and flung in their heavy kit. It was the beginning of a long, frightening and hellish exercise known in Special Forces jargon as 'escape and evasion'. One Unimog had been hit by enemy fire and was burning. Its passengers tried to pile into the back of the other, but that too was hit and it flared up.

The drivers bailed out and joined the retreating foot soldiers. The burnt-out hulks of the Unimogs were left for the Cubans to claim as war trophies.

The company literally ran at full speed to escape while the tanks and BRDMs closed in from both flanks, chasing them across the Karoo-like open veld as they pumped tank shells and machine-gun fire in their general direction. The situation looked grim. The only solution left was to bombshell — split up and go in different directions — which they did. This increased the number of targets and reduced their size, so the tanks had the perplexing problem of deciding which small group to go after. The tactic unexpectedly worked well.

Jan Hougaard had experienced some anxious moments. Mike could only make fleeting contact with him after he had gone ten kilometres or so. He briefed Jan and reported that 11 men were missing. Jan informed all levels of command — which inevitably caused the commanders and their staff officers to go into panic mode. The exception was Swart Hand Serfontein, who along with Jan remained confident that Mike would return with his company.

At one stage staff officers in Pretoria were demanding the names of the dead and missing — at a time when Mike was dodging tanks and having no idea how to regain control of his scattered company. In those circumstances, conducting a roll call would have been somewhat difficult.

Two days later the whole company reassembled at Calueque with not a wound to show amongst them, except that there were probably quite a few blisters on the feet of the whites!

*   *   *

Lieutenant TT De Abreu escorted an artillery forward observation officer to an OP within sight of the main Cuban deployment at Techipa. After that he took his platoon to the east to get away from an area that was a heaving nest of Cubans and FAPLA.

As fate would have it, their spoor was picked up by a tank unit which was soon hot on their trail. Nightfall brought relief and they broke contact. At sunrise they continued to move east, but one of TT's patrols reported that the tanks were back on their spoor and closing fast.

It became a hare and hounds scene, with the hare unable to stop long enough to call for the accurate artillery support which Jan Hougaard had on standby. TT eventually passed a short sitrep to Zulu Tac HQ, only to have a staff officer tell him that he was misinformed — he was actually being chased by South African tanks!

TT almost burst a blood vessel and told this senior but unidentified staff officer exactly what he thought of him. Coming from a black Angolan, as it did, this probably did not go down well at Tac HQ.

In the meantime, the very real enemy tanks had called for more tanks and armoured cars to cut off the platoon's escape. TT found he was being hemmed in on virtually all sides in terrain where cover was a rarity.

Jan was still standing by to let rip with the artillery. But TT was too pressured by events threatening to imminently overwhelm his platoon to be able to provide Jan with an accurate target reference. Eventually, as a last resort, he radioed his own locstat and asked for fire be brought down on the platoon. Despite reservations, Jan did as he was asked. It did the trick and in the confusion TT's platoon broke out. Miraculously, they escaped unscathed.

'It will only be God and our feet that will bring us home', TT told Jan on the radio.

*   *   *

On 26 June Jan Hougaard ordered the to gunners to saturate Techipa and its outposts with artillery fire.

The enemy had SAM-6 systems in the vicinity, but their positions were unknown. Jan thought of a clever ruse to get them to reveal their locations so they could be attacked and destroyed. Two Impala strike jets took off for a mock attack, but they pulled away fast and low before the enemy could fire missiles. As they did so the gunners released weather balloons towing radar reflectors made of tin foil. These rose rapidly and the enemy radar locked on to them. The over-eager Cubans assumed the echoes, which had been carefully calculated to represent Impalas, indicated a return strike coming in at low level.

In response they launched SAM-6 missiles at the balloons.

The South African gunners intently watching their cymboline radar screens quickly worked out the positions of the missile systems. There were a few sharp orders and moments later the MRLs and G5 155mm long-range guns rained down rockets and shells on the six positions plotted. They destroyed three, maybe four of the positions.

It was Techipa's turn next. The MRLS and G5s continually hammered the Cuban brigade concentrated there. The G2s and 120mm mortars, because of restricted range, concentrated on the advanced outposts.

Intercepts indicated that the devastation had been phenomenal. A large quantity of equipment had been destroyed and some 500 to 600 Cubans, FAPLA and SWAPO had been killed — many more wounded.

Major Pierre Franken had occupied an OP within sight of Techipa to control the massive artillery strike. He had to be infiltrated on foot with a 32-Battalion Recce team, well in advance of the Tac HQ's deployment. There was no UNITA presence in that area of Angola, so the locals along the infiltration route were classified as hostile.

50-Division's formations were newcomers to warring against the South Africans. They were relaxed and slack within their defended localities and had not expected a close interest in bases that they believed were well beyond the reach of artillery. So, in short, they had neglected to dig themselves in like good infantrymen.

Despite the devastating artillery barrage, or perhaps because of it, the Cubans set out to push the South African artillery south and out of range. To achieve this a Cuban regiment began an advance towards Calueque. Another advance from Xangongo to Cuamato had already begun, but it petered out after brushing against a hastily deployed rifle company of 201-Battalion.

The Cubans were over-cautious and they never succeeded in occupying Cuamato.

*　　　*　　　*

61-Mechanised Battalion had become a battle group, having been reinforced by Major Hannes Nortmann's force of ZT3 guided missile Ratels, a Ratel-90, a Ratel-20 — Hannes' command vehicle, a company of paratroopers and two rifle companies from the SWA Territorial Force. It also had, of course, its organic tank squadron under command.

Apart from his own vehicles Hannes had another seven Ratel-90s, 11 Ratel-20s and eight Ratel-81s. It was a formidable combat team, but still vulnerable to T54s or T55s if the Cubans handled them properly.

61-Mechanised Battalion moved forward to occupy high ground to the north of Calueque. Its orders were to stop the enemy's advance. The opposition had not been sighted by nightfall on 26 June, so the tank squadron decided to withdraw and establish a laager some seven kilometres to the rear.

The remainder of 61-Mech, perhaps feeling lonely, decided to join the tanks. They took a disgruntled Hannes along with them. The battalion had effectively abandoned the only decent tactical terrain close to Techipa that could be utilised to halt or delay the Cuban's advance if they decided to attack South African-occupied Calueque. The next morning they moved forward to reoccupy their old positions, but they were already too late. The Cubans had beaten them to it and were concealed in dead ground beyond the crest. They were obviously waiting for the South Africans to return so that they could clobber them at close range.

61-Mech used the Techipa-Calueque road as an axis of advance while Hannes advanced to the east of it. He approached the high ground he had vacated so reluctantly the previous day, fully expecting to have to fight to regain possession. He crested a rise and descended down the far slope that was thickly covered with bush. Lurking there were enemy tanks and a swarm of infantry armed with RPG7s, expectantly waiting to wipe out Hannes' Ratels. This particular Cuban commander, however, had never met Hannes Nortmann.

RPG7 rockets erupted at a range of 25 metres or less and a Ratel-90 was hit. Hannes and the other Ratel-20s kept the Cuban tank-hunting teams at bay by hosing the bush with long bursts of automatic fire.

A company of T54s appeared to take on Hannes and his vulnerable Ratels. The combat team had been trapped in a cleverly selected killing ground. To charge into the thickets would be an invitation to be shot out at close quarters by well concealed RPG7s. Retiring to the crest would expose the Ratels to overwhelming tank fire on the open slope. The Cuban commander was clearly aware of the advantages of a reverse slope defence — something we South Africans had tended to neglect in our military teaching establishments since World War-II.

Hannes and his men just had to stick it out, hoping to win the firefight or suppress the enemy fire long enough to break contact. The Ratel-90s shot out a T54 tank, two track-mounted ZSU-23 anti-aircraft guns and several trucks. Hannes called for assistance and the battle group sent a troop of tanks. The Olifants moved into hull-down positions behind Hannes' squadron and gave covering fire through which they could withdraw to safety beyond the crest. This allowed Hannes to send his Ratels to the rear in bounds. He covered the last few Ratels with the 20mm gun of his own Ratel.

Breaking contact was difficult, especially with Cuban infantrymen armed with RPG7s swarming around the Ratels. Hannes was badly wounded in the neck and hand, but he kept at it, firing long bursts into the swarms of infantry.

It was estimated that the South Africans killed about 60 Cubans, knocked out two T54s, two ZSU-23 anti-aircraft guns and an assortment of vehicles. The Cubans, thoroughly subdued, broke off the engagement and withdrew. The South Africans lost a Ratel and its commander, 2nd Lieutenant Meiring. Three of his crew were wounded.

The South Africans finally withdrew when it was reported that a stronger Cuban tank force was on the way.

Following this inconclusive action, the Cubans launched an air strike with six MiGs against the wall of the Calueque Dam. Sadly, a stray bomb, an 'over' killed 11 young National Servicemen who were brewing tea some distance from the intended point of impact. It also narrowly missed an armoured ambulance parked nearby containing Hannes Nortmann, now a category two casualty en route to 1-Military Hospital, Pretoria. He was reluctantly out of the war for good.

20mm cannons deployed in an anti-aircraft role to protect the dam wall damaged two MiGs and one crashed on its way back to base.

The Cubans again advanced on Ruacana shortly afterwards. 32-Battalion companies, however, had mined the roads extensively resulting in many casualties amongst the enemy's advanced patrols of mixed tanks and infantry which slowed them down. Having lost the momentum of their advance, they came under heavy artillery fire which forced them to break off and withdraw to Techipa.

By then, because of international political developments, 61-Mechanised Battalion also withdrew its forces back across the border to Ruacana in SWA/Namibia.

*   *   *

For almost a year a South African delegation comprising Foreign Minister Pik Botha, Defence Minister Magnus Malan, Foreign Affairs Director Neil van Heerden, SADF Chief General Jannie Geldenhuys, National Intelligence Service Director-General Neil Barnard, Joe Boshoff of the National Intelligence Service, Derek Auret and Andre Jaquet of the Department of Foreign Affairs and Major-General Neels van Tonder of Military Intelligence had been holding discussions, overseen by American Assistant Secretary for African Affairs Chester Crocker, with the MPLA and the Cubans to discuss a Namibian settlement and the withdrawal of Cuban and South African forces from Angola. The South Africans, backed by the Americans, demanded the two issues be linked. There could be no Namibian settlement without the withdrawal of foreign troops from Angola.

Meetings took place at such diverse centres as London, Brazzaville (three times), Cairo, Geneva (twice) and New York (twice), with numerous sub-meetings in Havana, Pretoria and Luanda.

Chester Crocker succeeded brilliantly in bringing a 22-year war to an end. Others had tried before, but they had all failed miserably.

When the last bomb was dropped — the one that killed the 11 National Servicemen — they were engaged in dotting the i's and crossing the t's on a cease-fire agreement that would lead to a peace accord and elections in SWA/Namibia.

The battle of 26-27 June 1988, for all intents and purposes, was the last direct confrontation between the SADF and SWAPO/FAPLA/Cuban military forces.

The long and drawn out bush war had started in August 1966 at an almost impossible place to find on the map called Ongulumbashe. The first contact was fought between SWAPO and a South African Police contingent bolstered by paratroopers commanded by myself.

UN Security Council Resolution 435, which under its various terms included the redeployment of combatants on both sides under supervision of a UN peacekeeping force, was designed to call a halt to the shooting and to bring peace to SWA/Namibia. Officially, the war came to an end on 31 March 1989. In terms of the resolution, 32-Battalion, together with other South African units in the operational area, were confined to their bases under the supervision of UNTAG (United Nation's Transitional Assistance Group) to help the peace process get under way. The SWA Territorial Force was disarmed and stood down.

The only SWA/Namibian security force in the field was the SWA Police. SWAPO were supposed to be confined to their bases in Angola north of the cutline. They were not, however, subjected to monitoring by UNTAG. They were able to move about and concentrate forces at will which allowed them to be ready for a massive armed incursion at a time and place of their choosing — comfortable in the knowledge that UNTAG either could not or would not stop them.

Not surprisingly the devious and cynical Sam Nujoma, the SWAPO leader, chose 1 April 1989 — the first day of peace — as his D-day. SWAPO gangs totalling 1 600 guerrillas swarmed across the Angolan border from Chitado in the west to Beacon 29 in the east. Their mission was to establish bases inside Owamboland to create the erroneous impression that they had succeeded in wresting control of vast stretches of real estate from the South African Security Forces. After many years of valiant struggle they had liberated Namibia from the hated racists in the south — or so they wanted the world to believe.

Ignoring the presence of the SWA Police — at least the ex-Koevoet part of it — was a fatal miscalculation. With awesome courage the police tackled these extremely well-armed gangs and wiped them out one after the other. But they suffered grievous casualties themselves and it was touch and go for a while. The SADF was in the process of unilaterally reactivating some SWA Territorial Force units. But it was unnecessary because the police had carried the day in spite of the odds being heavily stacked against them.

UNTAG provided barely concealed support and encouragement for SWAPO and avoided condemning Nujoma's arrogant breach of the cease-fire protocols. UNTAG also tried unsuccessfully to restrain the police from deploying forces against SWAPO. In the early stages, at least, they refused outright to sanction the release of helicopter gunship support into desperate contact situations where masses of SWAPO were threatening to wipe out — and sometimes did wipe out — small police patrols.

So SWAPOL (SWA/Namibian police in the shape of a thinly disguised Koevoet) would bring down the curtain on the bush war in those series of bloody engagements fought over a period of nine days from 1 to 9 April 1989. Perhaps it was a quirk of fate that what the police had started in 1966, they also had to finish in 1989.

SWAPO's treacherous armed incursion on 1 April 1989 caused only a slight stir in 32-Battalion's peaceful posture. Even this passed when the situation failed to escalate as many had predicted — and perhaps — hoped that it would.

Eventually, after free and fair elections under UN supervision brought SWAPO to power, 32-Battalion vacated Buffalo Base and withdrew to South Africa along with the rest of the SADF.

32

Move to Pomfret

A new era loomed for 32-Battalion. It would be an era of peace, something they were unaccustomed to. It filled the men with misgivings — even with a sense of dread. The unit had been forged in battle and had taken its shape in combat from its very beginnings. It was honed to a fine edge through a long and contentious war that had lasted from September 1975 to the end of June 1988.

What the impact of peace would be on the spirit, character and operational readiness of 32-Battalion was uncertain. In the minds of the black troops, at least, there was considerable concern for their personal well-being and that of their families.

They were still in the army, but suddenly they found themselves without the job they were used to. It is probably the same for most soldiers at the end of a war, but most soldiers go home when the fighting ends. That was not the case with 32-Battalion. They were being uprooted from a home they loved dearly, albeit in a strange land, to trek to a place even more foreign and farther away. Worse, they would have to live amongst people whose languages they could not speak and who had cultures that held no attraction for them. It meant the umbilical chord with their own Angola was being cut forever.

In the winter of 1942/43 an unknown German soldier scratched on a wall in the ruins of Stalingrad: 'Enjoy this war — the peace will be worse.' That war was indescribably awful and brought nothing but disaster, particularly for the surviving German troops who were marched off into 'liberating captivity' by the communists. The defeated German 6th Army vanished into the bitter cold of Siberia to be worked to death in Stalin's slave camps and mines. Many years later and long after the war had ended, a pitiful few of them, broken in mind, body and spirit, were returned to Germany by the Russians.

32-Battalion would also find that for them, the peace was worse. The real suffering was awaiting them in a South Africa that was on the brink of a new political dispensation. Despite the blood they had shed to make an honourable peace possible, no credit for that would accrue to them.

Several centres were canvassed as a new home for the Battalion. One of them was Madimbo on the Limpopo River about 100km east of Messina (now Musina) with a climatic environment similar to Buffalo Base in the Caprivi. It was also conveniently situated close to operational activity on a border regularly infiltrated by MK (*Umkhonto we Sizwe* — Spear of the Nation, the military wing of the ANC) through Zimbabwe from their bases in Zambia.

There was also a potential ally, the SADF-sponsored RENAMO resistance movement in adjacent Mozambique, that would be only too willing to fill the not-so-comradely gap left by UNITA. Madimbo was situated in a narrow strip under the control of the SADF. It was an established military base tactically positioned in a no-go area between the Nwanedzi River in the west and the Pafuri River in the east. It sat snug between a high double fence in the south enclosing several rows of sisal and the

Limpopo River to the north — truly an ideal place to tuck away a controversial unit like 32-Battalion.

Staff officers at Army Headquarters, however, chose an abandoned asbestos mine as its new home. It is called Pomfret and is 180km north of Vryburg, then a stronghold of the AWB (Afrikaner Weerstandsbeweging), the right-wing Afrikaner political movement. It was just outside the borders of the most remote part of fragmented Bophuthatswana, then a black 'Homeland State' of apartheid South Africa. Bophuthatswana authorities complained about the potential threat posed by 32-Battalion as its men had to pass through a fragment of 'President' Lucas Mangope's republic on their way to shop in Vryburg. The complaint was not surprising for the combat-hardened Buffalo Soldiers had been widely associated in the public mind with alleged horrific excesses in Namibia and Angola as the result of negative communist-inspired propaganda. The local Tswanas were frightened that they might become the victims of similar 'outrages'. After all, had they not been called the ' terrible ones' in Angola? Vryburg's white right-wing burghers were not happy either about the thought of armed black soldiers being located within their district.

Objections, however, made no difference and the troops were moved to Pomfret anyway. Vryburg was the nearest town, albeit far to the south, where the Battalion could do business. Its economy boomed virtually overnight because of the influx of new shoppers. The townsfolk also discovered to their amazement that these black combat soldiers — the old Boer generals would have turned in their graves at the thought — were actually superbly disciplined and well-behaved. What's more, the presence of the unit had a calming influence on fractious ANC-orientated elements in the locality.

The new 32-Battalion Pomfret Base, however, turned out to be a death trap for everyone — officers and men, women and children, black and white alike. I still cannot believe that the authorities allowed the unit to be settled at Pomfret when it was international common knowledge that the dumps on old asbestos mines spelt death, or at the least, the chronic incurable lung disease of asbestosis.

Was it ignorance that resulted in the selection of Pomfret, or was it sloppy staff work? I personally believe the choice was motivated by an official desire to move 32-Battalion as far as possible from South Africa's crowded urban centres in case a fuss was made over the army's Foreign Legion being settled in their midst. It was politics, as usual, that decided the issue. In the end, the relocation turned out to be a disaster for the unit that had done more than any other to further the National Party government's apartheid cause. When the political sun was shining and it seemed that nothing could go wrong, they were only to pleased to bask in 32-Battalion's military achievements. When it was sundowner time for apartheid, however, they did not want to know about its troubles.

Colonel Mucho Delport brought his command cadre, including his black officers and some NCOs, from Buffalo Base to have a close look at Pomfret. The units' officers and men had been assured that the move to Pomfret would only take place if everyone was satisfied with the place.

The army, however, gave them little choice. It was either Pomfret or demobilisation in SWA/Namibia, after which they could throw themselves on the unlikely mercy of SWAPO — after having fought them for all those years. The exercise was a token gesture. The army confidently expected that they would be satisfied. They were an unsophisticated and trusting people who were ignorant of the dangers posed to their health by asbestos fibres.

The white officers and NCOs were also unaware of its likely effects. The mining company, before passing ownership to the army, had spread the dumps and the general area with a thin covering of soil which they maintained would seal in the loose asbestos. It was, of course, only a dishonest move to smooth the way for them to palm the mine off on a gullible army. It had become a major liability when the bottom fell out of the asbestos market after it became widely known how dangerous the stuff was to human health.

The white soldiers trustingly accepted the word of their higher headquarters that the sparse layer of soil would mitigate the danger. They passed this information on to their men in good faith. The covering, however, made hardly any difference and the mining company knew it. The miserly few centimetres of soil would soon be blown away by the Kalahari winds or washed away by the rains.

So 32-Battalion was plucked from a paradise on the banks of the mighty Okavango River, with its flood plains and the majestic trees of its riverine forests, and dumped in the harsh wastes of the Northern Cape where not even the trickle of a stream softens the stark and arid scenery.

They would miss the mighty Okavango. They would miss the ambience of Buffalo Base and the *Kimbo*. But at least the SADF was providing concrete proof of its commitment made for the first time in 1976 by General Malan — then Chief of the Army and later Minister of Defence — and subsequently repeated on several occasions by others high up the ladder of power that 32-Battalion would not be left in the lurch. They had promised it would always be an integral part of the South African Army.

A civilian contractor was employed to move the Battalion, its equipment and personal effects by rail and by road. It was a well-planned move, somewhat better organised than Battle Group Bravo's shambolic departure from Angola in 1976.

Although they were members of the SADF, none of the Angolans were South African citizens, so their futures lay in the balance. Wives, in particular, viewed the move with misgivings. They were being uprooted from their homes where they had been looked after by the army with sympathy and compassion.

Husbands and an increasing number of their sons had been on arduous and dangerous missions and had returned to Buffalo Base to recuperate, rest and retrain. Too often many of them had returned in body bags, swelling the silent ranks of men laid out in neat lines in the war cemetery. Some had returned physically or mentally marred, often for life, to become a burden on their families and a liability to the unit.

Now they were leaving the place that had brought them so much comfort. Worst of all for the bereaved families of the fallen, they were leaving behind their warrior husbands and sons. They also expected the worst — that SWAPO would come along and desecrate the graves.

Nevertheless, for obvious reasons the unit could not stay in the Caprivi, so in June and July 1989 32-Battalion moved to Pomfret.

It looked the same as any other disused mining village. It had a small compound with houses and single quarters built from asbestos sheets for the black mineworkers and relatively comfortable houses built from asbestos bricks for the white mine officials.

There were not nearly enough houses to accommodate all the families. Most had to be put in tents — and this was in the middle of a severe winter. Much more accommodation was needed and a builder was contracted to put up 800 brick houses.

Only a few black families could be settled in the asbestos brick and board houses. The majority had to wait until brick houses became available. Eventually, the occupants were allowed to purchase both those and the older asbestos units. Many availed themselves of the opportunity, fondly anticipating that they would be remaining in Pomfret in relative comfort for the rest of their lives.

It was not long, though, before many of the new brick houses began to crack, a typical syndrome in sub-economic schemes where contractors are not particularly fussy about standards. Nevertheless, in the meantime the completed houses were taken over with great ceremony and the new township was grandly named Esperanza — Portuguese for 'hope'.

Some hope it turned out to be.

Apart from the mine dumps and the asbestos houses, the streets, playing fields, parade ground and all the open spaces were permeated with loose asbestos. The contaminated soil a few centimetres down was easily stirred by marching feet and the churning wheels of heavy army vehicles or was brought to the surface by the picks and bulldozers during building activity or when trenches were dug.

Asbestos particles got into everything. The stuff permeated bedding, carpets, clothing, the washing, eating utensils and even food. It clung to the skin and dirtied the hair. It got into noses and mouths and finally finished up in the lungs. The first symptoms of asbestosis would usually appear among the black troops and their families who were based permanently at Pomfret — the whites only passed through on rotation.

The school was reopened. Some teachers, however, were unceremoniously fired. In spite of many years of loyal and excellent service, they did not have South African qualifications.

The school, like its predecessor in Caprivi, gloried in the name of Pica Pau. This pleased me enormously because it commemorated Major Charlie Hochapfel, a fallen comrade who had been killed in an ambush some time after he left 32-Battalion.

During the settling in phase, it became necessary to placate a scandalised Department of Home Affairs. Several thousand black foreigners had arrived without notice in the hallowed land of the Republic of South Africa without the knowledge and consent of this implacable department. The solution, arrived at with the greatest reluctance, was to make all the black troops and their families South African citizens forthwith, breaking a whole plethora of iron-bound laws and stringent residential requirements. Someone at the top must have leaned on them heavily. My guess is that it was General Magnus Malan, scrupulously sticking to his word. Finally, acceptable conditions were arranged. One was that the so-called Portuguese troops and their dependants should be given a last chance to remain Angolan subjects — or opt for South African citizenship. It was not much of a choice. If they elected to retain their Angolan citizenship, Home Affairs would immediately arrange their discharge from the army and order their repatriation to Angola. It was made clear that the move would have to be done under their own steam, which meant trekking through SWAPO-ruled Namibia to get there. This posed a tremendous obstacle, considering the hatred that was felt for 32-Battalion by the new government in Windhoek.

Despite this, some opted to retain their Angolan citizenship and left for the north. Whether they made it home to Angola is uncertain. My guess is that most of them probably settled illegally amongst the Kavangos and Caprivians in north-east Namibia, with a few Kwanyamas joining the Owambos in the north-west.

While the unit was settling in at Pomfret, a team from the University of the Free State arrived to test the area for the presence of asbestos particles. They were aghast at the dangers their tests exposed and critical of the army for having settled the battalion in such a hazardous environment. Whether the army had expected the place to get a clean bill of health and was displeased with the report is unclear. It didn't take long, though, for the report's ominous indicators of a hidden, creeping sickness and early death to start having a negative effect on the morale of the troops and their families. Despite this, it appears that the army's high command did nothing and no waves were made by the staff at the unit. Apparently there was an attitude of pretence that nothing was amiss, so no consideration was given to moving the Battalion to a safer environment. It would remain at Pomfret come hell or high water, asbestosis or lung cancer.

A professor at the University of Pretoria told the author that making old asbestos mines safe involves five distinct phases. The first is chemical treatment to stabilise the soil — which would have been far too expensive — or covering it under a metre of uncontaminated topsoil — which was impractical. The second phase involves planting grass — which requires prodigious amounts of water, but there was hardly enough available at Pomfret for domestic use. Phases three, four and five call for the planting of various kinds of vegetation to bind the soil and act as windbreaks. Only then would Pomfret have become safe from wind-blown asbestos particles. No such reclamation work was carried out.

The SADF may yet have to face civil claims from former 32-Battalion soldiers and their family members who are suffering from asbestosis. The condition is irreversible and usually leads to early death.

The Battalion began attracting a flock of new arrivals anxious to don the coveted camouflage beret — without having to go through the selection cycle. Some were officers who had discovered that service with 32-Battalion looked rather good on one's curriculum vitae. In the past they had probably perished the thought of leaving the fleshpots of Pretoria for a unit where firefights were a way of life. Nor had the hostile tropical savannah appealed to them, what with the heat, thirst, fatigue, mosquitoes, mopani flies and the sheer discomfort of it all — to say nothing of the constant anxiety of operating deep behind the enemy lines in Angola for months on end. What was more, as a white commander, one had to communicate with black Portuguese-speaking soldiers who seemed to critically check one's every move against an invisible check list. And why did they have to learn Portuguese? What was wrong with the good old boeretaal (Afrikaans)? Even English would have been preferable to that.

There were others, though, who had been trying to get to 'the war' for years— who would have done almost anything to face the enemy shoulder-to-shoulder with the Buffalo Soldiers. But they never got the opportunity. For the Battalion, the war was over. In future it would be peacekeeping, a somewhat tedious affair and a difficult switch from their previous occupation of bush fighters.

The newcomers did their best to become integrated into the unit with some of them hoping, somewhat unreasonably, that another 'proper war' would soon come the way of 32-Battalion. Few of them had been tested in battle, so predictably, the troops regarded them with a critical eye. The situation was not helped either by some of them adopting a superior attitude. Instead of showing some humility at the honour of being enrolled in such a famous unit, they behaved as if they had done the unit a favour by joining it. Most came straight from the Military Academy or from infantry units comprised of National Servicemen where everything from training to discipline was conducted in the rigidly prescribed army way. It was the philosophy of the boot camp versus the unobtrusive, relaxed perfectionism and personal discipline found amongst combat veterans of many years standing. It was that mutual respect that had made 32-Battalion such a formidable fighting unit.

The rookies were let loose amongst a bunch of battle-wise warriors who had learnt the business of war the hard way — in the bush with blood, sweat and tears — not from text books and courses far removed from the real thing. Naturally the veterans resented the highhanded intrusion of a leader group that had not gone through the mill. The new boys also resented the barely concealed disrespect shown to them by the veterans, black and white alike.

To resolve this divisive situation, the commander eliminated the cachet and prestige of wearing the camouflage beret. Henceforth everybody was allowed to wear this coveted badge of courage and combat excellence — whether they were combat soldiers, base wallahs, cooks, bottle washers or whatever. It was a thoughtless move that did untold harm to the unit's esprit de corps, so carefully nurtured by previous commanders. The fighters were no longer set apart by a clearly identifiable badge or item of uniform, as is customary in elite units the world over.

Instead of uniting the unit, the new order caused the formation of cliques and the development of the 'us and them' syndrome. To rub it in, the HQ staff, mostly newcomers, added a laurel wreath to the unit's blazer badge — but only for those serving on the staff. From the times of ancient Greece and Rome, 'winning your laurels' has signified an outstanding military or sporting achievement. The high-handed action of nullifying this insulted the outstanding fighting contributions that the rifle and support companies had made over the years of armed conflict. It implied that their contributions were markedly inferior to those made by men who spent most of their time polishing the seats of office chairs with their backsides.

For the first time in the unit's history and perhaps because they were out of the firing line, racism crept into relationships between black and white. Perhaps it was due to a lack of communication and a careless disregard for the sensitivities of others, rather than through deliberate discrimination. The easy camaraderie, always present amongst those who had faced lead together, began to disappear.

When a white commander treats a black rifleman with arrogance and contempt, it inevitably leads to resentment. The black victim feels that his self-esteem as a person belonging to a particular race group has been attacked. This could precipitate a collapse of discipline which could escalate, through a series of insubordinate incidents, into a full-blown mutiny.

It must be pointed out, though, that the black soldiers of 32-Battalion had always been well disciplined. They were always ready to accept justifiable reprimands— even harsh ones at times — in good spirit as long as they came from seniors whom they knew and respected as caring commanders.

Fortunately, some of the old-guard white leadership accompanied the Battalion to Pomfret and a few remained with it right to the end. There was Major Louis Scheepers, a former artilleryman and an infantryman by choice; Major Tinus van Staden, commander of the troops who executed a brilliant night attack at Tumpu during the Cuito Cuanavale saga; WO1 Koos 'Crocodile' Kruger, famed for his wrestling match with a crocodile in the Okavango River; Captain Louis Lombard, who married Colonel Eddie Viljoen's only daughter; Commandant Jakes Jacobs, a former Recce who had served with Battle Group Bravo as a corporal in 1976 and Captain Martin Geldenhuys, who had taken a rucksack full of snakes for a swim in the Cubango River. Martin, sadly, was killed in a helicopter accident shortly after the Battalion's arrival at Pomfret.

By the time of the move to Pomfret, the old guard white leadership had been drastically whittled down and replaced by an increasing body of black officers. The real backbone of the unit, however, remained the black NCOs, both senior and junior. Most of them had been with the unit from the beginning and were the repository of its bush lore, combat experience and history.

The star of the old-timers was undoubtedly Sister Sakkie Korff. This remarkable woman was trusted implicitly by the men and their families. Not only was she a qualified nurse, capable of fixing any ailment or injury short of complicated surgery, but was also a psychologist, a marriage councsellor, a mother-figure and a strict disciplinarian. She had been known to wrathfully kick over a drum of illicit skokiaan, freshly brewed from anything that would ferment in an equally illegal shebeen. Sister Sakkie worked tirelessly and virtually single-handedly to hold families together — especially later when they came under tremendous strain after husbands were posted to other units in distant corners of South Africa after the unit was disbanded. Yet she is a slender and tiny woman, nothing like the Valkyrie that one might imagine. Sister Sakkie is now a much respected sister in charge of a clinic for expatriate South Africans.

33

A new kind of war

To understand 32-Battalion's contribution to the maintenance of law and order in the Republic of South Africa, a short overview of the prevailing internal and external threats is necessary. Such threats became more focussed against South Africa, which had always been the ultimate prize of the communist-directed liberation struggle, after Zimbabwe obtained its independence under the despotic and Marxist Robert Mugabe.

The ANC and its military wing *Umkhonto we Sizwe* (MK) had been allied to Joshua Nkomo's Zimbabwe African People's Union (ZAPU) and its military wing Zimbabwe People's Revolutionary Army (ZIPRA) long before Zimbabwe's independence. Both were supported by the Soviet Union and had rear bases in Zambia. Robert Mugabe's Zimbabwe African National Union (ZANU) and its military wing, Zimbabwe African National Liberation Army (ZANLA) were rear based in Mozambique and looked towards Red China for inspiration and support.

During 1967 MK cadres had joined ZIPRA in a major armed incursion into Rhodesia from Zambia, which was smashed by the Rhodesian Security Forces. In 1979, the final year of the Rhodesian War, MK guerrillas joined ZIPRA forces in Matabeleland to fight off ZANLA guerrillas who were encroaching into areas they considered to be their own.

After the 1979 Lancaster House Agreement, ZIPRA and ZANLA guerrillas were moved into assembly points under the supervision of British and British Commonwealth peacekeepers to give substance to the cease-fire and to prepare for the forthcoming elections. In Matabeleland MK cadres joined their ZIPRA comrades in a specially designated assembly point.

Robert Mugabe and his ZANU-PF party, not unexpectedly in some quarters but to the amazement of others, won the election hands down.

The assembly points were closed. After protests by South Africa, many of the MK cadres were weeded out by the British and flown back to Zambia. Others disappeared into the sparsely inhabited south-western corner of Matabeleland to settle and intermarry with the locals. They set up villages and created a potential base area from which the Messina District just across the Limpopo River could be infiltrated. The border, in any case, was so wide open at the time that many illegal farm workers commuted daily from their homes in Zimbabwe to work on South African farms.

From 1980 there were MK incursions into South Africa either from Zambia via Zimbabwe or from Zambia through the Tuli block in Botswana. They planted landmines and harassed the South African farming community eastwards as far as the Great North Road. White farmers, their black workers and family members fell as victims to mines at an increasing rate.

The collapse of Portugal's African empire in the mid-1970s had opened up infiltration routes for MK through Mozambique. Politically inspired troubles in the black townships of South Africa escalated and ran out of control. This brought about a blight of street committees and people's courts in the black townships. So-called trials by these kangaroo courts were short and unencumbered by the necessity of a defence. The guilt of those accused of cooperating with the government authorities was taken as read and sentences were arbitrarily and quickly executed, often with the horrific necklace — a car tyre doused in petrol, draped around a victim's neck and set alight.

Infiltration routes became increasingly well-trodden. The route from Mozambique via Swaziland carried a stream and that from Lesotho a trickle. The inflows from Botswana and Zimbabwe also multiplied.

There were other stress points on the South African political landscape. The IFP (Inkatha Freedom Party), under the leadership of Chief Mangosuthu Buthelezi, was at loggerheads with the ANC. In fact, Buthelezi had been targeted by ANC hit squads, as were most of the Zulu chiefs who supported the IFP. An internecine war erupted among the Zulu tribes that engulfed most of the old Natal Province (with Zululand, now KwaZulu-Natal). This war was carried up to the Witwatersrand area (now Gauteng) where hostel dwellers, mostly Zulus and IFP supporters, fought largely ANC-orientated squatter and township communities.

This gave rise to the establishment by the ANC of so-called SDUs (self-defence units). In reality they were a thinly disguised way of forcibly expanding ANC control over the black townships and the heavily populated rural areas of Natal.

There was also the UDF (United Democratic Front), a front organisation for the ANC in South Africa, while the ANC was in exile. It organised internal resistance against the apartheid government, especially among the youth.

On 2 February 1990 President FW de Klerk made his watershed speech unbanning the ANC and other black political movements. But instead of decreasing the tempo of unrest increased. It was the so-called Rubicon speech that the world had expected and President PW Botha had failed to make in the mid-1980s. Botha told the author that the speech he had ordered to be prepared, mostly by the Department of Foreign Affairs, bore no resemblance to the one handed to him shortly before he mounted the rostrum. The consequences of his failure to make that speech, whatever its contents might have been, are still with us today.

After the ban was lifted on the liberation movements, the ANC and the PAC (Pan Africanist Congress) tried to make the country ungovernable by encouraging mayhem and a climate of violence. White commercial farmers became prime targets for murder. The intention, it appears, was to cause the collapse of the National Party government or to force it to hand over the instruments of power to the only movement that could call a halt to the violence.

32-Battalion, formerly faced with the relatively simple confrontation of war, suddenly found itself in a grey area where everything was chaotic and every action was attended by numerous politically-inspired pitfalls.

In 1988, before the move from Buffalo Base to Pomfret, the commander of 32-Battalion had reorganised the Battalion into two separate operational groups — Ops Group 1 and Ops Group 2 — each comprising three rifle companies and combat support elements. This was a sensible arrangement since the unit often operated as two battalion-based battle groups on widely separated fronts. It became possible to rotate the two groups in a sensible manner between the firing line and rest and recuperation back at the base.

After the unit's move, the nomenclatures again changed, this time to Ops Battalion 1 and Ops Battalion 2. These designations were later changed to the more militarily acceptable 32/1 and 32/2-Battalions. At that stage the unit should have been changed to become the grander 32-Infantry Regiment to accommodate its organic infantry battalion sized units. This would have made the numbering of subordinate battalions acceptable by army custom. That it was not done created an anomaly where an infantry 'battalion' apparently had two infantry battalions under its command.

The first unit deployed operationally within South Africa was 32/1-Battalion, then still known as Ops Group 1. It was commanded by an old hand, Major Louis Scheepers, who would later be promoted to commandant. It deployed to the Soutpansberg Military Area (SMA) to interdict MK infiltration routes across the Limpopo River from Zimbabwe. Ops Group 1 achieved its first success when it intercepted a gang in transit in the area west of Vhembi, killing one guerrilla and wounding and capturing two more.

The SADF did not believe MK guerrillas matched the calibre of their SWAPO counterparts. Overseas military experts thought the same after analysing their achievements in the field. The British Army derisively labelled them the most 'ineffective liberation army in the world'. Their strong points were politics and 'psywar' coupled with their ability to intimidate, incite and politically mobilise the masses.

Apart from coping with escalating violence against the farming community in the Limpopo River border area, 32-Battalion also had to deal with illegal border crossings by Zimbabweans fleeing Mugabe's oppressive rule. In the early 1980s he had mobilised his North Korea-trained Fifth Brigade and launched it into Matabeleland to knock the politically opposed Matabele into subservience. 20 000 civilians, perhaps many more, were brutally murdered. Others were raped, robbed and beaten and whole villages were torched. After that the desperate, disillusioned and impoverished Matabele tried by every means to escape to South Africa. Those who made it were happy to obtain even the meanest of jobs — mostly as farm labourers — as long as they could get away from Mugabe's rampaging thugs and the spectre of famine, death and violence.

This mass movement became a Trojan Horse for MK infiltrations. It was the task of 32-Battalion to sort the genuinely distressed from suspected MK subversives. The unit did a splendid job because it was operating within a familiar physical and military environment. It would, of course, have been even more effective if it had been sent across the Limpopo River to hunt the MK before they crossed, but the political situation at the time was not conducive to such drastic action.

In April 1990 32/1-Battalion was withdrawn to Pomfret and placed on standby for possible redeployment in Kwa-Zulu Natal. In May there was a sudden flare-up of violence that could no longer be controlled by the police. 32/1 and 32/2-Battalions were rapidly deployed to the Pietermaritzburg area, then later to Umlazi near Durban.

In Umlazi and other townships close to Durban, the emphasis was on the confiscation of illegal firearms. The people possessing them were supposed to be arrested by the police and brought for trial, but despite large quantities of weapons being found, only a few of the culprits were convicted in court.

In the townships around Pietermaritzburg, free movement had been severely curtailed by running battles between ANC and IFP gangs which were fighting for supremacy over their own pieces of turf. Both parts of 32-Battalion were deployed to forcibly bring an abrupt end to these bloody clashes. The combatants, particularly the ANC, had not expected to be handled so robustly. To the dismay of both sides, they discovered that the 32-Battalion troops were immune to political indoctrination from whatever source because they had no tribal loyalties in South Africa.

Within a few days highly volatile townships like Ennerdale were brought under control. People could move about freely without the danger of being assaulted, robbed or raped. 32-Battalion troops continued their wary patrols and made friends with the locals while in the process of restoring law and order.

The battle-weary residents were ecstatic. The press, however, by and large, was highly indignant that Portuguese-speaking 'mercenaries' should be strutting the township's streets as if they owned them. Both the ANC and IFP warlords began to clamour for the withdrawal of these 'notorious and bloodthirsty killers' who had come from their own bush war in Angola. SACP/ANC negotiators at the CODESA talks also demanded their withdrawal. Even some negotiators from the ruling National Party began making disapproving noises. It was apparently a growing political reality of the time that appeasement of the ANC by returning 32-Battalion to its barracks had to be done — even if it meant a breakdown of law and order in an area.

The locals in the townships, however, drew up petitions that were signed by thousands, entreating the military authorities to keep 32-Battalion patrolling their streets. A withdrawal, they said, would again seriously jeopardise their safety. The government of the day nevertheless gave way under pressure and the troops were withdrawn.

So in spite of the SADF having achieved remarkable successes in the affected townships for the first time, the 32-Battalion troops were pulled out and redeployed in the rural areas of the Natal Midlands. They left behind bemused and frightened township dwellers who waited for the horrors to descend on them again, this time with a spirit of retribution by political activists from both sides. They had to brace themselves to absorb the next round of murders, necklacings, arson, beatings, rapes and looting as best they could. They were becoming mere strugglers for survival in a country that had begun to boast to the outside world that South Africa was about to give birth to democracy.

In the Natal Midlands it was another kind of war for the bush fighters from Angola. Instead of endless bush stretching forever in all directions with few signs of human life, they found themselves in a landscape with thousands of hills liberally scattered with kraals, all within shouting distance of each other. Patrolling was mostly done at a 45° angle, either climbing to the top of a hill to reach a kraal or sliding down a steep incline to start the a laborious climb to the next one. These kraals were only a few hundred metres apart as the crow flies, but for foot patrols slogging up and down the hills, it was heavy going.

The nature of the conflict was also different. It was bloodier, more straightforward and often in the nature of pitched battles between Zulu factions. The Battalion, in fact, had to deal with tribal and village animosities that were hundreds of years old. Such conflicts had only recently been decked out in ANC and IFP colours to justify their continuance in South Africa's violent landscape of the time. Fighting was a way of life — a part of Zulu culture since long before Shaka's time. Despite this, order was restored within a week at the most wherever the Battalion was deployed.

But elsewhere in the country the flames of violence were still raging. In the Witwatersrand (Gauteng) townships like Tembisa, Vosloosrus and Katlehong had become no-go areas and were fresh cauldrons of misery, murder and rape for the inhabitants. The police could not or would not cope and nor could the army — some units like the paratroopers and 32-Battalion excepted.

Many of the black army units had become highly politicised. 5-South African Infantry Battalion in Ladysmith, KwaZulu-Natal, was known as an IFP battalion. 21-Battalion at Lenz, near Johannesburg, was considered an ANC battalion. In the Witwatersrand townships, police were often seen carting around factions of the warring IFP from one battle scene to the next in their armoured Casspirs. They had also taken sides in this chaotic mess. The flames were fanned mainly to the advantage of the IFP, but the ANC also benefited, especially when units like 21-Battalion became involved.

It should be remembered that many people, the author included, were dubious about 32-Battalion's suitability in an environment far removed from the one in which they had lived and fought for so many years. They surprised us all, perhaps themselves too, by shaping up brilliantly. What's more, they became a bone of contention as various group commanders fought hard to get the unit deployed in their own particular areas of responsibility.

When 32-Battalion moved in to restore order on the Witwatersrand, it was like a breath of fresh air. They were there to do the job of restoring sanity without an ulterior motive. Their first deployment was to Group 41 at Heidelberg. From there they went to Kempton Park near Johannesburg where they stayed in a railway facility built by Italian prisoners of war during World War-II. The troops operated as reaction forces which meant they were called out mostly during the hours of darkness and over weekends when violence stalked the streets of the townships. Strong points were established in the affected areas from where the reaction forces could deploy and rotate from the main base in Kempton Park.

Within a few days of 32-Battalion's deployment, law and order was restored. The unit even went as far as disciplining belligerent school children who were running amuck — by getting them and their equally politicised teachers to clean up the mess they had created in and around their schools. At the request of the locals, tipper trucks were provided to help them clean up the streets. Some residents showed their feelings for politicians by dumping tons of rubbish on the stoep of an ANC big shot living in Thokoza. This, of course, did little to endear 32-Battalion to the ANC. The locals who had suffered badly from the ANC's intimidation, however, beamed at his humiliation. Once again they could go about their business in peace without fear of assault or molestation.

The ANC, in particular, were furious about 32-Battalion's obvious effectiveness in restoring law and order, while they were doing everything they could to stoke the fires of discontent. A showdown was inevitable. The ANC complained and threatened, insinuating that the Buffalo Soldiers were a 'third force' involved in the despicable acts of depravity that they themselves were inflicting on the people.

Others felt differently. The Municipality of Kempton Park expressed its gratitude for the unit's contribution towards the reestablishment and maintenance of law and order within its boundaries. It awarded 32-Battalion the Freedom of the City and on 21 September 1991 the unit exercised its rights by marching through the town with its colours flying, drums beating and bugles and trumpets playing. By right of ancient custom they could also march with bayonets fixed and swords drawn — but the South African army no longer had bayonets to fix or the officers' swords to draw.

In due course, the highly conservative town of Vryburg followed suit.

The crunch came in April 1992 when two 32-Battalion Buffel infantry fighting vehicles were deployed into Phola Park, Thokoza, to carry out a routine patrol. Phola Park, a squatter camp, was an ANC stronghold in the middle of Thokoza Township that harboured gangs of criminally inclined ANC comrades. It had been fenced off with razor wire in an effort to bring its belligerent residents under some sort of control.

The Buffels moved in and were fired on from some shacks with AK47s. In the way of trained soldiers, the troops disembarked, rapidly deployed into attack formation and returned fire in accordance with accepted counter-ambush drills. As they cleared up the ambush site, a sergeant was shot in the stomach.

Meanwhile the rest of the company had rushed to the scene of contact as a fireforce. Spreading out in an extended line formation they swept through the affected area. They came on some wounded civilians and a large quantity of expended AK47 cartridge cases. The ambushers, however, had managed to escape.

A skewed report of the incident burst like a bombshell before the assembled CODESA negotiators at Kempton Park. Biassed reporting continued in the media. Newspapers and the SABC shrieked hysterically about the barbaric hordes from the jungles of Angola who had raped a large number of women, sjambokked people and killed several innocents in Phola Park.

The bare back of a male victim crisscrossed with prominent welts, allegedly the result of a sjambokking by a 32-Battalion soldier raging out of control, appeared on a TV news bulletin. The film had apparently been made within hours of the incident.

Anyone, black or white, who has served in any of Africa's many wars is surely familiar with wounds left by sjamboks, canes or sticks. They bleed and suppurate for several days at least. If untreated they remain open and turn septic. Then they begin to heal and form a distinct greyish welt. After several weeks the scabs fall off. The welts shown on TV were several weeks old, almost totally healed and showed no evidence of suppuration or scabs. Yet the emotion-packed voice of the TV journalist informed viewers that the scandalous incident had occurred only a few hours before. It was termed 'investigative reporting' designed to expose the cruel face of apartheid brutality.

I believe it was an act deliberately staged as a propaganda exercise by the ANC and designed to mislead the public. There was another oversight. 32-Battalion troops, in common with other soldiers, were not issued with sjamboks.

Instead of leaping to the defence of his army and accepting the report back by senior officers on the spot who had investigated the incident, the government elected instead to pander to the calculated outburst of the ANC. President FW de Klerk immediately appointed a judicial commission of enquiry under Judge Richard Goldstone. South Africa waited expectantly for months for Judge Goldstone to report.

The men of Golf Company who were accused of rape were paraded in front of the alleged victims. What the complainants were unaware of, however, was that the company had been liberally salted with 75 men who had been hundreds of kilometres away in Pomfret when the incidents allegedly occurred.

The girls, nevertheless, obligingly pointed out a large number of the Pomfret 75 as their ravishers. They amounted to more than a third of the line-up. Judge Goldstone threw out the accusations. He found that Golf Company had been deliberately led into an ambush by third parties unknown and that it was they who were probably responsible for the killings, rapes and assaults. The judge was unable to find a shred of evidence that merited a criminal charge being laid against any of the officers and men of Golf Company. Not a single member of 32-Battalion was tried for the abuse of human rights — because it never happened. But to this day 32-Battalion has never been officially exonerated for the Phola Park affair.

Yet it is not that easy to sweep the whole sorry business under the carpet. Nobody tried to find out who the third party was and who set up the Battalion. Not even President de Klerk, as supreme commander of the SADF, felt duty-bound to order that someone should try to get to the bottom of this sordid episode. The media did not bother to withdraw their accusations. At the best they remained silent about Judge Goldstone's findings. Some accused the army of a cover up.

Phola Park came and went. The Goldstone findings stoked the fires of hatred against the battalion by the ANC and PAC. The IFP, at least, had the sense to back off. Demands for the unit to be disbanded became more strident. The ANC, in fact, insisted that all the Buffalo Soldiers be returned to Angola and handed over to the MPLA — whom they had defeated so frequently on some very bloody battlefields.

Meanwhile the 32-Battalion companies, unaware that the Sword of Damocles was hanging over their heads, continued with their task of stabilising out-of-control townships. Eventually they were recalled to Pomfret. Although the unit had been returned to its barracks, it remained as a reserve immediately available to deal with situations in townships that other army units or the police were unable to cope with.

34

Bolt from the blue

While the CODESA 1 Agreement was in the process of being implemented, the Security Police produced documentary evidence that implicated a strong ANC faction in a plot to destabilise KwaZulu-Natal. Armed insurrection had been planned on a large scale with the intention of forcing the National Party government to commit the full strength of the Security Forces in that province to prevent a meltdown. If the military combat potential could be swung in favour of MK, the way would be open for a political coup.

There was a powerful lobby within the SACP/ANC Alliance that maintained, in accord with Marxist-Leninist theory, that the final phase of a workers' revolution could be concluded only with a takeover by force of arms. They believed the CODESA negotiations were doctrinally flawed. At best they would lead to an unacceptable compromise. The Alliance believed that the winner should take all and that the ANC, as a liberation movement, should be prepared to resort to an armed takeover if negotiations did not produce the results they desired.

The second string to the ANC's bow was its top secret *Operation Vula*, designed to bring about a revolutionary and violent overthrow of the government. When the Security Police uncovered the operation, it produced considerable anxiety in the ranks of the National Party government. It also caused a stir in Security Force circles and in the IFP which would have been first to be attacked. An armed insurrection, however, could only succeed if the Security Forces were hamstrung to such an extent that they became largely ineffective in countering *Operation Vula*.

An orchestrated psychological offensive was launched to discredit the police and the army. The ANC made unsubstantiated allegations that a third force was operating in the townships with the object of killing the ANC's leadership element and intimidating the people. The murder of Chris Hani added much weight to these claims. And 32-Battalion was the perfect target for such a psychological offensive. Wildly implausible Goebbels-style propaganda designed to focus the general public's aversion towards the unit continued to be made.

It became clear that for the success of *Operation Vula* to be assured, 32-Battalion would have to be neutralised. This was the key to any successful counter-insurgency campaign in the townships. The unit found itself being portrayed as an important component of a so-called third force. The Phola Park incident was stage managed to assist with this scenario.

Rumours surfaced that the Battalion was being disbanded. They were stoked by continuing demands by the SACP/ANC Alliance that the 'Angolan mercenaries' be returned to their own homeland. Disappointingly for the Alliance, the National Party government's reaction remained noncommital at best, although there was the occasional undertone of sympathy for the ANC's stance. Yet this did not stop NP politicians from canvassing votes for the 1992 referendum from white members in the military base at Pomfret. This was despite the fact that the canvassing of votes by political parties within the bounds of a military unit, ship, aircraft or military installation had never been allowed in terms of very strict regulations under the old dispensation.

The black troops, by then, were naturalised South African citizens. At another National Party meeting at Pomfret, irregularly I must assume, a local politician assured the unit it would never be left in the lurch or disbanded. He said that rumours to the contrary were only malicious gossip designed to discredit the government of President FW de Klerk.

*   *   *

The multiparty negotiations at the World Trade Centre at Kempton Park had been struggling. A Record of Understanding drawn up during negotiations preceding CODESA 2 containing proposals for an interim constitution with a Bill of Rights, a democratically elected Constitutional Assembly and other elements, was finally signed by Nelson Mandela on behalf of the ANC and President FW de Klerk on behalf of the National Party government.

Unfortunately it was universally misunderstood. Key role players like KwaZulu's Chief Minister Buthelezi and the IFP were incensed at what they regarded as a bilateral deal between the ANC and the governing party and announced their withdrawal from the negotiations.

A month later Buthelezi joined President Lucas Mangope of Bophuthatswana, Brigadier Oupa Gqozo of Ciskei, the Conservative Party, the Afrikaner Freedom Foundation and the Afrikaner Volksunie in forming the Concerned South Africans Group (COSAG). They called for CODESA 2 to be abandoned and replaced by a more representative negotiating forum.

In mid-November the Goldstone Commission issued a dramatic statement that hit the government like a bolt from the blue. Judge Goldstone and his commission had made a surprise raid on Momentum Mews, an office building in a Pretoria suburb that was the headquarters of Military Intelligence's Directorate of Covert Collection (DCC). During the raid they seized files that they alleged indicated unacceptable activities — perhaps even a third force.

This resulted in the appointment of Lieutenant-General Pierre Steyn, the Chief of Defence Force Staff, as a one-man commission to investigate the SADF's intelligence activities. It caused deep dissatisfaction within the ranks of the SADF when 16 officers, including two generals and four brigadiers, were placed on compulsory retirement and another seven sent on compulsory leave.

The rights and wrongs of this action are still being argued, but whatever the case, it resulted in the ANC placing the question of a mythical third force into even sharper focus. It is significant that the National Party government had to hastily service out-of-court demands by a number of these officers for a redress of wrongs. Long after the 1994 election Major-General Chris Therion, one of those who had been subjected to compulsory retirement, commenced a court action to clear his name. The case was settled by Mr de Klerk publicly withdrawing allegations made in his biography that were considered to be false and unsubstantiated.

The National Party government was also at loggerheads with General Bantu Holomisa and the Transkei over PAC terrorists being harboured there. They had embarked on a campaign of murdering whites using Transkei as a rear base. This situation was compounded when a PAC spokesman announced in December 1992 that his organisation had declared war on white South Africans.

In January or February 1993 I became uneasy about the persistent rumours of 32-Battalion being disbanded and the somewhat unconvincing reassurances from government that this was not so. I asked an Australian friend to telephone the offices of Minister of Defence Roelf Meyer. I knew a call from me would remain unanswered as I had mounted a scathing attack in the press criticising restrictions placed on the disciplining of troops and I was, in any case, none too popular in government circles.

The minister was unavailable but he returned the call within 15 minutes. Meyer accused my Australian friend of being a troublemaker and a right-winger and said he was spreading false rumours about the disbandment of 32-Battalion when no such move was contemplated.

Meyer handed over the Defence Ministry to Eugene Louw about a week later. A few weeks after that President de Klerk, without prior warning to anyone in the battalions, announced on television and in the press, that 31- and 32-Battalions would be disbanded as soon as possible.

The shock and dismay in Pomfret, especially among the black troops and their families, can only be imagined. President de Klerk had almost indifferently wrecked the futures of well over 3 000 men, women and children.

As the founding commander I was thunderstruck. Promises made by generals and former heads of state had been broken without even a blush of embarrassment. The blood that had been shed by the men of 32-Battalion and the anguish suffered by the families of those who had fallen appeared to mean absolutely nothing to the president and most members of his government. The troops had been treated like pawns on a chessboard, sacrificed by the government to their SACP/ANC opponents when the negotiating process required a concession.

Major-General Daan Hamman, then the Deputy Chief of the Army, explained the background to me many years later. I had not asked him for an explanation at the time, as he was a good friend and I had no wish to embarrass him.

A South African delegation, led jointly by Foreign Minister Pik Botha and Nelson Mandela, had flown to New York to visit the UN. With the delegates was Major-General Jan Klopper, the Chief of the SADF's Director-General Operations. The purpose of the visit is unknown and why General Klopper was included is a matter for conjecture.

Was the government anticipating demands of a military nature by the UN before an agreement could be made to ease the sanctions that were strangling South Africa's economy? Was General Klopper there merely as an adviser on SADF matters to the delegation, or was he authorised to make decisions on behalf of SADF Chief, General Kat Liebenberg? Perhaps he had been sent by his chief so that somebody was on the spot to fight the battalions being disbanded. On the other hand, his mission could have been to provide his chief with an early warning as to which way the wind was blowing at the UN so that action could be taken to minimise the damage. It is unlikely that this will ever be known as both generals are now dead. Jan Klopper, a good soldier, committed suicide after his retirement and Kat Liebenberg died of cancer.

Whatever the case, it seems that someone phoned President FW de Klerk with the recommendation (or was it confirmation?) that 31- and 32-Battalions would be disbanded immediately. The person making the call might have been General Klopper, but this seems unlikely. Surely protocol would have demanded that it be done by the cabinet minister on the spot, Foreign Minister Pik Botha? The political implications and the reasoning behind the move are also unknown, but it was obviously at the behest of the ANC. Pik Botha was probably in agreement anyway as in later years he became a card-carrying member of the ANC.

Whoever it was, General Klopper first tried to phone his immediate boss General Liebenberg and then Army Chief General Georg Meiring. He later said he had failed to get through to either. Daan Hamman told me that neither were available because it was a weekend. The issue was important and with them being unavailable it was Klopper's duty to immediately get hold Hamman. I personally believe that if General Meiring had been tipped off about what was going to happen he would have ensured he was at home and available to fight the issue.

The State President's office made unsuccessful attempts to phone General Liebenberg and after him General Meiring. It was not to consult with them but to tell them that the decision had been made to disband 31- and 32-Battalions. General Hamman was the next in line and he was at home. He was ordered to go to Pomfret immediately and tell 32-Battalion that they were being disbanded. He was told to smother any fires of discontent as best he could. And so General Hamman told the stunned command and staff cadre of the Battalion that they would be disbanded by 27 March 1993. He told me he considered it the worst moment in his military career.

I believe that if either Kat Liebenberg or Georg Meiring had been consulted in advance by President de Klerk about the question of disbanding two such exceptional units, they would have strongly resisted it. I suspect that President de Klerk wanted to avoid a 'battle in the trenches' which was one of the reasons why he confronted them with a fait accompli. The other, I believe, is that President de Klerk was confronted with an ultimatum to get rid of the unit that resulted from Pik Botha's and Nelson Mandela's visit to the United Nations.

Georg Meiring had sent Daan Hamman to Pomfret only three weeks before to reaffirm to the officers and men that there was no possibility whatsoever of the Battalion being disbanded and that malicious gossip to the contrary should be treated with the contempt it deserved. Now he had been ordered by his president to face the same troops and tell them the 'malicious rumours' had become a reality. I am sure that Georg Meiring would not have sent Daan Hamman on that earlier mission unless he had been reassured at least at Defence Minister level that the troops had nothing to fear. Generals Meiring and Hamman are men of integrity and I am sure they were deeply distressed at being misled and misused.

It appears that the Minister of Defence, Eugene Louw, was not consulted either. I discussed this with former State President PW Botha. He told me that he had been highly upset and had personally confronted Eugene Louw about what he called 'the betrayal of my word' to the men of 32-Battalion and their families. Louw insisted that he had not been consulted and that the first he had heard about the unit being disbanded was on the SATV news.

The government's spin doctors went into action. A stream of justifications emanated from the president's office. They were routed via the Chief of the SADF, presumably to put distance between the president and these disgraceful happenings. The rationalisation given was that the military and its financial situation had changed so much that the army's structure had to be downsized. This transparently dishonest red herring was paraded for the consumption of a gullible public who were insufficiently well informed to be able to judge for themselves.

It would have been a severe crisis indeed if such an unnoticed fiscal threat had crept up on the government within the space of 24 hours — a crisis so serious that it had forced the government to implement an immediate cut back on its army. The reality is that it takes weeks, months and perhaps even years to arrive at a structured plan to reduce an army to more affordable proportions.

SADF channels also gave out that it would be in the interests of members of 32-Battalion to be posted to other units. It would improve their career prospects within the broader spectrum of the army, rather than within the narrow confines of the Battalion. Logic again applies. Why were the commanding generals and the 32-Battalion commander not consulted? Why the indecent haste? Had President de Klerk, as the Commander-in-Chief, experienced a sudden revelation that compelled him to take drastic steps without the necessity of relying on the expert advice of his commanders? And since when does a state president involve himself with the army's career planning by showing compassion for the career prospects of the troops affected?

All this indicates it was merely a dishonest attempt at damage control.

The fact was that the National Party government had caved in to SACP/ANC demands and intimidation at Kempton Park. Perhaps the president could have come clean and candidly explained why 32-Battalion had to go in spite of previous promises. This would at least have enhanced his integrity and he would have experienced at first hand the willingness of his fighting men to again make a sacrifice — their last — in the interests of the country.

Certain sections of the press as well as the SABC — which was appallingly servile to the government in power — lauded the State President. They seemed overjoyed that the 'notorious' 32-Battalion had been disbanded. The implication was that the 'third force' operators had been unmasked and removed before they did something worse. It is accepted in military circles that units acting in a disgraceful manner are arbitrarily dismissed from the order of battle. Disgraceful conduct includes the killing of civilians, running away in battle, shamefully surrendering to the enemy when still in full combat trim and mutiny or involvement in an armed insurrection against the country's rulers.

The Buffalo Soldiers had always been so highly conscious of their duty that they had always stood their ground with grim resolve — even when heavily outgunned and outnumbered. They were the best example of a professional approach to military duty and of exemplary conduct under fire in the whole SADF. Indeed, in South African military history they might have been surpassed in valour only by the South African brigade that was all but wiped out at Delville Wood on the Western Front during World War-I.

The valiant Battalion's abrupt disbandment by its supreme commander sadly carried with it an odour of disgrace so bad that people felt it best not to enquire too deeply into its passing. This is the unfair image of 32-Battalion that many people have been left with. Some in the all too forgetful media welcomed the passing of the unit and suggested it was just punishment. But just punishment for what?

* * *

At Pomfret the unit moved to give substance to its death sentence. Some companies were transferred to become part of 61-Mechanised Infantry Battalion at the Army Battle School at Lohatla. Some went to 111-Battalion, a Swazi unit based at Camden near Amersfoort. Those qualified as paratroopers were sent to 1-Parachute Battalion at Tempe in Bloemfontein. Koos Crocodile Kruger went with them. The rest remained at Pomfret to become part of the newly re-established 2-South African Infantry Battalion — formerly based at Walvis Bay — and were integrated with troops of coloured and Tswana extraction.

The soldiers were shocked and dismayed at the events that had so unexpectedly overtaken them. They were all offered the option of leaving the unit, but only with a meagre severance package. Many accepted the offer and ended up working for a private company, Executive Outcomes, fighting as mercenaries in FAPLA's war against UNITA. They had little choice as there were few prospects for them to make out in the new South Africa. They knew no other skills than soldiering. In any case the vast majority did not have the necessary educational qualifications to make it outside the comforting confines of the Battalion.

Most families remained at Pomfret while their menfolk went their different ways. It was a disaster in the making from which there was no rescue.

35

32-Battalion disbanded

My wife Ros and I attended what in the Royal Navy, where I served for five years, would have been called a 'decommissioning parade'. It was the first time I had set foot in Pomfret. We arrived the night before and stayed with Louis and Cheney Lombard, Colonel Eddie Viljoen's son-in-law and daughter. Eddie also stayed with them.

Eddie and I had much to reflect on regarding the treatment being meted out to our old battalion. We kept asking the same questions: 'Why had the men and their families been betrayed? Why had nobody kicked up a fuss? Why had there been silence from all quarters? There were no answers to these questions.

We attended the parade the following day, 26 March 1993. Eddie wore his uniform and I my 32-Battalion blazer. The VIP area was filled with former commanders, three or four generals, some civilians and the Battalion's command cadre. Everybody wore their decorations and medals.

The unit marched on parade, as smart as always, accompanied by a distinctly scruffy-looking army band. They trooped the national and the unit colours for the last time. It was an emotional experience for me. A few of them there were old-timers who had come back from *Operation Savannah* with me in December 1975. Many of the younger soldiers were sons of fathers who had served with the unit since the beginning. The soldiers of the first and second generations marched past, colours emblazoned with proud battle honours, watched by the somewhat embarrassed VIP spectators and subdued former members. There was a host of still younger sons and siblings looking on who would probably have been called to the colours later to continue the tradition.

It was 32-Battalion's last march. Their day of reckoning, in the eyes of some, had finally arrived.

Wives, mothers and children of those on parade sat around the perimeter. It was the last time they would see their menfolk wearing the coveted camouflage beret. For the last time we would hear the battle songs of the Battalion as more than 1 000 men expressed who and what they were and how they had fought their enemies in battle.

General Georg Meiring took the salute as the reviewing officer. He made a speech, the basic contents of which had probably been churned out by the President's spin doctors. But that was his duty — he had no option but to cover for the government. The president, our Commander-in-Chief, was not there as one might have expected and nor had he sent a representative. None of his cabinet ministers, including the Minister of Defence, had considered it important enough to attend this day when South Africa's foremost combat unit, an offspring of their own politically inspired 'border war', was dismissed from the army's order of battle. Neither President de Klerk nor any of his ministers sent messages to be read out to the troops thanking 32-Battalion for its services to South Africa in time of war.

During General Meiring's speech, Gert Kruger, formerly a lieutenant and a platoon commander with 32-Battalion, marched on parade and took up a dead-centre position facing the troops. He made a speech in Portuguese in which he berated General Meiring for his promise, made only a few weeks before, that the unit would never be disbanded. General Meiring, of course, had not been a party to the goings-on at top political level, nor could he have known what was happening in the mind of President de Klerk. Gert Kruger's impromptu address, however, showed all those present, especially the black troops, that many former members of the unit's combat leadership felt it was disgraceful the way solemn promises had been broken.

On the orders of Colonel Delport, the Military Police grabbed Gert Kruger and forcibly deposited him outside the gates of the unit. He was told never ever to return to Pomfret. So much for one man's bitterness and helpless anger. At least he had the courage to speak out.

There was a final farewell party, but it was more of a wake than a joyous occasion. Ros and I left after breakfast the following day because we could not stand the atmosphere of bitterness and despondency that hung over the heads of the battle veterans like a smothering blanket. The grim determination on the part of the unit's new leaders to see the instructions from on high fulfilled to the letter stuck in my craw. For them it was apparently just another order which had to be carried out dutifully and promptly. Most had joined the unit only when the war was on its last legs or after the establishment of Pomfret. They did not share the same empathy with the black troops as those who had faced hot lead side by side with them.

*   *   *

Despite having retired from the army, I still felt it necessary to express my feelings about the whole sorry affair. I initiated a collection of 30 silver rand coins from 30 anonymous officers, donating the first one myself. It was arranged that they would be handed to President de Klerk in Parliament on a suitable occasion. I had decided that the old and large rand coin was the right size to make the dramatic impact required.

During a Parliamentary debate on 20 April 1993, Dr Willie Snyman, the Conservative Party's spokesman on defence matters, stood up to address the State President. He asked a number of questions relating to the absorption of MK into the SADF.

Finally, Dr Snyman moved to the emotional topic of the disbandment of 31- and 32-Battalions. He began with an introduction and outlined the events preceding the battalion's decommissioning. He emphasised promises made by past presidents and generals both retired and serving. He spoke about the sacrifices, particularly in human lives and suffering, that the battalions had made. He detailed their fine military achievements on the battlefield.

Coming to the crux of the matter, he told President de Klerk that the officers and men of 32-Battalion believed that he had betrayed them. To express this sense of betrayal, 30 former officers of 32-Battalion had collected 30 silver coins and had requested he hand them to the president in parliament.

He stood up and left his seat — which was highly irregular — walked across to the government benches and dropped a bag containing the 30 pieces of silver in front of the highly startled president. Beside it he placed a scroll inscribed with the unit's Roll of Honour — those who had died in the government's cause.

President de Klerk, by all accounts, was furious. He sat speechless for a few moments, glaring at the bag in front of him. Never before had officers of the South African Army expressed their disgust at the actions of their supreme commander in such an insulting manner.

There was an uproar. The Speaker ordered Dr Snyman to retrieve the pieces of silver. Snyman refused, saying he had given his word to the officers concerned that he would carry out the task. The Speaker ordered him to leave the House.

A frantic and pathetic exercise in damage control followed. Newcomers to 32-Battalion issued a statement deploring the disgraceful action of 30 ex-officers of the unit who had demonstrated their disloyalty to the government of the day. They had brought the good name of the now defunct 32-Battalion into disrepute.

I was the only one of the contributors who was identified. The rest were ex-officers from the bush war days and a few of the old guard who were still serving.

Some believed that those who deplored our public gesture had little choice in the matter. Times had changed and they had to avoid being victimised. Their jobs were on the line and they had no wish to find themselves 'fired' in the media as had happened with certain other officers. There was no logic behind their statement anyway, as the good name of 32-Battalion had been irrevocably tarnished by its disbandment.

After that the issue was dropped and as far as I know, no attempts were made to identify the other 29 contributors. It was obvious that the government wanted to put the political embarrassment behind them. A can of worms had been opened and the less said the sooner it would be forgotten. They had no wish to have the humiliation become the subject of a vicious parliamentary slinging match between the National Party government and the opposition. Besides, enough damage had already been done to President de Klerk's personal image.

The major part of 32-Battalion — the Portuguese-speaking families still living in Pomfret around whose heads the battle had raged — gained not an inch of advantage from all the fuss. Ironically, when the elections came, most voted for President de Klerk and his National Party — those who had stabbed them in the back. Besides, they knew virtually nothing about other political parties because they had not been exposed to them. Pomfret, situated in arguably the remotest corner of South Africa, was barely accessible. None of the parties even bothered to go there to canvas for support — not even General Constand Viljoen. Maybe his conservative Freedom Front didn't want to attract black votes anyway — not even the votes of the black soldiers who had fought under his command when he was the Task Force and Army Commander.

*   *   *

I had no wish to see Pomfret again after the unit was disbanded. Nor did I want to look any of my old black comrades-in-arms in the eye again. As the founding commander of 32-Battalion and their leader in many battles, it was not easy to turn my back on their misery, but at least I could nurse my disgust, anger and bitterness alone. This was not so for 32-Battalion. As a disciplined unit they had to grin and bear it, while they rearranged their lives to cope with an uncertain future.

Ironically, the soldiers and their families found themselves confronting an almost identical survival problem to the one they had faced when they became refugees from a strife-torn Angola in 1975/76. This time the established social structure of the Battalion that had served as a comforting cocoon and safety net had been shattered.

Postings occurred and depleted sub-units departed for new units. Those posted to the Army Battle School, 1-Parachute Battalion and 111-Battalion had no option but to leave their families at Pomfret. Married accommodation was not available at their new postings.

Those who tried their luck in civvy street or with Executive Outcomes also left their families at Pomfret. Inevitably, fragile family structures began breaking down. Husbands posted to distant units could visit only infrequently. The families, now living outside the comforting orbit of a parent unit, were of little concern to the new command staff of 2-South African Infantry at Pomfret.

A sudden concern about the spectre of asbestosis manifested itself at Army HQ, despite its staff officers having shown little sympathy regarding the fate of the Buffalo Soldiers when they were in sole occupation. With commendable speed it was decided that 2-South African Infantry Battalion, as a 'proper' army unit made up of South Africans and not Angolan Mercenaries, could not be subjected to the creeping peril of death-dealing asbestos particles. So the unit was promptly resettled at Zeerust, but no married quarters were provided for the former 32-Battalion soldiers who had been posted to it. They had to leave their families behind to take their chances with asbestosis.

Over the course of time absentee husbands visited their home and families with less and less frequency. Some had taken girlfriends, a few took new wives and their families at Pomfret were neglected. The officers at new units, because of the distance, soon lost touch with the families. 2-South African Infantry, even before leaving for Zeerust, showed little compassion for the families of soldiers serving in other units. It was none of their business. Some abandoned wives and daughters were forced into prostitution, selling themselves to the troops of 2-South African Infantry to make ends meet. They also started to run shebeens. The formerly healthy social structure of the old 32-Battalion community began to collapse into a sordid heap of broken families, vice and delinquency.

Many who had taken the meagre package offered had squandered their money on buying cars. They returned to Pomfret penniless and squatted in their badly built brick homes, without jobs and with no means to support their families. Desperation mounted by the day. They were poverty stricken. Churches and other welfare organisations collected clothing, blankets and food for those once proud people.

Many of those who joined Executive Outcomes and fought in Angola returned with far less in their pockets than they had anticipated. Others made the return trip in body bags. They had fought in a war that was a mercenary affair.

'You either do the job, mate, or you're out. And to hell with your welfare or that of your family'.

Welfare considerations in the world of mercenary soldiering would reduce the vast profits for the heartless bosses who run such outfits. Former 32-Battalion men are still being recruited to fight as mercenaries in various parts of Africa — despite the practice having been outlawed by the South African government.

*   *   *

In September 2000 a planning and development consultancy conducted a feasibility analysis to seek solutions to the Pomfret situation at the behest of North-West Province. A copy of the report was forwarded to me anonymously by a friend of 32-Battalion. The contents, apparently, are supposed to be confidential — which does little to further the government's much vaunted policy of transparency.

It made recommendations in respect of regional and local economic development to ease the terrible plight of the Pomfret community. Judging by its performance in other areas, the North-West Province will be unable to deliver on most if not all of the recommendations. The report raised serious short and long term problems which emphasised my accusations of shortcomings by the former military and government establishments.

In the first place the vast majority of the community was found to be living in abject poverty below the bread line. They have been caught in a vicious loop from which there is no escape. It is, of course, possible to start small-scale manufacturing enterprises, but there is no market in which to sell the fruits of their labours. Once out of the gates of the old Pomfret base, the empty bush stretches for hundreds of kilometres with not a customer in sight. Furthermore, there is no public transport to get would-be entrepreneurs to even the tiny market at Vryburg. The availability of private transport is scarce because nobody there can afford to own and run a car anymore.

The only shop at Pomfret closed down when 2-South African Infantry moved out. A local farmer took over the old SADFI shopping facility with, one must assume, a reduced and more expensive stock holding. The next closest shops are in Vryburg. But with no transport and no money to spend, what does it matter? Effectively, Pomfret is cut off from the rest of South Africa and its population is relegated to an African Siberia.

The report lists these internal exiles as comprising 1 293 adults, 1 847 youths and 360 disabled men — the last figure includes 24 orphans. The disabled and most of the orphans can be directly attributed to the war in Namibia and Angola. In other words, they are the flotsam and jetsam of the Battalion's killed and wounded in action.

All the adults were jobless. Of them 27 were pensioners and 72 were the widows of the Battalion's war dead. There were 100 unmarried mothers and 94 divorcees.

The 3 500 people abandoned in this grim camp had little food on the table and no prospect of escaping the asbestos time bomb that is ticking down to catastrophe.

When 2-South African Infantry moved to Zeerust, they left behind a small detachment to support the community and operate their services. It has since been withdrawn along with the support services.

At the time of the survey the overburdened and unhygienic waste disposal installations showed signs of an imminent collapse. Effluent pipes were leaking so badly that running repairs had become impossible. One can imagine what the situation must be like by now. The only clinic had been shut down, which left the nearest one 150km away. With no transport, let alone an ambulance, it might as well have been on the moon. And with the village now a potential breeding ground for a wide spectrum of diseases and serious injuries resulting from rising violence, the consequences can be imagined. HIV/Aids has already got a death grip on many of the younger members of the population.

The town has no police station. Because of the health risks, members of the South African Police Service refuse to serve there. Desperately hungry people turn to crime to keep themselves and their families alive. It seems inevitable that an environment of violence and gangsterism will develop at Pomfret.

Only eight of the 18 boreholes are capable of delivering water for the community and they are operating on borrowed time. Until recently, many people had to go without water for days on end. The Public Works Department was supposed to service and repair the reticulation system, but found this beyond its capability. Now that they too have left one can only shudder for the people that remain there.

There is still the long-term ogre of asbestosis. The analysis did not examine this closely because it believed its team lacked expertise. It confirmed, however, that the danger is real and if it is proven to be hazardous to the health of the community, their relocation will be imperative.

Some families have resorted to dry-land subsistence farming which also disturbs the inadequate soil layer applied to cover the asbestos-polluted substratum. This leaves a choice: die of malnutrition now, or die of asbestosis later.

The people of the old 32-Battalion are already broken in spirit and their bodies are following rapidly. Their prospects are certainly far worse now than when I found them at M'pupa in southern Angola in 1975 as a rag-tag bunch of malnourished skeletons.

Then I could offer a future — now there is nothing ahead for them.

36

. . . And they died by the sword

There is an official war cemetery south of the old Pica Pau *kimbo* on the east bank of the Okavango River in Western Caprivi. It is on the exact spot where the first families found shelter from the relentless rains after they were forced to leave M'pupa in 1976.

Knowing the area as I do, I can be certain that the rank undergrowth is already reclaiming this last resting place of heroes and taking it back into the jungle. That, perhaps, is the lot of most soldiers who fall in battle in foreign countries, or even in their own countries. The fighting men who spill their blood so that others might live are too soon forgotten.

In Kohima in the Indian state of Assam, there is a small monument dedicated to the British and Indian soldiers who were killed in action while bringing the advance of the Imperial Japanese Army to a bloody halt — a desperate struggle in which they were vastly outnumbered. Perhaps that memorial, too, has disappeared into the wet jungles of Assam, a forgotten relic of the distant past that only military historians care about.

I cast my mind's eye back to the Caprivi where I see row upon row of white crosses, many of them marking the graves of men whom I knew intimately. There are hundreds of crosses, all identical, at heads of low heaps of the African soil on which the wives, children, mothers and friends of the fallen used to lay personal relics and bunches of indigenous flowers.

Apart from those buried at Buffalo Base, there are many other unmarked graves in Angola — those who could not be brought back because of the exigencies of war or those who died alone of their wounds and were classified as 'missing in action, believed killed'. Some died without a burial because the fortunes of war did not allow the time to scrape even a shallow pit. Some were buried in South Africa. The ashes of Sergeant Stewart were scattered at Buffalo Base on the banks of the Okavango River where he rests with the birds, trees and animals of what was once his Caprivi home.

Most fought for a cause they did not understand. But they did not die for that cause — they died for 32-Battalion and the men fighting on their left and right flanks — their comrades in arms, comrades in sorrow and comrades in laughter. But they also fell for you and me so that there could be a better life in a free South Africa.

Those who died were white and black. But what does skin colour matter? They were all heroes. In the Battalion, any colour was fine as long as it was not a cowardly shade of yellow.

We who came through it alive know what it is to have the spectre of death at our shoulders when going into battle. Having looked at it so often, we no longer shudder when we see it. We accept it because we can do nothing about it and sooner or later it will come to us all.

But, like the men who died at Kohima, the fallen of 32-Battalion should also be remembered — even if the memory is only dim, even if the graves in which they lie are reclaimed by the jungle, even if people should forget about that little cemetery in a country that no longer belongs to us — a cemetery that few of us will ever see again.

The words engraved on the Kohima memorial were copied from another monument erected by Xenophon's army of 10 000 Greeks 2 400 years ago after it fought its way back to the Black Sea through enemy hordes. The same words are also applicable to the sacrifices of another group of men — the soldiers of 32-Battalion — who fought just as bravely for us and for their unit:

When you go home one day
Tell them of us and say,
That for your tomorrow
We gave our today.

32-Battalion: Roll of Honour

1976

Rank	Initials	Surname
Rfn	J	Cardoso
Rfn	B	Domingos
Rfn	M	Mavuato
Lt	C J	Swart
Sgt	Danny	Roxo
Sgt	C	da Silva
Cpl	R	Ribeiro

1977

Rank	Initials	Surname
Rfn	J	Joaquim
Rfn	S	Henrique
Rfn	R	Pedro
Rfn	P	Paulo
Rfn	J M	Muquindia
Rfn	J A	Gracia
Sgt	B A	Minonambunga
Rfn	H M	Dos Santos
Rfn	J	Victor
2/Lt	G	Keulder

1978

Rank	Initials	Surname
Rfn	A	Cassamano
Rfn		Zagi
Rfn	A	Da Silva
Rfn	C	Esals
Rfn	N	Bernade
Rfn	S M	Chicoto
Rfn	R	Augusto
Rfn	B	Caquarta
Rfn	A	Mussungu
Sgt	CJ	Theron
Rfn	J	Linhawga
2/Lt	A L	Opperman
Rfn	L	Laurindo
Rfn	P P	Amorim
Rfn	J	Dumbo

1979

Rank	Initials	Surname
Rfn	A M	Tchizondo
2/Lt	S W	Coetzee
2/Lt	W A	De Vos

1980

Rank	Initials	Surname
Rfn	J	Miranda
Rfn	R	Alberto
Cpl	C C	Da Trindade
2/Lt	T C	Patrick
Rfn	M	Jenga
L/Cpl	A J	Falkus
Cpl	B Z	Gericke
2/Lt	P	van der Walt
2/Lt	J M	Muller
Sgt	S D	Braz
Rfn	S	Angelo
Rfn	J	Joao
L/Cpl	J	Kaumba
Cpl	M	van Wyk
Rfn	A	Caliango
Rfn	J	Miguel
Capt	C De J	Muller
Cpl	D H	Grobler
Rfn	B	Albino
Cpl	M C	Coetzee
Rfn	C	Marcelino
Rfn	J	Kambinda

Capt	A	Erasmus
L/Cpl	E	Sofia
Rfn	J	Matamba
Rfn	J	Francisco
Cpl	E C	Engelbrecht
Cpl	K	Vavala
Rfn	M	Augusto
Rfn	A	Edwardo
Rfn	A	Livingue

1981

Rank	Initials	Surname
Rfn	J	Joao
Rfn	A	Samba
Rfn	T W Z	Navaros
L/Cpl	J	Martins
Rfn	C	Cabonga
Rfn	F	Chameia
Rfn	A	Joaquim
Rfn	F	Dala
Rfn	D	Paulo

1982

Rank	Initials	Surname
Rfn	H	Naikako
Rfn	C	Evaristo
Rfn	Y	Joao
Rfn	A P	Manuel
2/Lt	P J S	Nel
Cpl	J	Conroy
Cpl	P T	Stewart
Rfn	D D	Donge
Cpl	M	Jose
T/L/Cpl	M	Bambi

1983

Rank	Initials	Surname
Sgt	A	Mande
Cpl	G H	Durand
Rfn	J D	Kativa
Rfn	J	Nambi
Rfn	E	Kasera
Rfn	T	Manganhes

1984

Rank	Initials	Surname
Cpl	A	Aurelio
Rfn	J	Dala
Rfn	I	Malongo

1985

Rank	Initials	Surname
Rfn	J A	Sachilombo
Rfn	A	De Almeida
Rfn	M	Muema
Lt	D G	Light
Cpl	M A	Kingeulele
Rfn	P	Jose
Rfn	J	Joaquim
Rfn	Z	Chipoya
Rfn	J	Chihamba
Rfn	K	Kalonga
Rfn	J	Fernando
L/Cpl	I	Dumba
Rfn	J E	Jamba
Rfn	B	Paulo
Rfn	P K	Kahete

1987

Rank	Initials	Surname
Rfn	D	Zumba
L/Cpl	M M	De Klerk

Rfn	K	Tolosi		Sgt	A	Batista
Sgt	J R M	Mananza		Rfn	L	Ntjamba
Rfn	G	Antonio		Rfn	J	Pedro
Rfn	M J	Kuyler		Rfn	J	Gonsalves
L/Cpl	E	Joao		Rfn	J R	Meyer
L/Cpl	W T	Chipango				
Rfn	G	Antonio		**1988**		
2/Lt	J R	Alves		Rfn	A N	Dinu
Rfn	F	Sikote				
Capt	A D	McCallum		**1990**		
Rfn	D	Cassela		Rfn	J	Vimango
Rfn	F	Maurico				
Cpl	B	Sokola		**1991**		
Rfn	C	Dala		Rfn	J A	Sampaio
Cpl	I	Vocolo				
Rfn	E N	Kapepura				
Rfn	P	Kapinga				

Another 100 men fell in battle before Battle Group Bravo was incorporated in the army as 32-Battalion. No records were kept of those combat losses because the men were regarded as FNLA soldiers. Later, after they had been abandoned by Chipenda, an attempt was made to rectify this matter, but without success. The unit's composition changed almost daily as newcomers arrived and others opted out. Included in the 100 are 84 members of Charlie Company who were cut off and shamefully abandoned to their fate at Ebo. They were decimated at leisure by an overwhelming Cuban/FAPLA force. Officially, they should not appear on a SADF roll of honour, but for those who fought alongside them, this attitude is not appreciated nor understood. They did at least as much as any member of the South African Army to halt the march of communism into southern Africa. For that, they too should be honoured. They lie in unmarked graves — if they were buried at all — out in the Angolan bush.

They are the unknown soldiers of our time.

Organisation and equipment: enemy forces

The enemy

1 South West Africa People's Organisation (SWAPO) — PLAN (People's Liberation Army of Namibia)
2 FAPLA (People's Armed Forces for the Liberation of Angola) — military wing of Angola's ruling MPLA (Popular Movement for the Liberation of Angola)
3 Cuban Forces

Enemy forces: organisation

FAPLA brigade	Three motorised/mechanised battalions. Each brigade had a battalion of artillery with three artillery companies per battalion.
FAPLA battalion	Three motorised/mechanised infantry companies, one company of tanks and usually several artillery/120mm mortar companies. Note: A company of tanks and a company of guns/mortars are equivalent to a squadron of tanks and a battery of guns/mortars in the South African Army.
FAPLA tactical group	Two companies of tanks and one mechanised infantry company.
FAPLA infantry coy	Three motorised/mechanised platoons mounted in lorries or BTRs/BMPs.
FAPLA tank company	Three tank platoons usually with a total of ten tanks.
FAPLA artillery coy	Three platoons of four guns each equipped with D-30, M-46 or BM-21 Stalin Organ MRLs (multiple rocket launchers) or a mixture of all three.
Cuban rifle regt	Three rifle battalions, each comprising three rifle companies, usually mechanised, and a tank company plus artillery.
Cuban tank regt	Three tank battalions each with three companies of tanks, possibly a mechanised rifle company and artillery. The tanks were Soviet T55s and T62s.
Cuban artillery regt	Three artillery battalions each with three gun or MRL companies.
Cuban composite air-defence regt	Probably consisted of three inflated air-defence battalions equipped with SAM-2, SAM-3, SAM-6, SAM-8 and SAM-13 companies as well as ZSU-23-4 self propelled anti-aircraft guns.
Cuban/SWAPO composite battalion	Probably comprised three motorised rifle companies.
Cuban 50-Division	Six rifle regiments, one tank regiment, one artillery regiment. one composite air-defence regiment and three composite Cuban-SWAPO battalions. Note: A Cuban regiment is the equivalent of a South African or a FAPLA Brigade.

Enemy Equipment: armoured fighting vehicles and other vehicles

BRDM-2	Amphibious armoured car mounting a 14.5mm heavy machine gun and a co-axial 7.62mm machine gun.
BTR-60	Armoured personnel carrier with carrying capacity for an infantry section of eight men. Mounts a 14.5mm heavy machine gun and 7.62mm machine gun co-axially in turret.
BMP-1	Infantry fighting vehicle, tracked and armoured and designed to carry a section of infantry. Armed with 73mm gun, a co-axial 7.62mm machine gun and Sagger missiles.
T34	World War-II medium tank (formerly Joseph Stalin) mounting an 85mm tank gun and a 7.62mm co-axial machine gun.
T54/T55	Post World War-II medium tank mounting a 100mm tank gun with co-axial 7.62mm machine gun in fully stabilised turret equipped with a relatively sophisticated fire control equipment.
P I 76	Amphibious tank armed with 76mm tank gun and co-axial 7.62mm machine gun.

Enemy Equipment: aircraft

MiG-19	Fighter-bomber.
MiG-21	Fighter-bomber. Maximum range 1 100km.
Su-22	Fighter-bomber. Operational radius 700km, bomb load 3 000Kg.
MiG-23	Interceptor but also used for ground attack. Armed with a 23mm gun, two AA-7 and four AA-8 missiles in air-to-air role and a selection of weapons for ground attack role. Combat radius of 900 to 1 300km in an interceptor role. Compared more than favourably with SAAF Mirages.
Mi-24 Hind	Gunship helicopter, with rockets and guns in pods.
MI-8	Troop-carrying helicopter, superseded by Mi-17.
Antonov 12, 22, 26, and 30	Cargo planes of various capacities.
Ilyushin medium bomber	Copy of British General Electric Canberra and on par with it.

Enemy Equipment: artillery/missile systems

75mm	Recoilless anti-tank gun.
82mm	B10 anti-tank gun, like the 75mm but can also fire high explosive shell.
Sagger	Wire-guided anti-tank missile, range 2 300 metres.
BM-21	Stalin Organ. Vehicle-mounted rocket system, range 21km. World War-II technology.
122mm D-30	Field gun also used in anti-tank role, range 15km.
130mm M-46	Medium field gun, range 27km.
30mm AGS-17	Belt fed grenade launcher, tripod or vehicle mounted, fires high explosive grenades at 65 a minute, range 1 750m.
Strela (Arrow)	NATO designation Grail or SAM-7. Shoulder-launched anti-aircraft missile, infrared homing, viable from a height of 50m to 2 000m.
SAM-6	Medium height anti-aircraft missile system. Can track and lock on to targets at range of 24km away at a ceiling of 12 000m.
SAM-8	As SAM-6 but more sophisticated. Self-propelled, can fire two missiles at a time at two separate targets. Viable from a height of 10m to 12 000m and as close as 1,6km from its firing position.
SAM-9	Short range anti-aircraft missile system mounted on BRDM-2. Viable from height of 50m to 4 000m.
SAM-13	Improved version of the SAM-9 mounted on a PT-76 tank chassis. Viable from height of 20m to 4 000m.

Enemy forces: equipment general

RPD	Light machine gun with drum magazine, calibre 7.62mm.
PKM	General purpose machine gun firing a rimmed 7.62 x 54mm cartridge.
AK47	Infantry assault rifle, 7.62mm x 39mm rounds. Also used extensively by own forces and UNITA.
PPSH	Sub-machine gun with drum magazine, 7.63mm calibre.
AP mine	Anti-personnel mine set above or below ground. Below ground: activated by a pressure plate. The 'Bouncing Betty' type is fitted with a propellant charge and a time delay that allows a mine to pop up and explode at eye level. The Pom Z is fitted to a stick and set above ground. It is activated by a trip wire.
AT mine	Anti-tank mine usually initiated by a pressure plate. TM46 is an example.
RPG-7	Recoilless anti-tank rocket launcher used extensively throughout the world and also by South Africa forces.
12.7mm	Anti-aircraft machine gun also used in a ground role. Like 50 calibre Browning.
14.5mm	Anti-aircraft machine gun also used in a ground role.
23mm	Medium anti-aircraft gun. Fires HE shells and tracer and can be used in the ground role. Sometimes mounted on tracked vehicles as ZSU-23-2 (twin barrels) or the ZSU-23-4 (four barrels).

Note: All enemy equipment and weapons were of Soviet origin.

Organisation and equipment: own forces

Own forces: organisation

Mechanised infantry battalion.

Two mechanised rifle companies, each with three platoons mounted in Ratel-20s, an armoured car squadron with three troops of Ratel-90 armoured cars, a support company with Ratel-81s in its mortar platoon, a Ystervark anti-aircraft troop and an assault pioneer platoon.

Tank Regiment

Theoretically it should have had three tank squadrons but in this war it had only two. The squadrons comprised three troops each with three Olifant (Elephant) main battle tanks and a mechanised infantry company.

Motorised infantry battalion.

In 32-Battalion it varied between nine and ten companies mounted in Buffels or Casspirs. Other battalions comprised the more usual three rifle companies. In addition each battalion had a support company with an 81mm mortar platoon, often a machine gun platoon and an assault pioneer platoon.

Artillery regiment.

Three batteries of guns or Valkyrie multiple rocket launchers. Each battery comprises three troops equipped with four guns or MRLs.

Battle group.

Could be either tank heavy or infantry heavy. A tank-heavy battle group comprised two squadrons of tanks, at least one mechanised infantry company, sometimes an armoured car squadron, perhaps a battery of 120mm mortars and almost invariably an assault pioneer troop. An infantry-heavy battle group comprised two or three rifle or mechanised infantry companies, the usual infantry support weapons, an armoured car or tank squadron, sometimes 120mm mortars and sometimes an assault pioneer platoon.

Combat team

An infantry or tank-heavy company/squadron could have a variety of permutations. A rifle or mechanised company could have an attached tank or armoured car troop. A tank squadron could have a mechanised infantry platoon attached. Tanks and infantry were often equally weighted with a squadron of tanks/armoured cars and an infantry company. If operating semi-independently away from its battle group, it would usually have attached support elements like 120mm mortars and assault pioneers.

Own forces: armoured fighting vehicles and other vehicles

Buffel

Mine-protected infantry fighting vehicle built on a Unimog chassis. Can carry an infantry section. South African designed variant.

Casspir

Mine-protected infantry fighting vehicle with excellent cross country performance. Can carry an infantry section. Has twin MAGs mounted in a roof turret and a second for a gunner next to the driver. The twin MAG's were replaced in some cases with a 20mm cannon. South African design.

Sabre

Any light 4x4 off-road vehicle modified for long range penetration operations behind enemy lines for extended periods. Has heavy calibre machine guns, 106mm recoilless anti-tank guns, mortars and a variety of weapons designed to give it devastating fire power. Used by the Recces and pathfinder company of 44-Parachute brigade.

Ratel-20

Armoured infantry fighting vehicle mounting a 20mm heavy machine gun. South African design.

Ratel-90

Armoured car and or tank destroyer, 90mm tank gun. South African design.

Ratel-81

Ratel with 81mm mortar. South African design.

Ratel-ZT3

Tank destroyer mounted with laser-guided anti-tank missiles effective to 5 000 metres.

Ratel-Command

With communication systems for commanders of mechanised units and formations.

Ratel-EW

Ratel with electronic warfare equipment for intercepting enemy radio traffic, fixing locations of radio broadcasts, jamming enemy radio transmissions, protecting own electronic security.

Eland-60

Derivative of French Panhard armoured car, 60m mortar.

Eland-90

Derivative of French Panhard armoured car with 90mm tank gun.

Olifant

Medium battle tank, 105mm tank gun with sophisticated fire control system. South African developed and upgraded British Centurion.

ARV

Armoured recovery vehicle built on the hull of an Olifant tank.

Wit Hings

(White Stallion) Mine protected recovery vehicle with armoured cab based on the SAMIL (South African Military) 100 cargo truck. An effective recovery system.

Plofadder

Rapid minefield breaching system comprising an explosive-filled hose dragged across the minefield by a rocket projectile fired from a Buffel infantry fighting vehicle. Designed to clear a lane wide enough for the passage of a file of tanks. South African designed.

Rinkhals

Mine-protected armoured ambulance for carrying stretcher cases and other casualties. Equipped to provide immediate stabilising treatment. South African design.

Own forces: aircraft

Impala

Versatile light strike aircraft used in a close air support role and as a trainer for conversion to Mirages. Italian design.

Mirage 111	Fighter/high level interceptor. The SAAF Cheetah is derived from the Mirage 111. French technology.
Mirage F1-AZ	Long range and versatile strike fighter. Maximum radius of action from 700km and 900km depending on weapons load and flight profile. French design.
Mirage F1-CZ	Fighter/high level interceptor carrying V3B infrared missiles coupled with a helmet sight. South African design.
Buccaneer	Low level medium bomber with radius of action of 950km boosted to 3 700km with additional fuel tanks. Maximum weapons load 7 257kg, including 1 000 pounder bombs, rockets and AS-30 (anti-submarine) air-to-surface missiles. British origin.
Canberra	Medium range high level medium bomber often used for photo reconnaissance. British origin.
Gunship	Alouette MK III helicopter, 20mm gun. French design.
Q car	Alouette MK III helicopter, .303 Browning machine gun, used for carrying a four-man infantry stick.
Puma	Troop-carrying helicopter that, depending on all-up weight, size and profile of landing zone, temperature and height above sea level, can lift a stick of 16 infantrymen. French design.
Oryx	Advanced version of the Puma helicopter. South African design based on French technology.
Super Frelon	Troop-carrying helicopter with a greater carrying capacity than the Puma and the added convenience of a tail gate. Designed for operations at sea level. Not effective in the high altitude and high temperature environment of the African interior. French design.
C130 Hercules	Four-engined medium range cargo aircraft. Also rigged for paratrooping. Carries two sticks of 64 paratroopers or 90 passengers. Maximum range 3 500km at maximum all-up weight. US design.
C160 Transall	Twin-engined medium range cargo aircraft, rigged for paratrooping. Range of 1 890km with maximum all-up weight. Carries two sticks of 64 paratroopers or 90 passengers. French design.
DC-3 (Dakota)	Veteran cargo and paratrooping plane. US design.

Own forces: artillery/missile systems

25 pounder	World War-II howitzer, fires 25 pound shells in close support role. Range 12 000 yards.
G2	World War-II 5.5 inch medium artillery piece firing a 140mm shell. Range 17 000 yards.
G5	Medium artillery piece. With rocket boosted ammunition fires 155mm shells to a true maximum range of 73km. South African design.
G6	As the G5 but motorised and mounted on an armoured chassis. Has superb cross country mobility. South African design.
Valkyrie MRL	127mm multiple rocket launcher (MRL) mounted on a Unimog chassis. Range 27km although officially given as 22km. South African developed from Soviet technology.
Entac	A drive-by-wire anti-tank missile system with 2 000m maximum range. French design.
Milan	Electronically guided anti-tank missile with maximum range of 2 000m. French design.
Stinger	Shoulder-launched infrared homing anti-tank missile claimed to be superior to the Soviet Strela. The Americans gave it to UNITA, but kept it away from the SADF who would have copied and probably improved it. US design.

Own forces: general equipment

GPMG MAG	General purpose machine gun of 7.62mm NATO calibre. Issued to the South African Army. One of the best machine guns in the field. Belgian design.
R1 rifle	7.62mm (NATO) calibre rifle issued to South African Army as the R1. It outclassed any other rifle including the R4 and the AK47. Belgian design.
R4 or R5 rifle	5.56mm infantry assault rifle issued to South African Army. R5 had a shorter barrel. Copy of Israeli Galil.
G3 rifle	7.62mm (NATO) calibre rifle issued to the Portuguese Army as the G3 and the South African Army as the R2. German design.
20mm AA gun	When mounted on Buffels in an anti-aircraft role it was called Ystervark.
20mm	Heavy machine gun mounted in Alouette gunships for air-to-ground application.
50 cal Browning	50 calibre heavy machine gun. World War-II vintage. US design.
30 cal Browning	General purpose 30 calibre machine gun. Stablemate of the 50 calibre Browning. US design.
Sten	9mm sub-machine gun. Designed for partisans in World War-II. British origin.
Uzzi	9mm sub-machine carbine. Israeli design.
M-79	Grenade launcher that fires 40mm shells. US design.
60mm mortar	Light infantry mortar, range 2 000m.
3 inch mortar	World War-II vintage mortar with a range of 1 000yards. British design.
81mm mortar	Range of 5 000m.
120mm mortar	Israeli designed version, range 10 000m.
3,5 inch rocket launcher	
	Shoulder-fired anti-tank weapon with maximum effective range of 300m.
Mines	Anti-tank, anti-personnel, claymore, etc.

Glossary/ Abbreviations

1-Military Area (MA):
Encompassed Owamboland, Kavango, Caprivi and the Kaokoland regions as well as 'shallow' areas beyond Angolan border; later subdivided into sectors.

A
ANC:
African National Congress of South Africa.
Artillery strike:
A sudden and heavy concentration of artillery fire brought down on a relatively compact enemy target.
AWB:
Afrikaner Weerstandsbeweging: Afrikaner resistance movement.
Axis of attack or advance:
A feature such as a road or valley or a bearing to give direction to an attack or advance.

B
Battle Honours:
Awarded to units distinguishing themselves in particular battles. Usually embroidered in gold on scrolls stitched to the unit colour. Each honour displays the name of the battle and the date.
Brewing:
Condition of a tank when it has been shot out and begins to smoke.

C
Callsign:
Elements from sub-unit level down are identified by callsigns rather than by their tactical denominations.
Chana:
Shallow grass-covered depression, usually saucer shaped, often with waterholes by its edges, scattered throughout the Miombo forest area of southern Angola and Owamboland in Namibia.
CODESA:
Convention for a Democratic South Africa
COMOPS:
Communication operations. It was controlled by Military Intelligence and focussed on psywar operations. It was also tasked to provide contingency cover stories to protect SA leaders from damaging propaganda.
Concentration area:
Area well to the rear where forces concentrate prior to a battle or a campaign, to be equipped and prepared for forthcoming operations.
Cooking:
A tank cooks or cooks off when it begins to burn and its ammunition starts to explode.
Coordination lines:
Lateral lines that are natural features on the ground used to coordinate the movement of flanking units or formations during an attack, advance, envelopment or withdrawal. Often also used as 'Report Lines' which require manoeuvring elements to report progress.
Counter-battery fire:
Used by own artillery, usually the long range version, to engage enemy artillery and mortars often well before H-hour to neutralise or disrupt enemy defensive fire plans or the support fire for their attacks.
Coup de main:
Taking advantage of a suddenly presented opportunity resulting from enemy neglect, panic or complacency, to grab a vital installation or well defended feature with forces at one's immediate disposal and at maximum speed before the enemy can recover from their surprise.

D
D-day:
The date on which an operation is launched.
D minus one:
One day before D-day.
Defensive locality:
Area occupied by a defending force to prevent an important terrain feature from falling into enemy hands. Characterised by defence works like minefields, trench and bunker systems, dug in guns, tanks and obstacles.
DGS:
Direcçao Geral de Sugurança — Portuguese security police.
DZ:
Dropping zone for paratroopers.

E, F
FAPLA:
People's Armed Forces for Liberation of Angola — MPLA's military wing.
Fire plan:
Supports the plan of manoeuvre. Developed to coordinate all available firepower within the manoeuvre and combat support elements.
FNLA:
National Front for the Liberation of Angola.

G
Gunner:
A general name for every artilleryman of whatever rank. It is also the lowest rank in the corps.

H, I, J
HAA:
Helicopter administrative area
H-hour:
Time an operation kicks off.
H minus one:
One hour before H-hour.
Infantry-heavy:
A battle group or combat team with more infantry than tanks.

K
Killing ground:
An especially selected area in which enemy forces are destroyed by a concentration of combat power.

L
Laager:
An all round protective formation adopted by armoured fighting vehicles and infantry fighting vehicles to rest, resupply and maintain their equipment.
Les Affreux:
'The terrible ones'. A derogatory term applied to mercenaries in the Congo in the 1960s. The MPLA's top structure applied the name to 32-Battalion because they maintained it was manned by treacherous Angolans recruited by the notorious American mercenary, Colonel Carpenter (That's me!). To this day the battalion is regarded as a former mercenary unit — despite it having been properly reflected as 32-Battalion in the South African Army's order of battle. The name rebounded on the MPLA by inspiring terror amongst its own troops.
Locstat:
Location status. A radio report of one's location on the ground. It can be indicated to aircraft by a white phosphorous or yellow smoke grenade.
LUP:
Lying up place or a hide for a small patrol.
LZ:
Landing zone for helicopters.

M
MK:
Umkhonto we Sizwe (Spear of the Nation) — ANC/SACP's military wing.
MAOT:
Mobile air operations team. A team deployed well forward to facilitate the incorporation, application and control of close air support in response to requests by the ground forces. It consists of a senior pilot and technical staff to handle communications.
MFC:
Mobile fire controller. Usually a mortar man with the assault formation who controls mortar fire.
MPLA:
Movimento Popular de Libertaçao de Angola — Popular Movement for the Liberation of Angola.

N
National Colour:
A silk and gold-tasselled banner reflecting the national flag and honouring units with distinguished records on the field of battle. Battle honours are not displayed on this colour. Only paraded on specific occasions.

O
Omurambas:
Long, narrow and slightly sunk valleys running between low forested dunes in south-eastern Angola, the Western Caprivi and Kavango. They become impassable mud traps in the rainy season. They are lined with strings of pans and covered with lush grass, acacias and other vegetation.
OP:
Observation post.

P
Phases of war
:
Not to be confused with the phases of a battle. There are basically five phases of war: advance to contact, attack, pursuit, defence and withdrawal.
PLAN:
People's Liberation Army of Namibia — SWAPO's military wing.

Q
Quartel
:
Portuguese for fortified barracks or garrison compounds.

R
R&R:
Rest and recuperation.
Registered target:
Artillery and mortars always register targets in advance for each phase of a forthcoming battle which allows them to bring down effective fire immediately the battle starts.
Ringmain:
A system that ties in a series of explosive devices with cortex or electrical cable to explode them simultaneously.
Rolling barrage:
A system of artillery fire support where fire closest to attacking infantry is lifted over the next line of fire in keeping with the pace of attack. This provides lateral lines of fire in depth which leapfrog ahead of the infantry.
RV:
A place on the map and on the ground where scattered forces rendezvous to establish or regain control.

S
SACP:
South African Communist Party.
SAP:
South African Police.
Start line (SL):
A linear feature on the ground or a marked line on which troops form up to begin an assault.
SWAPO:
South West African People's Union

T
TAC HQ:
Tactical Headquarters at the level of brigade and up. Deployed close to the battle area.
Tank-heavy:
A battle group or combat team with more tanks than infantry.
Tiffy:
A motor mechanic, auto electrician or armourer.

U
Unit Colour:
A silk gold-tasselled banner presented to a unit that has distinguished itself on the field of battle. It is an ancient military honour and is only paraded on special occasions.
UNITA:
National Union for the Total Liberation of Angola.
UNTAG:
United Nations Transition Assistance Group.

Index

1-Recce Commando-Regiment, 15, 16, 18, 24, 66, 86, 120, 124, 140, 204
2-Reconnaissance Commando, 137, 138, 140, 141, 147, 148, 150, 204
2-Military Area, Owamboland combat zone, 47
2-South African Infantry Battalion, 341, 344, 345
4-Reconnaissance Commando/ Regiment, 272, 306
4-South African Mechanised Infantry Battalions, 271,283, 285, 298
5-Reconnaissance Commando/Regt, 202, 229, 267
5-Regular Battalion, UNITA, 306
5-South African Infantry, 198
8-Brigade, FAPLA, 265, 310
13-Brigade, FAPLA, 268, 269, 298, 300
16-Brigade, FAPLA, 274, 275, 283-286, 288, 291, 298
16-Maintenance Unit, SADF, 138, 154
17-Brigade, FAPLA, 256
20-South African Brigade, 273, 278, 296, 298, 301, 305, 311, 315
21-Battalion (SA), at Lenz, 334
21-Brigade, FAPLA, 274, 275, 278, 279, 283, 284, 288-292, 299-302, 311
25-Brigade, FAPLA, 256, 265, 268-270, 282, 288, 296, 298, 303, 304, 306, 308, 309
28-Squadron SAAF, 255
31-(Bushman) Battalion, SADF, 182
44-Parachute Brigade, 66, 77, 124, 207, 209, 214, 220, 225, 238, 239, 341, 344
47-Brigade, FAPLA, 273, 276, 280-282
50-Cuban Division, 298, 308, 314, 321
59-Brigade, 273, 280, 282-284, 288, 291, 301, 302, 311
61-Mechanised Battalion, SADF, 273, 280, 282, 283, 289, 298, 303-305, 319, 322, 323
66-Brigade, FAPLA, 290, 291, 296, 298, 306
82-SA Brigade, 301, 305, 306
101-Battalion, SWA Territorial Force, 272, 274, 276, 288, 289, 291
111-Battalion, SADF, 341, 344
201 Bushman Battalion, 309, 321

A
Alto Hama, 95, 110
Aparicio and his ELP (Army to Liberate Portugal, 50, 60
Artur de Paiva (now Cuvango), 39, 93, 122
Aucamp, Lt,, 73, 74, 98
Auret, Derek, Foreign Affairs, 323

B
Badenhorst, Cmmdt Hank, 133
Baia Farta, 86, 88
Baixo Longa, 138, 143-147, 150, 154, 265, 312
Bale River, 243, 244, 249, 250
Barlow, Lt Eeben, 214, 238, 240, 241
Bastin, Maj Mike, 250
Battle Group Alpha (Operation Savannah), 33, 36, 37, 46, 68, 86, 92, 93, 98, 100, 107, 110, 124, 125, 182, 284, 288, 291, 300
Battle Group Alpha (in Operation Modular etc), 283, 284, 288, 291, 298, 300
Battle Group Bravo (Operation Savannah), 33-35, 40, 49, 51, 53, 55, 60, 62, 66, 67, 72, 74, 86, 92, 98, 102, 110, 112, 118, 121, 124, 125, 132, 134, 136, 142, 144, 145, 150, 182
Battle Group Bravo (Operation Modular), 283, 288-290, 296
Battle Group Bravo, (after Operation Savannah), 131

Battle Group Charlie (Operation Savannah), 50-52,
Battle Group Charlie (in Operation Modular etc), 283 274, 276, 280, 283-291, 296, 297, 298, 300-302
Battle Group Foxbat (in Operation Savannah), 59, 95, 96, 110, 115, 117, 119, 120, 125
Battle Group X-Ray, 115, 125
Ben-Ben, Gen, UNITA, 270
Benade, Col Vos, 223
Benguela, 56, 75, 77, 78, 80, 81, 83, 86, 88-92, 97, 99, 119, 126
Benguela Railway, 59, 92, 93, 96, 115, 133
Bestbier, Cmmdt Frank, 66, 74-76, 86, 88, 90, 95, 99, 101-103, 107, 119, 120, 209
Blaauw, Lt-Maj, Johan, 117, 125, 220
Blaauw, Maj Hennie, 1-Recce, 204, 205
Boshoff, Capt, 282
Botes, Lt Piet, 189, 204, 207
Botha, Foreign Minister Pik, 248, 323, 339,
Botha, Harry, 143
Botha, President PW, 183, 187, 332
Boucher, Sgt Trevor, 226, 228
Bouwer, Maj Smoky, 96, 100, 100, 101, 105, 106
Breytenbach, Lt, 291
Bridge 14, 114, 116, 120
Brink, Sgt Piet, 214
Brits, Capt Gert, 200, 201
Buffalo Base, 181, 182, 198, 200, 208, 252, 295, 297, 308, 309, 312, 325, 332, 347
Burman, Lt Des, 135, 147, 194, 195, 200
Buthelezi, Chief Mangosuthu, 332, 338
Butterfly Operations, 218

C
Cachueca, 249-251
Cahama, 51, 223-225, 228, 229, 237, 238, 240, 315, 317
Caimbambo, 81, 86
Caiundo, 37-40, 121, 122, 138, 142, 143, 150, 217, 242, 249
Calai, 25, 32, 34, 35, 40, 122, 129, 130, 134, 135, 222
Calueque, 51, 228, 297, 309, 317, 319-323
Caraculo, 62
Cassinga, 40, 203, 209, 210, 215, 217, 222, 237, 243, 244, 315
Castro, Fidel, Cuban dictator, 126, 252, 300, 301, 314, 315
Catengue, 69, 70, 75, 80, 81, 86, 97, 98, 119, 125
Catofé, 114, 117, 120
Caxito, 215, 216, 254
Caxito, UNITA intelligence officer, 215-217, 255
Cazombo, 133, 254, 255
Cela, 109, 110, 112, 114, 117, 118, 121, 125, 126
Chambinga heights, 270, 296
Chambinga River, 272, 282-285, 288, 289, 291, 296, 299, 303
Chana Bau, 194
Chana Chinoti, 209
Chana Eheki, 203, 205, 206, 209
Chana Hangadima , 149
Chana Henhombe, 209, 235, 235, 236
Chana Mamuandi, 150, 209
Chana Namixe, 235
Chana Namuidi, 203, 204, 209
Chana Omepapa, 209
Chana Umbi, 218
Charlie November, 32 Bn base, 198, 200
Chewalle, Gen, UNITA, 177, 243
Chipenda, Daniel, FNLA leader, 18-20, 22, 27, 29-32, 40, 44, 59, 66, 98, 103, 118,121,130, 132, 133
Chissombo, 148, 265
Chitado, 133, 134, 324
Chuangari, FNLA commander, 129, 141
CIA, 31, 123
Clack, Sgt Neville, 2-Recce, KIA, 205

Clifford, Sgt, 238
CODESA talks, 333, 335, 337, 338
Combat Formation Zulu (Operation Savannah), 33, 37, 39, 40, 45, 48-52, 56, 57, 59-61, 64, 67, 69-71, 73-76, 78, 86, 88, 93-95, 110, 112, 114, 115, 121, 123
Combat Group Piper (Operation Savannah), 137, 143
COMOPS (Communication Operations — SADF propaganda) department, 308
Conradie, S/Sgt Kenaas, 120
Corps of Engineers, 124, 137, 241
Coutado de M'pupa, 30
Coutado do Mucusso, 150-152
Crocker, Dr Chester, 316, 323
CSI's Special Tasks, 254, 265, 266, 292-294
Cuamato, 220-222, 317, 321
Cuando Cubango, 25, 130, 137, 138, 144, 146, 152, 155, 185, 191, 243, 255, 270, 295, 312
Cuangar, 26, 32, 36, 93, 129, 138, 139, 141, 143, 148, 160, 181, 222, 265
Cuatir River, 296, 299, 309
Cubal, 81, 83, 85
Cubango (formerly Artur de Paiva), 237, 243
Cuba/Cubans, 19, 52, 68, 76, 78, 82, 91, 92, 98, 100, 101, 108, 113, 117, 119, 120, 122, 124-126 133, 147, 191, 248, 265, 271, 277, 280, 297, 312, 317, 318, 320, 321
Cuito Cuanavale, 30, 121, 136, 144, 146, 150, 154, 155, 254, 255, 265-271, 284, 292, 295-303, 308-314
Cuito River, 19, 25, 30, 135, 138, 148, 153, 156, 255, 256, 268, 270, 272, 295, 298, 299, 301, 302, 304, 306, 308, 314
Cunene Province, 47, 149, 203, 216, 222, 249, 315
Cunene River, 20, 50, 51, 133, 223, 228, 229, 233, 236, 237, 247, 314, 315, 317
Cunjamba, 150-152, 255
Cuvelai, 40, 41, 43, 44, 93, 236, 239, 243, 245-248, 250, 315

D
Da Trinidade, Sgt Mac, 273, 282, 318
Dala River, 298, 300, 306, 307, 309
De Abreu, Lt TT, 320, 321
De Klerk, President FW, 332, 336, 338-341, 343, 344, 352
De la Rey, Lt Daan, 189
De Vos, Lt Tobias 'De Villiers', 286-288
Delport, Col Mucho, 297, 317, 326, 327, 343
Denard, Col Bob, French mercenary, 144, 146
DGS (Direcçáo-General de Seguranga — PortuguesenDirector-General of Security, 29, 65, 150
Diederichs, Cpl Diedies, 120, 126
Dippenaar, Capt Jack, 24, 25, 29, 32, 34, 36, 43, 46, 52, 61, 63, 68, 70, 72, 74-76, 81, 86, 90, 91, 101, 102, 104, 114, 224
Dippenaar, Cmmdt Dippies, 223, 224, 226, 227
Dippenaar, Dr Tony, 112
Dirico, 25, 153, 222, 266
Domingos, Commandante, FNLA, 21, 22, 29, 34
Dondo, 124, 126
Dos Santos, Maj Fonseca, UNITA, 146
Double O' or Oginga Odinga, FNLA, 29, 34, 137, 150
Dracula, Sgt, 32-Bn, 232
Du Plessis, Lt Duppie, 214, 215, 225, 231, 232, 313
Du Preez, Cmmdt Phillip 'Flip', 32, 130, 133, 135, 137, 144, 146, 150, 154, 155, 177, 215, 222
Du Toit, Cmmdt Boy, 95
Du Toit, Lt Kokkie, 1-Recce, 205

E

Ebo, 112, 117, 120
Eenhana Base, 192, 195, 204, 209, 218, 219
Ellis, Major Neall, SAAF, 213, 218, 229, 230-234, 239
Ennerdale, 32-Bn at, 333
Epelanca, UNITA commander, 155
Evale, 44, 45
Evelett, Gilbert, 282
Executive Outcomes, 341, 344

F

Fantome, FNLA commandante, 141
Ferreira, Col Deon, 211, 212, 213, 216, 218, 220-223, 225-228, 238, 240-242, 273, 279, 284, 289, 291, 298
Flechas, Bushmen, 20, 23, 33, 36, 117
FNLA, 17, 20-26, 29-34, 36, 38, 39, 44, 48, 58, 63, 66, 67, 94, 130
Fort Doppies, Recce base, 16, 200, 267
Fort St Michel, guerrilla training base, 251, 293, 294
Fouche, Col Paul, 298, 300, 301, 305, 306, 309
Fourie, Lt Herman, 154, 189
Fourie, Maj of Walvis Bay Commando, 154-155
Fourie, S/Sgt Piet, Fourie, 273, 274, 282, 318, 319
Franken, Maj Pierre, 273, 280, 281, 310, 311, 321
Frias, Gen Cintra, Cuban, 301, 302, 304, 307, 314

G

Gabela, 96, 104, 106, 108, 112, 114, 117, 124, 126
Gago Coutinho, 133, 144, 145
Geldenhuys, Capt Martin, 251, 330
Geldenhuys, Gen Jannie, 242, 251, 305, 323
Genis, Cmmdt Flip, 310
Geraldo, FNLA commandante, 66, 138, 141
Gleeson, Maj-Gen Ian, 187, 200, 201, 204
Goldstone, Judge Richard, 336, 338
Greeff, Maj Ken 'Wing Nuts', 139, 148
Greyling, Sgt Major Les, KIA, 205
Griesel, Lt, 189
Greef, Sgt Jack, 73
Grobbelaar, Capt Grobbie, 66, 73, 75-77, 81, 104,
Groenewald, Lt, 189
Guinea Bissau, Bravo Group soldier, 147

H

Hamman, Lt-Gen Daan, 339, 340
Harmse, Des, KIA, 86
Harris, Major-Col Jock, 66, 68, 98, 113, 271, 273, 297
Hartslief, Cmmdt Robbie, 274-277, 282, 290, 296, 297, 310,-312
Hayes, Sgt Alex, 214
Heap, Lt Sam, 189, 214
Hills, Capt to Cmmdt, James, 74, 75, 114, 227
Hochapfel, Maj Charles, 147, 148, 153, 156, 198, 328
Hodgson, Sgt Dave, 214
Holtzhausen, Major Hollie, 59, 95, 110
Hougaard, Capt to Cmmdt Jan, 214, 224-226, 228-231, 234, 249, 273, 281, 295, 297, 310, 312, 317-320
Humbe, 237, 240

I

IFP (Inkatha Freedom Party), 332, 333, 338
Ionde, 242, 243

J

Jacobs, Cmmdt Jakes, 330

Jamba, 152, 237, 243, 249, 254, 255, 269, 270, 281, 292, 294
Jamba (in Huila Province, not Savimbi's HQ), 243, 315
Jaquet, André, Foreign Affairs Dept, 323
João de Almeida, 51, 52, 61
JMC (Joint Monitoring Commission), 247, 248, 250
Joubert, Col-Brig Joep, 223, 225, 242,245, 246

K

Kambuta, UNITA leader, 30, 59, 133
Kashaka, Dr Vakulakuta, UNITA leader, 243
Katahale, Maj, UNITA, 39, 42
Katale, Johnny, UNITA, 32, 36, 155
Katitwi, 36, 37, 38, 121, 138, 143, 150, 249
Katzke, Capt Heinz, 219, 221
Kelly, Sgt Blue, 189, 207
Kempton Park, 32-Bn at, 334, 335
Keulder, Lt Gerhard, KIA, 188
Kingutu, Sgt, 232
Kioto, Commandante, 110, 133
Klopper, Maj-Gen Jan, 339
Koevoet, 191, 211, 315, 324
Korff, Sister Sakkie, 330
Kotze, Cmmdt Pale, 129, 134
Kotze, Cmmdt Willie,38, 56, 76, 115
Kruger, ex-Lt Jan, 342
Kruger, Sgt 'Fingers', 26-28, 46, 52, 73, 77, 84, 85, 115, 205
Kruger, Maj Polla, SAAF, 230, 233
Kruger, Major 'Uncle Sarel', 38
Kruger, Sgt Maj Koos 'Crocodile', 214, 225, 226, 230, 330, 341
Kruys, Cmmdt George, 112, 113, 117, 120
Kumleben Commission of Enquiry, 295

L

Lamprecht, Cmmdt Dan, 138
Laubscher, Koos 'Bom', 267- 269
Liebenberg, Lt Gen Kat, 300, 305, 306, 308, 339, 340
Liebenberg, Cmmdt, 300
Light, Lt David, KIA, 250
Linford, Cmmdt Delville, 36-40, 46,47, 49, 51, 53, 55, 57, 62, 63,68, 69, 74, 77, 78, 80, 86, 88-90, 92-95, 98-103, 107, 109,110, 115, 124, 125, 133, 135, 182, 191
Lobito, 92-98, 101, 113, 126, 128
Lomba River, 255, 273-275, 278-283, 310
Lombard, Capt-Maj, Louis, 330, 342
Loots, Maj Gen Fritz, 16, 18, 140, 202
Lopez, Portuguese pilot, 137, 144, 150
Lord, Col Dick, SAAF, 228, 256, 311
Lotter, Capt Jumbo, 189
Louw, Cmmdt Gerhard, 307, 308
Louw, Defence Minister Eugene, 339, 340
Luanda, 50, 59, 63, 109, 114-116, 117, 123, 126, 301, 308
Lubango (was Sa da Bandeira), 313
Lubbe, Staff Sgt Piet, 90, 98
Luengue, 137, 150-153
Lumumba, UNITA commander, 93, 94, 96
Lusaka Accord, 247, 248, 250

M

Macallum, Capt Mac, KIA, 277-279
Malan, Cmmdt Jan, 300
Malan, Gen, SADF Chief, Defence Minister Magnus, 182, 323, 327, 328
Malone, Lt Mike, 139, 154
Mangope, Pres Lucas, Bophuthatswana, 338
Marão, Staff Sgt Costa, 29, 45, 65, 66, 113, 120
Marienfluss, Kaokoland, 229, 230, 233, 234
Martins, Cmmdt Jan, 187, 189, 194
Masseca, 266, 267
Mavinga, 30, 137, 138, 144, 150-152, 254-256, 265, 266, 272-274, 279, 296, 298
McLoughlin, Col Pat, 301, 305

Meiring, Gen Georg, 269, 339, 342
Mendes, Sgt, 318
Menongue (was Serpa Pinto) , 40, 265, 266, 282, 295, 308, 310-313
Mentz, Maj Dave, 196
Meyer, Maj-Gen , 300, 305, 306, 308
Middlemost, Padre, 270
Miles, Lt Peter, 150, 151
Mindonambunga, Sgt Bernardo, 205
Mitton, Cpl, 286
Moçamedes (now Porto Namibe, 39, 59, 61-64, 66, 113, 126, 244
Moller, Cmmdt Hans, 48
Mongua, 50, 237
Moolman, Cmmdt Jules, 20
MPLA, 19, 20, 23, 30, 34, 36, 46, 63, 93, 131, 134, 142, 182, 247, 336
Mucusso, 138, 181, 222
Mulder, Shylock, 38, 61
Muller, Cmmdt Mike, 301, 305
Mulondo, 240, 251
Munanganga, SWAPO commander, 200, 202, 219
Mupa, 44, 227, 236, 313
M'pupa, 19, 20, 23, 25, 26, 30-32, 34, 35, 114, 121, 128-130, 134-137, 147, 149, 154, 346, 347

N

National Party government, 182, 332, 337, 338, 340, 344
Nel, Cmmdt 'Piet Graspol', 309
Nel, Cmmdt Gert, 17, 18, 182, 183, 198, 203, 204, 208, 211
Nel, Commdt Vossie, 37, 72
Nel, Sergeant Fanus 'Nella', 230, 232
Neto, Agostino, Angolan president, 19, 126
Niemann, Maj Boela , 242
Nienaber, Capt Tony, 214, 215, 224
Nkongo, 192, 193, 200
Nortje, RSM Piet, 235, 249, 250
Nortmann, Maj Hannes, 272, 274-278, 280, 282, 289-291, 297, 309, 322, 323
Nova Lisboa, 29, 59, 61, 66, 81, 98, 121, 126, 133
Nova Redondo, 98, 100-104, 106-110, 115, 125, 126, 134
Nujoma, Sam, SWAPO leader, 127, 324
Numa, Brig, UNITA, 268, 269, 271, 298

O

Okavango River, 20, 26, 34-36, 38, 39, 121, 122, 124, 138, 142, 143, 147, 148, 152, 153, 181, 314, 347
Omalapapa, 194, 195
Omauni Base, 185, 187, 189, 192, 194, 195, 197, 198, 207, 241
Omega Base, 182, 242
Ondangwa Air Base, 131, 201, 220, 229, 237, 242
Ondjiva (was Pereira de Eça), 215, 218-221, 223, 227, 228, 237, 239, 242, 243, 247, 249, 250, 315, 317
Ongulumbashe, 323
Operation Alpha Centauri, 270, 294
Operation Askari, 237, 243, 247, 248
Operation Cobra, 149
Operation Displace, 309
Operation Forte, 208, 237, 248, 251, 252
Operation Hooper, 252, 298, 299, 304, 305, 310, 311
Operation Kropduif (pigeon, 204
Operation Meebos, 237, 239
Operation Modular, 272, 273, 289, 295, 296, 298, 310
Operation Packer, 305, 308
Operation Protea, 215, 223, 228, 237, 239, 241
Operation Reindeer, 209
Operation Savannah, 43, 60, 110, 118, 120, 122-124, 126, 127, 128, 130, 131, 135, 137, 139, 160, 183, 184, 196, 209, 222, 243, 342
Operation Super, 233
Operation Vula, 337

Operation Wallpaper, 255
Oshikango, 317
Otjivelo, 223, 224
Owamboland, 26, 129, 149, 160, 179, 180,
    183, 191, 193, 196, 197, 200, 211, 213,
    223, 244, 247, 314, 316, 317, 324

P
Pereira de Eça (now Ondjiva, 38-41, 46,
    62, 87, 123, 126
Peu Peu, 51, 228
Phola Park, 32-Bn at, 335-337
Pica Pau kimbo (see Woodpecker)
Pomfret, 326, 328, 330, 332, 333, 336,
    338, 339, 341, 343-345
Porto Alexandre, 63, 64
Porto Amboine, 96, 104-106, 108, 124, 125
Porto Namibe (was Moçamedes), 313
Potgieter, Cmmdt Hap, 220
Pretoria Regiment, 298
Putter, Admiral Dries, Chief of Staff
    Intelligence, 294

Q
Quatir, 265, 310, 312
Quibale, 96, 114, 117, 124

R
Rabe, Lt Eric, 214, 240
Rademeyer, Sgt, 189
Rätte, Capt Willem, Recce Wing, 207, 211,
    213, 216, 224, 236, 239, 241-243
Reagan, Major Brian, 160, 177
Reconnaissance Commandos/Regiments,
    general, 117, 126, 205, 212, 216, 222,
    249, 288, 312, 318
Recce Wing, 32 Bn, 213, 216, 235-237,
    241, 247, 255, 279, 310, 317
Refugees, 34, 131, 133, 142
Regiment De La Rey, 306
Regiment Groot Karoo, 306
Regiment President Steyn, 306, 308
Renato, Brig, UNITA, 267-270
Retief, Cpl Anton, Recce, 60, 105
Ribeiro, Sgt Robbie, 45, 54, 56, 130, 137,
    143, 150, 152-154,
Riegaardt, Cmmdt Duncan, 5-Recce, 267
Rito, 147, 150, 154
Roberto, Holden, FNLA President, 31
Roçades, (now Xangongo), 48, 50
Rogers, Staff Sgt Mike, 189
Roper, Lt Barry, 151, 152, 156, 193
Rose, Lt Peter, 139, 147
Ross, Lt Jim, 214
Rossouw, Maj Gideon, 209
Rotunda, 51, 52, 56
Roxo, Sgt Danny, 29 43, 93, 116, 117, 120,
    130, 137, 138, 143-145, 150-154
Roza, Sgt Maj Carl, 185, 198
Ruacana, 26, 180, 191, 213, 229, 297, 323
Rudman, Cmmdt Les, 282, 305
Rundu, 19, 23, 25, 26, 30, 32, 34, 35, 59,
    89, 122, 124, 128-131, 134, 137-139,
    144, 146, 155, 185, 187, 193, 208, 241,
    242, 281, 293, 310
Rupping, Staff Sgt Riaan, 277, 278

S
Sa da Bandeira (now Lubango), 34, 38, 42,
    48, 53, 55, 56, 58-61, 65, 66, 68, 97,
    98, 119, 123, 124, 126, 133, 134
SAAF, 141, 143, 198, 204, 222, 223, 225,
    271, 281, 299
Sachs, Cmmdt Bert, 267, 270
Sadie, Lt Koos, 189
SAM-8 anti-aircraft systems, 281-283
Sanchez, Gen Ochoa, Cuban commander,
    314, 316
Santa Clara, 47, 48
Santa Comba, 112, 119
Savate, 138, 141-143, 215, 216, 218, 222
Savimbi, Dr Jonas, UNITA president, 19,
    32, 39, 59, 126, 130, 133, 134, 138,
    144-146, 154, 243, 249, 254-256,
    265-267, 269, 270, 272, 273, 281, 292,

293, 294-296, 310, 316
Savory, Lt Jim, 225, 226
Schalkwyk, Col Schalkie, 112
Scheepers, Maj Louis, 330, 332Scheepers,
Schoeman, Brig Dawie, 24, 32, 49, 51, 59,
    64, 80, 95, 103, 117, 118, 126, 137
Schoeman, Cmmdt Cassie, 301, 302
Schutte, Maj Johan, 249
Sector 10 HQ at Oshakati, 180, 184, 198,
    199, 211, 230, 231, 234, 237, 239, 242,
    315, 317
Sector 20 at Rundu, 148, 198, 208, 210
Serfontein, Cmmdt-Brig Chris 'Swart Hand',
    227, 315, 317, 320
Serpa Pinto (now Menongue), 39, 44, 64,
    66, 68, 99, 121, 126, 130, 133, 143
Sierro, Sgt Silva, 29, 43, 65, 113, 114, 130,
    137, 143, 145, 150, 153
Silva Porto (now Bié), 32, 126
Slabbert, Maj Toon, 50, 55, 61, 70, 73, 74,
    76, 82, 83, 86, 90, 92, 93, 95, 97, 103,
    110, 113, 115, 116, 118, 119
Slade, Sgt Maj Eugene 'Piet', 139, 147
Smit, Cmmdt Bok, 280, 297
Smit, Staff Sgt FL, 182, 281
Smith, Sgt, 238
Snyman, Dr Willie, Conservative Party, 343
Soviets, 26, 124, 126, 191, 223, 225, 227,
    247, 248, 265, 268, 270, 300., 314, 317
Spiller, Staff Sgt Charlie, 92, 137
Stewart, Sergeant, 347
Steyn, Lt-Gen Pierre, 338
SWAPO (South West Afriva People's
    Union), 24, 26, 32, 39, 48, 78, 94, 127,
    129, 137, 138, 142, 143, 149, 160, 180,
    182, 183, 190, 201, 218
Swart, Col Blackie, 112, 115, 120
Swart, Jeb, 240
Sydow, Sgt Kevin , 214, 238, 241

T
Task Force 101, 138, 139, 143, 147, 149,
    152, 156, 180, 181, 185, 200, 201, 204,
    211
Task Force Zulu, Ruacana, 317, 319, 320
Tate, Maj Pat, 138
Taylor, Lt John, 189, 196
Tchibemba, 51, 315
Techipa, 318, 319, 321-323
Tembisa Township, 32 Bn in, 334
Tetchamutete, 40, 236, 244, 247, 249
Thokoza, 32 Bn in, 335
Tippett, Staff Sgt Mike, 141, 143
Tumpo Triangle, 283, 284, 289, 291, 298,
    299, 301, 302, 305, 308, 309, 315

U
UDF (United Democratic Front, 332
Ueckermann, RSM, 217
Umkhonto we Sizwe (MK) , 331
UNITA, 17, 19, 20, 24-26, 30, 32, 33, 34,
    39, 41, 44, 48, 59, 65, 68, 93, 94, 121,
    126, 130, 133, 144, 149, 154, 155, 181,
    191, 215, 216, 228, 241, 249, 252, 254,
    266, 298, 314, 323
UNTAG (United Nation's Transitional
    Assistance Group, 323
Upton, Maj Coen, 20, 21, 23, 96
Uys, Piet, pilot, KIA, 86

V
Valentino, Dr, UNITA, 94, 96, 177
Van Achterberg, Commodore, 183
Van Coller, Maj Dries, 38, 55, 56, 68, 69,
    78, 81, 100, 101, 110, 115
Van der Merwe, Sgt Jan, 2-Recce, 145,
    146
Van der Merwe, Sgt Mecchie, 1-Recce, 62,
    63
Van der Mescht, Sapper, POW in Angolan
    hands, 227
Van der Spuy, Cmmdt Johan, 96, 135, 137,
    150
Van der Spuy, Cmmdt Sybie, OC 2-Recce,
    138, 141, 142, 144, 148, 150, 204

Van der Vyver, Major Jan, 249, 265
Van der Waals, Commdt Kaas, 32
Van Deventer, Gen André, 129, 133, 135
Van Heerden, Capt Piet, 38
Van Heerden, Col Corky, 32, 36, 38, 42,
    40, 47, 50, 53, 56, 60-63, 66-72, 74,
    76, 80, 81, 88, 89-91, 94-96, 100-103,
    107-110, 112, 114, 115, 125
Van Heerden, Foreign Affairs Director Neil,
    323
Van Niekerk, Cmmdt Gert, 48
Van Rooyen, Col Carl, 139, 185
Van Staden, Maj Tinus, 227, 297, 303, 304,
    306, 308, 330
Van Tonder, Maj-Gen Neels, Military
Intelligence, 323
Van Wyk, Lt Connie, 26, 29, 40, 44,-46, 48,
    61, 63, 64, 70, 75, 80, 82, 84, 90, 91,
    101, 102, 104, 113, 117, 118, 120
Van Zyl, Capt Piet Boer, 189, 279, 280,
    281, 283-285, 287, 288, 290, 295
Van Zyl, RSM Pep, 138, 151, 208
Van Zyl, Sgt Maj FC, 2-Recce, KIA, 205
Velthuizen, Capt Rooies, 224
Venter, Cmmdt Toutjies, 96
Venter, Maj, 135, 139
Verster, Cmmdt Joe, 1-Recce, 204
Verster, Major Koos, 187, 194
Vieira, Sgt Maj Tony, 189, 197
Vila Nova da Armada, 19, 135-138, 143,
    145, 147, 150, 156
Viljoen, Maj to Col Eddie, 185, 186, 194,
    198, 204, 209, 211, 216, 217, 224, 225,
    242, 243, 245, 246, 249, 250, 255, 256,
    266, 267, 269, 271, 273, 342
Viljoen, Gen Constand, 17, 149, 211, 303,
    344
Viposto, 282, 303, 304
Visser, Maj Nick, KIA, 59, 66, 86
Vorster, Prime Minister John, 123, 183
Vosloosrus, 32 Bn operations in, 334

W
Walker, Major Arthur , SAAF, 219
Walls, Sgt Brian, 2-Recce, 145
Walters, Maj Fanie, 139
Wannenburg, Sgt Wannies, 1-Recce, 120
Ward, Sgt-Maj Willy, 2-Recce, 138, 143,
    145-147
Waugh, Maj Peter, 255, 267
Webb, Commdt Eddie, 59, 95
Wessels, Platoon leader, 287
Williams, Lt Peter, 214, 241, 243
Woodpecker Base, (Pica Pau in
    Portuguese), 139, 143, 147, 148, 151,
    152, 154, 181, 347
Wooley, Capt John, 200

XY
Xangongo (was Pereira de Eça), 214,
    220-224, 228, 229, 237, 241, 243, 247,
    315, 317, 319, 321

Z
Zaïre, FNLA and 32 Bn soldier, 136, 137,
143, 200, 201
Zimbabwe African National Liberation Army
    (ZANLA), 331
Zimbabwe African National Union (ZANU),
    331
Zimbabwe African People's Union (ZAPU),
    331
Zimbabwe People's Revolutionary Army
    (ZIPRA), 331